THE SPRAY AND PRAY SQUADRON

3rd Bomb Squadron, 1st Bomb Group, Chinese-American Composite Wing in World War II

Margaret Mills Kincannon

Schiffer
Military History

4880 Lower Valley Road
Atglen, PA 19310

Other Schiffer books on related subjects

Chennault's Forgotten Warriors: The Saga of the 308th Bomb Group in China
Carroll V. Glines, 978-0-88740-809-0

Famine, Sword, and Fire: The Liberation of Southwest China in World War II
Daniel Jackson, 978-0-7643-4838-9

Blackboards and Bomb Shelters: The Perilous Journey of Americans in China during World War II
James P. Bevill, 978-0-7643-6264-4

Copyright © 2024 by Margaret Mills Kincannon

Library of Congress Control Number: 2023941037

All rights reserved. No part of this work may be reproduced or used in any form or by any means—graphic, electronic, or mechanical, including photocopying or information storage and retrieval systems—without written permission from the publisher.

The scanning, uploading, and distribution of this book or any part thereof via the Internet or any other means without the permission of the publisher is illegal and punishable by law. Please purchase only authorized editions and do not participate in or encourage the electronic piracy of copyrighted materials.

"Schiffer Military" and the arrow logo are trademarks of Schiffer Publishing, Ltd.

Designed by Christopher Bower
Cover design by Christopher Bower
Type set in Archer/Minion Pro

ISBN: 978-0-7643-6789-2
Printed in India

Published by Schiffer Publishing, Ltd.
4880 Lower Valley Road
Atglen, PA 19310
Phone: (610) 593-1777; Fax: (610) 593-2002
Email: Info@schifferbooks.com
Web: www.schifferbooks.com

For our complete selection of fine books on this and related subjects, please visit our website at www.schifferbooks.com. You may also write for a free catalog.

Schiffer Publishing's titles are available at special discounts for bulk purchases for sales promotions or premiums. Special editions, including personalized covers, corporate imprints, and excerpts, can be created in large quantities for special needs. For more information, contact the publisher.

We are always looking for people to write books on new and related subjects. If you have an idea for a book, please contact us at proposals@schifferbooks.com.

In CBI

For years to come when veterans meet
And tell the story of each feat,
They'll let you know and oft repeat,
They served in CBI.

Some spent long years in that war zone.
Each felt that he was alone.
No one had thought to bring him home
From far-off CBI.

Millions of Indians, there one sees,
Along with the quiet, sly Burmese
And four hundred million patient Chinese
Dwelling in CBI.

To reach this place took many a day
O'er waters deep and far away.
For hostile subs, a human prey
En route to CBI.

Then safe from dangers of the seas,
The tropics plagued him with disease,
Nor did the climate seek to please,
In the land of CBI.

A constant foe lurked in the sky,
The place where many brave men die,
Who flew with God, their sole ally
O'er hazardous CBI.

Some tramped the stretches of green hell,
Where reached the silent jungle spell,
Yet quite a few survived to tell
Of treacherous CBI.

There, they fought the wily Jap
And pushed him back on the rugged map.
The GI over the stronger chap,
Conquered in CBI.

Of our brave men, we lost our share.
With courage and faith, 'tis often rare
They died to make a dark world fair
Far off in CBI.

Now while they sleep across the sea
Awaiting the last great reveille,
Let all thank God most fervently
Safe home from CBI.

Pray that these souls died not in vain,
Nor lost be all this war's great gain
For which so many suffered pain
Out in CBI.

But back at home, safe with each friend,
Let every one of our brave men
Work for a peace that'll never end,
Veterans of CBI.

—Anonymous. Souvenir edition of "The Angel's Harp," vol. VII, no. XXI, SS *Marine Angel*, December 9, 1945

Contents

"In CBI" 3
Preface 6
Acknowledgments 9

Chapter 1	Wars and Rumors of Wars	12
Chapter 2	Scorching at Malir	24
Chapter 3	Training for Combat	38
Chapter 4	Mildewing at Moran	56
Chapter 5	Bombing in Burma	74
Chapter 6	Moving to Dergaon	100
Chapter 7	Evacuating from Kweilin	116
Chapter 8	Stagnating at Peishiyi	128
Chapter 9	Task Force 34 at Chihkiang	158
Chapter 10	Successes and Setbacks	184
Chapter 11	Relocating to Liangshan	206
Chapter 12	Defending Laohokow	230
Chapter 13	Last Airfield Lost	242
Chapter 14	Holding Chihkiang	262
Chapter 15	Turning the Tide	284
Chapter 16	End in Sight	310
Chapter 17	Victory in China	326
Chapter 18	Back to the ZI	356
Chapter 19	Aftermath of War	368

Appendixes

Appendix A: B-25s Assigned to 3rd Bomb Squadron 386
Appendix B: Chinese Air Force Personnel Listed in Movement Orders 390
Appendix C: Biographical Sketches 393

Endnotes 466
Bibliography 488
Index 504

Preface

> Under the leadership of Chennault, the planes of the smallest of all our Air Forces harass and smash relentlessly at the Japs. They support the ground forces of the fighting Chinese, deep in the hills where supplies are hard to come by and where Lend-Lease is unknown. In all sorts of weather, these pilots, both Yank and Chinese, continue the job of keeping China for the Chinese, strafing and bombing enemy columns, making sea sweeps, blasting military installations.
>
> —Excerpt from "'Flying Trapezists' Together in China," *CBI Roundup* II, no. 45 (Delhi, India), July 20, 1944

Such praise was common for Claire Lee Chennault, a major general in the United States Army Air Forces by this time in the war. Renowned as a brilliant strategist, he surmounted seemingly impossible odds to secure victory in the skies over China against invading imperial Japanese forces. This controversial commander known as "Old Leatherface" was beloved by the men who served under him, and esteemed in both the United States and China, but he often ran afoul of other military leaders, who lacked confidence in his innovative ideas and who favored their own agendas.

Born on September 6, 1893, in Commerce, Texas, Chennault spent his boyhood in Gilbert, Louisiana, and underwent Reserve Officers' Training Corps (ROTC) training while attending Louisiana State University. Afterward he became the teacher for a one-room school. At the onset of World War I, he graduated from Officers' School and transferred to the Aviation Division of the Army Signal Corps. His aim was to become a pilot, but hostilities ended before he received his wings—rejected three times because he did not possess the necessary qualifications to be an aviator, according to his superiors. On his fourth attempt, Chennault was accepted and received his first wings on April 9, 1919. Graduating from pursuit pilot training in 1922, he remained in the service after it became the Army Air Corps in 1926, and was appointed chief of Pursuit Section at Air Corps Tactical School in the 1930s.

During those postwar years, Chennault honed his skills as an aerobatic flier of biplanes. In the lead of a three-man team called the "Three Musketeers," he performed intricate aerial maneuvers at events across the country, including the National Air Races in 1928. In 1932, as a pursuit aviation instructor at Maxwell Field in Alabama, Chennault reorganized the team as "Three Men on a Flying Trapeze," which continued to perform for awestruck spectators below. By 1937, Chennault had served twenty years in the military but was repeatedly passed over for promotion. Citing health problems—chronic bronchitis and partial deafness from many years of open-cockpit flying—he resigned from the Air Corps with the rank of captain, and the aerobatics team was disbanded.

Soon afterward, he accepted an invitation from the Chinese Nationalist leader, Generalissimo Chiang Kai-shek (extended at the urging of Madame Chiang, the generalissimo's pro-Western wife), to go to China to survey the ineffectual Republic of China Air Force (ROCAF)—and thus began Chennault's second military career, for which he became best known. At that time, most Americans, including President Franklin D. Roosevelt, opposed all overseas military involvement.

When Chennault arrived in China in June 1937, he discovered that the occupying Japanese were committing atrocities against its defenseless civilian population that matched the brutality of Hitler's Nazis in Europe, plundering, torturing, raping, and killing with impunity. Japanese planes bombed Kunming and the surrounding area almost daily for target practice, and the Chinese air force could do little to deter them. It became Chennault's mission to transform the ROCAF into an effective fighting force capable of fending off the invaders. Under paid contract, he became Chiang Kai-shek's chief air adviser, training Chinese pilots according to the American model as well as participating in occasional scouting missions.

Chennault returned to America in 1941 and recruited a group of men from the Army Air Corps, Marines, and Navy that formed the American Volunteer Group (AVG). The mission of this small band of mercenaries based in Burma was to fly P-40s, using Chennault's tactics of "defensive pursuit" to shoot down Japanese aircraft in an attempt to aid the Chinese in their fight for survival. This was a new strategy that was met with great resistance by most military leaders at a time when bombers were generally faster than pursuit planes.

It was not until after the Japanese attack on Pearl Harbor in December 1941 that the AVG went into action in earnest. Within days, Chennault's airmen began attacking ground targets and engaging enemy aircraft throughout the China-Burma-India (CBI) theater. Their primary objective was to protect the vital Burma Road, but the unit also guarded Rangoon and other strategic locations in Southeast Asia and western China against Japanese forces. The AVG proved to be enormously successful and racked up a series of impressive victories over the invaders. Two weeks after their first mission came the earliest news reports praising Chennault and his fearless fliers, and soon Chinese newspapers, followed by the American press, began referring to them as the "Flying Tigers." Their exploits quickly assumed legendary proportions, and Chennault became a hero as their daring leader.

The AVG launched missions against the Japanese for seven months. Chennault, who returned to active duty in the United States Army Air Forces in April 1942 with the rank of colonel, was promoted soon afterward to brigadier general. Opposed to inducting his Flying Tigers into the Army, he feared that turning his group into a regulation military unit would reduce its effectiveness. However, top brass had no intention of supporting a private air force that functioned outside military channels after the US entered the war.

At midnight on July 4, 1942, the American Volunteer Group ceased to exist. Replaced by the China Air Task Force (CATF) and formally inducted into the USAAF, the group continued to be known as the Flying Tigers. Because of the Japanese occupation of Burma in early April, the mission of the CATF was to defend the air supply route over the Himalayan Mountains between India and China—known as "the Hump"—as well as to provide air support for Chinese ground forces. Stationed in India, the task force (flying both fighters and bombers) operated under Chennault's command as part of the 10th Air Force, which controlled supplies, personnel, and operations. With few resources available to fight a powerful enemy deployed across a vast front, the CATF achieved a combat record that proved it to be a worthy successor to the AVG.

The CATF was in existence for nine months. On March 19, 1943, it was disbanded and replaced by the recently established 14th Air Force. Chennault, now a major general, became its commander. The 14th Air Force, under his leadership, continued the Flying Tigers legacy and went on to win air superiority in China. Chennault remained in command until July 1945, when he again retired—forced out once more because of his controversial methods and outspoken criticisms. By the end of the war, the 14th Air Force had more than twenty thousand men and one thousand planes in China that played a vital role in the defeat of Japan. Key among them was the unique Chinese-American Composite Wing, which took Chennault's plan to assist the Chinese even further than his previous efforts.

After the war, Chennault returned to China. He purchased surplus military aircraft and established the Civil Air Transport (later known as Air America). These aircraft facilitated aid to Nationalist China during the struggle against Mao Tse-tung's Communists for political control of China in the late 1940s and were later used in supply missions to French forces in Indochina and the Kuomintang occupation of northern Burma throughout the mid- to late 1950s.

Chennault was finally promoted to lieutenant general in the United States Air Force on July 18, 1958, only nine days before his death on July 27 as the result of lung cancer. He was interred with full military honors at Arlington National Cemetery.

Without this unconventional and courageous leader, the events that unfold within these pages would never have been accomplished.[1]

United States Air Force

Acknowledgments

"My dad never talked much about the war." Those are words spoken to me repeatedly by sons and daughters of many of the men who served with my father during World War II.

Well, neither did mine. I had heard the story about the tiger that walked across the road in front of him while he was in India, and I had seen the spent bullet that struck his boot but caused no injury as he flew as tail gunner on a mission in China. My younger brother said he had heard the one about strafing a train in Burma. Although we had heard his stories of the benign variety, he never told us about the *real* war—about the extreme privations that he endured, the hours of tedium when gas and bombs were in short supply, the anxious waiting to finally take off on a perilous mission, or the heart-pounding suspense when approaching a well-defended target. He never mentioned the flak bursting in the air all around or the big guns firing from below to shoot down his plane. We knew nothing of the friends whose fate was uncertain for days after they crash-landed in enemy territory, and certainly not about those who never came back. It was only late in life that Dad finally began to speak openly about his service. He, as many others who fought in that terrible war, had shut away the memories that haunted him. They wanted to protect their families from knowing about the events they had endured, and they knew that only others who had "been there" could fully understand.

When I began to ask questions, Dad said that the only thing he could remember was that he was in the 14th Air Force and served under General Chennault, but I was curious to learn more. It was a personal quest. I wanted to share whatever I was able to discover with him, as well as with his sons (my brothers) and his grandchildren (my children, nephews, and niece). I certainly never intended to write a book. It was after my research began to yield such vast amounts of information, and especially after I began to find the families of other men who served in the 3rd Bomb Squadron with my father, that I realized I had to share all that I had learned.

Holdings of the Air Force Historical Research Agency (AFHRA) at Maxwell Air Force Base, Alabama, proved to be an invaluable source of data. Scanned and copied to compact disc, the monthly historical reports, special and general orders, operational reports, and other documents relating to the Chinese-American Composite Wing, the 1st Bomb Group, and the 1st, 2nd, 3rd, and 4th Bomb Squadrons have formed the "backbone" of this volume.

Many excellent books have been written about the war in China by those far more knowledgeable than I, and some were even written by actual participants of that war. I am not a historian, and I certainly have no personal experience with war. Because my strength as a retired English teacher is research, I have relied heavily on the writings of others to give historical context to the events described in these pages. Any errors are entirely my own.

To compensate for deficiencies that might arise from my reliance on others, I decided to make this not only about military history but more particularly about the men who lived it. From operational officers who got the glory to mechanics, orderly room clerks, and cooks, they were all crucial in the effort to drive the Japanese invaders out of the Asian mainland. In my attempt to provide a glimpse into their day-to-day existence in that "forgotten" theater of war, I have included many of the trivial, mundane events of their daily routine, as well as details of adrenaline-pumping raids as aircrews bombed and strafed enemy installations. All of it was essential to their eventual victory.

None of this would have been possible without the assistance of a great many people. I feel special gratitude toward my dad, who patiently endured hours of questioning as I attempted to rekindle memories and extract details. During one weekend we had spent a day together, talking about the people and events he remembered. When I returned the following morning, he told me, "I didn't get to sleep until almost three o'clock. I was reliving all of that." I am glad to have been able to spend that time with him, since this work, initially intended as a tribute to him, has become a memorial as well.

Others have additionally provided an abundance of valuable information. Robert Hugel, the squadron's final living American member, sent me a copy of the diary he used to record events following the crash behind enemy lines of a B-25 in which he was flying as tail gunner. He also shared with me photos of himself and the washed-out plane.

In addition, I have been in contact with the wives and widows, sons and daughters, brothers and sisters, nieces and nephews, grandchildren, and cousins of other men who served with my dad, and I feel a sense of kinship toward these people with whom I have exchanged letters, emails, and telephone calls. Many of them have shared photos, diaries, logbooks, letters, newspaper articles, discharge papers, and a variety of other documents that have been invaluable in putting this together. I extend my thanks to all those contributors.

Tony Strotman shared photographs and answered my questions that related to his father's 341st Bomb Group, 69th Composite Wing. Szu-meng (James) Peng shared photos of the silk banner presented to Capt. Robert C. MacNeil, 3rd Bomb Squadron engineering officer and later operations officer, from his extensive personal collection of World War II memorabilia. When he personally visited with Tu Kai-mu, former 3rd Bomb Squadron pilot who was a signer of the banner, he acted as my liaison and assured Mr. Tu that his story will form a significant part of this history.

Maj. Daniel Jackson has aided me in many ways. Author of *The Forgotten Squadron: The 449th Fighter Squadron in World War II*; *Famine, Sword, and Fire: The Liberation of Southwestern China in World War II*; and *Fallen Tigers: The Fate of America's Missing Airmen in China during World War II*, he has gone above and beyond by sharing relevant documents with me, critiquing my manuscript, and providing detailed suggestions for improvements.

This would not be complete without thanking my family. They have encouraged me through the years that I have worked to bring this book into being, and I am grateful to my husband of sixty years, Tom; my children, Jeff and Coleen; my children-in-law, Lisa and Lance; and my grandchildren, Sydney, Evan, Cameron, and Caroline. Their support and patience have been invaluable to me.

To those extraordinary men who served in the "Spray and Pray Squadron," I especially extend my deepest gratitude and respect. They were patriots who believed in the cause for which they fought and sacrificed their own ambitions and comforts—and sometimes even their lives—to win that war. We can only imagine how different our own lives would be if they had not succeeded.

Margaret Mills Kincannon
Flower Mound, Texas

CHAPTER ONE
Wars and Rumors of Wars

Enemy planes still swarmed in the distance.

"This battle has been going on for nearly three hours. . . . It is no joke. It is a real war!"

With microphone in hand, a reporter for radio station KTU climbed to the roof of the Advertiser Publishing Company building in downtown Honolulu and broadcast the first eyewitness account of the attack by the Japanese Imperial Navy that struck the US naval base at Pearl Harbor and then the city of Honolulu, ushering in one of the darkest periods of American history. It was a sneak attack that shocked an unsuspecting nation, exposing the lie behind ongoing diplomatic negotiations between Japan and the United States for the purpose of maintaining peace in the Pacific.

On a peaceful Sunday morning—December 7, 1941—the Japanese extended their reach and struck the American installation on the serene, tropical island of Oahu, territory of Hawaii. It was obvious that even as talks between the two nations took place, the Japanese were making elaborate plans for aggression in their attempt to drive Western interests out of the Pacific. Immediately following their raid on the Hawaiian Islands, assaults were carried out on other Pacific targets: Malaya, Hong Kong, Singapore, Thailand, Guam, the Philippine Islands, Wake Island, and Midway Island.

Many Americans heard of the ambush when their favorite radio programs were interrupted on an otherwise tranquil Sunday afternoon. An Associated Press bulletin first reported it to mainland news organizations and radio networks at 1:07 p.m. Eastern Standard Time. After confirming the initial bulletin with the government, the major networks broke into regular programming at 2:30 p.m., bringing reports of the attack, still in progress, to a stunned American public. Programming was interrupted with updates to the first sketchy information as more reports came in throughout the afternoon, bringing home to listeners across the United States the full impact of Japan's treachery.[1]

President Franklin D. Roosevelt called it "a date which will live in infamy" when he addressed a joint session of Congress the following day and asked for a declaration of war. Over the four years that followed, the lives of many hundreds of thousands of young Americans were disrupted and forever changed by the hostilities that had erupted half a world away.

James Henry Mills was one of them. Known to his friends as "Hank," he was eighteen years old when he learned of the attack. The news aired in his hometown soon after he and his sweetheart returned from church and were sitting down with her family for Sunday dinner. Hank soon experienced firsthand that this was, without any doubt, "a real war." He became one of more than sixteen million Americans who served in World War II, and almost three hundred thousand of those were casualties.

An unprepared America had not recognized the signs of impending aggression, yet they had been there all along.

The world was at war. The past decade had witnessed the rise of imperialism on a scale such as had never been seen before. Territorial acquisition through military invasion and conquest went unchecked. Expansionism spread across Europe and beyond.

Resentments had simmered since the conclusion of World War I, when provisions of the Treaty of Versailles in 1918 left many European nations with deep dissatisfactions. Among the results of these grievances was the rise of Italian Fascism in the 1920s. Under the leadership of Benito Mussolini, the Fascists sought to establish a New Roman Empire based around the Mediterranean. Italy claimed and conquered Ethiopia in 1936, initiating a policy of expansionism in Europe and North Africa. Fascists troops invaded Albania in early 1939 and Egypt, Greece, and British Somaliland in 1940.

The militant takeover of Germany by Adolf Hitler and his Nazi regime in 1933 initially sought to reclaim the "rightful" territories of historic Germany, but this soon became a drive to dominate all of Europe. Nazi Germany and Fascist Italy signed a treaty of cooperation in October 1936 that created the Rome-Berlin Axis. The Nazis took control of Austria in 1938. Aggression continued with the invasion of Czechoslovakia and then Poland in 1939. By the following year, Hitler's forces had marched into Denmark, Norway, France, Belgium, Luxembourg, the Netherlands, and Romania.

The Soviet Union under Joseph Stalin entered a nonaggression pact with Nazi Germany in August 1939. The agreement allotted eastern Poland, Latvia, Estonia, Finland, and Bessarabia (including parts of what are now Moldova and Ukraine) to the USSR, while western Poland and Lithuania went to the Nazis. Three months later, Stalin marched his troops into Poland, followed by the occupation of Finland, Lithuania, Latvia, and Estonia in 1940. After Hitler broke the treaty and invaded the Soviet Union in June 1941, Stalin shifted Soviet allegiance to the Allies (later called the United Nations), which opposed the Axis aggressors, although it was always an uneasy alliance.

As these events were unfolding farther west, the tiny island nation of Japan made its own grab for territory. The Japanese viewed all the lands of Asia to be the rightful property of the imperial Japanese government and the emperor. The goal of unifying or dominating the Asian lands had been deterred by the presence of foreign military forces in the Philippines, Hong Kong, Malaya, and the Dutch East Indies, although the vast Chinese mainland was virtually defenseless. The First Sino-Japanese War began in 1931, when Japan took advantage of the political fragmentation of China to create the puppet state of Manchukuo in Manchuria. Japan signed a pact with Nazi Germany in November 1936, with the objective of fending off Stalin's Communists. Japanese imperialist policy was renewed with an advance on China in 1937, launched by the bombing of cities such as Shanghai, Nanking, and Canton. Japan's goal was to dominate China politically and militarily and to secure its vast natural resources and other economic reserves, primarily food and labor, for its own use.

On September 27, 1940, Japan entered the Tripartite Pact with Germany and Italy to form the Axis Alliance. The aim of this unholy trinity was global domination. Bloodshed in Europe, Africa, and Asia continued, and hostilities escalated. With all these factors in operation, it was inevitable that American territories soon became targets for takeover.

The United States had long maintained neutrality but, with the bombing of Pearl Harbor, could no longer avoid being forcibly thrust into the conflict that was already raging. Young men across America rushed to enlistment centers by the thousands to fulfill their patriotic duty by signing up. In fact, such great numbers volunteered that there were insufficient resources to train them all, so many initially went into reserve units to await the time when they were called into active service.

Less than a year after America entered the war, Hank went to Little Rock and enlisted as a private on September 2, 1942. As he related those long-ago events, "Rather than be drafted, I enlisted and requested I be put in the Air Force, because I didn't want to walk on the ground and carry a rifle." He was inducted the next day at Camp Chaffee Army Base at Fort Smith.[2] "Passed exams & am in Army now," he proudly announced via a postcard to his family. A small-town boy, Hank had scarcely been out of Arkansas, but all of that soon changed.

Hank's experiences were in many ways typical of all who passed through the military's training programs. Basic training was at Keesler Field near Biloxi, Mississippi, under the direction of the Army Air Forces Technical Training Command. A standard period of indoctrination for those destined to become technical specialists included basic military general orders, military conduct, and close-order and open-order drill; familiarization with all standard weapons, assembly, cleaning, and utilization; rifle range qualification on the 30-caliber carbine rifle; gas mask training and procedures; physical training with obstacle course; and one week of field training.

Most often called "Mills" during his service, in compliance with military tradition and an occupant at this time of "Tent City" with other recruits, he wrote in a letter on the nineteenth: "I believe that this has been the hottest day that I can remember. We drilled and marched to-day. We march about a mile or over, I think, to the mess hall & back three times a day, that is six miles in all. Besides that, comes the regular drilling & marching." In spite of earlier complaints, he was adjusting to the routine. "We have been getting pretty good meals the last day or two. I guess I am just getting used to it though."

With basic training unexpectedly abbreviated by about two weeks, he was transferred the following day to Sheppard Field, north of Wichita Falls, Texas, where he began classes in general aviation mechanics applicable to "all types" of aircraft, according to Hank. He learned to work on airplanes and hydraulics and electronics and "any mechanical work concerning the airplane." Promoted to private first class and attending classes primarily at night, he began training to become an airplane crew chief.

"One day I realized what a fool I had been," he recalled of that time. Hank and his high school sweetheart, Nancy Risinger, had gone together for three years, and they had talked about marriage before he enlisted. Nancy wanted to get married right away, but Hank thought it was unfair to ask her to wait for him. "I knew if I got married, it'd be just a short time until I had to go in service, so I wouldn't." It was a decision he had come to regret. He called Nancy and told her, "You go to the courthouse and get a marriage license. I'm coming home this weekend and we're going to get married." Nancy, then employed as a grocery store cashier, bought her first wedding ring because Hank's meager pay of $54 per month did not permit him to pay for it.

He went AWOL and left base at 4:30 on Saturday afternoon, hitchhiking all night on Highway 82 to El Dorado, a distance of about 370 miles. "I had bad luck catching rides," Hank explained. He arrived just at sunrise on Sunday morning, October 18, 1942. After only a couple of hours sleep, he went to Nancy's home and together they went to "Sunday school" and church. Their families ate dinner together after the morning's services, and then they went to the minister's house, where Hank and Nancy were married in a simple ceremony at 2:00 that afternoon. After a brief visit with her cousin to announce the event, Hank kissed his new bride goodbye. "My daddy drove me to Texarkana and put me out." He hitchhiked back to camp and arrived just before roll call on Monday morning. "There I had gone all weekend, got married, no honeymoon, no nothing." Hank and Nancy did not see each other again for more than two weeks, when he was able to get a weekend pass and hitchhike home again.

The newlyweds had their first taste of married life at Wichita Falls, where Nancy arrived by bus on Christmas Day. "I am hoping she will stay several days. She will be about my only Christmas this year but next year we will spend it at home," Hank optimistically wrote to his mother. The couple rented a room in the home of a family who lived about 7 miles south of the base, and ate most of their meals together at the lunch counter of a Rexall drugstore located nearby. Nancy wrote to her mother-in-law, "This is the coldest place I ever saw. The wind blows all the time. Sunday Hank and I went to town, and the wind blew so hard I couldn't stand up, and we had to go in the doorway of a building and get stood up again." One day as they were shopping at the PX, Nancy and Hank were surprised to meet her uncle Elgie Risinger, who later flew cargo planes over the treacherous "Himalayan Hump" between India and China.

An 11:30 p.m. military curfew imposed a peculiar schedule on the couple. Going to bed at about five o'clock in the afternoon "so Hank can get some sleep," he then got up, ate supper, and left for camp at about 10:45. "I am by myself most of the night," Nancy explained. Once there, he slept again at the barracks ("#701/Upstairs") until time for his class, which extended from 3:00 a.m. until 11:00 a.m. Hank always wore his overcoat through the night because of the bitter cold of the unheated aircraft hangar in which classes took place. He was allowed a few additional hours off on New Year's Day, and then Nancy took the bus back to El Dorado on January 2. Following a grueling overnight hike in below-freezing temperatures as part of required field training, Hank graduated from that school on January 16.

Soon afterward, a press release that provided details was sent for publication in his hometown newspaper:

> Sheppard Field, Texas—Pfc. James H. Mills, son of Mr. and Mrs. James E. Mills of Route 1, Box 207, El Dorado, Arkansas, has graduated from an intensive course in aviation mechanics and is now prepared to blast the Axis. Sheppard Field, near Wichita Falls, Texas, is one of the many schools in the Army Air Forces Technical Training Command which trains the specialist technicians who maintain our bombers and fighter planes in perfect combat condition. He now is eligible to become crew chief on a bomber and to win a rating of corporal or sergeant.
>
> Before entering the school, he has trained at one of the basic training centers of the Air Forces Technical Training Command and learned to fight the Axis with other things besides the tools of his trade. Men trained by the Command are versed in the art of protection and offense as well as repair.

"Don't pay too much attention to what it says, it is just some free advertisement for the army," Hank reassured his mother.

A policy had recently been instated to send basic mechanics graduates to factory schools for additional specialized instructions. Hank went for that phase of training to Middle River near Baltimore, Maryland, where Glenn L. Martin Company manufactured the B-26 Marauders and provided practical experience in their maintenance and repair. He arrived on January

20, following a three-day train ride in Pullman cars, first class. His journey took him through Texas, Oklahoma, Illinois, Missouri, Kansas, Pennsylvania, Indiana, Ohio, and Maryland, passing through cities such as Kansas City, Chicago, Pittsburgh, and Baltimore. "We saw the Mississippi & other rivers frozen over & big chunks of ice flowing down the stream & breaking when they hit the pillars. We saw snow from Sunday night till last night, but there's none here. Must be too cold." He requested that his mother send heavy wool socks and one of his sweatshirts as additional protection against the frigid temperatures.

"The Army has a fenced[-]in area here where we live & there are trailers on two sides of us & the plant on the other side. The Army furnishes or rents the trailers to the workers. . . . The plant is camouflaged so well that you can't see it till you're pretty close up on it. The parking lots have big nets over them. I imagine the place is about invisible from the air." He was pleased with the accommodations. "The barracks are small & hold 34 men, and we don't sweep or anything. There are civilian janitors that sweep & keep the coal in the stove's fires; the stoves never go out. . . . The mess hall is run by civilians, the food is better than at any camp I've been in so far."

Hank was disappointed by his visit to Baltimore, which he described as dirty and "full of bums and tramps." Far more favorably impressed by Washington, DC, he wrote that he had visited the Smithsonian Institute, the Capitol building, and other buildings on Capitol Hill and had seen the White House. His view of the city and Potomac River from the observation tower on top of the Washington Monument was spectacular. Hank sent souvenirs back home from the nation's capital, including a pennant that proclaimed he was "SERVING OUR COUNTRY."

After seeing the sights, completing the Marauder factory training, and then graduating in late February, Hank received his certification as a B-26 airplane mechanics specialist.

Next, he was transferred to Rome, New York (about 15 miles northwest of Utica), where the Rome Air Depot provided advanced training in aircraft engine maintenance and repair throughout the war. A high point of that period was singer Kate Smith's broadcast of her popular radio variety program, *The Kate Smith Hour*, for an appreciative audience of GIs in a big aircraft hangar. Her stirring rendition of "God Bless America" was a favorite. Far less enjoyable was the weather. "I've heard people all my life say it won't snow because the weather's too cold. It was thirty-nine degrees below zero and snowing, so I don't believe that story about too cold to snow."

Hank quickly learned that it is never "too cold to snow" as he spent the winter attending technical schools in North Texas, Maryland, and New York. *J. H. Mills collection*

"I got paid today, my big $15.00. I have a total of about $25.50 now," he wrote in late March as training continued. By this time, Nancy had begun to receive her dependent allowance, consisting of $11.00 deducted twice monthly from Hank's pay, supplemented by $32.00 per month contributed by the government. "Well, I went up again today on the test flight. Everything works fine. I was pretty busy part of the time working on some of the electrical equipment." Hank graduated from the electrical course, designed to prepare students to maintain aircraft electrical systems, at the end of the month.

On detached service and unassigned, he spent the month of April at Hunter Field, Savannah, Georgia. "Nobody here understands our orders, why we are here or anything else. Nobody knows anything. It sure is a mess. They're trying to find out something though and until they do, they can't put us to work or anything else." He was "enjoying the southern climate very much" after enduring the miserably cold winter. "There are palm trees all over the place & green grass everywhere."

Still unassigned, Hank arrived by train ("a day coach, rough, old, dirty & smutty") at Plant Park, Tampa, Florida, on April 30, according to his Mother's Day greeting sent soon afterward. "Plant Park was originally a fair ground, one of the nicer ones with ballpark, stadium and midget automobile racetrack, and large permanent buildings. The army took it over, but it is not very well suited to be an army camp. It doesn't have the proper facilities to handle any number of men." He shared a barracks with about two hundred others. "We sleep on cots, no place to hang clothes."

After only a few days there, he reported for duty at MacDill Air Base, located 8 miles south of Tampa. Soon afterward, he was promoted to corporal and unexpectedly assigned supervisory duties. "They put me in charge of all the maintenance of the squadron on the night shift," he recalled. "I don't know why they had me do that because there were staff sergeants working under me." Hank had authority to assign work to them—"anything that was needed, although they outranked me." His natural aptitude for anything mechanical provides a probable explanation.

Although the primary purpose of the base was B-26 training during that time, the Marauders were not popular. These twin-engine medium bombers were intimidating to the pilots who operated them. Many of them considered the aircraft to be difficult to fly and land because of its short wings, fighter plane maneuverability, and high speeds required for takeoff and landing. When flown at speeds lower than those specified in the manual, the aircraft would stall out and crash. The high incidence of accidents involving early models of the B-26 earned it such nicknames as "Martin's Murderer" and "Widowmaker." Up to fifteen crashes or ditches were reported in a single thirty-day period at MacDill, prompting the exaggerated slogan "One a day in Tampa Bay." Perhaps in part because of negative publicity caused by these complaints, B-26 training was discontinued at the base a few months later.[3]

Promoted to corporal, Hank was assigned duty as a crew chief on the night shift at MacDill Air Base at Tampa, Florida. J. H. Mills collection

Hank explained that the pilots were usually young, just out of pilot's school, and they were afraid of those B-26s. As they were attempting takeoff, they would cut the throttles back when they reached the end of the runway, and it made the spark plugs misfire. "I'd tell them, 'Don't get down there on the end of that runway and cut those engines back.' I told 'em, 'Keep those engines running. Make 'em go!' Well, they were scared of those planes. It didn't matter that I was just a corporal. They did what I told 'em."

It was at about this time that movie star Ann Sothern visited the base. A versatile actress of stage, radio, and film fame, she was most popular during the war for her *Maisie* film series, in which she played a wisecracking Brooklyn showgirl who found herself in a variety of unlikely adventures. Sothern's visits to military bases were typically informal drop-ins rather than staged performances. She preferred to mingle with the GIs, sharing their chow in the mess hall, drawing articles of clothing from the supply room, and stopping by their workshops.

Nancy was with Hank in Tampa, where they spent almost five months together. They rented a comfortable room in a family's lovely home only a block from the bay and about 6 miles north of MacDill, later moving into a neighboring house when a small apartment became available. Determined to make the most of whatever time they had together, they enjoyed Sunday afternoon strolls along the bay, and they spent time with friends—particularly with Eleanor and Lloyd Jackson from Tulsa, Oklahoma. They had been married at Wichita Falls the previous November. The two men served together until the end of the war.[4] In early October, Nancy boarded a bus for her return to Arkansas when Hank received orders for yet another move, as MacDill made the transition from B-26 Marauders to B-29 Superfortress very heavy bombers.

Briefly stationed at Barksdale Field at Bossier City, Louisiana, Nancy again joined him. The base had its own slogan to illustrate the B-26's unreliable performance: "Two a day the Barksdale way." They spent about a month of uncertainty as Hank waited for orders, but with the expectation that he would soon be shipped overseas. The lodging available to them was not their dream home. "We lived in a rented place that I think was a chicken house," he reminisced. "It had a toilet with a water tank overhead, with a little chain that you pulled to flush the commode. And the floors went this way, that way, this way, that way. It wasn't safe to get up at night and walk on that floor." Their favorite outing was going to Morrison's Cafeteria in downtown Shreveport with the Jacksons.

From Barksdale, Hank was sent to Seymour Johnson Field, located southeast of Goldsboro, North Carolina. In addition to providing technical training, the base had a unit known as the Provisional Overseas Replacement Training Center that prepared officers and enlisted men for overseas duty. While there, he received transition training to familiarize him with the B-25 Mitchell medium bomber. On February 14, he (with Jackson and others) boarded a train from Goldsboro

While at Barksdale Field and waiting for orders, Hank and Nancy discovered that affordable housing was so limited that they lived in a converted chicken house. *J. H. Mills collection*

that took them to New York City. After a few days at Fort Hamilton, they boarded USS *Mission Bay*, an escort carrier bound for the China-Burma-India (CBI) theater to join in the defense against expansion of Japanese imperialism in that part of the world. The men on board knew only that they were destined for a secret location in the Far East.

Navy records reported that USS *Mission Bay* (CVE-59) and USS *Wake Island* (CVE-65) steamed from Staten Island on February 20, 1944, loaded with Army personnel and planes bound for Karachi, India (now part of Pakistan). The previous day, *Mission Bay* had received thirty-eight Army officers and 175 enlisted men and loaded fifty P-47s, fifty cases of aircraft parts, miscellaneous spare parts, and aviation supplies. The carrier steamed from Pier 14, Staten Island, at 1330 hours. *Wake Island*, moored at the US Army Port of Embarkation, Stapleton, Staten Island, had embarked twenty-seven US Army officers, 143 Army enlisted personnel, seven US Navy officers, thirty Navy enlisted personnel, and three US Marines officers, as well as fifty P-47s, boxed aviation material, and Army and Red Cross supplies. This carrier got underway at 1300 on the twentieth and rendezvoused with *Mission Bay*, which led Task Force Group 27.2 accompanied by destroyer escorts USS *Trumpeter*, USS *Straub*, and USS *Gustafson*.

Hank described *Mission Bay* as "a small aircraft carrier" that also transported the first P-47 Thunderbolts sent to the CBI. The defense of Allied airfields in India and China was a major concern because of their vulnerability to Japanese air attack, and the 14th Air Force was already short on fighters. At the request of the Army Air Force, the US Navy diverted two escort carriers from the Mediterranean to transport one hundred P-47s to India. Glenn ("Red") Burnham, another passenger aboard *Mission Bay*, described its hangar bays filled with pursuit planes. "The carriers were being used for transport only: the flight and hangar decks were loaded with P-47s," he recorded in his diary. He was assigned soon afterward to servicing the P-40s flown on missions by the 17th Fighter Squadron (Prov.), 5th Fighter Group (Prov.) of the Chinese-American Composite Wing, 14th Air Force. Burnham's unit learned that they were replacements for a CACW unit that had been lost when their ship was attacked and sunk in the Mediterranean.[5]

Fifty P-47s carried partially assembled aboard USS *Mission Bay* were among the first one hundred transported to the CBI. *National Archives and Records Administration*

Wars and Rumors of Wars

At sea for a biblical "forty days and forty nights," according to Hank's recollections, *Mission Bay* went down and around the coast to South America, crossed the Atlantic, and then steamed around the coast of Africa and up to the Arabian Sea. This circuitous route was chosen because it was less likely to attract the attention of marauding Germans than if the ship had steamed directly east across the Atlantic and then along the coast of North Africa, as was the case when the convoy that carried personnel intended for the CACW (referenced by Burnham) had been hit by Luftwaffe bombers the previous November on the day after Thanksgiving.

Accommodations were far from luxurious. Men aboard the carriers were assigned to cramped quarters with little to keep them occupied other than to read, play cards, and sleep. Closely spaced rows of bunks were stacked one above the other. Seasickness plagued many once they put out to sea, although Hank was fortunate to have never suffered from it. "Some of those men threw up their toenails," he recalled with a grin. Fierce competition ensued regarding use of the head located farther down the passageway, which soon reeked of vomit. Hank wrote some letters while he was aboard the ship, and he asked one of the sailors to mail them for him. It seems they were not sent because he never received any replies—or perhaps they were intercepted by censors.

The monotony was interrupted when the carriers crossed the equator (0° latitude, 38° W longitude, headed south) just after midnight on Tuesday, February 29, and a traditional line-crossing ceremony got underway to commemorate the occasion. It was a protracted

King Neptune, attended by his court, presides over the initiation of "pollywogs" as they prove themselves worthy to become "trusty Shellbacks." Andrew R. Allegretto stands behind "the pirate" and to the right of one of the P-47s, while Norman L. Long takes swats (but protected by a book in his pants). *A. R. Allegretto collection, courtesy of Mary Allegretto Henry*

TSgt. Robert N. Solyn's "Shellback Certificate" was granted after his initiation into "the Solemn Mysteries of the Ancient Order of the Deep" on February 29, 1944, while southbound "for a Mission of War." *R. N. Solyn collection, courtesy of Robert N. Solin*

affair that extended into the following day, when King Neptune and his court, sporting gaudy costumes, conducted a mock trial of the uninitiated. These "pollywogs" were required to undergo a series of ordeals that included taking swats before they were deemed worthy to become "trusty shellbacks." Each of the men who took part in the rite was awarded a "Shellback Certificate," and these mementos are now treasured by the families of then 2Lt. George P. ("Red") Wood, TSgt. Robert N. Solyn, and Pfc. Andrew R. Allegretto, who were also aboard. "I had one, but I don't know whatever happened to it," Hank remarked.

The convoy made its first stop for refueling and fresh provisions at Recife, Brazil, on the afternoon of March 1, and passengers were granted shore leave. Entrepreneurs, accustomed to providing services to men who had spent long periods at sea, welcomed them. As the GIs passed along the wide streets leading from the docks, prostitutes called to them from second-floor windows of the buildings from which they worked: "Come on up, boys. Come on up, boys."

Hank, who seldom passed up an opportunity for a practical joke, remembered an incident that involved another of the GIs who went ashore that day—a man from Los Angeles, California, with whom he shared quarters. "So, this Charles J. Sacky, he claims that he didn't have anything to do with any of those girls—and he drank some, but he wasn't drunk. So, when we got back to that ship, the shore patrol people accused him of being drunk and being with one of those girls." The MPs threw Sacky into a cold shower, clothes, and all, and he lost his voice. "And every time he'd say something, he'd sound like that [*whispers*]. And I'd say, 'Huh?' He'd do it again. And for about two weeks—his voice came back, and he could speak, but I had him trained. Every time he said something, I said, 'What's that?' And he'd say [*whispers*]. After he got it back, he didn't know he could talk, but I'd make him go through that, all the time, every day." After they reached Karachi, the two men were assigned to different units (Sacky to the 5th Fighter Group) and never saw each other again.

The convoy got underway again at 1640 the following evening en route to Cape Town, Union of South Africa (now Republic of South Africa), via a "great circle route." Hank recalled that just off the coast of Brazil, "All of a sudden [the destroyers] took off, and then in a minute a sub popped up and ran up an American flag. 'Hey, don't shoot me! I'm one of y'all.' Those destroyers were gonna get 'im."

The destroyer escort received orders to leave the convoy on March 5, and the carriers "commenced zig-zagging and continued during daylight hours" to avoid torpedoes from German U-boats that might be patrolling the vicinity, according to *Mission Bay*'s war diary. The carriers entered the channel at Cape Town on the morning of Sunday, March 12, and waited for a heavy fog to lift before mooring at New Basin that evening at 1820. The men were again given shore leave. "There was a big billboard as we went into town—'There will be no mixing of the races'—and they were serious," recalled Hank. Capt. Raymond L. Hodges Jr. took a tour of Cape Town. One of the attractions along the route was the home of Cecil Rhodes, creator of Oxford University's Rhodes scholarships. Hodges was served tea and scones before he reboarded the carrier.[6]

In Table Bay on the afternoon of the fourteenth, *Mission Bay* completed degaussing procedures for correction of the ship's magnetic field before getting underway again at 1700. Escort vessels of the British Royal Navy joined the carriers at Cape Town. The frigate HMS *Bann* took station screening ahead of *Wake Island*, with *Mission Bay* in column astern. The convoy rounded the Cape of Good Hope and then continued steaming along the coast as it traveled northward. A destroyer, HMS *Quadrant*, joined the escort on the nineteenth and HMS *Raider*, a patrol vessel, on the twenty-first before anchoring off Cape Diego, near the northern tip of Madagascar, at 1228 on March 22. The convoy was underway again at 1704 from Diego Suarez Bay after the refueling of escorts.

The convoy's status on the twenty-third was "Steaming as before. Zig-zagging during daylight hours." The carriers entered the channel at Karachi at 0700 on March 29 and anchored off the breakwater to await the end of a dust storm. At 1625 *Mission Bay* was "moored port side to dock, Berth 21, West Wharf" and began discharging passengers and unloading cargo. *Wake Island*, moored nearby, also disembarked passengers and offloaded cargo.[7]

It was a strange and exotic place to these Americans. Hank, as many other young men who traveled to this unfamiliar part of the world, experienced culture shock soon after arriving in Karachi. "The men had a strange custom there. Everywhere you'd see men walking around holding hands together. I wondered, what kind of place is this I've come to?"

Karachi's streets were filled with people, both Indigenous and foreign. Many of them were military, not only American but also British, Indian, Canadian, Australian, and Chinese troops. It was a city with a significant Muslim population, so activities stopped at specified times of the day while the devout unfurled prayer rugs and turned their faces toward Mecca to pray. Hank's recollections included hearing the keening of the Muslin call to prayer. "I never did like the sound of that."

Sgt. Kenneth W. Daniels of the 1st Bombardment Squadron (Prov.), 1st Bombardment Group (Prov.), Chinese-American Composite Wing, described his only visit to Karachi a few months earlier: "I drank in the sights, sounds, and smells for a few hours—camels pulling big carts through the crowded streets where sweepers crouched whisking a bundle of branches, spitting blood-like beetle-nut juice and the God-awful sound of sitar music. A sacred cow stood on the sidewalk eating from a food stand while I watched a cobra-mongoose fight, trying not to inhale the putrid odors." He was glad to get back to camp at Malir, explaining, "The air smelled much better out on the desert."[8]

CHAPTER TWO
Scorching at Malir

Originally built as a training camp by the British in 1942, when Rommel threatened to drive Montgomery's Eighth Army all the way out of the Mideast and back to India, Malir Field (24°58' N, 67°13' E) served as a subbase of the main air base at Karachi. An important feature was a staging area for equipment and supplies shipped across India by rail and then flown into China for use by Allied troops fighting against the invaders. The field featured sandbag revetments, gun emplacements, a big tin hangar originally intended for dirigibles, a stockade, a hospital, and even a Polish refugee camp.[1] A pilot's handbook gave the airfield's location as north of the Karachi Road and west of a dry riverbed. Its east–west concrete runway measured 4,899 feet long and 150 feet wide, while a northeast–southwest "fair-weather strip" extended 4,500 feet long and 600 feet wide.[2]

Malir was a "well-equipped base with several landing fields, a depot area with railway spurs, and the other physical equipment of a functioning base that could accommodate about 20,000 men, with concrete and tile barracks for about 2,000."[3] Well planned, the stucco living quarters of "H area" were austere but comfortable, with good ventilation. Glass-paned windows were always kept open during the day to catch any chance of a breeze, resulting in a coating of dust that covered all furnishings, but they were generally closed at night, when the desert's scorching heat turned chilly, and blankets were required for warmth. Doors left open invited daring jackals to dash through the buildings. Oil lamps provided lighting. Freestanding latrines and shower buildings stood conveniently near the barracks.

Officers and enlisted men had their own separate recreational clubs. Meals for all personnel were prepared and served by Indians in British open-air mess halls. Four mess halls consisted of one for American officers and another for American enlisted men, as well as for Chinese officers and Chinese enlisted men. The 1st Bomb Squadron's Sgt. Daniels reported a steady diet of biscuits and "corned willy" that was "the army's version of corned beef." He described it as "a salty delight" that was "served hashed, fried, baked, or camouflaged some other way but always tasted like corned beef."[4]

After his arrival at Karachi, Hank was also sent to the airfield located 15 miles northeast of Karachi in North Malir Cantonment, out on the fringe of the Sindh Desert. There he was attached to a military organization unlike any other in the world.

The 14th Air Force (formerly the China Air Task Force) was constituted on March 5, 1943, and activated on March 10 in Kunming, China. Claire Lee Chennault, former commander

"The Flying Tigers, famed nickname of the American volunteer Group which wrote air history in China before the United States entered the war, has been adopted as the official emblem of the AVG's successor, the Flying Tigers of the US Army 14th Air Force in China. The emblem is shown here as it was presented to Maj. Gen. Claire Chennault, commanding general, 14th Air Force, *center*, by Sgt. Howard Arnegard, its designer, and Sgt. Robert Naves, Hampton, New Jersey. It consists of a winged Bengal tiger, with bared teeth and outthrust claws, on a circular field of blue, beneath the star of the US Air Force." *National Archives and Records Administration photograph, published on Fold3, used by permission*

of the renowned American Volunteer Group that gained fame as the "Flying Tigers," was promoted to major general and appointed commander of the 14th Air Force, whose insignia featured a winged orange Bengal tiger with a star above its back on an azure background. The insignia was adopted in October 1943 with Chennault's approval and endorsement. Members of the 14th Air Force and of the CATF that preceded it continued to be known popularly as "Flying Tigers," although they were not a part of his original AVG. A "friendly rivalry" always existed between the original Flying Tigers and the Flying Tigers of the 14th Air Force as to who had "bragging rights" to the name.[5]

John H. Yee, interpreter for the AVG, can be considered the best authority on the subject. He explained the origin of the name soon after the arrival in December 1941 of the American airmen: "For the first time in their lives, the people of Kunming witnessed something beyond their wildest dreams as the Japanese killer bombers were shot down before their own eyes. They clapped their hands and jumped for joy. A local news reporter, so inspired by this unprecedented heroic event in reporting the air combat, described the AVG planes as acting like 'Flying Tigers in pursuit of a Japanese flock of sheep.'"[6] Taken from the Chinese newspaper article, the term *Fei Hu* was used as a simile to praise the prowess of the American aircrews and was not originally intended as a proper name applied to any specific unit, although that is how it came to be perceived by some.

Military forces in China at that time were divided into two hostile camps: the Nationalist army of the pro-Western Kuomintang government, commanded by Generalissimo Chiang Kai-shek, whose headquarters was in Chungking, and the Communist "Red" Army of Mao Tse-tung (Mao Zedong), based to the northeast in Shensi Province. A latent civil war between the Nationalists and Communists limited efforts to protect Chinese territory from foreign invasion. Although the two factions had agreed to fight the Japanese instead of each other, the ensuing alliance was at best a troubled truce, and attempts to coordinate their efforts against the invaders were markedly unsuccessful.

By this time, the Nationalist Chinese army—at war against Japan's superior troops since 1937—constituted a numerically depleted, poorly equipped, inadequately trained, and ineptly led fighting force. Its equally deficient air force, in which pilot's wings were awarded on the basis of political or familial connections rather than ability to fly, was incapable of providing adequate support to the troops opposing the occupying forces on the ground in "the Second Sino-Japanese War," as it was called in China.

For the purpose of rehabilitating the Chinese air force fighting under Generalissimo Chiang, head of the Republic of China, and providing good will and understanding between the Chinese and Americans for the future, Chennault proposed that an operational training unit be established in India and operated by the 14th Air Force for the purpose of training Chinese fighter and bomber crews for combat operations. In addition, he suggested that ROCAF mechanics, under AAF supervision, assemble the aircraft that were to be used, and that Chinese combat and maintenance crews train at the OTU with the units to which they were to be assigned. On completion of the training of a complement, the plan called for the American and Chinese officers who had acted as instructors to then serve as group, squadron, and flight commanders of the combat unit.

The plan was approved, and the assembling of personnel and equipment began. Under the direction of the Chinese-American Operational Training Unit (Provisional), the 1st Bombardment Group (Provisional) and 3rd Fighter Group (Provisional) were activated on July 31, 1943. Malir Airdrome, on the outskirts of Karachi, was chosen as the site of the OTU because planes and gasoline were more readily available there than in China. The city's location on the coast of the Arabian Sea, with its two large ports, allowed the Allies to ship equipment, supplies, and troops for use in the CBI.

Old-model P-40s and B-25s no longer of service for tactical deployment were brought in for use as trainers. Additional B-25s from the United States and P-40s from North Africa were later assigned. In early July, Chennault reported that Chinese and American personnel were arriving at Karachi and that the OTU was expected to be ready on August 5. According to the proposed schedule, the OTU would turn out eight fighter squadrons and four medium-and-light-bombardment squadrons, together with three group and one wing headquarters by March 15, 1944. The training program began as scheduled and was well underway by September 1.[7]

The Chinese-American Composite Wing (Provisional), organized under code name "Lotus," was formally activated at Malir on October 1, 1943. It was "composite" in that its aircraft comprised both fighters and bombers. Although designated as a wing, it never flew as a single unit; instead, its operational units were often billeted at bases located hundreds of miles apart across India and China. Originally commanded by Col. Winslow C. Morse, the CACW eventually consisted of the 1st Bombardment Group, equipped with B-25 Mitchells (two-engine medium bombers), and the 3rd and 5th Fighter Groups, equipped with P-40s, many of them painted with the iconic "shark mouth" of the original Flying Tigers. Although they were most often called "Warhawks," the toothy grin of these P-40 pursuit planes earned them the preferred name of "Sharks" in the CACW.

Each group was made up of four squadrons each: the 1st Bomb Group of the 1st, 2nd, 3rd, and 4th Bomb Squadrons; the 3rd Fighter Group of the 7th, 8th, 28th, and 32nd Fighter Squadrons; and the 5th Fighter Group of the 17th, 26th, 27th, and 29th Fighter Squadrons. These were Republic of China Air Force squadrons that had been assigned to the CACW and reorganized according to American military standards. Duplicate Chinese and American commands were established both for bomber and fighter groups. Col. John A. Hilger, second in command on Jimmy Doolittle's famous raid in April 1942, was chosen as the 1st Bomb Group's American commander, while Maj. Lee Hsueh-yen (also in records as Hsueh-yian) became the Chinese cocommander. Because he had been shot down in the Tokyo raid and the 14th Air Force had a policy that prohibited airmen from flying combat missions after they had returned through enemy territory, Hilger was replaced by Lt. Col. Irving L. ("Twig") Branch on September 21, 1943.[8]

The CACW's planes and other equipment were supplied through Lend-Lease. Authorized through an act of Congress and signed into law on March 11, 1941, the program supplied materiel and services to America's allies. Between its inception and the end of the war in September 1945, $50.1 billion worth of supplies were shipped to various theaters of operation around the world, and the Republic of China eventually became the recipient of $1.6 billion worth of these supplies and services.[9]

Chinese pilots, bombardiers, and navigators were trained in the United States before being returned for service in the CACW, which, although officially part of the Chinese air force, was administratively assigned to the 14th Air Force. These airmen, many of whom had been recruited as students at Chinese universities, were "the cream" and took great pride in being chosen for this elite organization. The wing's operational units, fighter and bombardment, were jointly commanded both by American and Chinese air force officers, and its aircraft were jointly manned by American and Chinese pilots and aircrewmen. Because the Chinese owned the wing's aircraft, each bore the Chinese Nationalist emblem, the blue-and-white twelve-pointed Kuomintang sun.

A binational unit such as this had never been attempted before. An Air Force press release found among CACW records explained the concept. "In the composite wing, Americans will not fight as units for the Chinese air force as the AVG did, but actually fly side by side with the Chinese." It explained that some planes would have American pilots with Chinese crews, but most would be flown by all-Chinese crews. "Occasionally, an American will be in the lead element, at other times in the wing elements, the idea being to give the Chinese squadron and group leaders the latest 'know-how' in tactics with American aircraft and to give them training in actual combat under the best American direction."

Lt. Col. T. Alan Bennett, in command of the 3rd Fighter Group ("Al's Assassins"), praised the Chinese airmen, stating, "You couldn't find a finer bunch of fliers anywhere. We think those guys are so good we're staking our lives on it. Personally, I'll go anywhere with them." He went on to explain, "This is, after all, in the nature of a great experiment, and it must not fail, and we know it won't fail as far as the human element is concerned." The intention was to eventually turn the unit over to the Chinese after they had become sufficiently experienced to operate without the Americans, but this goal had not been attained by the end of the war.[10]

Chennault's plan was for one bombardment squadron to be trained simultaneously with two fighter squadrons over a period of six weeks, with the Americans acting as mentors to the Chinese. When those three squadrons had completed their training, they would move to China as three additional squadrons began training. This process would continue until a bombardment group of four squadrons and two fighter groups with four squadrons each had been brought to combat readiness. Group after group of Chinese and American pilots and crews came into Malir from China and America. These men spent hundreds of hours flying B-25s and P-40s and in studying military tactics, motors, and equipment. American GIs in khaki fatigues worked side by side in a cordial atmosphere with the Chinese, clad in their dark-blue work suits.

This hitherto untried experiment of coordinating the efforts of two widely dissimilar national groups was not without challenges. Differing languages presented the most obvious and immediate difficulty, but complete disparities in ideology, philosophy, and culture also had to be addressed. "The blunt American manners clashed sharply with the Chinese ideas on face saving[,] and both Chinese and Americans found they had to modify their manners in order to get good results. Many Chinese pilots had to be persuaded that it was not cowardly to bail out of a badly damaged plane and that crashing with their plane served no purpose," according to a CACW report written early in the venture. Maj. Don Hummel, formerly an attorney in Tucson and now wing intelligence officer as well as historical officer, explained: "We mess around a bit in the wide chasm between two languages and two civilizations, but on the whole, we get along beautifully and are saved by a sense of humor on both sides for our mutual blunderings." He blamed the contrast between the Americans' drive and need for immediate results with the Chinese tradition of patience and "politeness" for the misunderstandings that did occasionally arise. Although both nationalities made efforts to accommodate their counterparts in the interest of achieving a common goal, some problems remained unresolved at the end of the war.

The first squadron that began training with the 1st Bombardment Group (M)(P) after its organization was designated at completion as the 2nd Bombardment Squadron (M)(P). Information that came in from numerous sources as the squadron's training neared an end forewarned that additional air strength would be required in China very soon. The Japanese occupation of the Asian mainland continued to move forward, and threats on all fronts appeared increasingly ominous.

Enemy reinforcements had arrived in the Canton–Hong Kong area and in "Indo-China" (now more commonly written as Indochina), while a sudden increase in activity around Hankow and farther north was also observed. In Burma and western China, Japanese reinforcements were making themselves felt in a twin drive from Myitkyina and Teng-chung toward the north and east. Should the Japanese launch offensives simultaneously in all these sectors, the 14th Air Force would be hard pressed to cling to its limited sphere of operation. If the Japanese were to launch drives south toward Changsha, northwest from Canton–Hong Kong, and northeast from Indochina, the eastern bases might be jeopardized, and if a drive across the Salween succeeded or if a northwestern drive from Indochina materialized, Kunming itself would be in peril. Although enemy land offensives had been checked in the past, the small air strength of the Americans would be spread too thin if several of them should come at the same time, and Chinese armies would be incapable of stopping any determined Japanese drives.[11]

The 2nd Bombardment Squadron of the 1st Bombardment Group and the 28th and 32nd Fighter Squadrons of the 3rd Fighter Group received movement orders on October 17, 1943, and became the wing's first increment to move to China. They flew their planes over "the Hump"—the name given by Allied pilots to the eastern end of the Himalayan Mountains—to provide air support for Chiang Kai-shek's ground forces in accordance with Chennault's plan, and it was not long before they went into action.

The 2nd Bomb Squadron ("Avengers"), with six B-25s under the command of Maj. Tom Foley, became the first CACW unit to reach China, arriving at Yangkai in South China on October 25, 1943. Within a few days the next contingent of three bombers, led by the group commander, Lt. Col. Branch, followed, and finally the remaining three. The CACW officially entered combat on Thursday, November 4, 1943, when three 2nd Bomb Squadron B-25s flew on a mission out of Erh Tong airfield at Kweilin down to the coast. In a joint raid with Mitchells of the 11th ("Sky Dragons") Bomb Squadron, 341st Bomb Group, 69th Composite Wing, 14th Air Force, this was a sea sweep to hit Japanese shipping at Swatow Harbor. Maj. Foley successfully bombed and strafed an enemy cargo vessel and sank it.

The November 12, 1943, issue of *CBI Roundup* praised the successful initial efforts:

14TH AIR FORCE HQ.—During the past week, the 14th Air Force rained destruction upon Japanese troops, installations, shipping, and Japanese-occupied towns. As a result of these missions, during which the newly arrived Chinese-American Composite Wing participated for the first time on November 4, six large enemy vessels were sunk and one more was probably sunk. On a raid against the Swatow Airdrome, three Jap fighters and one bomber on the ground were damaged.[12]

Unfortunately, this date also marked the first CACW bomber crew to be lost. A B-25D piloted by Lt. Kao of the 2nd Bomb Squadron was damaged by ground fire while attacking enemy cargo vessels in Swatow Harbor. Later that night, Lt. Kao's plane crashed south of Liuchow, killing all on board. No given name was provided in the 1st Bomb Group's monthly historical report, but he was perhaps 1st Lt. Kuo Huan-chang, on flying status in October 1943.

Other CACW squadrons did not remain long at Malir after training but moved on to China, according to Chennault's schedule. The 1st Bomb Squadron completed training and crossed "the Hump" to join the 2nd Bomb Squadron in mid-January 1944. With its B-25s flew P-40s assigned to the 7th and 8th Fighter Squadrons, 3rd Fighter Group. The 4th Bomb Squadron, with the 26th and 29th Fighter Squadrons of the recently activated 5th Fighter Group, was the next to complete training and make the move on March 17.

US newspapers and theater service publications persisted in their praise of CACW efforts and reported intensive activity over China battle areas. As CACW aircrews racked up success after success, *CBI Roundup* reported that two squadrons of Mitchell medium bombers had sent to the bottom 103 Japanese ships totaling 195,000 tons up to February 7, quoting from an announcement by 14th Air Force Headquarters. "The squadrons that set up this number of watery graves for the Nipponese vessels were the 'Sky Dragons,' which accounted for 73 totaling 113,800 tons, and the 'Avengers,' who got 30 for a mark of 81,200 tons. These do not include ships damaged and probably sunk."

The article further declared, "Jan. 24 turned out to be 'the day' for the 'Avengers.' They sank six ships, including one gunboat, a tender and four medium-sized merchant ships and probably sank a large freighter." Lt. Mark Seacrest, whose prowess benefited the 3rd Bomb Squadron soon afterward, was credited with six confirmed kills.[13]

Beginning on February 24, Mitchells of the recently arrived 1st Bomb Squadron added their might to that of the Avengers and Sky Dragons, initially concentrating their combined firepower on Kiukiang's marshaling yards and warehouses. Throughout the winter and spring of 1944, CACW bombers and fighters in China struck repeatedly at Japanese installations in Hankow, Wuchang, Kiukiang, Hong Kong, Canton, and any other targets they could reach within their limited range. The wing's various units were later assigned to locations throughout south-central and southwestern China from which they could launch their attacks. Throughout the war, the focus of B-25 operations in the CBI remained assault on noncivilian targets such as bridges, airfields, truck convoys, and ships used to move enemy supplies. The effectiveness of the 14th Air Force, whose successes earned it the moniker "the Fighting Fourteenth," prompted the Japanese to take more-drastic measures against the Allied forces in China, while the hard-pressed Chinese armies continued to rely upon Chennault's units for their airpower.

On February 22, 1944, while other elements of the 1st Bomb Group were making a name for themselves in China, the Third Bombardment Squadron (Prov.) was activated according to Paragraph #2 of General Order #3, Headquarters Chinese-American Composite Wing

(Prov.), dated October 9, 1943. Maj. Lyle L. Shepard (wing executive officer) was initially placed in command, and Cpl. Charles W. Richards (administrative and technical clerk) was attached as the only enlisted man. On March 1, SSgts. George Gruber (AAF radio mechanic) and Jack Holmes (supply NCO), along with Sgt. William T. Earley Jr. (personnel NCO), were the first to arrive for duty at Malir.

Capt. Chester M. Conrad arrived later that day. Known as "Chet" back home in Sikeston, Missouri, where he completed training as an aviation cadet at the Missouri Institute of Aeronautics in 1941, Conrad had picked up the sobriquet "Coondog" somewhere along the way (his radio call sign, according to Hank). Capt. Conrad, former 1st Bomb Group operations officer at Kweilin, assumed command of the squadron, and Maj. Shepard and Cpl. Richards were relieved from duty and reassigned to CACW headquarters. Cpl. Richards was promoted to sergeant that same day, and Maj. Shepard to lieutenant colonel on April 1.

Arriving with Conrad were Capts. John C. Hinrichs Jr. (supply officer) and Thomas S. Simpson (B-25 pilot / flight leader), along with 1Lts. Louis F. Graves Jr. (navigator) and George C. Cunningham (bombardier). All of them had been with the 1st Bomb Group since soon after its activation.

Appointed officer in charge of the New London State Armory, Hinrichs had volunteered for service in the Connecticut State Guard while also working as zone manager for Mack Motor Truck Company at the Hartford branch. In June 1941, he accepted a direct commission in the Air Forces. He had been overseas since June 1942. Before transfer to the 3rd Bomb Squadron, Hinrichs had served as group materiels, utilities, transportation, and mess officer, as well as engineering and technical inspector. His organizational and leadership skills made him invaluable in organizing the new squadron. Under his direction, quarters were secured, and orderly and supply rooms were set up.

ROC pilots, bombardiers, and navigators, many of them States-trained, began arriving that same day, while Chinese enlisted men remained at Karachi Airdrome undergoing training in the fundamentals of aerial gunnery and engineering. Capt. Sung Shou-chon (Song Shou-zhuang) (X-221) commanded Chinese personnel in the absence of the squadron cocommander, Capt. Wu Ch'ao-chen (X-510), who served with the 2nd Squadron until he received orders for transfer.

Others arrived for duty over the next few days, including 1Lts. Eugene H. Dorr Jr. (armament officer) and Charles D. Miles (B-25 pilot / flight leader); MSgt. Donald W. Grant (airplane flight chief); TSgts. John P. Hanrahan (AAF radio operator) and Frederick C. Libolt (A/P instrument specialist); SSgts. Joseph N. Shock (AAF radio mechanic) and James R. Summerville (A/P electrical specialist); Sgts. Paul E. Haines and Charlie H. Hoyle Jr. (both A/P armorers) and Ewell F. Wilkerson (A/P crew chief); and Cpl. William G. Duffin (administrative and technical clerk) on the second and third. Assigned on March 4 were 1Lts. William L. Daniels and Mark T. Seacrest (both classified as B-25 pilot / flight leader); MSgt. Grady B. Fuller (line chief); SSgts. Homer L. Chasse (AAF supply technician) and William Meikle (administrative and technical clerk); Sgts. William L. ("Shorty") Armstrong (AAF radio operator) and Frank T. Jakubasz and Maynard W. Rieks (both A/P crew chiefs); and Cpl. John P. Barge (A/P and engine mechanic). They brought with them orders for the promotion of Capt. Conrad to major and 1Lts. Daniels, Graves, and Cunningham to captains.

SSgt. James E. McCann (section leader) joined the squadron on March 5. SSgt. Gruber was reclassified as supply NCO to assist Capt. Hinrichs on the following day, and Sgt. Earley became the squadron's first sergeant at about the same time. Each man's classification was designated in squadron records by a "Service Specialty Number" or "SSN" (also called a "Military Occupational Specialty" or "MOS" code). These classifications were based primarily upon their preenlistment experience and specialized training after enlistment.

Earley's hometown newspaper praised him for "skipping three ranks in one leap" by his promotion from sergeant "over the ranks of technician 3rd class, staff sergeant, and technical sergeant" to first sergeant while serving with "Chenault's [sic] Tigers." With the rank of corporal during training at Ft. Logan, Colorado, he had achieved "a very high scholastic standing, and it was from the commanding officer . . . that his parents had the great pleasure of receiving two letters commending his excellent scholarship." After his arrival in India while attached to the 2nd Bomb Squadron, "Bill began the study of Chinese and now both speaks and writes in that difficult language."[14]

His duty as first sergeant was to act as deputy to Maj. Conrad, serving as intermediary between him and his men. As administrative and clerical assistant to the commanding officer, he handled routine correspondence and organizational records. Other responsibilities included coordinating the efforts of all NCOs, assisting and instructing them in the performance of their work, as well as leading the men in close- and extended-order drills whenever necessary. Earley's skillful management proved essential in keeping the squadron running smoothly through the months that followed.

Delays in the arrival of Task Force Group 27.2 had brought about revisions to the squadron's organization. According to the 3rd Squadron's first official monthly historical report, it was necessary to bring back American personnel from China because of "failure of designated personnel to leave United States in sufficient time to arrive and train the Chinese personnel." The 1st Bomb Group's report provided further details. Following "an animated discussion" between Cols. Morse and Branch on February 12 at Erh Tong, they decided to assign personnel from the group and the 2nd Bomb Squadron for duty in the 3rd Squadron because "original personnel coming over by boat will be tardy for training." Although originally intended for temporary assignment, many of these men thereafter remained with the squadron.

Because of the delayed arrival of some necessary personnel, the officers were required to perform supplemental duties. Capt. Cunningham was assigned, in addition to his other responsibilities, as temporary adjutant; Capt. Graves as censor and schools' officer, squadron historian, and public relations officer; and Lt. Miles, an airplane mechanic in Kansas before enlistment, as engineering officer and flight leader.

On March 7, Capt. Wu received orders to lead twenty-one Chinese officers and enlisted men from CACW HQ at Kweilin to Kunming and then on to Karachi. These included 1Lts. Mao Shang-tsen and Cheng Fong-yuh; 2Lt. Kuo Chien-tze; Warrant Officers Tsao Chi-fan, Chu Tao, Cheng Yuen-lung, and Tso Kuo-tung; and Sgts. Ho Gei-hung, Pao Teh, Kwang Dsao, Liang Mao-hwa, Hwang I, Lui Yeh-chi, Yei Chien-shun, Yuan Shi-seng, Chen Shui-I, Wang Tsen-chen, Wang Tze-yu, Lee Wei-seng, Chang Kuo-ying, Chow Geng-shun, Lui Chi-tzang, and Tsu Chih-wang. By separate order, Sgts. Cheng Tze-lok, Lee Sin-min, Kwan Chun-cheong, Wu Chu-ching, So Chai-yok, and Yo Kwok-shun proceeded by the same route. Ground school began the same day, using personnel from the squadron and the OTU.

Maj. Chester M. Conrad and Capt. Wu Ch'ao-chen, squadron cocommanders, stroll through the sand in front of the control tower at Malir as American airmen begin training their Chinese counterparts. *R. N. Solyn collection, courtesy of Robert N. Solin*

Capt. Thomas S. Simpson was an aviation cadet in 1942. He went on to establish a formidable record of service in the Chinese-American Composite Wing, serving with distinction in the 2nd, 1st, and finally 3rd Bomb Squadrons. *T. S. Simpson collection, courtesy of Larry Simpson*

An Iowa farmer before enlistment, Maynard W. Rieks was attached to the 2nd Bomb Squadron at its activation on September 9, 1943, as a B-25 mechanic and later as an aerial gunner. Typical of those who survived combat, he appeared uncomfortable when his sons asked about his experiences, but they remembered a few stories. One was about a transport plane on which he was scheduled to travel for R&R at Bombay. Rieks boarded and was ready for takeoff. However, because it was determined that the plane was overloaded, he deplaned to wait for a later flight. Word came down afterward that the plane on which he was scheduled to fly had crashed into a mountainside as it crossed the Himalayas, and all aboard perished. He felt "survivor's guilt" and always regretted the loss of his friends. *M. W. Rieks collection, courtesy of Bruce Ries*

Capt. Simpson, appointed squadron operations officer, recorded his experiences from January 14 through November 4, 1944, in the small leather-bound book titled "My Stretch in the Service." It was a gift from his wife, Marge, who lived with their young son in Santa Monica, California. The diary is an essential source of information for this period. Simpson wrote that he flew from Miami along a route that included stops at Puerto Rico, West Indies; Georgetown, British Guyana; Natal, Brazil; Ascension Island in the Atlantic Ocean; Accra, Gold Coast (Ghana); and Khartoum, Egypt. He arrived at Karachi in August 1943, along with Captains Conrad, Hinrichs, Cunningham, Graves, and others destined for service with the 1st Bomb Group. Whereas most of the officers traveled by air transport along a similar route, enlisted men often made the long trip by sea. However, according to records of Sgt. Rieks, he departed the US on July 21 and arrived in Karachi on July 29, 1943, suggesting that he made the trip by air. When 1Sgt. Earley took a similar journey, also by air, "he experienced something that he will never forget—hitting an air pocket and dropping 4,000 feet all at once."[15]

From January through August 1942, Simpson had received his early training in Texas: primary flight school in Corsicana, basic training at Moore Field in Mission, and advanced training at Goodfellow in San Angelo, where he received his wings and commission as a second lieutenant. After his arrival in the CBI, he was assigned first to the 2nd Bomb Squadron in August 1943 and then transferred to the 1st Bomb Squadron in October. As pilot of a B-25H, Simpson was credited with sinking two 50-foot vessels at Wuhu on February 25, 1944, soon before his transfer back to Malir on Leap Day to join the 3rd Bomb Squadron.

He wrote, "All together we had 15 officers and 38 enlisted men" assigned to the 3rd Squadron during those early weeks. It was Simpson's opinion that the primary reason for returning personnel from the 1st Bomb Group to Malir was the lack of facilities, supplies, and gas in China.[16] It was a situation that plagued Chennault's air force throughout the war.

Some of these men had served in other theaters of war before being transferred to the CBI. Most of them were intended for service in the 402nd Bomb Group (Medium), which had been activated on May 19, 1943, at Kunming but never became operational and never had any squadrons or aircraft assigned. It was disbanded on July 31, 1943, and all personnel were reassigned to other units. Conrad, Simpson, Seacrest, Cunningham, Dorr, Graves, Hinrichs, Seacrest, Daniels, Miles, Libolt, Shock, Summerville, Jakubasz, Wilkerson, Hanrahan, Holmes, Hoyle, Haines, Duffin, Fuller, Chasse, Gruber, Armstrong, Grant, Earley, Rieks, McCann, Wilkerson, and Meikle were among those who were attached to the 1st Bomb Group from the 402nd. Many of them had reported for duty to the 2nd Staging Squadron, Staging Area Replacement Depot, at the Floridian Hotel in Miami Beach, Florida, in late July and early August in preparation for their move to Karachi.

Lt. William L. Daniels (*top left*) served initially with the 2nd Bomb Squadron. Here he is with Lt. Guy H. ("Feets") Williams (*front left*), Lt. Edwin ("Rags") Ragland (*front right*), and an unidentified captain before his move to the 3rd Bomb Squadron to assist in training the squadron's Chinese student-pilots. *Edwin Ragland collection, courtesy of Terri R. Goodhart*

Lt. Charles D. Miles (*left*), another original member of the 2nd Bomb Squadron, was called "Howie" by the other officers. He was attached for temporary duty to the 3rd Bomb Squadron to facilitate training of the Chinese airmen when personnel intended for service were delayed in their arrival because of the extended time necessary to steam around the coast of Africa to avoid enemy attack. He returned to the 2nd Squadron on May 24, 1944, according to the 1st Bomb Group historical report. *W. L. Daniels collection, courtesy of Richard Daniels*

Scorching at Malir

These were seasoned airmen and technicians who brought their considerable experience and expertise to form the nucleus of this new squadron. Many of them had already proved themselves in aerial combat. In late November 1943, Lt. Miles was credited with damaging a 225-foot freighter, and Lts. Seacrest and Daniels with sinking a 300-foot passenger-freighter at Amoy Harbor. Capt. Daniels's B-25D received a hit in the hydraulic system, causing the wheels to partially extend. He flew on to the base at Namyung and circled until his fuel supply was depleted, when he made a forced landing. He was later awarded the Air Medal, presented either for a single incident of meritorious achievement while participating in aerial flight or for completion of twenty-five combat missions.

The citation that accompanied it praised Daniels for meritorious achievement in aerial combat between November 25, 1943, and February 13, 1944, in which period he participated in twenty-five missions. On his first mission in China, he took part as pilot, with thirteen other bombers, in a low-level attack on a Japanese airdrome. The formation destroyed forty-six enemy planes on the ground and damaged hangars and warehouses. "The actions and conduct of Capt. Daniels have brought credit to his own record and are in accordance with the fine traditions of the Army Air Forces."

Daniels's extensive experience qualified him for instructing the 3rd Squadron's Chinese pilots. After graduating in 1934 from Riverside Military Academy in Gainesville, Georgia, he had studied aeronautical engineering at the University of Alabama. He was employed by Eastern Airlines as a pilot before entering military service in August 1940. He originally served as a second lieutenant with the 2nd Armored Division at Fort Benning, Georgia, but transferred to the Air Corps in December 1941, when America entered the war. After completing primary training at Pine Bluff, Arkansas, basic at Randolph Field, and advanced at Kelly Field (both at San Antonio, Texas), he graduated with Class 42G and received his wings in August 1942. Postgraduate training was at Ellington Field, south of Houston, Texas. Beginning in September 1942, he was an instructor with the B-25 Operational Training Unit (OTU) at Greenville, South Carolina. Daniels was sent to the CBI and assigned to the 2nd Bomb Squadron in July 1943, and he had been training and flying with that squadron's Chinese pilots until reassignment to the 3rd Squadron.

When later asked to describe his most memorable wartime experience, he replied:

It was the Thanksgiving day, 1944 mission over Shinchiku, Formosa; or perhaps the night someone tommy-gunned through the ridge pole of our hostel quarters at Erh-Tong, much to the concern of the fighter squadron billeted where the slugs were falling; or was it the two B-25 sea sweeps with Squadron Commander Foley with five of the seven Japanese fighters chalked up and the only comment from the General being, "Why not all seven?"—but that's another story.[17]

Maj. Conrad had repeatedly proved his capabilities before assuming command of the 3rd Squadron. In December 1943, then Capt. Conrad and Lt. Seacrest had participated in a mission on which they successfully blasted the docks at Kowloon near Hong Kong. In January 1944, Conrad took off from Erh Tong in a B-25H to search for enemy shipping south along the coast. Near Maoming, he encountered a Japanese Sally bomber and a fierce exchange of gunfire ensued, with TSgt. Hanrahan operating the top turret guns. Because tracers from both turrets hit the Sally and it apparently never pulled up after diving away from the B-25, Conrad and his crew claimed it as probably destroyed. Hanrahan received credit for the kill,

MSgt. John P. Hanrahan, the 3rd Squadron's communications chief, was credited with shooting down a Japanese bomber as he was operating the top turret guns on a mission to Kowloon while serving in the 2nd Bomb Squadron. *R. N. Solyn collection, courtesy of Robert N. Solin*

qualifying him for membership in the "Pistol Packin' Papas": those members of the bomber group credited with shooting down an enemy aircraft.

During this same period, Lt. Graves was navigator on a low-level bombing mission flown by Lt. Col. Branch against targets at Yochow. Graves was awarded the Purple Heart after he received a slight wound to his forehead when the Mitchell's Plexiglas nose was shattered by flak from an enemy freighter.

On a separate mission, Sgt. Armstrong's Purple Heart, presented after his return to the States, was the result of his being knocked unconscious and receiving a 1-inch cut to his brow when the Plexiglas dome of the plane's turret was shattered by antiaircraft (AA) fire from a Japanese gunboat.

American enlisted men were paid for the first time on April 10. Chinese personnel attached to the squadron on the following day included two captains, thirty-seven first lieutenants, fifteen second lieutenants, six sublieutenants, and seventy-eight enlisted men (names not specified in the squadron history but likely including Capt. Wu and the men who moved with him from Kweilin). Col. Frank E. Rouse, in command of the 5th Fighter Group, acting for the wing and with temporary authority over the 3rd Squadron, called a meeting of American officers who were to work with both of the next two fighter squadrons (the 17th and 27th) and the bombardment squadron. Topics of discussion were transportation, training, and supply problems. On March 12, Sgts. Budd W. Evitts (administrative NCO) and Joseph W. Mroskey, Pfcs. Herman L. Burton and Stanley B. Rickman, and Pvt. Jack A. Trout (these four A/P and engine mechanics) joined from the 5th Fighter Group.

Orders issued for the transfer of Cpl. Harold G. Sarver and Pvt. Walter C. Egdorf at the same time were rescinded on March 18. Sarver served with the 4th Bomb Squadron for only about two more months, when a two-plane sea sweep from Erh Tong at Kweilin to the vicinity of Hong Kong was off on May 12. A 1st Bomb Squadron Mitchell piloted by 1Lt. Guy H. ("Feets") Williams led, and Sarver was in position as tail gunner of the following 4th Squadron plane flown by 1Lt. Leonard G. Shepard, a former Royal Air Force pilot.

Lt. Charles J. Portaluppi, the 4th Squadron's historical officer, described the tragedy. Having reached the South China Sea, they "searched fruitlessly for some time, the visibility being quite bad due to low ceiling and scattered rain." At approximately one o'clock they finally sighted a lone boat and decided to attack it. "Not until he had passed over the vessel, did Lt. Williams realize that they had made contact with either a Japanese destroyer or a gun boat. (Naval intelligence later tentatively identified it as a gun boat.) Lt. Shepard came down to attack in Lt. Williams' wake, but as he flew over the vessel at skip[-]bombing height, his right wing was either shot off by enemy anti-aircraft fire or sheared off by the mast of the gun boat." The plane fell into the sea in two parts, both of which "burned fiercely" for a few moments and then sank. With Lt. Shepard, TSgt. Alonzo H. Kerlin, Sgt. William A. Grimes, Cpl. Harold G. Sarver, and SLt. (Sublieutenant) Wu Wen Mo also lost their lives. The remains of all crew members were determined to be unrecoverable, and all were posthumously awarded the Purple Heart.

On the nineteenth, twenty-three Chinese personnel were attached from the 4th Squadron. Included were 2nd Lts. Huang Hsiung-sheng (serial number X-815) and Yang Hsin-kuo (X-816), as well as SLts. Chang Chang-keng (X-817), Chang Chi-lung (X-818), Chang Kwang-lu (X-819), Chen Chang-shiang (X-820), Cheng Yung-koen (X-821), Chiang Tung (X-822), Feng Hu-tao (X-823), Hsu In-kwei (X-824), Hu Tze-cheng (X-825), In Yen-san (X-826), Kiu Kwang-shih (X-827), Kuo Tung-I (X-828), Lin Yu-chow (X-829), Liu Peng-chung (X-830), Shiong Shu-kien (X-831), Tu Kai-mu (X-832), Tung Shih-liang (X-833), Wang Yung-siu (X-834), Wu Pao-yi (X-835), Yen Pao-san (X-836), and Yu Yu-tsai (X-837). Because most of these pilots had been trained in the States, ground schools for them were "abbreviated."

According to the squadron historical officer, navigators and bombardiers bore the brunt of the training, receiving instructions in navigation, bombardment, gunnery, intelligence, and other necessary skills. Among the navigators who arrived during this period was 1Lt. Ting Cheng-liang (丁振亮) (X-275), known to the Americans as "Daniel." Because he had attended a Christian missionary school in Shanghai and spoke fluent English, he acted as interpreter during training at Malir as well as in other situations when it was required.

Ting had come to the 3rd Squadron from the CAF and was stationed at Liangshan Airfield before his move to Malir. When his squadron received orders to move to India, he sent a message by telephone to his wife, "Lucy," a nurse at a hospital in Chengtu's city center. With her was their year-old son Cheng, since no daycare was available, and other nurses shared the responsibility of caring for him when she was busy with her professional duties. When she received the message, she was determined to see her husband before he left, so the resourceful young woman immediately found a babysitter for her child and hired a *hwagan* (similar to a sedan chair but made of bamboo). Conveyed by two coolies, she traveled about 270 miles eastward to Liangshan, much of the route along narrow mountain paths, so she could bid

Lt. Ting Cheng-liang ("Daniel") came to the 3rd Squadron from the Chinese air force as a navigator-bombardier. Because he was fluent in English, he also served as a translator whenever necessary. Here he proudly displays the "skunk patch" on his jacket, although the skunk is not indigenous to China and few had ever seen the animal. *Ting C. L. collection, courtesy of David Ting*

Lt. Tu Kai-mu was one of the Chinese university students recruited for pilot's training in the US, and he went on to establish an impressive combat record. His account of service in the 3rd Bomb Squadron forms a vital part of this history. *Courtesy of Tu Kai-mu*

farewell to her husband. When she arrived at the base and asked where she might find him, someone pointed to the sky and told her that he was "there in the airplane squadrons just taking off." Lucy realized she was too late. Overhead she saw the formation of airplanes, heading south toward Burma on their way to India. Despondent, she returned to Chengtu, where she and her son lived with her brother until their family could be reunited many months later.[18]

Although from an aristocratic family and a fourteenth-generation descendant of Genghis Khan, SLt. Tu (or Du) Kai-mu (都凱牧) was in many ways representative of the young States-trained Chinese airmen who served in the CACW. Born in 1922 in Manchuria (now northeastern China), he and his family moved from their home to escape the Japanese invasion in 1931. He studied in the economics department at the National Northwest University in Hsian (or Sian, now Xian) in northwestern Shensi Province and originally planned after graduation to become a bank clerk, at that time a highly respected and well-paid position. When agents of the ROC Air Force came to his university to recruit cadets for training in the United States, he decided to sign up—not from a desire to become a pilot but because the screening process included a physical examination. Tu considered it to be a good opportunity to have a chest x-ray, which would determine whether he had tuberculosis—a generally incurable disease at that time in China. He passed all the exams and was accepted into the program.

Because he was too embarrassed to drop out, Tu became an aviation cadet at the ROC Air Force Academy in southwestern China's Yunnan Province in 1941. He was one of about 150 cadets to be sent to Chanyi (Zhanyi) for basic training. About eighty-two of those completed the course and were sent to the United States, steaming aboard HMS *Sterling Castle* from Bombay to New York City by a route that was nearly the reverse of that later followed by *Mission Bay*. Tu was sent to Arizona and again received basic training, this time on the PT-17 trainer at Thunderbird Field at Glendale. He received primary training as a bomber pilot on the BT-13 trainer at Marana Army Airfield near Tucson, followed by advanced training at Williams Air Force Base at Mesa. While there, he was paired with Chang Kwan-lu (Zhang Guang-lu) on the AT-9 trainer. Tu received his pilot's wings (both USAAF and ROCAF) on October 1, 1943, before moving to La Junta Army Air Force Training Base, south of Denver, Colorado, to fly B-25s.

At each stage of training, increasingly more of the candidates "washed out" because of the stringent requirements. Many of these returned to China as navigators, bombardiers, or mechanics. In February 1944, those who had successfully completed training as B-25 pilots were sent by transport plane to Karachi, with stops at Natal, Brazil; Casablanca, Morocco; and Cairo, Egypt. They were assigned briefly to the 4th Squadron before transfer to the 3rd. While stationed in India, Tu often flew as Capt. Hodges's copilot; later he went on to fly numerous missions in China as a pilot.[19]

Attached at the same time was SLt. Yen Pao-san, who had arrived at Karachi in January 1943 and remained there for almost a year. Initially he and other Chinese airmen awaited the arrival of the B-25s to begin training of new personnel. Later he became an instructor for the 9th Bomb Squadron, 2nd Bomb Group, of the Chinese air force. After training for the 9th Bomb Squadron was completed in December, he was informed that he was to fly with the Americans. Because Yen preferred to continue serving in the CAF, he and two other Chinese pilots flew to Chungking to present their case. Their request was rejected, however, and they were assigned first to the 4th Bomb Squadron in January 1944, and then to the 3rd Bomb Squadron in March. Yen's name appears in later mission reports as Yen Pao-shen (X-478).[20]

CHAPTER THREE
Training for Combat

Flying began on the afternoon of Saturday, March 11, with five B-25s in commission, some of them "uncared for" and in poor condition. Pilots not scheduled for flight drew sessions on the Link Trainer, a flight simulator that taught them to fly "blind" on instruments, while navigators used the D-8 bomb trainer recently erected in the hangar. Lt. Dorr went to Karachi Air Base to retrieve equipment that had been removed from squadron planes, including some that had been stripped to supply parts to the 4th Squadron as it prepared for transfer to China.

That was also the day that officers and enlisted men of the softball club played their first game. With Cpl. Duffin pitching, the 3rd Squadron "whipped" OTU's Prides by a score of 5 to 3, and again the following day by 3–0. Duffin's speed and accuracy had opponents and spectators wondering, "Who is this guy?" As a senior, he had led his Cleveland high school team to win the Ohio state baseball championship in 1939, and he was signed by a semipro team after graduating. He continued as the squadron's pitcher until malaria set in a few months afterward, repeatedly sending him to the hospital and sapping his strength and stamina.[1]

SSgt. Holmes was another talented player on the enlisted men's team who later received praise for his skills as a "line drive hitter" and star player whose usual defensive position was center field. He went on after the war to play in the semipros at Salt Lake City.[2]

The streak continued with another win against the Royal Air Force team by 10 to 1, according to Capt. Graves, who had been a sports editor for the newspaper in his hometown of Texarkana before enlistment. He had served as historical officer for the 1st Bomb Group before his transfer to the 3rd Squadron and continued as its historian until his return to the US a few months later.

SSgt. Jack Holmes transferred in from the 2nd Bomb Squadron as a supply sergeant but was reassigned duties as a crew chief soon afterward. During recreational periods, the squadron softball team also relied upon him to bring in the runs. *Courtesy of Terry Holmes*

Seven planes used for training were in the air for most of the two flight periods on the fourteenth. Maj. Conrad; Capts. Simpson, Daniels, and Seacrest; and Lts. Miles and Potter (unidentified; perhaps with the OTU) "checked out" more than twenty Chinese pilots. Most of them were States-trained and had logged more than 125 hours flying B-25s, to their credit. Daniels logged 6.5 hours in the air that day—the longest duration entered in his flight log during that period, all of them as pilot of B-25Cs.[3] Ground schools continued. While American aircrews instructed their Chinese counterparts in effective strategies for aerial combat, Chinese mechanics were gaining practical experience working on planes under the guidance of American mechanics. Two jeeps were assigned to the squadron for use by nine officers and their various departments.

Although surrounding fields were used for transition, traffic congestion was increased significantly when two fighter squadrons and another B-25 squadron (the 341st Training Group Detachment) moved onto the field. Disagreements with Wing arose concerning assignment of some of the Chinese. SLts. Huang and Joung (or Young), both former B-25 pilots and instructors, received orders to join Chinese training commands. The two had been flying the squadron's B-25H that was used for training on the newer model. Col. Rouse wired his protest to Gen. Chennault, arguing that transferring them would be a waste of "good pilot material."

Many believed the B-25 Mitchell medium bomber produced by North American Aviation, named in honor of Gen. Billy Mitchell, considered to be the father of the US Air Force, to be the most versatile and reliable bomber in World War II. New H models began to arrive during this period to replace some of the older B-25Cs and Ds. The D model had several modifications that made it superior in combat to the B-25Bs used for Col. Jimmy Doolittle's renowned 1942 Tokyo raid. Improvements included the addition of Plexiglas windows for the navigator and radio operator, heavier nose armament, and deicing and anti-icing equipment, and these features were continued in the B-25H.

The H model replaced the standard-length transparent nose of the B-25D with a shorter, solid-metal nose. It also featured a redesigned cockpit intended to be operated by a single pilot. The copilot's station and controls were eliminated, with the seat cut down and used by the navigator/cannoneer. Waist and tail gun positions were added. The radio operator was moved to the aft compartment and operated the waist guns, and the dorsal (top) turret was moved forward to the navigator's compartment to balance the additional weight of the waist and tail gunner positions.

Intended for use primarily as a gunship, the B-25H boasted increased defensive firepower designed to improve its effectiveness in low-level attacks. A 75 mm cannon (type T-13) fired through the nose of the aircraft at a rate approximated as four rounds per strafing run. Because of its low rate of fire and relative ineffectiveness against ground targets, as well as a substantial recoil, it was sometimes removed and replaced with two additional .50-caliber machine guns as a field modification. In addition, the H model mounted four fixed forward-firing .50-caliber machine guns in the nose, four more in forward-firing cheek blisters, two in the top turret, one each in a pair of new waist positions, and a final pair in a new tail gunner's position. This made a total of "10 machine guns coming and four going," as well as the 75 mm cannon and "a brace of eight rockets and 3,000 lb. (1,360 kg) of bombs" according to manufacturer's promotional material, although no evidence of rockets has been found relating to H models used by the 3rd Squadron.[4]

Some of the B-25s were shipped partially disassembled, Simpson later explained. The wings were removed and then reinstalled after the planes had reached their destination. Simpson once climbed aboard one of the Mitchells that had arrived recently and then "started it up, rolled to the takeoff point, headed down the runway to rotate speed, pulled up on the yoke and nothing happened so he instinctively pushed down and the plane lifted off," his son related. "He turned to the right, but the plane went left. Managed to get back down using his flight skills." The reason for the reversed reactions was that the wings had been installed "bassackwards." No harm was done, although "someone got chewed out."[5]

As the 3rd Bomb Squadron was being organized and training began, the 4th ("Lucky Lady") Bomb Squadron left Malir and began the transfer to China. Accompanied by the 26th and 29th Fighter Squadrons, the 4th Squadron began its move on March 17. The fighter planes were able to cross the Hump without incident, but the bomb squadron's ten heavily loaded Mitchells were forced to turn back because of bad weather. They made their way across safely when conditions improved, landing at Chanyi before joining the 1st and 2nd Squadrons of the 1st Bomb Group at Erh Tong.

Flying for the 3rd Squadron was curtailed that morning as planes of the three squadrons bound for China got on their way, although ground schools continued. Maj. Conrad received a cablegram requesting the shipment of thirty-nine Chinese gunners to China. Lt. Graves wrote, "Apparently for the gunner-shy First Squadron[,] which apparently was shortsighted in this personnel phase, withdrawal of these gunners would leave this squadron without training material." Col. Rouse supported Maj. Conrad's objection and wired it to 14th Air Force wing and group headquarters.

As was customary on Sundays, the men were allowed to have the morning of March 19 off from duty assignments. Church services were held separately for Protestants and Catholics who were inclined to attend. Officers and enlisted men moved into quarters formerly occupied by 4th Squadron personnel. Officers moved from Cottage 9 to Cottage 8, which had better equipment and was considered more comfortable, while enlisted men moved from barracks near the officers' club to those containing the orderly room, "which most convenient." Flying resumed in the afternoon, when Chinese navigators first put their skills to the test aboard the new B-25Hs. Captains Simpson and Daniels both recorded two hours of flight time in their logbooks.

Eight planes were in the air for Monday's half-day flight period. Two were given to each of four flight leaders for use in training of the Chinese pilots. Maj. Conrad gave transition to Capt. Sung, vice commander. Capt. Simpson took up four Chinese navigators to familiarize them with the navigational system of a B-25H during a four-hour cross-country flight (Malir to Karachi and return to Malir). Lt. Edwin A. Senkbeil joined temporarily as

Eugene H. Dorr, Charles D. Miles, Mark T. Seacrest, and William L. Daniels (*left to right*), enjoy the companionship of an unidentified female (perhaps Dr. Edith Millican, daughter of Aimee Millican, who operated Kwan-sien Rest Camp). *E. H. Dorr collection, courtesy of Barbara Dorr Dent*

a pilot from the 22nd Bomb Squadron, 341st Bomb Group. Capt. Hinrichs and Lts. Dorr and Miles spent part of the day at Karachi Airdrome, checking for missing parts on planes that were turned over to the squadron. So many parts had been salvaged that Maj. Conrad was reluctant to accept the planes, despite assurances that requisitions for replacement parts had already been approved. Maj. Conrad held a meeting with the enlisted men late that morning to discuss working and living conditions and military discipline.

An unidentified man stands to the left of John P. Hanrahan, Charlie H. Hoyle Jr., and Paul E. Haines, others who came from the 2nd Bomb Squadron. G. B. Fuller collection, courtesy of Elizabeth Fuller Zea

On March 21, ten enlisted men were noted as attached, reclassified, and assigned duties: TSgt. John P. Hanrahan (from AAF radio operator to communication chief), TSgt. Frederick C. Libolt (from airplane instrument specialist to A/P inspector), SSgt. Jack Holmes (from supply NCO to crew chief), SSgt. William Meikle (from administrative and technical clerk to intelligence NCO), Sgt. Paul E. Haines (from A/P armorer to power turret specialist), Sgt. Charlie H. Hoyle Jr. (from A/P armorer to armament chief), Sgt. Frank T. Jakubasz (from A/P crew chief to flight chief), Sgt. Ewell F. Wilkerson (from A/P crew chief to flight chief), Cpl. John P. Barge (from A/P and engineering mechanic to crew chief), and Cpl. William G. Duffin (from administrative and technical clerk to personnel NCO). Chinese mechanics worked on red-lined (grounded) planes with American personnel while TSgt. Hanrahan instructed radio operators and maintenance men, working independently until a communications officer could be assigned. Pilots continued training, and navigators spent the first of two days on the firing range.

The squadron's first fatal accident occurred on the following day, when two Chinese B-25 pilots and two unauthorized passengers were killed. Lt. Miles had checked out SLts. Shiong S. K. and Lin Y. C. (both attached on March 19), who were "shooting landings" aboard a B-25D, serial #41-29909. He had instructed the pilots to land at 1030 after about two hours of flight, but they had not returned by the scheduled time. Investigation revealed that three members of "a transient P-40 squadron" had "climbed aboard to get flight time" without the knowledge or approval of the operations officer, Capt. Simpson. Erroneously named "2Lt. C. Youngham" in the subsequent report, 1Lt. Charles F. Yunghans was a pilot attached to the 91st Fighter Squadron, 81st Fighter Group, which had recently arrived from Italy for retraining on P-51 and P-47 aircraft prior to joining the 14th Air Force. The fourth fatality was Sgt. Charles F. Alton Jr., engineer-gunner for the 375th Bomb Squadron, which flew B-24s with the 308th Bomb Group.

The sole survivor, fighter pilot 2Lt. Webster Smith, disclosed the plane's fate when he was brought to the base hospital suffering from two broken ankles. He reported that the Chinese pilots were flying low over the water when "a scraping sound preceded the crash into the Indian Ocean about ¾-mile out at sea, southwest about twelve miles from Karachi." He gave this account of the experience:

Training for Combat

We took off about 0900. We flew around about half to three quarters of an hour, landed and the pilots changed seats. The first pilot [Lin] was a very good pilot. The second pilot [Shiong] flew around for a while and came in to shoot a landing—He made a sloppy traffic pattern and approach, but a good landing. We took off again—I was sleepy and did the thing that saved my life. I got in the crawlway with my feet forward. We flew around for a short while, then I heard something scrape—like an engine cut out. I took the hand-holes and pulled myself so I could see Lt. Youngham. He was tense and the plane was flying with one wing low. I didn't know if we were over water or land. Within 15 seconds of the first noise the scraping started again, but much more violent, and the next thing I knew I was covered with water. Thinking I was trapped inside the ship I imagined that was certain death—when it suddenly occurred to me, I had elbow room; which I didn't have in the passageway. With just a few strokes I came to the surface of the water.

The plane, about 50 yards distant from Smith, upended and submerged within a minute or less, with no sign of life. After attempting to swim and discovering that both ankles were broken, Smith discarded his shoes and trousers to reduce drag and then used two seat cushions as flotation devices as he paddled toward land, estimated as at least ¾ mile away. Four natives fishing on a small boat in the shallows rescued him about ¼ mile from shore and conveyed him to nearby Landhi Field, home of the China-Burma-India Fighter Replacement Training Unit. There, medics administered first aid and morphine and set Smith's ankles before moving him to the hospital at Malir. He was later sent back to his hometown of Omaha, where he remained hospitalized until August.

Although Smith was unable to provide full details, the investigation panel determined that "the airplane contacted the water, either the propellers or fuselage, skipped off and could not stay in the air due to damage of propellers or aircraft." The crash landing followed a few seconds later, hurling Lt. Smith through the nose tunnel and out through the nose of the plane; although he was thrown clear, his ankles were fractured. The aircraft sank in a few seconds, and "no other persons" cleared the wreckage. The channel at low tide is about ¾ mile wide and 3 miles long, and the plane sank in 30 to 40 feet of water. Because no parts were visible at low tide, the exact spot could not be determined, and the wreck could not be located.

Operations had forbidden all flights overwater, so the aircraft had no life raft or life vests at the time of the accident. General cause was recorded as "Negligence" and, more specifically, "Willful lack of care" and "Violation of restrictions." Bodies of the four who died were determined to be unrecoverable. Capt. Simpson signed the reports as operations officer.[6] On the morning following the accident, Maj. Conrad lectured the Chinese pilots about low flying and promised to dismiss any of them guilty of "buzzing" without authority in the future.

Word came that the additional American personnel intended to man the 3rd Bomb Squadron were expected to arrive soon, allowing some of those who had been transferred in for temporary duty to return to their units. A new policy was instituted on Sunday the twenty-sixth, when no flying or other training was scheduled for either morning or afternoon. "Headquarter decrees Sunday will be a full holiday," wrote Graves. On the following day, two additional H models were ferried in from Karachi Air Base and turned over to the squadron, making a total of five. When Lt. Miles arrived the next day with another H, the plane acted up both on takeoff and landing but checked out normally on the ground. Training intensified through the week, with instrument, navigation, formation, and transition missions; altitude and skip bombing; and night flying constituting the curriculum.

High winds and subsequent dust storms on Wednesday, March 29, delayed the arrival of *Mission Bay* at Karachi and curtailed flying at Malir. Flight time during the afternoon brought the squadron's total to 394 hours and 10 minutes to date. Graves, a flight instructor who had trained Chinese airmen at Luke and Thunderbird Air Bases before serving in the same capacity with the 1st Bomb Group, reported progress as "very satisfactory in all phases of training" and added that the training period had reached a point where "crews must be considered and gunnery, bombing, and navigation missions prepared." Maj. Conrad and Col. Rouse interviewed the just-received personnel the following day, with the intention of establishing an assignment roster that took into account their levels of expertise and experience. The squadron had been operating without an intelligence officer, communication officer, or adjutant, so they hoped that they could fill these positions from among the new personnel.

Earlier that day, Maj. Conrad had brought the squadron's first B-25J, welcomed as "a highly desirable addition to the squadron," from Karachi. Others came in through the next few days. Modifications were included to better equip the J model for medium-altitude attacks, returning it to a bomber role. The new J looked much like the earlier D model, having reverted to the longer nose. Also like the D, it had a copilot's position. The "less than successful" 75 mm cannon was eliminated. Some B-25Js were built with a solid-metal nose containing eight .50-caliber machine guns (called the "strafer nose"), while a greater number of them featured the earlier Plexiglas "bombardier nose" or "greenhouse nose" containing the bombardier's position. Regardless of the nose style used, all J models included two .50-caliber guns in a "fuselage package" located directly under the pilot's station, with two more in an identical package under the copilot's compartment. The solid-nose variant, which came into greater use near the end of the war as the B-25J-2, carried a total of eighteen .50-caliber guns: eight in the nose, four in under-cockpit packages, two in an upper turret, two in the waist, and another pair in the tail. This impressive firepower remained unsurpassed by any other bomber in World War II.[7]

It was at about this time that 1Sgt. Earley learned of another new arrival—his "heavyweight" son, weighing 10 pounds, 8 ounces, born on March 26 in Teaneck, New Jersey. Instead of having to endure the usual long wait for mail informing him of the birth to arrive by ship, Earley's father notified him of the good news by cable.[8]

On April 1, SSgt. Shock (an airplane mechanic and sheet metal worker in Little Rock before his enlistment in July 1940) was promoted to technical sergeant, and Sgts. Armstrong (reclassified to armorer-gunner), Jakubasz, Rieks, Wilkerson, Haines, and Hoyle to staff sergeants. Cpls. Barge and Duffin were promoted to sergeants. The men who had arrived aboard *Mission Bay* were officially attached to the squadron on the third. Officers included Capt. Howard M. Goeller (adjutant), Capt. Raymond L. Hodges Jr. and 1Lt. Reuben Ragland (both B-25 pilots / flight leaders), and 2Lt. George P. Wood (communications officer). Enlisted men attached at that time were TSgt. Robert N. Solyn (operations NCO); SSgt. Isabel G. Mier and Pfcs. Clyde L. Learn and Andrew R. Allegretto (A/P armorers); Sgt. William H. Whearty, Cpl. James H. Mills, and Pfc. James A. Wadlow (A/P crew chiefs); Pfcs. John W. England and Eril W. Peters (A/F radio operators); and Pvts. Lloyd E. Jackson (instrument specialist) and Norman L. Long (A/F radio mechanic).

Training for Combat

Lt. Paul L. Young, an American citizen of Chinese descent who served as intelligence officer, proved to be an invaluable asset to the 3rd Bomb Squadron with its racially mixed personnel. *P. L. Young collection, courtesy of Gerry Young Lim*

All attached to the Personnel Section (*left to right*), William T. Earley Jr. (first sergeant), Capt. Howard M. ("Pop") Goeller (adjutant), and SSgt. William G. Duffin (personnel NCO) enjoy some time away from the orderly room. *J. H. Mills Collection*

Along with others attached to the 17th or 27th Fighter Squadron, 5th Fighter Group, by Special Orders #23, Headquarters 5th Fighter Group (P), these new arrivals were designated as "Shipment AB-720-A," and orders were issued to pay them for the month of March. Attached from the 5th Fighter Group, 2Lt. Paul L. Young assumed duties as intelligence officer, and Capt. Daniels and Lt. Miles (both flight leaders) were released on the following day and transferred for temporary duty to the 5390th Gunnery School at Karachi Air Base. Both later returned to duty with the 2nd Bomb Squadron, stationed at Liangshan. Capt. Hinrichs was assigned additional duty as technical inspector, and Capt. Goeller as administrative inspector.

This was also about the time that 1Lt. Robert C. MacNeil joined the squadron as a B-25 pilot / flight leader. Soon afterward he was appointed squadron engineering officer, responsible for supervision of the ground duties of all airplane crew chiefs, aerial engineers, inspectors, and mechanics. From Minneapolis, his training in airplane mechanics had begun at Northwest Military & Naval Academy, but he discovered that his credits did not qualify him to become an aviation cadet. After failing the mental and physical examinations twice, he was so determined to become a pilot that he began an intense self-directed program of study and physical training. MacNeil, then a private in the 401st School Squadron at Sheppard Field, was accepted on his third attempt and began preflight training at Kelly Field, Texas, in mid-November 1941, continuing through standard USAAF schools.

After completing a year of college at Depauw University, Goeller had made his way in the summer of 1930 from Columbus, Indiana, to Galveston, Texas, where he signed on as a deck boy aboard *Edgehill*, giving his age as twenty-one instead of twenty. His thirst for adventure having been satisfied, he returned afterward to Indiana, where he found employment as an accountant. Following his marriage two years later, he tried his hand at farming. In addition, he owned and operated the St. Denis Hotel and Laundry with his brother Wallace in Columbus.

In early 1942, he applied for a commission in the Army and was administered an oral examination to assess his qualifications. Addressed to him as first lieutenant, a telegram arrived from the adjutant general's office in Washington, DC, in June, ordering him to leave on July 1 to report at the officers' training school at Miami Beach, Florida. After the completion of training, Goeller became base administrative inspector at Great Falls, Montana. In May 1943, he was named commanding officer at the Army Air Base at Glasgow, Montana, where he served until his move to the CBI.[9] His administrative experience qualified him to fill the position of adjutant and administrative inspector, tasked to distribute the commanding officer's orders and ensure their compliance. Other duties were overseeing the general well-being of squadron personnel and keeping them combat ready, as well as monitoring completion of the monthly historical report and other records. Because he was their senior in age, the other officers called Goeller "Pop."

The Chinese received additional personnel too. On April 4, these men were transferred to the 3rd Squadron: Haiso Yuan-tuan (X-1312), Li Shin-liang (X-1314), Li Chen-si (X-1313), Ho Wei-ch'ing (X-3115), Kao Chen-k'ai (X-1316), Liu Kwan-ping (X-1318), Li Chan-jui (X-1317), Li Lieh (X-1319), Wang Ching-chuan (X-1320), Tuan Tsai-pang (X-1321), Kuo Hsiao-yi (X-1322), Feng Chen-k'wan (X-1323), Kuo Feng (X-1324), Chang Kuo-wei (X-1326), Wang Chun-sheng (X-1327), Huang Tung-shou (X-1328), Chung Chuan (X-1329), Nieh Lien-yuan (X-1332), Yao Shu-chi (X-1330), Liang Yun-tien (X-1334), Wei Chang-su

TSgt. Manuel C. Smith joined the 3rd Squadron briefly to assist in training the Chinese gunners. He later fulfilled the same task at 1st Bomb Group Headquarters so successfully that he was awarded Chinese Air Force Wings. *M. C. Smith collection, courtesy of Pamela Smith*

Cpl. James H. ("Hank") Mills, a B-25 crew chief, trained Chinese mechanics in all phases of airplane maintenance and repair. *J. H. Mills collection*

Sgt. Ho Gei-hung was a Chinese mechanic whom Hank remembered particularly well. Ho was one of two men who taught him to communicate in their language. *J. H. Mills collection*

Training for Combat

(X-1335), Ho Wei-cheng (X-1337), Tso Jui-heng (X-1339), Ma Lung (X-1340), Liu Chung-chieh (X-1346), Mai Pei-chen (X-1345), Chow Kwan-yuan (X-1347), Chow Hsian-chen (X-1349), Wang Ying-ch'ing (X-1350), and Wu Kuo-yu (X-1348). These thirty men all were sergeants who had completed the gunnery course at Group. TSgt. Manuel C. Smith, classified as an intelligence specialist, joined from the 4th Bomb Squadron and was sent on detached service to Karachi to assist in training the next class of gunners.

Hank explained the situation at Malir: "There was a squadron of Chinese attached to our squadron to learn from us how to operate the American planes." He remembered that there were more Chinese than Americans. In fact, the Chinese outnumbered the Americans by a ratio of at least two to one and later four to one. Although culturally vastly different, the two nationalities worked well together. Soon they began to learn enough of each other's language to be able to communicate on a limited basis. Most of the Americans developed a Chinese vocabulary of about twenty to thirty words. Using a kind of "pidgin" or "pig latin" accompanied by gestures, they were generally successful in accomplishing simple tasks, although this kind of communication often broke down in emergency situations.[10]

Hank's recollections included many hours spent maintaining and repairing the B-25s with the squadron's Chinese mechanics. Two of them, Sgts. Ma Tian-you and Ho Gei-hung (Hank referred to him as Ho Fri-hung), spoke some English, and they often taught him Chinese words and phrases as they worked together. Seventy years later, he still remembered some of the expressions that he learned in their dialect. For instance, "The Chinese word for oil is *wy oh*," he recalled.

"The Chinese had a separate place—a building where they had their dining room," he explained. Although the Americans and Chinese trained, worked, and flew missions together, by mutual agreement they ate and slept separately. A mixed mess had initially been attempted, but both national groups found it unsatisfactory. Reasons for separate facilities included differences in dietary preferences such as preparation of the food and the order in which courses were served, as well as other cultural considerations. For instance, the Americans wanted their soup at the beginning of the meal, while the Chinese preferred it at the end.

The wing's various squadrons flew with mixed crews on early missions, but the language barrier created serious problems. Chinese crewmen sometimes misunderstood orders and bailed out. The result was loss or damage to the plane, although crew members were usually capable of walking out. Even pilots who spoke fluent English often reverted to Chinese when they became excited. Many of the Chinese pilots, such as SLt. Tu, had studied English and spoke the language well. Ray Hodges said that they often did so with a southern US accent since many of them had been trained in the American South.[11]

At other times, misunderstandings led to far-more-dire consequences than an unnecessary bailout. Capt. Moncure N. Lyon, a 4th Bomb Squadron pilot who later flew missions in cooperation with the 3rd Squadron, related an incident in which such a misunderstanding proved fatal. It happened on a river sweep down the Yangtze in search of enemy shipping soon after the move to China. When his B-25 was shot up by enemy fire, Lyon instructed his American bombardier to go back and instruct the three Chinese crewmen to bail out. The bombardier did his best to explain the situation to them. After the Americans found each other on the ground, they determined that the Chinese had misunderstood the order and gone down with the plane, although the deaths may have resulted from their concept of honor.[12] Later the CACW reverted to separate American and Chinese crews for missions because of multiple mishaps of the same nature.

Training at Malir increased in complexity through the following weeks, both in the air and on the ground. These tasks formed the curriculum for April 12:

> Cross[-]country navigation flights with a two-ship formation also skip bombing with gunners in turret getting dry runs. Navigators have also been assigned to ships, those not flying will be assigned to link trainer, bomb trainer or in class getting instructions on navigation. Gunners assigned to flights, and they will fly with these flights and start firing from the turrets. Four planes in commission today. Total 34:10 hours flown today, and all gunners were given examination on identification of friendly and enemy planes.

Lt. Reuben Ragland Jr. had always dreamed of being a pilot, he revealed in a 1994 interview. However, his early military experience with the Pennsylvania National Guard in Pittsburgh was as his unit's finance officer, as well as later at Fort Meade in Maryland. When he eventually arrived at Karachi, it was as a B-25 pilot and flight leader with the 3rd Bomb Squadron, thus fulfilling his vision. He flew with Capt. Simpson on the squadron's first bombing and strafing mission to Burma, followed by many other successful raids until his return home in April 1945. *Courtesy of John Ragland*

Reuben Ragland later related an incident that occurred during this period. Capt. Simpson was in position as pilot and Lt. Ragland as copilot of one of the new J models. It was a routine trip across the desert. Simpson insisted that he knew the terrain and did not need any navigational charts, but when they found themselves "looking down at nothing but water," Simpson admitted that they were lost and handed the controls over to his copilot. It was fortunate that Ragland was able to navigate by radio for a safe return to base—or was this just Simpson's way of testing the skills of his new copilot?

Ragland, from Jacksonville, Florida, had attended Virginia Military Institute, where he studied electrical engineering. After graduating in 1939, he took a job with US Steel in Pittsburgh and joined the Pennsylvania National Guard. Assigned to Battery B, 176th Field Artillery, at Fort Meade, he received his commission as second lieutenant in March 1940. He was called up to active duty two years later. After being transferred to South Carolina, where his duties included setting up camp and digging latrines, he decided to sign up for flight training. He was elated to be accepted a brief time afterward, recalling in later years, "I left that night!" Assigned to bases throughout the South, Ragland learned to fly fighter planes and twin-engine planes, later becoming an instructor in gunnery school. Afterward, stationed in Utah, he trained pilots and tested "war materials" that were dropped on Japan and Germany during the war.[13]

It was while he was in Utah that Ragland became impatient with being kept out of the war and one day announced to his companions, "I'm getting out of here!" A new aircraft had recently been brought in that allowed the colonel to fly to Salt Lake to see his wife, so Ragland and his buddies climbed aboard and took off. They flew around the field several times, buzzing the headquarters building until officers came out to see what was happening. As Ragland was landing the aircraft, something went wrong—perhaps a gust of wind—and the plane crashed. Everyone got out as fast as they could and ran—all except Ragland, who stoically maintained his position in the pilot's seat.

The adjutant came up to the window and asked him, "Is anyone hurt?"

Training for Combat

Lt. Ragland demonstrates a maneuver of aerial combat to Chinese student pilots. Tu Kai-mu is to the left of him, looking directly into the camera with a broad smile. *R. N. Solyn collection, courtesy of Robert N. Solin*

Lt. John F. Faherty joined the squadron as a bombardier. After serving as assistant operations officer for six months, he was appointed armament officer. *John F. Faherty collection, courtesy of Dennis Faherty*

"No, sir."

"Thank God," the adjutant replied. Then he turned and walked away. The very next day Ragland received orders that sent him on his way to the CBI.[14]

Despite his earlier impetuous behavior, Ragland proved to be a competent and respected pilot. "I always liked to fly with him," Hank commented many years later.

Sgt. Gruber returned to duty in mid-April after spending four days in the hospital for some unspecified illness. The following day, 2Lt. John F. Faherty joined the squadron from CACW HQ as bombardier and was appointed assistant operations officer. SSgt. Wilbur C. Dunlap, who had arrived aboard *Mission Bay* and initially been attached to the 27th Fighter Squadron as a crew chief, was transferred to the 3rd Squadron as bombsight maintenance technician. SSgt. Rieks was reclassified from A/P crew chief to A/P propeller specialist. Hank remarked that the official classifications had little meaning. "The only thing we knew about it was that we were just all mechanics."

There was, however, an acknowledged hierarchy. Assigned as a crew chief, Hank was a noncommissioned officer and the lead mechanic of a specifically assigned B-25 with responsibility for its line inspection, maintenance, and servicing. Throughout his service in the 3rd Bomb Squadron, Hank's primary responsibility was to repair and maintain the Mitchells, often working long into the night to correct problems and test out the repairs while the aircrews slept. His duties included diagnosing trouble, laying out inspection and repairs for his crew of mechanics, calling in specialists (electrical, hydraulic, instrument, power turret, and others) to address any unusual difficulties, and checking and giving preliminary approval of the work. His direct superior was one of the B-25 flight chiefs (at that time, MSgt. Grant and SSgts. Jakubasz and Wilkerson) who was responsible for all maintenance crews of a single flight of planes (three or four). In charge of all of them was MSgt. Fuller, squadron line chief, who in turn answered to 1Lt. MacNeil as engineering officer.

MSgt. Grant was "regular army" and "had been in the army a long time" before being assigned to the 1st Bomb Group, Hank recalled. Only three years old when his mother died,

SSgt. James R. Summerville works to correct an electrical problem in a B-25's engine compartment. He was one of the specialists whose expertise was required when the airplane mechanics and crew chiefs were unable to complete complex repairs. *F. T. Jakubasz collection, courtesy of Robert Jakubasz*

young Don had spent the Depression years in the care of a Salvation Army children's home. After reaching adulthood, he lived with his father in a San Francisco hotel, finding work where he could, including as a hotel doorman. A career in the military seemed an agreeable solution, so he enlisted in about 1934. Stationed at France Field, Cristobal, Panama Canal Zone, in 1940, he had attained the rank of sergeant by that time. Grant reenlisted in late 1942 and transferred to the Air Forces; he was sent to the CBI the following summer. Hank related, "They used to test-fire the guns before a mission." Grant, who most frequently flew as turret gunner but occasionally as waist gunner when he was with the 2nd Bomb Squadron, was verifying that the .50-calibers were operating reliably. "He shot off the gun and had it aimed too low. It shot out a little piece of Plexiglas and cut him. He got a Purple Heart for that."

Some changes were made during the same period by the Chinese: 1Lts. Chang Yua and Chu Shen-chun, with SLts. Chang Yi-sheng, Teng Chun-chin, and Cheng Shi-shen, were attached, and SLts. Liu Ping-chuan and Chao Chan-fu were released. The following day, one captain, two first lieutenants, three warrant officers, and twenty-two enlisted men (names not specified) were attached from the Chinese air force. Over the next few days, gunners fired from the turrets, radio mechanics were assigned to maintain equipment on specific planes, and pilots fired the 75 mm cannons.

It was while he was stationed at Malir that Hank and Nancy's first child was born on Friday, April 21. The squadron historian wrote on that day, "Dust storms no flying today." Nancy's letter sent to Hank through the Army Post Office system at APO 882 announcing the birth of a daughter took several weeks to reach him, since mail delivery was accomplished by a route similar to the one by which he had arrived. Aircrews flew increasingly more-challenging practice missions through the end of the month. Squadron records reported fourteen American officers and thirty-nine American enlisted men; 118 Chinese were reported as attached from the CAF.

As May began, SSgt. McCann was reclassified from section leader to A/P armorer, and Pvts. Jackson and Long were promoted to privates first class. Lt. Young left for detached service to China in preparation for moving 1st Bomb Group headquarters to Peishiyi, near Chungking. Orders specified that he was to proceed via air, rail, or motor transport (or a combination) to Luliang, where he was to report to the commanding officer of the 1st Bomb Group for temporary duty. As was usual procedure, Young was authorized to receive $6.00 per diem while traveling, except at points where temporary duty was performed and government quarters or billets were furnished, in which case per diem was $3.00. Where government rations and quarters were furnished, per diem was suspended.

At the same time, twenty-four Chinese sergeants from the CAF were attached for duty as gunners. Two days later, Capt. Goeller sent a request to wing headquarters for serial numbers of the following: Chen Yun-Hwa, Wu Yun-kui, Leh Wan-Chuan, Chang Sui-ann, Hsu Pen-yin, Kuo Pin-lin, Lin Yon-hwa, Yen Lin-kee, Chow Foo-seng, Yu Teck-jun, Lee Min-cheu, Chen Tee-seng, Fun Tee-foe, Chew Yu-kwan, Chua Chen-chung, Yin Sen-su, Huang Chan-teh, Veng Von-jea, Cheng Kong-chuan, Chang Feng-wu, Lin Tar-chin, Huang Chin-an, Liu Feng-fei, and Lee Feng-man.

Sgt. Mroskey was reduced in grade "upon recommendation of his immediate CO" to private, "with cause," in accordance with 1st Bomb Group HQ special orders dated March 18. He was released from the 3rd Squadron and transferred to the 310th Airdrome Squadron. With the Fighter Replacement Training Unit, their organizations were combined with those of the Flexible Gunnery Training Unit and HQ Army Air Forces, India-Burma Theater Training Command, which remained at Malir until the end of the war.

Orders were issued for Capt. Seacrest to receive the Oak Leaf Cluster to his previously awarded Distinguished Flying Cross for meritorious achievement in a combat mission on December 23, 1943, when he sank a 200-foot Japanese gunboat. "While on a sea sweep mission in a flight of two medium bombers in an area where rain and a low ceiling hampered visibility, he discovered the gunboat at anchor in a cove surrounded by high hills," according to the accompanying certificate. "Despite the hazards of heavy antiaircraft fire from the vessel and flying into a difficult location with poor visibility, Captain Seacrest pressed his attack to masthead height. A direct bomb hit in the boat's magazine sank the vessel in eight minutes. This display of aggressiveness and courage are in accordance with the highest traditions of the American military service." Well liked and much respected, Seacrest was one of the squadron's most popular officers, and recognition of his achievements was a source of pride for the men with whom he served.

Seacrest, then a first lieutenant, had been mentioned in an article that appeared in *Yank* weekly magazine at about the same time that he was transferred to the 3rd Squadron. He was pilot of a 2nd Squadron B-25, with Sgt. Shin L. C. as top-turret gunner. Shin earned membership that day in the "Close Shavers Club" as the result of "a freak near-tragedy that happened during enemy interception over Changteh." After Seacrest pulled up as he left the target area, Shin clambered up to the pilot's compartment excitedly displaying a red-tipped .50-caliber slug. Shin "burst out with a flow of Chinese words." The Chinese copilot

Lt. Faherty (*left*), Lt. Young (*right*), and an unidentified officer (*center*) stand beside the sign that marks the location of the Chinese-American Composite Wing Headquarters and Operations (*to the left*) and the Operational Training Unit (*turn right*) at Malir. *J. H. Faherty collection, courtesy of Dennis Faherty*

Capt. Mark T. Seacrest is pilot of "The Sylvister" in this photo. He came to the squadron as a B-25 pilot / flight leader but was soon appointed its operations officer and later commanding officer. *J. H. Mills collection*

GIs stationed at Malir escaped their dreary military existence as frequently as possible and fled to Karachi to enjoy its delights. Here Sgt. Frank T. Jakubasz, Sgt. Maynard W. Rieks, and an unidentified friend (*left to right*) pose in costume as maharajahs for a souvenir photo to amuse their families back home. *M. W. Rieks collection, courtesy of Bruce Rieks*

Training for Combat

finally calmed him down long enough to discover that the slug had come from the guns of an escorting P-40 that had "jumped a Jap fighter about to attack Seacrest's plane." The P-40 bullet, although spent in flight, crashed through the top-turret dome and hit Sgt. Shin in the chest, leaving him with an egg-size swelling 1 inch over his heart that was his "souvenir for the close shave."[15]

The squadron's new arrivals soon settled into the routine with its "old hands." Regardless of the heat and dust, Malir was the most comfortable and well appointed of the bases occupied by the 3rd Squadron during the war. To offer recreation in their spare time, the Red Cross provided separate on-post clubs for officers and enlisted men. Snack bars, reading rooms, barber shops, and athletic activities such as baseball, horseshoes, ping-pong, weightlifting, and volleyball were available. Outdoor movies were shown several evenings each week.

At other times when they had time off from duties and could get passes, Hank and his buddies went into town. There was regular train and bus service between Malir and Karachi, or they could make the trip by diesel car. Soldiers could get a haircut, buy articles for prophylaxis / birth control, or receive treatment for venereal disease (although brothels were off-limits and patrolled by the military). They might choose to worship at any of four Christian churches, view exhibits at Victoria Museum, read in the library at Frere Hall, watch a movie at one of several English-language "picture houses," or attend a dance sponsored by organizations such as the Birch Club. Other activities might include strolling through the Mahatma Gandhi Gardens, spending an afternoon at the Karachi Zoo, urging on a favorite horse at the Turf Club, or swimming in the sea at Clifton Beach.

Some shops in town, including those along Elphinstone (now Zaibunnisa) Street, catered to the needs of British and American military personnel serving in the vicinity. According to an "informational booklet" published by the US Army the following year, they could purchase English-language newspapers and books; leather goods such as boots and shoes; clothing of wool, silk, and cotton fabrics (ready-made or tailored to fit); pajamas; and hats in this popular commercial area. Customers could have their souvenirs such as carved ivory and sandalwood pieces conveniently shipped to the folks back home. Hank bought several pieces, including an ornately carved ivory necklace with a large elephant pendant for Nancy.

On one of these trips into town soon after he arrived, Hank bought a pair of handmade leather boots. "I stood on a pad and a man drew an outline of my feet. About a week later, I went back and got them. Those were good boots. They fit well, and I wore them for a long time." On another occasion, Hank bought a brown leather fedora that he wore for long afterward.

The men stationed at Malir particularly enjoyed taking a break from the chow served on base. For the Americans, Café Oxford, Café Rex, Café Ciros, and Café Rio on Elphinstone, as well as Café Grand on Victoria Road, were popular places to enjoy a meal. Equally recommended were the Allies Café, the Whitehouse Café, the World Café, and the International Café. Both the Chungking Restaurant, also on Victoria Road, and Victory Restaurant near the Paradise Cinema served good Chinese food.[16]

It was during this time that Hank received an invitation from one of the Chinese mechanics with whom he worked to go to one of these restaurants in town. He did not recall its name but remembered the experience fondly for many years afterward. "They had a partition in there with ropes on it, and two men pulled the ropes and made the air move, like a fan," he recalled. "And we went to that place, and we couldn't speak the same language, but he had me go there with him and he bought me supper, and I remember those Chinese people swinging that big fan. I was the only American there. All the rest of them were Chinese, and I was there as the guest of one of those Chinese men."

The dining room at the Killarney Hotel on Scandal Point Road had been the site of celebratory dinners of the 2nd Bomb Squadron the previous year and continued to draw patrons. The Bristol Hotel near Frere Hall, Carlton Hotel near Cantonment Station, Marina Hotel on Elphinstone Street, and North Western Hotel near Queen's Bridge were equally reliable for a satisfying meal. The Bluebird Hotel was a favorite of Hank and his friends. The dining room was upstairs. Because the people who operated it were Pakistani rather than Indian, it was one of the places in town where they could get a meal that included beef. Patrons were seated and then served "a good, broiled steak" with french fried potatoes. Dinner included homemade ice cream for dessert.

Although others sometimes accompanied him, Hank most often went into town with Barge and Wilkerson. The three men worked closely together and had much in common, including their southern heritage. Barge was, like Hank, a crew chief and married. Originally from Greenville, Alabama, before moving to Georgia, Barge had attended school with Maj. William B. McGehee, wing adjutant. McGehee occasionally sent letters back home to the local Greenville newspaper for publication and described his experiences, which included traveling across India by train, written from "Somewhere in China" on February 16. "The day after Christmas [1943] I ran into Corporal John Barge, who was also on the train," he wrote. They had not seen each other in at least five years, "so we really had a good talk." As soon as they reached Chabua, McGehee tried to get Barge transferred to the CACW, but he

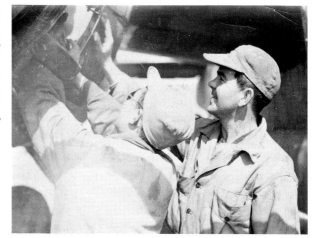

Sgt. John P. Barge, a B-25 crew chief, works here with another mechanic. Publicity photographs such as this were sent to hometown newspapers along with brief explanations of the CACW's binational operations. GIs additionally used them to exchange information that would allow postwar correspondence with friends. On the back Barge wrote his home mailing address: "209 13th Ave., Cordele, Georgia." *J. H. Mills collection*

Sgt. Ewell F. Wilkerson, classified as a flight chief, works on an engine of a B-25 H, A/C #717 (its "Chinese number" barely visible). Written on the back: "Route 2, Box 338, Biloxi, Mississippi." *J. H. Mills collection*

Training for Combat

was on orders to go to China. "So, when I got up here, I tried again and this time we were successful. He is now assigned to this outfit as one of our crew chiefs. So at least we have two Greenville boys in the Chinese-American Composite Wing. Most of our people are Chinese, so I don't guess any of them are lucky enough to claim Greenville as home."[17]

Frasier Wilkerson, a flight chief, was from Mississippi. "We always called him 'Wilkie,'" Hank recalled. "Wilkie used to tell me stories about the Old Testament. He was raised to go in—I think it was a Baptist church." Hank remarked that of all the men with whom he served, "He was my favorite."

Whereas downtown Karachi was clean and modern, there were slums surrounding the main part of town where locals lived in unbelievable poverty and squalor. These areas were off-limits to military personnel, yet beggars harassed the GIs wherever they went. Lt. Donald S. Lopez, who served in the 75th ("Flying Sharks") Fighter Squadron, 23rd Fighter Group, 68th Composite Wing, and in later life became the deputy director of the Smithsonian National Air and Space Museum, wrote an account of his visits to town. "Visiting the city was an unpleasant experience. Everywhere we went we were besieged by beggars of all ages, shapes, and descriptions. Most of them were so dirty that we hated to be near them, and many were horribly deformed and so grotesque that revulsion overcame pity. We were told that parents often maimed their children to prepare them for begging."

Frequently, gangs of youths would chase a man, wanting to shine his shoes. If he ignored them, they threw mud and horse manure on his shoes so he would need a shine. "Some of the beggars were imaginative and amusing in their pleas. In addition to the standard 'Baksheesh Sahib, no mama, no papa, no food, baksheesh,' they often added, 'No flying pay, no per diem!' While certainly a true statement, it usually brought a laugh and perhaps a rupee (worth 33 cents at that time)."[18]

Training progressed according to schedule into the month of May. Combined missions that included both pursuit planes and bombers flying in formation proved satisfactory. High-level bombing and dusk flights, overwater flights with navigation by dead reckoning, and overnight cross-country flights were accomplished too. Simulated bombing and strafing missions with all-Chinese crews were equally successful. Premission briefing was demonstrated and rehearsed. The projected curriculum was completed on May 15, and then the squadron waited for orders in anticipation of joining the other bomb squadrons in China. Soon afterward, someone strafed a herd of camels, three of them pregnant. The gunner's identity and nationality were never discovered, nor whether he fired from a fighter or a bomber.

Reshuffling of personnel continued, particularly among the Chinese. Capt. Wang Chih-lung (X-314); 1Lt. Mai Ku-teng (X-223); 2Lts. Kuo Chien-tze (X-328) and Tsao Chi-fan (X-329); and SLts. Yen Pao-san (X-836), Chu Tso (X-330), Cheng Yuan-lung (X-331), and Tso Kuo-tung (X-332), as well as twenty-four gunners (names unspecified), were released from the 3rd Squadron on May 22 and reassigned.

The following day, Pfc. Trout entered to the hospital at Karachi diagnosed with acute appendicitis and did not rejoin the squadron until after its permanent change of station. Capts. Seacrest and Hinrichs, assisted by SSgts. Jakubasz and Gruber, respectively, left on detached service to Moran Field in the northeastern state of Assam, India, to begin preparations for the move. Seacrest checked into the hospital soon after his arrival at the new base.

Delays allowed additional time for polishing necessary skills. Increasingly greater levels of responsibility were given to Chinese air and ground crews as the month neared its end. Simpson's flight log recorded training missions through May 26 (as pilot of a B-25H, flight time 1:45, local gunnery). At last, training was deemed complete. Graduation ceremonies for Chinese personnel were conducted in the aircraft hangar, and celebratory dinners were held, all attended by high-ranking American and Chinese officials. Brig. Gen. Morse congratulated the graduates, praised their hard work, and explained his expectations of them. Hank also remembered visits by Maj. Gen. Chennault and Generalissimo Chiang.

As the 3rd Bomb Squadron was being organized and trained, the Japanese were busily transporting supplies and troops south from Peiping (now Beijing) and Manchuria via railroad to the Yellow River bridge north of Chenghsien. Their intention was to push south to take the portion of rail line from the Yellow River (Huang He) to Sinyang—the last section of track between Peiping and Hankow held by the Chinese. Completing that rail link to Hankow would ease Japanese dependence on the Yangtze River for moving supplies. Moreover, it would ultimately threaten the entire network of 14th Air Force bases in eastern China.

The Japanese began pushing south of the Yellow River in several drives, and China-based CACW bombers and fighters were called upon to do their part in opposing this offensive. Airpower forged by Chennault's airmen provided the only weapon by which the poorly equipped Chinese had an advantage, and this small air group's P-40s and B-25s knocked out much motorized transport and gained air superiority between the Yellow and Yangtze Rivers.

Squadron personnel felt pride when they learned of the recent successes of other CACW units operating in China, particularly after receiving news of Maj. Gen. Chennault's commendation addressed to Col. Morse, wing commander, on May 10:

1. Your Chinese-American Composite Wing is highly commended for its very successful operations against the Japanese on 5 and 6 May 1944 in the Yellow River area.
2. I extend my sincerest congratulations to you and your officers and enlisted men, both Chinese and American, who played a part in the success of the operations.
3. These operations are in themselves a vindication of the Wing's formation of mixed Chinese and American personnel. The successes are a tribute to their efforts to overcome the handicaps of differences in language and background in achieving the necessary teamwork.
4. I feel certain that these triumphs are indicative of future accomplishments and that they will lend great impetus to our offensive against the Japanese.

Now, with training at its end, officers and enlisted men still at Malir anticipated joining the other CACW squadrons and doing their part against the enemy in the near future. Events, however, did not proceed quite as expected.

CHAPTER FOUR
Mildewing at Moran

After the completion of training, Conrad's combat-ready squadron began preparations for transfer to Moran, a distance of about 1,720 air miles almost due east. Simpson summarized the move in a terse diary entry: "We went to Moran, Upper Assam. Field was hacked out of jungles; had a 6,000' steel runway. We lived in tents."[1]

Moran Field (27°08'34" N, 94°54'15" E), just south of Moran Town (Moranhat) in the broad Brahmaputra River valley, served as a subbase of Chabua Airdrome. Located about 30 miles farther northeast and built on the Hazelbank Tea Plantation at the foot of the towering Himalayas, Chabua had served as the staging field for China-bound CACW units. It was used more commonly as the "jumping-off place" for planes ferrying vital equipment and supplies over the Hump to Kunming, where it was then distributed to Allied bases in China. Moran Field was used primarily for landings and takeoffs by Air Transport Command (ATC) on "Able route," which crossed the mountain chain's higher north end and supplied fuel to bases at Chengtu. Since Japanese occupation of Burma (now called Myanmar) in 1942 had resulted in the closure of the Burma Road and there were no Allied-controlled coastal cities, aid and materiel to China had been entirely cut off except for what could be flown in by cargo plane over the mountains, making these bases invaluable because of their relative proximity to the Chinese border.

Special Orders No. 100, CBI HQ, Air Forces Training Command (Prov.), dated May 26, 1944, listed personnel who were to travel by air transport: 1Lt. Dorr; 2Lts. Wood and Faherty; 1Sgt. Earley; TSgt. Smith; SSgts. Haines, Meikle, Summerville, Dunlap, Chasse, McCann, and Mier; Sgt. Evitts; Cpls. Mills and Hoke; and Pfcs. Burton, Peters, Wadlow, Long, Allegretto, Learn, Rickman, Jackson, and Trout. With them were fifty-seven Chinese officers and enlisted men led by Capts. Lee Yu-hwa and Tsuei Shiang-cheng (refer to appendix B, "Chinese Air Force Personnel Listed in Movement Orders," for details). Traveling by truck to Karachi and overnighting there on the twenty-ninth, they proceeded directly to Moran the following day.

By the same orders but to travel by military aircraft (the squadron's B-25s) were Maj. Conrad; Capts. Simpson, Graves, Cunningham, and Hodges; 1Lts. MacNeil and Ragland; MSgts. Fuller and Grant; TSgts. Shock, Hanrahan, and Libolt; SSgts. Rieks, Hoyle, Wilkerson, and Armstrong; and Sgt. Barge. TSgt. Smith and SSgt. Chasse, who had been on detached service at Karachi, rejoined the squadron and "thumbed a ride." With them were fifty-three Chinese officers and enlisted men led by Capts. Sung S. C. and Wu C. C. (refer to appendix B, noted above, for details).[1]

A separate detail lead by "Pop" Goeller and consisting of TSgt. Solyn; SSgt. Holmes; Sgts. Duffin, Jakubasz, and Whearty; and Pfcs. England and Jackson, as well as an unspecified number of Chinese, made the long journey by train.

Off Karachi at 0819 on May 30 through clouds of swirling sand, Maj. Conrad led the squadron's eleven B-25s, divided into four flights, to Agra. After a hurried dinner, they were off again by 1410 bound for Gaya. Capt. Simpson logged the flight's total time as six hours and thirty-five minutes. "Training days are definitely behind," noted Capt. Graves. All personnel—officers and enlisted, American and Chinese— slept on Army cots set up outdoors, while Sgts. Hanrahan and Armstrong "bedded down with the aircraft." The night was cool, and the men found their overnight accommodations to be comfortable.

The following day, "with an eye to the difficulties of steering a full formation around turbulent weather," the formation again divided into four flights led by Maj. Conrad, Capts. Hodges and Simpson, and Lt. Ragland. Trailing about three minutes apart, elements flew at low altitude below towering cumulus clouds up the Brahmaputra River valley to Moran Field, which "stood out clearly about fifteen miles east of the river, bounded by dense jungle, lying parallel to the railroad and main valley highway." Barely visible through the haze could be glimpsed the daunting barrier that was the Himalayas. Simpson recorded flight time as three hours and thirty minutes. Capt. Hinrichs, who had arrived earlier with SSgt. Gruber to set up mess and quartering facilities, guided the planes into revetments, "all fed by steel landing strips."

Conditions at bases in the Assam valley were primitive, and Moran's airfield was no exception. Living quarters and offices were a block of bipoled British tents with concrete floors, with only a few thatch-roofed wooden huts reserved for senior officers. Walkways were raised areas built about 2 feet aboveground, made "mushy" by heavy rain that signaled the advent of monsoon season. Officers were quartered in the first row of tents, enlisted men in the next two rows of five each, and the Chinese in the next four rows. Outdoor toilet and shower facilities were deemed satisfactory, regardless of their crude construction. Temporary headquarters was set up in the first tent of the area.

Located in a grove of trees about ¼ mile northwest of the revetment area and surrounded by jungle, the camp's occupants were under constant attack by ferocious insects of all descriptions. Screaming monkeys threw fruit at passersby and made frequent raids on the tents in search of food. "This was on a tea plantation, and every once in a while they'd leave one big tree somewhere," recalled Hank. "Usually there'd be one here, one here, one there. I never did understand why they left that one big tree."

Sgt. George Gruber (supply NCO), Capt. John C. E. Hinrichs Jr. (AAF supply technician), and Sgt. Homer L. Chasse pose in front of the supply shack (*left to right*). J. H. Mills collection

Lt. Ragland and Capt. Hinrichs monitor the weather as they stand outside the entrance to their tent on a typically overcast evening at their camp. *J. H. Mills collection*

SSgt. Isabel G. Mier, an airplane armorer, works with his Chinese counterpart to service machine guns in the nose of a B-25H. *J. H. Mills collection*

Pfc. Aubrey LaFoy, who served in the 51st Air Service Group with the medics, described the accommodations in the vicinity of Chabua to which he was assigned later that year: "The tent contained four canvas army beds, some blankets, mosquito netting and one weak light bulb hanging from the ceiling of the tent."[2] Hank shared a similar "double-top British tent" with Isabel Mier, who was known by others of the squadron as "Izzy." The two had become friends during their long voyage aboard *Mission Bay*. Mier often received letters from his father, who lived in Gonzales, Texas. The man always wrote in Spanish because he spoke little or no English. Izzy "claimed to be Spanish," Hank recalled. "I said, 'You're not a Spaniard. You're a Mexican. You should just say you're a Mexican.'"

The day after their arrival, Maj. Conrad and Capt. Hinrichs flew "bright and early" to Chabua to talk with officials at headquarters of the 10th Air Force's 5320th Air Defense Wing and to visit with Capt. Seacrest, who was in General Hospital recovering from an attack of "yellow jaundice."

Seacrest was awarded the Air Medal on June 1. The citation accompanying it stated that he had "distinguished himself by meritorious achievement in twenty-five combat missions" between November 25, 1943, and January 1, 1944, as a pilot and leader of Chinese personnel in medium bombardment aircraft. He displayed excellent flying ability and aggressiveness on various sea sweep missions on which he sank a seagoing tug, a tanker, and a large enemy passenger vessel. "During his attack on the passenger ship on December 26, 1943, the nose wheel door of his plane was shot off and antiaircraft fire damaged the right wing. Despite this damage to his bomber, he completed the attack, sinking the vessel. Lieutenant Seacrest's accomplishments are consonant with the finest traditions of the Army Air Forces."

As the month began, the squadron prepared for the possibility of enemy air raids. Lt. Ragland and crews that formed "A" and "B" flights stood alert all day. "Our squadron will follow the 90th [Fighter] and 83rd Bomber in taking off upon the alert signal (three machine gun bursts) and will fly due west across the Brahmaputra and circle in the foothills until 'pancake' or 'all clear' is sounded," according to Capt. Graves. Chinese personnel were briefed in alert procedure, radio communications, and the grid system used in flight control by wing headquarters. Capts. Simpson, Hodges, Graves, and Cunningham familiarized themselves with operational materials, while Lts. MacNeil, Dorr, and Wood had their respective engineering, armament, and communications sections at work on the airplanes. Engineering checked out squadron aircraft and determined that all were in good condition and ready for combat flight, although no operations were planned before June 3. Transportation arrived in the form of two jeeps and three weapons carriers.

Mechanics and specialists keep A/C #724 ready for missions. *Left to right, back row, standing*: James H. Mills (with his hand on machine gun), Stanley B. Rickman, Maynard W. Rieks, and James R. Summerville. *Middle row, kneeling*: John P. Barge, Lloyd E. Jackson Jr., James E. McCann, Ewell F. Wilkerson, Donald W. Grant, Joseph N. Shock, Frank T. Jakubasz, James A. Wadlow, Frederick C. Libolt, Grady B. Fuller, and Herman L. Burton. *Front row, seated*: unidentified Chinese, and Robert C. MacNeil, engineering officer (*far right with cigarette*). This H model was one of several that were still in service at the end of the war. Notice the Marston mats. *J. H. Mills collection*

The 83rd Medium Bomb Squadron, another B-25 unit stationed at Moran, provided orientation for the pilots and crews as they became familiar with local terrain, targets, and flight and communications conditions. Cpls. Hoke and Mills were promoted to sergeants, and Pfcs. Allegretto, Learn, Burton, Jackson, Rickman, and Trout to corporals. In a postscript to that busy day's activities, Graves wrote, "Someone killed a 5-foot hooded cobra about fifty yards from the last tent in the front row. Sweet dreams, Chillun!" During his time in India, Hank always took the precaution of checking his bedding for cobras before turning in at night, as well as his boots in the morning before pulling them on.

At night, the camp's occupants could hear the trumpeting of elephants used as beasts of burden by native workers. An added deterrent to sleep was the roar of tigers skulking nearby. Hank recalled that they made a sound like *haaah-YAOW*, with "a big noise right at the end." He always slept with a submachine gun and a Colt .45 pistol beside him in his cot in case one of the big cats came prowling too close.

Netting called "mosquito bars" enclosed all beds. One night soon after their arrival, Hank and Izzy were sleeping in their tent when they were awakened by an unusual sound. Hank grabbed his weapons, jerked back the mosquito bar, jumped out of bed, and turned on a light, just in time to see the back end of a large cat exiting the tent and disappearing into the night. He was not able to identify it—"just that it wasn't a tiger." Whatever it was, fear of the feline's return prevented the two men from getting much sleep for the rest of the night.

Making up the squadron at that time was a diverse cast of characters. Of those who received promotions on the first, Hank recalled that Burton was a bartender from Kentucky. He remembered Jackson particularly well because they met during training at Wichita Falls; were stationed at Tampa, Shreveport, and Goldsboro; and shipped out of New York for Karachi together. Both remembered Allegretto, from the Jersey Shore. Hank recalled, "He was Italian. There is a picture of him, and he had a tattoo of a naked woman on his arm. In the picture another man is holding a fire extinguisher, pointing at that tattoo." Hank said, "I asked him, 'Were you drunk when you got that?' I didn't even need to ask. I already knew the answer." After the war, Allegretto's wife and mother teamed up to persuade him to "get clothing" for the woman, so the tattoo was modified by the addition of a pair of shorts and small top.[3]

Hank remembered this about Hoke: "He was the one that was on a troop ship. The Germans sank it and he survived that sinking, but he was goofy in the head after that." Hoke had been aboard HMS *Rohna*, which departed Oran, Algeria, with two other ships, HMS *Egra* and HMS *Karoa*, on November 24, 1943. They joined a convoy headed east toward the Suez Canal that was to proceed to Karachi. At about 4:00 on the afternoon of the twenty-sixth, Dornier Do 217s of the Luftwaffe's Kampfgeschwader 100, stationed at

From Armament and clowning for the camera are (*left to right*) Lt. George C. Cunningham (squadron bombardier) aiming the fire extinguisher, Pfc. Andrew R. Allegretto (airplane armorer), with the tattoo, and Sgt. Clyde L. Learn (airplane armorer and cannon specialist) offering him a shirt to cover it. *J. H. Mills collection*

Marseilles, France, attacked the convoy with radio-controlled glide bombs. *Rohna* was struck amidships just above the waterline, almost blowing the ship in half. Hundreds of men perished in the explosions and the raging fires that resulted. Many others lost their lives when they jumped overboard to escape the flames. An estimated 1,200 died in the attack, and hundreds more were wounded. Of the 152 enlisted technicians bound for the CBI, only forty-eight survived, and twenty-eight of those were fit for duty. Hoke was among the survivors, his wounds consisting primarily of contusions to the thorax according to hospital admission records. He was later awarded the Purple Heart. Because of censorship restrictions, his mother, in Pennsylvania, did not receive assurance of his survival until the arrival of a letter from the National Jewish Welfare Board in late January 1944.[4] There is little wonder that Hoke was profoundly affected by the experience. He was assigned duty as a gun turret specialist after being attached to the 3rd Bomb Squadron and was not required to fly combat missions.

The CACW's adjutant, Maj. McGehee, was another witness to the devastation. He included his impressions of the experience in his February 16 letter to the Greenville newspaper. "We left Africa finally, and were on our way through the Mediterranean to this theater.... I think we were the first convoy to go through there for this theater.... There we got our first real taste of this war when a bunch of German bombers knocked the hell out of us twice." Although they sank only one ship out of the convoy, "it was certainly touch and go for a while." The ship he was on got through without damage, but quite a few friends with whom he had served at Eglin Field didn't make it. "It was a pretty rugged two days, but it could have been worse. I know now that the most helpless feeling in the world is to stand on a ship and watch a bomb coming down and hear it whistling. All you can do is stand there ready to jump and hoping it doesn't hit." He concluded that "those people who said the Mediterranean was 'an Allied lake' at that time didn't know what they were talking about."

McGehee wrote that he had finally arrived in India and described it as "a country of contrasts." He explained, "They have the brightest colors and the dullest, the richest people and the greatest poverty, the most beautiful buildings and the worst slums, some beautiful country and the most barren." Spending five days traveling on a troop train, he saw quite a lot of the country through the train's windows.[5]

The tropical climate at Moran was in complete contrast to the desert conditions to which squadron personnel had become accustomed at Malir. This part of India receives some of the heaviest rainfall in the world, with over 400 inches each year, and monsoon season ordinarily extends from early June through August. During those months, the bases became a sea of mud. Perforated metal strips called "Marston mats" that overlay the runways and revetments made it possible for the planes to take off and land, even during the rainy season.

High temperatures and humidity caused everything belonging to the men, including their clothes and shoes, to mildew within days. Drinking water

Stripped down to T-shirts as a concession to the heat, Capt. Louis F. Graves Jr. (squadron navigator and historical, censor, publications, and schools officer) and Maj. Conrad (commanding officer) consult at the line. *R. N. Solyn collection, courtesy of Robert N. Solin*

Mildewing at Moran

was purified by boiling or the addition of iodine. Dysentery and malaria were prevalent, here as they were later in China. Known without affection as "Annies," the malarial *Anopheles* mosquitoes flourished in the steamy, swampy conditions that prevailed in Assam during monsoon season. Hank recalled that the men took Atabrine as a precaution against the debilitating infection. Administered in the mess hall, GIs swallowed one tablet after breakfast and one after supper, twice per week. "It was yellow, and it'd turn your skin yellow after you had been taking it. I guess it worked, because I never did have malaria."

The Japanese had completely occupied Burma, geographically positioned immediately south and east of Assam, since early April 1942. The enemy had assembled a strong force at Myitkyina (pronounced MIT-chi-nah), the largest town in upper Burma, which was used as a base of operations. Their goal was to capture the Imphal plain and push into upper Assam to cut off air supplies to China over the Himalayan Hump. Such a move would be disastrous for the Allies because it would give the Japanese complete supremacy over China. The control of Imphal was, therefore, critical.

The crossroads city of Imphal in the Indian state of Manipur was the only practical approach by which the Japanese could invade India from Burma, because of the forbidding mountain range that ran along their shared border. To resist the incursion, British and Indian forces strongly fortified the Imphal plain and Manipur valley. Japanese forces laid siege to the city as the British and their Allies offered fierce resistance. Bombing of Allied strongholds had continued uninterrupted for two years by the time Conrad's squadron reached Assam. Lord Mountbatten had urged an assault into north-central Burma to capture Myitkyina and Mogaung, both strongly held by the Japanese. Myitkyina's airfield was taken on May 17, although the city still held, and Mogaung was under attack.[6]

As this situation was developing, Chinese forces succeeded on May 11 in crossing the Salween River as they advanced from China's Yunnan Province and were heavily engaged just west of Tatangtzu as well as along the Schweli River. While they waited for orders to proceed to China, the 3rd Squadron's fliers had hopes of taking part in some of the action in Burma.

Maj. Conrad and Capt. Hinrichs traveled to the supply depot at Jorhat and "made connections for the future" as June began, Graves wrote. Capts. Cunningham and Graves visited A-1 and A-3 (Personnel and Operations) at wing headquarters, where they received updates on the tactical situation, as well as a supply of intelligence information and materials. Operations and Supply each received a telephone, and electric lights were being set up for all sections. The following day, the two Chinese cooks assigned to the kitchen walked out. They had previously been supplied with Army rations but were now expected to provide meals using fresh meats, fruits, and vegetables, and the cooks apparently objected to any actual cooking.

"Typical monsoon weather forestalled any operation today, although work continued on the line," wrote Graves. "Heavy rains turned the tent area into a quagmire. Usually, the rains and winds are heaviest after nightfall. Few tent floors escape a thorough washing and mold is showing on articles of clothing."

As for the mechanics, they soon discovered that aircraft maintenance was a serious problem, not only because of the weather but also because spare parts were in short supply and working conditions were poor. There were no hangars, so Engineering did repairs and maintenance in the aircraft-parking areas. During monsoon season, work on the planes was performed primarily at night because of the brutal heat. Resourceful mechanics rigged makeshift covers to protect the engines during downpours so they could keep the planes ready to fly. Since aircraft that regularly crossed the Hump often flew well above their normal operating limits, concerns for safety increased the need for constant maintenance.

MSgt. Arthur Oxford, who had arrived at Moran in March with the 82nd ("Bulldog") Bomb Squadron, had this to say: "Soon our B-25s went into action to support both the Chinese drive in northern Burma and the British counterattack in Assam. They bombed the Jap bases like Myitkyina and Kumaing and Katha. They ripped up railway bridges and junctions. They caught Jap planes on the ground in raids on airfields. And then in June the four-month monsoon season set in to give us a new batch of trouble."

Continuing the narrative, TSgt. Charles A. Metcalf of the 83rd ("Black Angel") Bomb Squadron provided more details. "Trouble is right. The weather was so thick the birds could walk on it. Our planes were lucky to get a day clear enough to see the target. And even if they did, they still had to cross and recross the 9,000-foot-high Chin Hills, which were always blanketed in a few thousand feet or more of clouds," he said. "We ground men soon made some delightful little discoveries about the effect of constant rain and dampness on a plane. Metal parts, for instance, rust or corrode. Fabric rots and leather gets mildewed. Radio equipment goes on the blink and machine guns jam up."[7]

The four squadrons (81st, 82nd, 83rd, and 434th) of the 12th ("Earthquakers") Bomb Group, 10th Air Force, had flown against targets in Egypt, Libya, Tunisia, Pantelleria, Lampedusa, Crete, Sicily, and Italy before transferring to India. Since arrival of the 82nd and 83rd Squadrons, these experienced airmen had been flying their B-25s on primarily low-level bombing and strafing missions against targets in Burma.[8]

Maj. R. L. Patterson, in command of the 83rd Squadron, was distrustful of the abilities of the recently arrived and biracial 3rd Bomb Squadron. Before allowing the mixed Chinese American crews to "tack onto" his planes for missions, he insisted that 3rd Squadron airmen fly a practice formation flight with the 83rd to demonstrate their readiness for combat. After being presented with Maj. Patterson's demands on June 3, Maj. Conrad agreed, although he and the rest of the squadron were "slightly irritated at Patterson's belittling attitude." The following day, Capt. Hodges and "his Chinese boys, Lts. Tung and Yen," flew follow element to the 83rd Squadron's lead element. Capt. Graves later commented, "Our boys assembled and tacked on much quicker than the 83rd, who flew an extremely wide pattern."

Hodges, from Alabama, had been flying since 1938 and was far from inexperienced. Although he joined the Air Corps in September 1940 as a mechanic, he later qualified as an aviation cadet and completed the typical pilot's training curriculum, which consisted of ten weeks of preflight school (military protocol; classroom preparation for flight training), ten more of primary flying school (basic flying skills; more classroom instruction), ten of basic flying school (more-complex flight maneuvers), and ten of advanced flying training (preparation for single-engine or multiengine assignments), followed by ten weeks of postgraduate transition flying training (preparation for piloting the specific aircraft used by the unit to which student was to be assigned). As a test pilot, Hodges flew about fifty-five different kinds of planes during this period, including "some Navy, some foreign, some experimental planes." He became a training instructor at Turner Field in Albany, Georgia, and Eglin Field near Valparaiso, Florida, where he trained Jimmy Doolittle to fly the Mitchells he used on his raid. Since his arrival aboard *Mission Bay*, he had trained Chinese pilots and crews. While the 3rd Squadron shared the field with the 490th Bomb Squadron of the 341st Bomb Group, 10th Air Force, Hodges collaborated to perfect "glip bombing" against bridges. The technique proved so successful that the 490th gained fame as the "Burma Bridge Busters" and the 341st as the "China Glippers."[9] Hodges's wingmen, Tung and Yen, were almost equally well trained.

When Hodges's plane, A/C #713, bellied into a rice paddy after developing mechanical failure on a practice flight, it was soon surrounded by solicitous natives bearing fruit and water. *R. N. Solyn collection, courtesy of Robert N. Solin*

Capt. Raymond L. Hodges Jr. (B-25 pilot / flight leader), in the pilot's seat here, was one of the squadron's most experienced—and most highly respected—flight leaders. He later moved to the 1st Bomb Squadron and became its commanding officer. *J. H. Mills collection*

Mechanics examine Hodges's plane before determining that the damage was irreparable and consigning its usable parts to be salvaged. *Walter Contreras collection, courtesy of Bob Contreras*

After about an hour in the air, Capt. Hodges's plane (a B-25H, A/C #713) developed engine trouble. With 2Lts. Chang H. H. and Tu K. M., Hodges was flying at 5,000 feet in conditions of scattered clouds, ceiling about 7,000 feet, and unlimited visibility when the oil pressure on his right engine dropped to zero. Soon after Hodges turned back toward the field, his right propeller "ran away" and would not feather (turning the blades into the wind to eliminate drag). The plane was unable to maintain altitude, so at about 1445 he made a wheels-up landing in a rice field about 8 miles northwest of Moran Field. Flying on Hodges's right wing was 2Lt. Tung Shih-liang (X-833), who reported observing that the right engine caught fire and gas spurted out. He followed the lead plane down to tree level and saw the pilot and the two crewmen on the wing of the downed plane, waving their arms. Tung returned to Moran and reported the plane's location. Failure of the engine's internal lubricating system was blamed for loss of oil pressure, since oil lines were determined to be intact. Capt. Simpson signed the report as operations officer, as well as Capt. Seacrest and 1Lts. MacNeil and Ragland. SSgt. Rieks was noted as crew chief. The plane was turned over to the 52nd Service Group, China-Burma-India Air Service Command, for salvage.[10]

In his capacity as airplane armorer, SSgt. James E. McCann often wore heavy, insulated gloves to protect his hands and arms from the fierce heat generated by the machine guns after prolonged periods of continuous firing. *Courtesy of Mark E. McCann*

Capt. Hodges borrowed a bicycle from one of the locals ("the Chief," according to Simpson). As he started pedaling back toward base, he met his rescuers along the road. Capt. Graves wrote that when two trucks "drove through tea garden lanes" and arrived at the crash site, the rescue team found the plane surrounded by natives, who had brought "quantities of fruit and water" to the downed airmen and "gathered up airplane parts scattered in the wake of the crash." Graves praised Hodges for crash-landing "beautifully," with the least possible damage to the plane and no injury to personnel. "All hands" had returned safely to the airfield by 1900.

Because of his stocky build, Hodges had been given the nickname "Ponza" (meaning "portly" or "fatty" in Mandarin Chinese) by the officers, and some of them, such as Bob MacNeil, referred to him as "Fat Hodges." The enlisted men always called him "Captain" out of admiration and respect.[11] He went on to fly a multitude of successful 3rd Squadron missions.

Despite Graves's comment that no one was injured, the description of circumstances is very similar to a story told by Jim McCann about the crash in a rice paddy of a B-25 in which he was a crew member. The plane's fire ax dislodged and hit him in the forehead, knocking him out. As he was regaining consciousness, he looked up and beheld a strange sight. Approaching was a heavily bejeweled maharajah riding on an elephant. In his dazed and bewildered state, his first thought was "I'm dead, and God is an Indian." Doctors wanted to put a steel plate in his head, but McCann feared that the metal would cause an adverse reaction, and never allowed it.[12]

By this time, bombers assigned to the 3rd Squadron, each displaying the Kuomintang sun, also bore a Chinese air force number—in the range from 713 through 726 for bombers of the 3rd Bomb Squadron. On the nose of each plane was a roundel featuring the squadron's insignia: a black-and-white skunk with his tail raised in the "armed" position and a self-protective clothespin on his nose. Above his back was his target: a burnt-orange rising sun against a turquoise sky. Its design was the creation of Capt. Hinrichs.[13] The squadron mascot represented yet another example of cultural differences between the Americans and the Chinese, who were unwilling to characterize themselves as skunks and therefore referred to the animal as a weasel or ferret (*yo shu*).[14]

MSgt. Grady B. Fuller (line chief and later engineering officer) and TSgt. John P. Hanrahan (communications chief) point to the roundel featuring the new squadron insignia on this B-25H's nose. *G. B. Fuller collection, courtesy of Elizabeth Fuller Zea*

Capt. Hinrichs, creator of the squadron's insignia, proudly wears the "Spray and Pray" patch on his jacket. The pipe was his trademark. He was rarely pictured without one, and he collected dozens of them through the years. He is a major in this photo. *J. H. Mills collection*

This close-up of Capt. Simpson's patch shows it in greater detail. The black-and-white skunk against a turquoise sky had as his target a burnt-orange "rising sun" representing imperial Japan above his back. The background color for the leather patches was later changed to dark brown because the turquoise paint used in the earlier version was not durable. *T. S. Simpson collection, courtesy of Larry Simpson*

Later in the year, MSgt. Hanrahan called his outfit the "skunk-holding-its-nose-to-the-rising-sun" squadron, while "the Flying Skunk" squadron occasionally appeared in newspaper articles back home. The squadron's historical officer noted that they called themselves the "Spray and Pray Boys." The term "spray and pray" (generally used derisively) refers to the practice of firing an automatic firearm toward an enemy in long bursts without making an effort to line up each shot or burst of shots, yet hoping for accurate results. In the case of the 3rd Squadron, the name was chosen with a kind of tongue-in-cheek humor. B-25s flown by the 3rd Bomb Squadron can easily be identified by the skunk displayed on the nose, including Hodges's plane that crashed into the rice paddy. When asked in later years why they chose a skunk as their mascot, Simpson answered, "Well, we had to pick *something*."[15]

The squadron experienced its first alert at 0935 on June 5. Lts. Yen and Liu, Chinese pilots, were commended because their planes "got off the runway with an amazingly short take-off despite a bomb load." The all-clear was sounded before most of the Mitchells were even out of their revetments. The alert was determined to be a false alarm, and activities soon returned to normal.

The estrangement that had developed between the 3rd and the 83rd Squadrons "reached a crescendo at the evening meal" following Hodges's forced landing. Unsatisfied, the Black Angel Squadron's commander demanded a second flight to test the capabilities of 3rd Squadron airmen. This time Conrad objected, on the grounds that his squadron had already demonstrated its ability and that a second flight would be a personal affront to his men. Patterson's attitude was "inspired by an apprehension of the close formation the Third flies," according to Graves. "His comments are whimsy, not founded on any logic."

Conrad refused, insisting that his squadron would "merely await the arrival of the necessary fighter protection in Col. Rouse's outfit and the assignment of a lead airplane." Maj. Patterson appealed to Brig. Gen. John F. Egan, in command of the 5320th Air Defense Wing, who wired a message to Conrad demanding that he yield because the other officer outranked him as the "supreme commander." Conrad had no choice but to concede to the second practice flight, which took place on June 7. This time, Lt. Ragland's flight flew second element to Maj. Patterson's lead three elements. Once again, the Chinese pilots "made a wonderful showing," and Patterson called off the practice flight.

The 3rd and 83rd Squadrons were scheduled to fly their first mission together on the following day, but severe turbulence intervened to prevent operations. Maj. Gen. Howard C. Davidson, former CACW training chief and now in command of the 10th Air Force, held a conference that included representatives of both bomb squadrons and the 90th Fighter Squadron of the 80th Fighter Group ("Burma Banshees"), which shared the same field. Davidson's major points were his intention to remove the 83rd back to its group near Calcutta, as well as the 3rd Squadron's assuming the bombing role over Burma in support of Lt. Gen. Joseph W. ("Vinegar Joe") Stilwell's troops with protection by P-40s from the 90th and the CACW's 5th Fighter Group, which was scheduled to arrive soon. The 83rd departed on June 11, "leaving Upper Assam to the Third."

A trip to the 52nd Air Service Group's S-2 (Intelligence) at Jorhat produced equipment that included "jungle kits plus escape kit ingredients." Components varied, but a typical jungle kit consisted of a backpack or vest with pockets containing odds and ends that would come in handy in case of a crash landing. Items generally considered essential were maps, Burmese- or Chinese-language *Pointee-Talkee* books, a *How to Get Along* survival book, American flag "blood chit," compass, flask, whetstone, folding machete, saw blade, razor blades, fishing gear (leader, line, and hooks), matches, sewing needles and thread, and even toilet tissue. Always included was a first-aid kit that contained iodine, bandages, tweezers, and Benzedrine subcarbonate (a powerful amphetamine), in addition to such items as a few hard chocolate bars and bouillon powder. The Chinese had begun hearing lectures on bailout procedure, as well as jungle and escape procedures, and were getting calisthenics every afternoon.

Capt. Wu Ch'ao-chen, squadron cocommander, was promoted to major at about this time. Trained under the older CAF system, Wu was considered to be old-fashioned by those trained by the Americans, so tensions occasionally arose among the Chinese regarding his methods. No one could question whether the Chinese, regardless of their training, were awaiting the opportunity to get in their blows against the invaders at least as eagerly as the Americans.

There was uncertainty concerning the squadron's assignment as the 83rd Squadron was moving off base and the 3rd was assuming its role, according to Graves. "Rumor has it that the Tenth Air Force is to be moved to Kanjakoah replacing the Burma-bound 5320th Air Defense Wing. We will be directly under the wings of the Tenth apparently!"

Maj. Conrad's squadron continued to make preparations for joining the fight in Burma, but bad weather prevented its B-25s from flying any combat missions for more than two weeks. The same monsoon conditions that caused downpours in camp also produced treacherous storms over the mountains, creating even-more-hazardous conditions than usual. "It is imperative that air support be given troops surrounding entrenched Japs at Myitkyina, but insurmountable weather always intervenes," wrote Graves in frustration. Every day, 3rd Squadron flight crews were up early and stood by, "hoping for a clear report to warrant flying through the Himalayan Pass down to the battle area," but every night they returned to their tents "missionless." The closest they came to a mission was on June 13, when nine planes made it as far as the taxi strip before the red light flashed from the tower and a voice announced over the command set, "Mission inadvisable. Weather bad at pass." Graves noted, "The 'do nothing' period isn't attributing anything to morale."

Following the departure of the Chinese cooks, the 83rd Squadron had temporarily taken over duties in the mess hall, which it shared with the 3rd Squadron. When these "chefs" transferred out, Capt. Hinrichs took over responsibilities for cooking and serving. Capt. Graves wrote, "The kitchen personnel reads like a rated cast of characters—two captains, a tech, master and staff sergeant manning the ladles and stoves. To our unbounded surprise, the quality of dishes has improved fifty percent." It became common to see "officers and ratings sweating out a KP stretch."

Unlike at Malir, officers and enlisted men ate their meals in a shared mess hall. With morale at a low ebb, tempers were short. One day, as SSgt. Gruber was serving in the chow line, he "got into it" with Lt. Ragland over some trivial incident, according to Hank. Ragland reacted with "Do you want to take it outside?" Gruber declined the offer, and the two resolved their disagreement without a fight. Gruber's Jewish Austro-Polish family always called him "Joey," although his legal name was George. His parents had fled the Nazi threat and moved to Brooklyn, where his father found work as a tailor.[16] Gruber had worked as a shipping and receiving clerk before enlistment and served as squadron supply sergeant under Hinrichs since his transfer to the 3rd Squadron.

To alleviate the personnel shortage, kitchen help was urgently requested from wing headquarters. The Chinese seem to have heard about the improvements in the Americans' chow. Soon they lodged a complaint about their food and demanded American rations—"a problem Capt. Hinrichs must answer."

According to SLt. Tu, whose recollections are invaluable in understanding events from the Chinese point of view, it was at about this time that a disagreement arose that did lead to blows, and he described the incident in an interview more than sixty years later. One day a Chinese pilot whose surname was Xu (SLt. Hsu In-kwei, who was attached to the 3rd Squadron on the same date as Tu, per squadron records) and an unnamed American "mechanical sergeant" were performing routine maintenance inspections. Because Hsu's English was poor, he was unable to communicate effectively with the sergeant, who became increasingly annoyed. Tempers flared and voices rose. In his frustration, Hsu shouted, "You are a liar!" Tu's comment on the inevitable result: "From my several decades of experiencing interacting with Americans, I know that you can directly inform them of your complaints, but if you call them a liar, they will get mad, and a physical confrontation may result."

The sergeant struck the first blow. Simpson and Tu, along with several NCOs, rushed over to break up the fight, but not before Hsu got the worst of it. The sergeant punched him in the face, resulting in a black eye and bleeding from the teeth. Hsu gave the American a hard kick before they were separated. Afterward, the two made peace and apologized to each other.

However, the physical assault on a superior officer by an NCO was a serious offense that could call for a court-martial, so the incident was reported to higher levels of command. Gen.

George E. Stratemeyer, commanding general of the Army Air Forces' India-Burma Sector, paid a visit to Group to deal with the situation personally. Tu acted as interpreter. Gen. Stratemeyer first lectured the squadron leaders, Majors Conrad and Wu, on keeping discipline among their subordinates, and then together they discussed what should be done about the incident. Stratemeyer urged that consideration be given to the fact that it resulted from poor communication. Wu held that an NCO's striking an officer was inexcusable and deserved a harsh penalty, while Conrad argued that a court-martial was not necessary, and urged a lighter punishment. The NCO was ultimately sent back to the US but not court-martialed. According to Tu, the greatest challenge for the Chinese was that they must understand and communicate in English.[17] This incident was one of many that demonstrated the difficulties caused by differences in language and culture between the Chinese and Americans, but it also showed their willingness to work together to resolve their differences.

As squadron personnel waited for missions, they sometimes obtained passes and made their way into Dibrugarh, located about 20 miles north on the Brahmaputra River's south bank. Known as the "Tea City of India," it was an important business and industrial center for the region. An estimated 50 percent of Assam's tea production was shipped from the city. Temples abounded, and sacred cows wandered the streets unrestrained. There were shops and restaurants that catered to the British, Chinese, and American military personnel stationed in the area. Although there was an "American club" in town, eating in Dibrugarh was discouraged because of uncertain sanitation at most dining establishments. Nightly poker games back at camp were the principal form of entertainment for the men, supplemented by three "shows" per week "shown through the courtesy of the fighter squadron, projection owners and operators."

News that a CACW insignia had been authorized circulated in mid-June. A design submitted by Capt. Harry L. Kebric, CACW combat liaison officer, had been adopted by the War Department following extensive revisions. Maj. Hummel, wing historical officer, explained, "To make the dragon in his design look less reluctant, and to get a typical Chinese dragon into the composition, Capt. Kebric had the design further developed by Mr. Chen Yen Chian, an artist on the staff of the Kweilin Office of War Information, OWI." The Wing Insignia Selection Committee approved this final design before submission to the War Board. Hummel explained the significance of each element:

> The new Wing insignia and its symbolic significance might be described as follows: Centered in a blue, gold-bordered field, in bold relief against the blue background, are shown the gold Chinese dragon, representative of the Chinese Air Forces, and a tawnish winged tiger, symbolizing the 14th US Air Force. Between them, tooth and nail, they tear to shreds the Japanese flag, this signifying their joint objective, the ultimate victory over the common foe. Slight cloud forms in this blue field further symbolize the air, the operating medium of the air forces.
>
> Above the blue field, the red and white stripes arching down over the top half of the insignia are representative of the colors common to the flags of both nations. The symbolical flag is further developed by the blue of the keystone set in the top center of the striped arch; while the white sun and the white star set beside each other in the keystone indicate the aircraft symbols used by the two nations. Surmounting all, two golden, winged hands are clasped in a firm, hearty grip, and are intended to represent the hand of the CACW Chinese airman and the hand of a CACW American airman, gripped in mutual support and confidence.

Lt. Col. Irving L. ("Twig") Branch, in command of the 1st Bomb Group, was a favorite among the men who served under him. He took command in July 1943 and returned to the US in September 1944. During that period, he was awarded Chinese Air Force Wings as well as the Yun-Hui decoration. *R. L. Logan collection, courtesy of Katherine A. Logan*

Rain fell intermittently through the day on June 14. Late that night, "a mud-splattered jeep dragged to a stop outside the poker room in the orderly building." The voice bellowing for "Coondog" was that of Col. Branch, group CO, accompanied by Maj. Thomas F. Manion, group adjutant, and Capt. Dale Osborne, wing expediter on service at Chabua. Men of the 3rd Squadron were expecting to receive orders for their move to China, their "ultimate destination," as had the group's other three bomb squadrons immediately after completion of their combat training. However, it was not to be. Col. Branch brought details of the situation in China and passed along Gen. Chennault's decision to the squadron commander, informing Maj. Conrad that his men should expect to spend the summer in Assam rather than moving on to China, where the supply situation was so bad that another B-25 squadron could not be supported until fall. The bull session extended well into the night and ended with bacon sandwiches served at midnight. Discussion continued through the next day as the monsoon persisted.

"Our dubious status cleared amazingly today," reported Graves on the sixteenth. Along with Col. Branch and Maj. Manion, Conrad flew to Chabua for a visit to headquarters of the 5320th Air Defense Wing, 10th Air Force, which was responsible for defense of the airfields in the Assam area and protection of air traffic to China via the Hump route, as well as air support for Lt. Gen. Stilwell's ground offensive in northern Burma. Stilwell's aim was to reopen the Burma Road, which ran from Lashio in a northeasterly direction across the Burma/China border before meandering eastward to Kunming, as well as a new land route to extend from Ledo in Assam to intersect the Burma Road above Lashio. Later called the "Ledo Road" and then the "Stilwell Highway," this new passage was intended to allow increased access to supplies, equipment, weapons, and munitions required for Allied operations in China, but opening this route proved to be a monumental undertaking.[18] Stilwell's ground troops included the 5307th Composite Unit (Provisional), a deep-penetration unit organized as code name "Galahad" but which gained fame as "Merrill's Marauders."[19]

At 5320th Headquarters, Conrad was shown a dispatch from Gen. Chennault that gave a new assignment to his squadron. Providing air support for Stilwell in Burma put the 3rd Squadron under the command of the 5320th Wing. Simultaneously working directly with the 14th Air Force, it was to take over the role of B-24s of the 308th Bomb Group, which supported the Chinese offensive in the Salween area. Conrad was assured that B-25Js intended for lead ships would be provided for bombing critical targets along the Burma Road. Before leaving for China, Col. Branch offered further assurance that he would clarify matters in Kunming and then return to Moran to initiate a trip to obtain the promised airplanes from the factory at Bangalore, India. Capt. Seacrest, recently released from the hospital, flew with Maj. Conrad back to Moran later that day.

The following week, Maj. Conrad visited 10th Air Force HQ at Kanjakoa for more operational information. There he received orders to proceed to China to discuss the cooperation of his squadron with the 69th Composite Wing of the 14th Air Force, operating out of Yunnanyi. Coordinating the squadron's efforts at air-to-ground support of the offensive by the Chinese army's "Y Force" or "Yoke Force" was at the top of items under discussion. The 3rd Bomb Squadron expected to enter the war at last.

The Chinese National Revolutionary Army in Burma, with other Allied forces, had been forced to retreat when the Japanese invaded Burma in early 1942. Two divisions, the 38th and the 22nd, plus fragments of three others, retreated into India, where they were placed under Stilwell's command. Reequipped and retrained, they were designated "X Force" and formed the majority of Stilwell's front line when he advanced from northern India into northern Burma in October 1943, with the intention of reoccupying Burma and establishing a land supply line from Assam to the Chinese province of Yunnan. It was these two divisions of China's New 1st Army for which the 3rd Bomb Squadron was to provide air support.

The Salween drive was initiated in support of Stilwell's main offensive. A forward echelon headquarters of the 69th Wing had been set up in early May at a new field near Yunnanyi to direct the advance. On May 11, 1944, Chinese troops designated "Y Force" reentered Burma from Yunnan, crossing the Salween River in force at two points north of Teng-chung, about 75 miles southeast of Myitkyina, and making two lesser thrusts across the river opposite Pingka. The mission of Y Force was to drive down the Burma Road, taking Teng-chung, Lung-ling, Mangshih, and Pingka, and eventually to meet with the other attacking forces in central Burma, although Teng-chung, Lung-ling, Mangshih, and Pingka were still in enemy hands at the end of June.[20]

On May 17, Stilwell's Y Force and X Force, along with Merrill's Marauders, captured Myitkyina's airfield, used by the Japanese as a base from which to attack Allied aircraft flying over the Hump. One immediate benefit of clearing the enemy stronghold was that it provided the Allies with an emergency airstrip. A second, according to Lt. Lopez of the 75th Fighter Squadron, was that Hump aircraft were able to fly much farther south and thus at a lower altitude. New routes crossing "the Low Hump" were established, including those that connected through Myitkyina. Lopez explained, "In effect they were flying around rather than over the Hump. Within a few months the amount of tonnage carried over the Hump had doubled, and the Fourteenth Air Force supply of fuel and ammunition increased markedly."[21] Although the airfield had been captured, the heavily garrisoned town resisted the Allied advance, as small Japanese forces held on tenaciously to Myitkyina and other defensive positions.

Chinese and American forces were making steady progress down the Mogaung valley. The Chinese, short of artillery as well as almost everything else that they needed to engage the enemy, depended on mules and coolies to bring up supplies after they had been ferried across the unbridged river, and Chinese troops at advanced positions frequently ran short of food and ammunition. The mission of the 69th Wing in this campaign was to give close tactical support to the attackers, isolate the battlefield, and provide air supply. Brig. Gen. Frank Dorn, commander of the Yunnan force at his headquarters at Pao-shan, selected the targets.

An announcement issued by Adm. Lord Louis Mountbatten's headquarters explained the military situation in Burma as it existed in mid-June. The Chinese 22nd Army captured Kamaing, "the principal supply base in North Burma and the key enemy stronghold in the Mogaung Valley," on June 16, following a seven-day siege. "Farther to the south, the Chinese seized the town of Parentu, while in the main North Burma bastion of Myitkyina, Chinese and American troops continued to make gains in the north and west sectors." On the Salween front, a "token juncture" had been made between Stilwell's North Burma forces and Chinese guerrillas, who had captured Lauhkaum, well to the west of Hpmaw Pass and 60 air miles northeast of Myitkyina. It was the first China-Burma link since the Japanese occupation of Burma. During this period, the Japanese were reported to be "reinforcing the area they hold in the Mogaung Valley and around Myitkyina, but their railway lines were unusable, and the enemy was obliged to bring whatever fresh troops he could on foot."

An official headquarters spokesman stated that Allied progress in the area was slow, but a juncture by Chinese troops driving southward from Kamaing with airborne Chindits near the town of Mogaung was expected in the near future. Operations over the whole Burma-India front were likely to continue right through the monsoon, he predicted. "Japanese strength in Burma is now twice what it was at the end of the last monsoon, and enemy reinforcements were observed in the India sectors south of Bishenpur," where a separate Allied campaign was expected to attempt driving the enemy southward. The situation on the Imphal plain was "reasonably satisfactory."[22]

Although numerically inferior, the Japanese had developed strong defensive positions at every avenue of approach and were deployed to exact the heaviest possible casualties among the attackers. Reduction of each strongpoint depended on heavy air attack. The defending Japanese, although lacking air support, possessed superior lines of supply, so multiple bombing and strafing missions were directed against enemy staging areas and supply dumps. Interdicting the transport of enemy troops and supplies became the primary focus of the 3rd Bomb Squadron when it was finally able to join the fight.

As the month of June neared its end, squadron activities progressed as usual. Chinese and American crews at Moran were thoroughly briefed on a possible mission into the Hukawng Valley in northern Burma on June 18, but bad weather both in Assam and over the target prevented planes from taking off. As the 3rd Squadron waited to be ordered into action, Chinese driving a command car overturned and slid off the muddy road into a water-filled ditch, narrowly escaping injury. The wrecked vehicle was hauled to Chabua for repairs.

Native laborers cleared underbrush and repaired "dissipated" walkways between tents. Supervised by Lts. Wood and Faherty, they also completed the erection and furnishing of tents in the area allocated to Col. Rouse's fighter squadrons, due to arrive

Lt. George P. Wood, the squadron's communications officer, was a "jack of all trades" who flew eight combat missions and later served as assistant supply officer and assistant operations officer. *G. P. Wood collection, courtesy of Glynis Wood Jamora*

Lt. Faherty, bombardier, is in the pilot's seat of B-25H A/C #714 sometime before it crash-landed because of damage caused by enemy fire in August 1944. He, Capt. Seacrest, and their Chinese passenger and aircrew all survived with relatively minor injuries. *R. N. Solyn collection, courtesy of Robert N. Solin*

soon. A transport command unit flying C-47s moved onto the field temporarily and set up headquarters adjacent to 3rd Squadron headquarters at the line. Having also completed training, the 5th Fighter Group's 17th and 27th Squadrons arrived at Moran with their P-40s on June 24 and took residence in the block of tents immediately west of the 3rd Squadron. "It is questionable whether they will remain here or proceed to China for operations," wrote Graves.

Rain continued to fall, calling a halt to operations.

CHAPTER FIVE
Bombing in Burma

Early on June 25, 1944, Capt. Simpson once again briefed aircrews, and then he and Lt. Ragland went with them down to the flight line. There they stood by in alert shacks for hours, hoping for a chance to hit the enemy. Weather finally cleared enough to allow planes into the air for the 3rd Bomb Squadron's first combat mission late that Sunday afternoon. Simpson and Ragland flew two B-25Hs with three 90th Fighter Squadron P-47s as cover on a low-level raid against railroad bridges and rails between Mohnyin and Mawhun. The bombers each carried six 500 lb. HE (high explosive) bombs fused to eleven-second delay. Weather was "as briefed, viz, low broken and high overcast to Pass, thunderstorms along ridges in Valley, with ceiling 5,000 and unlimited visibility." The aircraft arrived over the first bridge (24°32' N, 96°12' E) at 1655 hours. Simpson went in at 200 feet true altitude, with Ragland trailing close behind. Bombs hit the abutment and destroyed the bridge. Because they still had bombs, the pilots flew on to hit a second bridge (24°27' N, 96°11' E), causing some damage. Then they followed up with one direct hit on the roadbed south and another north of Mawhun. Both pilots shot two rounds of 75 mm ammunition from the cannons. The formation encountered no enemy opposition either from the air or the ground, and results of the mission were "excellent." Simpson noted its duration as three hours and ten minutes. All aircraft returned to Moran safely.

The 90th Squadron's P-40s, featuring the Burma Banshee's distinctive nose art—a snarling, blood-drooling skull, were supplemented by this time with recently acquired P-47s. Each of these new fighters had an individual fuselage number (ranging from 70 to 99) and a blue ring around the hood; later diagonal black stripes were added to the tail section. In combination with the banshee wail of the fighter's engine as it came in low to provide increased firepower for dive-bombing or skip-bombing runs, it promised death and destruction to the enemy. Tasked primarily with providing combat air patrols for transports over the Hump to Kunming and conducting ground attack operations in Burma in support of troops in contact with Japanese occupational forces, the fighters lived up to their group motto, "Angels on our wings."

Following their return from this mission, as from others that followed, the crews gathered for debriefing, and details were recorded in the squadron's Flight Operational Intelligence Report. Observations noted by the aircrews attested to the successes of previous raids: "Railroad lines from Mawlu north to Mogaung badly damaged and not in service at present. In addition to bridges hit on mission, two more near Taungni observed destroyed by previous bombardment. Roundhouse at Mohnyin reported destroyed. Rolling stock observed online all bombed and out of service." Crewmen observed signs of recent repair work along the road, but not enough to permit usage.

Capt. Graves signed as acting intelligence officer for this and other mission reports in the absence of Lt. Young. In the operational summary for missions to Burma, details submitted by Graves included the total number and model of B-25s that took part but did not record serial or Chinese airplane numbers and did not list crew members.

Although not all the names of participants have been found, this was listed in Lt. Wood's Individual Flight Record as his first combat mission, with flying time recorded as three hours and ten minutes (in agreement with Simpson's flight log). He held a pilot's rating, but his position on the aircrew was not recorded. Wood had served as the squadron's communications officer since soon after his arrival aboard *Mission Bay*. Responsible for oversight of the operation, maintenance, and repair of all squadron radio, radar, telegraph, teletype, and directional equipment, he took part in this mission to verify that it all functioned as it should in flight (and perhaps for the adventure). When he had begun training as an aviation cadet, Wood told his mother, a restaurant manager, that he was training to be a cook, to prevent her from worrying. After attending the AAF Advanced Flying School at Stuttgart, Arkansas, in the fall of 1942, he was recommended the following January to attend the AAF Signal Corps' Officer Candidate School at Maxwell Field, Alabama. He graduated and received his commission as second lieutenant in April 1943. He was later stationed at Marianna Army Air Base, Florida, and Seymour Johnson Field, Goldsboro, North Carolina, before being sent to the CBI.[1]

Lt. Wood sits at his desk in Communications. On the back was written the caption that identifies him as "Red Wood." *J. F. Faherty collection, courtesy of Dennis Faherty*

The enemy's occupation force in Burma relied heavily upon the railroad system for transporting supplies from collection and storage points to its troops in the field. At Mandalay, all rolling stock was rerouted for ultimate destinations. One vitally important line moved out northeast to Lashio, where supplies for the Japanese Salween armies were processed and transshipped to motor conveyances. The heaviest traffic flowed west and north toward Yeu and Myitkyina. Just out of Mandalay this line crossed the Irrawaddy (Ayeyarwady) River via ferry and then entered Sagaing, passing from there a short distance into Ywataung. Here the line divided, with one branch winding west over the Mu River to Monywa on the Chindwin River and northward to Yeu. The main line continued from Ywataung north through Shwebo to Naba, where a short spur joined it to Katha on the Irrawaddy. Beyond Naba the line passed through Mogaung and thence to Myitkyina, 200 miles farther upstream on the Irrawaddy.[2]

During the seventy-eight-day siege to take the Japanese stronghold at Myitkyina, the railroad line south of the town by which the enemy received supplies was a primary target of the 3rd Squadron. Hank confirmed, "For a while we were making bombing runs over Burma," although after more than seventy years he did not remember the dates of those missions or their specific targets. His recollection of the squadron's missions in Burma and throughout the war: "We were always bombing bridges." The principle behind this was that bombing a bridge contributed more toward defeating the Japanese than bombing an enemy base, although the squadron's B-25s did that too. "Bridge busting" disrupted enemy supply lines and deterred the Japanese advance, even if only temporarily. As soon as the bridges were rebuilt, the bombers hit them again. The squadron's unrelenting pounding of bridges persisted throughout the war.

The afternoon of the squadron's first mission coincided with the arrival of two B-25Js with crews from the 83rd Bomb Squadron, "but [we] are awaiting a wire from Gen. Stilwell authorizing the return of those crews and assigning the planes to our use as lead aircraft for missions," wrote Graves.

The following day, Capt. Hinrichs; 1Lts. MacNeil and Chu S. C.; 2Lts. Chang C. K., Kuo C., and Liang K. Y.; SLt. Wang Y. S.; and SSgts. Chasse and Wilkerson took off on an administrative mission to Bangalore, where B-25s were assembled at the Hindustan Aircraft Factory. Although thunderstorms moved in and prevented any combat operations, the field at Moran was not lacking in excitement. Someone tossed a cigarette into a puddle of water that had a film of gas floating on its surface, igniting a fire at the armament "basha." Quick action prevented damage to supplies, although the thatched-roof bamboo hut sustained slight damage. Armament moved in temporarily with Engineering until repairs could be completed.

While some of the men were fighting the blaze, notification came stating that the wreckage of an airplane had been spotted about 25 miles southeast of Moran, right at the foot of the Himalayas. Rumor soon spread that it was one of the squadron's two B-25s that had recently departed for Calcutta on their way to Bangalore. A Stinson L-5 liaison plane's pilot notified Communications of the wreckage's location, and a rescue crew with three jeeps, a truck, and an ambulance set out over a muddy trail to the scene. According to the squadron history, "The journey was exhausting, and night fell before all vehicles reached the crash area. Here the fighter doctor relieved our worries by revealing that the plane was a B-29." The team found no survivors, although one native reported seeing one or more bailouts. "No bodies, only limbs, were found," Graves wrote. "Under the circumstances, it was felt best to postpone the search until morning, so the squad returned to Moran, mud-spattered, hungry and thirsty, after leaving one out-of-wack jeep near the crash scene."

Hank was with the rescue party. "It was the worst thing I ever saw," he recalled many years afterward. The heavy bomber had broken apart and been driven into the ground. "Little ol' scraps of metal were all that was left of that plane." The scene of the catastrophe was still clear in his memory. "It was just a big muddy spot with burned places and pieces of men's bodies there—a man's shoulder and arm—a leg sticking out of a boot—some other parts of bodies that I couldn't recognize. The worst thing was that smell. They say when you smell it, you'll never forget it." Vultures were perched in the tall trees all around the crash site. "They had been down picking at that wreckage, eating parts of those dead soldiers." It affected him profoundly. Several days passed before he was able to eat anything at all. "It would come time to eat, I'd sit down, and that scene would come. I couldn't eat. I didn't *think* about eating. You couldn't make yourself eat; it was so terrible. That smell—I will never forget that." Decades later he described it to his younger brother Ralph in a rare conversation about his military service while on a fishing trip, and he still remembered it as "a nightmare you could never get away from."

On June 15, Capt. Marvin M. Stockett and a full crew from the 45th Bombardment Squadron, 40th Bombardment Group, of the XX (20th) Bomber Command, had taken off from Chakulia, India, bound for Hsing-ching, China, which was used as an advance base for deployment of the Superfortresses in raids against the Japanese home islands. "Stockett's Rocket" (serial #42-6261), loaded with bombs for a scheduled attack on Yawata, Japan, was last reported at Jorhat on its way to fly over the Hump. All twelve on board, including eleven crewmen and one passenger, were killed in the crash. The cause was never determined, although overheating of the behemoths' engines was among the many problems common to these early B-29s. Official records still list the aircrew of Stockett's Rocket as missing, although the circumstances of that crash conform to what is known about the wreckage reported by 3rd Bomb Squadron personnel.[3]

Lt. Col. Robert D. ("Mac") McCarten and Col. Marvin L. Harding, 10th Air Force A-1 (Personnel) and A-2 (Intelligence), respectively, visited the squadron on June 27. Harding brought "batches of target information for intelligence files," according to Graves. McCarten, former CO of the 490th ("Skull and Wings") Bomb Squadron, which contributed toward retaking the Myitkyina airfield, had recently been assigned to 10th Air Force HQ. He "talked tactics with the pilots and later gave a lecture to the entire squadron on bridge-busting. (He had formerly been CO of a squadron that had 50-odd bridges to its credit.)"

McCarten outlined three principles of bridge busting: flying along the longitudinal axis of the bridge, flying at a height at least a mathematical 50 or 60 greater than airspeed, and using a 1,000 lb. bomb. After weeks of experimentation, the key to success for "glip bombing" was discovered to be a "hop technique" that included a shallow dive just as the bombs were released. "Both colonels made a favorable impression on the squadron and there is an expectancy of fine cooperation between the squadron and higher echelons." The following day, 10th Air Force A-3 (Operations) surprised the squadron's pilots and navigators with intensive briefing on a vital Myitkyina target that called for precise bombing and strafing. All crews "stayed alerted" during the afternoon, but weather failed, and the mission was postponed.

Orders dated June 28 brought even-greater numbers to the squadron's Chinese personnel, adding ten lieutenants and twenty-five sergeants. The new arrivals were Lts. Wong Yung-hang, Kao Wen-cheng, Kwang Tsu-hwa, Ching Kuo-lok, Chan Bing-chung, Wei Kwo-an, Kao Yao-hwa, Wong Hwen-lei, Chung Hun-cheng, and Lin Yak-chun, as well as Sgts. Chang Yi-ting, Ho Shung-han, Wong Tao-chang, Lee Hwa-kuo, Tsio Wei-chi, Wong Yi-hai, Sze Dien-wen, Lin Shih-sing, Chang San-ying, Ching Sun-shon, Chow Yang-hao, Wang Men, Lee Wen-ching, Tung Mao, Ma Pai-chang, Own Dun-yi, Chang Tio-hung, Ching Ding-chuen, Lin Kuo-chuen, Chen Chun-chow, Ju Kuo-hwa, Chang Siai-chi, Lee Hsien-yi, Tien Chung-ying, and Lee Ching-lin. No serial numbers were included.

For the 3rd Squadron's second mission, delayed until the twenty-ninth, Captains Simpson and Hsu flew two B-25Hs on a weather check, but Hsu turned back because of instrument trouble. Lt. Wood was a member of Simpson's crew. After reporting conditions at the Pass as hazardous due to low clouds and thunderstorms, Simpson flew on alone to hit the railroad line south of Mohnyin (about 100 miles southwest of Myitkyina) up to Naba. He was over the target at 1540 hours carrying six 500 lb. HEs fused to eight-to-ten-second delay. Only one of the bombs exploded, on a section of railroad tracks just north of Mawhun. The bombardier reported at least three others as duds. Crewmen spotted two unidentified small-engine aircraft near Mohnyin. When one of them turned toward the B-25, Simpson climbed into the low cloud base and headed toward home. The Mitchell was back down after three hours and ten minutes' flight time. Simpson's summary of the mission: "Chinese boy flew on my wing till we hit instrument weather. I got to the target alone, dropped 6 500# bombs and 5 of them were duds!"

The fuse (sometimes "fuze") was a mechanical device attached to the nose and sometimes the tail of a bomb before a mission. Its purpose was not only to detonate the bomb but also to ensure that the plane cleared the area before it exploded. Activated by the airstream when the bomb was dropped, a windmill-like "arming vane" turned a set of gears inside a cylinder that aligned a small charge of impact-sensitive explosive with the main bomb charge. The fuse was timed to a precisely calculated number of seconds so that the bomb traveled a predetermined distance before it was detonated. The fusing depended upon bomb type, altitude from which it was dropped, nature of the target, and other factors. For example, if an aircraft was dropping a bomb on a runway full of aircraft, fusing should be instantaneous. However, if the bomb was dropped on an aircraft hangar, there should be a small delay, so it did not detonate as soon as it hit the roof.[4]

It was the responsibility of the airplane armorer to fuse the bombs to the required timing and load them into the release mechanisms before a mission. Armorers were also expected to inspect, repair, and maintain all aircraft armament, including bomb racks and release mechanisms, cannons, machine guns, and auxiliary equipment. They kept all weapons in mission-ready condition by cleaning and oiling them after each use and replacing or repairing worn or broken parts. SSgts. McCann, Armstrong, and Mier and Cpls. Learn and Allegretto had this important assignment at the time, with SSgt. Hoyle as their chief. Armament officer Gene Dorr later described Hoyle as "the best I ever worked with" in a letter he wrote to Jim McCann many years later.

Lt. Ragland flew another weather reconnaissance mission in the early afternoon of the following day, and he remembered its details for long afterward. He was flying without escort on his way to bomb the rails south of Mohnyin when he was intercepted at 1410 by six Oscars in the valley south of Kamaing (25°26' N, 96°40' E). Ragland's B-25H was flying at 8,000 feet on a heading of 180°, and the enemy fighters were at 9,000 feet on the same heading, formed into two loose "Vs." He later related his shock when he looked up and saw them "above me to my left." The lead aircraft made a feint and approached to within 800 yards. "I thought, better turn and identify who they are before I go any further. So I turned over like this and all of a sudden they turned like this, and every single one of them had great big red balls on their wings! I wished I wasn't there! What in the world was I going to do? All I could say was 'Here come the Japanese.'" The second Oscar pulled away with the lead plane as if to follow with a similar attack from flight level at three o'clock, while the other four "milled confusingly," according to the mission report. None were within firing range at any time.

Ragland made a controlled turn away and "hit the deck," dropping to 2,000 feet according to the report, but he remembered going down to treetop level at full throttle before he "hightailed it out of there." He recalled, "I still had bombs in the plane, but I didn't even think of that." The plane returned home without dropping its bombload. "I landed that plane with the bombs in it. If they had bounced out, we'd have been goners. That's how scared it made me."[5] The Myitkyina mission crews remained on alert throughout the day, and "a general discussion was held about the Lt. Ragland episode." Col. Branch heard the story when he stopped for a brief visit to confirm plans for the promised B-25Js on his way to Bangalore.

Capt. Simpson, 2Lt. Hsieh W. W., and SSgt. Rieks left on June 30 on their way to Bangalore to pick up a B-25H as a replacement for Hodges's defunct plane. Simpson logged it as three hours and fifteen minutes from Moran to Calcutta, where the three stopped for the night. After learning that Capt. Hinrichs and Lt. MacNeil were there and staying at the Grand Hotel, Simpson made arrangements to share their room. "Flew on from Calcutta in the B-25J that was going to Bangalore," he wrote the following day. "Took us 5:20 from Calcutta. Arrived at 4:00 p.m. and left in my new C.A.C.W. plane for Karachi at 5:45. Got to Karachi about 11:00 p.m. Mostly instrument weather but Hsieh W. W. was a good navigator and we made it in fine style." After delaying departure the next day until 2:00 while waiting for weather to clear, the crew spent that night in Agra. "Bad weather all along the route. Rain all the way. Worst storm I've ever run into—no power on. I was going up 2,000'/minute and indicating 300 mph." The crew landed for lunch at Gaya on the following day before completing their errand and returning to Moran.

In North Africa before being transferred to the CBI, Rieks was a farmer from Iowa, and Hank remembered him as a good man and a good mechanic. He had an often-repeated expression: "If it rains before seven, it will quit before eleven." Hank recalled, "Maynard was the one that taught that to me. He had raised corn, and he knew." However, the Iowa farmer had reason to doubt the validity of his midwestern adage in monsoon-drenched India during this four-day administrative mission.

Sgt. Maynard W. Rieks, an airplane crew chief, works with two Chinese mechanics. He wrote "Alden, Iowa" on the reverse. *J. H. Mills collection*

Pfcs. Long, Peters, and England were promoted to corporals on July 1. Later that afternoon, the squadron flew its fourth and most effective mission to date, in spite of unfavorable weather. The mission's target was the railroad south of Mohnyin. Two B-25Hs each carried three 500 lb. HEs and four 250 lb. HEs, all fused to eight-to-eleven-second delay and dropped from 300 feet. Over the target at Naba at 1733, Capt. Seacrest dropped a 500 lb. bomb on a locomotive inside a railroad shed, while Capt. Hodges hit the roadbed (24°40' N, 96°14' E) with a string of 250-pounders. Seacrest scored a direct hit by another 500 lb. bomb on a bridge (24°34' N, 96°12' E), causing severe damage that made it unusable by the enemy for several days. Results were termed "good." Capts. Seacrest and Hodges flew out to check weather again on the following day, but both were forced to turn back at the Pass by a solid overcast.

Frequently serving during this period as Hodges's navigator, Lt. Ting kept a photograph after the war that included himself with Capt. Hodges and his Chinese air and ground crews grouped in front of A/C #714. He indicated two men and wrote characters translated as "catastrophe" and "perish" below, although he did not provide their names. He noted that the photo was taken at "Moran airport, India" and that they were ready for a mission to attack "Dianmian Railroad" (translated "Burma railroad"). A similar photo showed him with Capt. Seacrest and the same plane with Chinese personnel. Among his wartime memorabilia, Ting kept maps of Burma and Upper Assam printed on silk, as well as a Chinese flag with Burmese

Capt. Seacrest is the American seated here with his Chinese air and ground crews. Sgt. Li Chan-jui is standing, fifth from the right. A/C #714 seems to have been a favorite, since it appears in several squadron photographs taken during this period. *R. N. Solyn collection, courtesy of Robert N. Solin*

Bombing in Burma

Lt. Ting kept this photo with other military memorabilia. Taken at Moran, it depicts air and ground crews of A/C #714 before a mission against the railroad in Burma. Capt. Hodges is the American seated in the front row. The officer seated third from the right is not identified but may have been Ouyang Chun, a navigator-bombardier who failed to return from a mission on March 30, 1945. Ting is sitting in the center of the group, his face circled. *Ting C. L. collection, courtesy of David Ting*

inscription. When his son later asked if flying missions over Burma was dangerous, he answered, "Not much, because we had air superiority over the Japanese." Ting took part in 3rd Squadron missions until the end of the war.[6]

Capt. Seacrest was "one hell of a great pilot," and Tom Earley later described an event that proved it. While the bomb squadron with its B-25s was sharing the base with the fighter squadron and its P-40s, it was inevitable that disagreement arose as to which was the better aircraft, so a competition was arranged. Seacrest took off in his B-25, and the best of the fighter pilots took off in his P-40. The fighter plane should have had a clear advantage over the bomber because of its greater speed and maneuverability. Ten minutes or more passed as the men on the ground waited. Then the P-40 came "screaming past" with Seacrest in his B-25 right on the fighter's tail, "chasing the hell out of him."[7]

The *Pilot Training Manual for B-25* used by the USAAF during this period stated that the airplane pilot was responsible for the airplane and its crew, proper inspections and checks, hand and oral signals, proper maneuvering of the airplane, and proper operation of the engines and auxiliary equipment (when flying the J model, he shared some specific duties with his copilot). He must know how to fly the aircraft in all conditions, to be proficient in engine operation and to know what to do to keep the airplane running smoothly, and to fully understand the responsibilities of each of his crew members. He was involved with mission planning and preparation, including training of aircrew members when necessary. He provided premission briefing to ensure that aircrewmen fully understood their duties, but he was encouraged to allow them to exercise initiative, so they all worked together for success of the mission.

Instructions equally stressed the importance of maintaining good interpersonal relationships between the pilot and his crew, who were putting their lives in his hands every time they took off. As airplane commander, he must earn their respect and maintain discipline, which included immediate obedience to orders when they became necessary, while at the same time developing and keeping their trust and good will. Seacrest's prowess as a pilot and as a leader perfectly demonstrated his success in achieving these objectives.

The 3rd Squadron's ground crews had not been able to complete preparations and depart from Karachi until mid-June, traveling by train (a distance of more than 2,000 miles) to the base at Moran. If men of the 3rd Squadron followed the route taken by the 1st Bomb Squadron a few months earlier, the journey by train would take about ten days, including stops for water and "laying over on a sidetrack for hours at a time." Sgt. Daniels related that men of his 1st Squadron stayed overnight at Tistamuk Ghat, a British rest camp. The next day they embarked on a riverboat, where they spent two days before arriving at Randu Rest Camp. After about two days there, they traveled an additional two days by train before pulling into Chabua.[8]

A detail of the 17th Fighter Squadron took a similar route, traveling by train for about ten days and then "up to Lahore, over to Delhi, down to Calcutta." There they changed trains and made their way finally up to Chabua.[9]

Capt. Graves did not specify the route taken but wrote that the 3rd Squadron's ground personnel arrived at Moran on June 31, "after the twenty-day train ride across India's hinterlands." The men arrived "fagged and war weary" and "fed up on Army rations and impromptu bedding and bounded by rail confines." Nevertheless, all personnel arrived safely and in apparent good health, "a tribute to the efficiency of Capt. Goeller, squadron adjutant and travel master extraordinary who threatened many an Indian trainman with a 'kick in the ass' with success." The men who returned from "DS enroute to duty" with him were TSgt. Solyn, SSgt. Holmes, Sgt. Duffin, and Pfcs. England and Trout, according to the next day's morning report.

July 1 was the date that the squadron acquired a flight surgeon, Capt. James L. King (the "fighter doctor" mentioned by Graves), attached from the 5th Fighter Group ("temporarily, perhaps permanently"). Previously serving with the Army Transport Command in Alaska, "Doc King" had arrived aboard *Mission Bay* in March. He remained with the 3rd Squadron until after its transfer to China.

Hank was sent on the following day to Comilla, India, for unspecified detached service. Now officially "Cumilla" and the second-largest city in the eastern part of Bangladesh, Comilla Cantonment was at that time used as headquarters of the British 14th Army. Previously providing air support to British forces in Italy, the 12th Bomb Group's 434th Bomb Squadron (M) was at that time assigned to reinforcing the 10th Air Force in India by providing tactical bombardment support and had recently been moved to Comilla. The Engineering Detachment of the Eastern Area, India-Burma Service Command, and the Headquarters Detachment of the Combat Cargo Task Force (Prov.) were other organizations stationed there. Whatever his purpose, Hank completed his task and returned to Moran two days later.[10]

The situation caused by understaffing in the kitchen was relieved by the welcome arrival of four new additions. "We got in four cooks one time, and I don't remember a single one of their names. They didn't stay with us long but got transferred somewhere else," Hank related. Sgts. Elmer J. Thompson, Alvin A. Hall, and Allen B. Malone Jr. and Pvt. Philip Piecuch arrived to take over kitchen duties, to the relief of Hinrichs's team, who had been pulling KP.

Allen B. Malone Jr. was one of four cooks who transferred in to relieve Capt. Hinrichs and his kitchen crew following the desertion of two Chinese cooks assigned to the mess hall. A. B. Malone Jr. collection, courtesy of Jim Johnson

Sgt. Malone sports a borrowed pistol for this photo, taken in front of his tent at Moran. Holstered pistols were generally reserved for members of flight crews. A. B. Malone Jr. collection, courtesy of Jim Johnson

Sgt. Gruber (supply sergeant) and Pvt. Philip Piecuch (cook) go shirtless outside their tent, attempting to escape the relentless Upper Assam heat and humidity. F. T. Jakubasz collection, courtesy of Robert Jakubasz

Lt. MacNeil and party arrived from Calcutta, Maj. Conrad from China, and Capt. Simpson from Bangalore. MacNeil and Hinrichs returned with six airplane loads of engineering and photographic equipment, Simpson with a new B-25H, and Conrad with the latest news from the 14th Air Force and the 69th Wing at Yunnanyi. The squadron commander also brought back maps, photographs, and target data relating to the Japanese front along the Salween. The following day, Maj. Conrad and captains Seacrest and Graves went to 10th Air Force Headquarters and showed A-2 and A-3 the information acquired from the 14th and the 69th. Officials of the 10th Air Force were cooperative and made plans for reproduction of most of the material for the use both of the 10th headquarters and the fighter units in this area.

Squadron Mitchells flew two missions on Tuesday, July 4. Capt. Hodges and Lt. MacNeil took off on a weather check, flying low as usual through the valleys to prevent detection by enemy radar, and returned without incident. Capt. Simpson and Lt. Ragland flew a second

Capt. Simpson was the lead pilot of the unfortunate July 4 mission, only nine days after the squadron's first mission to Burma. He was later recognized for his composure and courage that allowed him and his crew to escape into the nearby hills, according to the certificate that accompanied his Silver Star. *T. S. Simpson collection, courtesy of Larry Simpson*

Lt. Eugene H. Dorr, the squadron's armament officer, manned the top turret gun on this mission until Simpson used it to decimate advancing Japanese troops. *E. H. Dorr collection, courtesy of Barbara Dorr Dent*

Capt. George C. Cunningham was A/C #721's navigator who made his way back to camp separately. Recurring attacks of high fever, chills, and other serious symptoms of malaria affected these three men for years afterward. *Courtesy of Jim Brahos*

weather reconnaissance mission along the Burma railroad, their objective to bomb railroad bridges south of Mohnyin. On the previous evening, Simpson and some of his buddies were playing a game of hearts in his tent. An experienced pilot at twenty-three, he had few concerns about the scheduled mission and ate an emergency candy bar from his survival pack out of boredom. It was an impulse he soon regretted.

Simpson's crew included Capt. Cunningham and 1Lt. Dorr. The three of them had served together since the 1st Bomb Group's inception and already had "history." In September 1943, Cunningham and Dorr were attending a twenty-day course in military intelligence at the British Field Security School, Intelligence Corps Depot, in Karachi. Because of the distance from their barracks at Malir, the two men were housed at the Killarney Hotel in town. Simpson, Cunningham, and Dorr attended the farewell party ("straight stag") for Col. Hilger, held on the thirteenth at the Gymkhama Club in Karachi, according to the group's historical report. "Lt. Simpson, suffering under the stigma of having scratched a PT-17's wing, found solace in the bottle. Was tucked in bed at the Killarney Hotel" by his more sober companions.

Originally from rural Kentucky, Cunningham had moved to Washington, DC, where he was a prelaw student at George Washington University while working as a bookkeeper/cashier for the Department of Agriculture. He enlisted in the Army Air Corps as an aviation cadet in September 1941 but was diverted to bombardier and navigator training. He later trained student bombardiers at Columbia, South Carolina, before reporting for duty with the training unit that became the 2nd Bomb Squadron. He had served as the 1st Bomb Group assistant operations and training officer as well as PX officer before transferring to the 3rd Squadron as bombardier.

Dorr, who had taught high school biology in Boston for a year before entering the Army Air Corps, later described his early military training in a letter to Jim McCann: "Started out as a flying cadet in Albany, Ga. but washed out and finished in armaments & bombsight maintenance at Lowry Fld, Denver on Dec. 5, 1941." He entered active duty from the Air Reserve on

December 8 (as President Roosevelt was calling for a declaration of war against Japan) and received his commission as second lieutenant the following week. "After a long stretch in the training command at West Texas bombardier training schools I ended up with the CACW." As the squadron's armament officer, he had responsibility for supervising the maintenance, loading, and repair of all armament equipment. Dorr, Cunningham, and Simpson, friends since the bomb group's earliest days, shared vivid memories of this mission for the rest of their lives.

When two Mitchells took off at 1015, ceiling was 110 to 300 feet and visibility was limited by scattered showers. The planes were last seen heading into bad weather at low altitude toward Mogaung. Subsequent reports provided details. Capt. Simpson flew a B-25H, Chinese A/C #721, with a crew made up of 2Lt. Wang Yung-sin (X-834) as copilot (per the Aircraft Accident Report, although the H model had no copilot position), Capt. Cunningham as navigator, 1Lt. Dorr as turret gunner, Sgt. Chiang Chue-shu (X-2178) as radio-gunner, and Sgt. Mai Pei-shun (X-1345) as tail gunner.

Because turbulence prevented them from reaching Bhamo as planned, the two bombers dropped 500-pounders on railroad targets at Naba Junction and Katha. "Had to fly with my side window open in order to see the tracks," Simpson wrote in his diary. He came in low on an attack of a bridge, about 10 feet above the bridge deck, when the Mitchell was hit by rifle and machine gun fire that knocked out its left engine. "I knew I was going down as soon as I took machine gun fire to my engine," he later told his family. He motioned to his wingman of his intentions by waving his arm in a gesture that he intended to indicate, "We're going down; we're going down!," but Ragland took the gesture to mean, "Bye bye; see you back at the base." The wing plane proceeded back to base alone. Simpson was annoyed when Ragland left him, although the other pilot could not have known that his help would be urgently needed.

Oil pressure dropped to zero. "Had all the crew put on parachutes." He asked the men if they wanted to bail out, but they said that they would "stick." The engine ran rough, and rpm fluctuated between 2,000 and 2,800. The left propeller would not feather, and the plane could climb to no more than 800 feet in altitude. White smoke began pouring from the engine and a small flame appeared from under the cowling. "Had to land or jump right away," Simpson concluded. "Everything was happening pretty fast," he later recounted in an interview. "Boy, I was scared! I must have prayed. I recall saying to myself, 'What will Marge think? What will happen to her and the kid?'" He had never even met their six-month-old son, Tommy Jr. (nicknamed "Sandy"), and feared that he never would.[11] It was a circumstance that he shared with the other two Americans, both of whom also had children born after they shipped overseas.

After four failed attempts at landing the plane, "I gave up and started looking for a place to sit down," related Simpson in an official report of the incident. Then he instructed his crew to brace for a crash landing. "It was raining so hard I couldn't see more than one[-]half mile ahead. The road was to my left and seemed fairly smooth, so it was there that I headed and set the ship down." The road was about 20 feet wide, and there was a good straight stretch before it made a turn to the right toward a steep cliff, and Simpson knew he had to put the plane down before that turn. As the Mitchell was skimming above the road, the second engine cut out.

"It came to me in a flash—the memory of a movie I saw 10 years ago." Using it as his inspiration, Simpson aimed the aircraft between two trees in an attempt to reduce forward momentum by knocking off the wings. "My flaps cut the speed from 200 to about 160 miles an hour. I flipped off the ignition. Then we hit. My left wing hit a tree and was knocked off, so the plane was straightened but . . . the right wing hit another tree." The tree trunks clipped about 10 feet off each wing. "We dropped down to about 100 miles an hour, but we were still eight or ten feet high. I shoved the stick forward and bellied in."

The aircraft was on the ground at 1320. "Could hardly tell when we hit the ground," Simpson wrote. "The plane came to rest, and the crew and I got out unhurt." Dorr stated in his evasion report that "we weren't too badly shaken up," although he later related that he had suffered an injury—a deep gash in his groin. The road on which the B-25 landed was the north–south Kamaing-Mogaung section of the Ledo Road, 12 miles west-northwest of Mogaung (Love Victor 2447 on grid map). SLt. Wang later stated that he had noticed lubricating oil oozing from the engine sill before the bombs were dropped, but did not report it because the instruments seemed normal. He observed that the plane "landed very well except that one[-]third of the left wing was knocked off the plane about fifty feet."[12]

Fearing an explosion, Simpson ordered his crew to clear the plane. They all scrambled out of the emergency hatches in time to see a group of about fifteen to twenty men approaching at a run along the road behind them from the south, with twenty to thirty advancing at about 200 yards from the opposite direction. "Someone's coming to save us," Wang said. Then they had "ten seconds of relief" before realizing that the "faint green" uniforms and white stars on the helmets of the soldiers identified them as the enemy, equipped with hand grenades and sidearms but no rifles. They were "Jap troops retreating southward along the west side of the Ledo Road from Kamaing," according to the historical report.

The advance party took up a position just behind the tail. "Our Chinese asked them to come up one at a time," but none understood Chinese. As the leader uncorked a grenade and drew back his hand to throw it, Dorr dropped to the ground and opened fire on them with sidearms from where he lay in the road. At the same time, Simpson sprinted back to the plane, leaped into the top turret, and tried the power switch. To his immense relief, the guns were still operational. Simpson turned the twin .50-caliber guns on the enemy soldiers and fired between the stabilizers, killing or wounding all in the first group before swinging around and mowing down those in the second group.

"They hit the ground, grabbing their bellies. I saw their grenades go off among them. Of course, I couldn't hear anything but the racket of those fifties," Simpson explained. "I cut down every one of them. I didn't fire in bursts. I just poured it on—like with a garden hose. Then I swung the turret to the north. It was all over in about two minutes. I must have shot about 600 rounds." Four were trying to escape by crawling into the brush to the side, so "I ran a stream of lead up the road on each one to make sure none was alive." Satisfied that the immediate threat had been neutralized, "I finished up by spraying the jungle all around us" before firing one final burst into the group straight ahead. He dispatched about fifty in dead or wounded, in addition to two that he said were killed by the right wing as the plane landed. Later reports by Chinese troops confirmed eighteen dead found near the plane. Simpson's actions provided a dramatic demonstration of the squadron motto, "Spray and Pray." Dorr, who estimated the enemy casualties as nearer seventy-five, commented in a separate interview, "Simpson cut down every one of them except those I got."[13]

As Simpson exited the plane, he threw out his parachute with jungle kit attached. He had always wondered if his parachute would work when he needed it, so "I did the damnedest thing," he explained. In an effort to create a diversion, he turned back to where it lay in the mud, grabbed the red handle of the ripcord, and pulled. The white nylon came tumbling out. Grabbing the emergency pack, "then I ran like hell." He and the crew made their escape into the brush and ran "some distance" before stopping to catch their breath and appraise their situation. As they sprinted across the road, "Japs spotted us" and started firing. They had one compass from the pilot's kit, so they headed north. They were trying to make it to the hills, where they expected to have a better chance of escaping.

They kept running, under constant fire, "Japs right at our heels." Shots hit close "every now and then," so they hit the ground and crawled until they were in the clear before running again. After two hours of evasion, they came to a stream. Simpson recorded that as they were running for their lives, "Dorr baptized me from a stream. Prayed as I had never prayed before." Dorr, a devout Catholic, also prayed. Through the years that followed, he kept his worn, mud-encrusted rosary in the same condition as when he wore it through those terror-filled days on the run.[14]

The Japanese brought up mortars and fired in the direction of the fleeing men all afternoon and into the night but were unable to find their quarry. "Got away from them and hid till it was dark. Crawled on hands and knees all night. Japs all around us," Simpson wrote in his diary. It was every man for himself, and Simpson became separated from the others. The Japanese had chased him to a big river (likely the Mogaung, which meanders through the valley of the same name), where he was trapped. As the enemy approached, they fired 1 lb. shells from mortar tubes that they carried on their backs. Just when they were about to overrun his concealed position, one of the mortar shells hit the tree next to him, knocking it down across the river, away from the approaching soldiers. Simpson scurried over the tree to the other side of the river and ran until they lost track of him. Simpson lost his .45 pistol in his frantic attempt to escape, leaving him defenseless..

One of the Chinese had been a guerrilla in North China, and his experience enabled him to lead them past Japanese positions. Sometime during the night, he volunteered to go ahead to scout for signs of the enemy. Shortly afterward, a loud crash shattered the silence. Since it was pitch black, Cunningham called out to the other man, "Are you okay?" The man answered from mere inches away. He had not even left yet. When they investigated, they found that the noise had been caused by a falling tree—perhaps the same tree that Simpson used to make his escape across the river.[15]

They continued their slow and cautious progress until five o'clock in the morning, when they finally stopped, posted a guard, and tried to get some rest. Then, concealed under banana leaves, they slept fitfully on a hillside beside "a Jap trail." The men remained in hiding until sometime during the afternoon before moving on. They discussed their situation and agreed that traveling primarily at night would decrease the likelihood of running into enemy patrols. Cunningham later explained that they also concluded that they would have a better chance of making it out if they split up.

By stolen native boats and forced marches, they continued to travel on Thursday in a generally northwesterly direction, experiencing more narrow escapes. Spotted once more by enemy patrols, again they ran and hid in the brush. Then they spent another night in misery. Their matches were wet, and they had nothing to eat other than a few carefully rationed chocolate bars (one per day for each of them, according to Dorr). Clouds of mosquitoes swarmed in the air around them. "We could crush whole handfuls simply by closing our fingers in the air around our heads." The leeches were just as bad. "The water was full of them. When you finished drinking, leeches would be sticking to your lips." Every day they removed their boots and poured out the blood that collected as they waded through water infested with the blood-sucking parasites. Jungle slime coated them from head to foot, and hunger became a gnawing agony.

Coming upon a deserted enemy camp, they sneaked past through a ravine. "Went right on through and ran into the Japs," wrote Simpson, who had managed to rejoin the others. Confronted unexpectedly by the enemy patrol, Wang reacted by firing off six shots from his

.38 revolver. The soldiers returned fire. Everyone scattered. Cunningham ran to the right and did not rejoin his companions. Wang made his own escape into the brush and became separated from the others. Simpson and Dorr, who stayed together, crouched in silence for two hours while the enemy soldiers beat the jungle for them.

They had all heard reports of torture of their captives by the Japanese. According to Dorr, Radio Tokyo had repeatedly and specifically threatened the Chinese-American Composite Wing: "We'll torture any Americans we find in that outfit." He and Simpson knew that capture would mean death—probably a slow and horrible death—so they "sort of reached an agreement."

Dorr proposed that if they were captured, "I'll shoot you and then shoot myself."

"That's okay by me," Simpson replied. They never spoke of it again.

Simpson, Dorr, Chiang, and Mai hid until midnight as their pursuers searched the jungle all around them and resumed their mortar fire. After the enemy patrol moved on, the fugitives went back through the camp and continued along the same trail, traveling on until they considered it safe to stop.

The four traveled all morning on Friday the seventh. "Heard Japs as we lay down to sleep so ran again. Came to the 2nd Jap camp. Crawled through. Water up to our shoulders." Simpson later explained that it was a fenced, heavily armed POW camp that held about four hundred US and British prisoners. The captives were naked and tied up in long rows by barbed wire that would slash them if they moved. Knowing there was nothing they could do to aid the miserable men, all they could do was keep running.

Later they reached a clearing near a village, where women were chopping wood. "Came to a native village and started to have a look when two machine guns cut loose at us. Just missed us by ½ foot!!!" The most likely explanation for their hostile reception was that the villagers mistook the Chinese crewmen for Japanese, although it is possible that they were themselves Japanese sympathizers. It was another close call. Once again, the men escaped into the brush and made their way farther up the mountain unharmed.

At about 4:30 in the afternoon on their fourth day of being pursued through swamp, river, and jungle, the starving and exhausted men came upon a Kachin village occupied by a tribe that had survived the Japanese slaughter by running away higher into the hills. Simpson said, "We were so worn out that we knew this was the turning point for better or for worse. Besides, we had smelled food cooking."

Hunger drove them to overcome their caution and approach. After struggling over a hilltop, they found themselves confronted by three hundred Kachins, not 50 yards distant, waiting for them with long knives, according to Dorr. The Kachins charged as the virtually defenseless and hopelessly outnumbered men stood there immobile. Then Dorr realized that one of the Chinese was still wearing an enemy soldier's helmet that he had picked up from the road near where they crashed. He knocked it to the ground and signaled to the Kachins that the Chinese were enemies of the Japanese. The leader scowled—smiled—and then expressed in sign language that Japanese infantry had on the previous day killed the village chief and beheaded his children. "We were about to cut off your measles at Lowry Field, Denver, heads too," the Kachin leader said with a grin.

With the issue of mistaken identity resolved, the Kachins proved to be friendly. After an exchange of ninety-six silver rupees from the emergency fund, the villagers conducted the men to a hut, fed them, and allowed them to rest for the first time since the crash. Simpson wrote, "Had a huge meal of rice, eggs, tea and soup. Slept there all night."

They were awakened at five o'clock the following morning. "Had breakfast in the village and started out for Chinese lines at 7:30. Came to their camp at 11:00." The men were escorted through the valley until they ran into a patrol from the 22nd Division, 1st Chinese Army. There they met Lt. Col. Dupree and waited by the road with him to be taken by jeep to the Chinese camp, where Simpson was conducted to 22nd Division headquarters to meet with the commanding officer. The Chinese then took them to a camp of Black American marines at Kamaing, farther up the Mogaung River valley. There they learned that Cunningham had been brought in the previous day and was already on his way back to Assam. "Ate like horses[,] then went to bed." Wang came in the following day. Simpson noted that Col. Dupree took him back to the plane. "Chinese had advanced to it by the 8th. Holes everywhere in the ship."

They remained at Kamaing for a day and a half, waiting for the next riverboat to take them to Warazup, the nearest airfield. As they waited, they saw about 150 Japanese prisoners who were being held at the camp. Then they boarded a "boat" made up of two pontoons lashed together and propelled by an outboard motor. Accompanied by five other such improvised craft, they traveled north along the river to Warazup. "Took us 8½ hours to go upstream to Warazup. Distance—20 miles. Colored boys ran the boats and we had quite a race. Our boat was first in. Rained all the way." At Warazup they were informed that the field was closed because of the incessant downpour. "I finally talked a fellow into coming down from Shadazup in an L1 [Stinson L-1 Vigilant, a three-man light observation aircraft] and picking us up one at a time. Arrived at Shadazup and flew from there to Tenjauk [Tingkawk] Sakan, an ATC base where I caught a C-47 and flew back to Moran. Got there at 11:30, first one to get back. Stayed up till 1:00 a.m. telling my story."

Although all six of the downed airmen safely made their way back to Moran, it was a bit more complicated for Sgt. Mai, who was somehow separated from the others. When he was found and brought to the Marine camp, Mai (who could not speak English) was initially held as a POW. The confusion was perhaps prompted by a souvenir Japanese helmet. Because he was also wearing Simpson's flight jacket at the time he was taken, someone decided to do some checking and determined that he was one of the missing aircrew.[16]

Simpson wrote in his log: "Shot Down Over Enemy Territory On Combat Mission" and "Landed Plane On Ledo Road." T. S. Simpson collection, courtesy of Larry Simpson

Sgt. Frank T. Jakubasz, flight chief, stands by to check out a mechanic's work on an engine. In addition, he sometimes took his turn as a gunner on missions. *F. T. Jakubasz collection, courtesy of Robert Jakubasz*

Official reports of the incident were signed by Capts. Simpson and Cunningham, 1Lt. Dorr, and 2Lt. Wang Yung-sin. Capt. Seacrest and 1Lts. Ragland and MacNeil signed the mission summary, and SSgt. Jakubasz was noted as crew chief. This was the first of the 3rd Squadron's planes to go down in combat. Unfortunately, it was not the last.

On July 5, as downed A/C #721's crewmen were making their escape, Capts. Hodges and Graves flew over the Hump to lead the rear echelon of Col. Rouse's 27th Fighter Squadron, 5th Fighter Group, across to Kunming. SSgt. Gruber went to the hospital. TSgt. Smith, who had joined the squadron at Malir, was transferred out. He had been attached to the 4th Squadron in late December 1943 and now returned to that unit. Reclassified as armorer-gunner in early August, he was placed on detached service to the 2nd Bomb Squadron, later transferring to the bomb group as gunnery instructor.

Sgt. William L. Armstrong, Army Air Force radio operator (*left*), and Sgt. Manuel C. Smith, attached as an intelligence specialist but proficient in gunnery (*right*), work on a B-25H's machine guns. *J. H. Mills collection*

Cpl. Clyde L. Learn and a Chinese armorer load .50-caliber ammunition and check out machine guns in the nose of a battle-worn B-25H. Although newer B-25Js came in to replace these old H models, several remained in service until the end of the war. *J. H. Mills collection*

Bombing in Burma

Two B-25Hs took off from Moran on the seventh, each carrying six 500 lb. HEs. Planes were over the target area at 1240. Bombs dropped at 300 feet fell on the railroad bed south of Naba Junction, scoring three direct hits on the tracks and disrupting rail traffic. The aircrew reported powerboats on the Mogaung River carrying "friendly troops," according to this report for mission #10.

On that day's second mission, two B-25Hs, each with a bombload of four 250 lb. and three 500 lb. HEs, were over the target at 1730 and hit the railroad south from Mohnyin to Naba. Although two bombs were direct hits on a bridge immediately south of Naba, neither exploded because of defective fusing. Eight were near misses that damaged the roadbed. Both aircraft were hit by machine gun and small-arms fire at a village ½ mile east of Naba Junction. Gunners strafed those positions, expending 250 rounds of .50 caliber.

On July 8, Lt. Ragland was the pilot of a B-25 (serial #43-3897) on a weather reconnaissance mission. He flew almost to Hsenwi, on the border between Burma and China, before turning back because of thunderstorms and towering cumulus clouds en route and in the target vicinity, with nine-tenths cloud coverage. Three bombers (two B-25Hs and a recently acquired J model in the lead) set to fly the primary mission "to plaster the rails again" from Hopin south to Mohnyin were also forced to turn back because of impassable weather, "plus motor failure on one craft." Lt. Wood was a member of the crew aboard one of the H models. Weather conditions were reported as "low bases and high ceilings, scattered rain and thunderstorms." A third "recce" with two B-25Hs reported identical results.

All squadron members—"Americans and Chinese, officers and men alike"—had been "sweating out news of the missing crew," according to Graves. He wrote two days after the crash that a 315th Troop Transport pilot had reported sighting a CACW B-25 crashed near Mogaung, apparently having effected a successful crash landing, since only a wingtip and props were damaged and the escape hatches seemed to be open. The transport pilot, Lt. Hatlock, stated that the aircraft looked as if it had been well crash-landed and as if all hands had a good chance to survive. "The aircraft was sighted in friendly territory but due to the scattering of friendly and enemy troops before and after the bomb line, it seems possible the crew bumped into Jap patrols."

When Chinese troops reached the B-25, they found Japanese ideographs scratched with a bayonet into the paint of the fuselage: "Here died a brave group of Japanese while trying to capture important booty." The Hump Rescue Squadron attempted to reach the damaged plane but opted to destroy it to prevent it from falling into the hands of the enemy. P-51s strafed it and set it ablaze.[17]

One of the downed crewmen of A/C #721 (Cunningham, although at that time believed to be Simpson) was reported to have made his way into Hukawng Valley Camp in far northern Burma on the eighth. "The rescue squadron with ATC" continued to search for the others. When word was received on the following day that all crew members had survived and been recovered, "The sigh that went through the squadron sounded like a tuba note." All were reported to be in safe hands at Kamaing and were expected to soon be returned by air transport.

Two B-25Hs took off on July 9 to check the weather and proceeded to bomb the railroad south of Mohnyin to Naba, each carrying six 500 lb. HEs. Over the target at 1530, they released bombs at 300 feet and scored two direct hits on the railroad bed immediately south of Naba, six hits on the embankment, and four near misses that twisted the rails. Gunners strafed and fired boxcars with four hundred rounds of .50 caliber. A fire that broke out in a previously damaged car suggested it was being used to store fuel or ammunition. The aircraft encountered small-arms fire from an area to the left of the railroad station and siding at Naba, which caused no significant damage.

On a second mission that day, a formation of six planes (five Hs with a J) attempted once again to get through to the Hsenwi bridges and came within 15 miles before being forced back by weather. The Mitchells proceeded to their secondary target—"the same old railroad"—arriving on target at 1650. Bombs dropped from 300 feet covered an area from Hopin south to Naba with thirty-six 500 lb. HEs and eight 250 lb. HEs. It was the best mission to date, knocking out two bridges by direct hits and heavily damaging two others, and aircrews reported at least ten direct hits on the rails. Machine gun posts were strafed and silenced. "Hasty repair work visible along railroad and increased A/A signify importance of rail communications. Opine the railroad will be out of commission at least three days," wrote Graves. Lt. Wood, who had taken part in three previous missions, also flew this one. The Mitchells were in the air for five hours, and all returned safely.

It was at about this time that Capt. Seacrest, as acting operations officer in Simpson's absence, put Hank on flying status. "They volunteered me." He explained, "I never did request flight duty, but they put a duty list on the bulletin board. I started to see my name on the bulletin board, that I was scheduled for the flight for the next bombing run." He flew his first mission the very next day. "From then on I was on flight status." Those on flying status were required to "participate frequently and regularly in aerial flights until released by competent authority." Although his only gunnery training had been for qualification on the submachine gun at Sheppard Field, Hank was assigned duty as an aerial gunner on combat missions. Since gunners were expected to be familiar with the coverage area of every gun position and to bring the proper gun to bear on the target as required, all of Hank's training was "on the job."

He did not remember the number of missions in which he took part but estimated that he flew about fifteen to Burma. During this period, "We flew every day, somewhere." He retained clear memories of the "big balls of fire coming out of the barrels of those big guns trying to shoot us down." When asked in an interview if he was afraid, Hank replied, "You didn't think about fear during the flight. Some of the people, after they first were put on flight duty, some of them said, 'I'm done'—said, 'Take me off flight duty. I'm not doing that anymore.' Well, I understood why they felt that way, but I didn't. I couldn't do it. I knew someone had to do it, and there I was. I wasn't scared. I knew if my time to die was there, then God would take care of that." As did many others who went into combat, Hank learned to focus on accomplishing the task at hand and set aside thoughts of personal danger. An added incentive: "Flight personnel earned 50% more money than anyone else."

The last of the squadron's supplies and personnel under the charge of Sgt. Whearty arrived by rail from Karachi on July 9. Listed in the morning report as "DS enroute to Duty" were Sgts. Chu Te-chao, Chang Kwei-ho, Lee En-hsiang, and Mou Lei. TSgt. Hanrahan returned to duty from the hospital on the same date. One of the new cooks, Pvt. Piecuch, was treated for enteritis, commonly caused by harmful microbes in food or water.

Shown here wearing his A-2 leather flight jacket, Hank was "volunteered" for flight status and continued flying missions as an aerial gunner until the end of the war. *J. H. Mills collection*

Sgt. William H. Whearty, an airplane crew chief, stands ready near the flight line. *R. N. Solyn collection, courtesy of Robert N. Solin*

Pfc. James A. Wadlow, crew chief, works with a Chinese mechanic. Written on the back, "Jimmy Wadlow and one of his boys." *R. N. Solyn collection, courtesy of Robert N. Solin*

Capt. Hodges, with three Mitchells, took a heading to Calcutta to pick up the remainder of recently secured supplies on July 10. With him went 1Lt. Hwang T. P. (X-273), 2Lt. Feng M. T. (X-523), SSgt. Chasse, and Pfc. Wadlow. Hodges, flying a B-25J, serial #43-3888 (no A/C number specified), made a normal landing at Barrackpore Airdrome (about 15 miles north of Calcutta) in the lead of the three-plane flight. After landing, he pulled off the runway to watch the other two planes come in.

Flying B-25H, Chinese A/C #717, 2Lt. In Yen-san (X-826) followed Hodges in and landed on the last half of the runway. In was unable to stop before rolling off the end into the mud. Crewmen of A/C #717 were 1Lt. Shen M. C. (X-130) and Sgt. Hieh L. Y. (X-1409). Despite the red light that was flashed at him from the tower, 2Lt. Hsu Tse-chong (X-525), flying the second B-25H, A/C #714, made a similar landing. Members of this crew were 2Lt. Hsu C. H. (X-132) and Sgt. Li S. L. (X-1393). Likewise unable to stop, Hsu rolled the aircraft off the end of the runway and into the tail of In's plane. Both aircraft sustained minor damage—A/C #714 to the side of the cockpit and #717 to the left fin, rudder, and horizontal stabilizer. Hsu experienced minor contusions to his face, but no other injuries were reported. Both planes were repaired and returned to service.[18]

The squadron hit its first target in formation at 1700, staging a low-altitude attack on enemy stores, supplies, and troops at Mohnyin with six B-25s (five Hs and one J). More than 90 percent of the thirty-six 500 lb. HEs dropped "at minimum altitude" fell in the target area. Crewmen observed a number of small fires, although no damage was visible because of the "sheltering terrain." Previous strafing by Thunderbolts had caused a large fire in damaged boxcars. A hail of scattered small-arms fire hit the plane but caused no significant damage.

Lt. Young returned on the same day from group HQ in Kweilin. Later that evening, the remaining crewmen of A/C #721 returned aboard a P-47 from their ordeal, "quite the worse for their grueling experience." The exhausted men "cleaned up, told their tales and hit the sack." They deserved their rest after traveling over 100 miles in seven days through the dense jungle of northern Burma.

It took almost two weeks for news of the crash to filter back through official military channels. Cunningham's wife, Laura, staying with her parents in Albuquerque, received a call from the War Office requesting that she come in for a conference. Accompanied by her father, she feared the worst. Conducted to an office, she was informed that a telegram had been received concerning her husband, who was reported to be "missing as a result of enemy action and presumed dead." As she sat there sobbing in inconsolable grief, she received the astonishing news that a second telegram had just arrived for her. It was from George, who assured her, "I'm safe." She confided in later years whenever she told the story, "It was the worst forty-five minutes of my life."[19]

Simpson wrote the day after his return, "Laid around all day. Hungry as a bear." He filled his leisure time with writing letters and reading. "Found a letter . . . saying all who had gone down in enemy territory and had been helped by friendly natives could no longer fly over the territory and if no other jobs could be utilized, the person involved could be sent home." He concluded, "Am going to try to be sent home, even if Conrad tries to stop me." The following day's entry: "'Pop' Goeller wrote the letter today saying it was recommended I be sent back to America under this regulation. Chet said he would sign it tomorrow. Started feeling tired. Running a slight fever. Doc gave me some pills." Subsequent diary entries demonstrate his rapidly deteriorating health as malaria began to take its toll. On July 14: "Felt lousy today. Fever 102." He wrote on the following day: "Doc said I had to go to the hospital when fever was 103 but I talked him into letting me stay till tomorrow. Fellows really flying missions. Feel bad. Mark Seacrest took over my job as operations officer."

The following year, Simpson was commended for his "gallantry in action" and awarded the Silver Star.[20] In addition, he received the Air Force Commendation Medal, and Soong Mei-ling (also known as Madame Chiang) personally awarded him the Hau Chow Medal for his heroism. She had given him a large piece of jade carved as a dragon with a monkey from her own collection in February 1944, only a short time before Simpson's assignment to the 3rd Squadron. Chiang Chung-cheng (original name of Chiang Kai-shek) awarded him the Breast Order of Yun Hui with Ribbon on January 21, 1946.[21] It was not until forty years later that Madame Chiang also presented Cunningham with a large green jade belt buckle.

These represent some of Simpson's most treasured mementos. Madame Chiang awarded him a jade dragon-and-monkey pendant at Kweilin before he joined the 3rd Squadron, and he was awarded the Silver Star in April 1945. *T. S. Simpson collection, courtesy of Larry Simpson*

The squadron's Mitchells continued to attack and destroy railroad targets in the Hopin and Naba areas that had been bombed earlier in the month. Its first mission against targets along the Salween River in support of Y Force and X Force troops was accomplished on July 11, when bombers finally succeeded in getting through to the Hsenwi Bridge, about 38 miles north of Lashio. Lt. Wood was a participant in the mission aboard a B-25H, according to his Individual Flight Record signed by Capt. Seacrest as operations officer. Six aircrews were briefed, but one turned back due to a mechanical malfunction. The remaining planes reached the target at 1205. This bridge was considered vital to Japanese communications and supply lines via the Burma Road, and at least three direct hits by 500 lb. HEs rendered it impassable. Bombs falling short damaged the roadbed, and overages started large fires in

Bombing in Burma

probable supply areas southwest of the bridge. Gunners "severely strafed" machine gun posts immediately surrounding the main bridge. The squadron's five B-25s returned safely after four hours and fifteen minutes in the air.

On the following day, on the 3rd Squadron's twentieth mission, Capt. Seacrest led a flight of four B-25s against a second Salween target that "hit the mud." Each plane carried six 500 lb. HEs. Bombs dropped from 300 feet on the target area at Mongyu on the Burma Road destroyed two bridges with six direct hits; twelve were near misses. When aircraft encountered heavy antiaircraft, machine gun, and small-arms fire at the main bridge, gunners knocked out all of those positions. Capt. Graves's recap of the mission as acting intelligence officer included this assessment: "Damage or loss: none (miraculously)."

Following the successes achieved by squadron missions, Maj. Conrad received a warm reception at 10th Air Force headquarters, where Cols. Hopkins, Harding, and McCarten acknowledged that "we were doing a fine job" according to Graves. Arrangements were made with Col. McCarten to provide fighter escort "to certain missions." Aerial photos of damage inflicted to the Hsenwi and Mongyu Bridges "bore out our destruction claims and boosted the squadron stock in the A-2 and A-3 offices of the Tenth Air Force." Copies were sent to Gen. Stilwell's headquarters in the Hukawng Valley. "To date the squadron has destroyed eight bridges in support of Stilwell's forces as well as the Yoke Force moving westward across the Salween from China," Graves noted.

The squadron's first medium-altitude mission on July 14 was "a complete success." Two 3rd Squadron Mitchells took part, with Capt. Cunningham flying his "initial bomb dropping from a lead ship." More than 90 percent of the forty 250 lb. HEs fell into supply areas at Mawhun. Crewmen observed two fires. The 2nd Bomb Squadron's Maj. Lawson G. Horner Jr. flew the wing plane on this raid.

With Col. Branch, Majs. Lloyd S. Smith and John H. ("George") Washington, Capt. William ("Tex") Waggaman, and four enlisted men, Maj. Horner had arrived from Bangalore the previous day, and flying a few 3rd Squadron missions provided an opportunity for him to gain combat experience while they waited to cross over into China to join the bomb group at Kweilin. All of them except Col. Branch had been attached to the squadron for rations and quarters, according to the July 14 morning report. Experiencing chills and fever, Branch checked in immediately to the 111th hospital, where Maj. Conrad and several others went to visit him. Maj. Smith, Group dental officer, joined the squadron with the intention of staying a month or so.

Maj. Lloyd S. Smith (called "Smitty" by the other officers), bomb group dental officer (*left*), and Maj. James T. ("Jim") Bull, 8th Fighter Squadron, 3rd Fighter Group (*center*), are pictured here with Capt. Lou Graves, the 3rd Squadron navigator (*right*). On the reverse was this regarding Smith: "Did you ever have him drill a tooth with that foot-powered contraption he used?" *R. L. Logan collection, courtesy of Katherine A. Logan*

"Bridge out—mission accomplished." *J. F. Faherty collection, courtesy of Dennis Faherty*

Three planes were off on a weather check the following morning and, despite unfavorable conditions, dropped eighteen 500 lb. bombs on railroad bridges and rails south of Mohnyin, with two direct hits on a bridge and four hits on the roadbed. This was Lt. Faherty's first mission as bombardier, and he recorded its duration as three hours and ten minutes in his personal flight log.[22] A thunderstorm ripped through the camp that night, leaving two fallen trees in its path but causing no serious damage or injury.

It was during this period that another serious conflict arose between Chinese and American personnel. This time it involved the squadron's adjutant and a Chinese sergeant. Omitted from the squadron's monthly historical report, the only details discovered came from Capt. Simpson's diary as related to him by Lts. Wood and Dorr after he returned from a hospital stay. "Pop Goeller had taken a Chinese boy by the nape of the neck and kicked him out of his tent. Big row—Chinese refused to fly. Conrad arrested Pop and confined him to his quarters—even has to have his food brought to him. What a life—Air Inspector from 10th A.F. came down. Pop is to be transferred to HQ 10th AF. Not bad for kicking a Chinese boy in the 'A,'" Simpson wrote in his diary after learning of the incident.

Faherty occupies the cockpit of a B-25H. Bombs with Chinese characters and the bridge painted below the window suggest eight aerial victories and one Hump crossing. *J. F. Faherty collection, courtesy of Dennis Faherty*

Bombing in Burma

The regrettable event likely occurred on July 15, since the following day's morning report noted that Sgt. Liu Ho-teh (X-2126) went from duty to the hospital. Previously signed by Capt. Goeller, morning reports for the sixteenth and extending through the end of the month bore the signature of Maj. Conrad.

Capt. Simpson and Lt. Dorr, suffering from malaria and "the effects of their recent escapade," were sent to the hospital the following day. Capt. Cunningham joined them five days later. "Doc insisted I go to the hospital today," wrote Simpson. "Fever 105 so this afternoon I was driven up to 111th Station Hospital at Chabua. Too weak to sit up even. They took a blood smear and told me I had malaria." On the seventeenth: "Ran a fever of 106 today. Was delirious. Hot as hell—can't eat a thing. Taking quinine right and left. Feel awful." His condition became so severe that he was unable to take the quinine by mouth so was administered quinine solution "in the arm—a quart at a time." Dorr, suffering similar symptoms, later commented that he lost 35 pounds during the ordeal. The "malarial trio" remained in the hospital until the end of the month.

Cunningham remembered "Doc Yeoh" who took care of them. Dr. Yeoh Seou-ting (X-864), a Chinese physician from Malaysia, was 1st Bomb Group flight surgeon, serving with the rank of second lieutenant. Accompanying the advance party that included Lt. Young when it took off from Erh Tong on July 1 to facilitate the bomb group's move to Peishiyi, "Doc Yeoh, Chinese Flight Surgeon" was "to care for our boys if they get sick en route." He continued to look after their health until the end of the war and maintained contact with several of them through the years that followed.

Recent squadron successes did not go unacknowledged. Maj. Conrad received the following citation from Maj. Gen. Howard C. Davidson, commanding officer of the 10th Air Force, dated July 17:

> I have noticed with great satisfaction the splendid results achieved in attacks by your squadron while operating with my command. The destruction of bridges and stores so vital to the enemy reflects not only a high state of training but also a fine esprit; which, inspiring cooperation resulted in the unified endeavor of all members of your Composite organization in overcoming hardships and trying field conditions. . . . It is my desire that you convey to each member of your organization this expression of my gratitude, and I wish you, collectively, further good hunting.

The Chinese had some changes during this period, beginning with 1Lt. Tu Pin-chow (no serial number recorded), attached in mid-July. Capt. Sung Shou-chon (X-221), 2Lt. Tsai Chang-an (X-280), and SLt. Liu Wan-jen (X-283) were dropped from squadron rolls and returned to China. Col. Branch, released from the hospital, was attached for rations and quarters to Conrad's squadron. With his traveling companions, he settled in to await the return of flyable weather suitable for traversing the mountains before returning to China.

Turbulent conditions once again grounded planes until the twenty-third, when a nine-plane formation hit the Wanting supply area. The Burma Road ran through Wanting (Wandingzhen), located just north of the Burma/China border in Yunnan Province and just south of the Shweli River. The Mitchells carried a total bombload of seventy 250 lb. HEs, fused instantaneous, and arrived on target at 1310. Bombs were dropped from 9,000 feet on Faherty's lead. Two hung up in the racks, while the remainder fell harmlessly west of the target area. Faherty had trouble with the PDI system (pilot direction indicator, used by the bombardier to specify heading changes to the pilot), which resulted in the error. Capt. Graves explained that it was his first lead mission, and he was understandably nervous and apprehensive of results. "The only hopes of damage lies in the possibility of there being camouflaged installation where the bombs fell."

As bombardier, his primary goal was to accurately and effectively bomb the target, and all other function was merely preparatory. With only one point in space at which a bomb could be released to hit a predetermined object on the ground, teamwork between the pilot and bombardier was required in determining ground speed, altitude, direction, etc. The bombardier must thoroughly understand his bombsight's purpose and function, and the operation and upkeep of his bombing equipment such as racks, switches, controls, releases, doors, linkage, etc., keeping it all in perfect operating condition.

Faherty gained expertise through experience in these and other capabilities as he continued in his capacity as bombardier, eventually assuming additional duties as the squadron's armament officer.

This was the squadron's first mission on which propaganda materials were dropped. Provided by the Office of War Information (OWI), these "informational leaflets" served a variety of purposes. Some of them, intended for the native population and printed in the local language, explained how downed American fliers could be identified and the steps to be taken to return them to their bases. Others provided vital information about the war situation, such as the need to evacuate particular areas. Printed in Mandarin, other leaflets were intended to encourage Chinese ground forces and assure them of air support as they continued their resistance against the invaders. Still others, written in Japanese, warned the enemy of the consequences of continued aggression and demanded their unconditional surrender, even encouraging them to turn against their superiors.

One of these OWI leaflets, CBA-31, depicted two B-25s flying overhead. Printed on both sides in Burmese, it was distributed across the countryside at about this time and served as a warning to the locals:

DANGER! BOMBS FOR THE JAPANESE!

These are American planes flying over your land. From this great height people down below look like small ants. That is why pilots cannot always tell friends from foe. To be safe, stay away from the Japanese. . . . For your own safety, when you hear the Japanese are coming, leave your village at once.

Do not return until three or four days after the Japanese have left.

A Message from the Pilot of the Plane Flying Overhead:

I am flying over your land to kill Japanese and to destroy their supplies. I have no other purpose here.

Before the Japanese attacked my country I lived peacefully at home. I had no desire for war. But Japan attacked the United States just as it attacked Burma. Now my comrades and I attack the Japanese wherever they are found. We shall not stop until the Japanese have been completely beaten. I do not want to harm you.

Stay away from roads used by the Japanese. Stay away from their railroad. Stay away from Japanese military places. Do not needlessly endanger your lives.

Another version of this leaflet written in the Shan dialect and coded XBSha-30 was disseminated by fighters and depicted a P-47 Thunderbolt flying over the landscape of Burma.[23] Thousands upon thousands of leaflets were dropped along with the squadron's bombs through the course of the war, in Burma and later in China.

Most of the missions through the month were flown with H model Mitchells, each equipped with a 75 mm cannon that was operated by the pilot. The cannoneer's seat was positioned where the copilot sat on other models. He removed a panel that covered an opening through the floor, and then climbed down into the compartment below, where the cannon was positioned under the pilot's seat. It was the duty of the cannoneer to load twelve live 75 mm shells, pointed upward, into the storage magazine under his own seat and then to keep the cannon loaded. When it was ready to fire, he reached up and tapped the pilot on the knee. The cannon's recoil momentarily stopped the plane in midair when it fired, causing it to drop about 200 feet before it could "catch up" and begin to move forward again.

Hank sometimes served as cannoneer and described one of these missions. "I was standing on the floor right behind and to the side of that cannon, and when it would fire, I'd reload it. And it fired. It wasn't supposed to fire." The pilot, who had not fired it, thought Hank had been responsible for the misfire. "He turned around and growled at me. I told him, 'I didn't fire that. You almost cut me in two with that thing.' When it recoiled, it came back."

"Well, don't load it. We won't fool with it anymore," replied the pilot, whose name Hank did not remember. "I don't know. I flew with so many." Malfunction of the cannon was such a common occurrence that the newer J model eliminated it altogether.

SSgt. Meikle was returned from intelligence specialist to his previous classification as intelligence NCO, while TSgt. Solyn was reclassified from operations NCO to intelligence specialist. The contributions of these two were essential to successful operations. Working as a team, their duties included constantly reviewing the general military situation in the squadron's area of operations by studying maps and reports as they came in. Responsible for gathering and analyzing available information regarding enemy dispositions, strengths, and movements, they passed the data along to Operations, to be used in planning tactical employment. They prepared maps to be used in the planning and execution of missions. As reports were received regarding any changes to the situation that might affect the success of a mission, they prepared and transmitted updates so decisions could be made on the basis of the most-recent developments.

The critical nature of Solyn's intelligence assignment, which also included overseeing the packing of parachutes because of his previous experience while serving in the Connecticut Air National Guard, would have ordinarily kept him on the ground.

TSgt. Robert N. Solyn, in his capacity as intelligence specialist, evaluates data at his desk. His extensive collection of photographs has aided in bringing this squadron history to life. *R. N. Solyn collection, courtesy of Robert N. Solin*

However, his sense of adventure overcame his caution, as well as the objections of his superiors, and he was given permission to fly a combat mission. Since the bomb squadrons were perpetually short on gunners, he filled in at one of those positions. He later related his memories of manning one of the B-25's .50-caliber machine guns and seeing ground fire coming from below, although the Mitchell was able to return to base with little damage. His curiosity having been satisfied, Solyn was thereafter content to remain behind his desk.[24]

The practice seems to have been relatively common, because 1Sgt. Earley told a similar story to his family, explaining that he once filled in on an aircrew that was short a tail gunner. Their plane was hit and disabled by antiaircraft fire, and the crew was ordered to bail out. After the aircraft failed to return, aircrew members were listed as missing, and it took over a month for them to get back to a friendly area with the help of Chinese civilians, according to his recollections.[25]

Because the name of neither Solyn nor Earley has been found listed among participants of any combat mission of the 1st Bomb Group, their participation either took place on missions to Burma when 3rd Squadron operational reports did not include names of aircrewmen, or it was kept as a carefully guarded secret.

CHAPTER SIX
Moving to Dergaon

The third week in July brought about some significant changes. Maj. Conrad learned that his squadron was scheduled to move to a new base at Dergaon (26°43'7" N, 93°59'26" E), about 80 miles west-southwest of Moran and 20 miles west of Jorhat, the nearest sizable town and site of a C-87 base used primarily as an ATC refueling stop. Recently vacated by a Royal Air Force fighter/bomber squadron, Dergaon's location was of strategic advantage because it provided easy access to the route over the "Low Hump," by which the Mitchells traversed the 9,000-foot Chin Hills to reach their targets.

There was a considerable amount of confusion regarding spelling of the new base, and several versions appeared in records. The squadron historian wrote on the twenty-fourth, "Doesn't make a damn how this was spelled on July 23, this is correct, see?" Graves wrote on the same date, "Col. Branch and party are still consuming our beans and hotcakes."

An advance detail that included Capt. Hinrichs; Lt. Wood; SSgts. Armstrong, Jakubasz, and Summerville; Sgt. Malone; Cpl. England; and Pfc. Wadlow left for "Deragon" as the end of the month approached. Capt. Graves, Lt. Faherty, and Sgt. Meikle made up a second detail that arrived the following day. Hinrichs inspected the facilities and found them acceptable. He reported that although there were no base functions or furniture, the field was better located and laid out than Moran. Mess halls and quarters (once again tents) were readied. Remaining personnel completed the move two days later, when a truck convoy brought supplies that were unloaded at the new base. The squadron was to share the field with the 89th Fighter Squadron of the 80th ("Burma Banshees") Fighter Group, which was setting up quarters in the basha area of the field. Graves described the situation: "No A/C on the field—just a handful of Uncle Sam's boys, a few Limeys, Wogs, and a helluva lot of cows."

As they were making the move to Dergaon, Hank had an encounter that remained indelibly in his memory. He was driving along a dirt road with the convoy in an open weapons carrier filled with supplies. With him were two Chinese officers as passengers. Unexpectedly, a full-grown Bengal tiger stepped out of the dense bamboo thicket into the road a short distance ahead. Hank stopped the vehicle. The unconcerned tiger ambled across the road and then reentered the vegetation on the other side. Hank turned to the Chinese pilots and asked, "Did you see that tiger? It's not every day that a real, wild tiger walks out in front of you."

"We saw it," they answered. The two officers jumped out and pulled their handguns. "They started shucking those little ol' pistols."

"What do you think you're doing?" he asked.

"We're going to shoot that tiger."

"You're not going to shoot that tiger. You better get back on board, 'cause we're leaving here right now. You're not going to make that thing mad and come in here and jump on us." The officers complied, and the three made their way to the new base without further incident.

Squadron aircraft arrived on the twenty-eighth. One had trouble with landing gear but managed to get down successfully after circling for about an hour. Squadron headquarters and organization officially relocated from Moran (APO 629) to Dergaon (APO 466) on that date; personnel were noted as on detached service from Headquarters 10th Air Force. Unloading of supplies continued throughout the day, in spite of a shortage of labor and rain that fell intermittently but persistently throughout the week. The remaining tents were erected, and general preparations continued satisfactorily. Conditions can be summed up in a succinct message that Maj. Conrad sent to his family in Missouri at about this time: "I am ok. The weather is hot and the mosquitoes bad."[1]

As they were settling into their new home, Capt. Graves cryptically noted, "The incident of 'who took the gin' presented a squadron headache for several days[,] and the veteran enlisted men took the long drill to the line twice per day to no one's satisfaction and the case petered out."

Hank provided more details. He explained that Maj. Conrad reported two bottles of "whiskey" missing from his quarters soon after the move. In an attempt to extract either a confession from the culprit or information regarding the crime, the enlisted men were required to march, morning and evening, from their living quarters to "the area where the planes were kept" and back again. As Hank remembered it, he did not march with the others, although he appears in a photo taken of the group. "I said, 'I didn't steal it, and I'm not going to march.' And I didn't." Lloyd Jackson, a corporal at that time, remembered marching to "a

Led by 1st Sgt. William T. Earley (*far left, front, dark pants*), enlisted men take "the long drill" from their tents to the flight line. *Column to the left*: Andrew R. Allegretto, John P. Hanrahan, Elmer J. Thompson, unidentified (face not visible), unidentified, Herman L. Burton, next two unidentified, and James A. Wadlow (wearing pith helmet). *Middle column*: Ewell F. Wilkerson, James H. Mills (white T-shirt, grinning into camera), unidentified (face not visible), Donald W. Grant, and George Gruber; last two unidentified. *Column to the right*: Clyde L. Learn, Alvin A. Hall, Lloyd E. Jackson, Philip Piecuch, James E. McCann, Homer L. Chasse, and William G. Duffin. *J. H. Mills collection*

made-up song" that went like this: "Somebody stole my gin. Somebody stole my gin. Didn't say they were leaving. Somebody stole my gin."[2]

Eventually the matter was dropped due to lack of evidence, although some of the enlisted men suspected that Sgt. Whearty, who had arrived with them aboard *Mission Bay*, was the guilty party. Before the war, Whearty worked for a dairy in Boston and had a delivery route that included a number of wealthy households, and he had boasted that he expected to retire within five years after returning to his route. Instead of dealing with the homeowners, he left the orders with their head housekeepers and charged about triple the price. "That's how he was gonna retire. He was stealing money from those rich people." Hank was also critical of Whearty's behavior toward the Chinese mechanics. "He shouted at them, and they didn't like him. He was unkind."

On July 30, Graves reported that the squadron was "all tented and mess arrangements made," although with a limited menu. The men were served a monotonous diet of pancakes and coffee for breakfast and "wieners and more wieners for lunch and dinner." They were pleased when new personnel were attached as a base command that specialized in housekeeping and servicing of the tactical units. Myitkyina's commander ordered withdrawal by his troops and committed suicide on the same date. The Japanese began their retreat down the Tiddim road the following day, as B-25s from other units pounded enemy troops in the Hopin area. Having settled in, "we are ready for operations," declared Graves.

Capt. Cunningham and Lt. Dorr returned from the 111th hospital. SSgt. Haines, who had spent a few days there for treatment of enteritis, returned with them to duty.[3] Capt. Goeller, waiting for orders reassigning him, was appointed to Summary Court-Martial "for such cases as may be brought before him." SSgts. Hoyle and Meikle were promoted to technical sergeants, and Sgts. Barge and Duffin to staff sergeants. Lt. Young returned from detached service on July 31 and took over responsibilities as squadron historical officer from Lt. Graves. Cpls. Burton, Rickman, and Trout were reclassified from A/P and engine mechanics to A/P crew chiefs, and TSgt. Meikle from intelligence NCO to air operations specialist.

Rolls specified that forty-one Americans and 171 Chinese made up the 3rd Bomb Squadron at the end of July. During this first full month of combat operations, with eleven B-25s, the squadron completed sixty sorties in twenty-six missions, totaling 193 combat hours. These totals were only slightly fewer than the 4th Squadron, operating out of Kweilin, with thirty-three missions. The 1st Squadron flew fifteen missions from Peishiyi, and the 2nd Squadron, operating out of Liangshan, completed only two.

Following their move, the 3rd Squadron was back in action with mission #27 on August 1. The target was the Pangkham Bridge, just south of the Loi-Wing Factory airdrome (23°05.0' N, 97°39.5' E), situated on a bend of the Shweli River near the Yunnan border. Formerly a privately operated American airplane assembly factory, it had been seized by the Japanese when they occupied Burma

A B-25H takes off from the grassy field at Dergaon bound for Burma. *R. N. Solyn collection, courtesy of Robert N. Solin*

and rebuilt as a maintenance and repair facility. A two-plane echelon arrived in the target area at 1730. Each plane carried three 500 lb. HEs. The wing plane was forced to turn back when its top-turret canopy blew off, resulting in minor injuries to the gunner, Sgt. Kan K. M., but the lead plane went on to complete the mission. The bridge's single-span truss construction made it difficult to inflict any significant damage. Although one bomb scored a direct hit on the bridge, it went through the flooring and exploded without visible damage to the foundation or span. However, because flooring was knocked out, the bridge was claimed as damaged and temporarily inoperative. A near miss to the side of the bridge may have caused damage. The mission report stated that the Shweli Bridge, 5 miles south of target, was still out of operations, and the Loi-Wing Factory strip, just inside Yunnan, was unusable.

Crews were briefed on the evening of August 3 to hit separate targets: the Pangkham Bridge, Wanting supply area, and Myitkyina. The B-25s carried an aggregate bombload of 24,400 pounds. The first element again hit the Pangkham Bridge, which was reported as completely destroyed. Lt. Young referred to the bridge as "the Bhamo bridge" many years later in an interview, although its location was about 35 miles southeast of Bhamo. "I was part of the 10th Air Force in Burma and participated as a navigator in a bombing mission to destroy the Bhamo Bridge," he recalled. "Previous attempts to destroy the bridge had failed. It was important to do this because it was a supply route for the Japanese. Our plane was one of three [two according to the operational report] flying at low altitudes. My crew had a successful hit and the bridge was destroyed. We were awarded Air Medals."[4] Young's summary of this mission in his first squadron historical report stated, "Photographs disclosed bridge completely destroyed."

The second element proceeded to the nearby Wanting supply area, but one aircraft failed to reach the target because of engine trouble. It was probably this mission that Lou Graves mentioned in a letter to Jim McCann many years later: "If my memory is sound, you and I shared a B-25 experience with an engine afire coming back from a low-level mission into Burma, with old Coondog Conrad at the stick. Obviously, we survived but there were moments I had doubts." The two Chinese gunners flying with them had doubts too. McCann told his family about this mission, on which one of the B-25's engines caught fire. Because the gunners spoke little English, they did not understand when he explained that the plane could fly with only one engine. As they repeatedly attempted to bail out through the escape hatch, he grabbed them by their harnesses and hauled them back in. His concern was that they might encounter headhunters if they succeeded in bailing out, since the plane was passing over Naga territory on its route back to base.[5]

It seems that his confidence in the plane's abilities was justified, despite warnings to the contrary. "One of the first missions in a B-25H proved the experts wrong. We were told the 'H' would never fly on one engine," McCann stated in an interview published in 1984. He explained that the pilot extinguished the fire and climbed from 100 feet on one engine. He feathered the prop and then ordered his crew to dump all unnecessary equipment to lighten the plane. After climbing to 500 feet, the Mitchell was barely able to "scrape back through the pass" but landed safely.

McCann was assigned to the 2nd Bomb Squadron at its inception in summer of 1943 to assist in training Chinese armorers and gunners. He was placed on flying status in mid-November. Since the 2nd Squadron was moving to China soon afterward, he "ended up in the base hospital at Malir with yellow fever." He was left behind and attached to the 1st Squadron when it began training. In early December, McCann was assigned to special duty as an instructor with the OTU at Malir, where he was responsible for providing gunnery training to

Chinese enlisted men of the recently activated 4th Bomb Squadron. He recalled, "We ... had trouble making the Chinese gunners understand the automatic cut-off on the interrupter system when the turret guns came in line with our own tail fins. They shot the tail fins off a couple B-25s before they understood the interrupter did not stop the guns when firing, except at their own tail." He rejoined his squadron at Kweilin but was sent back to Karachi in early 1944 to work with the 3rd Squadron.[6]

Hank recalled similar missions. He told his younger brother in one of their rare conversations about his service that "I can't tell you how many times we would finish a run and just hope we could get enough power to make it back over the mountains. Those engines would be popping and smoking, and our plane would be shot up with so many holes that we didn't know if we were going to get back to our base." As Conrad's plane limped back over the mountains toward home, the formation's second Mitchell flew on to complete the mission. In spite of nine-tenths cloud cover, all of its bombs hit within the target area.

The third element of six planes was over Myitkyina target #1 at 1750 and dropped thirty-six 500 lb. HEs. The lead plane had bomb release failure on the first pass, so the navigator-bombardier lined up the target to make a second run. The wing plane made four passes due to similar failures. All bombs, released "by select" from 200 feet, fell in the target area, except for six that hung up in the racks and had to be salvoed (i.e., released all at once). No fires or explosions were observed "due to nature of target." Although it was not specified in mission details, "Target #1" may have been the hospital, reportedly being used at that time as enemy headquarters, although the railroad terminal was another prime target.

Bomb racks were usually set to release either in train or in salvo. When set to drop in train, the bombs fell one at a time at predetermined intervals. The salvo setting dropped the entire bombload in one operation. When bombs hung up in the racks, the bombardier generally found it necessary to hit the salvo switch. Pilots were seldom pleased when bombs were salvoed, because the sudden loss of several hundred pounds caused the B-25s to "jump," making it difficult to maintain formation. A third option, releasing "by select," allowed bombs to be dropped individually by the pilot or bombardier.

Graves mentioned in his operational report that "Chinese ground troops apparently recognized insignia of our A/C as several waved flags and bits of clothing[,] and our Chinese personnel acknowledged recognition." Young wrote a similar account: "Chinese ground forces waved flags and caps as our planes passed low over parts of Myitkyina." MSgt. Hanrahan later related, "My outfit bombed Myitkyina down in Burma just 45 minutes before Chinese troops retook it. For three days before that, we flew low over Chinese lines so that the soldiers could see the Chinese insignia on our wings. They knew we were paving the way."

The once-prosperous city of Myitkyina, formerly a thriving river-trade and resort town but now burned and gutted, officially fell at 1545 hours on August 3, when Chinese troops who volunteered for the duty entered the city. Enemy stragglers and snipers, making a last stand, were wiped out the next day. The capture of Myitkyina completed the reconquest of about 10,000 square miles of Burma, and the prospect of joining the Ledo Road with the Burma Road was in sight. The next Sino-American move was projected to be toward Bhamo, to the south, and then on to Lashio and a junction with the Burma Road.[7]

Squadron planes completed two missions in the same vicinity on the fourth. Five B-25Hs arrived over the target area at 1140 and dropped a total load of thirty 500 lb. HEs fused at 0.1-second delay from 3,000 feet on a position between two smoke bombs placed by the ground force along a strip of the Sawmah Road, 22 miles southeast of Mogaung. Graves reported that all bombs hit within the target area outlined previously, but were 300 yards west of the last smoke bomb laid by ground forces. Contacted by radio, the ground forces then attempted to place smoke bombs at the extreme ends of the target, but "their efforts were erratic and not conducive to either a good bomb run for range or deflection. Because the target was concealed personnel, operational evaluation had to be withheld pending ground reports."

Low-lying clouds partially obscured the target, causing results to be inconclusive. The smoke bombs were repositioned, and four planes flew a second mission over the target at 1615. This time, bombs were reported by ground radio as "right on the nose." Crewmen observed two fires, followed by explosions.

A report of action for early August stated, "B-25 Mitchells hammered the area six days out of seven, inflicting great damage, in the heaviest attacks yet delivered by them," in spite of heavy rainfall that created hazardous conditions in the area.[8]

CBI Roundup offered praise to the 10th Air Force for its effective air support:

Maj. Gen. George E. Stratemeyer's Eastern Air Command . . . provided one of the outstanding examples of effective co-operation between ground and air forces in the history of the CBI Theater. All during the week, air activity was on a large scale throughout Burma. In the days preceding the fall of Myitkyina, dive-bombers of Maj. Gen. Howard C. Davidson's 10th Air Force carried out intensive and unremitting attacks to liquidate individual Japanese strong points in the town. When Lt. Gen. Joseph W. Stilwell's ground forces entered Myitkyina, they found that virtually every building in it had been destroyed or severely damaged by bombing or artillery fire. The B-25s of the 10th and Tactical Air Forces concentrated on the northern section of the railroad between Mandalay and Myitkyina. On one of these attacks, they destroyed a railroad bridge at Hopin and knocked out a span of another bridge at Mawlu. Another raid inflicted severe damage on railroad yards and sidings at Mawlu and at Bilumyo, four miles north. The Mitchells also bombed troop concentrations at Sawmah.[9]

Capt. Simpson was released from the hospital the morning of August 5 and hitched a ride by ATC to Jorhat, where Lts. Wood and Dorr picked him up. They regaled him with the story involving Pop Goeller and the Chinese sergeant on the drive to Dergaon by jeep. At this time limited to flying only administrative missions, he wrote on the following day, "Received orders today to report to Calcutta to pick up the plane damaged a month ago by Chinese, bless them!!! Took Lt. Hsieh, W. W., navigator, and a Sgt. Liu, C. C. Hsieh was the fellow who went with me to Bangalore the last time. As good a navigator as Lou." Simpson left on a combat cargo plane and stayed overnight at Rest Camp #1 since the Grand had no vacancies. With few responsibilities, he took time for shopping, sightseeing, and other forms of self-imposed rest and recuperation (called "R&R") before collecting the repaired plane at Barrackpore and returning to "Deragon" at about 6:30 p.m. on August 13. "Bad weather all the way but made the trip interesting. Nothing much had happened since I left. Pop Goeller has been transferred to 10th A.F. at Chabua as Asst. Air Inspector. Good deal for him. Maybe I should kick one of them where he sits down."

The squadron's planes continued to fly in support of ground troops after the city had been taken. Six B-25s hit Tsungni on the afternoon of the fifth, dropping thirty-six 500 lb. HEs. All fell in the target area but west of the aiming point in the city. Low-flying fighters and transports "milling about the target area" hindered bomb runs. Crewmen reported at least two large fires

Moving to Dergaon

when bombs hit either fuel or ammunition. Light, inaccurate 40 mm fire about 5 miles west-northwest of the target burst above and to the rear of the formation, and machine gun fire came up from a position southeast of Tsungni. No .50-caliber ammo was expended.

Squadron Mitchells again hammered the Hsenwi Bridge on that same date. Capt. Seacrest led a two-plane formation that was over the target at 1425, with Lt. Lui P. C. as his wingman. Each plane carried six 500 lb. HEs. The pilots dropped their bombs individually in six passes at low altitude, and three were direct hits that destroyed one end of the bridge. Planes encountered heavy machine gun fire around the bridge and from a nearby village. Although one aircraft received several hits in the tail section, no significant damage resulted. On the third pass, shrapnel hit Sgt. Li C. J. in the ankle, inflicting two wounds, according to the operational report, but Li later stated that his wounds were the result of ground fire. Shattered Plexiglas caused a cut above Lt. Young's right knee as he was removing Sgt. Li from the tail turret during the attack.

"Once our plane was shot, leaving a hole," Li Chan-jui (Li Zhanrui) stated in a 2015 video interview that was conducted in Mandarin and translated into English. "My foot was shot. American doctors operated on me, but there is still half a bullet in my bone that couldn't be removed." He explained that he was a cadet at the China Air Force Academy when he was chosen in 1942 for special training in India by the Americans. He still remembered hearing the American commanders as they called the aircrews together in English for premission briefings: "Everybody—everybody—flying man. Now you gather nine o'clock. Come on to here. Our mission—our mission . . ." He recalled that he "sat at all the positions" and stated, "I did it all. I was bombardier, I was navigator, gunner, and pilot" on missions "targeting tanks and bridges and cutting Japanese supply lines" until the end of the war.[10]

Young, an American citizen of Chinese ancestry, had demonstrated courage since before the war began. Volunteering for military service in the regular army in December 1940, he later transferred to the Air Corps. Young had been stationed for about three months at Wheeler Field on Oahu, territory of Hawaii, when the Japanese attacked the field at 7:35 a.m. before hitting Pearl Harbor, farther south. Initially trained as an aircraft mechanic, he was assigned to Hawaii Intercept Command and quartered in a tent beside runway #27. Both of his tent mates died that day. He credited his decision to attend a church service held about 3 miles from the field with saving his life. Young was wounded in his right leg during the second attack on the field while attempting to move undamaged fighter planes away from those that were burning, earning him the Purple Heart. An official document published by the Naval Institute stated, "During the air attack on December 7, 1941, Paul L. Young . . . with the Army Air Corps on active duty was the first American of Chinese descent awarded the Military Order of the Purple Heart in WWII."

Young spent twenty-three months with a heavy-bomb unit in the Southwest Pacific, where he completed twenty-seven combat missions. He was shot down over New Guinea but escaped with minor injuries, although he was sent back to the US and hospitalized because of repeated bouts of malaria. Young then attended Navigator School at San Marcos Airfield in Texas. "I was put on a ship to Karachi, where I trained Chinese crews on B-25s," he later stated in an interview.[11] He returned to the States for intelligence training and was subsequently assigned to the 3rd Bomb Squadron as its intelligence officer, flying an additional five missions. Young was an invaluable asset to the squadron with its mixed personnel, helping to relieve any friction that developed between the two very diverse national groups.

The Mohnyin supply area was the target on August 6. Weather conditions were noted as "scattered cumulous and thunder" but "storms were by-passed." Six Mitchells arrived over the target at 1405. Each dropped six 500-pounders on the city of Mohnyin, most falling in the area bounded on the west by the railroad tracks, east by the river, north by the road crossing the tracks, and south by an abrupt bend in the river. Only one failed to hit the target, due to a malfunction of the release mechanism. Results were noted as "good." Lt. Faherty was bombardier of one of the Mitchells and noted its duration as four hours.[12]

On the same afternoon, two B-25Hs took off at 1620 and dropped twelve 500 lb. HEs, completely destroying the bridge at Hsenwi with three direct hits. Two trucks were left burning on the road just beyond the bridge. Important installations such as this were often protected by machine guns that were concealed by the surrounding jungle, making it difficult to locate and eliminate them. When heavy ground fire caused severe damage (described as "numerous holes") to both aircraft, gunners strafed an emplacement located about 30 yards northwest of the bridge. Sgt. Chu H. P. was credited with knocking out the machine gun nest. Lt. Wood participated in this mission, with duration of four hours and twenty minutes according to his records. It was likely a mission in which Sgt. Jackson remembered taking part. He related that Capt. Seacrest, pilot of one of the planes, made twelve passes to ensure success in destroying the target. Seacrest's plane was able to return to base and land normally, in spite of damage that included about two hundred bullet holes that were later patched with sheet metal and rivets under the direction of TSgt. Shock.[13]

Capt. Graves reported a low-altitude mission on August 7, when Capt. Seacrest led a two-plane echelon to Naba Junction early in the morning. Wood was on the crew of one of the B-25Hs. The aircraft arrived on target at 0740 and dropped twelve 500 lb. HEs on a railroad bridge. Two bounded off but exploded, shifting the rails and damaging the foundation. One was a direct hit on the adjacent roadbed, while another bomb hit the bridge but did not explode. Crew members reported it as a dud. After dropping the bombload, they came across a train. According to the mission report, gunners strafed rolling stock, damaging an estimated fifteen railroad cars. A 40 mm post was in operation 300 yards west of the bridge, and a few bursts were sighted behind and above the planes. Both bombers returned safely to base after three and a half hours.

Encountering the train was an unexpected bonus. Trains usually moved at night, but occasionally one was spotted on the move in the daytime or being made up. The Japanese were pressed for locomotives and used diesel units interspersed throughout the trains. Because the power units in the trains were not visible, gunners strafed the entire length of the string of cars and stopped them that way.

Cpl. Earnest D. Johnson, who later flew fifty missions with the 2nd Bomb Squadron, provided his impression of similar missions in his memoirs. He recalled that strafing railroad trains was one of the exciting things about war. "We flew low along the tracks to take the trains by surprise. When we saw a train, we chased it down the tracks and tried to hit it with the 75 mm cannon in the nose of our B-25H Model. The trains were pulled by steam locomotives[,] and when we hit the engine's boiler, steam would blow it into a million pieces—a spectacular sight." Should the engine crew see the attacking planes in time, they let the steam out of the engine boiler so it would not blow up and could be repaired.[14]

The mission on this day was one Hank remembered particularly well. "I was top turret gunner. I rode up with the pilot." Seacrest told him, as Hank recalled, "We're gonna strafe that train" but warned against firing forward because the concussion from the guns could break the Plexiglas cover. The aluminum gun-slot shields were sometimes removed to improve forward visibility, but this practice caused the Plexiglas canopies to shatter from the air pressure, resulting in injury to the gunner's face.

The upper turret of the B-25H extended above the roof of the plane and carried two .50-caliber machine guns that were ordinarily fired by the flight engineer, who was expected to know more about the plane than anyone else on board. Working closely with the pilot, he sat on an elevated folding bicycle-type seat with foot platform, mounted on a pedestal located in the aft portion of the cannoneer's compartment. When in position, he sighted and fired the guns through an electrically powered Plexiglas dome that swiveled to provide the best angle of attack. The turret was operated by means of hand grips that had controls for speed, intercom, and trigger that fired both guns simultaneously. The twin guns were mounted on either side of the gunner's shoulders. Each gun was fed by an ammunition box that held 440 rounds of ammunition—enough for only a few seconds of continuous firing.

According to Hank, the pilot instructed, "When I get partway through, I'll pull up real steep and you shoot between the tails" (the two vertical stabilizers). Hank described what happened next: "I turned the guns around and he did what he said. He went in at an angle where he fired, then he pulled up and I put those tracers on that train and fired all the way down, and in a little bit one blew up and it made fire—smoke and flame you could see for 50 miles. So that's the only thing I know of that I did that affected anything." He felt pride in that mission. "I got a lot of satisfaction that day. That one day I hurt them."

Capt. Graves participated in a second mission that was off later that morning. Six B-25s took a heading toward Onsansiang, northeast of Bilumyo. It was scheduled to be a medium-altitude mission with bombs released at 5,000 feet, but tremendous storms and cloud formations with cumulus building up to 18,000 feet in the target area forced the planes to abort and return without hitting their target.

On the eighth, Maj. Conrad led the largest formation yet to be assembled by the squadron. Ten Mitchells took off with Shwekyina supply area (about 80 miles north of Bhamo) as their target, but this mission was likewise abortive because of the tremendous cumulus cloud formations that covered the target and surrounding area. Faherty flew as bombardier aboard one of the planes, their target Bhamo and duration four hours, according to his personal flight record.[15] Similar conditions prevented all except weather reconnaissance missions for the next week.

Bad flying weather delayed the arrival of Lt. Young, the squadron's intelligence officer, who flew in on the tenth. The squadron was "sweating out" his safe return with PX rations from group headquarters at Kweilin until conditions cleared later that day. "Happy day, they are here. Beers tonight and morale tops."

Cpl. Parker P. Collins joined the 3rd Squadron on detached service from 10th Air Force headquarters on August 12. Formerly assistant to the dean of men at the University of Washington and a social worker on the staff of the King County Welfare Department at enlistment, he had served in India and Burma for more than eighteen months by this time in the war.[16] His purpose in being attached—perhaps to deal with recurring conflicts between the Americans and the Chinese—was not explained in the records, but his tenure with the squadron was brief. His name did not appear on orders for the next change of station later in the month.

In mid-August, 2Lt. Wood was promoted to first lieutenant. Capt. Simpson, 2Lt. Hsieh W. W., and Sgt. Liu C. C. returned to duty from Calcutta following a week's stay. Sgt. Yuan Hsi-sheng returned from the hospital. A weather reconnaissance mission over Mohnyin and vicinity reported good weather for a scheduled medium-altitude mission, but information failed to reach base because of poor radio contact, and "the mission was unable to get off in time."

American members of the 3rd Bomb Squadron celebrated Chinese Air Force Day on August 14 with their Chinese counterparts. Held annually, this holiday commemorates the heroism and sacrifice of Chinese pilots in defense of their homeland on that date in 1937, when the CAF scored its first air-to-air victory over the invaders. The entire squadron participated in a flag ceremony at 0800, with two Chinese generals and staff as guests of honor. Banners to commemorate the occasion were presented to the squadron's American component. Speakers were Gen. Sun, division commander, as well as the two squadron commanders, Maj. Wu and Maj. Conrad.

"Attention!" With Earley out front, enlisted men prepare to participate in celebration of Chinese Air Force Day with their Chinese counterparts. *J. H. Mills collection*

Color guards raise the American and Chinese Nationalist flags as Hank looks on from the left. *J. H. Mills collection*

Chinese members of the 3rd Bomb Squadron gather with American enlisted men for a group photograph following the presentation of several silk commemorative banners. *J. H. Mills collection*

Moving to Dergaon

Hank was issued a "Motor Vehicle Operator's Permit" on the same day. *J. H. Mills collection*

Signed by Capt. Goeller, still officially squadron adjutant although working with the 10th Air Force as assistant air inspector, it authorized him to drive a variety of motor vehicles. *J. H. Mills collection*

That same day, Hank was issued a "Motor Vehicle Operator's Permit" (O.O. Form No. 7360). Signed by Capt. Goeller, the permit authorized him to drive half-track and passenger cars, motorcycles, tractors, cargo trucks (from ¼ ton to 4 ton and larger), wheeled combat vehicles, and "special."

Squadron Mitchells flew two missions that afternoon. Maj. Conrad, with two high-ranking Chinese officers along as observers, led a nine-plane formation that was over the target at 1540. They bombed and strafed the city of Mohnyin "with excellent results." Bombardiers dropped a total load of fifty-six 100 lb. fragmentation bombs from 5,000 feet. The bomb pattern began just south of the Buddhist temple in the heart of the city, where there was an important Japanese supply depot on the Mohnyin–Indaw line. Waist gunners heaved out packets of leaflets over the densely populated area. Four bombs hung up in the racks and were salvoed. Conrad's plane encountered some antiaircraft fire, although no significant damage resulted. A projectile shattered the Plexiglas structure in the rear turret, but no injuries were reported from it or from other enemy fire.

On previous missions, the B-25s had carried exclusively 250, 500, and 1,000 lb. high-explosive bombs, which depended on the blast effect to destroy targets. Hank recalled, "I used to see the flash that was visible—a colored flash when a bomb would explode. I only found out a couple of years ago that flash was named plasma." Even "near misses" could cause damage when the bombs detonated.

During this period, many of these bombs were "below par" and failed to explode when dropped on the target, but Simpson had recently brought in a new supply of bombs and fuses from Jorhat. In addition to being of better quality, a greater variety of bomb types began to be received. This mission was the squadron's first to use smaller, 100 lb. fragmentation bombs. Termed "anti-personnel bombs," they caused severe injury from shrapnel created when the bomb's thin outer shell blew apart, or fragmented. In addition to "frags," the squadron was supplied with general-purpose demolition bombs (GPs) and incendiary bombs.

Capt. Seacrest led the second mission of the day, also carrying two Chinese officers as observers. His objective was to skip-bomb a twin bridge about 4 miles northwest of Lashio, starting point of the Burma Road's south end. Skip bombing was always done at very low altitudes (usually 200 to 250 feet) at speeds from 200 to 250 miles per hour. A "stick" of two to four bombs, preferably fused to four- or five-second delay, was released by either the pilot or bombardier at an angle that induced them to "skip" over the water, similar to skipping a rock on the surface of a pond. Their hope was that bombs would bounce into the target and detonate, although odds were about equal that they would bounce over the target and miss.

Two B-25Hs took off at 1505 hours from Dergaon Field. Capt. Seacrest flew Chinese A/C #714, with 1Lt. Chang Huan-hsin (X-226) noted as his copilot, 1Lt. Chu Shin-chuan (serial no. not specified) as navigator, 2Lt. John F. Faherty as bombardier / tail gunner, Sgt. Chiu Hsien-pin (X-2115) as engineer, 2Lt. Hsu Hung-yi (X-287) as radio-gunner, and Lt. Col. Sing (given name and serial no. not specified) as passenger, for whom this was reported to be his first mission. On Seacrest's wing was SLt. Liu Ping-chang (X-830), pilot of Chinese A/C #722, with 2Lt. Hsieh Wu-wei (X-278) as navigator, Sgt. Wang Shih-fu (X-2177) as engineer, Sgt. Li Chen-si (X-1394) as radio-gunner, and Sgt. Yuan Chen-fang (X-2114) as tail gunner. Their target was a highway bridge on the Burma Road, 4 miles north of Lashio. Weather and visibility were recorded as good.

Upon reaching the target, they discovered it to be heavily defended by concealed antiaircraft weapons. Crewmen almost immediately spotted a convoy of trucks parked beside buildings near the bridge. Seacrest dropped in to strafe, and Liu followed on his tail. Then they reversed and attacked the trucks with a second strafing run. Both planes were hit by heavy small-arms fire on the second pass, but they followed up with four more strafing runs. After destroying seven of the trucks, Seacrest went in low at 1720 to skip-bomb the bridge, blowing up the south end. Later reports claimed it as completely destroyed. Seacrest was preparing to make another strafing pass when his navigator, Lt. Chu, pointed to Liu's plane and signaled that its left engine was smoking, having evidently been hit by some of the six or seven machine gun nests dispersed in the target area. Then operating the waist guns, Faherty reported by interphone that "the back end of the ship was quite full of machine gun holes and that he desired to leave the target area," according to a statement later submitted by Seacrest.

When the left engine of A/C #722 started smoking, Seacrest gave the signal for Liu to join formation "because we were leaving." After climbing to 4,000 feet and circling, he saw that the other pilot did not join formation but climbed to 6,500 feet, feathered his left engine, and headed for Assam. Chu pointed out that it would be impossible for the damaged plane to get past the 10,000-foot-high mountain range it must cross by that route back to base, and that the nearest friendly territory was just east of the Salween River, only about 80 miles away in the opposite direction.

Lt. Liu's plane began losing altitude. Seacrest overtook it after about four minutes (estimated as 15 miles from Lashio) and signaled the Chinese pilot to change course and follow him in the direction of Yunnanyi, where the most westerly of the bases operated by the 14th Air Force was located. When they reached the Salween, Liu reported that he could go no farther and made a forced landing on an open plateau on the west bank of the river, about 100 miles southwest of Yunnanyi. A/C #722 was damaged but did not burn, and all crew members were observed exiting the aircraft.

As Capt. Seacrest was circling at 100 feet to allow Chu to take a picture of the grounded aircraft, Faherty informed him that their own left engine had begun pouring out white smoke. Seacrest immediately gained altitude and turned toward Yunnanyi, but the engine began to run very rough, backfiring, smoking, and sputtering, and "nearly lost all of its power." Seacrest later stated that he feathered the engine to "save it for an emergency" and flew on the right engine for about thirty minutes. During that time, he fired all the ammunition out of the fixed nose guns to lighten the plane, while Faherty tossed out the two waist guns, additional ammunition, oxygen bottles, hydraulic fluids, and spare canvas through the side hatch. When everything "loose" was jettisoned, Seacrest instructed Faherty to buckle on his chute and wait for the bailout order because the plane was becoming increasingly unmanageable. A/C #714 continued to lose altitude at about 100–200 feet per minute, with full power on the right engine.

"At 1830, we were still on one engine at 6,000 ft. following valleys in the direction of Yunnanyi, when we noted some mountains about 12,000 ft. in front of us," Seacrest wrote. "I started the left engine again and although it was running very rough, we were able to climb to 14,000 ft. At 1845, I tried to switch on the instrument lights as it was getting dark. The instrument lights would not work, and we had no lights in the cockpit at all, probably due to a short in the wiring due to ground fire." He was able to maintain a fairly straight and level course for almost ten minutes, although with considerable difficulty. At about 150 miles northwest of Yunnanyi, Seacrest gave the order for the crew to bail out.[17]

In Faherty's postmission report, he explained that he went back to the hatch to open it and jump, but enemy fire had jammed the latch. He ran back to the radio and told the pilot the situation, stating that he would try the rear hatch. Seacrest agreed but warned Faherty to "hurry up; we cannot stay up much longer." Faherty returned to the tail end of the ship and pulled the emergency release. "The wind took the plexiglass [sic] cover off. I stood upright on the gunner seat facing the front of the plane and pushed myself out."

Amazed that he felt absolutely no sense of falling, Faherty estimated that he descended at least 1,000 feet before pulling the rip cord. When the chute opened, it gave "quite a jolt; knocked the wind out of me." Even then he felt no sensation of downward motion, but when he looked up at the chute, he realized that he was oscillating like a pendulum, swinging 15 degrees from side to side. "I could see that I was nearing the ground at this time. I estimated I had another 3 or 400 feet to fall when I hit the ground. (It was getting dark and very hard to see; that is why I miscalculated my distance)." Hitting the ground knocked the breath out of him again. By the time he assessed the situation and collected the chute off the bushes, it was too dark to see, so he rolled in the chute and went to sleep. On the next day, he started his six-day walkout back to civilization.

Omitted from the official report were other details that Faherty later described to his family. When he woke the morning after the crash and looked around, he discovered that he had landed very near the edge of a precipitous drop-off of almost 3,000 feet. If he had tried to move from his position during the night, he may have plunged to his death in the darkness. Equally disturbing was the fact that he felt something move inside his improvised sleeping bag. When he reacted, out slithered a 4-foot snake that had crawled in to share his warmth during the night. It harmlessly moved away along the path and into some bushes. The path seemed fairly well traveled, so Faherty decided to find where it led. He bundled up his parachute as completely as possible and set off along the path that wound down the mountain.

Faherty was confident that he was in friendly territory, on the basis of the direction and distance they had traveled after the plane was hit. His calculation was confirmed shortly after noon, when he came upon a Chinese village, although he approached it with some trepidation because his appearance was greeted with shouts from several men along the path. When he pointed to the American flag sewn inside his jacket, they crowded around him shouting, "*Meg-wa-zen! Meg-wa-zen!*" (their term for "American"). Soon he was surrounded by the entire village, including children and dogs. It seemed that they were expecting him. The network of "inter-village grapevines" had heard of the plane crash, and they even knew the location of some of the other crewmen. Food and drink were provided to him, including *lin kai shwei*: cooled, boiled water as he requested.

Over the following twelve hours, Capt. Seacrest and some of the Chinese crewmen were brought in. Others arrived the next day until the entire crew was together. When A/C #714 crash-landed, all made it out relatively unharmed. Faherty, Chang, Hsu, and Sing were not hurt, but Seacrest suffered lacerations to his hands caused by the parachute straps, Chu sprained his ankle and bruised his head upon landing, and Chiu pulled a ligament in his groin and suffered "contusions of the urethia," according to the official report. The village elders confirmed the direction they should take toward the base at Yunnanyi, and wished their new American friends a safe and speedy journey.[18]

After the two bombers failed to return from their mission, Maj. Conrad submitted a "Missing Air Crew Report" that listed the members of both aircrews. Air Transport Command (ATC), 20th Tactical Recon Squadron, and the 10th Combat Cargo Command were notified and began searching the area from Dergaon to Myitkyina, and ground troops searched from Myitkyina to Lashio. Not surprisingly, they found no evidence of the missing B-25s or their flight crews. Assisted along the way by cooperative Chinese, Capt. Seacrest and his crew traveled by horseback and on foot. They reached Untingtown two days later and were met at Langina by Capt. Gold of the Yunnanyi Air Base. Together they walked on to Yunnanyi and then traveled by transport plane to Kunming, covering a distance of about 130 miles in eleven days. The downed airmen were "feted enthusiastically" in the villages through which they passed, according to letters that Seacrest wrote to his wife and mother on August 25 at a Chinese air force hotel. Both received the letters sent via airmail two days after receiving notification from the War Department in Washington that he was missing in action.[19]

Lt. Liu and his crew began their walkout at about the same time and arrived safely at Kunming on August 17. The navigator, Lt. Hsieh, reported that thirst had inflicted a major hardship on the crew as they made their way through unfamiliar territory. He later developed a compulsion for hoarding water, "saving every drop" through the years that followed.[20]

Following an informal meeting of the officers held in the Recreation Hall, the Chinese sponsored a presentation of their favorite form of entertainment to culminate the celebration of Chinese Air Force Day. Enormously popular throughout China, a traditional form of drama and musical theater had developed over a period of more than a thousand years. The Chinese wanted to share the experience with their comrades, so they invited all American personnel for an evening of Chinese opera "with all the fixings." The second act began the following evening at eight o'clock. Capt. Cunningham; Lts. Dorr, Ragland, and Liu; and Sgt. Barge missed it because they took off for "Calcutter" to pick up much-needed equipment, returning four days later according to Young.

Capt. Simpson wrote in his diary that he had returned to Dergaon from a supply run to Chabua and had a 104-degree fever, so Doc King sent him to the 24th Station Hospital at Jorhat. "Took a blood smear and found I had malaria again, only a different kind. Started taking pills right away and was put in a special room again. Only one officer's ward here, about 30 patients. Most of them GIs." He, Cunningham, and Dorr suffered repeated malarial relapses. Cunningham brought back another "souvenir" from their crash landing in Burma—a spot on his right hand that he called "jungle rot." It would occasionally become irritated and inflamed and begin to itch intensely. The condition tormented him for the rest of his life.[21]

The squadron's airmen undertook two missions to Burma in the vicinity of Naba against targets at Indaw, where the Japanese had built two airstrips. Off on August 15 at 1710, six B-25s dropped seventy-two 100 lb. HEs on "H" area. Results were excellent, with 95 percent of the bombs falling in the target area. Crewmen counted at least six fires. One of the aircraft salvoed in a dive-bomb attack and started at least two more fires. "G" area was the target of five B-25s that were over the target at 1535 on the seventeenth.

Bombardiers dropped sixty 100 lb. GPs from 7,000 feet, with disappointing results. All fell northwest of the target and caused no observable damage. McCann's memories of flying a mission to "knock out Jap fighter planes" referred to this mission.[20]

As squadron planes executed their final Burma raids, Maj. Conrad at last received orders on August 16 for his squadron's movement to China. Capt. James C. Kelso Jr., a former general office clerk for United Aircraft, Pratt and Whitney Division (manufacturer of airplane engines), in Hartford, Connecticut, was attached and assumed duties as adjutant

Capt. James C. Kelso Jr., appointed adjutant to replace Goeller, works on personnel records at his desk. His efficient administrative management soon earned him the respect of squadron personnel. *R. N. Solyn collection, courtesy of Robert N. Solin*

to replace Capt. Goeller, who was officially released from duty on the same date. Fifty-five Chinese personnel on detached service to the 3rd Squadron were transferred to the 490th Bomb Squadron, stationed at Dinjan, India. Capt. Hinrichs instructed all ground personnel to ready their belongings for shipment. Motor transportation to Chabua that he had arranged "failed to show up" when expected, according to Young. Vehicles finally rolled in on the afternoon of the twenty-first. The convoy got underway the following day at 1300 and arrived at Chabua at 1735. A thorough inspection of all baggage and planes still at Dergaon began as soon as the trucks left the base.

While operating out of Assam, the 3rd Squadron had earned acclaim by completing forty-eight missions against targets in Burma, providing air support to war-weary Allied ground troops desperately battling the relentlessly encroaching enemy.

These battle-tested airmen knew what awaited them. News was coming in that described attacks on Hengyang, an important railroad junction on the Canton–Hankow line. After five weeks of bloody fighting that produced severe casualties on both sides, Japanese forces smashed into the city proper. Its capture opened the way for a drive down the railroad for the remaining 170 miles to join forces with the invaders in Kwangtung Province, to the south, and give the enemy an unbroken 1,000 miles of rail route, bisecting China from north to south. Other CACW squadrons were supporting the city's defenders, and the 3rd Bomb Squadron's airmen expected to soon be ordered into the fray.

CHAPTER SEVEN
Evacuating from Kweilin

Conrad's men were finally on their way to China. According to 1st Bombardment Group's Special Orders No. 89, fifteen American officers and forty-one American enlisted men of the 3rd Bombardment Squadron were transferred from "Deragon," India, to Kweilin, China. These included Maj. Conrad; Capts. Graves, Hodges, Seacrest, Kelso, Wood, Young, Cunningham, King, and Simpson; 1Lts. Dorr, MacNeil, and Ragland; 2Lt. Faherty; 1Sgt. Earley; MSgts. Grant and Fuller; TSgts. Libolt, Solyn, Hanrahan, and Shock; SSgts. Chasse, Gruber, Holmes, Jakubasz, Meikle, Rieks, Wilkerson, Armstrong, Dunlap, Haines, Hoyle, McCann, Mier, and Summerville; Sgts. Duffin, Hall, Malone, Thompson, Barge, Evitts, Hoke, Mills, and Whearty; Cpls. Allegretto, England, Long, Peters, Trout, Burton, Learn, Jackson, and Rickman; Pfc. Wadlow; and Pvt. Piecuch.

Thirty-five Chinese officers and ninety-seven Chinese enlisted men were transferred by the same order under the command of Maj. Wu C. C. (see appendix B, "Chinese Air Force Personnel Listed in Movement Orders," for details).

SSgt. Gruber received orders on August 22 to proceed from Chabua to Liuliang to finalize arrangements. With him went SSgt. Chasse and Sgts. Malone and Hall. "Doc King" was released and ordered to report to 5th Fighter Group Headquarters after arrival at Kunming. The men at Dergaon were divided into three groups and alerted to be ready "at a moment's notice" for transport by ATC, which was to ferry them over "the Hump" of the treacherous Himalayas, the highest mountain range in the world. Again, they waited as inspectors searched planes and baggage. The first group was off on the morning of the twenty-sixth. The other two were ready to leave at 1900, but one of the transports had engine trouble and was unable to get away until the following day.

Their route from the Brahmaputra Valley floor, 90 feet below sea level at Chabua, crossed the surrounding mountain wall that rises abruptly to 10,000 feet and higher. So steep are the peaks that transport pilots always circled two or three times before gaining sufficient altitude to surmount the first range. Flying eastward out of the valley, the transports first topped the Patkai Range and then passed over the upper Chindwin River valley, bounded to the east by a 14,000-foot ridge of the Kumon Mountains. From there they flew over a series of 14,000-to-16,000-foot ridges, separated by valleys of the West Irrawaddy, East Irrawaddy, Salween, and Mekong Rivers, before crossing the main Hump—the Santsung Range, 15,000 feet at its highest peaks—that lies between the Salween and Mekong Rivers. The terrain became progressively less rugged as they approached Kunming.

Flying the Hump took planes over rugged terrain, often through violent storms, sudden downdrafts, and snow and ice at higher altitudes. Hump flights were particularly perilous because most of them were made at night to avoid Japanese planes that patrolled the route. The lack of accurate navigational charts and absence of radio navigational aids increased the hazard. It was some of the most dangerous flying in the world—so dangerous, in fact, that every flight over the Hump was logged as a combat mission, due not only to these conditions but also because of the possibility that the planes might be attacked by enemy fighters, although this threat was diminished after the capture of Myitkyina's airfield.

The stretch that had to be traversed was relatively short—about 500 aerial miles—but more than seven hundred planes went down while attempting the crossing, with more than double that number lost in personnel. Wreckage that littered the slopes below was so dense that the route became known as "the Aluminum Trail," and those who survived a crash faced the added perils created by the craggy terrain, Japanese patrols, and even fierce Naga headhunters who inhabited the mountainous border region.[1]

When the first of the CACW's planes made their way across the "High Hump" in late October 1943, one of the C-47 transport planes went down. Lost were 1Lt. Adrian P. Stroud, five American enlisted men, five Chinese pilots, and five Chinese enlisted men (personnel of the 28th Fighter Squadron, 3rd Fighter Group), as well as a Chinese major general and his aide. Their bodies were recovered and buried by Chinese villagers. Hazardous conditions caused the 2nd Bomb Squadron's B-25s to delay crossing until conditions improved. Flying one of the 2nd Squadron's Mitchells, Seacrest attempted the crossing on October 25 but was forced to turn back to change out an engine. With a minimal crew that included Earley, he successfully reached Kunming the following day.

Lt. William L. Daniels, who later assisted in the training of 3rd Squadron Chinese airmen, was the pilot of one of the last three 2nd Squadron planes to make the move. He recorded the experience in his personal flight log / diary on November 3: "We took off from Chabua at 1000 this morning to cross the 'Hump' and for what counts as our first combat mission. The Japs patrol this section and have shot down a few transports. We climbed to 17,500 feet and then just missed some of the high ridges. The mountain ranges run north and south, and it is the most rugged country in the world." The compass of the lead plane stuck, taking them 50 miles off course. "About halfway over[,] my right engine began to foul up and smoke. I stayed with the formation until we arrived over Kunming. Then my engine quit, and I went in on one engine. The field is 6,000 feet high, and I landed downwind to avoid circling. Made it okay.... I will have to have an engine change here."[2]

Even when the planes did make it across without mishap, conditions for passengers and aircrews were far from comfortable. Those who had become accustomed to the steamy climate of Assam particularly suffered from the subzero temperatures as the aircraft made their ascent over and around the snow-capped peaks. Although the planes did have heaters, they were usually broken, so passengers and crew sat on their feet to prevent them from developing frostbite, according to Simpson. Because there was no oxygen supply to the passenger positions of the Curtiss C-46 Commando and Douglas C-47 Skytrain transports, it was administered as needed from portable units for those feeling the effects of hypoxia as they huddled in their cold, hard aluminum bucket seats.

Hank retained vivid recollections of the experience many years later and related, "We went over into China and landed at Kunming. We flew the Hump." Wujiaba Airfield (24°59'32" N, 102°44'36" E), on the north end of Tien Chen (Dianchi) Lake, was only about 2.5 miles southeast of Kunming. Formerly headquarters for Chennault's AVG and then the CATF, the base had also served as headquarters for the 14th Air Force until the previous month.

Evacuating from Kweilin

Flying the perilous "Himalayan Hump," the air route that led over the mountains between north Burma and west Yunnan Province of China, was a memorable experience for all who made the crossing. *R. J. Koss collection, courtesy of Barbara Koss Hughes*

Kunming, the capital and largest city of Yunnan Province, was an important commercial, cultural, and military center for the region. It was a city that created powerful first impressions by all who visited there. Fighter pilot Lt. Lopez, who made stops at many of the airfields later used by the 3rd Squadron, described his thoughts when he flew into Kunming the previous year: "Somewhere along the route we crossed, without fanfare or even knowledge, into China, and after about three hours we began letting down to land at Kunming, the China terminus of the Hump. Since the elevation at Kunming was about 6,000 feet, the letdown didn't take long." As the transport circled over Kunming, the terrain took on a checkered appearance. As it lost altitude, he recognized that the checkers were rice paddies in various stages of cultivation. "Men, women, children, and water buffalo became visible, all hard at work with primitive tools, straining to eke out a living from their small plots. I would see many more rice paddies before I left China, since the country was immensely cultivated, and rice was the primary crop."[3]

When Capt. Simpson arrived in Kunming with the 1st Bomb Squadron in January 1944, he and "all the boys" went into town for a steak dinner. "Kunming is the dirtiest of all the towns since I left Miami," he wrote in his diary. The next night he went with two others to a restaurant where they enjoyed a feast that included sweet and sour pork, baked duck, rice, fish, and sour bread, followed by a whole chicken surrounded by chicken soup. "Really good," he declared. The tab was $2,200.00 CN (Chinese Nationalist dollars). At the then-current black-market rate of eighty CN per US dollar, the meal cost $27.50 for the three of them—considered to be an unreasonably high price that reflected the out-of-control inflation for goods and services in this city that served as a vital wartime hub.

At about the same time that the 3rd Bomb Squadron arrived, 2Lt. James R. Smith, a P-61 radar observer assigned to the 426th Night Fighter Squadron, also flew into Kunming. He wrote this evocative description:

A city with a normal population of perhaps 500,000 people was now thronged with refugees, bringing the wartime population to over 7,000,000. The streets, day and night, were crowded so as to be almost impassable to our jeeps and difficult even for pedestrian traffic, with people moving in streams from sidewalk to sidewalk, selling clothing, jewelry, sex, food—exchanging money. Making things like jewelry, pasta, clothing, shoes, items out of wood, furniture, curios, boxes, crates. They also made mulberry wine, a delightful light beverage that took the place of everything from

Coca-Cola to vodka with most of us. The sound was a constant changing kind of clangor with bells, firecracker pops, horns, gongs, engines, sirens, shouts, arguments, day or night around the clock. And there were smells, powerful smells, interesting smells—garlic, incense, cooking, fireworks, kerosene, wood fires, exhaust fumes, open sewers, animal odors. Some good smells and some really bad smells![4]

Kunming had been the terminus of the Burma Road, used to supply Chinese Nationalist forces before the fall of Burma. Now it served the same purpose for most flights flown over the Hump, making it "the busiest airport in the world," Smith wrote. "Planes were landing and taking off 24 hours a day without pause. At times, incoming flights were stacked at 500-foot intervals up to 25,000 feet in several different zones around the field." The night fighters of Smith's 426th Squadron became a familiar sight to 3rd Squadron personnel since they occupied some of the same airfields during the war.

The 2nd Bomb Squadron's Cpl. Johnson, who arrived in Kunming two months later, described his own early impressions. "With my first breath of China, I smelled the pungent outhouse odor of human feces used for fertilizing crops. I wondered if I would ever get used to the smell, but I eventually did. On my first morning in China, I was fascinated by the prospect of learning this ancient land I had only read about. I was anxious to help save it from the Japanese."[5] His thoughts were likely shared by many of the young Americans who found themselves in this intriguing and unfamiliar land for the purpose of driving out a fast-advancing enemy.

The 3rd Squadron's B-25s did not move to China at the same time as the ground crews but stayed behind with personnel sufficient to maintain them and fly them over the Hump later, when weather conditions improved. Remaining behind were Maj. Conrad; Capts. Cunningham, Graves, Hodges, and Simpson; 1Lts. MacNeil, Ragland, and Dorr; MSgt. Fuller; TSgts. Hanrahan, Hoyle, Libolt, and Shock; SSgts. Barge, Wilkerson, Armstrong, and Rieks; Sgt. Whearty; and Cpls. Rickman and Trout. On August 26, Capt. Simpson, 1Lts. MacNeil and Dorr, TSgt. Shock, and SSgts. Rieks and Armstrong were directed to proceed to Bangalore "for the purpose of ferrying A/C to their proper sta[tion]." Simpson, released that morning from the hospital, wrote that they were waiting at Chabua to go on by ATC to Bangalore. "Mac and I went to see Pop tonight. He's Asst. Air Inspector for the 10th Air Force." They returned a few days later with three new B-25Js. Those, along with the squadron's other B-25s, were expected to go into action as soon as the crossing to China could be completed.

After a brief stay in Kunming, the men continued their move by ATC about 450 miles almost due east to Liuliang, where inspectors again searched baggage and confiscated a large amount of contraband. Lt. Wood and fourteen American enlisted men departed by ATC on August 30 for Erh Tong Airfield at Kweilin, about 60 miles farther northeast, and Capt. Kelso and Lt. Young accompanied thirteen American enlisted personnel on the thirty-first. The squadron's remaining American personnel, with thirty Chinese officers and enlisted men, completed the transfer on September 1.

Situated on the Li River in Kwangsi Province, Kweilin was one of the newest and most beautiful cities of Free China. It was, at that time of the war, "bloated with war refugees, informants, spies and fifth columnists." The city was known particularly for its prostitutes, many of whom had fled north when the Japanese invaded Hong Kong. There were three bases south of the city among its "Mars-like, sugar-loaf limestone hills: Erh-tong, with Li-chia-chen slightly to the south and Yang-tong to the west," according to the 1st Squadron's Sgt. Daniels. "The runways of all three were surrounded by shacks and hostels tucked in arroyos and clefts."[6]

"They called Kweilin 'the Paris of the Orient,'" Hank recalled. According to an article from *Time* that he kept with his photographs, the "battered but glamorous Kwangsi city" was noted for its "holiday habits and friendly girls" that "made Kweilin's name blessed among US airforcemen on pass." The big base had been "stripped and partly scorched" as the Japanese advance threatened it seven weeks earlier, but "the panic had died in a crackle of firecrackers when the Chinese Army and the Fourteenth's airmen had checked the enemy at Hengyang."[7]

"They changed the names of most of the places," he commented. Kweilin (now written as Guilin) was one of many Chinese cities and towns familiar to American GIs during the war to undergo changes in the spelling of its name. Hank was accustomed to the Wade-Giles system of transliterating Mandarin into Roman characters, which was used during the war and is generally used in this history. The revisions are due to the official phonetic system called pinyin, now used for transcribing the Mandarin pronunciations of Chinese characters into the Latin alphabet. Initially developed in the 1950s, it applies to personal names as well as place-names. Based on the dialect of Mandarin spoken in the vicinity of Beijing, *pīnyīn*—拼—literally means "spelled-out sounds."[8]

The men settled into hostels for their brief stay at Erh Tong. Lt. Lopez, whose 75th Fighter Squadron was stationed at nearby Yang Tong, described the living quarters as well interspersed among the mountains, so they were not good bombing targets. Typical of the War Area Service Command (WASC) hostels at most of the bases, each hostel included two clusters of buildings, one for officers and the other for enlisted men. The buildings were long, one-story wooden structures divided into six or eight rooms, with a washroom at one end. Each room had eight to twelve bunks, most double decked, with crisscrossed heavy cord supporting mattresses filled with some kind of straw. "The pillows were filled with rice husks and rice and were quite hard, but I suppose if we were cut off from food supplies, we could always eat the pillows," he wrote. Each bunk had a mosquito bar that was tucked in on all four sides. There were a few chairs and tables and some built-in shelves for storage. The rooms were heated with charcoal stoves and had electric lights. It was often difficult to read at night, since the generators did not run smoothly, and the lights dimmed and brightened continually.

The adobe-daubed buildings were sometimes painted, but the interiors and all the furniture were unpainted raw wood. There were usually two or three ceramic water jugs, full of *lin kai shwai* (cool boiled water), and matching glasses. "As you can imagine, it was not safe to drink unboiled water," Lopez wrote. The mess hall was in a separate building, and there were outside latrines, eight-to-twelve-holers, nearby for the officers and the unlisted men.

The latrines surprisingly served as "social centers of a sort," he added. Because so many of the men who served in China suffered intermittently from dysentery, they often spent long periods of time in the latrines and had "many long and interesting discussions in these unlikely settings."[9]

"To date our sleep has been interrupted for the past five nights by air raid alarms. As yet no enemy planes appear," wrote Lt. Young. Capt. Hinrichs requisitioned and was issued Thompson machine guns for use in the event of actual attack. At Kweilin and other 14th Air Force bases in China, a complex air raid notification system was used to warn of aerial approach by the enemy. Devised by Gen. Chennault, it depended on lookouts on the ground who reported movements of enemy aircraft to a central control center by way of a network of hand-cranked telephones operated by peasants in small villages. These observations, in turn, were relayed to the threatened airfield, and a signal was posted. One "ball" (usually a spherical red paper lantern) raised on a pole indicated that enemy planes had taken off from their base, two balls meant the actual approach of enemy aircraft, and three balls warned that attack was imminent. The men stationed at these airfields joked that no one ever saw a three-ball alert, because everyone had already taken cover by the time it went up.[10]

During this time, no Japanese planes struck in the vicinity of Kweilin during the day, but "they did keep us in the foxholes night after night," reported Sgt. Frank W. Tutwiler, attached to a combat camera unit, in an interview published by *Yank* magazine. He had been assigned to cover "the strafing, bomb-spattering raids of the 'Flying Tigers' B-25s and fighters against the Japanese columns moving on Chengsha, Hengyang, Lingling, and eventually toward Kweilin itself." Barracks boys shouted the warning *Jing bao!* ("Air raid!") as they ran from room to room, turning off lights and banging on washbasins to wake anyone who may have slept through the warning siren. In addition to the wailing of the siren was the beating of a gong, and the sleeping men could recognize the urgency of the situation on the basis of its tempo: a slow beat for a one-ball alert, a bit faster for two-ball, and a rapid, steady *rat-tat-tat* for three-ball.

At night, the B-25s were rolled into caves carved into the surrounding hills to protect them. When the alert sounded, men hurried to battle stations or took cover in slit trenches, caves, or any other place where they could find protection from the enemy's bombs. Even Chennault's command center occupied a large cave as protection from air raids. According to Tutwiler, "These *jing baos* didn't amount to much, but they kept people awake[,] and tired people can't work efficiently in the daytime."[11]

Sgt. Oswald Weinert, a B-25 mechanic and gunner assigned to the 4th Bomb Squadron at Erh Tong at this time, eventually tired of falling out for air raids and stayed in the bunkhouse, explaining that he would rather die in his bed than in a muddy ditch.[12] Hank preferred to err on the side of caution: "I'd always run for that muddy ditch."

By this point in war of conquest, Japanese military forces occupied about the eastern third of mainland China and controlled most of the main railroads and highways and all of the seaports. The undefeated, veteran China Expeditionary Army consisted of one armored division, twenty-five infantry divisions, and twenty-two independent brigades—eleven of infantry, one of cavalry, and ten of mixed troops. These forces were divided into three separate groups. The North China Area Army occupied the North China plain from the Yellow River to the Great Wall and kept watch, along with the large Japanese army in Manchuria (Kwangtung Army), on the Soviet forces in the Far East. Farther to the south, the 13th Army held the lower Yangtze River valley and the coast north and south of the port city of Shanghai. The 6th Area Army, immediately west of the 13th Army and extending south to Canton and Hong Kong on the coast, contained the elite of the Japanese units and operated against the Chinese and Americans in central China. Despite the large number of units, China's immense size and the absence of a well-developed transportation network immobilized much of the Japanese army and limited the extent of its operations.

The Japanese had launched a major offensive called Operation Ichigo in April 1944. Utilizing 400,000 men organized into seventeen divisions and supported by 12,000 vehicles and 70,000 horses, it formed a gigantic pincer movement designed to split Free China. The operation had three main objectives: improve routes of supply and communication by controlling the railroad between Peiping and Hong Kong, provide a link between Japanese forces in China and French Indochina, and eliminate the Allied airfields from which bombing raids were being successfully launched in southern and central China. In the initial phase, the 12th Army moved south from Kaifeng to join the 11th Army moving north from Hankow. The Japanese seized control of Henan Province in central China's Yellow River valley by the end of May and then marched south along the Hsiang (Xiang) River. The main thrust was then a powerful drive from Hankow by the 11th Army, designed to link up with a push westward by the 23rd Army from the vicinity of Canton. The enemy offensive was relentless, and the overwhelming force of the invaders crushed resistance by the understrength, demoralized Chinese defenders, who suffered heavy losses.[13]

By the time the 3rd Squadron reached Kweilin, the airfields at Hengyang and Paoching had been seized, effectively pushing back the reach of American airpower. On August 16—the same day that Conrad received orders for the transfer to China—the Japanese 11th and 23rd Armies, operating under command of the 6th Area Army, began to move into the northeastern region of Kwangsi Province. Chinese troops, who had recently retreated following the Fourth Battle of Changsha, were incapable of offering battle but engaged in a campaign to delay the enemy's advance.

SSgts. Armstrong, Jakubasz, Rieks, Summerville, and Wilkerson were promoted to technical sergeants and Cpls. England, Long, and Peters to sergeants as September began. Good Conduct Medals, awarded to all personnel who had completed one year of service following the Pearl Harbor attack and with no marks against them, were awarded that day to thirty-three enlisted men: 1Sgt. Earley; MSgt. Grant; TSgts. Armstrong, Hanrahan, Hoyle, Jakubasz, Libolt, Meikle, Rieks, Shock, Solyn, Summerville, and Wilkerson; SSgts. Barge, Chasse, Gruber, Haines, and Mier; Sgts. Hall, Hoke, Long, Peters, Thompson, and Whearty; Cpls. Allegretto, Burton, England, Jackson, Learn, Rickman, and Trout; Pfc. Wadlow; and Pvt. Piecuch. When asked about his conduct because his name was not on the list, Hank recalled, "It was always good" but commented wryly, "I guess I didn't measure up." According to his discharge papers, Hank did receive recognition of his good conduct prior to his arrival in the CBI.

Capt. Kelso picked up some PX rations and distributed them to the men, who were "in good spirit upon arrival at the new base." They did not receive mail while at Kweilin (APO 430) during their time there, however, as the Army postal service tried to "catch up" with them.

Those injured on the August 14 mission spent a few days recuperating in the hospital before rejoining their squadron in early September. The return of Capt. Seacrest and Lt. Faherty was met with "considerable pleasure and excitement" following their walkout. Since Seacrest's wife and mother, in Colorado, and his father, in Nebraska, had received news that he was missing only two days earlier, their anxiety was short lived. All had rejoined their squadron by the time the USAAF sent a letter dated September 23 to Faherty's parents in Wisconsin, informing them that their son was missing in action.

As was customary for airmen who had bailed out, Faherty sent his parachute home soon after his return. Because parachutes were made of silk or nylon—both rare commodities during and immediately after the war—it also became customary for brides to use the parachute material for their wedding dresses. When Faherty married his sweetheart, Verena, in 1946, she was unable to use his parachute for her bridal gown because his sisters had cut it up to make underwear from the highly desirable fabric.[14]

The squadron's B-25s remained behind at Dergaon until September 4, when they crossed the Hump and arrived at Kunming, completing the move of the last CACW unit to reach China. Loaded with equipment, they then made their way on toward Kweilin. Even as squadron aircraft were making their way to China, plans were being developed for their departure. Capts. Hinrichs, Seacrest, and Kelso attended a conference at Yang Tong on the fifth to discuss the most-effective procedures for evacuation. Lt. Wood logged a fifty-minute administrative mission on that date. There was some uncertainty as to whether the B-25s would even be moved to Kweilin because of the imminent enemy threat, but they all arrived safely at Erh Tong on the afternoon of September 8. That was the same day that the Japanese 11th Army overran Lingling, both the town and the airfield. Then began their advance on Kweilin.

Changes in command were taking place in the 1st Bomb Group as the enemy drew nearer. Col. Irving L. Branch was replaced as group commander by Lt. Col. David J. Munson, former wing operations officer. During the same period, 1Lt. Leo C. Baker was transferred from the 1st to the 3rd Squadron. Cpl. England received orders to proceed to Kunming for the purpose of attending radio school on VHF equipment, and Sgts. Hall and Malone were detached to Luliang. SSgt. Chasse arrived from Dergaon. Capt. Graves, just returning from a week at Camp Schiel (a rest camp built in beautiful mountainous country east of Kunming, on the north shore of Yangzonghai Lake), was transferred to 1st Bomb Group HQ and appointed group navigator and assistant personnel and training officer.

Cpl. John W. England, attached as A/F radio operator, became one of the squadron's VHF specialists. He was responsible for maintaining and operating radio equipment used to communicate between the squadron's aircraft and nearby ground stations. *R. N. Solyn, courtesy of Robert N. Solin*

On the Chinese side, seven navigator-bombardiers were sent to Peishiyi for temporary duty with the 1st Bomb Squadron. They were 1Lts. Wang Kuan-tze (X-953), Chen Fuo-wu (X-936), Wei Kwo-an (X-933), Kao Wen-wing (X-930), Wang Yung-hung (X-932), Huang Ysu-hwa (X-957), and Keo Yao-hwa (X-___). Near the end of the month, Maj. Lee H. Y. was replaced as 1st Bomb Group cocommander by Maj. Wang Yu-ken (X-114), and Maj. Chen Yu-fang (X-365) became vice commander.

During this time, the Nationalist government's WASC furnished living quarters and food, such as they were, but GIs had to fend for themselves in other ways. They found it necessary to buy charcoal for their stoves and peanut oil for their lamps at exorbitant prices on the open market, usually through a Chinese houseboy at a substantial commission. Houseboys were highly valued for their performance of services that eased the complexities of life in this often-incomprehensible situation. The preferred method of payment was generally in the form of cigarettes or other American goods that could be traded on the black market. As was common practice, Hank and the other men with whom he shared quarters retained the services of several houseboys, whose duties included such domestic chores as cleaning, laundry, shining shoes, and running errands. Houseboys were also informed as to where local females eager to sell their favors could be found on a particular night of the week, for those so inclined. In charge of them was a "No. 1 House Boy," who remained with the squadron until after its later move to Peishiyi.

The 3rd Squadron's recently arrived bombers flew only four missions before the evacuation of Kweilin, all against towns in the path of the enemy drive. Raids were flown in cooperation with the 4th Squadron, also directed to hit targets in the vicinity of Lingling. The first mission took off from Erh Tong at 1403 on September 10, when nine B-25s with an escort of four P-51s of "the 118th Fighter Squadron" (118th Tactical Reconnaissance Squadron, 23rd Fighter Group, 68th Composite Wing, 14th Air Force) attacked targets at Lingling. Each of its fighter planes boasted a distinctive yellow-and-black lightning bolt that extended along the length of the fuselage. Maj. Conrad led the formation to bomb the town located on the east bank of the Tan River. Each plane carried eight 250 lb. demos, dropped on the bombardier of the lead aircraft. A/C #718 accidentally salvoed its bombs due to a malfunction of the racks, but all bombs fortunately hit within the target area. Results of the raid were reported as good.

Nine Mitchells were off at 1440 on the eleventh on mission #50. Maj. Conrad, Capt. Hodges, and Lt. Ragland each led an element of three planes and bombed Luhungzsu. Five P-51s and two P-40s of the 118th Fighter Squadron escorted. Each Mitchell carried eight 250 lb. demos and were over the target at 1545 in echelon formation (diagonal). After making two dry runs from northeast to southwest, bombardiers dropped on the leader, releasing sixty-five bombs at 2,500 feet, but seven hung up in the racks and were returned. Release mechanism malfunction caused bombs of two of the aircraft to accidentally salvo on the second run. Only six entered the southwest corner of the target area but caused no obvious damage. The flight crews reported multiple small fires along the railroad that was the target of the 4th Bomb Squadron.

Lt. Wood recorded two administrative flights on that day—one of three hours from Kweilin to Luliang and another of four hours and thirty minutes from Luliang to Liuchow—as squadron personnel prepared to evacuate. He returned to Kweilin on the following day to wait for the evacuation order.

Squadron planes flew two missions on the twelfth, each with six B-25s. The first took off at 1150, when Capt. Hodges and Lt. Ragland each led an echelon of three bombers that flew in "V" formation javeliend down to the right. Each plane carried eight 250 lb. demos to hit the town of Tunghsiangkiao. Bombs were dropped on the lead bombardier at 3,000 feet. Two aircraft had bomb release malfunctions, and one plane salvoed on target. An estimated 70 percent reportedly hit in the target area.

Hodges and Ragland were off again at 1650, each leading a three-plane "V" javeliend down. Their target was the town of Huangyangshih, about 260 miles northeast of Kweilin, located north of Lingling and south of the Hunan Kwanusi railroad. Each plane carried eight 250 lb. demolition bombs. The leader was over the target at 1725 and its bombs were dropped at 3,000 feet. One aircraft salvoed north of the target due to a release mechanism malfunction. An estimated 85 percent of the bombs hit the target area. As with operational reports for missions to Burma, no crew lists and few aircraft numbers are available.

Hank's *Time* magazine article outlined reforms recently instituted by Generalissimo Chiang that included improved provisioning, medical care, and training of the troops, but these changes had yet to have any significantly favorable effect. The Chinese were described as "ill-nourished, ill-armed, [and] ill-clad" as they opposed 120,000 Japanese troops advancing toward Kweilin. This "underprivileged" Chinese army defended the city as "the Fourteenth's flyers hammered them desperately from above," even launching missions as demolition and evacuation took place.[15]

As enemy troops closed in, the dispirited Chinese offered little resistance but began their retreat to the south. The Chinese 93rd Army abandoned its defensive positions at Chuanhsien, 90 miles from Kweilin, early on September 13. The Japanese moved at will against the Chinese rear and past the miles of fleeing soldiers and civilians who were flooding out of villages and towns in the vicinity. No one knew exactly where the Japanese were, although marauding columns of cavalry were reported to be approaching the city within 40 miles, and rumors placed them only 10 miles away. The following day, Gen. Chennault and Gen. Stilwell made a visit to Kweilin for a final conference with Gen. Chang Fah-kwei and Brig. Gen. Clifton D. ("Casey") Vincent, in command of the 68th Composite Wing, 14th Air Force, to which the 3rd Bomb Squadron had been attached, as well as of the base. With Stilwell's approval, Vincent issued orders to abandon the airfields and destroy the stores of gasoline. Final evacuation and demolition procedures began immediately.

Brig. Gen. Clifton D. Vincent (left), in command of the three airfields at Kweilin, and Maj. Conrad (right) chat with a Chinese coolie carrying a pair of "yo-yo baskets" at Ehr Tong field. Courtesy of William D. Grubbs

Lt. MacNeil, who had stayed behind temporarily at Dergaon, considered Kweilin to be "an almost perfect airfield, before we were forced to abandon it[,] even leaving behind uniforms and a quantity of beautiful photographs that never could be replaced." While he was stationed there before his transfer to the 3rd Squadron, the generalissimo and Madame Chiang had visited the base, and she gave MacNeil "a carved jade seal with his name in Chinese," he stated in an interview soon after his return from the war. He recalled that at about Christmas 1943, the situation in China was looking "so black" that he and his fellow officers were issued an extra pair of shoes because they feared they might have to walk out through Russia.[16]

Listed in 1st Bomb Group Special Orders No. 81 were these 3rd Squadron members who were transferred from Kweilin to Peishiyi: Maj. Conrad; Capts. Graves, Hodges, Seacrest, Cunningham, Hinrichs, and Kelso; 1Lts. Wood and Ragland; 2Lts. Young and Faherty; 1Sgt. Earley; MSgts. Grant and Fuller; TSgts. Hoyle, Libolt, Solyn, Wilkerson, Hanrahan, Jakubasz, Meikle, and Summerville; SSgts. Chasse, Dunlap, Holmes, Mier, Barge, Duffin, Haines, and McCann; Sgts. Hoke, Mills, Thompson, Evitts, Long, Peters, and Whearty; Cpls. Allegretto, Jackson, Rickman, Burton, Learn, and Trout; Pfc. Wadlow; and Pvt. Piecuch. By the same order, Maj. Wu C. C. led a Chinese contingent that comprised thirty-four officers and ninety-seven sergeants (refer to appendix B, "Chinese Air Force Personnel Listed in Movement Orders," for details).

Later in the month, the list of Americans was amended to include Capt. Simpson, 1Lts. Dorr and MacNeil, TSgt. Shock, and SSgts. Armstrong and Rieks, who were on detached service at Bangalore when the evacuation took place. Also added were SSgt. Gruber and Sgts. Hall and Malone, who were at Luliang, and Cpl. England, at Kunming.

Preparations for evacuation had begun several days prior to the final order. Alerted and ready to evacuate since the seventh, each man was allowed a small bag for personal belongings needed for immediate use, while the remainder was packed into foot lockers to be transported by train. Capt. Kelso and Lt. Faherty were in charge of personnel evacuated by rail. They had been instructed to have the men ready to leave by 1530 on September 12, but trucks taking them to the train station did not depart from the field until 1900. Once aboard, they waited for many hours before getting underway because movement was blocked by a derailment up the line. On the tracks just outside the city and at the south station stood three stalled trains. Maj. Conrad and Capt. Seacrest came down to the train station to see the men off. They finally rolled out late the following day. Serving with a detail selected to assist with security during the long delay and the far-longer journey that followed, 1Sgt. Earley was later awarded the Bronze Star for his vigilant attention to the task.[17]

Almost the entire civilian population of Kweilin, carrying their meager possessions in pitiful bundles, made their escape before the advance of the Japanese 11th Army. Shops, hotels, brothels, cafés, and houses were boarded up and deserted. Some even set fire to their property to prevent it from falling into enemy hands. Soon nearly the entire city was engulfed in flames.

Pvt. Piecuch waves from the stairs while an unidentified Chinese soldier (*left*), Lt. Faherty (*center*), and SSgt. Haines (*right*) claim their places on board. *J. H. Mills collection*

Sgt. Jakubasz, a flight chief, joins two CAF airmen and Chinese evacuees urgently attempting to flee Kweilin by train, although he evacuated with the truck convoy. *J. H. Mills collection*

Piecuch and Solyn entertain other evacuees with their antics as they all endure the long wait for the trains to move. *J. H. Mills collection*

Refugees by the thousands clogged the dirt roads and packed every available train as they fled the city toward Liuchow, 100 miles southwest. Immobile passenger and freight cars were crawling with people, like bees in a hive, inside and outside, on roofs, and on the rods. They ate, slept, washed, and cooked as best they could near the tracks. Sanitary conditions were deplorable, and doctors feared a cholera epidemic. Still, people waited, mostly with stoic patience because they had little other choice, although some set out walking along the rails in their desperate search for safety.

The 3rd Squadron flew no missions on the thirteenth but spent the day preparing to evacuate. The air echelon led by Maj. Conrad, which had remained "until the last minute," took off for Peishiyi on the morning of September 14. Capt. Hinrichs and Lt. Young, in charge of the truck convoy carrying squadron equipment and supplies with a detail of eight enlisted men, left at about 2:00 that afternoon. The demolition of Erh Tong began as squadron personnel departed the field.

Every available transport plane had been brought in from India to assist in evacuating personnel, equipment, and supplies. All three airfields were abandoned after everything that might be of use to the enemy was either hauled away or destroyed by demolition crews in compliance with a "scorched earth" policy. Explosives were planted in holes dug in the runways and then detonated to prevent the Japanese from having immediate use of them. Exploding ammunition and tracer shells fueled the inferno that burned hangars, hostels, depots, and alert shacks, as well as equipment, extra supplies, and bombs stored in caves.[18]

McCann took part in the squadron's final missions and remembered bombing and strafing enemy troops in sampans on the Li River. "The last time we took off[,] we strafed them as the gear was coming up and our own people were blowing the field behind us."[19]

Even after the airfields were evacuated, reports stated that "B-25s led the attacks on Jap columns moving on the abandoned city along the two main highways from the northeast and southeast, strafing motor convoys, troop concentrations and supply dumps in the Chuanhsien and Tanchuk areas. Allied planes were unopposed by Jap airmen over the battle area."[20]

By the following week, the invaders were within 25 miles of the city, but instead of launching an immediate attack, Japanese forces unexpectedly paused for five weeks to regroup and regather their overextended supply line. Kweilin was converted to a fortress, and Generalissimo Chiang reportedly ordered his troops to hold it at all costs. Chinese forces dug in and waited. Advancing in a wide arc against the Kwangsi Province capital, by late October Japanese troops were within 6 miles to the east, 6 miles northeast, and 9½ miles southeast. Chinese defenders continued in their attempts to disrupt enemy supply and communications lines.

By November 1, the city's defenses had been breached. Three Japanese columns forced their way into the suburbs of Kweilin, and a fourth was within 2 miles of the city, Chinese high command announced. A reinforced Japanese column pressing from the east forced a crossing of the Kwei River and broke through Chinese defenses in the city's railroad station. Another column entered the northern suburbs of the town but was beaten back. A third column crossed the Li River south of the city and pushed to the outskirts. Still another column was reported within 2 miles east of the town. Fierce fighting was reported in progress.[21]

Chinese ground troops rallied and put up a stiff opposition, but Kweilin fell on November 11.

CHAPTER EIGHT
Stagnating at Peishiyi

All elements of the 3rd Squadron made their way from Kweilin to Peishiyi Field (29°29'46" N, 106°21'32" E), about 13 air miles northwest of Chungking (Chonqing) in Szechuan Province. Of vital importance, the city served as Generalissimo Chiang's provisional capital from 1937 to 1945. The nearby airfield at Peishiyi (Baishiyi), where headquarters of the CACW and the 1st Bomb Group had also recently been relocated, was used by the ATC as a resupply and evacuation stop within China.

Maj. Conrad's B-25J, A/C #715, bellied in on a sandbar in the Yangtze River at Chiuling Po after he discovered a malfunction of his nosewheel's locking mechanism. *J. F. Faherty collection, courtesy of Dennis Faherty*

After a brief stopover at Chihkiang, 3rd and 4th Squadron Mitchells came in at about the same time. The weather cooperated for a change. "The sun appeared on the job this morning for the first time in many a day," wrote Maj. Manion, the group's historical officer. Ten 4th Squadron planes touched down late in the afternoon of the fourteenth, and two planes of the 3rd arrived later the same day. When Maj. Conrad attempted to land his B-25J, A/C #715, he discovered that his nosewheel would not lock. Aware that a wheels-up landing on the crowded field would lead to disastrous results, he flew on toward Chungking and bellied in on the sandbar airstrip in the Yangtze River at Chiuling Po (Jiulongpo), south of the city center. There were no injuries to his crew, but Conrad's plane had significant damage in landing and remained there for repairs. SSgt. Barge, its crew chief, was left "to maintain a minimum crew" and repair the plane, according to a subsequent report.[1]

Sgt. McCann flew with Conrad and later recalled, "We crash-landed on an emergency fighter strip near Chungking. Our squadron was to be stationed at Peishiyi on the other side of the mountain."[2] The remainder of the 3rd Squadron's planes arrived on the sixteenth, except for one that was left temporarily near Chihkiang because of needed repairs.

With all the new arrivals from the 3rd and 4th Squadrons, housing and messing facilities were "pretty crowded," according to Manion. Even with the additional personnel, "our exceptionally good mess is holding up pretty well," although lines were long and seating was cramped. Old friends who had not seen each other for many months of separation were reunited, and "the bull flowed freely." Damp, cool weather brought out blankets and jackets, and some of the men began to think about making their own stoves from oil drums to heat the hostels.

The facilities were a disappointment. Previously used by the AVG, the base had stood in an abandoned and neglected state for about two years prior to its reclamation by the CACW. In early July, while Lt. Young was on detached service from the 3rd Squadron, he had visited there with an advance party to check out the base prior to the transfer of CACW and 1st Bomb Group Headquarters. The men were billeted in "an old AVG Hostel, which leaned a little toward the Spanish type of architecture, with a patio here and there, and an inside garden where flowers are abundant, with a lawn and banana trees lining the path," according to Lt. Benjamin Wu, the 1st Bomb Group's historical officer at that time. The detachment's personnel spent two uncomfortable nights "combating bedbugs and mosquitos."

Soon after Young's visit, Maj. Hummel, the wing's historical officer, described the airfield at Peishiyi. Consisting of a long, flat, grassy strip set among misty hills, it most resembled "a serene cow pasture," he noted. At the eastern edge of the grassy rectangle were "a few scraggly buildings, the operations building with its glassed cupola being the only adequate[-]looking structure, set next to some truck garages in a row of shacks—mere roofs on poles—suitable for storage of overnight freight." The airfield had no hangars and no adequate revetments, and the packed-gravel taxi strip down the center of the mile-long runway was overgrown with grass and weeds. It, like the rest of the field, looked "fit for nothing but grazing."

On the north and south ends, hummocks and minor foothills rose directly from the flat rectangle of the field. From the west side rose hills, the sides of which were utilized for a few small revetments and a gunnery school and range. To the east, a strong range of higher hills, lifting to an elevation of 2,300 feet, rose behind Peishiyi village, which ran parallel to the southern half of the airfield. Set on a commanding rise at the northern end of the village stood the CACW Headquarters building. The structure had formerly served as headquarters for the AVG and may have been the mansion of some overlord of Peishiyi village in the more distant past. Between the field and the mansion were rice paddies and farmhouses built around a central mud-packed courtyard that was used as a threshing floor at harvest time.

Little had changed by the time the 3rd Squadron's evacuees arrived from Kweilin. Officers were housed in the AVG-inherited hostels located about 2 miles beyond the village and headquarters building. Their spacious but austere rooms were furnished with wicker and bamboo chairs and rope-spring beds. A dayroom provided a place for poker games, bull sessions, and letter writing. The officers' compound was dense with banana trees that bore "never-ripening little green bananas above huge purple blooms."

New arrivals at Peishiyi discovered their quarters to be marginally more comfortable than their tents in India. Standing in front of their hostel are (*left to right, top row*) Isadore F. Hoke, Stanley B. Rickman, and Wilbur C. Dunlap; (*middle row*) Budd W. Evitts, James H. Mills, James J. Ryan Jr., and their "No. 1 House Boy"; and (*front row*) William G. Duffin and William Meikle. *J. H. Mills collection*

Enlisted men suspected that their dilapidated quarters, a half mile farther down the road, had originally been used to house coolies during construction of the airfield. Relegated to the lowest level on the Chinese social scale, coolies were laborers whose accommodations required no more than the most basic of necessities. Regardless of their original function, the hostels had been built in the traditional style that featured tile roofs with upturned eaves. Hank remembered that the design was the result of superstition. Because they believed that demons could travel only in a straight line, the Chinese constructed their roofs with an upward curve so any evil spirits that might fall from the sky would shoot back up into the air and be unable to enter the structure to harm its inhabitants.

Overcrowding (although not by airborne demons) led to uncomfortable conditions. Six or seven men bedded down in little rooms that should have accommodated no more than four. They slept on narrow army cots. Each room also held a dresser and a lone chair at a small table, on which stood a single candle for lighting. The glass had long since been broken or removed from windows, and the screening hung in tatters.

The ancient well that provided water was completely inadequate for their needs, according to Maj. Hummel, whose monthly historical reports typically provided informative and entertaining descriptions of wing activities. Drinking water was always boiled. Bathwater, scooped out in buckets by coolies, "had a tobacco-brown color, with much debris, twigs, scum, and moss, and indeterminate decomposed messes looking like frog entrails. Refuse soon clogged the showers. The water stank. Live little fish came spurting through the taps." The situation underwent some improvement when a platform supporting large storage barrels was constructed to provide water for daily showers, and heaters were even added later to warm the water.

Outhouses were equally primitive. Although they boasted "marblish" toilets, flushing was accomplished by a coolie who dipped a gallon grease can full of water from a barrel that stood outside the door, and then splashed the water into the toilet and liberally over the seat. If the paper inside the bowl clogged, he fished out paper and other solids with a split bamboo stick and deposited it on the floor. Other coolies periodically stirred the mess in the ditch behind the outhouse, dipped it up in buckets, and used it as fertilizer on the rice paddies.

Hummel provided a typically comprehensive account of Peishiyi Field's deplorable conditions after the arrival of the 3rd and 4th Squadrons:

The sudden influx of additional personnel complicated and crowded the hostel living conditions and mess hall eating conditions, but to Wing personnel already inured to the elementary life it merely made a more crowded elementary life. We jostled a little more in the washroom, trying to gain vantage points before the three distorted, weathered mirrors—two when the third fell down. We also jostled for the two farm-kitchen washbasins—the third had sprung a leak. We shared limited, sorry shower water among augmented personnel. We waited longer before the mess hall, and in the mess hall, while the limited staff of Chinese messboys, which had not grown with the growing clientele, slithered a bit more madly back and forth over greased paths that tracked out of the kitchen through the back entrance into the mess hall. . . . If the floors and kitchen shelves got greasier[,] so did the unchanged dish water in which our dishes were dipped and rinsed. Daily the rim of the coffee cup under the nostrils became a little more sourly corrupt—it smelled the way the sour-slick unwashed rags looked, with which day in [and] day out the waiters slithered coffee and crumbs and jam and gravy off the tables on to the mess hall floors.

When a drunken soldier threatened to "beat the living daylights" out of an overworked waiter, he reacted by walking out, followed quietly by all of his Chinese colleagues. "A few mysterious whispers, a few meaningful slant-eyed glances[,] and mess hall and kitchen were emptied of workers in a Chinese-version sit[-]down strike." It took an hour to put down the insurrection, as hungry, bewildered GIs sat patiently at empty tables.

A staff correspondent for *Yank* wrote during this period that "China is crowded and hungry." He described the food typically dished out in China mess halls as "not exactly sumptuous," and practically none of it was "GI from over the Hump." At one or two out-of-the-way stations where GIs were few, the food was tasty, well prepared, varied, and plentiful, but at other stations it consisted primarily of water buffalo meat, potatoes, rice, eggs, "strange local vegetables (including tons of cucumbers)," small, sweet cakes, and "indifferent coffee."[3]

At Peishiyi, as at other bases in China until the end of the war, "We ate Chinese food prepared by Chinese," Hank related. "Occasionally we'd get some C rations, which was canned food, made in America. Made in America—that was a treat." Of the food commonly on the menu in China, "Water buffalo was the worst meat," he said. "You'd take a bite of it and chew it till it would swell up so big you had to throw it out and get another bite, to get the juice." Bean sprouts were another new experience. "I never had heard of bean sprouts, but they were good to eat—and a *lot* of rice." After the war, Hank almost refused to eat rice because he had his fill of it in China. "I've had enough rice to last me a lifetime."

To relieve some of the overcrowding that resulted from the unexpected influx of personnel, Wing issued orders for planes and personnel of the 1st Bomb Squadron to move to Hanchung (Hanzhong), about 250 miles north. They packed up and planes began to leave immediately, although the remaining personnel and equipment completed the move later. Delayed by bad weather and the need to use the transports to evacuate other bases in the path of the relentless Japanese advance, squadron personnel did not complete the move until the end of October.

Capt. Hodges was transferred to the 1st Squadron and made the move with its personnel. Since his arrival aboard *Mission Bay*, Hodges had flown thirty-one missions with Conrad's squadron and was awarded the Distinguished Flying Cross and the Air Medal for his missions over Burma. Hodges was promoted to major and placed in command of the 1st Bomb Squadron in December. He completed thirty additional missions with the 1st Squadron and was awarded two more DFCs and another Air Medal, as well as the Chinese Silver Star.[4]

As the 1st Squadron was moving to Hanchung in Shensi Province, a mission that involved detachments of the 3rd and 4th Squadrons was being planned from the airfield to the north. Six B-25s were prepared to depart Peishiyi for Hanchung at 1600 on September 20 on a joint mission by the two squadrons, but one 3rd Squadron plane "bogged down" in the sand and could not take off with the others. Maj. William H. ("Bill") Dick, the 4th Squadron's commanding officer, led three B-25s in takeoff from Hanchung at 0840. With him aboard A/C #705 were Capt. Wilbraham A. Hoffson, Sgt. Rex A. Farris, SSgt. Edward F. Zeitler, and Capt. Arza D. Judd, photographer; #706 and #700 (both with Chinese crews) took wing positions. Following the 4th Squadron element, Capt. Seacrest piloted A/C #719, with Graves, McCann, and Hanrahan as his crew, and A/C #713 (2Lts. Chang Y. H. and Chen Y. K. and Sgts. Hsu S. S. and Chang C. H.) flew on his wing. All participating planes were H models. This was the "biggest" mission of the month, according to Young. The Mitchells proceeded to Hsian, where they picked up eight P-40s of the 7th and 32nd Fighter Squadrons, 3rd Fighter Group, to fly close escort and eight P-47s of the 312th Fighter Wing, usually assigned to protection of the B-29 bases at Chengtu, as top cover.[5]

Capt. Seacrest, pilot of A/C #719, led the 3rd Bomb Squadron element in a joint mission with the 4th Bomb Squadron against the infamous Yellow River Bridge. This was the first mission that provided details regarding crew lists and airplane numbers of the participants. *Walter Contreras collection, courtesy of Bob Contreras*

Maj. Conrad joins Col. Jim Bull, 3rd Fighter Group commanding officer from September through December 1944. Bull served in the Air Force Liaison Detachment at Hankow after the war ended. *R. L. Logan collection, courtesy of Katherine A. Logan*

Each B-25 carried three 1,000 lb. demolition bombs. Their objective was to cut the Yellow River Bridge (34°57' N, 113°32' E). This heavily defended, 2-mile-long railroad bridge, crossing the Yellow River about 150 miles east of the 90-degree bend that redirects the river's course eastward toward Shanghai, was an important supply route used by the Japanese that carried 3,000 tons of war materiel every day on the Peiping–Hankow ("Ping-Han") line.

Reports later stated that the P-47s repeatedly broke radio silence on the way to the target, and revealed the fact that they were escorting bombers. In addition, the formation inadvertently passed over the enemy-held Loyang (Luoyang) Airdrome on the approach. The bombers flew over the bridge at 200 feet in line abreast. The aircraft encountered automatic-weapons fire reported as intense but ineffective, especially from the south bank near the railroad yards and from two batteries west of the north end of the bridge. Over the target, Maj. Dick's bomb release jammed on the first run, but he fired one round of 75 mm HE and strafed heavily, silencing fire from the flak boxes. At least two bombs struck the piling piers and skipped through to the other side, stripped of fins. One may have been a direct hit on the north end of the bridge.

Seemingly appearing out of nowhere, ten Tojos jumped the formation. The P-40s did their job well and attacked the enemy fighters, preventing them from reaching the bombers, but the P-47s "dived to the deck" and abandoned the formation. After "mixing it up with the Tojos," the P-40s again took up position of close escort. The fighters returned to Hsian, and the bombers made their way back to Hanchung, on the ground at 1815 and proceeding to Peishiyi the next day. The B-25s flew in "V" formation javelined down to the right, as they had on the approach.

The infamous Yellow River Bridge, located 10 miles north of Chenghsien (Chengchow), was targeted repeatedly throughout the war and soon became the 1st Squadron's primary target. Although there were other bridges in the vicinity that crossed the Yellow River (China's second-longest river after the Yangtze), this one was always known by US airmen as *the* Yellow River Bridge. In reaction to repeated strikes, the Japanese made continuing modifications to strengthen the bridge's defenses, including the installation of cannons in caves cut into the high bluffs above the river. Despite frequent bombings, the bridge's construction made it simple to repair by teams of coolies who were pressed into service, allowing rail traffic to be reopened after only a few days.

Stagnating at Peishiyi

Sgt. McCann had flown many combat missions by this time, and he took part in this mission in his usual position as top-turret gunner. "The first Jap I ever shot was taking a crap in the woods," he ruefully related in later years. It always weighed heavily upon his conscience, although he knew he had no choice in firing on the man because it was his duty to destroy the enemy whenever presented with the opportunity.[6] The conflict between conscience and duty tormented many of these men through the war and the years that followed. It was one of the contributing factors that created the condition now known as posttraumatic stress disorder (PTSD), which many unwillingly took home with them from the war.

As the 3rd and 4th Squadrons opposed the drive from the north, Chinese troops were staging at Peishiyi Field to be sent by transport to fight the Japanese toward the west. This was the first of the troop movements to the area 100 miles west of Kunming, where these recruits—all malnourished and most of them suffering from a variety of diseases—were expected to halt the Japanese advance from Burma into Yunnan. So hopeless were the people of Peishiyi village for any chance of success that they held a symbolic funeral for the departing men. The following morning, the equally dispirited soldiers sat along the road in long triple files that stretched from headquarters to the airfield, a quarter mile beyond.

Hummel described their pitiable and unprepared condition: "They were a sorry lot. Bare-legged they sat at the road-side, straw-sandaled. And most of the bare, browned legs, and many of the faces were spotted with evil, putrid running sores." Each carried a canteen with a yellow towel knotted over it that "represented their only armament." The huge straw coolie hats that they had set on edge before their crossed knees "looked the most military—they looked like medieval shields and seemed to emphasize the medieval helplessness of their weaponless state." Only one man in about eighteen carried an ancient rifle. Marched by companies and packed fifty per transport, the miserable, frightened men were sent as "cannon fodder" to oppose the superior troops of their oppressors.

As September neared its end, 1Lt. Hsia Wei-wei (X-278), 2Lt. Liu Ping-cheng (X-830), and Sgts. Chien-fang (X-2114) and Lee Chen-si (X-1304) received orders to Chengtu for seven days of R&R. Maj. Conrad proceeded to Luliang on an administrative mission "on matters relating to 1st Bomb Gp." Lt. Baker and SSgt. Wilkerson received orders to proceed, with others assigned to the 1st Bomb Group, to ferry additional aircraft from Kunming to Peishiyi. In theory, each of the squadrons was to maintain a force of twelve B-25s on the line, but the reality was that they seldom had the full allotment. Planes were sometimes damaged or destroyed either on combat or administrative missions, and replacement aircraft were not always available because of deficiencies in supply. When replacement planes were available, it became necessary to reuse their "Chinese numbers" to keep them within the range assigned to each squadron. A/C #714, for example, has been associated with serial numbers of at least four B-25s assigned to the 3rd Squadron.

After evacuating from Erh Tong on September 14, the truck convoy that included Capt. Hinrichs, Lt. Young, and eight enlisted men had set up camp 3 miles south of Maling at 1645, after a run of 65 miles. They arrived at Liuchow (Liuzhou) to the southwest at 1925 the following day, "just in time for a two ball alert." The all-clear was sounded after forty minutes. There was "a mad scramble for cover" when three enemy planes bombed Liuchow Field at 0245 on the sixteenth and again at 0225 on the following day. No casualties were reported. TSgt. Jakubasz kept photos of the bomb-damaged planes.

As the truck convoy evacuating from Kweilin paused at Liuchow, enemy bombers struck and destroyed several planes on the field in night raids. *F. T. Jakubasz collection, courtesy of Robert Jakubasz*

Pfc. James A. Wadlow, ordinarily performing duties as a crew chief, was "the mechanic" who patched up the vehicles as the convoy made its slow progress. He praised Capt. Hinrichs for his care of the men traveling up to Peishiyi. *James A. Wadlow collection, courtesy of Stephen Jackson*

Pfc. Wadlow was a member of this detail. In a newspaper interview before his high school graduation in 1940, he revealed that he planned to join the Air Corps and study at Randolph Field to become a pilot, but his aptitude in mechanics led him to be trained as a B-25 crew chief.[7]

He sent a letter from Liuchow to his family in southwest Oklahoma that included details of his adventure:

Dear Folks:

I don't know much to write but this will tell you I am O.K. We have evacuated our home base and I am seeing China by jeep. There are ten of us with Captain in charge, four jeeps and a weapon carrier. We are more or less on a vacation. We are having a pretty tough time of it but I am enjoying it O.K. We have the best officers in the whole lot in charge of us and we are really seeing some pretty country. We stop and camp at night and go swimming every chance we get. The rest of the boys all went by plane and train. The Capt. picked us to go with him and we have the best way of all. We had to ferry rivers and things like that and really had a time, but it is fun. And the rest of the trip will be lots worse. We have 6 to 8 hundred more miles yet to go.

We had an air raid and they really dropped bombs. We have a radio and a phonograph with us and everything else to make it more pleasant, thanks to the Capt. He really takes care of us. We sleep in pup tents, and I don't mind it at all. I am more or less the mechanic on this trip. I patch the old jeeps up. We will go through Bandit

Stagnating at Peishiyi

country some of the way, but we have plenty of ammunition and weapons. So don't worry. We have really been over some rough country almost like the Burma Road, I guess. I saw some of the boys here that I came overseas with. They are all a swell bunch of boys. We are right between two Mountains. The Capt. is a cook. It may be a long time before you hear from me again because I move around so much. The news sounds good, and I hope it won't be long till I will be home. We have two Chinese house boys along with us and they help a lot. I have got to load my jeep down and be ready to go in the morning. We carry our gas and oil in the weapon carrier. (You would call it a pick up.) It is getting dark, and I have to get my bunk fixed to sleep in. I fixed two starters today and checked the jeeps all over. We don't have many parts so will have to wire them together with wire. We repaired a spring yesterday. Will have to close this and get busy. Please don't worry if you don't hear from me. I can take care of myself.

Your Son,
Love, Snooks
James A. Wadlow[8]

The trucks made their way northward by way of Nantan, Tuhshan, Kweiting, Kweiyang, Tungkangchang, and Lungtze. The men who had traveled by rail arrived at Kweiyan (Guiyang) by truck on the twenty-fourth ("looking rugged," wrote Lt. Young) and completed the journey to Peishiyi with the truck convoy.

TSgt. Solyn reported gunfire on the train that killed hundreds of the exposed passengers desperately clinging to the train, as well as attacks by snipers after he had joined the truck convoy. In this photo, the blackboard behind him shows all the squadron aircraft and their current dispositions. *R. N. Solyn collection, courtesy of Robert Solin*

TSgt. Solyn wrote a letter to his father and sister in Connecticut that was summarized in a local newspaper. It confirmed Young's assessment: "He was at Kweilin when the Nipponese took the advance air base in their all-out assault. He and six other American soldiers were the last to leave the field before it was blown up." According to the article, "They succeeded in getting to a train which was evacuating Chinese civilians. Under constant enemy gunfire during the trip through the tortuous mountain country, 600 of the Chinese civilians were killed. At times they were forced to take cover in the woods for protection against bombing. After twenty-four days of constant danger and hardships, they finally got through." They lost all of their equipment and "only had the tattered clothes which barely covered their bodies."[9]

Although no official reports have been found regarding any direct confrontation with the enemy as they made their way to the new base, Young related many years later that during the "final withdrawal before demolition from big China Kweilin Air Base," Japanese soldiers on horseback surprised the convoy from three sides and he "escaped by land after nine days with only the clothes on his back"[10] (part of this description may have been confused with earlier events in New Guinea).

Capt. Hinrichs told his family that during the evacuation, the jeep he was driving was hit by enemy rifle fire that shattered the vehicle's windshield, narrowly missing him.[11] Solyn told a similar story about a sniper. He thought that the man riding behind him had given him a hard kick until the back-seat passenger noticed that he was bleeding from a wound in his back. The bullet missed anything vital and only grazed him, leaving a long scar. He was later awarded the Purple Heart.[12]

The convoy proceeded without further reported incident, arriving at Peishiyi on the evening of September 28. It had covered more than 600 miles, stopping frequently along the way to check over the trucks for mechanical problems, make minor repairs, and change the tires. "With a long[,] tiresome[,] and rough trip behind them, the men needed no inducement to hit the sack early for the first good night sleep in sometime," wrote Young. Solyn and his comrades who traveled by train were sent to the base hospital for treatment and rest before they rejoined their squadron.

Young wrote on the following day, "We woke up to the pounding of rain on our tents. It is an indication that our arrival wasn't a minute too late." He noted conditions of cold, damp rain and "lots of mud" that allowed the men "to catch up on some well[-]needed rest." The downpour fell almost incessantly for the next three weeks. Accommodations both for officers and enlisted men were filled to overflowing, and many latecomers, including those 3rd Squadron men who had arrived by truck, were compelled to move into unwinterized tents that had been hastily erected in any available spaces between compound buildings. Among them were Lt. MacNeil and TSgts. Shock, Rieks, and Armstrong, who had been on detached service to Bangalore. According to Capt. Simpson's diary, he, "Chet," and MacNeil arrived by plane the same day. "Had to move into a tent—Conrad, MacNeil, Seacrest, and myself." Other new arrivals seeking accommodations included 1Lt. Frank P. Pulaski and 2Lts. Thomas H. Edgerton and Lois G. Bains (all B-25 pilots), who were attached that same day.

As the month ended, Sgt. Malone was transferred to the 2nd Bomb Squadron at Liangshan, and Sgt. Thompson was assigned to 1st Bomb Group headquarters as mess sergeant. Sgt. Hall, another cook who had joined the squadron at Moran, was transferred from the 3rd to the 1st Squadron at Hanchung. He was originally assigned to a unit that was sent to Europe and later fought at the Battle of the Bulge in late 1944 / early 1945. It had shipped out while he was in the hospital in New York. Hall was reassigned (likely to the 12th Bomb Group) and sent to North Africa and later to Sicily and Italy as the war accelerated in that part of the world. He then boarded a ship, thinking that he was going home. Instead, he found himself headed to the CBI. In later years, he told his family that he ran mule trains into Burma and India, and he also did preflight checks for Gen. Chennault's planes.[13]

Receiving promotions on October 1 were 1Lts. MacNeil and Ragland to captains; 2Lt. Faherty to first lieutenant; SSgts. Armstrong, Jakubasz, Rieks, Summerville, and Wilkerson to technical sergeants; Cpls. England, Long, and Peters to sergeants (by order dated September 1); Pfc. Wadlow to corporal; and Pvt. Piecuch to private first class. Lt. Dorr was sent to 95th Station Hospital at Kunming (about a mile from 14th Air Force headquarters) because of asthma, and Sgt. Peters checked in to be treated for malaria.

Sgt. Wendell E. Peters, an A/F radio operator, repeatedly volunteered as aerial gunner in addition to his other duties on some the squadron's most dangerous missions. *W. E. Peters Collection, courtesy of Linda Peters Colvard*

TSgt. Jakubasz provided some details of the journey by truck from Kweilin to Peishiyi. The convoy traveled more than 600 miles in two weeks. Here he wears the China-Burma-India shoulder patch in addition to sergeant's stripes. *F. T. Jakubasz collection, courtesy of Robert Jakubasz*

MSgt. Fuller, squadron line chief, qualified to receive a direct field commission. He became the squadron's engineering officer soon after receiving his commission as second lieutenant. *G. B. Fuller collection, courtesy of Elizabeth Fuller Zea*

When TSgt. Jakubasz sent news of his promotion to his father in Massachusetts, he avoided inclusion of details regarding the war situation, in compliance with censorship restrictions, and he made only veiled references to the recent Kweilin evacuation. "I wish I could write all I have been thru and have seen happen before my eyes. Only then would you understand that here in China 'the tea is very bitter,'" he wrote. "One night during my journey with one of the officers, we were given shelter and food at a hospital. No, we weren't sick, only very tired, and fortunate to find a place to sleep." He and other GIs in China had heard news from back home stating that shipbuilders and plane workers were already quitting their jobs because of progress the Allies had made in Europe, but "there is a battle going on over here."[14]

MSgt. Fuller left for Kunming to take his warrant officer examination. From a small town in Georgia, he had enlisted in the Air Corps in October 1939. He hoped to be accepted as an aviation cadet, but vision testing revealed that he was slightly color blind. Because the condition could prevent him from distinguishing colors on the instrument panel, he was disqualified from flight training.[15] Fuller was instead sent to Chanute Field and Scott Field in Illinois and then to Maxwell Field in Alabama to learn airplane mechanics. Promoted to master sergeant, he was a crew chief in the Engineering Department at Westover Field in Massachusetts before being sent in summer of 1943 to the CBI, where he was attached to the 2nd Bomb Squadron.

Since the war in Europe was the US military's primary focus at that time, the CACW found itself at the bottom of the totem pole when it came to receiving planes, replacement parts, gasoline, and other supplies. Of the supplies that were sent, only a small percentage went to airfields in China. The Ledo Road had not yet been extended across Burma, and everything the CACW received still had to be flown in over the Hump and then transported by some combination of cargo plane, river barge, and truck to its ultimate destination. The cost of gasoline was estimated at $20 per gallon by the time it reached one of the bases in China.

Ingenuity was often required on the part of the mechanics to keep the bombers ready for missions when weather permitted and gasoline was available. Replacement parts for the B-25s were almost nonexistent, particularly at forward bases later in the war. If a plane "bellied in" and could not be repaired, all usable parts were cannibalized and then utilized on other planes to get them back into the air. Because maintenance supplies and equipment were seldom available at the airfields in China, mechanics operating under the principle of "Make do or do without" learned to improvise. The 1st Squadron's Sgt. Daniels wrote that he once used peanut oil as a substitute for hydraulic fluid, and he purchased hairpins in town to use as "safety wire" to secure aircraft nuts, bolts, and clamps.[16]

SSgt. Chasse was one of many affected by the shortages. From a large French Canadian Catholic family, he had entered seminary but later explained, "Then I discovered women." He enlisted and served in the 2nd Bomb Squadron as a "door gunner" in aerial combat, according to family stories, although his name has not been found in operational reports.[17] Classified as an Army Air Forces supply technician since the 3rd Squadron's activation, he was responsible for keeping a stock of miscellaneous aircraft parts and replacement items such as hydraulic units, batteries, and electrical cables, issuing them as required when presented by properly authorized requisitions. He was also expected to maintain a supply of hand tools, mobile repair equipment, and small parts needed by the mechanics in servicing or repairing the airplanes and aircraft equipment. However, limited availability presented seemingly insurmountable difficulties that persisted until the war ended.

As the Japanese army continued to move forward with Operation Ichigo, there was little that Conrad's squadron could do to deter the drive to overrun 14th Air Force bases. The combination of dwindling gasoline supplies and deteriorating weather conditions resulted in little flying time for the 1st Bomb Group's B-25 crews stationed at Peishiyi in late 1944. Clouds that produced a steady drizzle kept the planes grounded for most of the month. "All operations are at a standstill," Young noted. At first, squadron personnel welcomed the lack of operational activity as an opportunity to "catch up" on unaccomplished tasks, and the various sections worked overtime on the chores that had been neglected because of the move from Dergaon to Kweilin and finally to Peishiyi.

A war correspondent visited the base at about this time and published an article that was reprinted in *Groop Poop*, "a bi-weekly publication of, by, & for the cogs of the Gambay Group" (the nickname given to the 1st Bomb Group a short time later):

> If you want to know what it means to fight a war on a shoestring, ask any American at this base in rain[-]sodden Sze-Chuan Province. These fellows not only are at the outer extremity of the tail end of the world's longest supply line, but they are living—existing would be a better word—in a climate that certainly is among the world's worst. Almost the only pleasure they get is in fighting the Japs, and the weather makes that less frequent than they would like. Day in and day out, for weeks on end, the boys never see the sun. There is a chronic drizzle. Mud is everywhere. The clammy cold sinks into their bones and refuses to be dislodged. Fuel is scarce and some of the boys are sleeping in unheated quarters.

Getting by with "next to nothing," the men had cigarettes, occasional magazines, and movies three times a week. "Otherwise, there is nothing to do but work, eat, sleep and try to keep warm." There was no Red Cross Canteen, and the dispensary doubled as a rec room. Mail was seldom received, because gasoline and equipment took most of the cargo space on incoming planes. Addressed to a GI at APO 627, a letter or package from home usually took from two weeks to two months to reach its intended recipient. "Little things count for a lot around here. Paper is so scarce that the commanding officer is obliged to post a notice warning that 'the practice of using mimeograph paper and typewriter paper for sanitary purpose must stop.'"[18]

At Peishiyi, as at other China airfields, the 1st Bomb Group felt the neglect of the US military in this "forgotten" theater of the war. "The war in Europe has always caught the lion's share of attention," Ray Hodges observed. "We were kind of the stepchild and got what was left. We ate off the land. We didn't get food and supplies until the war in Europe was over."[19]

Sgt. Norman L. Long attended VHF training at Kunming in October, and he, along with Sgts. England and Peters, became the squadron's VHF specialists. *N. L. Long collection, courtesy of Gordon A. Long*

Hank's recollections included visits by high-level brass at some of the bases. An occasion that prompted one such visit by dignitaries was the first anniversary of the Chinese-American Composite Wing. Because Gen. Chennault was scheduled to arrive soon, October 3 marked the beginning of "general policing of the field and especially the enlisted[-]men housing area." Personnel who had recently arrived by train and motor convoy were "ready to go to work," Young noted. Those who had been living in the muddy tents were ordered to move into the squadron supply room, where Sgt. Long set up lights. From Indianapolis, Long's expertise as a radio mechanic seems to have qualified him for the job.

Persistent rain in the vicinity had turned the base into a sea of mud, so three officers supervised the laying of a wide, raised walkway around the 3rd Squadron's hostel and tent area. This activity was determined to be more important than the dental inspection that had originally been scheduled by Maj. Smith, group dental surgeon. Maj. Hummel wrote this account of the work to improve conditions by personnel of the various squadrons:

The first free afternoon in October all the enlisted men were called out on a rock[-]heaving detail. Truck load after truck load of big and small rocks were brought from the Chinese quarries to the mud[-]bound EM hostel where the clerks formed long lines and chain-ganged rocks from hand to hand to pitch them in the mud for a path through the compound from rooms to mess hall to washroom, in winding sweeps around the tents, and in a long, graceful curve to the latrine. Drainage ditches were dug around each puddled tent, and little elementary culverts were built under the rock paths. The rock-brigade labors continued all the next day, but not even a handout of donuts and coffee could quite atone for the sting of being in the drizzle on a rock pile on a free afternoon. Indignant wisecracks flew faster than the rocks, there was much clever talk about our losing face before our coolie allies, and the rueful commentary went around that evidently the "PROV" following the title of the Chinese American Composite Wing must stand for: "Pave roads on vacations." The air was as full of half-bitter wisecracks as it was of drizzle.

As the base was being prepared for the CACW's anniversary celebration scheduled for Sunday, October 8, headquarters distributed a memo that called for the uniform to be "Class B, cotton sun tan, ties and garrison cap." (Brig. Gen. Morse further instructed, "FIELD JACKETS AND/OR OVERSHOES WILL <u>NOT</u> BE WORN" and that "All personnel not on emergency duty will attend.") It soon became evident, however, that only about half of the squadron's enlisted men were able to "scrape up a complete clean khaki uniform." Because most of their belongings had been left behind at Luliang, while other khaki components were yet to be returned from the Chinese laundry due to the wet weather, a decision was made to allow the men to wear either khaki or olive drab for the event.

Work stopped at 11:00 and vehicles took the men to their hostels to dress for the festivities. Dinner was served early, and all personnel assembled at the Station Master's Compound at 1400. Persistent rain prompted the celebration to be shifted from the airfield to the recreational hall of Chinese headquarters, which had a small stage. The Chinese had decorated the hall for the occasion. Large flags were placed at the front—Chinese on one side of the stage and American on the other. On the back wall of the stage hung pictures of President Roosevelt and Generalissimo Chiang on their respective sides. Chinese personnel filled one side of the compound and Americans the other, forming an aisle down the center. Hummel wrote that those in attendance were attired in "anything that could be considered a uniform." The casual, bare-headed appearance of the Americans stood in sharp contrast to the Chinese, who attended in full uniform.

Posters that adorned the whitewashed walls of the room appealed to the wing's binational character: "Friends at Peace," "Training Together," "Working Together," "Fighting Together," and even "Thinking Together." Maj. Hummel observed, "No doubt the Chinese poster designers had in desperation hit upon this silent form of mental telepathic communication, for whatever we were doing together, we still were not talking together." He explained, "Even the ceremonies of our first year of working and fighting and thinking together had still to be carried out bilingually and were considerably encumbered by the need to have all the proceedings cheated off in Chinese and hackled out in uncomfortable English by a hard[-]worked Chinese interpreter." Gen. Chennault and Gen. Chow Chi-jou, director of the Committee on Aeronautical Affairs, Chinese Air Force, were listed as guests of honor on the program, printed for the occasion in English and Mandarin.

Maj. Garner G. Collums, wing adjutant, called the men to attention and read the Order of the Day, signed by Gen. Morse:

1. Today the Chinese American Composite Wing (Prov), as such, is observing its first anniversary. A year is a long period in war time. This past one has presented many difficulties. Pilots have flown over difficult terrain; maintenance personnel have worked long hours; and administrative personnel have had to surmount personnel, intelligence, and supply problems peculiar to this theater. Because of different customs and language, the Chinese members have had difficulty understanding the Americans and likewise the American members have had difficulty understanding the Chinese.
2. Regardless of what has been required, each man has done his job, and together we have accomplished more than I believe was expected.
3. As your Commanding General, I wish to take this occasion to say "Happy Birthday" and to thank each officer and enlisted man for the part he has played in building this organization and reflecting credit on this Wing.
4. I wish you to know that I have every confidence in you and that I am sure that you will continue to serve with diligence, courage, and honor.

Maj. Gen. Chow Chi-jou, or "General Joe," whose official title was director of the Commission on Aeronautical Affairs, was in command of the Chinese air force. When the CAF began to falter after years of struggle against the superior forces of the Japanese, he traveled worldwide to make an intensive investigation of foreign aviation methods. *R. N. Solyn collection, courtesy of Robert Solin*

Maj. Conrad addressed the audience on the occasion of the Chinese-American Composite Wing's first full year of operations, congratulating them on their spirit of cooperation. Logan captioned this "The Coondog." *R. L. Logan collection, courtesy of Katherine A. Logan*

Maj. Seacrest, recipient of the Air Medal with Oak Leaf Cluster and the Purple Heart, was one of several presented awards that day. Three members of the 4th Bomb Squadron were awarded the Air Medal: Capt. Wilbraham A. Hoffson, Lt. Kenneth A. Elston, and M/Sgt. Peter L. Dodge. Logan noted on the back of this photo that Hoffson is on Seacrest's left. *R. L. Logan collection, courtesy of Katherine A. Logan*

Seacrest is pictured here with Chinese personnel who had presented an embroidered silk banner to the American members of the squadron. The large characters are translated "Destroy Tokyo," the smaller characters on the left as "New 6th Army, Leader Liou Yao Shion," and at the right as "Chinese air force in India, 1st Air Wing and 3rd Squadron." *R. L. Logan collection, courtesy of Katherine A. Logan; translation courtesy of David Ting*

Brig. Gen. Morse (commander of the Chinese-American Composite Wing), Maj. Gen. Chennault (commander of the 14th Air Force), and Lt. Col. David J. Munson (commander of the 1st Bomb Group) confer here regarding important military matters—or perhaps it was the weather. *G. P. Wood collection, courtesy of Glynis Wood Jamora*

Gen. Chennault and other notables then proceeded to the stage. Gen. Chow congratulated the men on the "splendid cooperation between the Chinese and American personnel." (TSgt. Solyn noted on the back of a photograph sent home to his family, "Gen Chow or as we call him General Joe. He is the Chinese High Minister."[20])

Gen. Chennault read a lengthy letter in honor of the day that began "Just a year ago, October 8, 1943, a significant event took place. This event was the flight to China of the first units of the Chinese-American Composite Wing and the establishment of its base of operations in the forward area of combat." In looking back at the CACW's achievements, "we find a record of which to be justly proud and an inspiration to officers and men to carry on their excellent work in the future," he stated.

He outlined the wing's accomplishments through the past year, offering the usual praise to its two national components for working "shoulder to shoulder" and as "brothers-in-arms" and providing statistical evidence of their cooperative operations. "So you have succeeded in large measure, in overcoming apparent insurmountable obstacles which have no parallel in air operations in any other theater of war. The year has recorded a series of successes in which you and the members of your Command, as well as the Chinese people and the USAAF[,] may well take pride." All the proceedings were, of course, translated for the audience.

Stagnating at Peishiyi

Maj. Seacrest was called forward, and Brig. Gen. Morse awarded him the Air Medal with Oak Leaf Cluster and the Purple Heart, followed by presentation of the Air Medal to three members of the 4th Squadron. Then Gen. Chennault presented Gen. Morse with the Distinguished Flying Cross and the Air Medal for meritorious service, numerous missions, and a vast accumulation of air hours and combat flying over rough and poorly mapped terrain. Capt. Simpson, recently transferred to the bomb group as assistant operations officer to Lt. Col. Austin J. Russell, group executive officer, was not favorably impressed. "Pretty sorry affair if you ask me—giving away honor awards to a man just because he has rank," he confided to his diary.

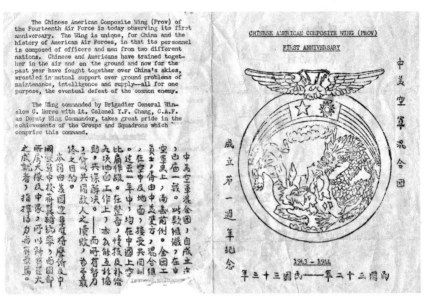

This bilingual program was prepared in recognition of the first anniversary of the Chinese-American Composite Wing, celebrated on October 8, 1944, at Peishiyi. *T. S. Simpson collection, courtesy of Larry Simpson*

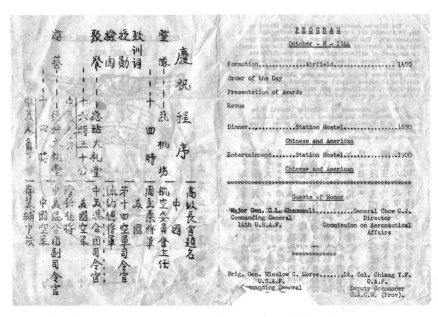

Reverse: Special events extended from early afternoon into the evening.

While CACW notables were gathered, representatives from major US magazines such as *Life* and *Post* interviewed the squadron's officers, with the intention of publishing accounts of some of their missions. Recognizable here are Seacrest and Faherty, only recently returned from their walk-out, with Gen. Chow (*these three seated at the far side of the table*), and Hodges and Ragland (*seated across from them*). Tom Simpson later told his family that he had expected a magazine write-up about his walkout from Burma in the *Saturday Evening Post*. *R. N. Solyn collection, courtesy of Robert Solin*

Camp Show #99 formed part of the evening's entertainment. Shown here (*left to right*) are Gene Emerald, Jack Cavanaugh, Joe Tershay, and Basil Fomeen at Yangkai during their tour of China. *TSgt. Eugene Wozniak collection, website maintained by Tony Strotman, courtesy of Tony Strotman*

All the officers, both American and Chinese, attended a Chinese banquet and "Gambay party" at the Station Hostel that began at 1630. "As usual it seemed to become a contest between the American and Chinese Officers with the Chinese 'ganging' up on us," wrote Lt. Young. Hummel commented that the banquet was "typically crowded with a menu of much variety, unending toasts, much and deep wine drinking which soon obviated the necessity of an interpreter—if we weren't thinking together we could at least do a thorough job of drinking together—the signing of numerous autographs, and the mutual, ceremonial exchange of commemorative scrolls." Simpson wrote, "Brother did I get stinky!!!! Started drinking from small cups—wound up with a soup plate—how did I guzzle that stuff. Tasted like hell. Wound up giving it all back to nature, oh how I did give it back!"

The dinner was followed by an excellent and varied program of entertainment that began at 1900 with Maya Rodowitz, an interpretive dancer from the Polish embassy at Chungking. Unfortunately, the Americans responded to the invitation by "staying away in droves," perhaps because many of the enlisted men had spent the afternoon having their own celebratory drinking parties. The largely Chinese audience, with "a sprinkling of American officers and a handful of GIs" who had remained sober, appreciated not only the dancer's versatile artistry but also her sheer gown, according to Hummel.

Next on the agenda was entertainment by USO Camp Show #99. Made up of four veteran vaudeville performers, it featured Gene Emerald (master of ceremonies and guitarist), Basil Fomeen (accordionist), Joe Tershay (magician), and Jack Cavanaugh (cowboy roping tricks). Although these were not "big name" entertainers, this troupe gave more than six hundred performances enjoyed by GIs in Italy, Africa, the Persian Gulf Command, and the CBI.[21] An orchestra from the Children's Conservatory of Music completed the day's celebration. The music was performed by war orphans who played native instruments. "The quality of their playing rounded off a full evening for the appreciative, if thin, audience," wrote the wing historian.

Lt. Dorr and MSgt. Fuller missed it all. Both were sent the previous day to the 95th Station Hospital at Kunming. The squadron's morning report noted SSgts. Duffin and McCann as sick in quarters; both were hospitalized for malaria soon afterward.

The order that attached 2Lt. Lois G. Bains to the 3rd Squadron in late September was rescinded on October 8. He served with the 2nd Bomb Squadron until his death on May 26, 1945, when he was the pilot of a B-25 that went missing and was later determined to have crashed, killing all on board.

Sgt. Long gives a lesson in radio maintenance to a Chinese radioman. *N. L. Long collection, courtesy of Gordon A. Long*

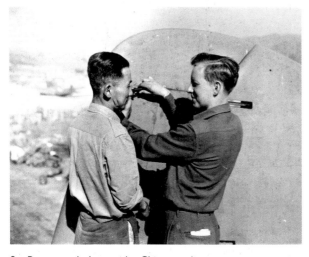

Sgt. Peters works here with a Chinese radioman on some exterior equipment. *R. N. Solyn collection, courtesy of Robert N. Solin*

"Blue Monday—guess why—couldn't even go to work today," noted Capt. Simpson on the day following the celebration. "Lay around with a head the size of a tub." Sgts. Long and Peters were sent to VHF (very high frequency) radio school in Kunming, where they learned to repair and maintain equipment that sent and received radio waves ranging from 30 to 300 megahertz, usually employed in two-way land mobile systems. The squadron's Engineering Department, tasked to keep the Mitchells in flying condition in the event that weather should improve, took advantage of the rain to change out two engines. Later that day came the most welcome event of the week, when mail delivered to the men stationed at Peishiyi brought news from home. Another concert was presented that evening, this one in observance of Chinese Independence Day. Called "Double Ten Day," this holiday is held annually on October 10 to commemorate the onset of the Wuchang Uprising, which led to the overthrow of the Qing dynasty in 1911. An "all-girl" Chinese orchestra traveled from Chungking along muddy roads, and the men enjoyed the rendition of many American favorites, which included "Swanee River."

Capt. Kenneth P. Wilson from CACW headquarters attended the concert and described it in a letter to his family:

> The 10th of this month (tenth month) is called the double tenth here in China is a national holiday (same as our July 4th)—seems that 33 years ago China became a republic. Anyway it was a big day—and in the eve I went to a symphony concert given here in honor of the C.A.C.W. and the double tenth—it was China's finest orchestra, finest musicians—can't compare with American stuff, but was good. . . . These people came from our nearest large town in rain via truck over roads in which they got stuck 3 times—three trucks for 34 people and instruments—even had to bring their piano—40 people were to take part—only 34 instruments were playable when they got here. The piano was a mess—never was much good I guess, but the Chinese girl was a good sport about it—was nice looking and a very good player—probably the best musician was the violinist. The kettle drum had a dollar bill size hole in the bottom of it. They sure went to a lot of trouble to put this thing on. The trip here took over ten times as long as a correspondent trip would under normal bad weather conditions in the states.[22]

Maj. Hummel wrote that for this performance, it was the officers who "stayed away in droves," either because of their too-enthusiastic celebration at the Chinese banquet the evening before or because the event had been "poorly and haphazardly announced" by the Chinese. "The result proved uncomfortably embarrassing for allies who worked and fought together but who evidently weren't thinking too well together, since the carefully thought-out program was ceremoniously climaxed with the presentation to the Chinese American Composite Wing of a beautifully inscribed silk banner." It soon became apparent that no officer of suitable rank was present in the hall to accept the banner. After "a short eternity of embarrassed silence," Col. Chiang, wing vice commander, "had to step into the breach of etiquette, hastily double in brass as Wing's American representative, and accept the banner for his non-thinking allies."

All officers and enlisted men reported to the dispensary for tetanus, typhoid, cholera, and smallpox vaccinations. By the following day, "the arms of all personnel beginning to take the effect of itching and sore due to shots taken yesterday morning," wrote Lt. Young. Every time the men were given injections, they had to take the rest of the day off. Hank explained, "They gave us twice the normal dosage each time because they said since the serum was made in China it wasn't as good as if it was made in the States." Because of the unhealthful conditions that prevailed, immunizations were administered semiannually. Capt. Cunningham and SSgt. Haines were noted as "sick in quarters," both suffering from bouts of malaria, and Haines then spent a few days in the hospital for treatment.

Later that day, representatives from the 3rd and 4th Squadrons volunteered to study the feasibility of establishing an officers club on the base. Capt. Graves, still waiting for transfer back home, was appointed to the court-martial board. The group's public-relations officer organized a contest to determine a moniker, and "Gambay Group" was the favored option. *Gom bey*, an often-used toast literally meaning "dry cup" but equivalent to the American "bottoms up," in this case had a double meaning that warned the enemy that the fate of their shipping or other targets would also be "bottoms up."

That evening, officers of the 3rd and 4th Squadrons hosted a reception to welcome Lt. Col. Munson, the 1st Bomb Group's recently appointed commanding officer, and Lt. Col. Russell, new executive officer. At the party, "Chinese version of our 'Tom Collins' (Chinese gin, lemon powder, and water) flowed freely and a fried chicken dinner was provided," wrote the 3rd Squadron historian. Capt. Simpson commented that Munson was "not a bad sort of a guy but far from Branch." He exercised restraint this time. "Gin galore but I stayed sober remembering yesterday. Sang all the old songs and a few fairly new ditties I'd never heard before. 'Please Don't Tear Our Back House Down' went over big."

He wrote again on the following day: "Even the transports haven't landed here in three days—the ceiling has been so low. Strictly weather for ducks. Half day and I'm now sitting in my room writing this and listening to records."

With weather conditions curtailing missions, many of the men relied on reading and rereading the books and magazines in circulation to fill their leisure time, while others engaged in the seemingly endless games of poker, hearts, and other card games. On movie nights they usually went to see whatever film was featured, regardless of what was showing and how many times they had seen it before. There were generally two showings, one in the officers' hostel and one at the enlisted men's mess hall. "It, well, it was something to do," commented Maj. Manion, group historian. Maj. Hummel wrote that overcrowding often made it necessary for the men to view the films "on the hoof." The audience gladly stood in the jam-packed hall "while having their morale boosted by strictly Grade E movies—the only type that seemingly could get to us over the 'HUMP'—no doubt because of their feathery lightness of artistic and entertainment content." He surmised that their enthusiasm was motivated primarily by the opportunity to view the female form on screen. On nonmovie nights, the enlisted men's mess hall doubled as a reading, writing, and recreation room since there was no additional space available for such activities.

During this time of operational inactivity, Hank and others sometimes ventured into town, as well as nearby villages. The most conveniently located was Peishiyi village, described in the group history as having "a long street about one mile long, with only a few turns, many shops, and admiring youngsters generally giving a 'Ding How' all along the way."

Hank was surprised by the clothing typically worn by the younger children, whose pants had the seats conveniently removed. Even more astonishing to him were the practices of adults, who also relieved themselves when and where they felt the need. He once observed a woman giving birth as she worked in a field. After the infant was delivered, she wrapped it against her chest with a wide strip of cloth and then continued with her work.

Under the tutelage of the two Chinese mechanics who taught him some expressions, Hank learned enough of the language to make himself understood when conversing with the locals. "They were always teaching me Chinese words. I used to go into villages and dicker with them and buy stuff." He still remembered some phrases: "*Nee jee mengsa si shi ma*. That means, 'What is your name? *Nee jee* . . . you . . . *jee* is possessive. *Mengsa* is name. *Si shi ma* is question mark. Well, I used to could talk that stuff. Those Americans would go with me in those villages, and I could talk with those Chinese."

Impressed with his ability to communicate with the locals, Hank's buddies would ask, "Where did you learn to speak like that?"

"I'd tell them, 'I just picked it up.'"

Hank, sharing the opinion of most Americans, liked the Chinese people, who were generally pleasant, friendly, and hardworking. When the Chinese encountered an American soldier (called *meg-wa-zen*), their usual reaction was a greeting of *ding how* ("very good"), accompanied by a big grin and a "thumbs-up" gesture.

This roadside store that Hank visited was operated by a Chinese family. He spoke enough of the local language to be able to bargain with shopkeepers, thanks to two mechanics with whom he worked. This photograph is one of many depicting life in China that he sent home during the war. *J. H. Mills collection*

Maj. McGehee, wing adjutant, wrote: "So far, I like China better than any place I have seen. There are more people here than in India, it seems, and just as much poverty, but not nearly as much begging. The people here are far more industrious than the Indians, are much friendlier, and have a good sense of humor, which was something I had not seen before I got here." The shouted greeting of *dinghow* meant "of the best," or very literally "You're o.k.," he explained. "It really makes you feel good, for it's such a definite reflection of what they are taught at home by their parents. The US is really building up a tremendous amount of good will everywhere I have been, especially here."[23]

In spite of often-harsh conditions, Hank had good memories of his time in China and of the Chinese people. "They thought Americans were the greatest thing in the world." His recollections included dealing with shopkeepers. "The main thing I remember is when you went to a Chinese business, the first thing they did was bring you in and made tea. You drank tea first. Then you discussed business. You haggled. They'd start out with double what they would expect to get. You'd start out with about half of what you expected to pay, and you met as close to the middle as you could."

"Things were cheap," he recalled. "I bought some Chinese embroidered silk bedspreads. I sent one to my mother and one to my wife.... They were pretty." He also sent home other beautifully embroidered articles, including silk scarves, handkerchiefs, and a child's cape and shoes, as well as hand-painted silk fans. "I've seen children working in those places. They didn't have any child labor laws. All children worked."

Although locally produced goods were relatively inexpensive, prices of most imported products were greatly inflated. A GI could buy a one-dollar Brownie camera for twelve dollars in American money, and a ten-cent pocket comb cost him two dollars and fifty cents. A bottle of good scotch could be purchased for $250. If he wanted a simple but well-prepared restaurant meal, he had to be prepared to pay two to four dollars or even more for it.[24]

During the month, a cholera epidemic in Peishiyi village killed twenty-five, including soldiers of a Chinese battalion stationed there. Houseboys were hastily inoculated to protect them against the disease. The thoroughly immunized Americans were unaffected, although hardly any of them escaped colds and respiratory infections prompted by exposure to the damp chill, and some suffered from malarial relapses. Names of several of the officers and enlisted men appeared on morning reports during this period as "Dy to sk in qrs," followed a day or two later by "Sk in qrs to dy."

The rain stopped for long enough to allow the first glimpse of blue sky in more than a week. TSgt. Solyn was ordered to Chengtu for "dental treatment" in mid-October, according to the squadron's monthly historical report, although hospital admission records indicated health issues involving "Male Genital Organs, disease of (non-venereal)." TSgt. Holmes returned from treatment for an ulcer on his cornea.[25] McCann and Duffin returned from the hospital to duty. A one-ball alert was sounded at 1110 on the fourteenth, sending alert crews to stand by their planes to take to the air, if necessary, but no enemy planes appeared.

The following day, "the sound of four engine bombers flying over our field" caused great excitement. A formation of B-29s was returning from southern Formosa (Taiwan), and one of them landed to refuel. It was one of 104 China-based Superfortresses that had taken part in a successful raid against an aircraft plant at Okayama. Men poured onto the field from every direction to get a look as the big bomber pulled into position. The monster's 1,000-gallon requirement severely taxed the resources of the gasoline-depleted field, and the laborious process of hand-filling the tanks was not completed until after darkness had fallen. Overnight, its 90,000 lb. weight sank into the waterlogged field, requiring all of the CACW's resources in weapons carriers and 6×6s to pull its wheels out of the mud and onto the hard strip the following morning. "All hands were on hand to watch the B29 taking off from our field and were amazed at the short run made," wrote Lt. Young.

Shortly after its takeoff, the men experienced another one-ball alert. Fighters took off but were called back after forty minutes. Once again, no enemy planes appeared. Later that day, Capt. Graves, squadron navigator, was transferred to 1st Bomb Group headquarters in preparation for his return home.

On the afternoon of October 16, the enlisted men gathered at Group to hear the articles of war, as well as a "Sex Morale" lecture. Because of the high incidence of venereal disease among the local population, warnings were issued frequently against exposure to it in its many and varied forms. Films that illustrated affected genitalia, both male and female, accompanied the lectures in an attempt to discourage unprotected sexual contact. Those who ignored the warnings were urged to seek immediate medical care. "A pretty nice PX ration was distributed immediately afterward and was welcomed by everyone."

When the skies briefly cleared on the next day, Maj. Conrad ordered the squadron's eight planes currently in commission out for formation flying. While taxiing into his parking space, Lt. Pulaski applied the brakes but slid across the slick, muddy ground into a small pile of bombs. The propeller of his left engine was damaged slightly.

Hoping to be on his way back home by this time, Capt. Simpson had noted in his diary about two weeks previously: "Found out my application to go home had been not favorably considered at this time by 14th AF. Have to wait for the letter to return and then I'll be put in as 'war weary.' Hope to God it goes through as such." Approval had been granted three days earlier to leave the bomb group in preparation for his return to the States, and Simpson logged this practice mission as pilot of a B-25J as he waited for orders.

Pfc. Piecuch was placed on detached service to the 2nd Squadron at Liangshan, where Sgt. Malone had been sent in late September. Their services were not required at Peishiyi, where a complete kitchen staff was already in place. Cpls. Rickman and Allegretto were briefly hospitalized for unspecified maladies.

On October 19, 2Lt. Wayne H. Senecal (two-engine A/C pilot), Sgt. Loyal L. Fox (A/P armorer-gunner), and Cpls. Alfred J. Magyar (radio operator–mechanic–gunner) and James J. Ryan Jr. (A/P mechanic–gunner–flight engineer) were transferred in. MSgt. Fuller returned

Sgt. Loyal L. Fox was attached as an airplane armorer-gunner for seven months and flew many successful missions in China. *Courtesy of Darlene Fox Blair*

Cpl. Alfred J. Magyar was attached as a radio operator–mechanic–gunner at the same time. Allegretto captioned this one "Al Magyar and Chinese radio man." *A. R. Allegretto collection, courtesy of Mary Henry*

Cpl. James J. Ryan Jr., airplane mechanic–gunner–flight engineer, was the third enlisted man attached in October. *James J. Ryan Jr. collection, courtesy of Kenneth Lancaster*

All recent arrivals, Frank P. Pulaski, Thomas H. Edgerton, and Wayne H. Senecal (*left to right, standing*) and Loyal L. Fox, James J. Ryan Jr., and Alfred J. Magyar (*kneeling*) pose for the camera. *A. J. Magyar collection, courtesy of Lynn Magyar Zwigard*

from headquarters after successfully passing his physical examination for warrant officer. Both Capt. Hinrichs and MSgt. Grant were transferred to wing headquarters. The clear weather ended later that afternoon, grounding planes again.

SSgt. Gruber, accompanied by Cpl. Wadlow, arrived from Kunming with sad news concerning squadron and personal equipment left behind during the transfer. Most of it had been left out "at the mercy of the weather," and thieves had broken into personal equipment and stolen everything of value. Lt. Wood returned from detached service at Kunming.

Taking a break: (*left to right, standing*) Loyal L. Fox and "No. 1 House Boy"; (*kneeling*) James H. Mills, Ewell F. Wilkerson, William G. Duffin, unidentified but perhaps Charlie H. Hoyle Jr., Sgt. Ho Gui-hung, and (*reclining*) Norman L. Long. *J. H. Mills collection*

Hank and others of his hostel were disappointed when they lost their "No. 1 House Boy," who had evacuated with them from Kweilin. Although others continued the task of caring for the GIs and their quarters, the men had come to rely upon his efficiency and enjoyed his company.

Lt. Dorr, suffering from recurring bouts of malaria and asthma, was transferred in grade to Detachment of Patients, 95th Station Hospital, at Kunming. He had not made the move with the rest of the squadron and explained it in a letter to Jim McCann almost forty years later:

TSgt. Joseph N. Shock, who preferred to be called by his middle name, Ned, was an airplane mechanic and sheet metal worker before his enlistment in 1940. In the CBI since July 1943, he was initially attached to the 2nd Bomb Squadron. Ned had completed a radio course and joined the 3rd Bomb Squadron as a radio mechanic at its activation, and he often participated in missions as an aerial gunner. He was promoted to master sergeant in May 1945. *Courtesy of Susan Shock Garfield*

When the 3rd Bomb went up to China after being in Assam, I was left behind at Chabua with malaria again. Hospitalized 11 times with it before I finally got over it a few years later. Got up to Kunming and was held there since Kweilin was being evacuated. Tom Manion came thru and told me that the outfit was pulling together at Peishiyi and that if I could get there, he'd take care of any paperwork. Actually, they had been planning to have Charlie Knight [2nd Bomb Squadron; KIA on May 26, 1945] and me to take a convoy there from Kunming. So I bummed a ride on a transport and got to Peishiyi. Tom and George had been sent state side but since I had the ground MOS's I wasn't on the way home with them despite the Burma walk-out.

Malaria hit again, and the flight surgeon sent him to the hospital in Kunming, where he was processed back to the States. "I expected to get home for Thanksgiving of '44 but started coming down with malaria again between Karachi and Casablanca. Some RCAF ferry pilots gave me quinine[,] and I held it in check until we had to remain too long in Casa and off to the hospital again. Got home in time for Christmas." Damage to his spleen caused by the repeated attacks of malaria eventually led to Dorr's retirement from the Air Force on disability.

A break in the rain allowed two of the squadron's bombers into the air for test flights, but inclement weather created hazardous conditions that contributed to the crash of one of them. Capt. MacNeil, TSgt. Shock, and SSgt. Barge had been ordered to Chungking "on matters pertaining to 1st Bomb Gp." On October 22, Capt. MacNeil was assigned to "test hop" A/C #715, which had been left at Chiuling Po for repairs to its nose gear the previous month and to ferry the plane on to Peishiyi. He took with him TSgt. Shock as engineer. Weather conditions were recorded at takeoff as "overcast at 1,000 to 1,500 feet, clouds topping mountains, visibility five to seven miles below overcast." MacNeil's preflight check showed the aircraft's fuel level at 100 gallons in the right tank and 140 gallons in the left. The command set (radio equipment used for short-range communication with the tower or with nearby planes) was out, but the plane seemed to be normal otherwise. In flight, he discovered that the main gear would not retract, the radio compass was out, and the flight instruments were very inaccurate. "After take-off I circled Chungking checking the landing gear," MacNeil later reported. "A check of the gear at this time showed 70 gallons in the right tanks and the necessity of a field suitable for a wheels[-]up landing at once."

Chiuling Po, on Chungking's outskirts, had only a small, undeveloped fighter strip that ended abruptly at the river. Since facilities at the field had proved inadequate for making all the needed repairs, MacNeil flew the plane on to Peishiyi in spite of the low ceiling. "I flew a heading of 243° and entered the overcast at about 2,000 feet leveling out at about 3,000 feet. I flew past the E.T.A. to Peishiyi without finding a break in the overcast. I made 180° and could not find Chungking. I circled and finding no holes climbed to 5,000 feet and bailed TSgt. Shock out." At that time the right tank had about 30–40 gallons indicated, but they had been in the air thirty minutes and had preflighted the ship on the original 100 gallons. Assuming that there was less gas than was indicated, MacNeil circled and let down to 3,100 feet for ten to fifteen minutes and then bailed out. As he was floating down, he saw the aircraft break out of the overcast and hit a mountain, apparently with a dead right engine.[26]

TSgt. Shock's report stated that during the flight, the nosewheel came up and locked but the main wheels came up only about three-quarters of the way and stayed there. He believed that the main radio compass was out of commission, but otherwise the airplane was "flying and operating in fine condition." After he had bailed out and landed safely, he could hear the plane circling for about ten or fifteen minutes and "then I didn't hear it anymore." The bomber was reported as "washed out and completely wrecked" near Kweintown, about 60 miles southeast of Chungking. MacNeil and Shock were returned to Chungking the same night, and Maj. Conrad was notified of their safety at 2300.

When MacNeil later wrote about the incident to his parents in Minnesota, he added more details. "I flew around looking for a hole until the gas gauge was knocking on zero. Then I climbed out. I must have knocked myself out when the chute opened, because I was floating in a big overcast the next thing I knew. A couple [of] seconds later the plane came busting out of the clouds and blew up against a mountain." It took about three minutes for him to hit the ground, he wrote. "I could see the rice paddies and I started yelling all the Chinese I knew. It must have scared them because there was only one who would come near me. He led me into a village. I was the first American who had been seen in their town."[27]

In subsequent investigation, Capt. MacNeil was held "wholly responsible" for the loss of the plane because "he used poor judgement in entering an overcast known to rest on the mountains en route not knowing whether or not the radio compass and command set were inoperative and with insufficient gasoline to reach better weather." No recommendations were made for discipline because of his previous excellent record as "an ambitious and conscientious" engineering officer and combat pilot. A report of the accident and findings of the inquiry was signed by Lt. Col. Russell (president), Lt. Col. Percy H. Sutley of the Medical Corps (flight surgeon), and Maj. Dick, 4th Bomb Squadron (aircraft accident officer). Capts. Seacrest and MacNeil and TSgt. Shock filed additional certificates.

When Ned Shock recounted the incident to his family in later years, he added details not revealed in the official reports. He said that when he and MacNeil found each other after the crash, he was so angry that he punched the pilot in the jaw because MacNeil was drunk when he took off. Shock described MacNeil as "flamboyant" and said that he often took unnecessary risks.[28]

As a crew chief, Hank worked closely with MacNeil, the squadron's engineering officer and test pilot, and described him as "a good pilot and a friendly fellow." He said "Mac" often came to him and inquired, "How's number so-and-so?"

"It's ready to go," Hank would reply.

"Go get you a chute and let's take it up and twist its tail."

"He got a 'Dear John' letter while he was over there," Hank recalled, although MacNeil and his wife, Barbara, were still together after the war. Perhaps the need to drown his sorrows because of marital discord explains the allegation that he was drinking before takeoff.

The CBI's "top brass" were engaged in a bitter dispute regarding a great number of issues, many of them having to do with the distribution of Lend-Lease materiel, and Chennault and Stilwell were in open competition over the limited supplies coming into the theater. The conflict arose, in part, because Stilwell insisted that the war would be won by troops on the ground, while Chennault was equally adamant that it would be won by the air forces. Each of them believed that his claim to supplies held the greater validity.

The distribution of these supplies was under control of Stilwell, who served as commander of all US forces in China, Burma, and India, as well as deputy commander of the Burma-India theater under British admiral Louis Mountbatten and as chief of staff to Chiang Kai-shek, commander of Nationalist Chinese forces. Mutual animosities persisted regarding who was to blame for the loss of Allied bases as a result of Operation Ichigo. Stilwell blamed Chiang and Chennault for loss of the eastern China bases, and the generally accepted reason he had rationed supplies to the 14th Air Force was his openly expressed dislike for Chiang (whom he called "Peanut" and "G-mo") and his disdain for Chennault. When Chennault requested an increase in shipment of supplies needed to counter the Japanese offensive in China, Stilwell refused, protesting that the supplies were required to combat the enemy in Burma. Stilwell accused Chiang of making unreasonable demands, as well as hoarding supplies for his Nationalists to use against Mao's Communists. When President Roosevelt suggested in August 1944 that Stilwell (by then a four-star general) be given command of the Chinese forces, the generalissimo adamantly rejected the proposal.[29]

Blaming Stilwell for the Japanese successes, Chiang urged US high command to recall him. In October, Roosevelt did just that, dividing the CBI in the process. On October 24, 14th Air Force HQ was reassigned from US Army Forces, China-Burma-India theater, to US Forces, China theater. Maj. Gen. Albert C. Wedemeyer, who had previously served tours of duty in the Philippines and in China, became chief of staff to Chiang Kai-shek and commander of US Forces, China theater. At the same time, Lt. Gen. Daniel Sultan became commander of US Forces, India-Burma theater. In reality, these organizational changes had little practical effect on the men at bases scattered across the former CBI.

Before his departure, Gen. Stilwell praised the 14th Air Force in a parting message, which was relayed by Gen. Chennault on November 6:

> As I relinquish command of this theater, I wish you to know of my confidence that you will continue to prosecute your mission on the same high plane as you have in the past. I have watched your fortunes closely, and I have taken great pride in your achievements even though the exigencies of the service have precluded a closer association with the officers and men of the Fourteenth Air Force. Despite its discouraging condition, you have carried the ball with great success. You have cut the Jap air force in China to the vanishing point. You have struck him on the sea and on the ground. You have won the admiration and respect of the Chinese. In closing I extend my best wishes for a speedy return home after your final victory.

Sent to commanders, all units, 14AF.
By Chennault.

Leaden skies persisted in leaking a steady shower. Mud became so deep in the vicinity of Peishiyi that it threatened to shut down the base completely. The roads from the hostels to the line and those around the field were flooded and impassable. Maj. Hummel described the situation in typical style: "The slime on the roads worked itself deeper, became porridge, became soup. There was no sound bottom, and vehicles stirred and pushed the mire, dug themselves deeper ruts, lurched axle deep out of water holes only to be led helplessly into the next water hole by the imprisoning ruts," he wrote. "Soft shoulders of the narrow roads slid toward the flooded rice paddies, and often jeep, weapons carrier, or Chinese station wagon slid with them into the paddies and had to be winched out again with great slitherings and mud slidings and concerted groans of hundreds of coolies heaving their shoulders under the vehicle."

Beginning on October 23, all officers and enlisted men not absolutely required at headquarters were assigned to road-repair duty. All vehicles were commandeered to haul rocks from Chinese quarries to fill the sinkholes in the road. Shovels, like everything else on the base, were in short supply. While enlisted men heaved rocks into water-filled holes, the officers—using their boots as digging tools—scraped out drainage ditches. "They solemnly dug their five[-]inch[-]deep ditches using the toe of the boot as a scoop, and with the sole as a trowel plastered the bottoms of the runnels a little smoother. . . . The whole helpless effort looked almost as silly as it was pathetic," declared Hummel.

TSgt. Libolt devised an innovative approach to difficulties caused by working in the mud. In an attempt to increase traction and prevent himself from slipping, he wrapped his boots with wire as he went about his duties. From Indiana, Libolt had enlisted in the regular army in May 1940 as a mechanic's helper and later transferred to the Air Corps. He was one of the 1st Bomb Group's original members, serving as A/P instrument specialist before his transfer to the 3rd Squadron and assignment as an instrument specialist and later the squadron's airplane inspector.

Brig. Gen. Morse addressed the officers regarding the care of vehicles and the importance of good roads, although repairs had already begun. The next day's efforts were concentrated on the section of road leading to group headquarters. Lt. Pulaski directed 3rd Squadron road crews on the twenty-sixth. After three days of labor that produced only minor improvements, the effort was abandoned.

A detail working to improve facilities at Peishiyi included Sgt. Solyn (*wielding the sledgehammer*) and Sgt. Fox. Their supervisor wearing his leather flight jacket brought along refreshments, if the bottle in his pocket is an indication. His face is not visible, so he cannot be identified with certainty. Sgt. "Izzy" Mier appears to be amused by the situation. *R. N. Solyn collection, courtesy of Robert N. Solin*

TSgt. Frederick C. Libolt, who served as a mechanic in the infantry before his transfer to the Air Corps, was one of the CACW members who reported for duty at headquarters of the 2nd Staging Squadron at the Floridian Hotel in Miami during the summer of 1943. He was first assigned to the 3rd Fighter Group but moved to the 1st Bomb Group and was attached to the 2nd Bomb Squadron. While later serving with the 3rd Bomb Squadron, Libolt's name appeared frequently in mission reports as a top-turret gunner. *Courtesy of Jodi Libolt Shannahan*

Squadron personnel received their pay for the first time in two months. The situation was improved when Capt. Kelso was appointed class "A" finance officer for the purpose of paying squadron vouchers and payrolls. Later that day came some good news in the form of encouraging reports of American successes in the Philippines.

Without combat missions to keep them occupied, many of the men looked forward to payday as incentive to take part in a game of chance. Hummel noted that the much-used playing cards were worn and dog-eared, and men resorted to solitaire when they lost all their money. Sgt. McCann seldom passed up a poker game and was one of the lucky (or perhaps skillful) ones who frequently came out ahead. On one occasion, he and several of his buddies played all night and then all the next day. McCann won big and sent a check for $1,000 back home to West Virginia. Because he won frequently, his wife, Helen, suspected that he was getting the money by dealing on the black market, so she was hesitant to spend it until convinced of the legitimacy of its source. "It's always better to hide things in plain sight," she often said, so she concealed it in a frame holding a picture of their son Jack, born after Jim had shipped overseas.[30]

Lts. Faherty and Pulaski inspected, oiled, and repaired the squadron's typewriters late in the month. Pulaski's preenlistment occupation in Connecticut as a bookkeeper / office clerk may explain his skills in servicing office machines, but it could not predict his proficiency as a pilot on many later 3rd Squadron B-25 missions. Faherty was appointed armament officer to replace Lt. Dorr, and Lt. Wood became acting supply officer to fill in for Capt. Hinrichs.

Weather again cleared enough to allow planes aloft. Sgts. Peters and Long returned from Kunming after completing a course on VHF radio equipment. Col. Russell and Capt. Seacrest took off to ferry two B-25s up to the 1st Bomb Squadron at Hanchung. Heavy cloud overcast and "tremendous cloud covering" in the proposed target area caused cancellation of missions to be led by Maj. Conrad scheduled for October 30 and 31. Hank was admitted to the hospital for treatment of acute nasopharyngitis (more commonly known as "a bad cold") and was released after a few days.[31] End-of-the-month morning reports specified forty Americans on the roster: nine officers and thirty-one enlisted men. No figures were provided for the Chinese.

It was at about this time that Sgt. Li Chan-jui was transferred out, although a search of squadron and group records has produced no evidence. His name has not been found after the evacuation of Kweilin. Li remembered that after he returned to China, he was granted leave to visit his family, whom he had not seen in eight years, and the only photograph from his early life was taken with his father while on that visit. Clearly visible on his jacket is his 3rd Bomb Squadron skunk patch. His recollections of bombing and strafing missions until the end of the war included daily raids against Bangkok, Thailand's capital city, which had become an important command center for the Japanese on the Southeast Asian front. Major targets of the 10th Air Force during this period of the war were the newly completed Port of Bangkok and the Thai railway system. "Once we bombed a train carrying armaments, all bombs, machine guns, pistols, and bullets exploding," Li recalled. Although advancing age had severely diminished his eyesight, he could still clearly visualize the explosions many decades later.[32]

Capts. Graves and Simpson and Lieutenant Edgerton returned to Peishiyi from Kunming with a B-25H replacement. Simpson logged his "Last Flight In China" as three hours and ten minutes from Peishiyi to Kunming and back to Peishiyi. By this time, some of the American pilots had completed their tours of duty and received orders to go home, and Capts. Graves and Simpson were among those allowed to return to "Uncle Sugar Able." Simpson wrote, "Can hardly eat or sleep I'm so excited. Will try to go tomorrow." The two men "said goodbye to all the fellows" and left Peishiyi aboard a C-47 for Kunming on October 30 for the first leg of their journey.

After crossing the Hump and stopping for fuel and food at Chabua, Jorhat, Lilimar Hat, Gaya, Delhi, and Karachi, they continued their hopscotch journey toward the west. They filled spare time by sightseeing and shopping on stopovers at Abadan, Iran, Cairo, Egypt, Benghazi, Libya, Tripoli, Tunisia, Algiers, Algeria, and Casablanca, French Morocco, before crossing the Atlantic. Simpson's final journal entry, written at Casablanca and dated November 4: "No planes again this morning. Lou and I played basketball and then had a shower. It's now 1200 and time for lunch."[33]

CHAPTER NINE
Task Force 34 at Chihkiang

While 3rd Squadron Mitchells remained grounded at Peishiyi, it became clear to observers that Japanese forces coming from the north were moving toward a junction with troops advancing westward toward Nanning from Canton. As the enemy's attempt to drive Allied forces from bases across China moved forward, even Kunming, headquarters of the 14th Air Force, came under threat. Although this vital military complex was never taken, airfields fell like dominoes over the next few months. Chinese ground forces, with the support of Chennault's airmen, opposed the enemy's relentless advance in central China, especially the regions south of the Yellow River and immediately west of the Ping-Han Railway, and as far east as the Nanking-Shanghai area.

Col. John A. Dunning, in command of the 5th Fighter Group at Chihkiang (Zhijiang), had put in a request in October for four B-25s with crews to run missions in close conjunction with his "Flying Hatchet" fighters to resist the Japanese drive. His pilots had found that daytime targets were scarce and scattered because the enemy was moving troops and supplies primarily at night, so that was when he intended to strike. Called "Task Force 34," its participants were to be detached from the 3rd and the 4th Squadrons, which had some night-flying experience from the period that it was operating out of Kweilin.

On October 30, two 3rd Squadron bombers (both J models) formed up with two from the 4th Squadron (an H and a J) and proceeded from Peishiyi to Chihkiang (27°21'01" N, 109°35'24" E), about 375 miles east-northeast of Chungking. Capts. Cunningham and Ragland, 1Lt. Baker, 2Lts. Edgerton and Senecal, SSgt. McCann, Sgt. England, and Cpls. Allegretto, Burton, and Jackson were the first Americans to be assigned from the 3rd Squadron. Of the Chinese taking part, 1Lts. Ouyang Chun (X-277) and Sheng Chiu-jang (X-225), SLt. Chang Kuang-lu (X-819), and Sgts. Liu Teng-wen (X-2131), Ho Wei-ching (X-1395), Wang Ching-chuan (X-1400), Wang Tsung-cheng (X-2294), Teng Chiu-sheng (X-2133), Tso Jui-chen (X-1414), Taun Ysai-pang (X-1401), and Su Chai-yu (X-2305) were sent to join their American counterparts.

Col. Dunning and Col. Rouse (who had been with the fighter group since training began at Malir but was awaiting orders back to the States) were eager to begin operations immediately. They proposed a mission that very night, but discretion prevailed and they delayed night operations for a few days to allow the bomber crews to become familiar with the airfield and the surrounding terrain. Members of Task Force 34 spent their first week getting organized. As ranking officer, the 4th Squadron's Capt. Moncure N. ("Monty") Lyon was placed in command, and Capt. Ragland was assigned as operations officer. For the 3rd and 4th Squadrons, only the detachments operating out of Chihkiang were capable of joining in the action through the following month because of ongoing rain and shortages at Peishiyi.

In June, Capt. Sam Carran of the 26th Fighter Squadron, 5th Fighter Group, had described Chihkiang Field as "a picturesque spot." Situated at the western base of the Paima Shan Mountains, "it lies in a small, fertile valley formed by the Hung Kieng River as it flows about the feet of the surrounding mountains," he wrote. "Heavy rainfall keeps the valley green.... Colors are vivid and contrasting, sudden strange fogs and brilliant sunsets are frequent. The rugged, off-shaped peaks, with clouds floating through them, form an eerie backdrop for a 'Land of Oz'-like scene."

He wrote that the mountains presented "a formidable obstacle, with the consequence that many and varied weather as well as navigational difficulties daily confront our airmen." The narrow taxi strip was "carved off the top of a hill," with the revetments in which the planes were stored at night "down in a kind of rice paddy area away from the main part of the runway."

The airfield's runway consisted of about 3,200 feet of gravel with a short dirt overrun on the north end. The south end sloped down at about a 30-degree angle and ended abruptly with a precipitous drop of about 100 feet down to mudflats that extended for several hundred yards to the river. The following January, this hazardous configuration led the pilot of a 341st Bomb Group B-25J to miscalculate and overshoot about two-thirds of the runway, causing the bomber to drop off the end and crash into the rice paddy below. As the plane burned, the flight engineer's leg was trapped under the heavy armor plate, and flames began to reach him. After repeated desperate attempts to pull him out, Col. Dunning mercifully shot the doomed man in the head.[1]

About a mile away from the revetments were the living quarters, with the Chinese in one area, American enlisted men in another area, and officers in yet another. The quarters were initially wooden barracks, although winterized tents were added later. According to Jim Bennie, crew chief of the 17th Fighter Squadron, also stationed there, the barracks had potbelly stoves that were put into use when the weather turned cold, as well as electric lights and bunk beds. "The beds were two by fours with cords slatted between them and net mattresses, just a cotton pad. You had your two blankets and a mosquito net, which was obviously used to keep out mosquitoes but also to keep out rats. Rats were always a problem." In addition, there was an orderly room and a medic's clinic. The mess hall was arranged with the kitchen in the middle, and dining rooms on one side for enlisted men and officers on the other. The food provided was "caribou" and the invariable water buffalo, rice, and bean sprouts, with eggs for breakfast.[2]

The ongoing combination of limited fuel and almost continuous mist or light rain with low clouds prohibited aerial operations out of Peishiyi. Aircrews of the 3rd Squadron had been accustomed to flying almost daily before their move to China, but now the pace of life slowed. Boredom brought about by inactivity soon caused an inevitable slump in morale, which seemed to be in direct proportion to the number of missions completed. Fortunately, a USO troupe that featured model/actress Jinx Falkenburg, dancer/contortionist Betty Yeaton, and singer Ruth Carrell arrived to entertain the troops, the majority of whom had not seen a white woman in six months or more. These three entertainers, with actor/comedian Pat O'Brien as emcee, singer/guitarist Jimmie Dodd (husband of Ruth Carrell), and singer / piano player Harry Brown accompanying them, appeared in USO shows at forward bases in China and later in India from October to early December 1944.

The men stationed at Peishiyi enjoyed the two-hour performance of Camp Show #374 on October 30 in the Chinese Recreation Hall (where the anniversary celebration was held), which had dressing rooms in addition to its stage. Capt. MacNeil later commented that Jinx "couldn't do much but look pretty," although he, and likely the other audience members, considered that to be "quite enough."[3] Hank brought home several photos of the entertainers (the females, that is) and remembered them well. Lt. Young commented the following day, "The boys are still talking about the show we saw here yesterday. It was really something to talk about for a while and we could stand more of the same type of entertainment, especially the singing and dancing. Even seeing a civilian these days makes you feel funny."

The 1st Bomb Group historical officer, 1Lt. Howard T. Chenoweth, included his own praise and recapped the show in the month's historical report. He wrote that Pat's Irish stories, impersonation of famed Notre Dame football coach Knute Rockne, and accounts of the great coach's life were received with great enthusiasm. Jinx was "very decorative and also received a big hand." Ruth Carrell and Jimmy Dodd "really stole the show." He played the guitar, and they both sang many late songs and were "much in demand" by their enthusiastic audience. Ruth was "one of the loveliest entertainers it's been our pleasure to view." Harry Brown "sang several nice songs and had a very good voice." The other member of the troop, Betty Yeaton, "literally tied herself in knots for us. She too was very lovely and received a big hand for her efforts in our behalf."

In addition to their pleasure at viewing the three attractive females, audience members particularly enjoyed O'Brien's humorous stories, and Young chronicled several. Some of them involved ethnic humor, which was not considered offensive at that time but represented good, clean fun.

One favorite was about a battalion that stood review every day. The major in charge stepped out in front each morning and roared the command "'ATTALION ATTENTION!" This went on daily until one day as he called out "'ATTALION ATTENTION!," a little guy way down in back started walking around and kicking up dirt. Again the major gave the command, and still the little guy walked around kicking up dirt and talking to himself. The major instructed his aide to bring the soldier forward. "What's the matter with you, soldier?" asked the major.

"You always so a pick on me," said the little guy. "Every day, I'm a da guy you so holler at."

"But," said the major, "I've never picked on you."

"Da hell a you don't," replied the little guy. "Same a thing every day always, 'ITALIAN ATTENTION!'"

Left to right: Jinx Falkenburg, Betty Yeaton, and Ruth Carrell, female performers of Camp Show #374, were well received by their appreciative audience. Hank occasionally mentioned them in the years that followed, and his wife, Nancy, always seemed a bit jealous because of his enthusiastic comments. *J. H. Mills collection*

The Hollywood troupe received high praise, not only for their performances but also for their positive interaction with the soldiers whom they entertained. This stood in marked contrast to the negative publicity garnered by actress Ann Sheridan and her entourage in August, when the performer had voiced her dissatisfactions concerning scheduling and accommodations. In a review published in *CBI Roundup*, a New York drama critic wrote, "The players gave every indication of having a good time, as well as providing one, and that adds decidedly to any audience's fun." He concluded, "All in all, the O'Brien-Falkenburg Co. gave not only a good show but accomplished considerably more than that. . . . They showed themselves good sports and good fellows, everyone here liked them enormously and the GIs will go back home feeling better about the theater and its people."[4]

Mier and Magyar pose with a group of Chinese that includes Sgt. Ho (*standing, second from left*) and others (*unidentified*) in front of a B-25H, A/C #717. *R. N. Solyn collection, courtesy of Robert N. Solin*

Most events into the following month were routine. Capt. Seacrest, Sgt. Whearty, and Cpl. Trout missed the big show, off on an "XC [cross-country] flight" for detached duty to Hanchung and returning the following day. Sgt. Fox and Cpls. Ryan and Magyar were placed on flying status. SSgt. Duffin, whose duties as personnel NCO required him to maintain current individual service records, morning reports, and sick reports, was assigned responsibility as squadron mail orderly in addition to his other duties. TSgt. Hanrahan was promoted to master sergeant, Sgt. Hoke to staff sergeant, and Cpls. Learn, Rickman, and Trout to sergeants. Lt. Young was sick in quarters with his third bout of malaria since he had been attached to the squadron, and Lt. Pulaski and SSgt. Haines were others noted as sick in quarters. Capt. Kelso was appointed administrative inspector to replace Capt. Goeller, and Lt. Faherty was appointed fire marshal as Lt. Dorr's replacement.

Kelso's efforts as finance officer evidently paid off, because the men received their pay according to schedule on November 1, with "no waiting like last month." A mass was conducted in the enlisted men's hostel by a priest, J. M. O'Connor, who had made his way through the mud. "If you could but see the roads they have to travel you would appreciate more the work these missionaries are doing in foreign countries," Young commented.

As the month progressed and rain continued its daily drizzle, the weather turned colder. The hostels had no stoves, so some of the men made their own charcoal-burning stoves similar to those used at Kweilin. Lt. Chenoweth noted, "We still haven't received the stoves for our quarters, and many are buying charcoal to burn in improvised stoves, made from cans. It helps a great deal." Enterprising Chinese entrepreneurs reacted predictably to the increased demand. Three days later Chenoweth wrote, "We might have expected it. The Chinese have raised the price of charcoal on us since so many have been buying it to heat their rooms, in their home-made stoves." Some of the men made an effort to winterize their quarters by nailing cardboard over broken windowpanes, but their attempts to drive out the damp chill met with limited success.

The list of men awarded the Good Conduct Medal was amended to include Capts. Cunningham and Ragland, 1Lt. Baker, 2Lts. Edgerton and Senecal, and SSgt. McCann. Several Chinese officers and enlisted men were added by the same orders: 1Lts. Ouyang Chun and Shen Chiu-jang, SLt. Chang Huang-lu, and Sgts. Liu Ting-wen, Ho Wei-ching, Wang Ching-chuan, Wang Tsung-chang, Teng Chiu-cheng, Tso Jui-chen, Tuan Ysai-pang, and Su Chai-yu. Capt. Seacrest, Lt. Pulaski, MSgt. Hanrahan, and Cpl. Trout left for Bangalore to pick up another new plane.

Movie nights continued to provide a welcome diversion, and *Swing Fever*, starring Kay Kaiser, was one of the "shows" that the men enjoyed during this time. A break in the weather permitted five planes into the air for formation flying on the eleventh—the first time that month. The film for the following evening was *Government Girl*, starring Olivia De Havilland. A three-ball alert was called at 2314. The all-clear was given after an hour and six minutes, allowing the tired men to return to their beds. Classified as aerial gunnery instructor, 2Lt. Jerome G. Cantor was attached in mid-November. Cpl. Piecuch returned from Liangshan but was transferred to the wing about a week later. TSgt. Shock was detached on special service to the 1st Bomb Squadron at Hanchung. Col. Russell organized softball teams in the 3rd and 4th Squadrons and group headquarters the following week, in an attempt to boost morale. Games were usually played on Wednesday afternoons, when the men were given a half day off, and on Sunday afternoons.

Maj. Archie H. McGray, group intelligence officer, conducted orientation for new aircrew personnel recently assigned to the 3rd and 4th Squadrons as November drew to a close. "As always with new personnel, they are eager to get in their lick at the enemy," wrote Lt. Chenoweth. Lt. Wood was assigned additional duty as assistant operations officer, and Lt. Cantor as assistant gunnery officer. Explaining the frustrations associated with instructing Chinese enlisted men in the intricacies of gunnery, Cantor said in an interview soon after his return home to New Jersey: "We did it with interpreters—or tried to. It was pretty discouraging to talk for several minutes to the students, stressing the points which needed to be stressed, and then have the interpreter go over the same ground in four or five sentences. You just knew he could not have told them everything you had said."[5]

More replacements arrived and were attached: 2Lt. Robert L. Logan as B-25 pilot, 1Lt. Willard G. Ilefeldt as B-25 pilot / flight leader, and Cpl. Robert E. Schlicher Jr. as A/P mechanic–gunner–flight engineer. Another three-ball alert interrupted the men's sleep, although no enemy planes ever materialized. Maj. McGray gave the first of what became weekly summaries of war events that had occurred through the past week in various theaters.

The establishment of the new China theater under Maj. Gen. Wedemeyer the previous month had brought no immediate or revolutionary changes to the wing's rank and file, although some administrative changes were instituted that had to do primarily with expenditures, reports, issuance of orders, and other procedural matters. A new directive insisted that medals be awarded as "recognition of the performance of duty or an act of heroism above and beyond normal expectations" and not passed out as freely as in the past.

"The unit was not anything like you see on TV," Hank reminisced. "There were just a few officers. I think there was a total of fifty-two people, enlisted and officers. And there was none of that jumping up and saying 'Sir' every time an officer came. We spoke with one another just like friends. They called me 'Hey, Sarge.' I called them 'Lieutenant'—'Captain'—that's all. There was none of that military stuff like you see in the movies. It was a different outfit. We were all friends." Although Chennault insisted on perfection in the air, he had never been a stickler about protocol or regulations in his command. Wedemeyer, who commanded his outfit "by the book" and required the same of those who served under him, intended to change all of that.

It was at about this time that the men stationed at Peishiyi began to notice a new emphasis on matters that had become merely routine, beginning with directives on military discipline, military courtesy, and proper uniform and military appearance. The salute between enlisted men and officers, long fallen into disuse, was reinstated. The casual attitude toward dress and familiarity between officers and enlisted men began to disappear with the appearance of the snapped salute. The inevitable caste system of the army, which "had been worn rather smooth by long months of close in-living and by long daily hours of working together in crowded hostels and in an overcrowded headquarters," began to reassert itself, according to Maj. Hummel.

"Inevitably at a working forward base such as this, a comradery grows up, perhaps merely because the facilities for maintaining the separate life in proper style with proper military swank simply do not exist. Struggling through the same mud, eating the same food, and grubbing in the same dirt and grime brings men together," he explained. "However, the transition was effected, after several explanatory lectures by different officers, which, it was noted, struck somewhat the apologetic 'Mother-knows-best' keynote of 'You're not going to like this, but it is good for you.'"

Chungking (27°26'29" N, 109°41'59" E), perched on mountainous terrain at the confluence of the Chialing (Jialing) and Yangtze Rivers in Szechuan Province of central China, had been heavily bombed earlier in the war. Evidence could still be seen in the "jerrybuilt" houses that gave it the appearance of "a vast sprawling slum." Unbearably hot and humid in the summer and bitterly cold in the winter, it was reputed to have the worst climate of any city in the world. "For seven months of the year it is buried beneath a constant dirty fog with almost an unbroken drool of rain that covers the Yangtse river like an evil pall," wrote a wartime visitor.[6] Yet, the city held attractions to the men stationed at Peishiyi whose interest had little to do with the weather forecast.

The 30-mile trip from Peishiyi to Chungking was usually accomplished via weapons carrier over rutted and pitted mountain roads. Fertile valleys far below that could be glimpsed from under the canvas cover did not quite atone for the "teeth-rattling misery of the ride," and the "over-crowded, war-torn, and pauperized town" was a disappointment, according to Hummel. The promise of steaks, ice cream, mixed cold drinks, and women provided the enticement to make the uncomfortable trip for the deprived and bored GI who was "tired of fried eggs and buffalo meat, tired of guzzling vodka in his monastic compound."

Passes, carefully and judiciously portioned out among all personnel, were granted for overnight visits to Chungking, as described in the 1st Bomb Group historical report. "A little town, only two torturous hours from Peishiyi, where is situated the war time capitol of China. A quaint town is Chungking with its little rickshaw pullers to haul the heavy Americans around. There we can get our fill of Ice Cream (at a price of course) (costing 900N or the equivalent of $2.25 at the legal rate of exchange or almost $ .50 at the rate that is obtainable at the Black Market)." An excellent dinner of steak and french fried potatoes was also available to visitors, as well as fresh fruits that included watermelons, apples, pears, peaches, plums, and bananas if they looked hard enough, he wrote. "Oh yes, and then the best part of it is we can get ice cold drinks. Ice in our drinks of lemon soda and Vodka! That and the Ice Cream is worth that long, dirty, and tiresome ride from Peishiyi to Chungking."

Wilkie and Hank enjoy a rickshaw ride on one of their visits to the city, as a photographer from the Ru Ru Photo Co. (*in the background*) records the event. J. H. Mills collection

Hank related an incident involving the rickshaw boys in town. "I remember one time in Chungking, coolies were pulling a rickshaw and had a big man in there." Because of the passenger's size, it took three of them to pull him. They started laughing and calling him *da biza*, meaning "big nose," Hank recalled with a grin. "And they were laughing at that man they said was 'big nose'—*da biza*." The term was used not only to describe a facial feature of abnormally large size but also as a humorous reference to a foreigner. The big GI had less appreciation for the joke since he had no understanding of Mandarin, but Hank laughed at the humor of it decades afterward.

Some of the men from his squadron "went out on the town" and "went to the places where the girls were." He explained simply, "I didn't. I was married." Typical of all towns in proximity to military installations, Chungking had a thriving red-light district, and many GIs made the long, miserable trip to go "catting." Considered to be slightly less sordid than the typical row of dirty huts where the "you-say-how-much girls" plied their trade were the bathhouses, where GIs could satisfy their sanitary requirements as well as their hormonal urges. Each basement room of the bathhouses had not only a large tub, but also a narrow bed. After scrubbing the back of her client, the prostitute retired with him to the bed to complete the transaction.

Hummel wrote that those who did not go "catting" generally divided their time between the Victory House, where they could obtain meals in a patio at awninged tables, or they could sit on tall stools at a little bar inside the Sino-American Club, which similarly provided a restaurant, reading room, and a dormitory. At the Sing Sing, GIs could enjoy ice cream (more nearly resembling sherbets or ices) of whatever flavor happened to be on hand, and tall, cool glasses of orange juice were available too. The Russian Café, across from the Sing Sing, was a basement restaurant set in a courtyard back from the street where customers could order thick, juicy steaks for a reasonable price, although a cup of coffee cost the same as a filet mignon. The Friends of the Allied Forces was a hostel that provided "clean sleeping quarters, a neat restaurant, an expansive, rather elaborate courtyard with a stage from which occasionally movies, concerts, and programs of interest to Chinese and Americans were given."

The Chialing House, which took its name from one of Chungking's rivers that intersects the Yangtze, was probably the most sumptuous hotel that the GIs visited in the city. Its bar featured a larger selection of liquors and mixed drinks than any other nightspot in Chungking. It also served excellent food. An added attraction was that it was a favorite among white women who were employees of the embassies perched high on the South Bank near the headquarters of Generalissimo Chiang. Other than these, who were in great demand, stateside women in the area consisted almost exclusively of Army nurses, Red Cross workers, and missionaries.

"Two men that I was friends with, we went out together some," Hank remembered. He had been friends with Barge and Wilkerson since they began working together at Malir, and the three often planned outings to break the monotony of camp life whenever they had the opportunity. It was during this period of inactivity that they decided to go into town. Hank described the outing: "I remember, one day Wilkerson, Barge, and me, it was outside of Chungking, and there was a mountain between Chungking and this base where we were, and we decided to go to Chungking to get something to eat." Rather than taking the long trip by weapons carrier, they hired coolies to convey them by sedan chair. "And those coolies had carriers with long poles with a man on each end—a man with a long pole on each side with a seat in the middle—and they carried us from there across a mountain to Chungking. And they'd walk these—kind of a little levee between the rice paddies, and we'd be up there." He described the coolies who carried the sedan chairs as "nothing but just looked like muscles, just skin and muscle, and they carried us over that mountain and down to Chungking, and they did that all for pennies." Hank and his buddies enjoyed their meal, "and of course, we had to ride back with some more coolies that had us on those seats."

Hank retained clear memories of his visits to town: "I used to see dog hides nailed up on the side of the houses. They ate dog or cat. You'd be walking down the street and see someone coming and think they had a couple of cats in their arms. It wasn't a couple of cats. It was a couple of cat's-hide gloves. Cats were valuable. They kept a string tied around their necks, tied to a chair or the table. They didn't run loose. They were rat catchers."

Cats were pampered and often lived much better than some humans. In Chungking, a full-grown cat was worth $2,500 CN or more each. "They were so scarce that a peddler with a basket-cage or two full of snarling, spitting beasts sells them all in a street or two of walking," a service publication reported. In the daytime, the owner of a cat kept it tied near him on a long, heavy string to prevent it from being stolen or from wandering away. At night it was free to wander around the locked-up house to "do its duty against rats."[7]

Most of the men, after making the arduous trip to Chungking a few times, chose to return only rarely or not at all. The shops were generally poorly stocked and unimpressive, and prices were scandalously out of proportion to the worth of the goods available. The GIs had ridden in the rickshaws and bought their souvenirs, and they had made the rounds of the restaurants, bars, and whatever other attractions that appealed to them. After having satisfied their curiosity, many chose to remain thereafter at Peishiyi.

Task Force 34's first combat mission took off from Chihkiang at 0720 on November 9. Capt. Lyon, with a 4th Squadron crew, was in the lead of three Mitchells, each carrying twenty-two 100 lb. demolition bombs fused instantaneous at the nose. No serial numbers, "Chinese numbers," or model numbers for the aircraft were provided in mission reports, although they included the two 3rd Squadron B-25Js, according to the squadron's historical report. They can be identified as serial #43-27809, A/C #714, and #43-3939, A/C #722. Capt. Ragland flew one of the wing planes with 2Lt. Senecal as his copilot, Capt. Cunningham as bombardier, 2Lt. Young C. H. as navigator, and SSgt. McCann and Sgts. Tso J. C. and Taun Y. P. as gunners (all 3rd Squadron except Young). Lt. Baker was pilot of the third Mitchell, with Capt. Shen C. J. as copilot, 2Lt. Edgerton as navigator, Cpl. Allegretto as turret gunner, Ho W. C. as waist gunner, and Wang C. L. as tail gunner (all 3rd Squadron). Operational intelligence reports for Task Force 34 during its brief period of operations provide evidence that most missions involved crews that were "mixed" to include not only both nationalities but also members of both squadrons, although some missions were made up of single-nationality or single-squadron crews. Missions were credited to the squadron represented by the pilot of the lead plane.

The objective of this mission was to bomb storage areas near Yiyang (Jieyang), northwest of Shatow (Shantou) in Kwangtung Province. Twelve 5th Fighter Group P-40s flew escort. Lyon's navigator had difficulty in locating the exact target, since it was on a dike beside a stream, and the area was flooded and covered with a network of dikes, streams, and canals. Incendiary bombs that were dropped to mark the target failed to explode, and there was no other satisfactory checkpoint. The Mitchells came in on a south-to-north bomb run at 6,000 feet indicated at 190 mph ground speed and intervalometer set at 150. As the lead bombardier was attempting to pick up the target, he accidentally tripped the release mechanism (set to drop in train), and the others dropped on his lead. Sixty-one of the bombs fell short, inflicting only minor damage to a village south of the target. Five bombs that hung up in the racks and failed to release were jettisoned. The planes were back down without mishap at 0930. McCann later explained that in addition to being extremely dangerous, returning with bombs that could not be dropped on target meant that the mission had not been completed and its participants were not given credit for it.[8]

A second mission, with the 4th Squadron's 1Lt. Portaluppi flying the lead plane, Capt. Lyon as his copilot, and 2Lt. Edgerton (who listed this as his fourth combat mission) as navigator, was off at 1137 on the ninth. The formation, flying without escort, again included the two 3rd Squadron Mitchells. Lt. Baker was pilot of the first wing plane, with SLt. Chang K. L. as copilot, 2Lt. S. A. Lipira as navigator (the crew's only 4th Squadron member), and Cpl. Allegretto, Ho W. C., and Wang C. C. as gunners, while 2Lt. Senecal flew in second wing

Lt. Charles J. Portaluppi, Task Force 34 historian and flight leader (*center*), and Moncure N. Lyon, its commanding officer and flight leader (*right*), chat with an unidentified GI in front of their hostel at Chihkiang. The three were 4th Bomb Squadron personnel. *M. N. Lyon collection, courtesy of Kelly Lyon*

Cold weather prompts Sgt. James E. McCann to wear his flight jacket, with its "skunk patch" clearly visible. Here he wears a CAF cap that was a gift from a Chinese friend. *Courtesy of Mark E. McCann*

Lt. Leo C. Baker, 3rd Squadron pilot (*left*), and Lt. Salvatore A. Lipira, 4th Squadron navigator-bombardier (*right*), stand in front of their hostel at Chihkiang. *Alfred A. Magyar collection, courtesy of Lynn Magyar Zwigard*

Lt. Thomas H. Edgerton, navigator-bombardier, flew many successful Task Force 34 missions from November 1944 to January 1945. He later transferred to the 4th Bomb Squadron and continued to fly missions out of Chihkiang. *T. H. Edgerton collection, courtesy of Wendi Borst*

position, with Capt. Ragland as his copilot, Capt. Cunningham as bombardier, 2Lt. Young C. H. (4th Squadron) as navigator, and SSgt. McCann and Sgts. Tso J. C. and Taun Y. P. as gunners. Each plane carried twenty-two 100 lb. demolition bombs. The objective of the mission was again to hit the storage area near Shatow, which was located this time without undue difficulty. Because of "the extreme narrowness" of the target, the bombers made two passes, both from north to south. The first was a practice run. Bombs were dropped on Edgerton's lead on the second run at 1301 from 5,700 feet at 185 mph indicated air speed. The gyroscope of his bombsight failed, resulting in an error in deflection of 200 yards to the right. Most of the bombs fell east of the storage facilities, and the only damage was to a house at the extreme edge of the target area, reported as destroyed. Crewmen observed meager and inaccurate automatic-weapons fire over the target, 1,500 feet below and trailing. The return flight was without incident except that one plane experienced minor engine trouble caused by defective spark plugs. All were down at 1405.

Maj. Hummel wrote that the "relative flop" of these early missions was because the crews were "out of practice, over-anxious, and tense" after two months of enforced idleness. Lt. Portaluppi, who was the task force's historical officer as well as flight leader, explained:

> As soon as the weather broke, the Fighters were more than eager to have Bomber Task Force 34 . . . do some bombing for them. Coming in the wake of almost two months dreary inactivity, this was welcome news to us. However, much to our dismay, the first two missions proved to be slight duds due to a combination of factors: smallness of the target, tenseness on the part of inexperienced navigator-bombardiers, and bombsight malfunctions. On both occasions we missed the target and felt rather bad about it. We were afraid that our stock would be lowered in the estimation of our confreres in peashooters, and we became even a trifle overanxious to prove ourselves.

On high-altitude bombing missions such as this, the Norden bombsight significantly increased accuracy for dropping the B-25s' bombs. This device used a mechanical analog computer made up of motors, gyros, mirrors, levels, gears, and a small telescope. The bombardier input the necessary data (airspeed, altitude, etc.) and the bombsight calculated the trajectory of the bomb to be dropped. Near the target, the aircraft flew on autopilot to the precise position calculated by the bombsight and released the ordnance. When using a correctly functioning bombsight, bombardiers could drop their bombs within a 100-foot circle from an altitude of well over 20,000 feet.[9]

On a third mission that included 3rd Squadron personnel on that date, Lt. Baker took off aboard a B-25J at 2025 with seventeen fragmentation bomb clusters to alert and harass motor vehicle traffic in the Hsiang valley. His copilot was SLt. Chang H. L., with Capt. Cunningham as navigator-bombardier, Cpl. Jackson as turret gunner, Sgt. England as waist gunner, and Sgt. Ho W. C. as tail gunner (all 3rd Squadron crewmen). The general purpose of this mission was to test the feasibility of night operations without moonlight. On the outbound flight, the bomber let down from 10,000 to 2,500 feet after reaching Siangtan (Xiangtan) and turned north.

Crewmen sighted the lights of a convoy of from twenty to thirty vehicles near Lukow. By the time the plane could make a 180-degree turn and come back, nearly all the lights had been extinguished. Cunningham dropped six clusters, setting ablaze at least one truck and probably destroying or damaging several others. Baker continued north, bypassed Changsha to the east, and proceeded to Siangyin. There he turned south on the west bank of the Hsiang to Siangtang and then turned north again over the same route. Northeast of Changsha, crewmen spotted the lights of a convoy of about ten vehicles. The pilot dropped four cluster bombs on a south-to-north run at 2,500 feet parallel and very close to the convoy, probably inflicting heavy damage. Baker again turned south on the west bank of the river "because time was running short," encountering intense fire from a variety of small arms and automatic weapons north of Yoloshan opposite Changsha, so he turned to drop the seven remaining clusters on a run toward the south at 4,000 feet. Fire was silenced. AA and ground fire of varying degrees of intensity came up from many points along the river on the return, but Baker put the plane down safely at 0010.

Portaluppi praised Lt. Baker for this and later night missions. "Subsequent night operations proved successful[,] and although both Capt. Lyon and Lt. Portaluppi had achieved some highly gratifying results on several operations, it was to Lt. Baker of the Third Squadron that most credit was due. He continued to amaze us by his unusual night vision and by his propensity to dropping frags right on top of trucks in a convoy[,] thus starting many a fire."

An auto mechanic in Indianapolis before enlisting in the Air Corps in late 1940, Baker was trained as an aviation mechanic and served in the Panama Canal Zone for twenty-two months. Following training as an aviation cadet, he received his commission and wings in late August 1943 and arrived in the CBI later that year. Originally attached to the 22nd Bomb Squadron, 341st Bomb Group, one of his early combat missions was as pilot of a B-25H on April 15, 1944, to hit a railroad bridge 15 to 20 miles northeast of Hanoi. His bombardier-navigator, James M. White, described him as "probably the best 75 mm gunner in the Air Corps." Although weather was "abominable"—rain, sleet, hail, and heavy turbulence—Baker spotted the river through a hole in the clouds and started a tight, spiraling descent. "The pucker factor was high as we knew the valley through which the river flowed to be no more than two to three miles wide with mountains rising on both sides," White wrote. "From time to time the clouds completely obscured our vision. It was cold in the cockpit but, looking over at Lee, I could see beads of sweat running off his nose. As for me, I could feel a steady stream running the length of my spine." Despite heavy ground fire and "tracers whistling past us," Baker took out a "rapid-firing, multi-cannon type [of] antiaircraft installation" and a machine gun emplacement with the cannon and then destroyed one span of the bridge and seriously damaged the other with 1,000 lb. high-explosive bombs on two passes. "Needless to say, the brass of the 22nd Bomb Squadron were highly skeptical when told of our results," White wrote. It was only after confirming photographs were submitted that they received credit for the destruction.

Many years later, Baker described these early missions undertaken by young, inexperienced aircrews: "A bunch of kids in a hot rod is what it was." He remembered a bailout soon afterward, when it took thirty days for the crew to walk back to their base. A boy no older than thirteen led them around Japanese emplacements and back to American lines, he said. "The boy would only accept a fountain pen for his service," Baker recalled in a newspaper interview conducted in the mid-1970s. He admitted to being terrified, in spite of speaking casually about bailing out and moving behind enemy lines.[10]

Baker's November 9 raid was the first of many "moonless night missions," initially suggested by Col. Dunning, to be undertaken by Task Force 34. Col. Dunning concluded that these were not only practical but profitable in spite of the added risks involved. As a result, most of the succeeding missions were night single-plane strikes at river, rail, and road traffic in the Hsiang valley and from Hankow to Kweilin. Although night missions had been accomplished prior to this, none had been attempted without moonlight. On these moonless night missions, total darkness and extremely limited radio-homing facilities made it imperative that the navigator never lose track of the plane's position. These missions proved so successful that they became a specialty of Task Force 34. An often-lamented disadvantage was that crews were seldom able to determine the extent of damage caused by the raids because they consistently encountered severely limited visibility.

On any mission, the navigator was considered to be the most critical member of the crew because it was his responsibility to find the target and then guide the plane back to home base. His duties in accomplishing this goal included calibration of instruments such as the altimeter, all compasses, and airspeed indicators, and alignment of the astrocompass, astrograph, and drift meter, as well as checking his watch and sextant for correct function, monitoring weather conditions, preparing a flight plan in close cooperation with the pilot, and keeping a flight log. It was essential that he be aware of the exact position of the airplane in relation to the earth at all times, determining geographic positions by means of pilotage, dead reckoning, radio, or celestial navigation, or any combination of these methods. Even under the best conditions, he had to overcome difficulties created by charts that were often inaccurate and lacked detail, no radio homers except around a few bases (and these were often distorted by the mountains), no radar or other navigational aids, and incorrect weather forecasts (especially upper winds). These limitations were multiplied on night missions without moonlight, when the navigator had to rely even more heavily on instruments. So dangerous was this kind of flying that a 4th Squadron B-25 later crashed into a hillside only minutes after takeoff from Chihkiang. 2Lt. Salvatore A. Lipira, detachment navigator who participated in the task force's second mission with Lt. Baker and many others, was one of a six-member crew who lost their lives only six months after this first moonless night mission.

Skies at Peishiyi were clear and bright on the eleventh—Armistice Day, then commemorating the end of World War I and now celebrated as Memorial Day—so Capt. Ragland flew in that morning to pick up spare airplane parts, maps, mail, and other needed items before returning to Chihkiang later in the day. Lt. Chenoweth wrote, "We all pause to think of [the day's] significance and renew our determination to keep faith with our comrades who have given their lives in the cause of freedom." The discouraging news came that Liuchow (Luizhou), 100 miles from Kweilin, had been captured by the Japanese 23rd Army as it moved west.

Two Mitchells, including #43-5049, A/C #710, piloted by Lt. Portaluppi, in the lead, followed by the 3rd Squadron's #722, were off Chihkiang at 0945 on November 16. Sgt. Liang Y. T., turret gunner on the wing plane, was the only participating member of the 3rd Squadron. Each plane carried six 500 lb. demos to attack the railroad bridge north of Chuchow. The Mitchells were escorted to the vicinity of Hengyang by eleven 75th Fighter Squadron P-51s and then on to the target by four of the fighters. The bombers were over the target at 1122 and made separate runs, all from south to north at about 250 feet and nearly parallel to the bridge. On his first run, Portaluppi dropped three that were over, one of them close to the end of the bridge. On his second run, the other three were near misses, straddling the bridge and falling in the river. Lt. Chao made four runs. On the first three, bombs hung up in the racks; on the fourth pass he salvoed and all were near misses into the river. Gunners strafed twenty railroad cars south of the bridge, camouflaged with green branches, followed by strafing of houses around the bridge and two 30-foot sailboats opposite Chuchow. Escort and bombers returned to base, down at 1240.

Two crews were briefed on November 16, but Lyon's plane, the 3rd Squadron's A/C #714, was unable to take off. Ragland was off aboard the 4th Squadron's B-25J, #43-36069, A/C #711 (with Senecal, Cunningham, Young, McCann, Jackson, and Wang C. C. as his crew), at 1645 with twenty-two 100 lb. M47A2 incendiary bombs. His objective was to destroy enemy stores and installations at Isuho, about 30 miles south of Changsha, and then to harass motor vehicle traffic in the vicinity, but he turned back a short distance out because of failure of the remote compass.

Lt. Edgerton's flight log listed two missions on November 17. He was Ragland's navigator aboard the 3rd Squadron's A/C #722, off at 0945 in the lead of a four-plane formation. Others of the crew were 2Lt. Chao S. T., 4th Squadron copilot, as well as Cunningham, McCann, Jackson, and Wang C. C., all 3rd Squadron. Following were A/C #710, the 4th Squadron's B-25H (2nd Lts. Chiu S. C. and Hu H. T., Sgts. Shia P. K. and Liang Y. T., and Cpl. Chang Y. C.; all 4th Squadron except Liang); A/C #711, the 4th Squadron J model (Baker, 2Lt. Chang K. A., 1Lt. Sze E. C., Cpl. Yue C. K., England, and MSgt. E. C. Bradley; 4th Squadron crew except Baker and England); and A/C #714, the 3rd Squadron's second J (2Lt. Chang K. L., 2Lts. Tu K. M. and Young C. H., and Ho W. C., Tso J. C., and Taun T. P.; all 3rd Squadron except Young). They flew in diamond formation to the target, carrying a bombload of forty-four 100 lb. demolition bombs, seventeen M41 stabilized fragmentation bomb clusters, four 500 lb. M69 incendiary bomb clusters, and two 100 lb. M50A1 incendiary bomb clusters. The bombers were escorted and covered by eleven P-40s of the 27th Fighter Squadron. The target was enemy installations, stores, and personnel in the easterly section of Hengshan.

On their first approach, the bombers overran the target and Cunningham was unable to release. They flew past the target and then turned 180 degrees and made a bombing run at 1015 from the opposite direction, releasing the demos and frags. More than 95 percent were on target, the pattern lying between the waterfront and the principal street parallel to it. The incendiaries failed to release, so Baker reversed and made another pass that resulted in a good dispersion. Crewmen reported five or six small secondary explosions, and smoke rose to 2,000 feet. The fighters left the formation after escorting the bombers out of enemy territory. The B-25s returned to base and were on the ground at 1115.

McCann, Ragland's top turret gunner on this mission, provided details of operations during this period in a postwar interview. Their B-25Js were "all silver (not camouflaged)," he revealed. "We started doubling up the bombload by using wire snappings to hold a second bomb on the bomb hooked off the station," he stated, and they did not salvo any bombs with the arming wire still on the bases. "All of our arming wires were wired to the bomb shackle so that everything we dropped was live. If the weather was socked in on the primary target, we tried the secondary, and if that was socked in, we brought our bombload back and never salvoed any bombs, but landed with them in the bomb bay because they were a scarce commodity." It was sometimes impossible to close the bomb bay doors with the double loads, but "we flew anyhow," he said. "A lot of times on the short fighter runways we would put up the gear, and it was either fly or belly it in the rice paddy. Our pilots made 'em fly anyway."

McCann explained, "We were the crazy ones. We flew the missions no one else wanted. We landed up and down the valley or you flew into a mountain. We learned to trust the Chinese navigator." Referring to raids against enemy supply movements, he said, "The Japs just couldn't learn to drive a truck at night without lights."[11]

On a second mission that day, the detachment's four Mitchells were off at 1500 and flew in two elements to hit separate targets. Flying A/C #711, Ragland led one flight, with Tu, Young, Cunningham, Jackson, Wang, and Taun, and #A/C #714 (Chang, Chao, Tze, Tso, Ho, and Shia) followed. The H model carried twenty-two 100 lb. M30 demolition bombs, and the J, seventeen 100 lb. M41 stab-frag clusters. Their target was a storage installation consisting of a group of several buildings outside Nanyo.

Scattered to broken clouds drifted at 6,000 feet as planes arrived over the target area at 1615. Capt. Ragland's element made a dry run to identify the target and then dropped three demos to the west at 3,000 feet. All were direct hits, although incendiaries of the wing plane failed to release. Both aircraft salvoed their remaining bombs on a third pass, and all hit the target. Crewmen reported fires and smoke rising to several hundred feet, but their view was cut off by the mountains as the Mitchells headed back to base.

The other element—led by Capt. Lyon aboard A/C #710, with Edgerton as navigator and England as tail gunner, and A/C #722, with Portaluppi as pilot and Senecal as copilot—carried twenty-two 100 lb. M47A2 incendiary bombs on the H and seventeen M41 stab-frag clusters on the J to attack a barracks area near Nanyo. Following a dry run, Capt. Lyon's element dropped all its bombs on the second pass. A good coverage of the barracks area resulted, although some overshot into nearby rice paddies. There were no fires, but crewmen observed substantial damage to the buildings. Both aircraft then strafed the area. Lyon fired one round of 75 mm HE on six to eight tanks spotted on the Hengyang Road, and his crew observed many strikes from .50-caliber fire. He then shot up a "probable motor pool" in a grove of trees. The aircraft attacked a number of large buildings in the area, Lyon with four rounds of 75 mm HE and then collectively firing several hundred rounds of .50 caliber. The only opposition was inaccurate machine gun fire from two positions. The Chinese tail gunner of Portaluppi's aircraft reported seeing a single enemy fighter at some distance while over the target. The flights returned to base separately, and both were down safely.

On the following day, Baker led four B-25s off at 1352, loaded with sixty-six 100 lb. M30 demolition bombs and twenty-two M47A2 incendiary bombs. Flying A/C #722, his aircrew was made up of Senecal, Cunningham, Edgerton, Jackson, and Ho. Completing the formation were A/C #710 (Chao, Tze, Shia, Chang, and Yue), A/C #714 (Chiu, Tu, Hu, Wang, Tso, and Taun), and A/C #711 (Portaluppi, Chang, Capt. Wei H. S., Lipira, Bradley, and Wilkins). Their objective was to destroy buildings and stores at Isuho Ferry, south of Siangtan. The bombers were escorted by eleven 17th Fighter Squadron P-40s that additionally dive-bombed targets at Chuchow (Zhuzhou).

The formation approached the target area "somewhat to the north" but corrected after a few minutes, making the bomb run at 10,200 feet. Except for two "drifters," all bombs were on target. Because of the conservative 100-foot interval, the pattern was good but "rather concentrated," parallel to the riverbank and extending 1,500 to 2,000 feet up to the Hengshan Road. Two fires, one reported as large, were observed as the formation left the target area, and smoke rose to about 2,000 feet, visible from 10 miles away. Fighters returning later reported several good fires. Antiaircraft fire ranged from moderate and inaccurate to accurate for range and deflection. Five or six bursts were in or near the formation, and twenty to twenty-five bursts trailed. The return flight was without incident.

Lt. Portaluppi wrote about these missions that "full vindication came as Captain Cunningham of the Third Squadron planted our formation's bombs squarely in the middle of a target at Hengshan and later at Isuho. Fighters returning from these missions are enthusiastic in their praise of our work."

Task Force 34's eleventh mission was off at 1908 on the eighteenth. Because the pilot of A/C #711, 2Lt. Chiu S. C., was assigned to the 4th Squadron, the mission was credited to that squadron, although the copilot, Lt. Chang K. L., as well as gunners Wang C. C., Ho W. C., and Tso J. C., were 3rd Squadron crewmen. This was another moonless night mission, its objective to harass motor vehicle traffic and alert the enemy between Siangtan and Changsha. Nearing Hsiang, crewmen spotted a large fire in a village about 25 miles west of Siangtan. Three large fires were burning at Isuho, which had been bombed in midafternoon, and Lt. Chiu released four M41 stabilized frag clusters around the fires to further harass the area and to discourage firefighters. He then moved to the vicinity of Changsha, an important commercial center and capital of Henan Province. Observing no activity there, he returned to the vicinity of Lukow. There the aircrew saw a long string of lights on a road or railroad and immediately attacked it, dropping all thirteen remaining bombs. Five large fires broke out, each apparently involving more than one vehicle. They then scouted the valley from Chutin to Changsha but found no more profitable targets, so they returned to base at 2215. Because of showers and thick overcast between 7,000 and 8,000 feet, the pilot had trouble landing and circled the field for two hours before letting down.

Capt. Ragland was off at 1815 on November 19 as pilot of A/C #722, carrying twenty-two 100 lb. M30 demolition bombs. Other crew members were Baker, Young, Allegretto, and Taun. They flew without fighter escort, as was customary for night missions. Their objective was again to harass motor vehicle traffic and to alert the enemy in the Hsiang valley. After Young navigated by instruments through heavy overcast to find the river, the Mitchell let down to search the vicinity from Siangtan to Changsha and then south of Chuting before turning north again. Baker attacked three truck convoys spotted along the Liling–Anjen road and dropped all bombs from altitudes ranging from 2,500 to 4,000 feet. Fires flared in each convoy. An explosion observed in one was probably from a gasoline tank truck. Gunners strafed a fourth convoy found on the road to Lukow. When the right engine cut out because of fuel pump failure on this pass, made at 1,500 feet, Ragland broke off the attack to gain altitude. After engaging the booster pump, he was able to return to base.

The 17th and 27th Fighter Squadrons, 5th Fighter Group, had trained with the 3rd Squadron and were operating out of the Chihkiang base and flying cover for Task Force 34 missions during this time. A fire that burned down the BOQ (base officers' quarters) and Barracks C on the eighteenth forced fighter personnel to find other accommodations until their quarters could be rebuilt. Japanese fifth columnists reported in the vicinity were suspected of starting the fires. Little was salvaged from the blaze, but the inconvenience did not prevent the fighters from continuing their task of protecting the bombers on missions.

Jerome G. Cantor kept this photo that he captioned "Task Force 34 'Briefing,' Chihkiang, China." It captured informal preparations for a mission against supply facilities on November 20, 1944. According to a notation in the 4th Bomb Squadron historical report, the first two men at the left are MSgt. E. C. Bradley and SSgt. L. L. Fulmer (turret and waist gunners). Next is Lt. S. A. Lipira (navigator), who is pointing out the target on a map. Cpl. A. R. Allegretto (tail gunner) is between him and Lt. W. H. Senecal (pilot), and Lt. C. J. Portaluppi (copilot) is at the far right. Notice the heavy padded jackets and sandals worn by the onlooking Chinese guards. *J. G. Cantor Collection, courtesy of Ronnie Cantor*

On Task Force 34's fifteenth mission, Ragland led a formation of two Mitchells that took off at 1310 on the twentieth to hit enemy stores and installations at Anjen. He flew A/C #711, with Edgerton and Wei (both noted as navigator), Cunningham, McCann, Tso, and Taun as his crew, and Senecal was pilot of A/C #714, with Portaluppi, Lipira, Fulmer, Bradley, and Allegretto. Eleven 17th Fighter Squadron P-40s flew escort. One Mitchell carried twenty-two 100 lb. M30 demos, and the other carried twenty-two M47A2 incendiary bombs. Clouds over the target area forced bombing altitude to be decreased to 4,200 feet. An excellent pattern resulted. All bombs fell on the target and covered most of the city area along the waterfront of the river for 1,500 feet. Black smoke that turned to gray and white rose to 500 feet and could be seen for 15 miles at 5,000 feet.

Lt. Baker, with 2Lts. Senecal and Edgerton as his copilot and navigator and two 4th Squadron gunners, again pounded convoys in the Hsiang valley on the twentieth. Baker took off at 1815 aboard A/C #722, carrying seventeen M41 stabilized frag clusters. When crewmen spotted a truck convoy north of Changsha, Edgerton sighted for range and deflection and Baker dropped four bombs individually, resulting in a large fire that could be seen from 35 miles at 3,000 feet. Moderate and accurate small-arms and automatic-weapons fire hit the bomber as it passed over the convoy, causing minor damage. About 30 miles farther north, the pilot dropped eight clusters on a second truck convoy. When crewmen observed about fifty trucks near Nanyo, he toggled the remaining bombs, producing an excellent pattern. Gunners strafed a fourth convoy of about thirty-five vehicles before the Mitchell returned to base.

Capt. Cunningham returned to Peishiyi from duty with Task Force 34 on November 21, and Sgts. England and Peters were again detached to Chihkiang. At 2005 on that date, Lt. Ragland was off in the same B-25J and carrying the same bombload as on the mission of the previous day. Flying as copilot was 2Lt. Tung S. L., and Cpl. Jackson and Sgt. Chow K. Y. were gunners (all 3rd Squadron). Both listed as navigators, 2Lt. M. A. Doran and Young C. H. made up the 4th Squadron component. It was a typical mission targeting enemy convoys. Ragland made four releases over Changsha, starting three small fires. He hit a convoy south of Siangyin, one fire resulting, and then attacked another north of Changsha as gunners strafed. Intense to moderate small-arms and machine gun fire encountered along the river and railroad at Changsha was inaccurate. Ragland took up a homeward course at Siangtan, down at 2350.

Carrying twelve M41 stabilized frag clusters, Capt. Lyon took off in the 3rd Squadron's A/C #722 at 1805 on the twenty-second. With him were the 68th Composite Wing's Maj. A. T. House as observer and copilot and a crew that included Sgt. Peters and Cpl. Allegretto as waist and tail gunners, as well as the 4th Squadron's Capt. Wei as navigator and SSgt. Weinert as top-turret gunner. They had volunteered for this hazardous mission without knowing the specifics of what it entailed until the briefing just before takeoff. It was a joint mission with the 68th Composite Wing that included twenty-two B-24s of the 308th Bomb Group (H) and two P-51s of the 75th Fighter Squadron, 23rd Fighter Group. Weather en route and over the target was noted as "CAVU" ("ceiling and visibility unlimited") with "good moonlight." Their destination was Hankow-Wuchang ("Wuhan"), an important transportation and distribution hub formerly used as headquarters of the Kuomintang government but now occupied by the Japanese. Its factories, warehouses, and stockpiles were the target of countless 14th Air Force raids throughout the war.

Portaluppi provided details and noted in the 4th Squadron's historical report the following: "To us who had previously considered Hankow safe only at 8,000 feet or above, the mission had every earmark of a semi-suicidal venture." The goal of the mission, flown at the request of the 14th Air Force and the 68th Composite Wing, was to test the feasibility and effectiveness of a B-25 to support heavy-bomber night operations against searchlights. The target area was heavily defended by antiaircraft, searchlights, and night fighters; their specific objective was to attack the searchlights on the Wuchang side and interdict their use during bombing runs. Two P-51s were assigned to the Hankow side. The searchlight tactics varied between master control, apparently mechanically pointed, and control by a single directing light. There was no scissoring and little independent searching. Their operators' reaction to attack was to put out all the lights at once. After the first pass, the searchlights were turned out and then immediately turned on again. Lyon promptly attacked them again, and again they were turned out. He then circled out of range, taking constant evasive action.

The "heavies" approached the target and made their runs singly or in small groups, dropping their 500-pounders. Each time the searchlights were illuminated in an attempt to pick them up, the Mitchell attacked the lights again. Lyon "devised tactics which made full use of the fire power of the Mitchell within the limitations of its maneuverability and yet kept risks to the aircraft at the minimum," while at the same time pressing the attack with aggressive determination. In addition to uncounted passes and maneuvers to bring the turret and waist guns to bear, he made fourteen forward-firing passes on searchlight positions. During three of the bomb runs, the searchlights were turned out when the Mitchell turned into the lights, and the lights were not turned on at all on one pass. It was impossible to completely prevent interference by the searchlights, since some bomb runs were made as the Mitchell was turning away from the target. The conclusion drawn from the experience was that the use of a Mitchell to support heavy-bomber night operations by attacking searchlights was both feasible and effective.

According to Task Force 34's operational intelligence report for mission #21, the aircraft remained in the target area for an hour and thirty minutes after the last heavy bomber appeared. No fires or secondary explosions were observed in the target area. Lyon dropped the Mitchell's frag load at 900 feet on revetments at Wuchang Airdrome, and gunners silenced meager light automatic-weapons fire. He released the two remaining bomb clusters as the aircraft passed over Pailochi Airdrome at 1,200 feet on the return flight. Encountering only slight opposition, gunners shot up those positions and a radar installation 3 miles southwest of the airdrome, expending 1,100 rounds of .50-caliber ammunition.

Return through the Yangtze valley was at minimum altitude and with constant change of course and altitude because the flight crew saw tracers of a night fighter as the aircraft was leaving the Wuhan area. Lyon flew the Mitchell on to Yiyang, where it was to have rendezvoused with the P-51s, and circled with lights on. No answer was received to radio calls, and it became evident that the fighters had taken advantage of the good visibility to go directly home. A/C #722 flew on to Chihkiang, where it was down safely at 2315. Volunteering for and successfully carrying out this hazardous mission earned Lyon the Distinguished Flying Cross.

The 4th Squadron's Sgt. Oswald Weinert, turret gunner on this Wuhan raid, later composed a detailed firsthand account of the mission. He wrote that the Japanese held a strongly fortified depot area at Hankow-Wuchang in two areas about 5 miles apart, where they stored ammunition and fuel. The towns were on the mouth of the river leading to the Tungting [Dongting] Lake. It was an important depot area from which other transportation distributed supplies. "Several other units (P-40, P-38, A-20s) had unsuccessfully attempted to destroy the searchlights in the area and some even died. We were aware how difficult it would be. The mission was to go in advance and shoot out their big searchlights so the B-29 and B-24 heavy-duty bombers could finish the strike. Major Lyon was one of the best pilots there was to lead the mission." There were five crew on the B-25: one pilot, one navigator, and three gunners, he wrote. "I was the only gunner from the 4th while the others were from other squadrons to volunteer. I was the crew chief as well as gunner."

It was Weinert's opinion that Lyon had "certainly earned the Silver Star that night." Although he had been recommended for the Distinguished Flying Cross for this mission, Weinert did not follow through with the paperwork necessary to receive it until many years afterward.[12]

Sgt. Oswald Weinert stands with a sign marking the location of his 4th ("Lucky Lady") Bomb Squadron's barracks at Chihkiang. He took part in many Task Force 34 missions as a gunner and crew chief, often flying with 3rd Bomb Squadron participants. He later qualified to receive the Distinguished Flying Cross. *Oswald Weinert collection, courtesy of Ossie H. Weinert*

Although Cpl. Allegretto, armorer-gunner on this mission, did not learn the exact target until soon before takeoff, he later stated that he "had prior knowledge of the heavily defended target area and knew that the weather to and from the target was poor, that icing conditions were prevalent and that enemy night fighters probably would be in evidence." Afterward he confided to Hank and other buddies that he would not have volunteered if he had known how dangerous the mission would be. Nevertheless, Allegretto did his duty and was later promoted and awarded the Air Medal for his participation. The citation that accompanied it read, in part, "Throughout the entire mission Sergeant Allegretto displayed superior technical skill as well as aggressive courage. His expert airmanship and his profound devotion to duty at a time of extreme personal danger denote outstanding achievement in aerial flight and exemplify the finest traditions of the US Army Air Forces." News of his award and recognition of his valor was published by the local newspaper of his hometown in New Jersey.[13]

Sgt. Peters, who also served as armorer-gunner on this mission, later received the Air Medal along with Allegretto, and the citation that accompanied his medal was identical to Allegretto's. He was raised in Nocona, Texas, about 80 miles north of Fort Worth and just below the Oklahoma border, and his award was announced in a Wichita Falls newspaper.[14]

Despite the many hazards, all returned safely. On November 23, the men stationed at Chihkiang sat down to their Thanksgiving dinner "with gratitude in our hearts for the unequaled opportunity that had been offered us" and with satisfaction to be "again [fulfilling] our obligations in the combat theater." Lt. Portaluppi concluded, "But above the petty considerations of personal pride in our work and satisfaction for the meeting of duty, we gave humble thanks to God who had so far spared us." Capt. Ragland, who spent the holiday at Peishiyi, returned to Chihkiang the following day.

Capt. Lyon led a formation of the detachment's four B-25s that was off Chihkiang at 0935 on the twenty-fourth to bomb stores and installations at Siangyin. Lt. Edgerton flew as his navigator, and Cpl. Jackson and Sgt. Taun as gunners. Lt. Baker was pilot of #43-5056, a new 4th Squadron Mitchell, and SSgt. McCann was his turret gunner. Another 3rd Squadron pilot, 2nd Lt. Chu K. S., flew A/C #722 with Sgts. Tso and Wang as gunners, and Sgts. Liang and Ho were gunners aboard A/C #714. The J models each carried twenty-two 100 lb. M30 demolition bombs, and the H carried twenty-two M47A2 incendiaries. Ten 5th Fighter Group P-40s flew escort.

Strong south winds carried the formation north of its intended course on the outbound flight, so planes arrived too close to the target to drop on the first approach. Edgerton was unable to line up on the target on the second pass. The formation then turned 180 degrees and made a run in the opposite direction, dropping from 9,000 feet. All were on target except two that drifted to the right into the river. The pattern was about 1,700 to 2,000 feet in length by 150 to 200 feet in width and lay along the riverfront on the west side of the town. Thick smoke and dust drifting back over the target prevented an estimate of fires or other damage. Heavy antiaircraft fire was probably from automatic weapons, moderate in intensity, and apparently accurate but mostly out of range. Crewmen counted more than twenty bursts, five or six of them from a position south of the town, "and these uncomfortably close." Most of the others were slightly below and behind.

Another night mission to support heavy bomb operations by interdicting use of enemy searchlights at Hankow-Wuchang (mission #26) was off at 1900 on the twenty-fourth. Lt. Baker was the pilot of A/C #722, with a volunteer crew that included Allegretto, Jackson, and Peters as gunners. The aircraft reached the target area south of Wuchang, and the navigator, Lt. Young C. H., brought the pilot around to the Hankow side in a wide circuit, arriving exactly at 2100. Baker circled north of Hankow for nearly an hour, but it was evident from the fires burning in the twin cities that the heavies had already bombed. He then circled back to the Wuchang side and made a bombing pass near a fire spotted in Wuchang, dropping twelve M41 stabilized frag clusters at 7,500 feet on a run to the north. Another fire broke out, observable from 10 miles away. Immediately ten searchlights illuminated, momentarily catching the aircraft in the beam, but the pilot dived out of the lights and evaded them before heading back up the Yangtze.

Baker soon became aware of two unidentified aircraft flying virtually wing position to the Mitchell. They promptly followed moderate change of course and altitude, and he was able to shake them off only by abrupt dives and turns. Thereafter the aircraft were seen frequently, and tracers flashed by from time to time as they tried to draw fire. The night fighters persisted in their attempt to pick up the Mitchell, but Baker took cover in a patch of overcast encountered near Tungting Lake and lost them. He proceeded homeward but encountered difficulty in locating the field because of extensive cloud cover. He finally found it after flying a search for ninety minutes and put the aircraft down at 0115.

The duties of Sgt. Jackson, classified as airplane instrument specialist, included inspecting, testing, maintaining, and repairing or replacing a variety of electrically, mechanically, or gyro-operated aircraft navigation and engine instruments such as compasses, gauges, and meters. Although specialists were seldom required to take part in combat missions, Jackson volunteered for this "second suicide mission," as he later described it to his family, because Allegretto and Peters had returned safely from the mission against the Wuhan searchlights two days previously and had volunteered again for this one. His assessment afterward: "It wasn't so bad."[15]

Worth noting is an account by Sgt. Weinert of a similar mission conducted on the previous night by a 4th Squadron crew. In addition to supporting heavy-bomber night operations by strafing the searchlights, a secondary objective of mission #25 was to test the effectiveness of the 75 mm cannon. Capt. Lyon was the pilot of B-25H #43-5056, A/C #711, with Weinert at the turret guns and Bradley and Goff at the other two gun positions. The plane had recently been brought in to replace A/C #710, lost on November 19 due to bad weather, although its 4th Squadron four-man Chinese crew survived.

Weinert related that in order to reach the target, it was necessary for the bomber to traverse "a long narrow lake." To avoid radar detection, the Mitchell flew in so low that its props "picked up water" as it skimmed just above the surface on its way to Wuhan. The fighter planes that supported the bombers flew in ahead of them to take out the searchlights but did not get them all, so Weinert strafed them as the plane pulled up from its bombing run. He provided these details of the mission:

> On the second night mission to the same area [Wuhan] we were flying low so we could not be detected by radar; about 300 miles in Japanese lines. During the pilot's rapid maneuvers, the one gunner became air-sick so I traded with the waist-gunner for the top turret gunner. The tail turret would not work. I tried to repair that while the other gunner stood ready. Then we were ready with both gunner spots ready. We were in continuous contact with the enemy lines and made fourteen individual strikes to short out the search light installations. This would help deter the Japanese

to detect our incoming planes. We had no idea when the other planes would be coming because of the radio silence. We knew we were on-our-own for this mission. We were in this seemingly impossible dangerous area around this large lake for 1 hour and 30 minutes before we were successful. This did allow the rest of the squadron to complete the bombing mission.

Nausea caused by the plane's motion was a common problem among aircrews. Weinert later told his family that he sometimes became airsick when operating the strafing guns and carried a can along to use in case he needed to throw up.[16]

Off at 1920 on the twenty-sixth, Lt. Portaluppi flew another recently assigned 4th Squadron plane, a B-25J, serial #43-3900, A/C #701, to destroy stores and installations at Lingling. Sgt. Peters flew as top-turret gunner and Sgt. Liang as tail gunner. Capt. Wei sighted for three M69 incendiary clusters that Portaluppi dropped individually in a good pattern extending 300 feet by 1,200 feet along the riverfront on the first run. He dropped the remaining M69 and two M50 incendiaries on a second run on the east section of the town. The M69 hit the target with good dispersion, but the M50s were mostly overs "due to differences in trajectory for which insufficient allowance had been made." The pilot then continued south to Kweilin, reducing altitude to allow gunners to strafe lighted vehicles estimated to total fifty, but he considered strafing to be ineffective because of "insufficient guns" on the new plane, which, in addition, continually jammed. Chihkiang's new homing station was ineffective beyond ten minutes from the field, but Portaluppi was down at 2215.

Off at 1935 on November 26 to once again hit stores and installations at Lingling, Baker was the pilot of A/C #722, and Lt. Col. Russell, the group's executive officer, who had recently joined the task force, was his copilot. Russell had heard good things about their successes and came to take part in a few missions to see for himself. Cpl. Magyar (who had returned to Chihkiang only the day before), as well as Sgts. Ho and Shu, all were 3rd Squadron gunners. They came upon a small convoy on the approach to the target, and the pilot released two M30 demos. Ho, tail gunner, reported that one was a near miss. Baker then made two bombing passes on Lingling, dropping six bombs that burst in the east-central section of the town and then fourteen more toward the north. Crewmen thought all of them were duds, since "no result whatever was seen of this attack" and "it was established that the fins were fueled, and the arming wires were on the racks on return." They observed little activity that made good targets for strafing. Baker's assessment of Chihkiang's new homing station agreed with Portaluppi's. The signal and identification could be heard, but no definite bearing registered until the aircraft was within ten minutes of the field.

During the month of November, crews of the 3rd and 4th Squadrons on detached service to Task Force 34 at Chihkiang flew nineteen missions, eleven of them night missions. Lt. Edgerton's flight log indicated that all of his missions were against targets in the Hsiang valley. Personnel and planes rotated to and from Chihkiang as needed through early 1945.

Thanksgiving on November 23 was not a memorable occasion for the men stationed at Peishiyi. Lt. Wood wrote to his mother in a message delivered by V-mail, "All I can see is buffalo meat for dinner; would sure like some cranberries." Because some of the extra supplies that were ordered for the holiday feast had not arrived, the menu included duck and not turkey, which was promised later. Maj. Hummel complained that the local duck was "a particularly stringy, muscular variety, never guilty of going to fat," and blamed their lack of plumpness on an "athletic life" caused by the Chinese farmers' practice of herding them frequently from one rice paddy to another in search of food.

Lt. Young omitted any mention of the celebratory feast in his monthly report, perhaps because the Thanksgiving holiday was not a part of his Chinese heritage. He commented that rain compelled Maj. Conrad, 2Lt. Logan, and MSgt. Fuller to postpone their trip with two old B-25Ds to Bangalore for the purpose of exchanging them for new aircraft. When they tried again two days later, they discovered immediately after takeoff that the electrical system of one of the planes was out of commission, so the trip was delayed once again. Wood commented that he "took a ride with the major" and that Conrad "had a difficult landing to make but he sure put it on the button." The planes intended for trade-in finally got away after a three-day delay.

A three-ball alert that sounded at 1945 on the twenty-third lasted about thirty-seven minutes. Hank recalled, "During moonlight periods in China, the Japanese would send bombing planes over to bomb our bases, and part of the time they would transfer part of the squadron, me included, to Chengtu." Allied planes had been frequent targets at Kweilin, but no actual attacks had occurred since the move to Peishiyi, in spite of repeated alerts. Now that the moon was waxing full, concern arose that it would be only a matter of time before enemy bombs hit the field. When the weather eventually cleared in late November, Maj. Conrad received orders to move six of the squadron's Mitchells farther back to Wenkiang (Wenjiang) in the western suburbs of Chengtu (Chengdu), capital of Szechuan Province. "Brass" considered them to be safer there from night attack, and the shortage of gas prevented them from flying missions, regardless of their location.

On November 25, Capt. MacNeil, 2Lt. Ilefeldt, TSgts. Jakubasz and Wilkerson, SSgts. Barge and Mier, and Sgts. Long and Mills flew to Wenkiang for temporary duty. With them went twenty-six Chinese officers and enlisted men: Capt. Sun S. C. (X-221); Lts. Huang T. P. (X-273), Chang C. K. (X-817), Ching K. L. (no. not listed), Teng C. C. (X-374), Kuo P. H. (no. not listed), Chiang T. (X-822), Shen M. C. (X-130), Ching H. C. (no. not listed), In Y. S. (X-826), Liu P. C. (X-882), Chen Y. L. (no. not listed), Cheng Y. K. (X-821), Chen S. C. (X-748), Chang C. C. (X-137), Pai J. S. (X-274); and Sgts. Chen P. E. (X-2176), Liao K. T. (X-2149), Wie C. S. (X-1417), Chang S. N. (X-2157), Hsiao T. P. (X-2179), Yong C. L. (X-2145), Chung C. (X-1408), Chiu C. L. (X-2141), Kuo E. Y. (X-1402), and Pao T. (X-2286). Six B-25s were off at 1546.

In a broad valley about 100 miles wide, Chengtu is situated about 60 miles east of the Himalayas. During the winter months, frigid mountain air blows down into the valley, where it mixes with warmer valley air to produce a "pea soup overcast" that can be as much as 10,000 feet thick. The 426th Night Fighter Squadron's Lt. Smith wrote at about the same time that the weather was always cold and damp, and that his squadron "lived in tents that were also cold and damp with mildew added. We stood alerts during the winter, but there was no enemy activity directed toward Chengtu. In that strange weather none was expected."

Smith recorded his impressions of the city: "Chengtu was an old place, in the sense that you could be sure it had been there a long, long time, but there were no signs of antiquity, like ruins or old temples," he wrote. "It was, however, a principle [sic] Chinese city of maybe a million people. But unlike Kunming, there were clean, wide, uncongested streets, and a feeling of quiet with little traffic—some trucks and ramshackle buses, but mostly carts, rickshaws, and our trucks and jeeps."[17]

While the squadron's B-25s were kept safe, their crews went to a rest camp operated by an American missionary. Far removed from the stresses of battle and providing opportunities for physical and mental relaxation, several of these camps had been established in the western part of China for men who were showing signs of "war-weariness." Available to officers and enlisted men in an anxiety-free environment were a variety of optional activities, as well as the finest food that was procurable in China. Kwan-Sien Rest Camp, "within easy driving distance" of Chengtu, was in a valley surrounded by the rugged Kwan-Sien (Qingcheng) Mountains just north of the city.

An article in the *China Lantern* provided a description of the facility's attractions: "Nestled in the center of one of China's most scenic areas, the new camp provides all the equipment for complete recreation including ball fields, tennis courts, a swimming pool, horses for riding, and extensive hunting and fishing facilities." For the "more sedentary" there was an opportunity for "a complete rest in comfortable quarters under the shade of stately cedars, fine food in the camp's mess hall and limitless possibilities for interesting scenic camera shots."[18]

Maj. Hummel offered high praise for its many benefits:

The Chengtu climate, high, dry, and handsome, almost in itself was enough release from snuffling, fog[-]dripping Peishiyi valley to have recuperative value. Even more the opportunity for ambling about in a house of many rooms, sleeping in a bed with springs, lounging before a crackling fireplace, and eating breakfast cereal flooded with genuine Holstein milk direct from the herd pastured on the campus lawn of Chengtu University, provided a week of non-military rest camp. For a week the GI soul, if not his body, was in mufti. For a week he saw American civilians, even though they had spent nearly all their lives in China, and more important, for a week he was not surrounded by military personnel and the soul[-]deadening khaki hanging from their frames and figuratively entered into their blood and bone.

Hank described it as "kind of like a hotel" that was "operated by the government for soldiers." Soon after his arrival, he learned that vitamin tablets were available, and he decided that he needed some. He had always believed that if a little will do some good, a lot will work wonders. "Since I hadn't had any for a while, I took a handful, and in a few minutes, I felt like I was *on fire*. I had to go to my room and start taking off my woolen clothes. Those vitamin pills hit me. I had more than enough!"

After the week of R&R at Kwan-Sien, MacNeil and his men moved into transient quarters at one of the B-29 installations that had been built in the vicinity of Chengtu. Hank explained, "Chengtu was the first B-29 base. The coolies built it. They leveled a place out and put large rocks down, then some smaller-sized, smaller-sized, on up to it was smooth. The first B-29s that came over sank through that. They were too heavy."

These B-29 Superfortress very heavy bombers of the 20th Bomber Command were based at four airfields—Kwanghan, Kuinglai, Hsinching, and Pengshan—in different areas of Chengtu's suburbs, all constructed as part of Operation Matterhorn (code name for the systematic bombing of Japan) and intended for use as bases from which to stage long-range attacks on industrial centers of the Japanese home islands. All four of those at Chengtu (as well as at other bases throughout China) had runways built over rice fields by thousands of Chinese villagers from the surrounding area who labored as their contribution toward defending their homeland against Japanese occupation. The herculean task of building the runways was completed by Chinese laborers working without mechanized equipment, first hauling the rocks from the riverbeds to staging areas where they were sorted into piles and then on to the sites where runways were to be built. Long lines of Chinese resembling lines of foraging ants moved thousands upon thousands of rocks with nothing but "yo-yo baskets": straw baskets suspended from each end of bamboo poles carried across their shoulders. Other workers then took the rocks and, using small wooden mallets, pounded away irregularities to form an almost-smooth surface before laying the rocks to construct the runways. Finally, massive stone rollers were used to compact and smooth the runway's surface, readying it to support the massive bombers. Men, women, and children worked from daylight until dark in return for twenty cents and a bowl of rice per day. The bases served their purpose but were discontinued for use by the "Superforts" after Allied forces secured the Marianas and operations were transferred there.[19]

Hank, Barge, and Wilkie went into the city for sightseeing and took photos to document their visit. Hank sent home a photo captioned "One of the gates in wall around Chengtu, China." Chengtu was one of the most attractive of Chinese towns, with wide streets and modern buildings. There were high-quality restaurants with excellent Chinese cuisine, as well as others that catered to American tastes. Directed toward "the eternal souvenir acquisitiveness of the GIs" were its "silk streets and silver streets, and jade-and-junk streets," according to Hummel.

"One of the gates in the wall around Chengtu," Hank noted on the reverse. This was one of several photographs of the city that he sent home. *J. H. Mills collection*

On the twenty-fourth came alarming reports that the Japanese had taken Nanning, 150 miles farther southwest of Liuchow. By the end of November, many of the major airfields used by the 14th Air Force and the 20th Bomber Command had been captured, and communication between Manchuria and Southeast Asia had been established. Gen. Wedemeyer, in command of American forces in China, expected the Japanese to drive toward Kunming or to push westward past the Yellow River bend toward Chengtu—or perhaps both.

Chinese forces had performed poorly in attempting to halt the Japanese offensive. Wedemeyer recognized that before the Chinese army could be successful, at least part of it had to be transformed into an effective fighting force. To implement his plan, called "Operation Grubworm," two American-equipped and American-trained Chinese divisions (the 14th and 22nd) were returned to China from Burma and India as reinforcements, and more troops began training to take part as Japanese forces shifted their advance westward toward Kunming and Chungking. Both cities were critical. If Kunming fell, the Hump aerial supply line would be cut. If Chungking, Chiang's wartime capital, was lost, the blow to Nationalist prestige and authority might be fatal. Always reluctant to relinquish any degree of authority, Chiang had little choice but to concede, although he imposed limits on the number of divisions the Americans were permitted to train, and kept many of his best soldiers in reserve near Chungking in the event his old enemy Mao decided to make his move.[20]

Activities at Peishiyi continued to be routine through the end of the month. Capt. Seacrest, Lt. Pulaski, MSgt. Hanrahan, and Sgt. Trout, who had left to ferry two B-25s to Bangalore, returned to Peishiyi with replacement D models. Capt. Seacrest assumed command of the squadron in the absence of Maj. Conrad, who had left for Bangalore with Lt. Logan and MSgt. Fuller in an old B-25D to "trade in" for another new plane. Logan was designated as a flight leader. Previously a bank employee in San Francisco, he had satisfactorily completed the typical course of training and received his commission at Kearns, Utah, in April 1944, soon before being sent to China. Capt. Kelso appointed Lt. Young as class "B" agent "for the purpose of acting as custodian for funds drawn for money belts of this squadron." Money belts, stocked with currency of the territories over which missions were to be flown and issued to pilots before takeoff, were intended to encourage cooperation by locals in case of a bailout. The value of emergency funds had been proved on Burma missions. Young was additionally appointed squadron security officer as November drew to a close.

The morning report's tabulation of personnel indicated twenty-seven present and thirteen absent of the forty Americans currently assigned. The delayed traditional Thanksgiving dinner was served at the midday meal to the men at Peishiyi. The menu comprised not only the long-awaited turkey (canned), but also roast duck, dressing, mixed green salad, french fried potatoes, asparagus, and blueberry pie. Afterward, a softball league made up of CACW officers and enlisted men and 1st Bomb Group personnel was informally organized. They played two games that afternoon. Wing clerks defeated both officers and bomb group teams. Gen. Morse played first base for the officers' team. Scores were not recorded.

TSgt. Armstrong had particular reason to be thankful when he received orders on that day to proceed to "the Zone of Interior." He departed for Kunming the following morning to begin his return home. Although no proof has been found, his early departure back to the US suggests the possibility that he was the "mechanical sergeant" engaged in the altercation with SLt. Hsu.

Born in Canada to American homesteader parents, Armstrong moved with them to Idaho as a child and grew up working the family farm. He later supported himself as an auto mechanic, finding work in Idaho, Montana, and California before enlisting in the Air Corps in December 1942. He was attached to the 1st Bomb Group soon after its inception and was transferred from the 2nd to the 3rd Squadron as an AAF radio operator when it was activated.

After returning to the States, Armstrong was sent to a convalescent hospital in Santa Ana, California, where he remained from February to June 1945. While there, he was diagnosed with chronic tonsillitis and "internal derangement of knee, old" (perhaps caused by a "hard kick"). Treatment included a tonsillectomy, but no treatment was recommended for his knee because it was "not a traumatism."[21] He did not receive his Purple Heart earned on the 2nd Squadron mission of January 25, 1944, until February 1946, while stationed at Fort George Wright in Spokane, Washington. A farmer at heart because of his early upbringing, Armstrong kept a 1-acre garden at his home during that time. He was, in addition, placed in charge of a "tighten-the-belt garden" cultivated on unused parade grounds in an effort to increase domestic crop production that would allow commercially grown food products to be shipped to starving people overseas.[22]

CHAPTER TEN
Successes and Setbacks

Although rainfall had diminished, mornings in early December continued to be shrouded by fog, with the days overcast and the nights clammy and dank. Mean temperature ranged between 40 and 50 degrees. Maj. Hummel concluded, "It was the humidity, not the cold that made us blossom out in red, leaky noses." The respiratory infections, although common, were "as mild as the temperature, and as unexciting." Morning reports continued to mention those who spent a day or two sick in quarters.

Roads were still muddy. "A jeep in a rice paddy became almost as common a Peishiyi sight as the family pig in the drawing room of the Peishiyi mud villas," he wrote. Improvements were being accomplished, however, despite the lengthy red tape required. "A plethora of coolies swarmed over our mud roads to build a crushed[-]stone road from Peishiyi Airfield to the main highway to Chungking." The handmade road was completed, rock by rock, by basket-carrying coolies who patiently placed the rocks and then stuffed mud into the interstices, often working long into the night with the aid of lights that had been set up for the purpose. New hostels were also being built by Chinese workers, but these were not completed until after the 3rd Squadron had moved on.

Supply shortages persisted into December. Two more months of labor were required before Allied forces in Burma were finally successful in reopening a land route that allowed delivery of aircraft, spare parts, ammunition, fuel, and other essential supplies to bases in China, although heavy reliance upon air transport continued until the end of the war.

As the month began, encouraging news was relayed to squadron personnel grounded at Peishiyi concerning recent Allied successes in the Pacific. US submarines had sunk an additional twenty Japanese vessels, including a light cruiser and a destroyer. American bombers with fighter escort flying out of Saipan were hitting targets as far eastward as Iwo Jima in the Volcano Islands. Updates regarding the war in Europe and the Pacific came in through the month, providing the men with some sense of connection to the war.

Closer to home, tragic news spread on the afternoon of December 2, when a C-47 transport crashed 2 miles south of the field after leaving Liangshan with eleven passengers. The aircraft, off at about four o'clock, crashed against the side of a slope and broke in half as it neared Peishiyi. A Chinese lieutenant colonel died of head wounds, and four injured American enlisted men were treated at the base dispensary.

The routine continued through the end of the year, although there were rumors that Peishiyi would soon be evacuated, as Kweilin had been in September. For security reasons, all base personnel were required to learn a series of seven passwords as a precaution against fifth-column infiltration such as was reported at Chihkiang. Hummel explained: "Such simple phonetics as koko, and something that sounded like 'Keyhole,' words suggesting condiments and hardware and other weird concoctions, became passwords because these simple phonetics could be mouthed by Chinese guards and wandering GIs alike." In spite of the apparent simplicity of the scheme, confusion arose. Neither nationality seemed capable of remembering which password was appropriate for which day. The Americans soon discovered that if they simply shouted the all-purpose greeting, *ding how*, cheerfully and heartily, the Chinese guard usually "did nothing more vicious than bare his teeth in a delightful grin." The use of passwords was discontinued when it became clear that Peishiyi and vicinity were safe from invasion, at least for the near future.

Capt. Seacrest was promoted to major, 2Lt. Young to first lieutenant, SSgt. Chasse to technical sergeant, and Cpls. Burton and Jackson (now a crew chief) to sergeants as the month began. Lt. Young was noted as sick in quarters with his seventh recurrence of malaria. A one-ball alert was sounded at 1955 on the sixth and lasted thirty-two minutes before the all-clear was given.

Hank captioned this photo "Task Force 34" and wrote their names on the reverse. Representing both the 3rd and 4th Bomb Squadrons, they are (*from the top down and then left to right*) Lloyd E. Jackson, James E. McCann, Lavaugn M. Wilkins, Oswald Weinert, Eugene M. Kearney, George R. Goff Jr., Herman L. Burton, Wayne H. Senecal, and Thomas H. Edgerton. *J. H. Mills collection*

Both from Oklahoma, Sgt. Manuel C. Smith (*left*), now back with the 4th Bomb Squadron, and James A. Wadlow (*right*) were glad to find each other in China. *A. R. Allegretto collection, courtesy of Mary Allegretto Henry*

Once again, no combat missions were possible except by the detachment at Chihkiang. Lt. Senecal, SSgt. McCann, and Cpls. Burton and Jackson, followed by Lts. Cantor and Pulaski; TSgts. Hoyle, Rieks, and Shock; and Cpl. Wadlow, all went to Chihkiang during the first week of the month. One of the photos that Hank sent home was taken at about this time. He wrote this notation on the back: "Lieutenants Senecal, Edgerton, Burton, Goff, Carney [Kearney], Weinert, Wilkins, McCann, and Jackson, Task Force 34." Of these, SSgts. Lavaughn M. Wilkins, George R. Goff, and Oswald ("Ossie") Weinert and Sgt. Eugene M. Kearney have been identified as members of the 4th Bomb Squadron, while the others were detached from the 3rd Bomb Squadron. Although McCann had returned there, his name appears in no later Task Force 34 operational reports.

December 7 brought memories of the Japanese attack on Pearl Harbor three years earlier, as well as a renewed determination to defeat the aggressors in the approaching year. The date held particular significance for Lt. Young, who had been an eyewitness to the devastation. He wrote, "No one needs to be told that today is the third anniversary of the outbreak of the Pacific war. The event was one of sharp personal significance, heralded not by the excited voice of a radio announcer but by the wailing, this time unquestionably authentic, of sirens and the whine and explosion of bombs." Soon afterward, a "friendly" baseball game between bomb wing officers and 3rd Squadron enlisted men took place, with the squadron's team losing by a score of 9–2.

Command of the CACW passed on December 6 from Brig. Gen. Morse to Col. T. Alan Bennett. Morse, who was flying to Europe on an assignment that involved bringing needed troops to China, took with him Maj. William J. Dierks as copilot, as well as MSgt. Donald W. Grant, former flight chief with the 3rd Squadron, as his crew chief. Lt. Col. Munson received his orders home and was replaced as 1st Bomb Group commander by Lt. Col. Russell.

The Japanese had gained partial success in establishing railroad facilities between their northern supply areas and French Indochina and were busy building and repairing bridges and tracks destroyed by the Allies. A great amount of activity was observed in the Yellow River bend on the northern war front, where a reported 200,000 Japanese troops were being moved in, new branch railways leading to the river were being built, and airfields were being improved and runways lengthened. Through the month, the 1st Squadron, operating out of Hanchung, and the 2nd Squadron, from Liangshan, flew missions in this area against supply routes that were feeding much-needed war materials to enemy forces in the south. However, the usual shortage of gasoline and bombs limited their raids against Japanese positions.

For Task Force 34, the first few days of the month brought great anxiety caused by a report that Col. Dunning received from headquarters at Kunming. It warned against the concentration of Japanese paratroopers in preparation for launching an airborne attack against Chihkiang. A schedule that would begin evacuation within twenty or thirty minutes of an alarm was circulated, but no paratroopers appeared. "As most people suspected, the thing was a complete fizzle and soon even the rumors ceased," wrote Portaluppi. After a few tense days, life and operations returned to normal for the men stationed there.

On December 3, Col. Russell led a four-plane diamond formation with mixed crews on Task Force 34's mission #30, takeoff time 0830. Russell flew A/C #711 with Lyon, Edgerton, Jen, and Ma, followed by A/C #722 (Jen, Lee, Tze, Liang, Chang, and Ho), A/C #701 (Senecal, Rich, Doran, Weinert, Tso, and Shu), and recently assigned #43-5051, A/C #718 (Tung, Chu, Wang, Cho, and Tong) on this 3rd Squadron B-25H's first Task Force 34 mission. Ten 75th Fighter Squadron P-51s flew escort. Their target was the storage area on the river northeast of Sintsiang. All the 100 lb. demos (twenty-two per plane) were dropped on Edgerton's lead from 9,000 feet in a pattern that began near the end of the bridge and extended through the middle of the storage area. Crewmen reported no fires, although severe damage caused by blast and fragmentation was probable. A single burst of AA was to the left of the formation as it recrossed the Hsiang River after hitting the target. The raid seemed to have surprised the main defenses in the target area.

The 3rd Squadron's A/C #722 again took off at 1815 on the following day (Baker, Chu, Shio, Zeitler, Shu, and Chow) carrying seventeen stabilized frag clusters to harass enemy motor vehicle traffic in the Hsiang valley between Lingling and Kweilin and to alert the area. At the target, Baker let down through 2,000 feet of overcast and so alerted Lingling. He flew a short distance south but, unable to see anything on the ground, returned northward. He plastered the hostel area with frags from 3,000 feet, extinguishing lights. The aircraft encountered a moderate amount of fire from automatic weapons and small arms, and aircrew members heard one hit, probably from small arms. After flying farther to the north for about ten minutes but finding no targets of interest, the pilot returned to base.

Baker later described the difficulties that he experienced when flying with Chinese aircrews. He recalled, "I've flown missions where I couldn't understand one word they were saying, and they couldn't understand one word I was saying." Briefings were conducted in both English and Chinese, and the Chinese navigators were usually able to communicate well enough with the American pilots to give headings and estimated times of arrival over targets. Dealing with the differences between the two cultures was equally difficult, he said. For example, while later assigned to the 4th Bomb Squadron with the rank of captain, he was given the temporary rank of colonel so Chinese superiors flying with him on missions would not lose face. Regardless of the annoyances, he admired the Chinese as people and as soldiers. "They were real fine people," he said. "They were faithful; they'd do anything for you. I'd trust them with my life[,] and believe me, they weren't afraid of the devil."[1]

As far as observable results were concerned, Task Force 34's most effective raid to date was carried out on the seventh. Four B-25s took off at 0802 and flew in diamond formation, again with Col. Russell leading. Baker flew as Russell's copilot aboard A/C #711. Edgerton, his bombardier, logged the mission (his sixteenth) as two hours and fifteen minutes in duration. Portaluppi flew as pilot aboard A/C #722, with Pulaski as copilot. With them were A/C #701 (Tung, Wang, Shio, Ho, Wang, and Shu) and A/C #718 (Jen, Sze, Chow, Jen, and Ma). Carrying an aggregate load of forty-four 100 lb. M30 demos, six 500 lb. M58 demos, and eighteen 100 lb. M50 incendiary bomb clusters, the aircraft took a heading to Tushan. Their objective was to destroy it and deny its use to the enemy. Russell's navigator, Wei, had some difficulty in finding the target, and then Edgerton released his bombs, #722 and #701 dropping on his lead for range and deflection and #718 releasing individually by select. An estimated 90 percent registered in a pattern that extended across the southern end of the town. A light and a heavy demo fell into the river, and two clusters fell short. Crews reported one secondary explosion and two fires—one described as large and giving off "much gray smoke," while the other was smaller.

The same four Mitchells, led by Capt. Lyon, were off in diamond formation later that day at 1200 to hit the town of Sankaio. Wadlow and Peters were Lyon's gunners aboard A/C #711, and Shock, Hoyle, and Magyar flew with the 4th Squadron's Lt. Rich as his gunners aboard A/C #718. The other two Mitchells, both J models and carrying all-Chinese crews, were A/C #722 (Chu, Tung, Cheng, Ho, Tso, and Shu) and A/C #701 (Lee, Hu, Sze, Liang, Chang, and Jen). Fourteen 5th Fighter Group P-40s flew escort. The Mitchells carried sixty-six 100 lb. M30 demos and seventeen 100 lb. M41 frag clusters. Because of unfamiliarity with the region, the formation first flew to Tushan and, using it as a point of departure, took up a nearly reciprocal course to Sankaio. After some course corrections, the planes made their bombing run. All bombs were away on the lead bombardier from 7,800 feet. A very good pattern covering two-thirds of the irregularly shaped town resulted in about 90 percent hits. Two or three bombs fell short and three or four were over. A sharp, flashing secondary explosion was followed by a large fire likely fueled by gasoline. Aircrews also reported several smaller fires. Smoke ("chiefly black") rose to 2,000 feet, visible from 25 miles away at 7,500 feet.

Afterward, a disagreement arose between the bomber and fighter crews as to whether Sankaio was the town that had actually been hit, although the 4th Squadron's Chinese navigator was confident in his identification. Capt. Wei, an experienced navigator who was using a Chinese map, had no doubt that he had successfully guided the planes to their target. "However, to obviate any future controversies or grave errors it was then decided to forego the bombing of those small towns on which pictures could not be obtained or which could not be positively identified by other means," noted Portaluppi.

Lt. Portaluppi took off at 1730 on the same date, with TSgt. Rieks as his turret gunner and Sgts. Wang and Liang as waist and tail gunners. His objective was to hit the Hengyang Airdrome and to restrict enemy operations by harassing supply movements in the Hsiang valley. Poor visibility at the river near Hengyang made it impossible to find the airdrome, so Portaluppi turned south to orient himself on the river. When he spotted the lights of a convoy, the pilot toggled four M28 butterfly frag clusters, knocking out the lights. These hypersensitive, delayed-action bombs being dropped by 14th Air Force planes were armed upon impact, so they were discharged by the slightest movement, even the vibrations set up by men walking nearby.

Continuing south and then turning north on the river, the pilot was able to locate the airdrome. He dropped two clusters on a bombing pass to the south, two more on a reverse run, and a final cluster on a third run to the southwest. Portaluppi then released the remaining nine clusters when crewmen spotted the lights of another convoy of about thirty vehicles north of Hengyang. A quick turn revealed three small fires burning in the approximate position of the convoy. Turning north again and nearing Siangtan, he found a third convoy. After some deliberation because of poor visibility, the pilot decided to drop down and strafe it. The first bursts were over, but those following scored many good hits. Continuing north until his navigator could determine a definite fix at "DD24" (Isuho), the aircraft then proceeded on course to Chihkiang.

Another mission credited to the 3rd Squadron was off on the seventh at 1810; its objective was to harass enemy supply movement, DD24 and north, and to alert the enemy in the Hsiang valley. A/C #722 (Baker, Pulaski, Lipira, Allegretto, Peters, and Cantor) carried seventeen M41 stabilized frag clusters. Arriving at the river at Changsha, Baker turned north to Tungting Lake but, finding nothing of interest, returned south. He dropped five clusters on a small convoy near Siangtan on the west bank, extinguishing the lights. When crewmen spotted a large convoy on the east bank 5 miles northeast of Siangtan, he dropped down to allow gunners to strafe it, then released the twelve remaining clusters. A fire broke out at once in the middle of the convoy and increased steadily in size, visible for 40 miles at 3,000 feet. Turning toward home, they discovered another convoy 5 miles southwest of Siangtan, apparently headed south. The pilot dropped down to attack it by strafing. Lt. Cantor, in position as tail gunner, fired on the last two convoys. Meager machine gun fire came up from one of them. One air burst was reported near DD24. About 5 miles farther northeast, crewmen observed two bright-green tracers that burned out at more than 7,500 feet.

Credited to the 4th Squadron on this seven-mission day was another raid on supply movements that was off at 1915. Flying the 3rd Squadron's A/C #718, Lyon (with Edgerton, Hoyle, Goff, and Magyar as his aircrew) carried seventeen M41 stab-frag clusters and took a heading to the Hsiang River. As he flew through the valley, darkness and progressively heavy overcast began to set in, and strong winds carried the aircraft considerably south of the point where the pilot expected to arrive on the river. When Lyon let down, he could not determine his position and, at 1,500 feet, suddenly realized that he was flying along the face of a mountain. Climbing to a safe elevation, he proceeded northward for nearly thirty minutes before Edgerton fixed their position north of Hengyang. Soon they spotted the lights of a convoy through the haze, and Lyon released eight clusters. The lights went out. Farther to the north, he dropped five clusters on another convoy, with identical results. He dropped the remaining bombs around a fire started by the previous mission in a convoy northeast of Siangtan. The characteristic inconclusiveness of night missions was compounded by December's cold and by strong winds that prevented strafing to follow up bombing of the blacked-out convoys. Antiaircraft and small-arms fire of varying intensity and accuracy came up from several positions along the river on the return.

Three missions out of Chihkiang were recorded on the eighth. The four Mitchells, accompanied by eight 75th Fighter Squadron P-51s, took off at 1043. Lt. Col. Russell flew in the lead to attack the town of Lipo, reported to be occupied by the enemy. Each of the bombers carried a mixed load of demos and incendiaries. Flying with Russell were Portaluppi, Wei, Edgerton, Shock, and Wadlow aboard A/C #711. Rieks, Hoyle, and Magyar were gunners, with a 4th Squadron pilot, Lane, and navigator, Doran, aboard #718. A/C #722's crew consisted of Tung, Lee, Shio, Jen, Liang, Chow, and Hu; aboard A/C #701 were Chu, Cheng, Ma, Tso, and Taun. Wei once again had difficulty in locating the target, and Edgerton was unable to "make his gyros settle down," so no bombs were dropped on the first two runs because of disagreement between the two concerning the formation's position. "Due to the excessive smallness" of the target, about 40 percent of the bombs dropped on Edgerton's lead on the third run hit the western edge of the town. All of #701's bombs fell in woodland north of the town due to pilot error. Aircrews saw no fires, although smoke rose to 1,000 feet. They observed a secondary explosion 500 feet north of the town, likely caused by a drifting bomb. Following this unsatisfactory performance, Edgerton noted in his log that the plane was in the air for two hours and twenty-five minutes.

Capt. Lyon led the task force's fortieth mission, with all four B-25s that took off at 1600 to attack an enemy cavalry unit reported at Nantan. He was the pilot of A/C #711 (with Cheng, Wei, Doran, Farris, and Goff), followed by A/C #701 (Rich, Wang, Sze, Chang, Shu, and Wang). The 3rd Squadron's H, A/C #718, was crewed by Jen, Cheng, Ho, Ma, and Jen, and the J model, A/C #722, by Pulaski, Baker, Lipira, Peters, Zeitler, and Allegretto. Excellent coverage estimated at 95 percent was achieved, with 100 lb. M41 stabilized frag clusters (seventeen per plane) dropped in train from 8,000 feet on Doran's lead, starting at the south end of town and running through it, crossing the stream and into the village on the far side. Two fires broke out at once in the central part of town. A secondary explosion in the northern section near the river was followed by a large fire that appeared to be fueled by oil or gasoline.

A single plane flown by Capt. Lyon with Col. Russell as his copilot was off at 1950 with twelve M28 butterfly bomb clusters to harass enemy supply movements and to alert the enemy in the Hsiang valley. They attacked convoys northeast of Yochow and north of Changsha and then bombed a very large convoy north of Siangtan. Rieks, Peters, and Wadlow "fired at every opportunity," extinguishing lights. Poor visibility and a gun malfunction prevented strafing of a second large convoy south of Isuho and another near Nanyo.

On the following day, Lt. Baker led a formation of Task Force 34's B-25s on a mission that took off at 1145 to attack Hochih. TSgt. Shock was his waist gunner aboard A/C #711. Lt. Pulaski, with Magyar and Cantor as waist and tail gunners, piloted A/C #718. Chinese crews flew A/C #701 (Wang, Tung, Cheng, Ho, Ma, and Tso) and A/C #722 (Chu, Lee, Shio, Jen, Chang, and Liang). Each plane carried twenty-two 100 lb. demos, released in train at 7,000 feet on the lead bombardier, but the bomb run was "not too effective." It started short and ran across the southwest side of town, scoring about 60 percent as hits. A secondary explosion in the southwest part of town resulted in a large fire, perhaps fueled by gasoline. Before returning to Chihkiang, the planes flew to Nantan to assess damage from the previous day's bombing.

A/C #711 was airborne at 1950. Carrying seventeen M41 stab-frag clusters, Baker again headed to the Hsiang valley, with Rich, Edgerton, Shock, Hoyle, and Cantor as his aircrew. They spotted a small convoy north of Paoching and observed considerable antiaircraft and ground fire at 9,000 feet. When they reached the vicinity of Siangtan, two enemy aircraft began following the bomber, "trying to make contact." There was no ground activity in this area, so the Mitchell turned north. Opposite Changsha, crewmen spotted the lights of a convoy northeast of the town, so Baker "turned over to them."

There they discovered a novel situation. Eight or more convoys, each of normal size (thirty to fifty vehicles) and separated from those before and after it by about ¾ mile, approached through the darkness. All were lighted and did not turn out their lights even when attacked. Enemy aircraft, probably totaling four and each carrying a red light, were patrolling the area. Baker made a pass on the first of the convoys, with Edgerton attempting to use the bombsight, but he was dissatisfied with the "run-up" and made another attempt on the next convoy in line. This, too, was unsatisfactory, and Baker moved to the third convoy, this time dropping by the customary approximate sightings used at night. Results were excellent. Bomb flashes appeared along the entire length of the convoy, knocking out the lights of many of the vehicles, and at the end of the convoy a large fire broke out that was observable for 35 miles at 5,000 feet. Poor vertical visibility and the presence of the enemy aircraft prevented any attempt to strafe the trucks. One followed the Mitchell back to the vicinity of Siangtan before it could be "shaken off." A considerable volume of automatic-weapons fire came up near DD24, although most was inaccurate, and it apparently drew off the enemy aircraft. There was no further sign of enemy activity, and the return flight was without incident, although the plane's heaters were inoperative, and the crew later reported extreme discomfort because of the cold.

Another mission by Task Force 34 to support heavy-bombardment operations over Wuhan took place on December 10. Lt. Young wrote in his monthly historical report, "For the first time Liberators of the 14th USAAF and units of the Chinese American Composite Wing (including two B-25s of our squadron) coordinated their attacks with those of the B-29s of the 20th Bomber Command. They followed the attacks on Hankow and Pengpu with a force of 200 B24s, B25s and P40s."

Off at 1710, Portaluppi flew A/C #718 (Doran, Farris, Goff, and Magyar as his navigator and gunners). He let down through layers of overcast and arrived over the target at 1905, carrying twenty-two M47A2 aimable incendiaries. The glow of fires became visible twenty minutes out of Hankow, making it apparent that the 308th Bomb Group B-24 Liberators had again started bombing ahead of schedule. When Portaluppi attacked the searchlights on the Hankow side of the river, a change in the enemy's searchlight tactics immediately became evident. Only seven lights were operative, and these were searching independently, in contrast to the fifteen to twenty-five master-controlled lights noted on the initial November raid. The pilot made more than ten strafing passes in an effort to render them inoperative. At first the lights were turned on to illuminate the Mitchell at every pass, but eventually they were turned out whenever the plane approached or fired a burst of tracer.

Portaluppi then made three bombing runs at 3,000 feet over an industrial plant on the Han River, southwest of the airdrome. He dropped two incendiaries on the first pass, and a large fire erupted but burned out rapidly. He dropped ten bombs on the second pass, igniting two more large fires. A smaller fire that burned fiercely with secondary explosions was determined to be on a barge or lighter in the river. Ten bombs dropped on the third run produced no effect. During that pass, four searchlights came on. These illuminated and held the Mitchell until another B-25 (the 3rd Squadron's J) that was covering the Wuchang side rushed over. This plane made a head-on pass on the lights on the Hankow side, destroying one and forcing the others out, "thereby relieving an acutely embarrassing situation for the first Mitchell," according to the mission report. Portaluppi fired five rounds of 75 mm HE "for harassing effect." One burst struck near a searchlight, which may have been knocked out by the cannon but more likely by .50-caliber fire, according to the pilot. Accurate and intense enemy antiaircraft fire was of "all calibers," and machine gun and light automatic-weapons fire that included bright-green tracers from one or two was "particularly hot." On the return flight to base, Magyar reported an enemy night fighter coming in fast at five o'clock and slightly below. Portaluppi took sharp evasive action, and the enemy plane was not seen again. All members of this volunteer crew were later awarded Air Medals.

In what was reported as a separate mission, Baker was off at 1711 aboard A/C #722 with Pulaski, Wei, Hoyle, Peters, and Cantor, carrying a bombload of twenty-two 100 lb. M30 demos to attack searchlights on the Wuchang side. While circling east after the heavies finished bombing, he saw that A/C #718 had been "caught suddenly by the lights while making a bomb run over the west side of Hankow." He immediately advanced straight across the target area through heavy antiaircraft fire and, in a head-on strafing pass at low level, shot out the lights behind the warehouse area on the Hankow side, "thereby relieving the other Mitchell from a highly dangerous situation."

Soon afterward, because his left engine had been running rough and occasionally cutting out during the entire time the aircraft was in the target area, the pilot turned on course for home without attempting to do any bombing in the area. He dropped eight bombs on a village ten minutes out, but all were misses. Crewmen later spotted the lights of a convoy. When Baker prepared to attack it, Wei erroneously informed him that the plane was over friendly territory, so they returned fourteen bombs to base. Most of the return flight was accomplished on instruments, as icing conditions and steadily increasing overcast closed in, restricting visibility. Poor radio conditions added to the difficulties of navigation, and Baker located the field only after extensive searching. The quick-thinking pilots narrowly averted a collision of the two Mitchells as they were making an instrument letdown. Both landed safely. Recommendations by the crews for improvement on similar future missions included better communications and coordination between the heavies and the Mitchells.

Cantor described this and other missions in a postwar interview. "Sometimes I flew as an observer, sometimes as a navigator, and several times as a bombardier," he related. "The American officers with the unit were few, so we had to double as brass." He had volunteered for this mission and operated the guns in the tail turret. He stated that the B-25 "hovered over the air throughout the attack and shot out Japanese searchlights" and that they were "over the target for an hour and a half." Cantor was awarded the Oak Leaf Cluster to his previously awarded Air Medal for this mission, which was one of forty-two he completed in thirteen months with the CACW. Details of this and other missions came as a shock to his wife and parents, since he had told them only of his duties as gunnery instructor to the Chinese.[2]

Cantor captioned this one "Barracks, Chihkiang, China, 1944." His jacket suggests cold weather, which coincides with Task Force 34's period of operations. His letters home that accompanied his photos regaled his family with stories of training the Chinese gunners but omitted references to his combat missions. *J. G. Cantor collection, courtesy of Ronnie Cantor*

On the same date, Lt. Col. Russell flew A/C #711 on a night mission that was off at 1930 against truck convoys in the Hsiang valley north of Changsha. Lyon flew as copilot, Lipira as navigator, and Allegretto, Wadlow, and Weinert as gunners. The Mitchell carried twenty-two 100 lb. M30 demolition bombs. Because of heavy overcast and haze, neither the river nor any other recognizable landmark could be found to determine the plane's exact position. Two large brush fires fortunately seen burning somewhere south of Tungting Lake were used as a point of departure, allowing Lipira to find the target area. Russell dropped all bombs on a convoy estimated at forty to sixty vehicles discovered near the lake, and all lights went out after the detonation of the second bomb. The string ran along the line of trucks, and small fires, one visible for 20 miles from the target at 6,000 feet, were observed after the bombs fell. Russell returned to the vicinity of the brush fires and took a course reciprocal to the outbound heading, encountering icing and lowering overcast along the way. After flying out the ETA, he established contact with "Soda," who relayed messages to "Deacon," attempting to get a bearing. After some time, the radio compass began to "settle down," and somewhat later a bearing was received from "Deacon," who informed them when they were over the field. The plane landed safely back at Chihkiang just before midnight. "All pilots out tonight" described conditions on these missions as the worst in their experience.

The main Japanese attack through December was concentrated along the Kweichow-Kwangsi Railroad from Liuchow toward Kweiyang and south to Nanning, which had fallen in late November. By mid-December, the Japanese had outrun their supply lines and were forced to halt their advance. The thrust westward went as far as the vicinity of Tuyun in Kweichow Province, where Chinese ground troops turned it back. This drive was never a big one and may have been intended only as a "feeler."

In a "friendly" softball game between bomb wing officers and 3rd Squadron enlisted men played at Peishiyi on December 9, "our team emerged second best with the sad ending of 9 to 2." In addition to results of this rivalry, the squadron history included a report of the 21st Bomber Command's fourth and most recent attack on Tokyo in less than two weeks. B-29s had hit although not destroyed the "great Musashima aircraft factory," which produced planes for the Nakajima works, with the loss of only one of the Superfortresses to enemy action. The men were also encouraged by other war news detailing advances in the

Pacific and Europe, as well as developments in China. "Chinese fresh troops from northwest China have been rushed to the aid of Kweichow Province. A communiqué said that Chinese troops have recaptured Pachai, deepest enemy penetration point in Kweichow," Young quoted. "Enemy troops in that area were bombed by the 14th AAF, which also struck Hochih and Tachang, enemy positions in French Indo-China, Thailand and the Salween River area, where it supported Chinese troops."

The second in a series of orientation hours jointly sponsored by the 3rd and 4th Bomb Squadrons took place in mid-December under the direction of Lts. Young and Smith of the two squadrons. The detachment led by Capt. MacNeil returned from Wenkiang after some much-appreciated R&R. Lt. Wood and TSgt. Chasse went to Chiuling Po Field to supervise the shipment of supplies. Cpls. James J. Morris Jr. (radio operator–mechanic–gunner) and Joseph P. Supsic (A/P armorer-gunner) joined the squadron, and Cpl. Schlicher was placed on detached service at Chengtu. The first wet snowflakes fell onto the muddy ground at Peishiyi and collected in the mountains around Peishiyi Valley.

On the eighteenth, 1Lt. Gerald J. Winter was attached as squadron supply officer. Capts. MacNeil and Ragland and SSgt. Holmes went to Ondal, India, for detached service, and Maj. Seacrest, Capt. Cunningham, Sgt. Fox, and Cpls. Morris and Schlicher to Hanchung for a scheduled mission.

A subsequent accident report stated that a three-ship formation led by Capt. Ragland, with Maj. Seacrest and SLt. In Yen-san in wing positions, took off at 0730. Poor visibility prevented them from landing, and all three aircraft returned to Peishiyi. At 0900 hours, Maj. Seacrest led on takeoff. SLt. In lost sight of the lead plane in the area of Chungking, so the formation was dismissed, and he flew on to Liangshan, landing there at about 1020. His plane was refueled with assistance from 2nd Bomb Squadron ground personnel, and In and his crew visited the mess hall for dinner before attempting another takeoff. At about 1230, a two-ball alert went up, and all planes on the field were ordered to vacate immediately.

SLt. In (X-826), with an all-Chinese crew of a B-25H, A/C #720, was cleared from Liangshan in overcast conditions and visibility of 3 miles in haze by the Chinese commanding officer of the 2nd Squadron. In's aircrew consisted of 2Lt. Chang Chao-ching, navigator (X-137); Sgt. Kuo Hsiao-yi, engineer (X-1402); Sgt. Chang Tsai-hwa, radio-gunner (X-2183); and Sgt. Yao Shu-chi, tail gunner (X-1410). Both SLt. In and 2Lt. Chang lacked experience in flying with instruments and became lost in the dense overcast. Unable to find the field at Peishiyi, they remained lost for more than six hours on a flight that would ordinarily take forty to forty-five minutes.

In explained in his official report of the incident:

Flew the heading 225 degrees[,] tried to make landing at Peishiyi. In that time the weather was bad enough. I couldn't see any ground mark, so I flew the instrument flying through those heavy and thin clouds. Sometimes met icing conditions. I flew at the altitude of 4,000 feet, I circled near the area of Chungking trying to make a landing, but the visibility was very poor. I couldn't see any landmark on the ground. Therefore, I only circled there. At the time 1810 I reached over the field, but I couldn't see any identification light and communication. Radio compass all running out. Therefore, I couldn't land Peishiyi field. I still flew circle the local area. Forty minutes later this ship already running out of gas.

When In realized that the aircraft's fuel level was dropping dangerously low after circling for forty minutes, he climbed to 8,000 feet near Chiangcheng (about 20 miles northwest of Peishiyi) and ordered the crew to bail out before jumping himself. In his report, Chang confirmed details reported by In, stating that the pilot "noticed the entire crew bail out." The navigator noted that after takeoff from Liangshan, he was unable to find Chungking but used dead reckoning to lead the ship over Peishiyi Field. When fuel levels dropped dangerously low and In ordered the crew to abandon ship, "I was the second one leaving the ship[;] after few minutes I land in a mud place." The plane went down, resulting in a "complete washout."

As Sgt. Yao made his exit from the tail gunner's compartment, he was knocked unconscious by the tail end of the plane and never opened his parachute. He died in the crash, and his body was discovered near the wreckage. In was unhurt, and the other three crewmen suffered only slight injuries. The Chinese crew's inexperience and "communication difficulties inherent in an organization where mixed nationalities are responsible for the coordination of clearances, PXs, and general operations of control tower" were cited as reasons for the loss. The investigative panel, consisting of Lt. Col. Russell, Lt. Col. Sutley, and Maj. Conrad, recommended "better coordination of Chinese and American personnel operating control towers."[3]

Two 3rd Squadron planes, Maj. Seacrest flying in the lead, went on to take part in a combined mission that included Mitchells from the 2nd, 3rd, and 4th Squadrons. (Of the seventeen initially committed, only fourteen planes reached the target.) Seacrest was the pilot of a B-25J, A/C #715, with Capt. Tsuei H. C. as copilot, Capt. Cunningham as bombardier, 1Lt. Hwang T. P. as navigator, Cpl. Schlicher as engineer, Sgt. Fox as radio-gunner, and Cpl. Morris as tail gunner. On his wing as In's replacement was 1Lt. Hsu I. K. as pilot of B-25H, A/C #716. This crew consisted of 2Lt. Kuo C. as navigator, Sgt. Yuan C. F. as engineer, 2Lt. Lee S. C. as radio-gunner, and Sgt. Chao K. P. as tail gunner. Their aggregate bombload was forty-six 100 lb. M30 demos, fused instantaneous and 0.1-second delay.

The bombers took off at 0930 on December 19 and rendezvoused over Laohokow (pronounced lo-HO-ko by the Americans) with their fighter escort: twenty-four P-40s of the 3rd Fighter Group. Their target comprised the oil and gas tank farm, railroad yards, and locomotive shed and repair shops at Pengpu, Anwhei Province, about 150 miles northwest of Nanking. As they approached Pengpu, the planes separated into two flights. Four 4th Squadron B-25s, Maj. Bill Dick leading, hit the tank farm. Maj. Seacrest and Lt. Hsu, with a B-25 from the 2nd Squadron flown by Lt. Lois G. Bains as second wingman, followed the element led by Lt. Col. Lawson Horner, now 4th Squadron commander. The formation proceeded to the railroad repair shops and buildings.

Horner's element approached the target area from the west. He led his formation east beyond the tank farm, turned north to the railroad tracks, flew west along the tracks, and then hammered the railroad yards and the locomotive shed and repair shop with 100 lb. and 500 lb. incendiary clusters. An explosion immediately erupted in the center of the yard, and large fires produced heavy volumes of black smoke.

Seacrest and his two wing planes were echeloned behind and to the left of Horner's planes to provide complete coverage, including the locomotive shed and repair shop in the southwest corner. They made the bomb run at 7,450 feet on a heading of 260 degrees at 200 mph, interval set at 80 feet. This echelon was credited with igniting the northeastern corner of the locomotive shed and covering several spur lines running into the shed.

Because of a malfunction of the release mechanism, Hsu salvoed his bombs, the greatest number falling across the river into an open field. Three bombs overshot, but others fell on target in a pattern parallel to the railroad yards. Antiaircraft fire over the target was moderate for range and deflection. Eight to ten bursts were near the formation; fifteen to twenty bursts were below and trailing. All were black and round in shape. Ground fire came from heavy and automatic weapons near the foot of the bridge on the east bank of the river.

All bombs were away at 1330, and the formation headed home. One white smoke column observed as the formation left the target area rose to about 200 feet and could be seen from a distance of 3 miles. Fighters returning later reported two secondary explosions on the railroad yards caused by elements of the 2nd Squadron, and one large fire on storage dumps by the 4th Squadron on the east bank of the river.

The two 3rd Squadron planes returned to Laohokow along with four from the 4th Squadron, but one of the 4th Squadron Mitchells ran low on gas and bellied in. No injuries were reported. The 4th Squadron's Sgt. Weinert later expressed his preference to fly with American pilots because the Chinese were hesitant to pull out of a fight and sometimes ran out of gas on their way back to base.[4] Four planes of the 2nd Squadron and three of the 4th proceeded directly back to Liangshan. The two 3rd Squadron planes remained overnight at Laohokow and returned to Peishiyi the following day.

Although aircraft encountered no enemy opposition, one of the fighters went down on the return trip. Lt. Col. William N. ("Bill") Reed, an AVG ace and at this time in command of the 3rd Fighter Group, led the fighters on this important mission. As he was returning to base at Liangshan, enemy bombers struck to avenge the previous day's raid on Hankow. The airfield blacked out and he was unable to land. As he waited for the lights to be turned back on, Reed circled his P-40 until it ran out of gas and crashed. He bailed out but, as Sgt. Yao had, hit his head as he jumped and did not survive. He was found near the wreckage with his parachute unopened. The highest-ranking member of the wing to be killed during the war, Reed had completed seventy-five AVG missions and sixty-six more with the CACW.[5]

Chennault's airmen had begun a systematic assault against Japanese supply centers and railways to prevent the accumulation of supplies to support Japanese offensives, and the December 19 mission was part of a huge, coordinated attack conducted by the 14th Air Force. Eighty-four B-29 Superfortresses flew out of Chengtu to strike Wuhan's main warehouse district along the river front in seven waves, ten minutes apart, while five others hit alternate targets. About 80 percent of the bombs were incendiaries, and the remainder were HEs. It was the first mass firebombing by B-29s.

Two hundred 14th Air Force planes flew in support, targeting surrounding airfields to prevent enemy planes from escaping or intercepting the big bombers. That same day, thirty-three B-24s carried out attacks on barracks and administrative buildings at Hankow, while twenty-three B-25s hit Wuchang and seven others bombed barracks and a bridge at Siaokan (Xiaogan) Airfield, located 30 miles farther west. Fighter support for the raids was provided by 149 P-40s and P-51s that claimed forty-two enemy aircraft down and destroyed on the ground. Raids flown day and night pounded airfields, railroads, supply dumps, and other targets in a drive to smash this vital link in the Japanese supply lines. Fires burned in the vicinity of Wuhan for three days, gutting docks, warehouses, and other shipping facilities. According to Sgt. Daniels, whose 1st Squadron did not take part in this mission, "The raid created a huge firestorm in the Hankow area and a total of sixty-four enemy aircraft were claimed destroyed[,] with a loss of only three American fighter planes."[6]

By this time, many of the P-40s of the fighter squadrons were being replaced with P-51 Mustangs. Said to be "fully 50 mph faster than the CACW's P-40Ns and capable of operations at much[-]higher altitudes," they also possessed a greatly increased range. The P-40N, used earlier in the war, boasted a respectable 750-mile range, which had made it a favorite of General Chennault, but the new Mustang's range was 900 miles, and later models exceeded that figure to 1,000.[7]

War correspondents were informed that aerial assaults would be carried out against every Japanese-held supply port on the Chinese mainland with "the maximum tonnage of bombs and the greatest number of planes which can be obtained," and combined raids such as the joint attack on Hankow by B-29s and planes of the CACW and other 14th Air Force units would continue for as long as necessary. Chungking radio appealed to Chinese civilians to immediately evacuate the principal cities of occupied China, Manchuria, and Formosa; to shun Japanese military establishments; and to avoid travel on any Japanese-controlled vehicle. During the same period, American planes dropped leaflets that warned the Chinese—especially those in or near Japanese-held supply ports, concentration areas, and airfields—to leave the area.[8]

Foul weather had grounded aircraft for a full week, but skies finally cleared enough to allow Task Force 34 operations to resume. A one-plane night raid was off at 1845 on the nineteenth, despite problems on takeoff with the right motor that threatened to scrub the mission. Carrying seventeen M41 frag clusters aboard A/C #722 (with Lane, Lipira, Weinert, Wadlow, and Magyar as his crew), Baker proceeded to the Siangtan area and turned north at the Hsiang. Between 10 and 15 miles south of Changsha, crewmen spotted the lights of a fifty-to-sixty-vehicle northbound convoy, some of them forming double lines along a stream. Determining that the vehicles were being ferried across the stream, Baker dropped ten clusters. One produced a secondary explosion with considerable lateral flash, starting a large fire, and another caused a smaller fire. He dropped the rest on a second convoy spotted at Fulimpo. He then dropped in to attack a third convoy of about fifteen vehicles west of Changsha by strafing, with many good hits.

Pulling up from the strafing run, the startled pilot narrowly avoided collision with a Japanese night fighter. Almost immediately, crewmen reported four others coming in from several directions. They appeared to be converging on the convoy and may have been attracted by the strafing. The enemy aircraft were not visible except for their position lights, and there was no indication that they had detected the Mitchell. The promptness with which the night fighters had arrived suggested excellent air-ground liaison, but they seemed to lack effective airborne radar. Although one generally followed for about ten minutes, there was no contact and no decoy firing. Chihkiang homing and radar facilities were excellent that night, and the plane was down without difficulty.

Aboard a 4th Squadron raider, A/C #711, off at 1900 this night, Sgt. Peters flew as Capt. Lyon's tail gunner. The river that meanders through the broad Hsiang valley was identified by its faint glimmer reflecting the moonlight, after more than an hour of searching for a checkpoint. The flight crew observed no enemy activity, so the pilot sought out Pailochi Airdrome. He released all seventeen M41 stabilized frag clusters over revetments parallel to the runway, but no effect other than the flash of their explosions was visible, and there was no reaction from the enemy. Crewmen observed lights of an aircraft on the return flight. A small amount of inaccurate A/W (automatic weapons) fire came up from the vicinity of Yiyang.

Lt. Edgerton logged a mission to harass enemy supply movements in the Hsiang valley on the night of December 20 as his eighteenth combat mission. Capt. Lyon, Edgerton, and gunners Shock, Hoyle, and Cantor took off aboard A/C #718 at 1900 in good weather, with some light from the early moon that allowed them to find the Hsiang River easily. Even before reaching it, they saw the lights of several convoys moving north in a 6-mile stretch of the Isuho–Hengshan road. They attacked the convoys at once, and Lyon released all seventeen stab-frag clusters in three passes from 2,000 to 1,500 feet. The accuracy of the bursts was from good to excellent, and all were well within the lethal radius of the bombs. Although no fires resulted, very heavy damage and casualties were probable.

Turning north, the pilot saw many lights, and since there was no indication of night fighters, the B-25's gunners strafed all lights at will. Near Changsha, they heavily strafed a small convoy, resulting in many strikes. Then they shot up a compound and started a fire south of Changsha. When the Mitchell later returned to the vicinity, they found that at least two buildings were in flames. As the plane continued south, crewmen observed the lights of two small convoys near Isuho. They strafed those vehicles "with many good hits" and forced out the lights.

At Peishiyi, nothing more menacing occurred than a one-ball alert that sounded at 1841 on the nineteenth. Its duration was three hours and four minutes. Although no enemy planes were spotted over the field, the men were once again kept from their beds. Lts. Young and Smith conducted the third in the series of orientation programs for personnel of the 3rd and 4th Squadrons, "with the complete coverage of the war news and operations" for the previous ten days. "The men of both the squadrons enjoyed the orientation program tremendously."

Squadron personnel had sent holiday greetings to their families in late November via V-mail to ensure arrival before Christmas. Hank wrote to his parents on a form provided by the 14th Air Force: "This isn't much of a Christmas card but it's the best thing there is. Wishing you a Merry Christmas and Happy New Year. Love, Son." Now, as the holidays approached, men stationed across China made plans to celebrate with whatever festivities they could manage.

Thanks to the efficiency of the APO system, packages began to arrive at Peishiyi during the week before Christmas. According to the CACW historical report, mail came in at 2,000 pounds each day, and on some days two such "morale-boosting loads" were delivered. The men had received a great many packages from home, so most had "lots of good things in their rat hole," wrote Lt. Chenoweth. The mess hall took on a festive appearance, decked

Still at sodden Peishiyi, Hank sent a Christmas greeting to his parents. The "Chinese characters" seem to be decorative and have no meaning. *J. H. Mills collection*

Successes and Setbacks 197

out with holiday red and green. So many tidbits were coming from home that GIs began experimenting with cooking weird concoctions of food on the little hostel-room stoves. "Whatever culinary horrors were achieved, they always tasted better than that produced in the mess hall, since it came from loved ones," Hummel noted. The gifts kept streaming in, some of them appropriate, as well as "strange, bemused conceptions of what constituted proper gifts for our hinterland existence," he wrote. "Flashy silk drawers, refined neckties, and even compasses were found in the lot. . . . Ill-conceived, even such gifts brought happiness. Morale had no ceiling this week before Christmas."

Packages from Nancy typically included candy (Hank's favorites were chocolate fudge, peanut brittle, and divinity), fruitcake, brownies, and oatmeal-raisin cookies, all made from ingredients that were strictly rationed and hoarded for special occasions back home, as well as such wartime luxuries as one or two apples and oranges. "It smells like Safeway sure enough," he gratefully wrote home.

Although the holiday held no particular significance to the Chinese, many of them gave small gifts to their favorite Americans. Because the pay of the Chinese, even officers, was so much lower than that received by American GIs, these gifts represented a sacrifice, and even the smallest was appreciated. In return, the Americans presented surplus toilet articles, gum, mints, and soap to their Chinese houseboys and others whose work they valued.

Maj. Seacrest was awarded the Distinguished Flying Cross and Maj. Hodges (now with the 1st Squadron) and TSgt. Armstrong the Air Medal, and Capt. Graves received both the Distinguished Flying Cross and the Air Medal (these last two now back in the States). December 22 marked the return of Maj. Conrad, Lt. Logan, and MSgt. Fuller from Bangalore, bringing with them supplies intended to enhance holiday cheer. TSgt. Solyn was sent to the hospital at Kunming and treated for a throat infection with penicillin (only recently in common use), and SSgt. Dunlap was admitted because of "eye trouble." From West Virginia, Dunlap had enlisted in the regular Army in January 1940 and attended Air Corps Technical Schools later that year. He had served as a maintenance technician at Maxwell Field, Alabama, at Southwest Proving Grounds, Hope, Arkansas, and Eglin Field, Florida, before steaming aboard *Mission Bay* to Karachi and assignment as a crew chief with the 3rd Squadron.

Maj. Seacrest, Lt. Wood, MSgt. Hanrahan, and TSgt. Libolt took off for Enshih. Lt. Senecal, Sgts. England and Jackson, and Cpl. Ryan left for detached service at Liangshan. All of them returned on Saturday the twenty-third, when everyone was given the afternoon off. That evening, the Wing's Chinese officers hosted a dinner-dance at the Chialing House in Chungking for all American officers. "Many beautiful Chinese girls turned out and everyone had a big time except for the long ride to and from town" in an overcrowded weapons carrier, according to the 1st Bomb Group's historical report. Lt. Senecal's son is now in possession of the printed formal invitation presented to him.[9]

Base personnel not required for duty also had a full day off on Christmas Eve, and a party was given for wing enlisted men that evening. It began formally with a brief speech by Col. Bennett before he hurried away on business of his own. Alcohol was consumed in abundance. Even the Chinese houseboys were made drunk by GIs too generous with their holiday cheer.

Afterward, some of the men made their way to the Chinese Recreation Hall for high mass. Priests, organists, and a choir leader had been imported for the occasion from Chungking. The mass was well attended. Since Protestants and Jews had no chaplain and no service, many of them took part as well, likely because they were feeling homesick and melancholy as a result of being separated from their loved ones by so many thousands of miles during the holidays. Some even sang in the choir. Although a party atmosphere had prevailed throughout the day and evening, the service was reverent and soothing.

MSgt. Hanrahan, with the 4th Squadron's MSgt. Everett C. Bradley, who had returned from Chihkiang, spoke on the NBC *Coast to Coast Army Hour*. Sponsored by the War Department, the series featured interviews with Army personnel serving in various theaters of the war. In order to reach its audience "live" on Christmas Eve back home, the broadcast was transmitted over Chungking Station XGOY at 0245 on Christmas morning and "beamed direct to the States." When questioned by the master of ceremonies regarding his duties, Hanrahan answered, "I'm communication chief for my squadron on the ground . . . and a top-turret gunner when we're in the air."

"What did you say the name of your squadron was, Sergeant?"

"I didn't say. It's a little tough to get out in one mouthful, but I'll try. It's the 'skunk-holding-its-nose-at-the-rising-sun' squadron." Hanrahan said that he had completed twenty-five combat missions by that time and explained, "We have to look for the Japs over quite a hunk of territory. You could drop the United States down into our hunting ground and have room left over for a sizable slice of Canada."

"Do the Chinese and Americans in your outfit celebrate occasions like Christmas together?"

"Sure, we team up on parties like everything else. We invite the Chinese to celebrate Christmas with us. . . . They'll have us in for their Chinese New Year festivities."

When asked about the past year's activities and hopes for 1945, Hanrahan related that the squadron's bombers had flown low over Chinese ground troops to encourage them before they retook Myitkyina, and expressed the hope "to be flying low over Chinese troops just before they march back into Kweilin and Liuchow . . . and Canton and Shanghai and Hongkong and Peiping."

Airfields across China received this greeting on December 25:

FROM GEN. WEDEMEYER'S HQS., CHINA—From Maj. Gen. A. C. Wedemeyer to his troops in the China Theater: Christmas 1944 finds us all half a world away from home, engaged in one of the greatest struggles in the history of mankind, such a terrible struggle that few of us can be home this Christmas. For us, Christmas must carry its spiritual message, the same message it has carried to men of good will for more than nineteen centuries—the message of "peace on earth." And those whom we love, those who wait for Christmas as we begin to celebrate Christmas Day, know that we in far-off China pray in one voice with them that peace through victory will be attained in 1945.

Gen. Chennault sent his own message of hope, praising his men's courage and endurance and expressing his confidence of victory in the coming year. "Working together with patience and fortitude will inevitably bring the dividends of victory and our early return home. With this full confidence, I extend to you all my most sincere greetings. Let us work together unceasingly to fulfill our pledge."

Christmas at Peishiyi was not "white," despite a few snow flurries during the previous week. In fact, Christmas Day was so warm that the men did not even need their jackets. They once again had the entire day off, and most started it by sleeping late. That morning, each of them received a gift of four cans of beer. China was one of the few US stations where troops were not supplied with a beer ration, because airfreight space over the Hump was much too limited for hauling beer, so this was a special treat. Still more mail and packages came in, and reveling started all over again. Christmas dinner was served at 2:00 that afternoon and consisted of canned turkey, roast duck and goose, dressing, cranberry sauce, mashed potatoes, salad, and apple pie. Although some of "the usual trimmings" were missing, Lt. Young noted, "We enjoyed it just the same." A dance was held that evening for the officers at the Chinese Recreation Hall, and truckloads of Chinese girls were brought in for the occasion.

A longing for home and a hope that the war would soon come to an end—these were the thoughts and emotions shared by men of the 3rd Bomb Squadron and servicemen around the world as 1944 neared an end. President Roosevelt's greetings were relayed to the men stationed at Peishiyi on the twenty-sixth. "We would not cheapen your hours of heroism by wishing you a Merry Christmas, but we wish you to know that we are with you in spirit, in comradeship, and in faith," he wrote.

SSgt. Dunlap, who had spent Christmas at the 95th Station Hospital in Kunming, returned to Peishiyi two days later.

Officers on detached service to Task Force 34 brought the spirit of the holidays to Chihkiang by the addition of an evergreen tree decorated with materials on hand and greeting cards from their families. Posing for the camera are (*left to right, front row, sitting*) Lt. S. A. Lipira and Lt. T. H. Edgerton; (*middle row, kneeling*) Lt. J. G. Cantor, Capt. C. H. Condon, Lt. E. E. Lane, Lt. M. A. Doran, Lt. F. P. Pulaski; and (*back row, standing*) Capt. M. N. Lyon, Lt. C. J. Portaluppi, Lt. J. H. Rich, Lt. L. C. Baker, according to an entry in the 4th Bomb Squadron monthly historical report for December 1944. *M. N. Lyon collection, courtesy of Kelly Lyon*

Among the 3rd Squadron officers assigned to Task Force 34 at Chihkiang during the holidays were Lts. Baker, Cantor, Edgerton, and Pulaski. With officers of the 4th Squadron, they erected an evergreen tree and decorated it with cotton "snow" borrowed from the dispensary, paper chains from materials acquired from the orderly room, and holiday cards received from home.[10] The fact that some of them were Christian and some Jewish did not prevent them from uniting in their celebration of the season.

Lt. Baker left Chihkiang for Kunming to pick up "some supplementary rations and above all some beer and jungle rations" that had been accumulating for the men of the bomb squadrons assigned to Task Force 34 and those of the 5th Fighter Group. He returned to Chihkiang on the twenty-fourth, to the relief of those who were eagerly awaiting his arrival. "The mission had been a huge success[,] and the whole base proceeded to celebrate it with frequent libations. Christmas eve was the witness of much hilarious merry-making in the best of American tradition," wrote the 4th Squadron's historical officer. Dinner on Christmas day was "excellent" and included "as many of the traditional foods as could be obtained."

The holiday season did not halt operations. Task Force 34 approached the end of the year rather unproductively by flying three one-plane raids on December 26, regardless of decidedly bad weather. The first (mission #50) was yet another raid against convoys in the Hsiang valley. A/C #718 (Portaluppi, Wei, Hoyle, Magyar, and Wadlow) was off at 1915. They spotted one or two lights in the vicinity of Hengyang, so Portaluppi dropped four of the twenty-two 100 lb. M30 demos on the chance that they might be part of a convoy. Coming across Hengyang Airdrome, he decided to "pay his compliments" by dropping four bombs that hit west of the runway, followed by eight more over a convoy south of Changsha. Next, he attacked the island opposite the town by dropping the remaining bombs and making five strafing passes, during which Portaluppi also fired three rounds of 75 mm HE. Finally, gunners hit vehicles on railroad cars about 10 miles south of Changsha with machine gun fire while the pilot blasted them with the cannon.

Failure of the plane's radio compass caused by a malfunction of the loop mechanism made it impossible for the pilot to locate Chihkiang, since dense overcast had settled over the area. He was eventually able to find the field through cooperation from another Mitchell that circled and flashed its landing lights at regular intervals. At one point, as Portaluppi was letting down through 1,700-foot cloud cover, he "received a very nasty shock when by mischance he broke out headed directly away from the field." Just as he was about to pull up again and was making a slight turn, he spotted a flare fired from the field and "promptly made for it, where to the great relief of all concerned, the aircraft was down at 2400 after nearly five exacting hours."

A/C #722 (Baker, Jen, Edgerton, Rieks, Farris, and Shock) was airborne at 2000 with twenty-two M30 100 lb. demos. Observing no enemy traffic because of heavy overcast in the immediate vicinity of Changsha, the pilot proceeded to Ikiawan, a town on the railroad about 15 miles south of Changsha. He dropped all bombs on a run to the south at 4,500 feet. Bombs struck in the town and dust rose in the moonlight, but no fires or secondary explosions were visible. Continuing south to Siangtan, Edgerton (who logged the mission as his seventeenth) plotted a course to Chihkiang, and Baker landed at 2310.

A 4th Squadron J, A/C #701 (Lane, Pulaski, Lipira, Cantor, Peters, and Aspgren), took off at 2045 with seventeen frag clusters, on the prowl for targets in the Hsiang valley. Finding no enemy activity as far north as Tungting Lake, the pilot turned south again to attack Changsha, where he dropped two bombs from 6,500 feet on the storage and docks section along the riverfront south of the town. Although the pattern of bursts ran through the area, no effect could be observed. On his way back home, Lt. Lane encountered Portaluppi's plane and aided him to locate the field. Soon after the other plane had let down safely, Lane's radio compass also failed. The plane drifted 40 miles north of the field before he began flying a reciprocal heading. A short distance from where the field was estimated to be, the crew saw a glow through the overcast. The pilot let down but found he was over a large brush fire. He located the field when flares were shot up from below.

On the final mission of the year—#53—Portaluppi (with Cheng, Doran, Farris, Rieks, and Wadlow) led in takeoff on December 27 at 1405 aboard A/C #722, followed by A/C #718 (Wang, Shio, Liang, Wang, and Ma) and escorted by eight 5th Fighter Group "Hawks." The bombers each carried twenty-two 100 lb. M30 demos to attack Ishan "in order to restrict its use by the enemy and to inflict casualties." En route the formation passed into clear weather conditions, but visibility remained limited. As briefed, aircraft met the railroad line west of the target and turned east. Portaluppi made one pass across the town to verify the target, and then the bombers turned 180 degrees and made the bombing pass at 2,800 feet, dropping on Doran's lead. Unfortunately, the intervalometer failed for several seconds before releasing the bombs, causing a severe error in range. Nearly all fell outside the "thickly built-up area" of the town, and only minor damage was inflicted to a few scattered houses. The only other damage reported was caused by one of the fighters that dive-bombed a village immediately east of Ishan, with considerable accuracy.

Through the month of December, operations by Task Force 34 opposed the Japanese advance in the Kweichow-Kwangsi area, where the heaviest action took place that month. Sixteen missions were credited to the 3rd Squadron and nineteen to the 4th Squadron. Six of them were against Japanese concentrations in small towns along their advance west from Liuchow. Considerable damage was inflicted on the enemy as a result of these raids. Eleven were night missions, ten against supply movements in the Hsiang valley from Yochow to Hengyang, where the task force took a heavy toll on the enemy in spite of bad weather and icing. The most effective nocturnal strike was against the searchlights of Hankow on the tenth. Five of the night missions were in support of B-24s at Hankow. Low-level bombing and strafing attacks by the B-25s aided greatly in reducing antiaircraft fire directed at the B-24s, and deterred the numerous searchlights from picking them up.

Girls were again to be imported for a dance held at the Chinese Recreation Hall for the enlisted men at Peishiyi on December 28. Maj. Hummel described the preparations. "About the GI hostel that evening there was preparatory spit and polish, shoes were shined, faces were scraped pink, medals, down to the conduct ribbon, were pinned across the chest, all to impress the promised truckloads of Chinese beauties. This time the customary outlandish ration of one man to 20 women would not pertain." Every man was to have his own dancing partner "to knead and maul and haul around the floor." Alas, when the truck appeared, only two girls were on it. The officers party of two nights before "had not left a sweet savor." Most of the girls had been unable to stand the rough ride by weapons carriers over the mountains to Chungking, and "most had heaved their pretty guts." None were in the mood for further manhandling by GIs and GI trucks. The dance was called off, and the disappointed GIs removed their finery and got sullenly drunk. "Our excessive holiday spirit was backfiring; everybody was satiated."

Americans may have had their fill of celebration, but the Chinese had more entertainment in store. They wanted to again share their favorite diversion with their American comrades, so for three consecutive nights they presented an extravaganza of Chinese opera. Hummel described the elaborate presentation:

> Officers and enlisted men were the honored guests, with specially-reserved front seats. The five hours of opera—three distinct protracted musical plays—were presented each evening in a cavernous barn-like Chinese airplane factory, drafty and damp and cold. The benumbed GI spectator huddled up in his overcoat tried to follow the endless gyrations of an involved cast of performers in a bewildering series of entrances and exits to the deafening clanging of cymbals and kettles, and the thunderous beating of drums. The cold of the cement floor stole up his feet to further benumb his addled brain from making any sense out of the wild evening on the stage. Chinese

opera seemed most athletic. The tearing in and off stage was interspersed with long chants in an affected falsetto tremolo to the accompaniment of stately gestures, pirouetting, and hand and finger posturing wherein every delicate toss of the hands supposedly held interpretive significance. The involved tortuous gyrations of an enormous cast on a tiny stage, disporting itself in wild leaps and snaking convolutions before it poured at top speed off stage, was meaningless to the western mind, but was so full of glittering color, resplendent costume and wild banshee action that for a while it held the attention of the huddled spectator.

The first of the plays was "a delicate fantasy," the next "an honest slapstick comedy," and "a bombastic historical drama of ancient battles and invasions" climaxed the marathon. "A little of this would have been interesting for sheer tantalizing curiosity. But a lot of it on top of the benumbing cold added up to a totality of boredom for the GI turtlenecked in his overcoat." Hummel concluded, "Numb with opera we recreationally ended the year 1944."

As the year came to a close, the 3rd Squadron received more additions to personnel. The monthly historical report stated that the "Spray and Pray Boys" welcomed 2Lt. Allan Mikola as squadron navigator, as well as Flight Officer Barton L. Wherritt (B-25 pilot), Sgt. Loren E. Gaffney (A/P mechanic–gunner–flight engineer), and Cpls. John J. DeFabritis (radio operator–mechanic–gunner) and Robert G. Hugel (A/P armorer-gunner), all of whom had arrived on Christmas Day. These last two additions were New Yorkers from the city's inner suburbs, DeFabritis from Westchester County and Hugel from the Bronx, immediately to the south.

Flight Officer Barton L. Wherritt, attached as a B-25 pilot, was one of several replacements who arrived in late 1944. He soon earned the respect of operational officers with whom he flew, despite the fact that he had not been granted commission as second lieutenant. *Courtesy of Terry Godfrey Healy*

Sgt. Loren E. Gaffney, attached at the same time, was a skilled welder and flame cutter who patched up the Mitchells in addition to his duties as an airplane mechanic–gunner–flight engineer. *L. E. Gaffney collection, courtesy of Terry Kasparek*

SSgt. B. F. Thomas Jr., found in civil records as Bert Franklin Thomas Jr., became the squadron's radar specialist. *R. N. Solyn collection, courtesy of Robert N. Solin*

Cpl. Robert G. Hugel, armorer-gunner, was another of those attached on Christmas Day. *Courtesy of Robert G. Hugel*

As a university student, Mikola had been recognized as an outstanding senior accounting major and granted a leave of absence from school to accept a position with a public accounting firm in Chicago. After graduating with a bachelor of science degree in business administration, he was employed as an accountant in his hometown of Paterson, New Jersey. After enlistment, his military training began at the Finance Replacement Training Center, Fort Benjamin Harrison, Indiana, in February 1943. He was transferred soon afterward to the AAF as an aviation cadet but was redirected to navigator school. Mikola completed navigation training and received his commission as second lieutenant in July 1944. He had served as 2nd Bomb Squadron navigator since his arrival in China.[11]

SSgt. B. F. Thomas Jr., a radar specialist from the Communication Department at Group, joined the squadron soon afterward. Formerly a radio mechanic, he had completed a radar course at Kunming in September. Cpl. Allegretto returned from the hospital in Kunming, where he had spent more than a week. Hospital admission files state that he received penicillin therapy for some undisclosed infection.[12]

All American officers and enlisted men stationed at Peishiyi were invited to attend new year's celebrations hosted by the China National Federation of Industries, the Association of Factories Removed to Szechuan, the Southwest Industrial Association, the Association of Merchants and Manufacturers of China Products, and the Chungking Chamber of Commerce. They held separate parties—for officers on Saturday evening, December 30, and for enlisted men on Sunday evening, New Year's Eve. Both events took place at the Victory House in Chungking and included buffets and music. In addition, "many girls of all nationalities were present and available for dancing."

Hank, who attended with Barge and Wilkie, recalled the evening. "We went to that place, and a man came out and invited us to come to a big auditorium-like room with a bunch of Chinese—the ruling class. They had been to school in Germany and different places over the country. They spoke English." He remembered that they ate a meal together, "and they kept jumping up and having a toast to Eisenhower, a toast to Chiang Kai-shek, in little bitty containers, and they put some of that rice wine in there, and that'll make you crazy, that rice wine." Not a heavy drinker, he preferred to remain sober. "One time I went outside and put my finger down my throat and threw up so I wouldn't have that stuff in me. We told them finally that we didn't want to hurt their feelings, but we were going to have to leave—and that's all I remember about it."

Lt. Young had been the squadron's historical officer for the past five months. He wrote, on December 31, in his final entry: "To all the new officers and enlisted men who joined our squadron in the last two months, we put our best foot forward in the hope that they will enjoy being with us as much as we enjoyed being with them." He wished good luck to Capts. Thomas S. Simpson and Louis F. Graves, 1Lt. Eugene H. Dorr, and TSgt. William L. Armstrong, who had returned to the United States during the year, and added, "May fortune be as generous with them as it has been in giving us such friends."

Through December, the 3rd Squadron flew thirty-five sorties in eighteen combat missions totaling fifty-eight combat hours (including the sixteen missions credited to the detachment at Chihkiang) and expended 6,210 rounds of .50 caliber; five rounds of 75 mm cannon shell; 291 M50A1, M47, M47A2, and M41 incendiary clusters; and 506 M30 100 lb. demolition bombs. As the year ended, the 3rd Squadron comprised nineteen American officers, forty-four American enlisted men, eighty-eight Chinese officers, and 137 Chinese enlisted men. Aircraft assigned to them were eight B-25Hs and three B-25Js.

CHAPTER ELEVEN
Relocating to Liangshan

As the new year began, wing headquarters announced estimates of damage inflicted upon the enemy. Unofficial totals included 190 enemy aircraft destroyed in the air and 301 more on the ground. In addition, 1,467 vehicles were listed as destroyed, 131 probably destroyed, and 1,074 damaged. CACW bombers and fighters had additionally sunk several hundred thousand tons of shipping and taken a heavy toll on enemy ground troops, facilities, railroads, and bridges. Since its first combat mission in November 1943, thirty-five fighters and eight bombers had been lost to enemy ground fire, and twenty fighters had been shot down by Japanese aircraft. The fact that not a single CACW bomber had been lost to enemy interceptors was attributed both to the abilities of the B-25 pilots and their crews and the quality of the escort protection provided by bomb wing fighter pilots.

January 1 was a day of leisure for the "imbibers of Chunking gin," affectionately known as "jing bao juice" (although other fermented or distilled concoctions that included rice wine and plum wine shared this appellation). Most members of the squadron stayed in bed until noon. Many later lined up outside the "doc's office" for something to alleviate the inevitable headaches and other symptoms of overindulgence.

The year-end excesses were put behind and activities returned to normal. Lt. Mikola, new squadron navigator, began a course for the Chinese student navigators on January 3. Capt. Jack M. Hamilton (B-25 pilot) and 1Lt. Robert E. Banger (navigator) were attached, and Sgt. Dunlap was ordered back to the 95th Sta. Hospital at Kunming for observation and treatment. SSgt. Gruber was promoted to technical sergeant, and Sgt. Evitts to staff sergeant.

Evitts, administrative NCO since the squadron's activation, oversaw activities of the clerks in the orderly room. His duties included replying to routine correspondence, routing incoming correspondence to higher

Capt. Jack M. Hamilton, a veteran B-25 pilot who had proved his worth against targets in North Africa and Europe, joined the 3rd Squadron in early January 1945. His cheerful demeanor soon earned him the moniker, "Smilin' Jack." *Courtesy of John Hamilton*

Lt. Robert E. Banger, a competent navigator-bombardier, joined at the same time. *Robert E. Banger collection, courtesy of Beth Banger Meehan*

Lt. Willard G. Ilefeldt, a B-25 flight leader, flew many 3rd Bomb Squadron combat missions and served as its historical officer until the end of the war. The "bombs" indicate thirteen aerial victories when this photo was taken. *W. G. Ilefeldt collection, courtesy of Christine Ilefeldt Hance*

authority whenever necessary, and supervising the publication of all orders, bulletins, letters, instructions, and commendations. During leisure time, he was a reliable player on the enlisted men's softball team.

Ilefeldt, known as "Tex" because of a drawl acquired during an early childhood spent in Texas, took over duties as squadron historian. Called a "dumb kid" because he was dyslexic and hyperactive, and labeled a troublemaker because of his frequent fights, he had been sent to a private boarding school intended to teach boys who were unsuccessful in traditional educational settings to become productive adults capable of supporting themselves. In addition to learning to accomplish a variety of practical chores and to take responsibility for completing those that were expected of him, he received a basic education using nontraditional teaching techniques that enabled him to overcome his disability and learn to read and write. Ilefeldt graduated from high school in Boston and went on to study acting and music, following in the footsteps of his opera-singer father, who had died when Willard was very young. He became an actor in summer stock, wrote plays, and sang with dance bands. So successful was he in conquering his condition that Ilefeldt later studied for the ministry, and he became a published author after retirement.[1]

Initially attached to the Massachusetts Army National Guard, based in Boston, he had enlisted in the infantry soon after the Pearl Harbor attack and gave details in his memoirs:

> I was inducted into the 26th Division, called the Yankee Division [at Camp Edwards, near Cape Cod]. We were told it had acquitted itself rather honorably against Germany during the first World War, doing its part "to make the world safe for democracy." After Pearl Harbor, when we were actually doing battle with an enemy and all the isolationists had turned quiet and I saw I was "in for the duration," I figured I better do something about it: I went to OC and became an infantry officer. Later (for the "convenience of the government," it was called) I transferred in grade and became a pilot and ended up as a flight leader flying combat with the Chinese Air Force under Chennault. But that is a story for another time.[2]

Relocating to Liangshan

Before shipping out to the CBI, he had married Janet Shaw, an actress whom he met at the Long Beach Municipal Airport while she was working on *Ladies Courageous*, a film about women pilots who ferried planes during the war.[3] "His wife knew some of those Hollywood women movie stars like Bette Davis," Hank recalled, and she had appeared in films with other stars such as Vivien Leigh, Susan Hayward, Clark Gable, Tex Ritter, Robert Taylor, and Humphrey Bogart as well.

The Chinese Orphan's Organization presented yet another Chinese opera. Everyone in the CACW stationed at Peishiyi attended—some out of genuine interest but most because attendance was a direct order from Col. Bennett. Maj. Hummel disclosed: "No better method has as yet been devised for securing a full, even if unwilling, house." As he had detailed in the December history, everyone who had the slightest curiosity about Chinese opera had already been "thoroughly satiated for three evenings of it," and "those who had no interest in the first place were now also herded to the Chinese airplane-factory-opera-house and had a long evening of opera rammed down their throats. It was the usual protracted historical fare . . . sighing for the heroics by gone days."

The hours-long performance was spectacular, with superb sword dancing, artful makeup, and exquisite costumes, according to the 3rd Squadron's new historian, who had not been subjected to any of the previous operatic programs. When the gorgeous "heroine" appeared—"a thing of beauty, with a high-pitched and strangely exotic voice that thrilled every soldier to the point of embarrassment"—men in the audience were shocked to discover that the "her" was actually a boy.

Hummel complained that the Chinese lacked the foresight to prepare even the sketchiest of synopsis to explain what signified "the off[-]key–falsetto wailing, and effeminate gestures on the stage." He noted that the uncomprehending and unwilling audience "could not be held" but "exuded surreptitiously through the doors" as the performance progressed. Enlisted men sneaked out the back until guards were posted to prevent further defections. Officers seated in the exposed front seats were urgently called out by accomplices on prearranged emergencies. When gaps appeared in the ranks, their Chinese hosts began to look strained and offended. "This lamentable evening ended our opera season, and unless the Chinese have short memories it is doubtful, after our calloused behavior toward their revered opera, we will ever be invited again—much to our relief."

The situation in China grew more troubling as 1945 began. As men of the 3rd Squadron languished at Peishiyi, the situation was looking grim. The Japanese were poised with heavy concentrations of troops and supplies in the Hengyang-Lingling-Leiyang triangle, from which three separate drives were possible: to occupy the Canton-Hankow Railroad corridor, to force the evacuation of 14th Air Force bases in Southeast China, or to strike toward Chihkiang, located northwest of Lingling. Two of these drives were launched before the end of January.

Soon after the year began, Japanese command made a decision to seize the railroad lines between Hankow and Canton. This objective was culminated with "lightning speed," thus achieving complete control of an inland supply route from bases in North China and the Yangtze basin to Canton and Hong Kong in the south, according to 1Lt. Robert N. Eisner, acting historical officer of the bomb group. This occupation greatly increased the mobility of the Japanese in moving men and equipment, especially to sites along the China coast where they anticipated that Allied landings might occur.

Regardless of the usual bad weather and shortages of gasoline and bombs, planes of the 1st Bomb Group attacked whenever presented with the opportunity. Most of the missions undertaken during January were aimed at the destruction of trackage, bridges, yards, and trains. As a result of these concentrated strikes, the Japanese were unable to use the rail lines between Hengyang and Kweilin or the airfields of those cities. Small detachments from the 3rd and 4th Squadrons remained at Chihkiang and continued their night raids on motor convoys in the Hsiang River corridor when weather conditions permitted, thereby depriving enemy troops of essential supplies.

Lt. Portaluppi expressed his opinion that the attitude of the military toward the supply situation in China at the time was generally one of apathy, since the primary focus was on the final Allied drive in the Pacific. Throughout the month, life at Chihkiang and Peishiyi continued along the same somewhat monotonous routine to which the squadron had become accustomed since its departure from Kweilin in September, he wrote. The weather was again responsible for holding operations to a minimum.

Through January, the only organized activity on the base at Peishiyi came in the form of occasional movies. Even Peishiyi village was declared off-limits after cigarettes and other government-provided items—even blankets and uniforms—were found for sale in some of the shops. A package of PX cigarettes bought for less than a dollar could be sold to a shopkeeper for $15. Since the ration was four cartons per man per month, a GI could easily add $45 to $60 to his monthly pay.[4] To discourage such black-market infractions, wing headquarters issued directives prohibiting the resale or barter of any items acquired from the PX. GIs were reminded that such items were intended exclusively for the personal comfort and pleasure of US soldiers and for no other purpose.

In addition, military discipline and courtesy came under increased scrutiny, especially in Chungking. Gen. Chennault issued a letter to all unit commanders of the 14th Air Force in which he referenced a recently received radiogram from Gen. Wedemeyer: "The CO was very much displeased with lack of discipline and general sloppy appearance of all ranks and grades." He urged all personnel under his command, both officers and enlisted men, to be properly dressed while outside their quarters in the prescribed uniform, according to the type of duty to be performed or the social activity in which they were engaged, and that they "avail themselves" of the facilities provided for shaving, although facial hair had previously been overlooked. "Poor discipline reflects directly on combat and operational efficiency." Chennault warned, "Such comments on the state of discipline of this command as quoted above are a source of embarrassment to me[,] and I expect every commander to take immediate vigorous corrective action to prevent a recurrence of this criticism."

Reports that ranged from failure to salute officers and incomplete or improper uniform to public intoxication and coercing local young women to accompany GIs to the photographer's shop had been received at CACW headquarters. Col. Bennett, in a letter that was distributed to all units under his command, conveyed this directive: "It is my desire that all American personnel of the Chinese American Composite Wing conduct themselves in a manner such that this organization will be an example to all others in the United States Armed Forces in China. We have a lot to be proud of, so let's show it in our dress and conduct." Officers came under even-greater criticism than enlisted men. They, too, had become accustomed to the relaxed, informal relationship brought about by sharing overcrowded facilities over a long period of time, and many did not even return a salute when it was occasionally delivered.

Hummel contended that these infractions were committed by personnel of non-CACW units on the base, which "kept us from such meager metropolitan life as Peishiyi's one, narrow, stinking, crooked street provided. It had been little enough; now we had nothing."

Even Chungking, now "increasingly stiffly militaristic, overcrowded, almost void of any provisions for sleeping quarters for the visiting soldier, and with its better eating and drinking establishments being off limits, at least to non-officers, while theoretically still on our three-day-pass visiting list[,] was actually more inconvenience and disappointment than the horrendous mountain ride warranted."

The weather finally cleared enough in the vicinity to allow planes into the air. Captains MacNeil and Ragland returned from India on January 6 with another new B-25J. Even more important to the men of the squadron, they brought with them "many delicacies and luxuries that under more[-]favorable conditions might be called necessities," according to Ilefeldt. They had made a visit to the American commissary and stocked up on as much as they could carry.

On that same day, six planes (one flight of three led by Maj. Conrad and the other by Maj. Seacrest) left Peishiyi and flew to Liangshan (now Liangping), which was to be used as the staging field because it was closer to the enemy action. Bad weather moved in again and delayed the mission for more than a week, prompting the flight crews to regret their failure to bring the necessary cigarettes, toiletries, and change of "undies."

Cpl. Allegretto works with two Chinese armorers to clean their weapons with A/C #715 visible behind them. It was one of the new J models that had recently been brought in to replace the older H carrying the same number. *A. R. Allegretto collection, courtesy of Mary Allegretto Henry*

The long-awaited mission finally took off from Liangshan on Monday, January 15. Nine B-25s from the 2nd Squadron, six from the 3rd (four H models and two Js), and three from the 4th were off at 1050. Conrad led the 3rd Squadron element with A/C #714, with Hamilton (copilot), Cunningham (bombardier), Banger (navigator), and Fuller, Long, and Hugel (turret, waist, and tail gunners), as well as Maj. V. B. Miller (observer). Seacrest was the pilot of the second J, A/C #715, with Sung S. C. (copilot), Mikola (navigator), and Libolt, Supsic, and Morris (gunners), and Wherritt flew #724, with Ilefeldt (listed as copilot) and Trout, Allegretto, DeFabritis, and Ryan (all gunners). Chinese crews flying A/C #716 (Chiang T., Kuan H. C., Hsiao T. P., and Weng C. K.), #717 (Teng C. C., Kao W. F., Yuan C. F., Ku C. T., and Ho W. C.), and #723 (Liu P. C., Liu P. C., Wei C. S., Liu T. C., and Lee J. S.) also participated, the last four all H models. The bombers flew to Laohokow, where an escort of twelve 3rd Fighter Group P-40s and four 16th Fighter Squadron P-51s joined them.

The formation flew on through clear skies to Kwangchow, to Shihkweiyao, and then to the Hankow storage area on the north bank of the confluence of the Han and Yangtze Rivers. The 3rd Squadron's planes were echeloned behind and to the left of the 2nd Squadron formation, which took the lead. Each carried eight 500 lb. GPs fused nose and tail to 0.1-second delay. All but three of the bombs, dropped at 7,450 feet on Cunningham's lead, successfully blanketed the target, falling in a pattern parallel to the railroad yards. A/C #716 salvoed its bombs due to malfunction of the release mechanism. Of those bombs released, 100 percent were credited as hits. Crewmen reported large fires and columns of heavy black smoke billowing to 6,000 feet. The successful Hankow docks raid was the only mission flown for the month by the 3rd Squadron, officially stationed at Peishiyi, and it served as a fitting final mission for Capt. Cunningham—his forty-seventh. He received his orders to return to the States three days later.

For Cpl. Supsic, who joined the squadron a month previously along with Cpl. Morris, this was his first and final combat mission. He received word soon afterward that his twenty-year-old brother, Army staff sergeant Peter Supsic, had been killed in action at Luxembourg during the Battle of the Bulge only two days prior to this mission. As one of three surviving sons of their widowed mother serving in the military, two of them in the AAF and one in the Navy, Supsic was thereafter required to fly no other combat missions but continued in his role as armorer.

Majs. Conrad and Seacrest returned to Peishiyi on the sixteenth and received orders for the squadron's permanent change of station to Liangshan (30º35' N, 107º50' E), situated about equidistant between Chengtu and enemy-held Ichang. They stayed overnight to finalize arrangements while Capt. MacNeil flew back with the news. The move, which was ordered in anticipation of a possible Japanese attack in the vicinity of Chungking and to position 3rd Squadron planes to better strike at the enemy's advance if an assault materialized, was well received by all personnel. "This transfer is welcome news to the squadron, for it promises an end to the squadron's 'ground fatigue,'" rejoiced Ilefeldt.

When Conrad and Seacrest returned to Liangshan the following day, they brought with them a new pilot, 1Lt. Frederick H. Greene Jr., from the 17th Fighter Squadron. His navigator, 1Lt. Robert J. Koss, was assigned by the same order but remained behind temporarily at Peishiyi. The squadron's Chinese contingent added some new personnel as well: SLts. Young Wen-peng (X-5016), Young Pao-ching (X-5017), Tsui Wen-poo (X-5018), Chen Kwo-chuan (X-5019), Szen Sze (X-5020), Kiang Ju-mao (X-5021), Chen Yi-poo (X-5022), and Tu Nan-li (X-5023).

Lt. Frederick H. Greene Jr. was attached to the squadron as a flight leader in mid-January. His experience with the 3rd Bomb Squadron included two bailouts. F. H. Greene Jr. collection, courtesy of Sibyl Greene Cryer

A navigator-bombardier, Lt. Robert J. Koss, joined at the same time. Both he and Greene had been attached temporarily to the 17th Fighter Squadron, 5th Fighter Group, before transferring to the 3rd Bomb Squadron. R. J. Koss collection, courtesy of Barbara Hughes

Lt. Edgerton explains the upcoming mission's target to a Chinese officer. He served with the 3rd Squadron from late September 1944 until May 24, 1945, when he transferred to the 4th Bomb Squadron. *R. N. Solyn collection, courtesy of Robert Solin*

Lt. Edgerton, still with Task Force 34, wrote in his diary on January 13 that he flew to Peishiyi to pick up mail for members of the 3rd and 4th Squadron detachments at Chihkiang. There he received news that had taken more than a month to reach him. "Found out today that Letitia Ann was born Dec. 5th 6:05 p.m. . . . Went to Peishiyi for mail or still wouldn't know I'm a father."[5] When he returned the following day, he flew aboard the new 3rd Squadron B-25J that had arrived from India on the sixth.

January 14 marked the first mission of the year out of Chihkiang. The new J model, serial #43-28164, was off at 1905 to attack supply movements in the Hsiang valley with seventeen M41 stab-frag clusters. Copilot to Capt. Lyon, Lt. Baker flew with an otherwise 4th Squadron crew. Heavy fog made it difficult to follow the river. Aircrewmen observed little activity north of Changsha, and the few groupings of loosely associated lights were extinguished as the aircraft approached, suggesting that they were on boats rather than vehicles.

When crewmen sighted lights in Changsha, the greatest number of them in the north-central section of town, the bombardier sighted for fifteen frag clusters. Flashes burst on the target. A second B-25J arrived and joined the attack on the central section and east of Changsha. Lyon then dropped the two remaining clusters on a convoy of twenty to thirty trucks south of the town. Although all bombs fell in the target area, heavy night haze obscured results. Lyon returned to Isuho and Siangtan with the intention of strafing but discovered that both had been blacked out. With no other observable enemy activity, the plane returned to base.

After Edgerton returned to Chihkiang on the fourteenth following his mail run, he participated in a mission that was off that evening at 1933. A/C #722 (Rich, Portaluppi, Edgerton, Rieks, Wadlow, and Magyar) followed the same course as Lyon's Mitchell and reported the same limited visibility near the river. When Rich saw the flashes created by the other Mitchell's bombs at Changsha, he joined in the attack and dropped six clusters on the south-central part of the town, although it had been blacked out as the result of Lyon's attack. He released six more clusters on the central section, but all seemed to be duds. The remaining five clusters, dropped farther east, burst on the target. With no further enemy activity observed, Rich returned to base. The crews of both planes reported "severe discomfort" as the result of the night's extreme cold.

Assigned to Task Force 34 in early 1945, Lt. Robert L. Logan, Lt. Thomas H. Edgerton, unidentified (likely 4th Bomb Squadron), an unidentified 26th Fighter Group officer, and Lt. Frank P. Pulaski pose for a picture in front of the Chihkiang barracks. *J. H. Mills collection*

Sgt. Gaffney, a mechanic-gunner-flight engineer who specialized as a welder and flamecutter, works with a Chinese mechanic on the engine of a B-25J, identified by its serial number, barely visible on the fuselage at the far right, as A/C #715. *L. E. Gaffney collection, courtesy of Terry Kasparek*

Lt. Faherty captioned this photo of Sgt. Learn "Pop cleaning 50 cal." Although he was noted as a cannon specialist, Learn continued in his other duties as an airplane armorer. *J. F. Faherty collection, courtesy of Dennis Faherty*

Sgt. William H. Whearty poses with 4th Bomb Squadron personnel. Standing (*left to right*) are Lt. Charles J. Portaluppi with Capt. Moncure N. Lyon beside him. Whearty is just below Portaluppi, the only one without a hat, and the other three are unidentified. *Courtesy of Richard Whearty*

Lt. Cantor and Sgts. Hoyle and Shock returned to Peishiyi in midmonth, and Lt. Logan and Sgts. Wilkerson, Gaffney, and Learn were detached to Chihkiang at the same time. Gaffney, assigned to the squadron as an airplane mechanic–gunner–flight engineer, had trained to be a welder and flame cutter in a program at Cessna Aircraft before enlistment and now aided in patching up the planes that were holed by enemy fire. Learn, called "Pop" by other squadron members, both officers and enlisted, and noted as a cannon specialist, was praised soon afterward in his hometown

Lt. Logan, only recently appointed a flight leader, was sent on detached service to Task Force 34 and soon found himself put to the test in combat. He is wearing his Chinese Air Force Wings as well as his AAF wings here. *R. L. Logan Collection, courtesy of Katherine A. Logan*

Relocating to Liangshan

newspaper for his "cheerful efficiency" that "has done much to strengthen the friendship between the peoples of the United States and China."[6] Unknown to any of them was the fact that wing headquarters was considering plans that would soon put an end to Task Force 34.

The 4th Squadron's A/C #701 took off at 1925 on January 15 carrying seventeen M41 stab-frag clusters. It was another night operation without moonlight. Sgt. Gaffney, on his first 3rd Squadron mission, flew as top-turret gunner with an otherwise 4th Squadron aircrew that included Lt. Lane as pilot. Finding clear weather with visibility restricted by haze at the river south of Changsha, Lane turned toward the town and there discovered the lights of a convoy. He released six clusters that resulted in a good pattern. Farther south, he dropped three clusters on lights around installations at Isuho ferry. Continuing to the south, crew members observed the lights of a convoy of more than twenty-four vehicles entering Hengshan from the west and north. Four strafing passes produced two fires described as red in color and "large and long as if several vehicles were burning." The aircraft continued its southward progress, and the pilot dropped the remaining eight bombs on the lights of a convoy of moderate size spotted north of Hengyang Airdrome. A small secondary explosion followed by two fires was the result. Lane then turned on a course for Chihkiang.

Another one-plane mission was off at 2000 on this night. A/C #722 (Portaluppi, Wang, Wei, Wadlow, Rieks, and Peters), carrying the same bombload and following the same course as Lane, dropped five clusters on installations at Isuho ferry. Seven clusters fell on a convoy estimated as twenty vehicles on the Isuho–Henshang road. Portaluppi bagged a third convoy 4 miles south of Hengyang Airdrome with the remaining clusters. Although a good pattern was reported for all bombs, the usual limited visibility of night missions prevented determination of results.

Off at 2050 on the fifteenth, the recently acquired B-25J, serial #43-28164 (Chinese number not specified), flew out of Chihkiang alone, carrying seventeen M41 stab-frag clusters, "to harass enemy supply movements" and to reconnoiter for reported enemy activity south and east of Hengyang. The plane's nickname was "You Say How Much" (a phrase used by local prostitutes) or "Filthy" (pilot's code name). Its pilot was 1Lt. Baker, and Capt. Lyon was his copilot, with 2Lt. Edgerton as navigator, TSgts. Farris as top-turret gunner, Wilkins as waist gunner, and Wilkerson as tail gunner. Three were members of the 3rd Squadron, and three flew with the 4th Squadron. Capt. Lyon recorded the mission as his fiftieth and Lt. Edgerton as his twentieth. Although many details were included in the subsequent Missing Air Crew Report and in 3rd and 4th Squadron historical reports for January, the most thorough account was submitted by the 5th Fighter Group, compiled from interviews later conducted and attached as supplemental to the operational report for Task Force 34's mission #58.

After taking off under clear conditions with visibility restricted by haze to 2 or 3 miles, Baker proceeded to the Hsiang River at Siangtan and turned north. Visibility in the target area was poor. Almost at once, crewmen sighted a convoy of forty to fifty vehicles through the overcast east of Siangtan, and Baker moved in for the attack, but bombs failed to release. Lights blacked out immediately as the Mitchell passed overhead. Baker found another convoy west of Changsha and attacked, but again bombs would not release. A check of equipment revealed that the intervalometer had been inadvertently set at "train," and the second convoy had also blacked out by the time the error could be corrected. Baker then attacked a group of lights south of Changsha that he believed to be those of parked vehicles, with five clusters. There was no immediate effect, although a good pattern resulted and considerable damage was later reported as probable.

The pilot turned south toward Hengyang, but neither he nor his aircrew observed anything of interest on this leg of the flight. After running out the ETA, he was unable to locate Hengyang and turned the aircraft north again. Visual contact with the Hsiang was lost and never reestablished as visibility became increasingly poor.

During this northbound leg, he attacked a convoy of more than thirty-five vehicles with seven clusters at an undetermined location. No immediate effect was observed, although the bombs again appeared to burst squarely on the convoy. Baker continued north and flew ten minutes longer than the south leg but could recognize nothing. However, believing that they were in the vicinity of Changsha, he flew a search, with all crewmen watching for landmarks. While on the east leg of this search, they spotted another convoy, and the pilot released the remaining clusters at a right-angle turn on a road at another unidentified location. Once again, there were no fires or secondary explosions, but an excellent pattern probably resulted in heavy damage. He then continued to search, but efforts proved unavailing. Still operating under the assumption that they were in the Changsha area, he took up a course of 260 degrees at 2400, with the expectation that when the ETA (0055) had been flown out, they would at least be able to establish radio contact with Chihkiang.

At 0100, however, they had made no radio contact whatsoever and had seen no recognizable landmarks, so Baker turned the IFF (identification friend or foe) to the emergency station. Assuming their position to be north of Chihkiang, on the basis of Edgerton's calculations, the pilot flew south for twenty minutes without results, then east for ten minutes. From about 0030 and continuing until just before the aircraft was abandoned, Baker and Lyon alternated in attempting to establish radio contact with any station on any of the channels in use, as well as in attempting to acquire a radio compass heading. They heard no station in the Chihkiang area. Although "Alloy" (Chengtu) and "Drawbar" (Peishiyi) were heard "R5 S5," no contact could be established. They followed a radio compass bearing on Liangshan (LM) that brought some hope for ten minutes, but the needle began to hunt and to circle. A later report stated that although the plane made no further confirmed radio contact after takeoff, a fragment of a radio transmission received by the air-ground station at Chihkiang at 0145 was thought to have been from the pilot. No contact could be established, and the identity of the message remained unverified.

By 0145 it had become obvious to those on board that the aircraft was completely lost and out of contact, with the added complication of a diminishing gasoline reserve. Edgerton checked the main compass against the magnetic compass in the tail, and the pilot took up a course of 330 degrees to ensure that the aircraft was over friendly territory if a bailout became necessary. During this flight, crewmen spotted lights on the ground that may have been a village, so Baker took the Mitchell down and circled, only to be greeted with small-arms and machine gun fire. The gunfire increased when he flashed on his landing lights, and he turned back on the course he had been flying.

As the gas level dipped lower, Edgerton called all members of the crew forward and checked their parachutes as Baker climbed to 13,000 feet. Soon the fuel in the forward tanks was down to 20 gallons, and 40 to 60 gallons in the rear tank could not be transferred. Immediately the pilot gave the order to bail out and reduced airspeed to 130 mph. Farris "coolly" raised the trap located aft of the bomb bay and dropped the outside hatch, according to the mission's supplemental report. "Its 'whoosh' was promptly followed by that of Sgt. Farris. He was followed in rapid successions by Sgts. Wilkins and Wilkerson." Edgerton told the pilot that the enlisted men were off, and then jumped through the forward hatch. Lyon waited until Baker had gotten clear of his seat and then left the aircraft.

When Lyon later told the story to his family, he added details omitted from the official reports. Lyon said that he had stayed at the controls while Edgerton made sure everyone got out. When he turned back to jump, Lyon noticed Wilkerson hanging from the rear hatch. Unable to persuade the reluctant man to let go, Lyon stomped on his hands until he freed his desperate grip and dropped through, finally opening his parachute. After they had all found each other and started the walk back, Wilkerson commented that he must have hurt his hands in the jump because they were so painful. He had no memory of events as they had actually occurred, or of the extreme measures employed to force him to release his hold.[7]

Occupied as he was with operating the aircraft, Lt. Baker did not see Capt. Lyon's wave of farewell, nor did he see him leave, and Baker hesitated momentarily in doubt about whether the copilot might have gone aft for some reason. In that moment the right engine cut out. The Mitchell was on its back in an instant, and Baker was thrown down behind the copilot's seat. As the plane started down into a spin, he fought his way to the controls and, cutting back the power on the left engine, succeeded in righting the aircraft. The right engine caught again, and Baker promptly shoved everything forward. Knowing he had lost altitude and had no time to waste, he steadied the plane for a moment, then stepped back and dropped straight through the open hatch behind him. The Mitchell flew on briefly before it started a whining, diving turn. Within thirty seconds it crashed and exploded on a mountainside.

When Sgt. Farris made his exit, he delayed opening his parachute several seconds to be certain of clearing the aircraft. When it popped, he experienced a severe jerk but was not hurt or rendered unconscious. He drifted down in the darkness through a layer of overcast, beneath which there was a freezing mist. Just as he became aware of the outline of hills rising around him, a flare of light from the aircraft's impact illuminated the ground, and he was down on an ice-covered mountainside. Receiving "a bad shock" on landing and injuring his back and ankle, Farris was unable to get up for about ten minutes. There was no wind, and the parachute spilled at once without trouble. After some time, he picked himself up and began walking back and forth in an effort to keep warm.

At 0530 the following morning there was enough light to travel, so Farris bundled up his chute and started down the mountain. He soon came upon a trail and within a ½ mile found a farmhouse. There he approached an elderly woman and attempted to communicate with her with the aid of his *Pointee-Talkee* booklet, which contained English phrases with their Mandarin translations. Either illiterate or unfamiliar with the Mandarin dialect, she was unable to read the *Pointee-Talkee* but pointed along the road while saying, "Kaiyang." Farris followed the trail. After walking for a while, he saw a telephone line and from it a lead into a large house a short distance from the trail. There a coolie was working, and Farris approached him with the *Pointee-Talkee*. The coolie motioned him to wait and quickly returned with two English-speaking Chinese, who brought him into the house and made him comfortable. Farris at once gave them a message that contained all "essential particulars" to be forwarded to Chinese and American authorities. Presently his hosts informed him that the others were in the village (which he assumed to be Kaiyang) 5 miles away, and at 0830 he sent a runner with a message to them. That evening, a banquet held in his honor was attended by the mayor of Kaiyang. The following morning, Farris, in a sedan chair and accompanied by armed guards, was conducted to join the others at the village.

When Sgt. Wilkins left the aircraft, he opened his chute as soon as he was clear. There was a sharp jar that knocked off his glasses, and he later found that his nose had been cut. He landed fairly hard in scrub growth, hurting his feet and bruising his knees and shins. Finding that he was on a hillside and that everything around him was ice covered, he decided to remain where he was until daylight. He stretched out on the chute and pack seat, covered himself with the canopy, and attempted to sleep. At dawn, he climbed to the top of the hill, from which he could see a road and a village. After watching the road for some time and seeing no "unfriendly activity," he walked in the direction of the village for 4 or 5 miles and there met Edgerton and Wilkerson at 0930.

When Sgt. Wilkerson exited the aircraft, he fell clear. Preparing to pull the ripcord, he found that he was unable to grasp it with one hand and was forced to use both. The chute opened with only a moderate jerk. Just before he hit, he saw the ground rushing toward him in the flare of the exploding aircraft. After landing on his back at the edge of a dry rice paddy, he lay there long enough to catch his breath and assess the situation, determining that his injuries consisted of several bruises and a "skinned" leg. Getting to his feet, he discovered that his hands were numb, and he had lost a glove. After some time, he hid his parachute and concealed himself under low pine boughs as protection from the freezing mist, keeping with him the seat pack that he had cut off. There he remained until daylight, when he crawled to the top of a nearby hill from which he observed a road and a village. After watching it for a while without noticing anything suspicious, he went down to the road and soon met a Chinese man whom he approached and showed his identification flag. The man pointed ahead and said, "Kweiyang." Wilkerson walked along the road in the direction indicated for about a mile and at 0900 met Edgerton near the village.

Lt. Edgerton, having checked the enlisted men out of the aircraft, gave the pilot and copilot a farewell poke, said, "Well, the others have gone; I think I'll go too," and dropped out. He blacked out for a few seconds when he popped his parachute. After coming down through a thin overcast he landed on a hillside, severely wrenching his left ankle. Since the ground was slippery and he could see nothing through the darkness, he wrapped up in his parachute and dozed until about 0530. Edgerton kept a diary of events during the walkout and wrote this succinct entry: "Went on mission to the valley. Got lost. Bailed out 3:15 a.m." The following day he wrote that the plane had run out of gas, and added, "Slept on the mountains in weeds covered with ice."

At daylight, a road about ¼ mile away became visible, and he limped over to it. A group of passing Chinese were civil and friendly, and a second group came along a few minutes later. One of them told Edgerton that there was another member of the crew in the village, and accompanied him back partway until they met a coolie who had been sent to bring Edgerton into the village. There he found Lyon at about 0730.

When Capt. Lyon saw that Lt. Edgerton was away and that Lt. Baker was clear of the seat and apparently ready to jump, he dropped out after dealing with Wilkerson's hesitation. Lyon opened his chute without undue delay and promptly experienced a very bad jolt that, although his harness had seemed very tight, injured and temporarily blinded his eye, wrenched his neck and shoulders, and caused severe pain in his groin. He heard the engine noise of the plane receding and then whine up as if in a dive. It cut off momentarily, and then he heard the props overrunning as the engine again turned up to full power. After a few seconds he heard the aircraft again go into a dive and shortly thereafter saw it crash in a sheet of flame that lit the countryside. The hills rose around him, and a moment later he landed fairly easily on his back in an ice-skimmed rice paddy.

Wading out, Lyon ascended the dike at the edge of the rice paddy and removed his harness. Then he walked toward a hamlet of five or six houses dimly visible in the distance. Dogs began barking and he heard people talking within, but although he pounded on the doors, called out, and burned a flare, none of the inhabitants opened up. He went back to collect his parachute, returned to the village, and huddled under "a sort of lean-to porch," but the shelter provided little protection from the cold. Because his feet and clothing were wet from the rice paddy, he removed his boots, shoes, and socks to dry and rub his feet. His socks promptly froze stiff.

Lyon remained huddled and shivering, occasionally rousing himself to pound fruitlessly on the doors until daylight, when a man appeared from a nearby house. He approached and, pointing up, inquired, "Fei-chi?" (translated "to fly"), according to the report, although *fei-ji* (translated "airplane") may have been more accurate. He then clucked solicitously and motioned for the suffering stranger to follow him to his house, where he stirred up a fire and allowed Lyon to warm and dry himself. Some of the village elders came in and, after inquiring if Lyon spoke Chinese, began to discuss prices (earlier the man had apparently assured his wife that there would be "money in it").

After eating a breakfast of fried eggs, Lyon set out to find Baker, since it was obvious that he had remained in the aircraft longer than the copilot had expected. Soon he saw Edgerton limping toward the village. After returning to the house together, Lyon gave instructions that Edgerton be given something to eat. Leaving him there, Lyon again went out and walked a circular route of about 4 miles. He encountered many woodcutters but discovered no useful information. On his return to the hamlet, he found that Sgt. Wilkerson had just arrived. At about the same time, a green-uniformed courier arrived and informed the crew that he wished to conduct them to the next village, where there was a telephone. Following some discussion, Lyon set out for the village, accompanied by a man who could speak a little English. En route he met Baker.

When Baker left the aircraft, he opened his chute as soon as it was clear. Unfurling easily, it swung him without a jolt. Baker heard the aircraft dive into a turn and worried for a moment that it might return and cause him harm, but then he witnessed its fiery crash. Drifting down, he attempted unsuccessfully to light a cigarette. As he was putting his lighter back into his pocket, he plunged through the branches of some small pine trees and struck on his feet, severely twisting his right ankle. His chute was caught in the trees, so he climbed down and left it there. The pain was so severe at first that he thought his leg was broken, but after a brief time he managed to get to his knees and then tried walking. After hobbling around for a few minutes, he concluded that his injury was a sprain rather than a fracture and his leg was "OK." He sat down again but grew cold and walked about until daylight, when he started down the mountainside.

From the crest of a ridge at about 0800 he saw a road below him. As he stood watching it for signs of activity, he saw Capt. Lyon. Shouting, "Hello!" to him, Baker made his way down and joined Lyon on the road, and together they went on to the village. There they found "no phone and no mutual understanding, and there was much talk at cross purposes." Then Edgerton, Wilkins, and Wilkerson arrived with the cooperative courier, who had paid for their breakfasts. There was "much speech making" and presently they were taken to the mayor's house, where with the aid of the *Pointee-Talkee* they were given a place to rest until lunchtime, when they were fed at the local jail at part of the compound in which the mayor lived. At 1500 the message from Farris arrived. Baker sent a reply to him, instructing him to remain where he was until the next day, when, according to the mayor, a truck would arrive to take them to Kweiyang (Guiyang). That night they slept on boards and trestles in the mayor's storeroom. Edgerton wrote that despite the rustic accommodations, "Thank God the whole crew was safe. Slept about 14 hours."

Farris arrived the morning of the seventeenth, completing the crew. Because of his sprained ankle, Edgerton's rescuers had built a litter to aid in transporting him, but all were deemed sufficiently recovered from their injuries to be able to travel. The arrival of the promised truck was put off at two-hour intervals; the roads were later found to be impassable for vehicles. Lyon acquired a fragment of a postal map that showed their location and the distance to the next village (6 miles), so at 1500 they abandoned the idea of the truck and set out on foot. They walked for three hours "at a good clip," according to Edgerton.

At nightfall they arrived at a Chinese military garrison, to which they were conducted by five soldiers they had met on the road. The commanding officer agreed to notify Chinese and American authorities "after much business with the *Pointee-Talkee*." They were provided a meager supper of five boiled eggs each (although the Chinese valued eggs for their nutritional content and may have been providing the best that they had) and inadequate sleeping accommodations that were marginally improved only after Lyon complained to the Chinese commanding officer. "All of us dead tired," wrote Edgerton. "Drank gallons of boiled water (cash wey). Slept on boards covered with straw."

On the following morning, the men were served more hard-boiled eggs for breakfast and advised to expect a truck to arrive and pick them up "in two hours." Edgerton noted the date as his ten-month wedding anniversary. Escorted on a sightseeing tour around the village by the commanding officer, they returned to find that many articles of equipment had been stolen during their absence from the room in which they had slept. Becoming restless, and with repeated inquiries about the truck eliciting the same reply, "in two hours," they informed the CO that if the truck had not arrived by 1100, they would proceed again on foot—"and this they did."

One of the guards who had arrived with Farris accompanied them throughout their journey. Lyon reimbursed this man, who made all necessary arrangements and paid off their bills, from the "E funds." They walked along the road and made fairly good progress, in spite of stopping to rest every hour. All of the party were in better condition and in excellent spirits. They had tea and rice cakes in villages through which they passed, and drank water purified with halazone tablets. About 3 or 4 miles out of Kweiyang, the guard attempted to arrange for a truck when they had reached a passable section of road, but the truck in question could not be started. Meanwhile, they heard another truck approaching. They stopped it and discovered that it was loaded with pigs. "Nothing loath," the crew climbed on. A "recalcitrant coolie" in the cab was "soundly booted" by the guard and "penitentially sat among the pigs" during the triumphal entrance into Kweiyang. Edgerton provided a typically terse summary of the experience: "Truck supposed to come at 10 a.m. 12:30 no truck. Walked 2 hours. Got ride on truck load of hogs the last 3 miles."

It was after dark when they arrived at headquarters of the Eastern Air Command (formed by cooperation of the British Royal Air Force and the American 10th Air Force). There a sergeant agreed to put them up until the detail of beds was mentioned; he then drew himself up and righteously thundered, "But where are your cots?" The arrival of a Lt. Col. Lyle prevented bloodshed. The colonel kindly arranged for a message to be sent to the 5th Fighter Group, suggested that the crew could receive better care at the SOS (Services of Supply) hostel, and arranged for transportation.

At SOS headquarters in the Kweichow Province capital, they were referred to Capt. Smith, who sent them to the hospital, where the captain in charge entered the crew as exhaustion cases. After luxurious hot showers, the weary men turned in to comfortable beds with clean sheets and had their first proper sleep in three nights. Edgerton summarized the evening: "Went to an Am[erican] hostel in town. Asked if we had our cots with us. Jackass. Took us to SOS. Slept in hospital for the nite. After a shower, clean sheets & good bed, oh boy."

The following day, after a restful morning and the unheard-of indulgence of breakfast in bed, the men were issued "clean shorts, Limey sox & hat." Then they "went into town [and] had a steak." They also got haircuts and shaves while in Kweiyang. That night they slept on cots in a tent at the "Army camp," where Edgerton wrote that he "like to froze to death." On the twentieth, they received an order to report to G-2 (Intelligence) at EAC headquarters, who had mistakenly been informed that the crew had gone down in the Paoching area.

The next day, after a conference during which they gave the G-2 such information as they were able to provide, Lyon sent a message to 5th Fighter Group headquarters asking that a Mitchell be sent to pick them up. The weather closed in at Kweiyang that morning, making it impossible to send the requested plane to retrieve the crew. Edgerton wrote that he attended mass at "Queyang" on the twenty-first, no doubt to express gratitude that he and the rest of the crew had survived their ordeal. Later in the day, Captain Lyon learned that a motor convoy was scheduled to leave for Chihkiang the following day. He thereupon sent a message stating that the crew would proceed to Chihkiang with the convoy.

The following three days were spent en route with the convoy and "were a blend of hard riding and discomfort, spectacular mountain scenery, equally spectacular displays by Chinese drivers (the crew concluded that flying combat was less disconcerting and probably safer!), hauling out foundered trucks and getting them started, removing wrecks from the road, eating in Chinese villages." On their first night they stayed at a Chinese hotel and "slept on boards again."

"Beautiful day & beautiful country," Edgerton wrote on the twenty-third. They spent that night at Chenyuan at a US Navy station, whose personnel were most hospitable and made every effort to ensure the comfort of the crew. Edgerton was favorably impressed with the coffee served by the "Navy outfit" and declared it "ding how."

At 2200 on the following night, January 24, the crew arrived back at Chihkiang in a cold, drizzling rain, "thus concluding the mission begun ten days earlier."

The six aircrew members had been reported as missing in action when they failed to return to base at the expected time early on January 16. According to an official report of the incident, Lt. Portaluppi led a search of an area 50 miles north of Chihkiang, where radar reported plotting an unidentified aircraft showing IFF at 0430, but they found no evidence of the plane or its crew.[8]

Crew members were soon discovered about 500 miles west-southwest of Chihkiang by local Chinese, who took them in hand and conducted them to military authorities as instructed. Baker and his crew were fortunate to have gone down in Allied-controlled territory, where the threat to their safety was slight. Word was received at 5th Fighter Group headquarters on the nineteenth and relayed to 3rd Bomb Squadron headquarters on the following day that all were safe and walking out in the vicinity of Kweiyang.

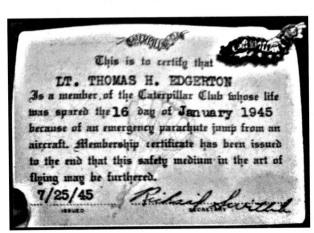

Lt. Edgerton's Caterpillar Club pin was awarded along with a certificate stating that his life had been spared "because of an emergency parachute jump from an aircraft," and the certificate was issued "to the end that this safety medium in the art of flying may be furthered." *T. H. Edgerton collection, courtesy of Wendi Borst*

In July, Edgerton received his pin and card granting membership in the "Caterpillar Club," the informal organization made up of men whose lives were saved by use of a parachute when jumping from a disabled airplane. Since parachutes were originally made of silk, the organization's name refers to the silkworms that were essential to early parachute production.

When Edgerton later told his family about this mission, he explained that the plane got lost in the darkness and ran out of fuel, forcing the crew to bail out. As the Mitchell's navigator, he always felt responsible for their misadventure. He also remembered the incident of Wilkerson hanging from the escape hatch.[9]

On January 16, Task Force 34 crews had as their objective the same targets as on other recent missions. Airborne at 1900, A/C #701 (Rich, Jen, Doran, Magyar, Liang, and Chang) carried seventeen M41 stab-frag clusters on this routine raid. When Rich bombed a convoy found near the Isuho ferry, a large fire was the reported result. When he blasted a second convoy near Siangtan, a good pattern resulted and fires broke out. Returning to Isuho to bomb the ferry produced no observable results. The Mitchell received light, inaccurate A/W and small-arms fire from both sides of the river but returned safely to base.

Pulaski, aboard A/C #722 (with Lane, Lipira, Bovard, Chow, and Shu), was off at 1930, carrying the same bombload as on the previous mission. He dumped all of them on a large convoy south of Isuho from 4,000 feet, with good results. A fire broke out at once, seemingly fueled by gasoline or oil "as it burned in one large mass with scattered burning patches around it." A dark column of smoke was visible for more than five minutes, despite poor visibility in the area.

A three-Mitchell formation led by Portaluppi flying A/C #722 (with Logan, Lipira, Levy, Wadlow, and Goff), followed by A/C #701 (Jen, Lee, Chang, Liang, Taug, and Shu) and A/C #718 (Wu, Kou, Shio, Chang, Chow, and Ho), was off at 1300 on January 17. Escorted by six 5th Fighter Group P-40s, their objective was to destroy ammunition and gas stores that had been reported in a small (600 by 300 feet) village immediately west of Hengshan. Capt. Chester F. Condon, Task Force 34 intelligence officer, accompanied the crew of the lead plane as an observer. The 3rd Squadron Mitchells each carried twenty-two M30 100 lb. demos, and the 4th Squadron plane carried seventeen M41 stab-frag clusters.

After one pass to identify the target, the bombers made a run to the west, but Lipira, blinded by a sun flash in the sight, was unable to release. The formation then made a 180-degree turn and dropped all bombs on the leader at 4,500 feet on the third pass, but only 40 to 50 percent were hits. The lead plane's demos cut through the north end of the target, producing mostly near misses, but the fragmentation bombs of the aircraft flying on #722's right wing were all on target. Demos of the plane on his left wing were not dropped because the bomb bay doors failed to open, presumably due to pilot error. The plane then left the formation to make an independent run. Bombs were dropped after some maneuvering but missed the target by several miles, striking the side of a mountain. No fires or secondary explosions observed in the target area proved unlikely the presence of gasoline or ammunition. The escorting fighters went on to attack targets around Hengshan with frags and by strafing. Two large barges were burned in the Hsiang off Hengshan, and at least one direct hit by a frag cluster damaged a compound at the railroad yards, from which a considerable amount of light automatic-weapons fire was observed. Lt. Logan recorded this as his first combat mission.

That evening, A/C #722 (Lane, Logan, Wei, Gaffney, Peters, and Tso) was off at 1845 to again hit enemy convoys. Lane released only one stab-frag cluster over vehicles on the move south of Isuho, and a later mission reported a fire at that location. After repeated attempts to drop them on convoys proved futile because of bomb-release malfunction, Wei salvoed the remaining sixteen bombs over installations at the Isuho ferry, all in the target area.

Mission #63 proved to be Task Force 34's final mission, although participating members were unaware of the fact at that time. Airborne at 1900, Pulaski flew the 4th Squadron's A/C #701 (with Wang as copilot, Doran as navigator, and Egdorf, Rieks, and Liang as gunners) and proceeded to Changsha, where he dropped stab-frag clusters on a line of trucks discovered near the town, another several miles to the southeast, and a third found farther west and nearer to the river on the same road. When they spotted a large southbound convoy on the east bank of the Hsiang northeast of Siangtan, visibility was too poor for strafing. Crewmen observed a fire south of Isuho that they believed to be the result of the previous raid. The aircraft turned on course for Chihkiang from the vicinity of DD24 and landed at 2235.

Through the month of January, the 3rd Squadron detachment flying out of Chihkiang was credited with six night missions and one daytime mission. The 4th Squadron also managed seven missions. Their joint purpose had been to disrupt traffic by bombing of trackage, bridges, rail yards, and other installations along the Hankow-Canton Railroad, ranging from Siangyin in the Tungting Lake area south to Hengyang, and to destroy truck convoys in the Hsiang valley. Despite a shaky start, Task Force 34 had gone on to establish an impressive record against the enemy, accomplishing this goal in its brief period of operation.

Lt. Jack H. Rich, who flew a number of these missions and later replaced Lt. Portaluppi as 4th Squadron historical officer, described the dangers and successes of Task Force 34's night missions. "Total darkness and extremely limited radio-homing facilities made it imperative that the pilot and navigator never lose track of their position. After the bombs were dropped on a convoy, if the terrain was known to be favorable, repeated strafing passes were made on the target[,] which was generally a large convoy of trucks," he wrote. As a result of these night attacks, coupled with 5th Fighter sweeps in the daytime, the Japanese lost great quantities of supplies destined for their drive to Kweiyang and Kunming and found it extremely difficult to advance during the subzero weather of winter in only cotton summer uniforms. "Quite possibly their winter uniforms[,] which never arrived[,] were burning somewhere along the road near Hengyang or Changsha or Youchow—or was it Hankow?"

On January 18, 1st Bomb Group headquarters announced plans for the reorganization of Task Force 34. Renamed "Fourth Bomb Task Force" and commanded by Maj. Dick, it was thereafter composed entirely of 4th Squadron personnel, and planes and personnel that had previously remained at Peishiyi supplemented the detachment at Chihkiang. Those from the 3rd Squadron no longer took part in its operations but received orders to move to Liangshan to join squadron personnel relocating there from Peishiyi. No further missions were reported by either the 3rd or the 4th Squadron through the remainder of the month as changes were being implemented for both organizations.

Sometime during early January, Lt. Cornelius Van Zwoll visited Peishiyi to evaluate the base's quality and condition. His report, dated January 26 and forwarded to CACW headquarters, disclosed: "It was learned that the CACW units do not operate from Peishiyi. Personnel are removed from time to time to operational bases elsewhere in China to perform missions. A stroll thru the barracks area confirms this impression gained from information of American military personnel on the base." He concluded that the damp, muddy base functioned merely as a "rest camp."

Maj. Hummel voiced his adamant protest against the accusations of this "dutch spy," who was administrative assistant to the China theater signal officer at Chungking, in typical fashion:

> How he acquired his findings was as mysterious as his whereabouts during his stay here, certainly he never contacted any responsible unit or officer in CACW headquarters. It was not until long after he left, that a transcript of his report reached Headquarters and we learned to our indignant open-mouthed surprise that we were a rest camp. It seems according to the intelligence report, that we had more men than we knew what to do with. Thus the secret agent on a quiet stroll through the hostels found many men in their sack.... What he observed, of course, was Third and Fourth Bomb Squadron personnel, stagnating here at Peishiyi because there was no effective station to which they could go to fly combat, nor gasoline or ammunition with which to combat should they find such a station. Thus hamstrung and cheated by conditions beyond their control, they moldered in mildewed Peishiyi, bemoaning their idleness.... There is little that is so conducive to strain, and little that so hammers down the morale as protracted enforced idleness, especially when imposed by outer conditions, and when it does not come as a reward at the end of a hard period of combat or work. In an empty hole such as Peishiyi, void of all civilized living, there is little escape except in unconsciousness of sleep. If these men slept, they slept to escape awareness of our Peishiyi rest camp. In dank Peishiyi, in winter, unless you have work to do, it is best to be unconscious. Thus, even while CACW was castigated for the sins of Third and Fourth Bomb Squadron personnel, these men were not sinning, but merely escaping from intolerable idleness and intolerable Peishiyi.

At the time that data were being collected for the report, 1st Bomb Group personnel at Peishiyi comprised only twelve officers and twenty-seven enlisted men of the 1st Squadron, three officers and twelve enlisted men of the 3rd Squadron, and eight officers and twenty-seven enlisted men of the 4th Squadron, in addition to the CACW headquarters contingent. Van Zwoll seems to have performed his anonymous surveillance during the time that most members of the 3rd Squadron were, indeed, serving in detachments at Liangshan, Chihkiang, and other fields because of the small numbers reported, and Van Zwoll's depiction of inactivity certainly applied to the squadron for most of its tenure at the sodden base.

Capt. Cunningham received his orders to return to the US on January 18. Two days later, the 3rd Squadron began its move to Liangshan. The airfield (30°40'46" N, 107°47'10" E) was located about 45 miles due west of Wanhsien (Wanzhou), the largest nearby town on the upper reaches of the Yangtze, and just north of a small mountain range. The men who were already there began to set up Operations, Intelligence, and Engineering, and Lt. Young and Sgt. Meikle arrived by jeep to complete the setup of Operations and Intelligence materiel on the following day.

Capt. Ragland and Lts. Wood and Koss, with details of enlisted men, left Peishiyi on the twenty-first to transfer squadron equipment and supplies by truck, sampan, and river steamer. For Hank, the most memorable part of the trip was transporting maintenance equipment and supplies by river. "We were moving to a new base, and we carried equipment by sampan," he recalled. "We rode a long way in that thing and then went and got on board a ship in the

Relocating to Liangshan

[Yangtze] river." It was crowded with local people, many of them traveling with livestock. "They'd have chickens with a string fastened to them, three or four of them at a time, out there on the open deck of that steam ship." Hank, who was always frugal, recalled traveling with Capt. Ragland, who often borrowed money from him. "I was his banker" was Hank's amused comment. All of them completed the transfer by truck, traversing the mountains via winding, switchback roads and arriving at the new base on the twenty-seventh.

Soon afterward, Lt. Koss described the move in a letter to his mother. "We took a two-day trip on a river steamer and sampan and really got to see China. I can't tell you where we went as yet but it was interesting," he wrote in his travelogue. "You cannot go a single block in China anywhere without running in to a house or village or city. Evy [his personal contraction for *every*] little bit of land is cultivated[,] even on the steepest mountain side, mostly rice paddies. We shot wild ducks on the way down. We are planning on going dove hunting here and if we get time we will go deer hunting too."[10]

After squadron personnel made their way from Peishiyi to their new base at Liangshan, Hank sent home several photos of the sampans that they used to transport personnel, equipment, and supplies. This one is identical to a photo that Lt. Koss sent home to his family, with the caption "I rode in one like this."
J. H. Mills collection

Koss sent home a photo that he captioned, "Sampan shoots the rapids. I rode in one like this." It was identical to a picture that Hank sent to his wife, Nancy.

Special Orders No. 12 issued by the 1st Bombardment Group, dated January 5, 1945, listed twenty-one American officers and forty-five enlisted men who were assigned to the new base: Majs. Conrad and Seacrest; Capts. Cunningham, Kelso, Ragland, Hamilton, and MacNeil; 1Lts. Banger, Faherty, Wood, Baker, Winter, and Young; 2Lts. Cantor, Logan, Mikola, Senecal, Edgerton, Ilefeldt, and Pulaski; FO Wherritt; 1Sgt. Earley; MSgts. Hanrahan and Fuller; TSgts. Gruber, Jakubasz, Libolt, Rieks, Solyn, Wilkerson, Chasse, Hoyle, Meikle, Shock, and Summerville; SSgts. Duffin, Evitts, Hoke, McCann, Mier, Barge, Dunlap, Haines, Holmes, and Thomas; Sgts. England, Gaffney, Long, Peters, Whearty, Jackson, Fox, Learn, Mills, Rickman, Trout, and Burton; and Cpls. DeFabritis, Magyar, Schlicher, Wadlow, Allegretto, Hugel, Morris, Ryan, and Supsic. At the time the orders were issued, Capts. Ragland and MacNeil and SSgt. Holmes were noted as on detached service in India, and 1Lt. Baker; 2Lts. Cantor, Edgerton, and Pulaski; TSgts. Rieks, Hoyle, Wilkerson, and Shock; Sgt. Peters; and Cpls. Magyar and Wadlow were still on detached duty at Chihkiang. Both recent arrivals, 1Lts. Greene and Koss were omitted, although other records verified that they moved with squadron personnel. Movement by Chinese personnel was by separate orders.

As the rest of the 3rd Squadron was moving, Lts. Baker and Edgerton and Sgt. Wilkerson, with Capt. Lyon and Sgts. Farris and Wilkins, returned to Chihkiang from their walkout at 10:20 on the night of January 24. The exhausted men wanted nothing more than sleep following their ordeal, but Lt. Edgerton wrote, "McCullar sleeping in my bed. Boo yow" (the 4th Squadron's 1Lt. J. M. McCullar had created this Goldilocks predicament). A party was given in their honor the following night. "Had a big party for us. We sat at the table of honor. 39 at the party. A ding how party."[11] Col. Dunning, with Maj. Charles C. Wilder Jr., both of them representing the 5th Fighter Group, attended the festivities. Col. Dunning expressed his great pleasure at having them all back safely, and used the opportunity to congratulate all of Task Force 34 for the "outstanding work" it had accomplished. Baker, Edgerton, and Wilkerson joined their squadron at Liangshan two days later and told their stories again.

Cpl. Johnson, whose 2nd Bomb Squadron had moved to the base a few months before the 3rd Squadron's arrival, wrote an account of his early impressions upon approaching Liangshan by air: "We turned west over a range of 7,000-foot-high mountains that were steep and barren except for a fringe of pine trees on their tops. The mountainsides were terraced with rice paddies high up, giving them a three-dimensional appearance. The flat Liangshan valley was covered with rice paddies, making it look like a large, shallow lake." Liangshan village stood near the western end of the valley, its narrow dirt airstrip running east and west along the north edge of the village. Scattered throughout the valley among the rice paddies stood "clumps of gray-tiled or thatch-roofed peasant farm buildings." The farms were accessible only by narrow, slippery foot paths on the mud dikes that separated each family's farm plot. "On a few low hills were situated the more substantial dwellings of the landlords and warlords who controlled the area. These redoubts were surrounded by high brick or mud walls to protect them from peasant uprisings or attacks by bandits or rival warlords."[12]

The village of Liangshan was typical of those in the interior of China that the CACW came to know so well. Maj. Hummel had described it the previous summer as "a nine o'clock town." He explained, "There were no streetlights, no modern buildings, and after nine there was no life. It was friendly but primitive. The town consisted of a single twisting, narrow street with a few alley-like offshoots." Unlike in most Chinese towns, the houses were constructed not of clay but were largely modern tile structures. "Bombings in the early war years had left unreconstructed ravages among the buildings. Long war had pauperized the town. . . . It was strictly a Chinese town, full of little Chinese restaurants. Odors of food at all times filled the narrow, crooked street."

Johnson painted vivid word pictures through his portrayal of people and places he encountered in China. Among them were rich details provided in his descriptions of village life that initially appeared strange and exotic to new arrivals but soon became commonplace to the men stationed nearby. He wrote that the village of Liangshan was surrounded by a high stone-and-dirt wall, broken down in several places. Tall ceremonial arches with heavy wooden ironbound gates where the roads entered the village on three sides were closed and locked at night to keep out bandits and thieves. "The walls were incapable of keeping out determined armies or bandits armed with cannon or explosives, but they did deter honest folk," he wrote. One long main street that branched at the eastern end ran through the village itself. One road went up over the mountains via a switchback dirt road to the Yangtze River canyon and the town of Wanhsien, and the other branch led to the airfield and the mountains beyond.

In town, most buildings were of unpainted wood or had a timber frame covered with bamboo matting and gray plaster, although a few government buildings and the local bank were constructed of "dun-colored brick." A few buildings were thatched with straw, but most had gray-tile roofs. Small shops along the main street displayed their wares to attract customers. "They offered everything: apothecaries with dried herbs and glass jars of medicines, wine shops, candy stores featuring peanut candy and cookies, and shops selling locally made clothing, shoes, and stockings. Tantalizing aromas came from small, open-air cafés, their customers seated on wooden benches eating noodles, drinking tea, and gossiping."

Civilians wore faded blue cotton trousers and jackets or long blue robes. Middle-aged women hobbled along on tiny bound feet. "Their huge thighs, developed as a result of their bound feet, were apparently sexually attractive to Chinese men of former generations," he surmised. Everywhere could be heard "the sounds of people chatting, babies crying, hawkers touting their wares, chickens and geese squawking, mourners wailing and the repeated explosion of firecrackers as funeral processions and wedding parties passed by."[13]

On an inspection tour conducted the previous summer, then Col. Morse had described the nearby airfield as having an established grass landing strip with another under construction. There were only about six revetments large enough to accommodate B-25s, with a dozen or so smaller ones scattered around the desolate-looking field. Fifteen more were being built for P-40s. The only permanent structure was a wooden building topped by a little glass-enclosed control tower. A 100,000-gallon gasoline dump was less than half full. The radio equipment was "very primitive." Hostels and mess halls were under construction but unfinished at that time. By the time the 3rd Squadron arrived, "straw-covered" barracks had been completed. Their floors were packed dirt. They had no electricity, and candles, lamps, and flashlights were used for lighting, although the mess hall and airfield tower were powered by generators.[14]

Regardless of these primitive conditions, it seemed that everyone was pleased with the facilities, which were newer and in better condition than those at Peishiyi. Living quarters were "quite adequate," according to Ilefeldt. Enlisted men occupied a new building, and officers had separate barracks all to themselves. The orderly room, Operations, and Intelligence occupied one building. It was arranged with the orderly room at one end and Operations and Intelligence sharing a room at the other end. Between them and accessible to both was a spacious briefing room. There was also a large supply house and an equally large engineering shack. A dispensary

Rice paddies stairstepped all the hills surrounding Liangshan, and Hank sent home several photos of them. This one is a duplicate of another that Koss sent home to demonstrate the terraced landscape at his new home base. *J. H. Mills collection*

All arable land was utilized for raising the villagers' crops, even in Liangshan village. Barely visible to the right is a well-built house. *J. H. Mills collection*

Squadron personnel quickly settled into the facilities and made Liangshan their home. *R. L. Logan collection, courtesy of Katherine A. Logan*

Logan captioned this photo "Hoy (our houseboy)" and noted that it was taken in January 1945. *R. L. Logan collection, courtesy of Katherine A. Logan*

provided general medical services, although serious cases were usually sent to the big American military hospital at Chengtu or sometimes to Kunming.

The 1st Bomb Squadron's Sgt. Daniels related that when he was there, everything at the Liangshan airfield was "muddy and dirty and there was no such thing as an operating shower." Food served at the base was consistently "cabbage-soup the color of dishwater and the same leathery, cardboard[-]tasting water buffalo. We suspected the buffalo weren't butchered until they had died of old age." These animals were the primary beasts of burden used by Chinese farmers, who were hesitant to slaughter the buffalo until they had lived out the full extent of their usefulness. The condiments served alongside contained "rat droppings, bamboo splinters, or simply didn't exist."[15] When GIs sat down to eat, they first performed a careful examination of the food on their plates and sorted through it to remove rice hulls, stems, pebbles, insects, and worms before consuming whatever remained that was determined to be edible.

Lt. Tu, who recalled that the most famous local product was its grapefruit, related that the Americans and Chinese lived separately at Liangshan, as at other bases. "However, the Americans would come to the Chinese mess hall to have some Chinese food, and we would also sometimes go over to enjoy some American meals," he revealed. Near the air base was an Allied forces recreation center improvised from a school. "It was basically a club for aircrewmen to relax and have fun. We could throw darts and drink there, but the spaces for officers and NCOs were separated. In addition to aircraft crew members from the 1st Group (only the bomber groups had NCO aircraft crew members), flight duty officers from the 3rd [Fighter] Group also used the club. Sometime the USO gave a military appreciation performance with American celebrities." They occasionally showed some of the latest American movies, including ones that had not yet been shown in the US, he said.[16]

Liangshan's geographical position as the eastern gateway to the Szechwan basin was of great significance, since it provided advantageous access to Hubei and Hunan Provinces. C-47 transport units used its airfield to carry supplies, troops, and equipment within China. Situated about 350 miles west of Wuhan, it was further utilized for flying unarmed P-38 photoreconnaissance planes to gather intelligence over Japanese-held territory, while the 426th Night Fighter Squadron, flying P-61 interceptors, defended against enemy aircraft attacking in the Chungking area. Hank remembered that the P-61s had twin stabilizers like the B-25s. Early one morning, as he was walking past a Black Widow that had returned during the night from a mission, he noticed bloody brain matter encrusted on the leading edge of the right stabilizer. The plane had flown so low that it collided with something living, either an enemy soldier or a large animal of some kind.

Weather at the new base was miserable, with dense clouds obscuring the tops of nearby hills and "raining intermittently between snow flurries," according to the 3rd Squadron history. The 2nd Bomb Squadron and most of the 1st Bomb Squadron were already at Liangshan. The base was so crowded that the 1st Squadron's officers were billeted in the 2nd Squadron's infirmary, while enlisted men "sloshed around our tents, ankle-deep in mud and ice water."

Soon after the move was completed, Lt. Young was transported to Kunming to be hospitalized for yet another recurrence of malaria, followed by Sgts. England and Whearty, who were ordered to the hospital for observation and treatment. Although his name is not listed in orders, Hank joined them soon afterward. He remembered being with England the first time he was hospitalized for dysentery. England, who had arrived with Hank aboard *Mission Bay*, was from Boston. Hank commented that when he accepted an invitation to go with England to church as they were recovering, it was his first experience with attending a Catholic service.

Sgt. England works on equipment affixed to an airplane stabilizer with the aid of a Chinese radioman. *R. N. Solyn collection, courtesy of Robert N. Solin*

Working with a Chinese mechanic, Sgt. Whearty checks out repairs on a B-25. *R. N. Solyn collection, courtesy of Robert N. Solin*

"I ate at some Chinese café in some village, and there were chickens hanging up by the neck. They didn't have refrigeration," Hank recalled. "I ordered some oxtail soup, and I thought when I ate that, there's something wrong here, but I ate it, and that's what gave me dysentery the first time." He was treated "at a local doctor's office" on base, but after initial efforts to control the problem with medicine from the dispensary proved ineffective, Hank was sent to "a big hospital that had white nurses from the States." Commonly used remedies for the ailment included paregoric and bismuth subcarbonate tablets, generally administered four times per day.

Food prepared or stored under unsanitary conditions and sometimes in combination with impure water often led to bloody diarrhea accompanied by fever. Another common cause of this malady was the use of human excrement to fertilize crops. "I used to see the prettiest tomatoes and watermelons in those villages. We couldn't eat 'em because the Chinese used human fertilizer on their crops. Disease will pass out of food into whoever eats it, so we couldn't eat those pretty watermelons or tomatoes or anything. They'd make you sick."

All meats, fruits, and vegetables served on the bases were thoroughly cooked as a precaution against contamination unless there was absolute certainty regarding their safe source. However, a particularly unpleasant form of amoebic dysentery known on some of the bases as "the Yellow River Rapids" plagued the men at airfields across China, sometimes passed along to the Americans as the result of faulty hygiene on the part of Chinese cooks and messboys.[17] Despite his precautions, Hank was hospitalized twice because of dysentery while he was stationed in China.

As the squadron was settling into new quarters, Imperial Headquarters in Tokyo revised its China policy in response to recent setbacks in the Pacific. With the Philippines and other island strongholds in imminent danger of falling into Allied hands, Japan feared that these strategic locations would become staging bases from which to launch an amphibious attack along the China coast. Beginning in late January, the primary focus of the Japanese army was shifted to warding off the expected coastal invasion, and forward American air bases were to be occupied to prevent their use in providing air support. Other than that, the plan called for only small forces to be permitted to launch raids into the interior. Instead, Japanese command intended to strengthen its forces in central and South China, particularly in the lower reaches of the Yangtze River between Shanghai, where it spills into the East China Sea, and Hankow, which lies about 430 miles inland. To execute the new plan, three divisions were tasked to reinforce the defenses along the coast of China, while remaining units were concentrated in the interior.[18]

Thus began the forced evacuation and destruction of the last strongholds of the 14th Air Force at Suichwan, Namyuing, Kanchow, and Hsinching, together with such staging strips as Kienow in Fukien Province. These bases had made it possible for aircraft to launch successful raids against Japanese coastal shipping, sinking millions of tons of valuable cargo bound for Japan. Eradicating them would interdict their use in providing air support to Allied coastal invasions and significantly reduce the effectiveness of the 14th Air Force. No move had yet been made toward Chihkiang, although the strong threat remained. While the enemy continued to concentrate troops along the Peiping-Hankow Railroad, no indications of operations had yet been observed.

The 3rd Squadron detachment operating out of Chihkiang was credited with seven sorties against the enemy through the first half of January, all for the purpose of rupturing enemy transportation and communications facilities along the Hsiang valley and the Hankow-Canton Railroad, running from Kweiyang to Siangyin in the Tungting Lake region. Six sorties flown by the main contingent of the squadron were medium-altitude formation bombardments of enemy railroad marshaling yards at Hankow. A total of 133 bombs were dropped—eighty-five 120 lb. fragmentation clusters and forty-eight 500 lb. demolition bombs.

As the month ended, 3rd Squadron personnel comprised twenty-two American officers, forty-five American enlisted men, eighty-eight Chinese officers, and 137 Chinese enlisted men. B-25s assigned to the squadron included eight H models and three J models. One J had arrived from India on January 6 and was lost on the sixteenth (the fifteenth, according to the report, although it actually went down early the following morning).

CHAPTER TWELVE
Defending Laohokow

Completion of the ground transport highway through Burma prompted a renewal of optimism. The first convoy departed on January 12 from Ledo in the state of Assam and traveled south through Myitkyina and Bhamo before intersecting the Burma Road near the China border. It reached Kunming on February 4 after covering a distance of 1,079 miles. The expectation was, as a logical result, that Allied bases in China would experience significant improvement in the supply situation as huge columns of trucks filled with supplies moved from India to China to carry on the war against the Japanese. Aircraft, spare parts, ammunition, fuel, and other essential supplies could now be delivered directly to Kunming and subsequently distributed to bases where they were needed.

Soon afterward, the 14th Air Force assigned USAAF service groups to CACW bases to distribute essential supplies and services. In theory, since servicemen no longer had to depend upon the corrupt Nationalist government's War Area Service Command for their logistical support, they could receive what they needed when they needed it. However, wing personnel soon learned that theory does not always conform to reality. In fact, there was very little change in their living conditions, and most of the squadrons continued to "live off the land" until the war ended.[1]

Promotions announced during this period included 1Lt. Baker to captain and 2Lts. Edgerton and Senecal to first lieutenants. They had been sent to rest camp at Chengtu and were still there when their promotions came through. TSgt. Libolt was treated at the dispensary for nasopharyngitis. The orderly room "finally arrived" at the field on February 4 and "immediately set up for work," wrote Lt. Ilefeldt. Capt. Ragland returned from Wanhsien, and Lt. Cantor arrived with a truckload of much-needed supplies on the same day. Sgt. Lu Hsueh-wei (X-1796) was attached as a radio operator a few days afterward.

On the fifth, Maj. Conrad received the startling information that he was scheduled for immediate return to the United States. The news was a shock to him, as well as to the entire squadron, since they had all been under the impression that he would remain for at least another year. He left the following afternoon for Peishiyi to assume duties as acting group commander until his orders came through to start home. Before his departure, Maj. Conrad wished the assembled men luck and success and thanked them for their cooperation. He left for the US soon afterward by way of Casablanca.

He was awarded special recognition for his service in cooperation with the CAF three months afterward. The accompanying certificate was translated as follows:

April 13, 1945

Honor Certificate (Tiger no. 446)

The Republican Government has honored Major Conrad with the medal of special award, based on the provision no. 6 of the awarding rules for the Army, Navy and Air Force.

President

Chiang Kai-shek[2]

Mark Seacrest, recently promoted to major, assumed command. Praising Maj. Seacrest for his "quiet efficiency and inspiration," Ilefeldt expressed confidence that he would "keep the squadron on the same level of effectiveness" that it had always enjoyed. Originally from Nebraska, he had moved to Colorado, where he graduated from high school. He attended New Mexico Military Institute in 1939 and Colorado State University the following year, when he also registered for the draft. Ten days after the attack that plunged America into war, Seacrest received orders to report to Kelly Field, Texas, as an aviation cadet. After completion of training at Ellington Field, Texas, he served as an aviation instructor at Greenville, South Carolina, before being transferred to the CBI, where he was attached to the 2nd Bomb Squadron at its activation.

Seacrest had flown nearly seventy missions as of mid-January 1945, according to an article in his hometown newspaper. The accompanying photograph featured Seacrest with a "Chinese friend," easily recognizable as Lt. Tu Kai-mu, although he was not identified in the article.[3] Seacrest's dedication and experience made him a logical choice to serve as commanding officer at the departure of Maj. Conrad.

In early February, Seacrest led a 3rd Squadron detachment called "Nimrod Detachment" to Laohokow (Laohekou) in Hubei Province, near the Henan border. The airfield (32°23'9" N, 111°40'5" E), on the north bank of the Han River, was situated about 220 miles northeast of Liangshan. The detachment was composed of two 3rd Squadron B-25s and two more of the 22nd Bomb Squadron, 341st Bomb Group. Aircraft of the latter were equipped with radar gunsights. The purpose of this detachment was to fly daytime river sweeps along the Yangtze from Hankow to Nanking; day and night missions along the Tsingpu Railroad, concentrating on trackage and bridges; and sea sweeps from Shanghai to Kioochow Bay later in the month. The remainder of the 3rd Squadron, operating with the 2nd Squadron out of Liangshan, was expected to run nighttime intruder missions on the Ping-Han corridor, concentrating on convoys and trains; day missions on the Ping-Han Railroad, concentrating on trackage and bridges; and light-of-the-moon missions on the Wuhan area to alert the Japanese and restrict the number of night raids on Allied bases.

Laohokow was at that time the most easterly of the 14th Air Force bases. Even more primitive than Liangshan, its grassy airstrip had functioned primarily as a safe haven for emergency landings by disabled planes before it began to be used to launch raids to disrupt Japanese supply lines north of the Yangtze River. The town of Laohokow was enclosed on three sides away from the river by a high mud brick wall that was in disrepair and had fallen down in several places, wrote the 2nd Squadron's Cpl. Johnson of a stopover there caused by engine failure. "The center of town was a large park-like square with flower gardens and lily ponds with goldfish. A gazebo for plays, concerts, and speeches was shaded by elm trees. On the adjacent parade ground, young children played games with sticks and balls while older children practiced Tai Chi and soldiers in uniform marched in close-order drill formations." Surrounding the square were shops, government offices, and a children's school. A museum offered wood carvings of local scenes. "A Lutheran Mission operated by a young Norwegian missionary and his wife offered a free medical clinic. Two Roman Catholic priests headed a French Catholic Mission and fermented excellent wines." It was a tranquil place, except for occasional raids by Japanese Zeros.[4]

The 426th Night Fighter Squadron's Lt. Smith flew into Laohokow earlier that year and provided his own observations: "We knew nothing about Laohokow except where it was on the map, some 450 miles east[-]northeast of Chengtu. What we found was a dirt airstrip only 2,800 feet long, way too short for fighter plane operations, no hangar, a dilapidated gas truck, a radio shack made of mud brick with a tin roof, and a worn-out 6 × 6 GI truck." Improvements that included extending the runway's length and width had been made by the time Nimrod arrived.

Smith went on to describe an air raid at the Laohokow airfield one night. This area was too remote to be covered by Chennault's telephone network at work in other parts of China. "The early warning system was called the 'Bamboo Telegraph,' and it literally was that. Within a perimeter of about 100 miles around the airfield, when bogies flew into the air space, rice paddy peasants would signal by rapping two sections of bamboo together." The sound on a still night would carry for miles, until the next rice paddy picked up and repeated the signal, he explained. "Nothing fancy about it, but it worked. When the sound of the bamboo drumming reached us, it would be swelled so that you could hear maybe 10 or 20 drummers. We would then know that we had only about 15 minutes to scramble."[5] It was a system that was used frequently during Nimrod's tenure at the field.

Lt. Koss and a Chinese navigator discuss the best approach to the target. *R. J. Koss collection, courtesy of Barbara Hughes*

Cpl. Robert E. Schlicher Jr., attached as a mechanic-gunner-engineer, flew as Greene's tail gunner on the Hsuchang mission. *R. E. Schlicher Jr. collection, courtesy of Charles L. Schlicher*

Sgt. Fox, an armorer-gunner, leads his Chinese counterpart through the process of cleaning an aircraft's machine guns. *R. N. Solyn collection, courtesy of Robert N. Solin*

Laohokow was then the home of the 8th Fighter Squadron, 3rd Fighter Group, which sometimes flew in support of Seacrest's missions. On February 11, eight B-25s took off from Liangshan at 1030 on the 3rd Squadron's fifty-sixth mission and picked up three 3rd Fighter Group P-40s as escort at Laohokow. Their target was the foundry and railroad yards at Hsuchang (Xuchang) (34º00' N, 113º48' E) in central Henan Province. Two of the planes, A/C #721 (Chen S. C., Yuang C. H., Liu C. T., Liu S. C., and Hu M. C.) and #724 (Chang Y. H., Ouyang C., Chen Y. C., Wei C. S., and Chung C.), returned to the field shortly after takeoff because of mechanical problems. Chen reported flight indicator failure, and Chang had problems with landing gear. The remaining six formed into two flights of three each. MacNeil led the first element, flying A/C #720, with Tsuei H. C., Mikola, Banger, Fuller, McCann, and Long. Flying on his wing was 2Lt. Chang K. L. as pilot of #716, with Liu C. C., Chu S. P., Feng C. K., and Su J. (Liu and Su were "borrowed" from the 2nd Squadron), as well as Wherritt piloting #718 and Faherty, Gaffney, DeFabritis, and Mier as his crew. This was Faherty's first combat mission since the August 14 bailout. The first three planes, carrying eight 500 lb. demos each, dropped their bombs west of the foundry, with no apparent damage.

Greene, pilot of A/C #714 with a crew that included Hamilton, Koss, Hanrahan, Hoyle, and Allegretto, led the second element. Ragland took position on his wing, flying #719 with Pulaski, Barge, Jakubasz, and Schlicher as his crew, and Senecal flew in third position aboard #722, with his crew that comprised Ilefeldt, Cantor, Fox, and Mills. These last three B-25s, carrying twenty-four 100 lb. bombs per plane, hit the foundry rather than the railroad yards as briefed. Hank, back on flying status, was tail gunner, and Fox was waist gunner on this mission. They strafed a building and "almost cut it in half," Hank recalled. As they were pulling up, Fox remarked, "If there was anybody in that building, you got 'im." Great volumes of gray and white smoke rose from the foundry, but crewmen observed no antiaircraft fire or enemy aircraft. Planes of the second element returned directly to home base, but those of the lead element landed at Laohokow and remained there until the following day before flying on to Liangshan.

Defending Laohokow

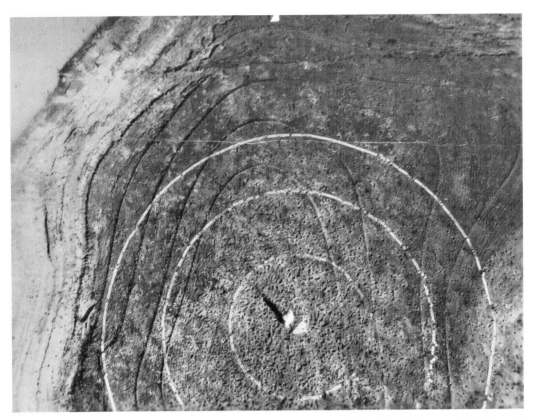

Lt. Koss, Maj. Hamilton's navigator-bombardier on this mission, captioned this photo "Hit target." *R. J. Koss collection, courtesy of Barbara Hughes*

This was the first of many 3rd Squadron missions in which Lts. Greene and Koss took part. Both men had enlisted in 1941 before America's entry into the war, Greene on January 16, in Buffalo, New York. His training prepared him to be a pilot, and he later trained aviation cadets to fly at Columbia Army Air Base, South Carolina, before receiving orders to the CBI.

Koss had enlisted in Chicago on April 9. The youngest of a large Slovenian family and born a month following his father's death, Koss had moved with his mother and several siblings in 1933 to Chicago from their farm 70 miles east of Pittsburgh. Mrs. Koss had generously extended credit at her general store during the Depression, causing her to lose the store and farm when needy neighbors were unable to pay their debts. He was initially attached to an infantry unit before acceptance as an aviation cadet. After the completion of training as a navigator-bombardier at Roswell, New Mexico, Koss was attached to the 378th Bombardment Squadron, 309th Bombardment Group, which trained B-25 pilots and aircrews at Columbia Air Base prior to their assignment to combat units overseas. It was likely there that he met Greene. After the unit was inactivated in May 1944, Koss was offered another training assignment in the US, but he wanted to be "in it" and declined. He was sent to Karachi and trained Chinese airmen with the OTU. At about Christmas 1944, he received his orders to China and was attached to the 17th Fighter Squadron before transfer to the 3rd Bomb Squadron. He did not at first inform his widowed mother or older siblings that he was assigned to an operational unit. They knew that he was in China, but he had told them he was flying supplies over the Hump to aid the Chinese.[6]

Four B-25s took off from Liangshan at 1215 on February 13, again with the foundry area at Hsuchang as primary target. Riverboats observed south of Hsuchang on the eleventh constituted their secondary target. Lt. Greene again led with A/C #714 (with Hamilton, Koss, Hanrahan, Hoyle, and Allegretto making up his crew), followed by Pulaski flying #713 (with Magyar, Fox, and Mills), Ilefeldt aboard #721 (with Cantor, Shock, and Trout), and Logan in #722 (with Senecal, Barge, Jakubasz, and Schlicher). The Mitchells picked up four P-51s over Laohokow, but the fighters turned back because of unsatisfactory weather conditions. Visibility over the target at 1445 was from 1 to 3 miles. All bombs were dropped in the target area on Koss's lead, except for three that hung up in the racks and had to be jettisoned on the way back to home base. The remaining bombs "walked up" the target area. Two fell short, and there was an explosion about 500 feet north of the target. Aircraft encountered no enemy aircraft or antiaircraft fire. The planes separated and went after sampans on the river south of Hsiangcheng, strafing between fifteen and twenty. Each aircraft made two strafing passes at about 50 feet before returning home.

An article in *China Command Post* published in mid-February reported, "The Chinese Army wrested the initiative from the Japanese attacking along the Canton-Hankow railway, throwing the lie to the Jap claim that the railroad is completely under their domination. Not only had the Japs failed to seal it but lost two points to counter-attacking Chinese who also smashed into Pingshek, about 170 miles north of Canton." Although the Japanese had sent reinforcements to the Shanghai area and to northern Indochina as a precaution against the expected American landing on the coast, a Chinese spokesman offered this opinion: "After failing to prevent the invasion of Luzon, the Japanese haven't the slightest hope of preventing an American landing in China with its very much longer coastline." He added that if the Japanese were planning an invasion of Yunnan to cut the terminus of the Stilwell Road to India, they were too late.[7]

Regardless of these optimistic remarks, Allied success was less certain in other parts of China. It was only a few days later that counterattacking Japanese, attempting to close a gap in the Canton–Hankow railroad, recaptured Pingshek. The enemy struck in the mountainous region between Pingshek and the nearby town of Ichang (Yichang) in Hunan Province. While one enemy column retook Pingshek and pushed northward, another struck toward the railroad east of Ichang. In Kiangsi Province, Chinese troops continued their attempts to sever the Japanese supply line from Hengyuang to the lost air base cities of Suichwan and Kansien. Chinese units attacked Japanese positions 9 miles south and 18 miles southeast of Lienhwa, one of the key points on this supply route. The Chinese also threw back a Japanese counterattack 9 miles south of Yungsin, another key point farther east where the Japanese line bent southward to Suichwan and Kanhsien. Enemy troop movement was observed along the Ping-Han Railroad between Chenghsien and Hankow. Fighting continued east of the Canton–Hankow railroad town of Chenghsien, as Japanese forces there were battling to safeguard their grip on the line.[8]

A detachment led by Capt. Hamilton proceeded to Hanchung on the fourteenth to strike the Japanese drive from the north. Nine B-25s left Liangshan and flew to Chengtu, where they were loaded with gas and bombs. Lt. Ilefeldt was favorably impressed by the convenience of the process and wrote: "The rapidity with which the bombs were spotted and the convenience of the gas pumps so close to the taxi strips certainly filled us with joy, and a little wonder. Those B-29 bases really have a beautiful set-up—stateside, in fact. To load a plane with gas, all one has to do is to taxi up to a pump, cut the engines, and say, 'Fill 'er up.'" The process was far different from that to which those stationed at Peishiyi and Liangshan were accustomed. "We have very primitive methods in comparison, for we have to pour our gas from a drum into little five[-]gallon buckets, then hand it up to a man on the wing, who pours it into a funnel, that is, after the gas has been strained. Eventually the tank is filled, but the work is done by Chinese coolies,

This demonstrates the protracted process that Lt. Ilefeldt described for filling the planes' gas tanks from buckets carried by Chinese laborers. *R. N. Solyn collection, courtesy of Robert N. Solin*

The method used for loading the planes with bombs was equally primitive. Here a team of coolies carry the heavy bombs that will be dropped on enemy targets. *R. N. Solyn collection, courtesy of Robert N. Solin*

Using brute force, bombs were then hoisted into position, where the armorer armed and secured them in the shackles. *R. N. Solyn collection, courtesy of Robert N. Solin*

making the task a slow one at best." He added that the coolies also carried the bombs by hand, "while at Chengtu there is ample transportation to satisfy the most critical, and we are anything but critical, in fact, we were green with envy."

After a layover caused by "lousy weather," the Mitchells flew on to Hanchung. Ilefeldt praised the living conditions and mess as "the best to be found in China" and added: "The coffee the cooks brew actually tastes like coffee, and with it they even serve milk, an item that is quite rare at our base. They serve butter with every meal, and sometimes they even serve honey and jam for the delicious pancakes at breakfast." Despite taking part in two missions out of Hanchung, "Everyone considered it the nearest thing to a rest camp he had seen."

Sgt. Daniels, whose 1st Squadron was stationed there, considered it to be "a big improvement over Liangshan and Peishiyi." He later wrote about the base: "Hanchung nestled in a bend of the lazy Han River. Five-thousand-foot mountain ranges ran east-to-west, one southeast and the other northwest of the city. The most prominent structure in the city was the bell tower of Bishop Mario Civelli's Wei-hwei Cathedral, topped by a pole where the jing bao lanterns could be raised." He added that enlisted men were billeted in a former mission dormitory behind "the Italian Cathedral," while the squadron's officers occupied a separate compound down the street.

This was a walled city with a normal population of about 50,000, but refugees flooding in from the east had increased its population to nearly double that number. The encircling wall was a typical earth-filled stone bulwark 25 feet high and 30 feet thick at the base. "Someone had built a crude wooden shack that looked like an old 'outhouse' on top of the southwest corner of the city wall which served as a control tower," wrote Daniels. The field's single grass-covered runway extended to the east and west, while revetments for the Mitchells spread to the south on its far side. The flight line, along with tents and buildings that housed operations, supply, and the orderly room, lined the west wall of the city.

Hanchung boasted a small park with tennis courts but with no nets, racquets, or balls. Its swimming pool was used by locals, although most squadron personnel considered the swimming hole on the Pau River, reached by means of a dusty truck ride, to be a better choice. The town had a few good open-front Chinese restaurants, but "we enlisted men couldn't afford to eat there very often." Daniels remembered a favorite restaurant that featured a tub of live fish next to the blazing-hot cookstove in the front. "You pointed to the fish you wanted and the proprietor would grab it out and sling it across the floor to be cleaned, filleted, and thrown to the cook. . . . Fast food was an oxymoron in China, but you knew the fish was fresh."[9]

By February 16, thirty B-25s from all four squadrons of the 1st Bomb Group converged at Hanchung for a huge raid that Col. Russell, bomb group commander, had planned on the North Railroad Yards at Shihkiachwang (Shijiazhuang), capital and largest city of Hopeh Province. This was an important railroad junction that served the strategic supply line running through northeastern China to Peiping. The raid was prompted in part by recent intelligence that reported damaged locomotives were being hauled to yards in North China for repairs.

The plan was, on the following day, for the planes to take off alternately every forty-five seconds from both ends of the runway until all of them were airborne. In this way, all thirty of the B-25s would be in the air within about twenty-three minutes. It was executed as briefed, except for one flight of planes that took off in the wrong direction and almost caused a midair collision. Despite poor visibility caused by clouds of dust as the planes took off, all but one of the B-25s were off safely by 0800 and headed for Hsian, where they were to rendezvous with their fighter escort of fourteen P-51s of the 311th Fighter Group Detachment. The bombers circled the field three times, but the fighters failed to come up because of a failure in communications.

The bombers, nine of them 3rd Squadron planes, then flew to a point north of Hanchung, where they separated into two elements. Lacking fighter escort, they diverted to alternate targets at Yunchen and Linfen, both located in the big Yellow River bend. The 1st and 4th Squadron planes turned south to attack Yunchen, where the situation rapidly deteriorated. Maj. Hodges,

Lt. Logan, a San Francisco native, stands with Lt. Senecal beside A/C #719 that has been personalized by the addition of "MY FRISCO JOE!" *R. L. Logan collection, courtesy of Katherine A. Logan*

Defending Laohokow

former 3rd Squadron pilot, flew in the lead of eight 1st Squadron B-25s that made up "Benton" flight. Three 3rd Squadron planes were to join three from the 4th Squadron to form "Charlotte" flight, but Lt. Logan, flying A/C #713 with Schlicher, Trout, and Mills as his gunners, was unable to take off because of mechanical failure of the right magneto. Another 1st Squadron B-25 with an all-Chinese crew took its place in the formation, which also included A/C #722 (Hamilton, Ilefeldt, Banger, Jakubasz, Mier, and Schlicher) and #719 (Chang K. L., Yang C. H., Chiu S. P., Fang C. K., and Liu S. C.). By this time, A/C #719 had been personalized for Lt. Logan with "MY FRISCO JOE!" in recognition of his San Francisco origin, although he did not fly it on this mission. Cpl. Schlicher is listed with the crew both of A/C #713, which did not take off, and #722, that did. He may have moved from one plane to the other.

Loaded with 500 lb. demolition bombs fused to 0.1-to-0.025-second delay, planes were over the target at 0955. They made bombing passes on railroad yards from south to north at 7,000 feet and at 5,700 feet, dropping on the lead bombardier. Nearly all the bombs missed their targets and landed in rice paddies or small villages outside the target area. Aircrews reported heavy ground fire. "A discouraged and bitter group of airmen returned from this fiasco and there was plenty of blame to go around," wrote Sgt. Daniels, who took part in the raid with his 1st Squadron.[10]

The 2nd Squadron and remainder of the 3rd Squadron that formed "Akron" and "Detroit" flights, respectively, were more successful. This formation turned north and attacked railroad yards at Linfen, about 220 miles northeast of Hsian. The formation approached from the southwest and picked up the Tungpu Railroad below Linfen, making two bombing runs up the tracks from south to north. The 2nd Squadron's lead bombardier was not ready to drop on the first run over the target, although two Chinese-crewed B-25s dropped sixteen 500 lb. demos. Some fell in the southern barracks area east of the railroad yards, while the others fell in a line north toward the northern barracks. On the second run, both flights dropped a total of seventy-eight 500 lb. demos that fell across the southeast end of the yards and into the vicinity of the turning wye (a triangular rail junction), tearing up trackage southeast of the yards.

Capt. Ragland, flying #720 (with Pulaski, Edgerton, Rieks, Hanrahan, and Hoyle), led the 3rd Squadron element, which also included #721 (Cheng Y. K., Liu P. C., Liu C. T., Wu C. S., and Ho W. C.), #723 (MacNeil, Tsai T. C., Fuller, Shock, and Long), #714 (Greene, Maj. V. B. Miller, Koss, Barge, and Allegretto), hastily repaired #713 (Wherritt, Cantor, Gaffney, DeFabritis, and Hugel), and #716 (Senecal, Faherty, Wadlow, Magyar, and Fox). The 3rd Squadron crews sighted two small enemy airplanes in a pattern landing at Linfen. They reported minimal antiaircraft fire: one black and two white bursts. Crews of the 4th Squadron observed four small airplanes and two medium planes "believed to be Lillies." All planes of the formation were down at 1200.

Another big mission was planned on the nineteenth to support Chinese troops fighting in the vicinity of Ichang. Mitchells of the 1st Bomb Group were to join in the action while all of them were assembled, but a front moved in that kept them grounded. Only the wing's fighters were able to take part in the attack on enemy rail lines, river communications, and ammunition dumps. As aircrews waited for the return of flying weather, many occupied their time by playing baseball or poker, duck hunting, and drinking liquor and eating provisions that had been stashed away by their 1st Squadron hosts. "Crowded conditions and squadron rivalries were getting on everyone's nerves," wrote Daniels, whose quarters had been invaded by the unwelcome "southern guests."[11]

The weather cleared enough to fly on February 21. Hank recalled, "They got us up early, and for breakfast that morning they fed us pork chops, fried eggs, and pancakes made with the best homemade sorghum syrup, made by those Chinese. I always remember that breakfast—a real American breakfast." It was customary to serve the men a substantial cooked breakfast before they headed out on a dangerous mission, Jim McCann later told his family, although a superior mess was common at Hanchung.

Twenty-one B-25s, four of them 3rd Squadron planes, were off by 0800. Twenty-four were scheduled to take part in the raid, but one 2nd Squadron plane had an accident caused by poor visibility while attempting takeoff, and two 3rd Squadron aircraft could not take off because of mechanical problems (a faulty induction vibrator on one, and difficulty with gas flow on the other). Eight from the 2nd Squadron ("Ashville" flight) flew in the lead, followed by four from the 3rd Squadron ("Butler" flight), and nine from the 1st Squadron ("Carter" flight). A fourth flight, "Delaware," was made up of three each from the 1st and 2nd Squadrons. Hamilton led "Butler" with A/C #719 (Ragland, Banger, Jakubasz, Mier, and Hanrahan as his aircrew), followed by #718 (MacNeil, Senecal, Shock, Hoyle, and Faherty), #716 (Logan, Schlicher, Trout, and Mills), and #714 (Cheng Y. K., Liu P. C., Chen Y. T., Wi C. S., and Ho W. C.). Each plane carried eight 500 lb. GPs. Passing over Hsian, the Mitchells picked up fourteen P-51s of the 311th Fighter Group, which had received the telegram this time.

Visibility at takeoff was limited to 1.5 miles but improved to 8–10 miles over the target: the railroad and machine shops at Taiyuan, capital and largest city of Shansi Province. A report of activity in the target area noted that Taiyuan appeared to be extremely active. Crewmen reported the railroad yards east of the city to be handling a capacity quantity of rolling stock. Incomplete photo coverage of the shop area from the airplanes on the mission showed them to be servicing "numerous cars and possible locomotives." The shops themselves seemed busy, with smoke pouring forth from all the chimneys in sufficient quantity to partially obscure the target, "making the bombardiers' problem all the greater."

The lead bombardier of each flight had a separate aiming point and bombed from a different altitude. Approaching from south to north, pilots followed the lead plane of each flight, and bombardiers dropped on the leader. Each flight hit its briefed target. When 3rd Squadron bombs were released from 6,500 feet, results were "very accurate," hitting almost all the large buildings within the shop area and producing secondary explosions accompanied by large orange bursts of flame. Crewmen reported antiaircraft fire, the heaviest after the target had been hit and planes had turned away. White bursts were several thousand feet below the formation; black bursts were accurate for altitude but slightly inaccurate for deflection. Six or more airplanes were parked in the revetments on Taiyuan North Airdrome, but some crewmen reported that they may have been dummies.

Hank related, "I remember one Japanese field that we flew over, and they had planes—not real planes but dummy planes to make you think they were—and I thought, how do they think those old things out there would make you think they were real planes?" The Japanese "used paper and sticks, made little frames—just a poor excuse for a plane. You could tell from a long way, that's not an airplane."

The formation passed south along the Tungpu Railroad on the way back to Hanchung. Barracks and railroad yards were extremely active at each town en route. All planes were down at 1300. Eager to return to home base, 3rd Squadron bomber personnel took a heading back to Liangshan soon after this mission was completed.

Maj. Seacrest received his orders to return to "Uncle Sugar" on February 26. It came as no surprise, since he had been put in rotation to go home soon before taking command of the squadron the previous month. Lt. Ilefeldt wrote that Seacrest "certainly deserved to go home, for very few men in this theater can claim as impressive a record." Overseas since July 1943, he had completed sixty-four combat missions and had 305 combat hours to his credit, and the amount of tonnage he had sunk while operating in the China Sea totaled among the highest of any other B-25 pilot in any theater. "Maj. Seacrest is indeed a resourceful combat pilot, for on several occasions, he has made as many as seven passes to knock out a very hot target, such as a Japanese gunboat. . . . Maj. Seacrest's exploits as a combat pilot are well known in this theater, and he leaves many admirers behind."

Capt. Hamilton, a recent addition to the squadron, was appointed its commanding officer. His extensive experience as a B-25 pilot / flight leader with the 489th Bomb Squadron, 340th ("Avengers") Bomb Group, 57th Bomb Wing of the 9th and later (from August 1943) 12th Air Force, more than qualified him to lead the 3rd Squadron. Initially sent with the 489th to the Mediterranean theater in March 1943 and stationed at El Kabrit, Egypt, he participated in primarily high-altitude bombing missions, both day and night, in support of the British 8th Army in Tunisia and Egypt. As Allied forces advanced, the squadron moved on to Italy, flying missions throughout Italy, Sicily, Yugoslavia, Albania, Bulgaria, and Greece. Its targets included airfields, railroads, bridges, road junctions, supply depots, gun emplacements, troop concentrations, marshaling yards, and factories. On February 14, 1944, while stationed at Pompei, Hamilton completed his sixtieth combat mission, in the lead of a six-plane formation against the east choke point of marshaling yards about 4 miles southeast of Perugia, Italy, earning a seventh Oak Leaf Cluster to his Air Medal. He returned to the US the following month and was stationed for some period at Baltimore and at Columbia. He had been in China since December 1944.[12]

When asked to compare the two theaters of operation, Hamilton's response was recorded in the 3rd Squadron historical report. "The weather is always good in North Africa, while in China, the weather is always bad it seems." The supply situation was much better in North Africa, and "the intelligence set-up" was much more elaborate than in China, he said. "But however much better supplied and equipped North Africa was, the work that the Fourteenth Air Force has done and is doing, the tremendous obstacles it is overcoming in order to hit the enemy, the amount of energy expended to do the great task it is doing, is indeed greater than that of any other theater."

Hamilton felt fortunate to have never been wounded in his three and a half years of service. The closest he had come was on a mission in North Africa when he brought in his crippled plane with forty-six holes in it.

The men at Liangshan enjoyed springlike weather during late February but were unable to run combat missions because of unfavorable conditions at potential targets in other parts of China. Sgt. Hwang Tung-shou (X-1407), was attached as aerial gunner. Capt. MacNeil, with FO Wherritt and other Americans who made up the aircrew, together with a Chinese crew, left with two of the squadron's planes for Laohokow, where they were scheduled to stage for a few weeks. Lt. Faherty's flight log specifies administrative missions between Liangshan and Laohokow from mid-February to early March. While he was there, he purchased a collection of beautiful photographs of Laohokow's residents engaged in typical activities: washing clothes in the river, weaving cloth, making rope, repairing shoes, selling spoons, getting a haircut, and others.[13]

Situated in a deep plain on the Han River, Laohokow was in a "pocket," with Japanese-controlled territory on three sides, to the north, east, and west. Its accessibility from the Yangtze River and the Peiping-Hankow Railroad—the two main arteries of supply and troop movements used by the Japanese in China—made it especially vulnerable to movement by the enemy. Hummel wrote, "Always at the back of the mind through all the months of CACW occupancy had been the knowledge that once the Japanese decided to drive down from any of their troop concentration points in Central China, Laohokow would fall—and fall in a few days."

Called "Pete" by friends and family, Wherritt had enlisted in February 1943 and was sent for pretraining to Rockhurst College in Kansas City, Missouri, and then, classified as an aviation cadet, to San Antonio, Texas, for primary training. Basic training was at Waco, Texas, then back to San Antonio for advanced training. When he graduated from there and received his wings, it was as a flight officer rather than second lieutenant. After spending time as an instructor at various bases throughout the US, he was sent in November 1944 to China. Being placed in command of Nimrod Detachment indicated the high regard he had earned while serving in the 3rd Squadron.[14]

During this period, all the Gambay Group's bomb squadrons were active against the enemy. The 1st Squadron sent a detachment to Hsian to operate under control of the 14th Air Force's 312th Fighter Wing against the Tsing-Pu Railroad, at the same time launching missions out of Hangchung against bridges along the Ping-Han Railroad. The 4th Squadron's detachment continued operations out of Chihkiang against enemy transportation in the Hsiang River corridor, while its remaining planes were maintained at Peishiyi to be available on call for special tasks and large-scale attacks.

Nimrod Detachment, initially headed by Maj. Seacrest, was tasked to run low-level missions on railroads, bridges, riverboats, and sea sweeps from Laohokow. The detachment operated from this unprotected position until the airfield was abandoned to the Japanese, while the 3rd Squadron's remaining planes operated with the 2nd Squadron out of Liangshan and flew night intruder missions against trains and convoys in the Ping-Han corridor, day missions against trackage and bridges along the Ping-Han Railroad, and light-of-the-moon missions against targets in the Wuhan area.

Lt. Eisner, the bomb group's acting historical officer, explained that enemy activity through the month "was reduced to the cleaning up of their drive against 14th Air Force bases in Kiangsi Province." The Japanese occupied Kanchow on January 30 and carried out consolidation around Suichwan. Their intentions appeared to be an intensified preparation of their defenses along the China coast and below Hanoi in French Indochina. Redeployment of troops was continued as part of these defensive measures, while extensive efforts were made to develop and maintain adequate transportation facilities in China, he wrote. "There was little offensive action on the Japanese part, but their capabilities of moving where they wished remained." Toward the end of the month, the Chinese launched a vigorous counteroffensive against Suichwan that seemed likely to succeed at least temporarily.

Lt. Young's name was dropped from squadron rosters as of February 28, after he was once again hospitalized for malaria. The move to Liangshan had been completed during the month, including the arrival of all Chinese personnel. "The latter part of February gave us a touch of fair weather, and a promise of better weather to come, which will allow us to operate against the enemy much more frequently," Ilefeldt optimistically concluded. Everyone was looking forward to the prospect after so many months of enforced idleness.

The squadron flew twenty-two sorties during the month, all of them on daytime medium-altitude bombing missions. Targets were along the main arteries running from north to south against foundries, railroad yards, and railroad engine repair shops. Planes dropped 224 bombs on enemy installations, including 152 500 lb. demos and seventy-two 100 lb. demos. Personnel consisted of twenty-one American officers, forty-six American enlisted men, seventy-eight Chinese officers, and 137 Chinese enlisted men. B-25s assigned to the squadron were eight H and three J models.

CHAPTER THIRTEEN
Last Airfield Lost

On March 1, squadron personnel at Liangshan assembled on the field and posed for photographs with A/C #714, in the best condition of the B-25Js, positioned behind them. The first included all but a few of the Americans assigned at that time, and then they separated for pictures of only the officers, only enlisted men, and the softball team. TSgt. Solyn kept copies but later explained to his family that he did not appear in them because he was the photographer. An unidentified Chinese child was seated with them. He was perhaps one of several orphan children who lived in an old kiln near the barracks, as described by the 2nd Squadron's Cpl. Johnson. It was common practice for the tenderhearted Americans to "adopt" orphans in war-ravaged China.

All personnel present at Liangshan on March 1, 1945, gathered on the field for squadron photos. This one included officers and enlisted men, and copies were distributed to all of them. They are identified individually in the photos of the squadron's officers and of enlisted men. Notice the Chinese child seated in Sgt. Dunlap's lap, behind Capt. Hamilton. *J. H. Mills collection*

Officers: (*left to right, standing*) R. J. Koss, G. P. Wood, R. L. Logan, F. H. Greene Jr., J. C. Kelso Jr., W. G. Ilefeldt, R. Ragland, B. L. Wherritt, F. P. Pulaski; (*kneeling*) J. G. Cantor, T. H. Edgerton, W. H. Senecal, M. T. Seacrest, J. M. Hamilton, R. E. Banger, J. F. Faherty, R. C. MacNeil. *J. G. Cantor collection, courtesy of Ronnie Cantor*

Enlisted men: (*left to right, standing*) J. J. DeFabritis, J. J. Morris Jr., R. E. Schlicher, I. F. Hoke, J. A. Wadlow, M. W. Rieks, J. H. Mills, F. T. Jakubasz, N. L. Long, E. W. Peters, H. L. Burton, W. G. Duffin, J. J. Ryan Jr., R. G. Hugel, L. L. Fox; (*middle row, kneeling*) J. P. Supsic, B. W. Evitts, L. E. Jackson Jr., C. L. Learn, W. H. Whearty, A. J. Magyar, S. B. Rickman, W. C. Dunlap, J. P. Barge, E. F. Wilkerson, J. A. Trout, W. Meikle, A. R. Allegretto, L. E. Gaffney; (*front row, seated*) J. Holmes, J. W. England, P. E. Haines, I. G. Mier, H. L. Chasse, C. H. Hoyle Jr., J. P. Hanrahan, W. T. Earley Jr., G. B. Fuller, G. Gruber, J. N. Shock, J. E. McCann, B. F. Thomas Jr., J. R. Summerville. Here the Chinese child sits between Gruber and Shock. *J. F. Faherty collection, courtesy of Dennis Faherty*

Squadron softball ball team: (*left to right, standing*) J. J. DeFabritis, J. W. England, P. E. Haines, R. L. Logan, W. Meikle, A. J. Magyar, and J. J. Morris Jr.; (*kneeling*) J. P. Supsic, J. Holmes, G. Gruber, W. T. Earley Jr., A. R. Allegretto, W. G. Duffin, J. C. Kelso Jr. The Chinese child with Duffin holds up a slingshot that was likely crafted for him by one of the Americans. *G. B. Fuller collection, courtesy of Elizabeth Fuller Zea*

Later that day, Lt. Koss wrote a letter to his brother Frank, explaining that he had been "moving around so much the past few months" that he had "lost count" of his correspondence. "I don't remember if I ever wrote and thanked you for the Christmas package. I received it a few days before Christmas and needless to say made good use of it. The Nestles came in handy in China." Observing an unofficial code of silence generally practiced by GIs, he made light of the discomforts and dangers that he endured in letters to his family. "As I told Mom[,] combat flying is mostly like I had expected[,] not much different than flying back in the States. However, that shot of mission whiskey hits the spot. You see the army gives us an ounce and a half after evy mission and it helps." A neutral topic being the weather, he commented, "The weather the past few days has been nice[;] the sun came out and that's something here in China."

He suggested that his family watch the movie *Dragon Seed* (based on the Pearl S. Buck novel), to better understand the situation in China; "of course the smell of China is not there." Koss closed by requesting another package to include "small cans of fruit, spam etc etc," as he often did in his letters to family.[1]

Cpl. Piecuch, who had been with the squadron in India, was transferred back to the 3rd Squadron for duty as mess sergeant on March 1 to oversee the Chinese cooks in an attempt to overcome deficiencies in the kitchen. Early in the month, 2Lts. Pulaski and Ilefeldt were promoted to first lieutenants, and 1Lt. Charles W. Jeffries was attached as Young's replacement as intelligence officer.

MSgt. Fuller, the squadron's line chief, received orders for a direct field commission in mid-March. Lt. Ilefeldt explained the process:

> There is more to being made a 2Lt. than meets the eye. An enlisted man must first be discharged from the army before he can receive his commission and be sworn in. Now, just how does one discharge a man overseas? We asked ourselves the same question, and then by the simple process of looking up regulation after regulation, (ah, regulations!) the discharge of a soldier is found to be a very simple one, indeed. So simple, in fact, that it could easily become habit-forming were it to get out of hand. Lt. Fuller was a civilian for a day; the first time in five years for him. We all wish Lt. Fuller the best of success, which is most deservedly his. Lt. Fuller is a soldier.

Recognized for his efficiency and outstanding performance of duty, Fuller was appointed the squadron's engineering officer to replace Capt. MacNeil, who took over as operations officer. Hank remembered Fuller as "head of the maintenance people." After receiving his commission, he was required to move out of the enlisted men's quarters and into the officers' quarters. "The officers didn't treat him well. They thought they were better than him," Hank recalled.

By this time, thirteen 14th Air Force bases in China had been lost: Hengyang, Lingling, Kweilin, Liuchow, Poaching, Suichwan, Tanchuck, Nanning, Tushan, Namyung, Sincheng, Nankang, and Kanchow. Intelligence indicated that the Japanese army was conducting large-scale activities and gathering their troops in southern Honan and central and northern Hupeh. Now a renewed Japanese offensive began with an attack westward on a broad front between the Yellow and Yangtze Rivers. The primary objective of this drive was to overrun the Allied bases at Laohokow, Hsian, Ankang, Hanchung, and Chihkiang in the same way they had at Kweilin and other bases the previous year.

Laohokow was the first of those intended for capture. Located on the central plain between the Yangtze and Yellow Rivers, it was vulnerable to ground attack since there were no natural mountain barriers or large rivers to stop the enemy. Only about 200 miles northwest of Hankow, the airfield was strategically situated for hammering the enemy supply and communication arteries in central China and could additionally be used to strike the China coast and the Shanghai and Shantung Peninsula areas. By Laohokow's fall, the Japanese would interdict the coordination of 14th Air Force coastal attacks from inland with seaborne coastal attacks by Pacific forces, just at the crucial period when the Pacific battle was reaching toward the mainland.

Strategy for the Laohokow campaign was simple. It began on March 1, when an estimated four thousand Japanese troops struck west and southwest from Lushan. Almost simultaneously, three additional columns of from three thousand to five thousand each thrust west from Paoanchen, Shengtien, and Shahotien, lying between Lushan and the Ping-Han Railroad. For the two previous months the enemy had been concentrating troops, supplies, and armor in the Hsuchang-Hsiangcheng-Wuyang triangle, and a fifth column was moved from Yehsien and Wuyang north along the Han River on Laohokow. Another independent drive started west and southwest from Loning. The converging drives were spearheaded by tanks, armor, and horse cavalry. Instead of moving down roads, as had been almost standard practice on their part in previous campaigns, the enemy swept cross-country, thereby eliminating any Chinese counterdefense. Demoralized by earlier defeats and suffering from a scarcity of troops, supplies, and weapons, the Chinese elected to hold out in strongpoint towns. The

Japanese, by avoiding the use of roads, simply bypassed the towns and their Chinese defenders. The minimal amount of fighting that did occur was confined to a few of these towns, and the countryside lay open and unobstructed to mounted and motor sweep by the enemy.

The 3rd Squadron, in cooperation with others of the 1st Bomb Group, entered the action a week following the initial advance and focused on knocking out enemy supply lines and communications in an attempt to slow the drive. Often flying in winter conditions that would have ordinarily kept them grounded, the bombers destroyed bridges and hit truck convoys, locomotives, supply dumps, and troops wherever they could be found.

Two B-25s took off from Liangshan and proceeded to Laohokow for mission #60 on March 7. Ragland took the lead, flying A/C #715 with Greene, Edgerton, Hanrahan, Hoyle, and Magyar as his aircrew, and #722 (__, __, Chen Y. K., __, Cheng C., and Wei C. S.; some names illegible) flew on his wing. Lt. Edgerton listed it as his twenty-second mission. From Laohokow, the plan was to intercept the Peiping-Hankow Railroad 5 miles north of Siaping, but the Mitchells hit the railroad south of the target and proceeded 50 miles farther south to Changtuikwan before turning back north. Crewmen observed no enemy activity along the track, although they noticed light ground fire south of Kioshan. At the railroad bridge north of Saiping, bombs were dropped by pilot release from 500 feet. Ragland's demos fell short and walked up the track, and two hit the north end of the bridge. The wing plane's bombs hit in a field 500 yards left of the track, the misses attributed to a bombsight malfunction. An estimated 40 percent of the bombs hit the tracks and 10 percent hit the bridge, and smoke and debris from explosions rose to 3,000 feet. The formation encountered moderate and inaccurate ground fire along the railroad track, and crewmen observed gun emplacements north and south of the bridge.

That same day, Wherritt flew A/C #718 (with Yang C. H., Gaffney, DeFabritis, and Hugel), off from Laohokow at 1025 carrying two 500 lb. GP demos, AN-M43, fused at the nose to four-to-five-second delay. This was Nimrod Detachment's mission #L-1, executed in coordination with the 3rd Squadron's mission #60. The target of this B-25H was the section from Sinyang (32°06' N, 114°05' E) north to Hsuchang along the Peiping-Hankow Railroad. Ceiling was unlimited and visibility 1–3 miles, with haze both at takeoff and over the target. Approaching a bridge 15 miles north of Sinyang, Wherritt reduced altitude and released at 300 feet to skip-bomb, but one demo failed to explode and a second hit 50 feet to the right of the bridge. At 8 miles north of Changtuikwan, he fired eight 75 mm HE shells from the cannon, scoring a direct hit on another small bridge that resulted in twisted rails and damaged stringers. A mile south of Kioshan, he came across a train with boxcars on the main track and a locomotive in a revetment, so he dropped in for strafing. Damage from 3,400 rounds of .50 caliber included holes to the boiler, through which crewmen reported escaping steam. The aircraft encountered light, inaccurate AA at a bridge at Hingkiang, as well as from Changtuikwan and Kioshan, but no damage was inflicted to the Mitchell, back down at Laohokow at 1325. Lt. Banger signed the report as Nimrod Detachment's intelligence officer.

Six planes flew from Liangshan to Laohokow and then on to Hsuchang on the eighth. Although most details in the mission report are illegible, it can be determined that MacNeil took the lead as pilot of A/C #714, and Ilefeldt flew A/C #722 (with Wilkerson as tail gunner). Other pilots were Hamilton, Tung, and In Y. S. (with Ouyang C. as his navigator); no other names or A/C numbers can be determined. The formation split into two elements, with four planes turning toward the railroad bridge 1.5 miles east of Chungmow. Hamilton successfully dropped his bombs on the bridge, but those from following planes dropped long, hitting two trucks and a house at the end of the bridge. The two planes going up the railroad made long sweeps along the tracks but did not find the railroad bridge 7 miles northwest of Chengsien that was their target. Instead, they bombed several smaller bridges and strafed a section of rail where they had discovered thirty-five cars. Crewmen observed some ground fire as they flew over the Yellow River Bridge, but all planes returned safely.

On a second mission conducted on the eighth, three planes took off at 1330 and flew from Liangshan to Laohokow and then on to destroy highway bridges at Hsiangcheng and Chowkiakow. Lt. Senecal flew the lead plane, A/C #715, with Pulaski, Koss, Magyar, Hoyle, and Shock as his crew. It was a new J model that had not yet received its CACW markings. The 1,000 lb. bomb toggled over the Hsiangchen target at 100 feet, skipping off the bridge and into the main street of the town. Bombs released by the other two planes also landed in the street, killing an estimated 100 to 150 people. As Senecal was pulling out of the dive, his bomber clipped a building of rock construction, damaging his vertical stabilizer and rudder. In addition, the wingtip was ripped off and the propeller blade was bent. Despite the damage, he gained altitude and jettisoned the remaining two bombs. The wing planes were A/C #719 (Chang C. K., Tu N. I., Kao W. C., Wei C. S., Chow K. P., and Shu S. S.) and A/C #723 (Tu K. M., Chen K. C., Chen Y. K., Lee S. C., Yuan C. K., and Cheng C.). A/C #719 was hit by antiaircraft fire that knocked out its hydraulic system. Lt. Tu Kai-mu's gunners strafed a train north of Siping and inflicted significant damage to the boiler. All planes reached Liangshan and were down at 1800. Hank recalled that as Senecal climbed out of his badly damaged plane, he calmly inquired of those standing nearby, "Anybody got a cigarette?"

Tu provided details regarding missions during this period. "We adopted several modes of attack," he said. "Apart from conventional level-flight bombing, we sometimes launched dive-bombing attacks or even used our 75 mm gun to strafe ground targets. All ball turret

Extensive damage to A/C #715 resulted on March 8 when Lt. Senecal pulled up sharply after bombing a bridge at Hsiangchen in Honan Province. After their return, its flight crew was photographed beside the damaged plane: *(left to right, standing)* F. P. Pulaski, R. J. Koss, W. H. Senecal; *(kneeling)* J. N. Shock, A. J. Magyar, C. H. Hoyle Jr. *A. J. Magyar collection, courtesy of Lynn Magyar Zwigard*

gunners also strafed the ground randomly in order to suppress Japanese antiaircraft fire, which was still a serious threat to us." He explained that escort was seldom considered necessary. "While out on a short-range mission such as our raids in Hubei, we judged that it would be almost impossible for us to encounter Japanese interception, so we tended to not have escorts."[2]

Lt. Greene and Lt. Teng briefed their crews at Liangshan for a mission on the morning of March 9. They took off at 0955 and proceeded to Laohokow, where they picked up a fighter escort of one P-51 and two P-40s and then attacked a railroad bridge 2.3 miles north of Jungtze. Flying A/C #713, Greene (with Mikola, Hanrahan, and Jakubasz as his aircrew) dropped his bombs and hit the north end of the bridge, but those of the trailing plane, A/C #723 (Yang W. P., Chang Y. C., Lu S. C., and Wang S. F. as flight crew), fell into the river and onto the left bank. On the return trip the bombers encountered fifteen to twenty freight cars and went in for strafing, severely damaging several.

Another glip-bombing mission by two B-25Js carrying thousand-pounders that were off at 0958 on the same day was even less successful. Targets were bridges at Yehsien and Junan. Lt. Logan, pilot of A/C #714 (with Ilefeldt, Edgerton, Whearty, Morris, and Ryan), dropped a 1,000 lb. GP at 300 feet at Yehsien that overshot the target. The bomb of the wing plane, A/C #724 (Liu P. C., Chen Y. S., Ouyang C., Tsao C. C., and Hsiao T. P.), could not be released. They flew on to Junan to hit the bridge on the east end of the town, but the leader again missed, hitting to the right. The trailing plane's bomb also fell into the river to the right of the bridge. Moving to the bridge on the west end of Junan, Logan hit the bridge, but the bomb caused only slight damage to the railing. The bomb release mechanism of Liu's plane once again failed, and Ouyang, his bombardier, kicked them out on the way back home.

Off on a solo raid on the same date, Nimrod Detachment undertook a mission to skip-bomb the highway bridge at Chowkiakow. FO Wherritt again flew A/C #718, off at 0920 with a crew that included Yang C. H., Wadlow, Long, and Schlicher. He released two 500 lb. GP demos on each of two runs. The first two bombs were over, and the second two hit the northwest end of the bridge, with no apparent damage. It was Wherritt's opinion that the bombs were too small to damage the concrete bridge. His gunners then strafed railroad tracks to the south, although the aircrew observed no enemy movement along the tracks. Wherritt fired four 75 mm shells that hit the tracks. The aircraft encountered small-arms fire, and damage to the plane's fuselage, left engine nacelle, left flap, left wing, right rudder, and elevator consisted of scattered bullet holes. The Mitchell was able to return to base in spite of the damage.

Two 22nd Bomb Squadron B-25Hs took off at 1205 on March 10, on Nimrod Detachment's mission #L-3. Capt. M. M. McCarthy led, with 1Lt. W. C. Van Voagt on his wing. They made a sweep along the railroad from Nanking to Tientsien and from Penypu north to Suchow before turning west to Kaifeng. They encountered small-arms fire at each village over which they passed. After the planes had dropped their bombs and fired the 75 mm cannons, Van Voagt's Mitchell crashed about ¾ mile west of the railroad and burst into flame. All died in the crash. Although no 3rd Squadron planes or crew participated in the mission, Lt. Banger completed and signed the report.

Winter conditions shut down operations at Laohokow from March 12 to 21, and no further Nimrod operational reports have been discovered. The Japanese 11th Army took advantage of the snow and freezing rain to launch an advance on the base that began on March 20 as bombers and fighters remained grounded by winter storms. The Japanese army, with 80,000 troops, crossed the Yellow River at night and assembled on the south bank before striking southwest from Lushan. A second column advanced north along the Han River valley in a pincer movement. The first ground fighting of the campaign was reported at Ichang, only 118 air miles from Laohokow. Beginning on March 22, fighter planes out of Laohokow struck repeatedly against the enemy as they pushed toward the airfield, while CACW aircraft incessantly pounded the enemy drive on raids launched from Liangshan, Ankang, and Hsian.

On the evening of Friday the twenty-third, returning 426th Night Fighter Squadron pilots reported seeing a large concentration of enemy vehicles about 30 miles northeast of Laohokow. Positioned bumper to bumper, the line extended for 12 miles. CACW headquarters issued orders on Saturday morning to begin evacuation of all nonessential personnel.

As preparations were being made to relinquish Laohokow, the 3rd Squadron received a new navigator when 1Lt. Thomas A. Kilian transferred in from the 11th Bomb Squadron, 341st Bomb Group. One of only two survivors of a crash on January 18 at Chihkiang as they returned from a mission, he had just emerged from the navigator's compartment in the B-25's nose, which was flattened. He was still recovering from a broken leg but expected to be back on flying status soon.

A new pilot, 1Lt. Donald J. Davis, transferred in at about the same time. Born in Iowa, he had moved from place to place with his nomadic family, living in Nebraska, California, Oklahoma, and Colorado. He registered for the draft in October 1940 in Enid, Oklahoma, specifying his mother, in Palisade, Colorado, as his contact person. From the Air Reserve, he enlisted in the Air Corps as an aviation cadet at Los Angeles in March 1942 and went on to graduate from advanced training with Class 43-C from AAF West Coast Training Center in March 1943, at Stockton Field, California. Davis completed forty-four missions while assigned to an AAF unit in New Guinea. After completing his tour of duty, he requested service in the CBI and left for China in mid-December 1944. His mother died on Christmas Eve.[3]

Lt. Baker, now with group HQ as operations officer, was awarded the Air Medal by Brig. Gen. Morse on March 24 for completing more than one hundred missions, adding it to his previously received DFC and the Purple Heart. When Baker informed his parents in Indiana of the recent award in a letter, he cautioned them to be patient because the current phase of the war in China was "not over," regardless of recent advances in Europe.[4]

That was the same day that the Japanese reached Nanyung. Fancheng—only 20 miles northeast—also fell, and a column approached Siangyang (Xiangyang) on the Han River, 40 miles southeast of Laohokow. Squadron planes flew missions from Liangshan throughout the day, in a desperate attempt to deter the enemy's advance. The first was by a single B-25H, A/C #717, carrying twenty-three M47 incendiary bombs. Lt. Greene, with Koss, Holmes, Morris, and Cantor as his aircrew, was off at 0910 to hit Yehsien, where bombs were seen to "string out about halfway across the town." Crewmen observed an estimated twelve to fifteen cavalry horses tied up outside a building of a small, unidentified village nearby, so Greene delivered a direct hit by a 75 mm shell. His gunners strafed many horse-drawn carts. On one of the strafing passes, SSgt. Holmes, top-turret gunner, swung the guns around and fired forward over the nose of the aircraft. The concussion shattered the Plexiglas over the pilot's seat. No one was injured, and the plane returned safely to base.

Off Liangshan at 1020 on a low-level mission to bomb and strafe the town of Wuyang, two planes climbed up through overcast to 11,500 feet and proceeded to Laohokow, where they began letdown through clearing conditions. Each carried twenty-three M47 incendiaries. Hamilton, flying A/C #722 (with Sung S. C., Chu S. C., Hanrahan, and Trout), attempted to drop bombs, but all hung up in the racks. Lt. Tung S. L., pilot of A/C #713 (with Kiang J. M.,

Huang C. N., Ku C. C., Wei C. S., and Hwang T. S.), dropped short. They circled and made a second pass at 1,000 feet. Bombs of Hamilton's plane salvoed when he attempted release, all falling short. Gunners of both planes strafed heavily. On the return, they strafed twenty to thirty wagons, all heavily loaded. Smoke rose from the vicinity of Yehsien, likely the result of the previous mission. Three kinds of propaganda leaflets totaling 19,520 were scattered. Both planes were hit by small-arms fire, one in the engine cowling and the other in the left wing, but they returned to base despite the damage.

Three crews were off at 1105 and bombed the town of Lushan, which appeared abandoned. Flying #714, Davis took the lead (with Senecal, Liu P. C., and Hoyle), and #719 (Chang K. L., Young P. C., Lee S. C., Feng C. K., and Chang T. H.) and #716 (Chang Y. S., Tsui W. P., Chang C. C., Chang C. C., Lee L., and Yuan C. S.) took wing positions. The pilots dropped all bombs on the town at 200 feet, starting fires, but aircrews noticed no activity of any kind.

Hamilton was off at 1948, flying A/C #714 (with Davis, Mikola, Ryan, Magyar, and Fox), scouting for targets of opportunity in the vicinity of Nanyang, Hsiangcheng, and Wuyang. When small-arms fire hit the plane at an unidentified village south of Hsiangcheng, Hamilton released twelve frag clusters at 200 feet. More ground fire came up in the vicinity of Wuyang. Thousands of leaflets were dropped on this mission, as on many others.

Another mission was off at 1120 to bomb and strafe the towns of Chiutien and Lengshuichen. Over the first target, Ilefeldt (with Mikola, Fox, Ryan, and Magyar) dropped twelve bombs from A/C #724. Flying the wing plane, #721, Lt. Cheng Y. K. (with Tu N. L., Ouyang C., Lu M. C., Mao C. M., and Hsiang T. P.) dropped twenty-three bombs, reported to "walk up through the town." The aircrews observed fires and smoke in both target areas. Leaflets were dropped.

On the final mission for that day (mission #70) in defense of the beleaguered airfield, Greene (with Senecal, Koss, Barge, Morris, and Whearty) took off at 2000 and flew A/C #721 to search for targets of opportunity in the vicinity of Yehsien and Wuyang. When crewmen thought they spotted a convoy through the haze, although visibility was so poor that identification could not be confirmed, the pilot released twelve frag clusters. As gunners strafed the road between Poyang and Chaohochen, ground fire hit the plane. Taking evasive action, Greene pulled up sharply, and Cpl. Morris, waist gunner, was caught off-guard. His left leg twisted under him, fracturing his ankle. He hit his head on the gun as he fell, opening a cut over his right eye that later required three stitches. Lt. Koss administered first aid, and Morris was taken to the hospital as soon as the plane landed.

Three missions were reported on March 25 as Japanese forces closed in. Two planes took off at 0845, with Ilefeldt in the lead with A/C #713 (with Chu S. C., Libolt, Peters, and Fox) and 2Lt. In Y. S. flying #716 (with Chang C. L., Lu H. C., Ho W. C., and Chow K. Y.) in wing position. Each carried seventeen 100 lb. M41 frag clusters. When they made a bombing pass on the southeast barracks area at Hsiangcheng (33°50' N, 113°25' E), Ilefeldt's bombs hit the target, but In's overshot. On the second run, four bombs of the leader and nine of the wingmen hit the northwest barracks area. The Mitchells then circled and made a run on the town, Ilefeldt dropping six bombs. Gunners of both planes strafed on the fourth run.

Two planes, both with Chinese crews, took off at the same time to bomb the town of Wuyang (33°24' N, 113°36' E) and strafe roads in the area. The leader carried incendiaries and the wing plane carried stab-frag clusters. When they came in on the first run, bombs of the lead plane, A/C #724 (Lt. Tung C. C., pilot, with Shen W. C., Chen Y. C., Chu S. S., and Chao K. P.), hung up in the racks, but the wing plane, #722 (Yu Y. T., Szen S., Kao W. C., Ku C. C., Feng C. K., and Chang T. S.), dropped all of its frags on the city. On the second run,

Tung succeeded in dropping all his bombs while Yu's gunners strafed. Crewmen observed white smoke in the target area. Before heading home, both B-25s strafed the roads and "a large round building" north of the town.

On the day's third raid, Senecal flew A/C #719 (with Liu P. C., Ryan, and Magyar making up his aircrew), off at 0915 in search of targets of opportunity in the vicinity of Nanyang, Yehsien, and Wuyang. Crewmen spotted eight to twelve trucks near Paoanchen, and Senecal dropped nine M47 frag clusters. He dropped eight more in a glide from 2,000 to 1,000 feet on a small village south of Powang before turning for home.

In response to the Japanese cavalry column that had appeared to the northeast, evacuation of Laohokow by air began the same day, as personnel, baggage, and equipment were packed into planes. Seventy-five officers and 207 enlisted men abandoned the field, including three officers and eight enlisted men of the 3rd Squadron.

Then began the demolition of anything that could not be transported. Ten planes that included three B-25s, one transport, three P-51s, and three P-40s (units not specified) were torched to prevent them from falling into the hands of the enemy. That evening, what remained of the gasoline (almost 80,000 gallons, according to detailed reports by Capt. Herbert Martin, base commander, but about half that amount per CACW revised estimates) was ignited. Then the last of the base's personnel fell back by motor convoy to Ankang along roads "crowded with refugees, ox carts, broken-down Chinese trucks, wheelbarrows, and Chinese troops, all streaming to the west." Among the refugees were the Norwegian and French missionaries, as well as the 2nd Squadron's Cpl. Johnson, who described the scene: "The rickety pontoon bridge crossing the Han River was clogged with refugees heading for safety in the mountains across the river. Fishing boats were also ferrying passengers across. From there, they would walk upstream to another of our airbases at Angkang."[5] The convoy arrived at Ankang in the late afternoon of Wednesday, March 28.

Still the Japanese inexorably advanced, averaging 22 miles per day. Enemy troops moved almost exclusively at night, in an attempt to escape the intense aerial attack delivered by aircraft of the 1st Bomb Group, the 3rd Fighter Group, and other combat echelons, all throwing everything they had against the enemy. The goal was to make the occupation of Laohokow as costly to the Japanese in lives, equipment, and supplies as possible. Resistance against the enemy movement continued until the end of the month, with the 1st Bomb Group described as "quite busy during this period, flying nearly all of its 158 March missions during the final week of the month." Aircrews of crippled planes in search of a safe place to land particularly felt the loss of Laohokow, which proved to be the final 14th Air Force base to be captured by the Japanese.

Hank seems to have been on detached duty with Nimrod Detachment during this time, although records are incomplete. He recalled flying for a short time out of an airfield in Japanese-controlled territory but could not remember its name. "The reason I was on so many bases in China was that the Chinese army was supposed to prevent the Japanese from overrunning the bases." Hank explained, "The Chinese army was ineffective, and [the Japanese] chased us out of one field so we had to fall back to another one, at different places. They kept us moving. We'd evacuate just before they captured a place." According to him, "The only reason we ever moved from one place to another, the Japanese were taking over more and more and more and more. They ran us off." Chinese ground forces in the vicinity of Laohokow were among those that had been withheld from Wedemeyer's strategy of reorganization and retraining, and Chiang's ineffectual troops were able to offer little resistance as enemy forces moved forward.

Lt. Ilefeldt reported the last week of March as one of fierce operational activity. Sgt. Daniels, whose 1st Squadron also took part in the intense action, called it "hell week."[6] After Laohokow was abandoned, missions continued to be launched from 14th Air Force bases that included Hsian, Hanchung, Liangshan, and Ankang.

On March 26, 3rd Squadron planes flew sorties against targets of opportunity in the vicinity of Kingman (30°52' N, 112°03' E) that included villages believed to be harboring Japanese troops. Logistical units ensured that supplies of fuel and ammunition were available for the attacks. Capt. Hamilton took off on the day's first mission at 1000, flying A/C #714 in the lead (with Ilefeldt, Koss, Ryan, Fox, and Magyar as his aircrew) and with 2Lt. Chang C. K. (with Yen P. S., Wei K. F., Wang S. F., Li L., and Yuan C. T.) as pilot of #713, on his wing. The planes became separated in the overcast and were not able to get back together. Chang's plane returned to home base, while the lead plane proceeded to the target. Hamilton released seventeen M41 100 lb. stabilized frag clusters over a small village north of Ichang, and then his gunners shot 2,400 rounds that caused damage to a large compound in the village.

Off at 1045, prowling for targets of opportunity in the Kingman area, 2Lt. Liu P. C., aboard A/C #724 (with Tsui W. P., Shen M. C., Ho W. C., Chung C., and Huang T. S.), bombed the town of Ichang with the same load as carried on the previous mission. Machine gunners shot seven hundred rounds. When the plane's hydraulic system began to malfunction, crew members believed that ground fire encountered over the target was responsible for knocking it out. They employed emergency measures to lower the wheels and landed at 1600. Subsequent inspection determined that shrapnel from the plane's own bombs had caused the damage.

On mission #75, Davis flew A/C #723 with Ouyang C. as navigator, Trout as engineer-gunner, Peters as radio-gunner, and Cantor as both bombardier and tail gunner. They were off at 1205 and bombed and strafed fifteen to twenty sampans on the river south of Ichang. Cantor dropped seventeen M41 100 lb. frag clusters, seen "walking down" the line of boats. Strafing expended three hundred rounds of .50 caliber.

At 1330, Greene took off aboard A/C #722 (with Tsuei H. C., Huang T. P., Libolt, England, and Whearty), carrying the same bombload as the previous three missions, and bombed and strafed first the town of Ichang and then a village believed to be Shihchiol, resulting in a number of large fires.

On the same date, two planes, A/C #723 (Chang Chang-kiang, Yen Pao-sen, Wei Kue-ka, Wang Shi-fu, Li Leih, and Yuan Chen-king) and #719 (Tu Kai-mu, Meng Chi-ming, Wang Kwan-tsai, Lee Chi-chen, Mao Chien-hai, and Keiao Tsu-pei), took off in clear weather and good visibility at 1240 and 1255, respectively, both with Ichang as their target. A/C #723's crew was the same as aboard A/C #713, which was lost in overcast and returned to base earlier that morning. Carrying napalm bombs (a mixture of incendiary oil and 100-octane gasoline) and frags, their objective was to bomb Japanese depots and troops from Ichang to Chingmen (Jingmen).

Tu later explained that during that time, "most of our guns were controlled by the pilot and copilot, so bombardier and gunners were responsible for loading ammunition for the guns. The radio operator would communicate with the base by telegraph if the pilot and copilot were unable to keep contact with the tower." On this day, radio contact was lost soon after takeoff, and no communication was reestablished. Both crews were listed as MIA when they failed to return at the expected time. Out of numerical order, it appeared in operational reports as mission #87. During this period, several missions were sent out that were entirely led by and composed of Chinese. "These Chinese flights were successful in every respect, except for two planes that did not return," Ilefeldt commented.

Chapter Thirteen

Both crews were soon reported by Chinese militia to be walking out. One plane was said to have crash-landed near Laohokow, and the other farther south, near Ichang. "Due to the rugged nature of the terrain we must fly over in order to hit the target, all indications point to the possibility of each plane flying on single engine," Ilefeldt wrote. "We believe this to be the case, for the only two possible avenues of return in a plane on single engine is [are] through the Yangtze River pass and through the other pass leading to Ankang. Both planes are reported at the north of these passes." Local Chinese authorities at Kunhsien reported on the twenty-seventh that A/C #723 had crash-landed nearby before reaching the target. Radio-gunner Lee Chi-chen (Li Xi-zhen according to Lt. Tu's later account, using the *pinyin* system) was seriously injured and later died as a result. Other crew members were recovered safely, according to later records.

Two days later, a report came in stating that A/C #719 had crash-landed near Changyang, and four of the six-man crew had been injured. Lt. Tu Kai-mu's plane was hit by antiaircraft fire, and the crew bailed out above Chingmen in central Hupeh Province. Tu later provided details:

After we arrived at the target airspace, we proceeded to dive-bomb and strafe the target and we hit all our targets. Because we executed this mission at low altitudes, however, we were at risk of being hit by Japanese ground fire. Due to the heavy armor of the B-25, we would not feel hits unless the aircraft was struck by large shells. We completed the mission, and, just as we were about to pull up to a higher altitude, cross the Daba [also Dabie or Ta-Pieh] Mountains and return to Liangshan, we suddenly discovered the right engine was on fire. As we were flying above Dangyang, Hubei, the engine made "Bang! Bang! Bang!" sounds, indicating a major malfunction. My copilot and I could not figure out where we had been hit, but it might have been when we were flying over Jingmen. I therefore activated the engine fire extinguisher and climbed higher.

The fire was soon extinguished, but then the starboard engine shut down. Although the B-25 was designed to continue to fly with only one engine, it would not have enough power to climb to a higher altitude. As Tu was attempting to find a suitable location to land, the port engine began leaking fuel where it had been hit by small-arms fire and continued to lose power as the aircraft descended. He immediately ordered the crew to bail out. According to Tu's narrative, the bombardier, Wang Guan-ze, bailed out first, followed by the copilot, Meng Ji-min, who exited via the escape trunk under the cockpit. Then the two gunners, Mao Jian-Hai and Xiao Zu-pei, and the radio operator, Wang Xi-zhen, jumped off through the side door. Tu bailed out last. All crew members were away from the disabled plane within four or five minutes.

The weather was quite clear when they bailed out, he said, and soon their parachutes popped open. Tu was separated from the others as they landed, and he came down in a forest. His watch indicated the time as 1313 hours. "Gales blew my parachute away, and I rolled over a few times." Although not injured in the parachuting process, he twisted his back during the landing. "I cut parachute lines, folded up the parachute, and took a good look at the area. I only knew that when I bailed out, we were somewhere above Dangyang. But since everyone bailed out at different times, I had no idea where this forest was, and I could not find my way out of the forest." However, all aircrewmen carried survival packs containing matches, field rations, knives, and the so-called Power pill, a stimulant. They also wore a leather flight jacket, which kept them warm in cold weather. "Short[-]term survival was therefore not a problem. . . . At night, I slept in the forest. Hearing animals howl and insects buzz in the pitch black of darkness sent shivers up my spine."

Early the next morning, he cautiously began the walk down the mountain. "After I had walked all day, dusk was approaching. I suddenly saw a man walking with a mule. I immediately tried to find somewhere to hide, but I heard him shout, 'Pilot! Comrade! I'm Borough Chief Li. I'm here to find you!' Hearing that was rather comforting. He then shouted again, 'Are you surnamed Du or Meng?'" Tu remained hesitant to answer. The premission briefing had informed crew members that the towns and cities of the Jingmen region were under Japanese control, while rural areas were still controlled by Nationalist and Communist guerrillas, as well as the army under Wang Jing-wei, a puppet regime supported by Japan, and the Japanese army sometimes sent troops to patrol the rural area. "That was why I still hesitated. I managed to sneak into him but also loaded my .45 pistol just in case." The man finally convinced Tu of his good intentions and identified himself as Li Ren-shan. He had brought the mule for the pilot to ride. "Knowing that someone was here to rescue me and ensure my safety, I immediately clasped and hugged the man as tears welled out uncontrollably."

Li took Tu to his house in nearby Yuya Township, Dangyang County, and Li's wife prepared food. "She made some noodles, and I ate them voraciously. This was, after all, the first hot meal that I had eaten in three days!" He remained there for three or four days. People sometimes came at night to discuss plans for getting the pilot back safely. Unsure of their identity, Tu took the precaution of hiding in the mountains behind the house during these visits. Kuo Jen-shan was one of Yuya Township's security leaders who came during that time. Working for the Bureau of Investigation (Kuomintang Military Intelligence Service), headed by Maj. Gen. Tai Li (Dai Li), he did not reveal the fact that he was a secret agent for Chiang Kai-shek. Eventually his protectors decided to send Tu first to Chinese-controlled Sandouping, upriver from Ichang, but it promised to be a dangerous undertaking. Before leaving, Tu gave his watch, .45 pistol, Chinese money, American dollars, sewing kit, first-aid kit, and "Power pills" to Li as an expression of his appreciation.

Li and other agents disguised Tu as a farmer and darkened his skin with firewood ashes mixed with water to make him appear tanned by the sun, and they warned him not to speak, because his northern accent would betray him. Then Tu and Li joined a group of five or six people carrying loads of farm products to market at Sandouping, but there were some tense moments when the group was questioned at a checkpoint by several of Wang Jing-wei's guards and two Japanese soldiers. Tu suspected that their cooperation in permitting the group to pass unchallenged had been bought. Then Li and the others gave him into the care of Commissioner Luo, the regional governor for several counties in the region, who had an office in Sandouping. Luo told Tu that he was lucky to be alive, and informed him that other aircrew members who had landed in friendly territory were already on their way back to the air base.

Because no river steamer from Sandouping to Szechwan was available for several days, they took him on to Dangyang. As Tu, Luo, and his entourage were walking toward the city center, civilians ran out from houses by the roads outside the city and set off fireworks to welcome him, shouting, "Long live the pilot! Long live the pilot!" Walking on, they found the streets clogged with people who came out to greet him. Tu gave a speech for the faculty and students of an elementary school in which he described his combat experiences and bailout, praised the courageous actions of the Chinese air force, and offered assurances of imminent Japanese defeat.

After a few days in Dangyang, Tu boarded a steamer at Ichang and traveled upstream on the Yangtze to Wan County in Szechwan, arriving there the following day. A jeep was sent to collect him, and he returned to base for debriefing. Later he was sent to the American military hospital at Chengtu for a physical examination. Tu was granted a twenty-day pass and allowed to take an American transport plane to Hsian to visit his family for the first time in four years. Decades later, Tu still remembered with enormous gratitude those who helped him return to his base. "Many downed American and Chinese airmen were able to return to the friendly lines safely because of the contribution and sacrifice of those brave Chinese citizens."[7]

The prohibition against allowing airmen who had walked out through hostile territory from flying subsequent combat missions would have ordinarily prevented Tu's name from appearing in later operational intelligence reports. However, circumstances changed soon afterward, allowing him to return to flying status.

At 0935 on the twenty-seventh, five B-25s took off on a low-level mission to bomb and strafe the town of Fangcheng, with "CAVU weather all the way to the target and back." Three P-51s from the 26th Fighter Squadron, 3rd Fighter Group, flew top cover. Pilot of A/C #716, one of the squadron's original H models, Senecal led the formation (with Banger, Gaffney, Fox, and Magyar). Following were 2Lt. Tung S. L., flying a second veteran H model, #713 (with Chen C. S., Chu S. C., Ku C. C., Wei C. S., and Huang T. S.); 1Lt. Chang Y. S., #714 (Wu P. Y., Kuo W. H., Chen Y. C., Shu S. S., and Tung N. C.); Wherritt, #718, a third original H (with Koss, Wadlow, Hugel, and DeFabritis); and 2nd Lt. Wang Y. S., #715 (Tu N. L., Ouyang C., Chiu H. P., Liu C. C., and Lu H. C.). Pilots released seventy-nine 100 lb. M41 stab-frag clusters and forty 100 lb. demos on Senecal's lead. An estimated 70 percent reached the target area, 10 percent fell short, and 20 percent overshot. The lead plane strafed after dropping its bombs, expending a thousand rounds of .50 caliber.

Two planes, A/C #717 and #724, took off at 1515 on the same date with an escort of two 26th Fighter Squadron P-51s. Hamilton's A/C #717 flew in the lead with Yang C. H., Ryan, Allegretto, and Long. The landing gear of the trailing plane (Teng C. C., Szen S., Liu P. C., Ahao K. F., Wang C. C., and Feng C. K.) failed to retract after takeoff because of hydraulic failure, so Lt. Teng returned to land. Hamilton, carrying ten 100 lb. demos and twelve 100 lb. stab-frag clusters, followed the road south to the target at Anlu, in east-central Hubei Province. He dropped only one bomb on the first run because of a hang-up of the racks. The problem was resolved, and he released the remaining twenty-one bombs on the second run. All hit the warehouse area. Gunners expended 500 rounds of .50 caliber, and Hamilton shot one round of 75 mm before returning to base.

Soon afterward, three B-25s were airborne at 1645 to again hit Anlu. Davis flew A/C #714 in the lead, with Senecal, Koss, Gaffney, and DeFabritis as his aircrew. Each plane carried thirty-four M41 stabilized frag clusters. A short distance out of Laohokow, the aircraft began a gradual dive to 3,000 feet. Davis lost contact with his left wing aircraft, #718 (Cheng Y. K., Tsui W. P., Chang W. C., Lai H. L., Chow K. Y., and Tso J. C.), in the increasing darkness just before reaching the target. Davis and 2Lt. Chang K. L., his remaining wingman, flying #716 (with Chen K. C., Shen M. C., Chen Y. L., and Ho W. C.), dropped their bombs on the first run, but heavy ground haze prevented an assessment of damage. Both Mitchells returned to Liangshan, down at 2035. The pilot of A/C #718, 2Lt. Cheng Y. N., later reported that his radio compass went out and he was unable to find home base. He followed the radio beam into Chengtu and landed at A-2. After an overnight stay, pilot and crew returned to Liangshan the following afternoon.

At 1940 on the twenty-seventh aboard A/C #722, Greene, Banger, Cantor, Hugel, and Magyar took off in search of targets of opportunity in the vicinity of Nanyang and southeast along the road to Piyuan. A light blinked along the road below, so Greene dropped four

M41 100 lb. frags and four 100 lb. demos (fusing "contact"). When crewmen observed activity at a compound 10 miles west of Fangcheng, he released an additional four bombs of each type, scoring hits on the compound. When another light blinked along the road 20 miles east of Nanyang, he dropped an additional four frags and three demos. Very heavy ground haze obscured results.

Likewise, on the prowl for targets of opportunity in the Nanyang area, Ilefeldt flew A/C #715 (with Wherritt, Chen Y. K., Rieks, Schlicher, and Peters), off at 2000. He followed the road from Nanyang to Yehsien to Wuyang to Nanyang and then along the road to Siangyang. Crew members observed no activity along the roads, so Ilefeldt instructed Sgt. Chen, specified as bombardier-navigator, to drop the bombload (ten 100 lb. demos and eleven frag clusters) on a small village south of Laohokow. Once again, ground haze prevented observation of the results.

On the final mission on the twenty-seventh, 1Lt. Teng C. C. with an all-Chinese crew (Szen S., Liu P. C., Chao K. P., Wang C. C., and Feng C. K.) took off at 2030 aboard A/C #713 on a low-level bombing mission against targets of opportunity from Nanyang to Kioshan and southeast along the road to Piyuan (the same crew, aboard A/C #724, had failed to take off because of hydraulic failure earlier in the day). Teng proceeded to Laohokow and then bombed the village of Piyuan, dropping ten 100 lb. demos and twelve frag clusters. No enemy activity was observed along the road back to Nanyang, although crewmen sighted the running light of an unidentified aircraft that they believed to be a night fighter. They reported fires burning in Laohokow. The plane blew a tire as it returned to base, but Teng corrected and landed without damage.

Two planes were in the air at 0820 on March 28 to bomb Ichang. In the lead was 2Lt. Hu T. C., aboard A/C #717 (with Young W. P., Hwang C., Chen Y. K., Ho W. C., Liu H. T.), with Davis, aboard A/C #715 (with Wherritt, Chu J. C., Trout, Hanrahan, and Hoyle), on his wing. Both aircraft let down to 4,000 feet a few miles before reaching the target and then dropped twelve stabilized 100 lb. frag clusters by pilot release at 2,500 feet. All hit in the target area. With the war going on around them, Chinese farmers were working in their fields. Although they saw grass huts with the roofs burned off, crewmen noted no enemy activity. They reported several P-40s flying south.

Three crews took off at 0830 and crossed the mountains to Nanyang and then followed the road north to the target at Paoanchen. Senecal led, flying A/C #714 (with Pulaski, Koss, Wadlow, England, and Mier), with 2Lt. In Y. S. as pilot of #716 (with Chang C. K., Hsiang H. T., Shu S. S., Chang Y., and Wang M. T.) and 2Lt. Kiang J. M. aboard #722 (with Liu P. C., Ouyang C., Liu P. C., Chen Y. C., and Luei M.) in wing positions. They carried an aggregate load of thirty-six 100 lb. frags and thirty 100 lb. demos. Koss covered the town center with his bombs. Hsiang and Liu P. C. dropped from the center to the edge of town, but about 30 percent of them overshot. Crewmen reported inaccurate small-arms fire.

That day's final mission took off at 1525. Seven planes in two elements approached along the river to bomb supply houses at Kingman from medium altitude. Weather throughout was CAVU. Maj. Hamilton led the first element as pilot of A/C #714 (with Sung S. C., Banger, Gaffney, Hanrahan, and Hoyle), and #723 (Yu Y. T., Chen S. C., Chen Y. K., Lu H. C., Tung N. C., and Chung C.) and #715 (Wang Y. S., Chen Y. P., Chang C. C., Chang T. H., and Wang C. C.) followed. They were briefed to hit the east-central part of town. Greene led the second element, flying #722 (with Chang H. H., Koss, Schlicher, Magyar, and Hugel), followed by Ilefeldt aboard #716 (with Ryan, DeFabritis, and Fox), and #717 (Chen C. S., Young P. C., Kuo W. H., Chiu H. P., and Feng C. K.) and #713 (Tung S. L., Chen K. C., Kao W. C., Ku C. C., Wei C. S., and Huang T. S.) completing the element. Their objective was to hit the west side of town.

Hamilton's element dropped on Banger's lead, with 1Lt. Chen Y. K. and 2Lt. Chang C. C., bombardiers of the wing planes, following suit. They released eighteen 500 lb. GP bombs on target, starting a large fire. Flames were orange with white smoke that turned black. When Koss, lead bombardier for the second echelon, accidentally dropped his bombs short of the target, Ilefeldt (flying without a bombardier), 1Lt. Kuo W. H., and 2Lt. Kao W. C. (both bombardiers) followed his lead and released before reaching the target area. Because crewmen observed no enemy activity in the vicinity of Kingman Airdrome, no strafing followed.

A communiqué issued by Chinese high command dated March 28 disclosed that one Japanese force had driven to within 43 miles of Laohokow, reaching the village of Sinyeh, to the northeast, before being wiped out. Chinese forces were "counterattacking on both banks of the Lo river, north of Laohokow; that Chinese had attacked and killed 200 Jap cavalrymen at Chenping, 62 miles northeast of Laohokow; and that the enemy attacking toward the highway city of Nanyang, 71 miles northeast, were repulsed." The Japanese at Chengping had driven 28 miles southwest from Nanchao, and the Nanyang fighting represented an enemy advance of 25 miles from Fanchang. Enemy troops at Nanchao had been repulsed, and the Chinese air force was active in that area. In the Ichang sector on the Han River, 49 miles below Laohokow, heavy fighting continued. Enemy forces were "driving toward the big American air base."[8]

Four crews were briefed on March 30 (mission #88) and took off at 1230 from Liangshan to hit "the large railroad bridge across the Yellow River at Chungmow" (34°41' N, 114°02' E). Although important, this was not *the* Yellow River Bridge at Chenghsien but was rather a 2,000-foot rail bridge that crossed the river a few miles farther east. Greene flew in the lead with A/C #722 (Pulaski, Koss, Ryan, Magyar, and Fox as his aircrew), and 2Lt. Tung S. L., in #723 (with Chen W. C., Liu P. C., Ku C. C., Huang T. S., and Feng C. K.), flew on his wing. Leading the second element, Wherritt flew A/C #715 (Davis, Banger, Schlicher, DeFabritis, and Hugel), with 2Lt. Chen C. S., in #717 (Young W. P., Kao W. C., Liu C. C., Chang Y., and Chiu H. P.), on his wing. Each carried three 1,000 lb. GPs. The B-25s picked up an escort of four P-40s at Ankang. Visibility in the target area was poor. Lt. Greene later reported making three passes on the target from south to north, but bombs failed to release on the first pass. He released two on the second run that struck the north end of the bridge, and another hit in the center, knocking out a 75-foot span. His wingman, Lt. Tung, dropped two that hit near the bridge. The bombs of A/C #715 hit the first span, and those of #717 hit the north end, "making a hole." Aircraft encountered moderate ground fire, and A/C #717 received four holes.

On the third run, A/C #722's remaining bomb also hit the north end. Although Greene's aircrew observed no ground fire, Sgt. Fox reported several bullet holes in the aft part of the fuselage following this final pass, as well as smoke coming from the left engine. "I saw a .30[-] caliber hole in the leading edge of the ring cowling of the left engine and a fairly large quantity of oil leaking behind the inboard cowl flaps," Lt. Greene later confirmed. He climbed to 15,000 feet, hoping to gain enough altitude to clear enemy territory before the left engine froze. Greene took a heading to Ankang, the nearest friendly field, accompanied by two P-40s until they were out of hostile territory. Oil pressure began to drop about twenty-five or thirty minutes after leaving the target, and the plane lost altitude.

In an attempt to stay in the air, the crew salvoed five machine guns, about three thousand rounds of ammunition, the liaison radio, and all other loose equipment. As much gas as possible was drained from the left to the right engine, but the right tank registered empty before the plane could reach the field. Greene gave the order for the crew to bail out 35 miles east of

Ankang. Ryan (engineer / top-turret gunner) jumped first, followed by Fox (tail gunner), Koss (navigator), Pulaski (copilot), Magyar (radio / waist gunner), and finally Greene. The plane went into a steep spiral to the right and then crashed and burned on a sandbank in the Han River. Local militia located all crew members of A/C #722 within three hours.

The Chinese had developed a most efficient system for rescuing downed airmen, even deep in enemy territory. "If one was able to get to a peasant, the peasant would get him to one of the organized guerrillas, many of them former troops of the local warlords, or to another peasant who knew how to contact the guerrillas," according to Lt. Lopez. "If the pilot was down close to the Japanese, the guerrillas were skilled at hiding him until the search was over. Then they dressed him as a Chinese peasant and took him back to friendly territory." Lt. Tu was experiencing the validity of these remarks at about this time. "They were risking their lives by helping us, because the Japanese would have executed them out of hand if they were caught, but that did not deter them. It was reassuring to know that we had a good chance of making it home if we had to bail out or belly in." Downed airmen had about a 95 percent probability of returning to their units with the help of these courageous Chinese civilians, many of whom died because of their efforts.[9]

All members of downed A/C #722 escaped injury except the pilot. When Greene landed on a hillside, he hit the ground hard and sprained his ankle. Inhabitants of a small, remote village found him and took him in until he could be reunited with the others to begin the walkout. Greene later recounted to his family the memories of sitting down to a simple dinner with the elderly grandfather of the kind and hospitable family that took care of him as an honored guest. He also described his discomfort at being bathed by young women in a hut that served as a public bathhouse. The water, probably prepared especially for him, was "boiling." Standing at 6 feet, 4 inches tall and very blond, Greene presented quite a spectacle to these villagers, who had never before seen a Caucasian. As he endured the ordeal, all the village children peeked in and giggled at this towering, blue-eyed foreigner.[10]

Pulaski ordered pilots of the other three planes that took part in this mission to return to home base when Greene began preparations for his forced landing, and Lt. Tung, pilot of A/C #723, returned as instructed, down at 1750. Wherritt, flying A/C #715, stayed with #722 until the crew bailed out and then turned toward Liangshan. He landed at 1840 with only thirty minutes of gas remaining. Lt. Chen, pilot of A/C #717, misunderstood the command and stayed with #715 and #722 until he ran low on gas. He landed at Ankang for refueling at 1740.

Two night missions were additionally off on March 30, the first by an all-Chinese crew. A/C #718, #43-5051 (Teng C. C., Chen Y. P., Ouyang C., Chow K. Y., Lui H. L., and Lei M.), took off at 1830 carrying seventeen M30 stabilized frag clusters, in weather reported as "poor," to blast the town of Hsuchang. Radio contact was lost soon after takeoff. When the plane was overdue for return, the control tower made radio contact with the pilot, who had become lost in the dark. The radio operator believed that the plane was within a radius of about 30 miles of the field, so he attempted to guide it in. Teng reported that he had only about 30 gallons of fuel and was flying at an altitude of 8,000 feet, so the tower instructed the pilot and crew to bail out. The plane crashed and burned 38 miles west-northwest of home base. One crew member was known to have gotten out safely. No information regarding the remaining crewmen has been found in American records, although others were listed as participants on subsequent missions except for 1Lt. Ouyang Chun, navigator, and Lui H. L., waist gunner. Ouyang may have been the officer noted as "perished" in Lt. Ting's photograph.

The second night mission (the squadron's #90) also had Hsuchang as its primary target, with Anlu as an alternate target. Senecal was airborne aboard A/C #714 with Ilefeldt, Chu C. S., Gaffney, Hanrahan, and Rieks at 1915. Visibility was poor, caused by a thick ground haze. The engines started "acting up" a short distance out, so Senecal decided to hit the secondary target. He made only one bombing pass and dropped seventeen M30 stabilized frag clusters at 2,000 feet. The crew reported multiple small fires in the target area. The plane returned safely to base. Mechanics later determined that the engine trouble had been caused by the use of 70-octane gasoline, although 91 octane was recommended for the Mitchells.

Sgt. Rieks, tail gunner on this mission but often in the position of turret gunner, was one of the mechanics who worked miracles to keep the planes flying, originally with the 2nd Bomb Squadron before transfer to the 3rd Bomb Squadron. In later years he remembered that he frequently flew with a "cocky" pilot on missions in China. Some of the others did not like him because they considered him to be arrogant, but Rieks said, "I was used to him." When returning from a successful mission, this pilot "would do all kinds of crazy things" to celebrate as he came in for a landing, often flying in low over the shacks of Chinese laborers working to extend or maintain the runways. As the plane buzzed the shacks, the blast of air created by the propellers blew off the straw roofs, and the workers' few possessions were scattered in all directions. Coolies ran outside, shouting and gesturing their displeasure. Although he felt sympathy for them, Rieks always chuckled whenever he told the story to his family.[11] Like Hank, he flew with many different pilots. Operations reports listed Sgt. Rieks on 3rd Squadron missions piloted by MacNeil, Ragland, Ilefeldt, Davis, and Senecal, to name a few. It is likely that most of them could be described as "cocky," since a highly developed self-confidence was essential to being a successful pilot in combat.

When asked about buzzing the coolies' shacks, Hank recalled, "I know we all used to do that some. We'd come back and there'd be a whole gang of coolies working on the field right at the end of the runway, and they ought to know when the plane turns and that prop blast hits them, it's gonna blow them and knock them onto the ground. They didn't learn from that. They'd do the same thing for the next plane."

Rieks described another unfortunate incident, when a Chinese pilot overshot the runway and "plowed into" coolies working on the runway. Several were killed as the plane sent dismembered bodies flying in all directions. Wives and friends came running out of the shacks, crying and shouting at the returning airmen.

The 2nd Squadron's Cpl. Johnson related a similar event that took place at Liangshan during this period, but one that was caused by superstition rather than by accident. When any kind of a vehicle approached, Chinese men and occasionally women would line up on each side of the road, ready to dash across in front of it just before the vehicle reached them. Their belief was that a near miss would kill any evil spirits following that person. "On one occasion, a B-25 in which I was riding was coming in on its final landing approach," he recalled. "Standing in the cockpit behind the pilot, I observed a Chinese man waiting at the edge of the runway. He began his dash across in front of our airplane. Seeing that he had misjudged our speed, he turned and ran straight down the runway in front of us. We were unable to miss him, and our propeller sliced him into four pieces."[12]

A joint mission that included six 2nd Squadron B-25s in the lead, followed by four planes of the 3rd Squadron and two of the 4th Squadron trailing, was off Liangshan on March 31 at 0940. Each plane carried eight 500 lb. GPs. The Ping-Han east railroad yards at Sinyang (32°08' N, 114°05' E) constituted the target. Hamilton's A/C #715 took the lead of the 3rd

Squadron element (with Davis, Banger, Hoyle, England, and Schlicher as his aircrew), followed by #724 (Cheng Y. K., Tsui W. P., Hsiao H. T., Chen Y. L., Wang M. T., and Chang C.), #716 (Wherritt, Shen M. C., Allegretto, Cantor, and DeFabritis), and #723 (Hu T. C., Kiang J. M., Huang C., Chen Y. C., Tung W. C., and Ho W. C.). The plan was for the first element, led in by the 2nd Squadron's Lt. Col. Horner, to bomb the barracks area while the second element went after the railroad yards.

The Mitchells climbed to 10,000 feet over the mountains and proceeded to the target. On the first two runs, heavy "yellow haze" obscured the target until it was too late for Lt. Banger to sight and release his bombs. The two Chinese wing planes dropped bombs at 8,000 feet as they passed over the target, but all fell into rice paddies north of the yards. Banger was again unable to sight on the second run at 7,000 feet, so he released no bombs. On the third pass, twenty bombs were dropped at 6,000 feet by all except the lead plane. Three or four hit the rail yards, while the remainder fell to the left in the building area. The lead plane still had its bombs, so Hamilton made a fourth pass over the barracks area. Although visibility remained too poor to sight, Banger dropped twenty-four bombs. Very heavy haze and smoke prevented observation of results. Because instantaneous fusing was used, it was unsafe for the planes to bomb at lower altitude and better visibility.

A 2nd Squadron mission report submitted by Horner stated, "While on course someone in the formation called the lead plane and stated that one of the B-25s had spun in. The lead plane then jettisoned its bombs and turned to search for the bomber. However, it did not spin in although it did spin out of a cloud in a spin." All planes were down safely at 1425.

Ilefeldt summarized the war situation in his March historical report. He wrote that the Japanese were still bringing in troops and supplies into the Shanghai area in anticipation of the threatened landing on the mainland of China from the Pacific. Manchurian troops had made a drive from the north, surrounding Nanyang and forcing the evacuation of the base at Laohokow. Another drive stemming from the south around the Kingman area had surrounded the twin cities of Shanyang and Fangchenchang. A join-up of those two drives was expected. "During the latter part of March, our squadron has run many missions in the areas mentioned above, knocking out the communications in an attempt to slow up the drive on Laohokow. Bridges were knocked out, truck convoys, locomotives, troops, and supply dumps were hit by us with relentless regularity both night and day, many times in the very worst of flying weather."

"The month of March was by far the best the First Bomb Group as a whole has ever enjoyed from an operational standpoint," wrote group historian Lt. Chenoweth. The bomb squadrons completed 158 missions during the month, and all but a very few were flown in the last week of the month. "It is with great pride that we view our accomplishment. It is definite proof of what our organization can accomplish when weather is favorable, and supplies are available."

As the battle was being waged for possession of Laohokow, changes were occurring at wing headquarters. Brig. Gen. Morse, who had been placed in command of the CACW upon its activation in October 1943, received orders back to the US and was replaced as its commanding officer. When he was sent to England and Italy to investigate ways and means of redeploying air forces from there to China, Col. Bennett, 3rd Fighter Group CO, became acting wing commander in December 1944. Gen. Morse returned temporarily from his liaison trip to Europe on February 15, 1945, but soon afterward received his orders to return home. On March 24, all wing personnel at the base marched in reviews on the airfield, and officers of his staff hosted farewell banquets in Morse's honor. Col. Bennett, who had been appointed wing deputy commander after Morse's return, resumed command.[13]

Bennett's cocommander was Lt. Col. Hsu Huan-sheng, one of the most experienced medium-bomber pilots in the CAF. He had been flying with the Chinese air force since 1927. In May 1938, the then Capt. Hsu led the first air raid to be flown over Japan. Instead of dropping bombs, however, his 14th Squadron dropped leaflets that promised leniency to Japanese civilians and urged cooperation between them and the Chinese army. He carried far more deadly ordnance on later missions and eventually advanced to commander in chief of the Nationalist air Force.[14]

Personnel assigned to the squadron through the month were twenty-three American officers, forty-eight American enlisted men, eighty Chinese officers, and 137 Chinese enlisted men. Details regarding other statistics, including aircraft assigned at that time, are illegible.

CHAPTER FOURTEEN
Holding Chihkiang

Spring brought with it warmer temperatures and the promise of more "flyable" weather in the near future. In early April, 2Lt. Cantor was promoted to first lieutenant, SSgt. Barge to technical sergeant, Sgt. Mills to staff sergeant, and Cpls. Wadlow and Allegretto to sergeants. Lt. Mikola was ordered to take the first available military transport to Chengtu to check into the station hospital for observation and treatment; he returned about a week later. Lt. Young was released from the 3rd Squadron and transferred to the 95th Station Hospital, Detachment of Patients, order effective February 26. Sgt. Thomas V. Coury joined from group HQ as clerk nontypist. A meningitis epidemic rendered Liangshan village out of bounds and kept the men on base for a while.

The enemy's drive that began in late March extended into the month. The 1st Bomb Group's four squadrons continued to chalk up mission after mission against enemy storage points and truck columns and to destroy bridges and trackage on the Ping-Han Railroad. "However, lack of satisfactory liaison made effective air support for front line Chinese troops impossible," wrote Lt. Chenoweth. "Since up[-]to[-]the[-]minute information on Jap and Chinese ground force positions was not obtainable, we had to hit storage areas and other targets far enough behind the line to assure ourselves that we were not hitting Chinese positions. We did our best and we feel that it was not without great value."

Six B-25s took off from Liangshan on April 1 at 1215 on a low-level bombing and strafing mission against Sinyang. One B-25, A/C #702 (L. J. Lalka, Size M. C., L. M. Wilkins, S. P. Gibson, and K. M. Bryan), was from the 4th Squadron, and the other five were 3rd Squadron planes: A/C #714 (Senecal, Ilefeldt, 4th Squadron navigator S. A. Lipira, Gaffney, and DeFabritis), #715 (In Y. S., Young P. C., Kuo W. C., Chang T. H., Ho W. C., and Liu H. T.), #716 (Liu P. C., Chang C. C., Chen Y. C., Chao K. P., and Chung C.), #723 (Davis, Chu S. C., Schlicher, Peters, and Rieks), and #724 (Tung S. I., Ku C. C., Shien M. C., Huang T. S., and Feng C. K.). It was a reunion of sorts, since several of the participants had flown together as members of Task Force 34. Because their target required crossing a series of mountains, winter conditions at high altitudes caused the route to be particularly hazardous. The Mitchells climbed to 14,000 feet but were unable to surmount the front that hung over the mountains, so the mission was aborted.

On the following day, Lt. Baker (now bomb group operations officer) was off aboard A/C #722 at 1845 with Hamilton, Banger, Hoyle, Wadlow, and Hanrahan. On the prowl for targets of opportunity at Nanyang, they were also forced to abort, this time because of heavy overcast in the target area. Baker let down to 4,000 feet as he approached the target area but was unable to break out of the cloud cover. On his return over the mountains, the radio compass went out, so he called in on the radio for a bearing. He made his way to the vicinity of the field but could not land because of heavy cloud cover. After circling for some time, he managed to find the field and was on the ground at 2400.

Three planes off at 0930 each carried eight 500 lb. GPs and targeted a railroad bridge at Sinyang. Hamilton led aboard A/C #714 (with Tsuei H. C., Banger, Hanrahan, Cantor, Schlicher, and Chu S. C.), and A/C #716 (Liu P. C., Chiang C. C., Chen Y. C., Chao K. P., and Chung C.) and A/C #715 (In Y. S., Young P. C., Chang T. H., Ho W. C., and Liu H. T.) took wing positions. Bombs of all three planes missed their target. Those released by Banger were "very near misses" to the left, while bombs of the other two overshot and hit even farther to the left.

Two planes were off at the same time and accompanied these three as far as Sinyang for mutual protection before turning to hit a railroad bridge at Mingkiang. Ilefeldt, the leader, flying A/C #723 (with Liu P. C., Hoyle, Gaffney, and DeFabritis), let down to 4,000 feet on the approach and then made a wide circle to locate the target. Diving to 1,500 feet, he released his bombs. Three 500 lb. GPs hit the bridge (reported as "definitely out of action"), and five more walked up the tracks. Eight bombs released by 2Lt. Tung S. L., pilot of #724 (with Szen S., Shen S. C., Ku C. C., Huang T. S., and Feng C. K.), missed the bridge but hit the tracks, causing extensive damage. Gunners expended six thousand rounds of .50 caliber, and Tung shot one round of 75 mm, but results were not recorded.

On the first of three missions off on April 7, a trio of B-25s were in the air at 1245, carrying a mixed load of M1 frag clusters and 100 lb. GPs. In the lead, Davis flew A/C #714 (with Ilefeldt, Mikola, Rieks, Hanrahan, and Allegretto), and A/C #724 (Chang Y. K., pilot; others illegible) and A/C #723 (Wherritt, Faherty, Trout, Peters, and Mier) flew in wing positions. Davis sighted cavalry about 10 miles south of Sichwan and went in for the kill. After dispatching ten to twelve horses by bombing and strafing, the Mitchells turned south down the river, where they hit an undetermined number of camouflaged tanks. All planes continued north to Sichwan and bombed the town. Wherritt then bombed the small town of Shatoying while the other two planes' gunners strafed more cavalry north of Sichwan. The Mitchells successfully completed the mission in spite of icing.

A mission that included two planes, A/C #715 (Wang Y. S., Tsuei S. C., Liu P. C., Chen Y. C., Ho W. C., and Ho W. C.) and A/C #716 (Yu Y. T., Chen S. C., Hsiao H. T., Tung N. C., Chao K. P., and Wang C. C.), took off five minutes later to hit Neishing. Searching for the target, the pilots circled but could not find a break in the clouds. "Rhine [rime] ice" accumulating on the aircraft at low altitude forced them to abort, so they returned to base without dropping their bombs.

Two B-25s were off at 1305 and dropped forty-eight M1 frags and forty 100 lb. GPs on the eastern section of Nanchang. Hamilton led with A/C #722 (with Chu S. C., Schlicher, DeFabritis, and Gaffney) and Lt. Tung S. L. followed in #720 (with Shen H. C., Hu C. C., Huang T. S., Feng C. K., and Li K. T., noted as "Chinese Army correspondent"). Machine gunners of both aircraft strafed many small boats on the Han River near Ichang. Crewmen spotted a crashed and burned B-25 with "silver collar" on the southwest side of the river between Ichang and Wuangen. As planes were landing back at home base, Hamilton circled five or six times before getting the wheels down because of a leak in the hydraulic system.

The tired crew of downed A/C #722 (whose Chinese number had already been reused) were back at Liangshan that evening following their walkout. Lts. Greene, Pulaski, and Koss; Sgt. Fox; and Cpls. Ryan and Magyar received a warm welcome. After debriefing, all of them were ready for food and a bed. Each man brought back a piece of his own silk parachute as a souvenir, and Al Magyar's daughter still treasures his, as well as his Caterpillar Club pin and certificate awarded soon afterward.[1]

After their safe return to Liangshan, some of the crew members of A/C #722 spent a week at rest camp before resuming their duties. Here (*from top to bottom*) are A. J. Magyar, J. J. Ryan Jr., T. H. Edgerton, L. L. Fox, and C. W. Jeffries. *A. J. Magyar collection, courtesy of Lynn Magyar Zwigard*

"Their plane was shot up over the target, and Lt. Greene, pilot, flew the crippled plane on single engine along the Han River to within seventy-five miles of the field at Ankang. The crew were forced to bail out when the plane finally ran out of gas," Ilefeldt recapped. "The importance of Laohokow is felt by us, for three planes in trouble during March could easily have been saved had Laohokow still been in our hands. We have used Laohokow on several occasions as an auxiliary field, and now since its unfortunate evacuation, we must sweat out an additional hundred[-] odd miles to bring in a crippled plane to safety." Lt. Greene, accompanied by Lt. Kilian, was ordered to Peishiyi for meetings at group HQ the following day.

Three missions took off from Liangshan on the ninth. With an escort of four P-51s, two bombers flew a river sweep from Hankow to Kinkaing, but both were forced to return to base because of mechanical problems: a faulty carburetor on one and cylinder trouble on the other. A/C #722 (Davis, Hamilton, Koss, Ryan, Hanrahan, and Schlicher) and #720 (Liu P. C., Chang H. H., Shen S. C., Wang M. T., Chen Y. C., and Chow K. P.) took part in this aborted mission, down at 1255.

For the squadron's one hundredth mission, three crews were briefed on a pontoon bridge on the Tan River between Likuanchiao and Sichwan. The planes took off at 1100 and headed to Laohokow, where they picked up the river but failed to find the bridge. Capt. MacNeil, flying A/C #714, took the lead (with Wherritt, Mikola, Hoyle, England, and Rieks), carrying twenty-two 100 lb. M30 GPs, and #717 (Wang Y. S., Tsuei S. C., Liu P. C., Chen Y. L., Ho W. C., and Ho W. C.) and #716 (Chiang T., Chu S. C., Chang T. C., Huang T. S., and Feng C. K.) flew in wing positions, carrying a total of twenty-four 100 lb. GPs and twenty frags. The formation continued to Sichwan and bombed and strafed three villages, including one where crewmen spotted a number of "good looking" saddle horses. Then they strafed sampans estimated as forty between Sichwan and Likuanchiao.

On the day's final mission, Lt. Senecal, flying A/C #715 in the lead (with Ilefeldt, Faherty, Cantor, Long, Holmes, and Schroeder), and #723 (Chang K. L., Yen P. S., Chang Y. C., Ku C. T., Liu H. T., and Shu S. S.) following were off at 1130 and climbed to 10,000 feet over the mountains. Letdown started at Laohokow, dropping to 2,000 feet over the target. Each plane carried twelve 100 lb. GPs and ten M1 frags. Senecal and Chang first bombed four small towns north of Likuanchiao, igniting fires in each. One of them was again Shatoying, according to Faherty's mission certificate. Results of one of the bombs began with white smoke but burst suddenly into orange flame that rose to 300 or 400 feet. Smoke from the fires could be seen from 10 miles away. The Mitchells went on to strafe small boats on the river, with gunners expending two thousand rounds before returning to base.

Cpl. Edmund Schroeder had recently joined the squadron as aerial photographer to document mission results. A graduate of Photography Training at Lowry Field in Denver in July 1943, he had taken part in three combat missions with the 2nd Squadron in late March and went on to fly twenty-five missions totaling 124 hours and fifteen minutes with the 3rd Squadron by the end of hostilities.[2]

Cpl. Edmund Schroeder joined the squadron as aerial photographer to document damage from bombing enemy installations and troop and supply movements. *Edmund Schroeder collection, courtesy of John Schroeder*

Lt. Paul L. Young stands between Sgt. Robert N. Solyn (*left*) and Sgt. William Meikle (*right*). Both had worked with him in Intelligence. *R. N. Solyn collection, courtesy of Robert N. Solin*

After another period of hospitalization caused by repeated malarial relapses, Lt. Young returned to Liangshan to collect his belongings and say goodbye to his squadron mates. Here he stands beside the veteran B-25H, A/C #716, with personnel from Engineering and Intelligence: (*left to right, standing*) P. L. Young, R. E. Schlicher Jr., J. H. Mills, S. B. Rickman, J. Holmes, W. Meikle, J. P. Barge; (*kneeling*) J. N. Shock, M.W. Rieks, R. N. Solyn, F.T. Jakubasz. Notice the prevalence of pipes in this photo, likely as a tribute to Young, who was seldom seen without one.. *J. H. Mills collection*

Holding Chihkiang

Lt. Young, after another stay in the hospital at Kunming, returned to collect his belongings. He left for the US on April 10. By this time, he had experienced between fifteen and twenty recurrences of malaria.

The 8th Fighter Squadron had joined the 7th and 28th Squadrons, 3rd Fighter Group, at Ankang on about the first of the month, moving from Liangshan to make room for 1st Bomb Group headquarters. By midmonth, group personnel were settled into tents, and office functions were set up in nearby buildings. Their accommodations were "very comfortable except for the heat at midday," and high winds occasionally flipped off the tent tops.

The transfer of group HQ to Liangshan was considered beneficial because it significantly reduced the long delays previously experienced in communications. "Here we have adequate space and more[-]pleasant surroundings so that we can do a better job than was possible in our cramped quarters at Peishiyi. S-2 [Intelligence], S-3 [Operations], and S-4 [Supply] with Armament and Air Inspector occupy a large well[-]lighted building on the line where we are handy to our squadrons and Base Operations," wrote the 1st Bomb Group historian. "Our Commanding Officer, S-1 [Personnel], and Communications occupy another building close by. Our Medical Department has a fine set-up in the hospital in the hostel area," he explained. "We are all happy to be again on an active base where we can see our planes take off and return from dealing death and destruction to our enemies. This way we have a better understanding of our part in the war and a stronger feeling that we are doing our part in licking the Japs."

After the loss of Laohokow, Chihkiang became the most easterly of the bases operated by the 14th Air Force. About 20 miles from Huaihua City in southwestern Hunan Province, it was the largest base south of the Yangtze and held great strategic value because it controlled the vital Hsiang River valley. The success of raids launched from Chihkiang, including those conducted earlier by Task Force 34, made it the next target for seizure by the enemy. In addition to being a practical base for the bombing and strafing of the Hengyang–Changsha corridor, it lay in the heart of one of China's richest rice-producing areas and served as a point of supply for the 4th Area Army and other Chinese forces stationed in the area. Perhaps of even greater importance, its capture would lay open Kweiyang and thus the approaches to Kunming and Chungking. On April 10, the Japanese initiated a 60,000-troop, three-pronged offensive on Chihkiang airfield that claimed the full attention of the 3rd and 4th Squadrons.

The enemy's main thrust moved west along the highway from Paoching, which served as their headquarters and supply depot during this operation, to Chihkiang, and much of the fighting took place along this route. The first of three flanking movements in support of the main drive advanced from Yuankiang, 180 miles northeast of Chihkiang, and led to the occupation of Yiyang. The second flanking movement was directed toward Sinhwa. This drive began with a strong show of force but dwindled to insignificance within five days, stopping 15 to 20 miles short of its objective. The third came from Tunganhsien and took Sinning (Hsin-ning) in the south. At that point the offensive split into two columns that moved north toward Chihkiang through three valley approaches. One drove almost as far as Wawutang, 58 miles from Chihkiang, and the other reached as far as Tangchiafang. The two columns then joined the main drive west from Paoching.

The Chinese, with more than 100,000 ground troops and even more in reserve, possessed a numerical advantage that had never previously proved sufficient to offset the superior equipment and training of the enemy, but the defense of Chihkiang demonstrated their renewed resolution. "Though they gave ground at first, the Chinese fought back with a stubbornness that made every *li* (roughly one-third of a mile, Chinese measure) expensive to the Japs," wrote a war correspondent regarding defense of the threatened base. Dramatically illustrating the renewed spirit and determination with which the Chinese fought was the fact that "the American-trained and equipped Chinese New Sixth Army, made up of veterans of the victorious Burma campaign, was near the field of battle but was not needed and was held in reserve." Flown back to China the previous autumn, these Burma-trained reinforcements were airlifted from Chihkiang at the battle's height, directly to the area of battle.[3]

When called upon to enter the fight, the New Sixth Army spearheaded the drive on western Honan Province. A publication by the India-China Division, Air Transport Command, provided details: "The defensive action would not have been possible without the reserve support of the 14th and 22nd Divisions of the Chinese New Sixth Army. This complete army, including military supplies, rations, ammunition, mules, horses, and other equipment, was transported to the combat zone by planes of the ICD under the direction of the China Wing."[4] Regardless of contributions made by reinforcements, it cannot be denied that Chinese regulars in the field fought with greater determination and skill than ever before. Chinese commanders were later praised for their aggressive spirit, and the troops for their bravery.

CACW defenders received their share of praise. "Contributing magnificently to the ground defense were the activities of the 14th Air Force, which played a conspicuous part in the defense of its own base," wrote the war correspondent. "Lacking air cover, the enemy had little defense against forays by planes of the Chinese-American Composite Wing. Jap lines of supply were harassed, his personnel were struck with demolition and firebombs and strafed. As Jap supply lines lengthened and striking power correspondingly diminished, it became increasingly obvious that the enemy effort was doomed to failure."

Ground liaison tactics used during the battle contributed substantially toward Allied successes. Nine ground radio teams, working closely with Chinese forces with the aid of panels and radios, produced astonishing results. The teams, each equipped with a 40-pound transmitter and receiver and assisted by interpreters to communicate directly with the fliers, spread out in a ring around the threatened base with the Chinese advance units to direct air strikes by CACW fighters and bombers, which had never before been able to strike with such accuracy and immediacy. In constant radio communication with the air bases and with the planes in the air, the teams directed fighters and bombers to the targets, many times at the request of Chinese commanders. The direct tactical support provided by the 3rd and 4th Bomb Squadrons and the 5th Fighter Group proved to be critical in beating back the enemy in the attempted seizure of this vital base.[5]

Missions on the tenth were initiated by a six-plane formation off at 0708 that had the railroad between Sinyang and Saiping as its target. The expected fighter escort failed to join them at Ankang, and the Mitchells flew on without escort. Wherritt led with A/C #714 (MacNeil, Mikola, Hoyle, DeFabritis, and Fox as his aircrew), and #723 (Ho T. C., Tsuei S. C., Huang C., Chang Y., Wang C. C., and Chung C.) and #724 (Cheng Y., Meng C. M., Shioa H. T., Liu T. C., Lai H. L., and Shu S. S.) were his wing planes. Pulaski followed as pilot of #720 (with Ilefeldt, Faherty, Hugel, Hanrahan, and Wilkerson), and #717 (Chiang T., Liu P. C., Ku C. T., Wang M. T., and Chow K. P.) and #716 (In Y. S., Chu S. C., Chen Y. L., Liu H. T., and Ho W. C.) took wing positions. At Kioshan, they separated into two flights. Three planes flew north and three turned south. The proposed strategy was to space 300 lb. bombs along the tracks about 2 miles apart, but one of the planes of Pulaski's element salvoed all eight bombs at once on the southern section of track. The other two scored eight hits along the rails. Wherritt's element, attacking the northern portion, dropped their bombs according to plan. Those planes encountered light ground fire at Mingkiang and light to moderate AA at Sinyang. All aircraft reassembled at Nanyang to search for strafing targets. Eight types of leaflets totaling 108,635 copies were dropped.

Four planes flew a similar mission off at 1410 to hit the railroad between Hwayuan and Sinyang. Led by the squadron commander, the formation consisted of A/C #714 (with Senecal, Koss, Ryan, Hanrahan, and Cantor) and, on his right wing, #724 (Yu Y. T., Chen S. C., Chang Y. C., Ho W. C., and Chang T. H.). Davis followed Hamilton aboard #720 (with Pulaski, Faherty, Libolt, Magyar, and England), with #716 (Wu P. Y., Tu N. L., Chang C. C., Liu C. C., Hung T. S., and Feng C. K.) in right-wing position. Each carried twenty-eight 300 lb. GPs. One plane dropped eight bombs on the track at once, while the other twenty were spaced as briefed. The bombs, all released at 300 feet by pilot release, caused bulges or broke the track.

The squadron registered two missions on April 11. Flying A/C #720 off at 1330, MacNeil (Wherritt, Koss, Hoyle, Whearty, and DeFabritis as his aircrew) targeted the Hsihsianssuchi area. Crew members sighted troops and cavalry 10 miles west of town, and Wherritt dropped ten 100 lb. GPs and ten M1 frags. Then he dropped in to allow gunners to strafe five trucks traveling with them. They observed many camouflaged foxholes along the ridge, at the same time spotting a panel displayed below after the bombs were released. White with a red band across the center and a red square on one end, it had the Roman numerals "IV IV" on one side, probably for the Chinese 44th Division.

Lt. Wang Y. S., in a second B-25, A/C #724 (with Yen P. S., Huang C. C., Chen Y. L., Liu K. T., and Ho W. C.), was airborne at 1345 and targeted the Hsihsianssuchi and Neisiang (Neixiang) area with twelve 100 lb. GPs and ten 100 lb. M1 frag clusters. His crew spotted a large fire with white smoke at Hsihsianssuchi, presumably the result of the previous raid. He then bombed and strafed the Neisiang area. Leaflets were dropped.

A/C #715, with MacNeil as its pilot and Senecal, Koss, Rieks, Hanrahan, and Cantor as crew, was off at 1300 on the twelfth. Icing in the clouds forced Koss to navigate around some of the mountains on the way to the target rather than taking the usual route over them. Despite poor visibility in the target area, MacNeil hammered Likuanchiao and small surrounding villages with eleven M47 incendiary bombs. Crewmen observed a number of fires in the town. Before heading home, the gunners strafed sampans on the Tan River, one of them loaded with enemy troops.

Three Mitchells off at 1410 flew a second mission. One plane with an all-Chinese crew reported engine trouble and returned to base, although no malfunction could later be found. The other two flew on to blast the railroad yards at Hsuchang. Hamilton flew A/C #716 (with Col. Russell as his copilot; Banger as navigator; Gaffney, Magyar, and Fox as gunners; and Maj. Maurice Barrett, group flight surgeon, as observer), and In Y. S., in #724 (with Chang W. L., Hsiao H. T., Chang T. H., Chang Y., and Mao C. H.), followed. Banger's bombsight "tumbled" on the first run, the bomb release mechanism malfunctioned on the second pass, and on the third all sixteen 500 lb. RDX fell south and west of the tracks. "Research Department Explosive" (RDX) bombs had only recently become available to the bomber crews. The formula for these highly effective bombs contained cyclotrimethylenetrinitramine, a chemical compound even more powerful than TNT. Ground fire came up from the vicinity of Tinghsien, and crewmen observed seven single-engine fighters on the Hsuchang airfield.

Capt. Ragland received his orders to return to "Uncle Sugar" during that day and set out immediately. He had served with the squadron for fourteen months and completed thirty-seven missions, but a back injury had called a halt to active duty sometime after his participation in the February missions out of Hanchung. As he went to board the plane for Calcutta and a connecting flight home, he inexplicably changed his mind. "All of a sudden, the words came out of my mouth, 'I don't believe I'll go. If it's okay with you, I'll wait until tomorrow,'" he told the sergeant on duty. "I hadn't planned to say it." When he returned the next day, he learned that the plane on which he was originally scheduled as a passenger had crashed, killing all on board. He later declared, "That was God saving my life, by making me say those words."

Other reminiscences included his good fortune in meeting Gen. Chennault. In a 1994 interview, Ragland recalled, "The last thing I did before I left China was to go into his office to meet him. He gave me a picture. I still have it today. He was a nice fellow." When he reached Calcutta, Ragland insisted on making the remainder of his trip home by ship instead of by plane. "I'm not going another inch by air," he insisted. Many years later, he learned that the plane from Calcutta had also crashed, leaving only one survivor.[6]

As Ragland began making plans for going home came the unexpected announcement of President Roosevelt's death on April 12. During the days following, American and Chinese dignitaries attended memorial services held at Kunming and other facilities across China. FDR's successor, Harry S. Truman, pledged his support toward continuing the former president's policies and ideals, including insistence on nothing less than the unconditional surrender of America's enemies.[7]

Hank was in the hospital when he heard the news about Roosevelt. His name does not appear on flight crew lists during March or early April because he was again on sick leave as a result of dysentery (confirmed by hospital admission records), this time far more serious than his earlier bout. Its effects troubled him for the rest of his life. Although dysentery was a perpetual affliction for many of the men, it presented particular discomfort to those who were required to spend long hours in the air, and it occasionally reached a degree of severity that required hospital care.

One of the two places where he was hospitalized was "way to the north," Hank recalled. Although he did not remember where he went for hospital care, circumstances he mentioned suggest that he was first sent to Ankang before being transferred to the military hospital at Chengtu. He related, "The last time I had dysentery, they sent me to another hospital a long way off from us, and I think they specialized in circumcision." Throughout the war, it was the policy of all branches of the military to urge uncircumcised men to submit to the operation, in an effort to improve personal hygiene and reduce the occurrence of venereal disease. Some of the men with whom he shared the latrine had undergone this procedure, and "they were in *pain*," Hank commented.

Medical staff at Ankang, one of the 14th Air Force's fighter bases, were known to encourage the procedure. Located 155 miles north-northwest of Liangshan, the base was at that time the home of the 3rd Fighter Group. Maj. Edward A. Kelly, awarded the Silver Star for his courage and dedication in treating the wounded in the *Rohna* tragedy, was the fighter group's flight surgeon. The previous October, with Capt. John Forgrave, he had performed this "minor" surgery for several members of the 26th Fighter Squadron of the 5th Fighter Group, stationed at Chihkiang.

Maj. Glyn W. Ramsey, who served in that squadron, gave this account: "The next morning early I walked into those guys' room to hooray them a little bit, and I saw some sick guys. Their faces were pale, and they were lying out flat on their beds, and they were not moving around." He later told acquaintances, "It's maybe a case similar to having a tonsillectomy: when you're little it may be okay, but when you're a grown man it's something else. I wouldn't recommend it to anyone, because those guys were tough—that is, they thought they were tough. But they sure were pussycats that next morning."[8]

At about the same time that Hank was in the hospital, Maj. Hummel reported that a similar odd phenomenon that he called "a circumcision craze" was occurring at Peishiyi. "It became quite fashionable, and in the mode, this removal of surplus flesh and hide. What induced it is hard to say, perhaps the new base surgeon wanted to keep his hand surgically competent, and to the patient, all enlisted men, the week-long rest on the back while the sore—oh so sore—trimmed appendage healed may have seemed inviting." Lt. Col. Sutley, who had recently taken over responsibilities as wing surgeon at Peishiyi, had previously served as flight surgeon for the 1st Bomb Squadron at Peishiyi and then at Hanchung.

According to morning reports, Hank returned from the hospital at Chengtu on April 18 after an absence of more than a month.

Squadron planes flew one mission on April 13, its duration six hours. In a jointly conducted raid, Mitchells of the 1st, 2nd, and 3rd Squadrons took off at 0900 to bomb the Kaifeng rail yards (34°47' N, 114°23' E), situated about 300 miles north of Wuhan and 5 miles south of the Yellow River. The yards served as a junction of two vital railroad lines—the Ping-Han, running north and south, and the Lung-Hai, running east and west—that supplied troops down the entire length of the enemy-held corridor.

Six 3rd Squadron B-25s took part in the raid, flying as second element behind five 2nd Squadron planes. MacNeil led the 3rd Squadron element, flying A/C #720 (with Davis, Edgerton, Ryan, DeFabritis, Hugel, and Schroeder), and #715 (Chiang Y., Chen K., Liu P. C., Ku C. C., Huang T. S., and Feng C. K.) and #724 (Chang W. L., Tsuei S. C., Hsiao H. T., Chen Y. I., Ho W. C., and Ho W. C.) flew on his wings. Senecal followed MacNeil in #722 (with Wherritt, Banger, Schlicher, Long, and Hoyle), with #717 (Yen P. S., Chen P. K., Lai H. L., Kao C. K., and Chin W. P.) and #716 (Cheng Y. K., Li K. T. as a civilian "Chinese reporter," Chang C. C., Cheng Y. C., Chung C., and Tung W. C.) in wing positions. The bombers picked up eight fighters at Ankang. The engine of one 3rd Squadron plane cut out about 10 miles before reaching the target, thought to be the result of ground fire encountered around Chenghsien. The pilot turned back after jettisoning bombs. He then discovered that the left engine had run out of gas, so he transferred gas from the right tank and landed the plane safely at Ankang. Over the target, the squadron's remaining planes dropped forty 500 lb. demos. All missed the target but hit buildings reported to be storehouses beside the tracks. Bombs dropped by 2nd Squadron planes all were misses. Two aircraft from the 2nd and two from the 3rd landed for refueling at Ankang before joining the others at Liangshan, the last down at 1715.

Lt. Koss, who had returned with the crew of #722 on the seventh and was back in the air on the ninth, flew no missions that day. He wrote another letter to his brother Frank that included the usual chatty, inconsequential observations but offered no hint as to the ordeal he had recently endured. "Right now, Frank[,] we have plenty of reading matter and don't send *Readers Digest*," he wrote. Other relatives had sent subscriptions and he ordered one, but none had yet arrived. "The army supplies us with all the latest books and best sellers. On our bookshelf right now is *Chad Hanna, Storm over the Land, The Robe, Moscow Date Line, The Keys of the Kingdom, US Foreign Policy, Report from Tokyo*, etc. etc. From that you can see the army has a good supply, O yes, and *A Tree Grows in Brooklyn*."

He provided details of a humorous incident that provided yet another example of the diversity in thought processes between the Americans and the Chinese:

My house boy put clean sheets on my bed today and I couldn't find the dirty ones. So I asked him in my best Chinese (Where the G__ d___ h___ did you put my dirty sheets) and he tells me in his best Chinese and when we gave up talking in our best Chinese and started using our hands and pigeon English, he shows me that he put the clean ones on under the dirty ones, thus keeping the clean ones clean[;] damn clever these Chinese. It also saves on laundry bills.

He added the usual plea for a package from home. "Would it be possible to send me some Cocacola syrup or Pepsicola syrup. We have the charged water."

Koss enclosed a copy of "Leaflet OWI/CA-117," dropped from the squadron's planes to gain assistance for US airmen who might come down in occupied territory. An illustration on the front showed a wounded American airman being carried in an improvised litter by

The Office of War Intelligence provided many hundreds of thousands of informational leaflets that were distributed across the countryside by AAF bombers and fighters. Lt. Koss sent this copy of CA-117 to his brother following his return from the March 30 bailout. *R. J. Koss collection, courtesy of Katherine Koss Schaar*

Reverse

Holding Chihkiang

two Chinese peasants. In the distance was a fallen plane. Beneath the airman was a facsimile of the CBI patch and Air Force star, with a line reading, "Look for the American insignias," followed by "AMERICA WILL NEVER FORGET." On the back were detailed instructions. Koss included a translation of the Mandarin text:

Chinese Friends:

The American airforce in China is daily increasing its powerful attacks upon the Japanese. Since where there is gain there is loss, some US airmen will inevitably fall, perhaps in your vicinity. Should an airman be forced down[,] remember he is your friend. Remember too he came to help keep the Japanese from bombing your villages and towns.

Should you find one of these airmen[,] you may wonder what to do. You may even have a moment of hesitation, fearing it is dangerous to help. But remember that China is a vast country, that the Japanese control only what is under their hobnailed boots, and that they are having increasing trouble controlling even that.

This is how you can help against the enemy of China and America:

First hide the American airman in some safe place. Lend him Chinese clothes so that he will not be recognizable from a distance. At night, or some quiet time, lead him towards free territory by unfrequented routes. You will find many men eager to aid you in this gallant work.

Chinese Friends, aid this airman in every way possible so he can return to fight again.

Remember he is battling to drive out the plundering Japanese. America will never forget those who help!

"THESE WORK," Koss wrote at the bottom of the page.[9]

At 0600 on April 14, A/C #720 (MacNeil, Banger, Ryan, DeFabritis, and Jakubasz) took off to check weather conditions along the railroad from Saiping to Sanyang and to destroy as much track as possible. MacNeil dropped eight 500 lb. GP bombs, which caused breaks in the track over a span of 10 miles.

Two crews from the 3rd Squadron and four from the 2nd were off at 0635 with the Yellow River Bridge as the target on mission #110. A/C #715, Hamilton as its pilot, led the 3rd Squadron element (with Senecal, Koss, Gaffney, Magyar, Hoyle, and Schroeder), and #724 flew on its wing (Hu T. C., Huang C., Chow K. P., Chen P. C., and Wang C. C.), on a heading from Liangshan to Ankang and then on to the target. Crewmen sighted five single-engine aircraft at Loyang, where a railroad bridge was out. Each B-25 carried eight 500 lb. GPs. All bombs "fell safe" (unarmed), although one span of bridge may have been damaged by the impact. Ground fire came from the vicinity of the bridge, but planes returned safely.

Following the route taken earlier on the weather observation mission along the railroad between Saiping and Sanyang, four 3rd Squadron planes were off at 0730. Davis flew in the lead of the box formation with A/C #722 (Wherritt, Faherty, Wadlow, England, Fox, and Cantor as his aircrew), followed by #716 (In Y. S., Li K. T. again as "Chinese reporter," Hsiao H. T., Chen Y. L., __, and __), #723 (Cheng Y. K., Chang K. L., Chen L. K., __, and __), and #717 (__, __, Chu __, Ku C. C., __, and Feng C. K.); some of these names are illegible. Their objective was to "tear up as much track as possible." Twenty-four 500 lb.

GP bombs were dropped along the tracks by pilot release, resulting in eleven hits on the rails and two on a bridge at Saiping. Davis then turned north and dropped twelve butterfly bombs in bomb craters along the tracks. Automatic-weapons fire received around Kioshan caused no damage.

A 2nd Bomb Squadron B-25J leaves the target area after bombing the Yellow River Bridge. It was the target of countless 14th Air Force operations throughout the war in an attempt to deter transport of troops and supplies to enemy battle areas. *National Archives and Records Administration*

During this time, reports came in that the Japanese were using "human detonators" to rid airfields and other places of the hypersensitive, delayed-action butterfly bombs, according to a service publication. "It is now learned that the Japanese have on occasion 'bribed' Chinese coolies to pick up these bombs. Naturally the promises of such things as rice never have to be fulfilled. It is also reported that the Japanese have tried to clear 'butterflyed' areas by forcing the Chinese through them at gun-point."[10]

Mission #112, on April 16, was conducted in cooperation with the 1st and 2nd Squadrons. Kaifeng was once again the target. Participating planes on this medium-altitude mission, led by the 1st Squadron and with four B-25s each of the 2nd and 3rd Squadrons, took off at 0600 from Hanchung. Three veteran H models and one J made up the 3rd Squadron flight. A/C #723 (Wu P. Y., Kuo Y. H., Lee K. T., Kao C. K., Liu C. O., and Liang M. H.), followed by #724 (Chen S. C., Hsiao H. T., Huang T. H., Loi M., Chang F. T., and Chung C.), #716 (Chang C. L., Yen C. S., Shen M. C., Chiu H. P., Chang Y., and Shu S. S.), and #720, the J model (Hamilton, Wherritt, Banger, DeFabritis, Jakubasz, and Hugel), made up the element. The bombers picked up their escort of four P-51s at Ankang, and the formation proceeded to the target in box formation. One of the 3rd Squadron's planes had bomb-release problems and dropped only two of its 500 lb. GPs on target and salvoed six in the town. The remaining aircraft dropped all bombs with an estimated 80 percent accuracy, resulting in large columns of black smoke rising to 1,000 feet that could be seen from 10 miles away. No strafing was done, and no leaflets were dropped due to an exhausted supply. Planes were back down at 1150 and made their way to Liangshan, with their flight crews accompanied by TSgt. Shock and Sgt. Trout. This mission was in coordination with a combined force that dropped one hundred 500 lb. bombs in about fifty major hits that day. Kaifeng was repeatedly targeted until the end of the war, resulting in eventual destruction of 70 percent of its yards and five warehouses.

Holding Chihkiang

On the same date, seven Mitchells were off to blanket Loyang with incendiary bombs. All went wide to the north and landed in rice paddies. Crewmen spotted ten aircraft at Loyang, seven of them obviously dummies. The other may have been operational. They observed more than seventy-five cars in Loyang's railroad yards, and two trains of twenty-five cars each on the railroad between Loyang and Tungkuan. This was listed in the squadron's operations report as mission #112A, but airplane numbers and crew lists were omitted from extant records.

"Smilin' Jack" is visible below the pilot's window of A/C #714 after it was irreparably damaged in a takeoff accident on April 16. *J. M. Hamilton collection, courtesy of John G. Hamilton*

Fox and Long inspect the damage before salvage operations begin. *R. N. Solyn collection, courtesy of Robert N. Solin*

Because the squadron had recently lost three planes, Lts. Pulaski and Ilefeldt and Sgt. Rickman had left on the twelfth to pick up another new replacement B-25J. They returned on April 17. Ilefeldt noted that as they were landing, they saw A/C #714, "one of our newer planes ... in a rather unflyable condition on the side of the runway." The previous evening, the plane was taking off on the Loyang raid when a tire blew out, tearing the undercarriage from beneath it and taking an engine with it. It then slid to a stop a short distance off the runway.

Associated with serial #43-27809 (sometimes written as #43-2709), this A/C #714 was first mentioned in mission reports while assigned to Task Force 34 the previous November and again in January, when Maj. Conrad led the 3rd Squadron element on the successful Hankow Storage Area raid. It appeared in the March 1 squadron photos at Liangshan. Considered to be "the least shot up" of the squadron's B-25s, it had been personalized soon after Capt. Hamilton was placed in command as recognition of his expertise as a bomber pilot and his popularity among the men. Dubbed "Smilin' Jack" (hero aviator of the long-running comic strip) because of his cheerful disposition, Hamilton's moniker had been painted below the window on the pilot's side of the cockpit.[11] Although it was designated as "his" plane, other operational officers took it up with equal frequency. No one was hurt in this incident, although the squadron was back to eight planes. Its reusable parts were salvaged, and its Chinese number was reassigned to a replacement plane soon afterward.

Members of the CACW were pleased when the word "provisional" was finally dropped from the names of its units effective April 12. Pfc. Raymond L. Outen was attached as a bombsight mechanic and Cpl. Edmund Schroeder as a photo lab technician, although he continued in his role as combat photographer. Sgt. Coury, who was being treated at the infirmary with penicillin for chronic sinusitis, was released and transferred back to 1st Bomb Group HQ. Cpl. Rae M. Delahoyde was attached as clerk nontypist in the orderly room to replace Coury but was subsequently assigned duties as intelligence NCO. From Detroit, he had previously served as clerk-typist at group HQ before being transferred to the 4th Squadron in about August 1944. Lt. Mikola left for the hospital at Kunming because of unspecified ailments, and Lt. Logan for treatment of dysentery.

Mid-April brought encouraging reports that American troops had landed on Iwo Jima and Okinawa, islands strategically positioned to provide staging bases for strikes against the Japanese home islands as well as on Chinese coastal cities. It appeared inevitable that the Allies would launch a full-scale attack against one or both of those targets, in an effort to force Japan into submission, but it was yet uncertain where efforts would be focused. However, because the Japanese believed they would retain the capability of sending their air force to the Asiatic mainland, they expected "the final battle" to take place in China.

The high level of operational activity continued for CACW airmen throughout the month, although the Japanese advance past Laohokow was waning. The wing's fighters and bombers flew day and night, attacking enemy troop and cavalry concentrations, gun positions, ammunition and supply dumps, convoys, and anything else that flew the flag of the rising sun. So successful was the opposition against the enemy in the Chihkiang campaign that it proved to be the last major offensive by the Japanese in China.

The 2nd and 3rd Squadrons ran a great number of missions from Liangshan during this period, and the increased level of activity produced some unexpected results. Because Combat Cargo and the ATC had been bringing in increased shipments of supplies of all kinds, including large quantities of gasoline and ammunition, no thought had been given to the

The method used for filling the gasoline tanks underwent some improvement. Here gas is being transferred to a plane using a pump. Fox and Rieks are assisting in the process (*on the wing at the left*), while Faherty and an unidentified Chinese officer supervise (*on the wingtip*). Faherty captioned the photo "Refueling the B-25." *J. F. Faherty collection, courtesy of Dennis Faherty*

possibility that it might end soon. "It took us all by surprise, as none of us had even considered the gas situation," wrote Lt. Ilefeldt. Temporary relief came in the form of an increase in shipments, but "another spurt of operational activity reduced the gas supply to nil, and we were informed that there was very little gas in the field for at least another month, in fact there was very little gas anywhere in China for that matter." As a result, the squadron's planes flew fewer missions and with formations that included fewer planes through the end of April. Ilefeldt lamented, "If it's not the weather it's the gas."

Two planes off at 1200 on the first of two missions on April 20 had Neisiang as their target. Greene (with Koss, Schlicher, Hoyle, and Magyar) was off aboard A/C #723 and led #719 (Wang Y. S., Sung S. C., Chu S. C., Chang F. T., Lee L., and Liu T. C.). The pair dropped twelve thermite bombs that crewmen observed "walking completely through town" on the first run. On the second run, the pilots released twelve napalm bombs, causing three large fires with secondary explosions and four small fires reported to be "burning good." Each plane dropped a red flare near Laohokow, and ground forces displayed panels pointing to the town of Laohokow, on the west side of the river.

A second mission that took off at the same time targeted Luchou. Two planes—A/C #722, piloted by MacNeil (with Senecal, Edgerton, Gaffney, Long, and Ryan), and #724, flown by Lt. Chang K. L. (with Hsiao H. T., Ku C. C., Tung M. T., and Chang T. H.) on his wing—made three bombing runs on the town. They released twelve thermite clusters along the main street on the first pass, followed by six napalm bombs on both the second and third passes that resulted in a number of fires throughout the town. Gunners strafed carts on the roads around Luchou before the formation returned to base.

Lts. Senecal, Koss, and Ilefeldt, accompanied by FO Wherritt and Sgts. Burton and Wadlow, went to Kunming and returned in late April with two new "strutters," as well as service equipment and supplies. Lt. Mikola returned from the hospital at about the same time. After twenty-two months and forty-two missions, MSgt. Hanrahan, communications chief, received orders to begin his journey back home to Rhode Island. He had been awarded the Distinguished Flying Cross, Air Medal with Cluster, and Bronze Star for his exemplary service.

During the last week of the month, Maj. Michael P. Henneck, bomb group engineering officer as well as technical and administrative inspector, and Maj. William L. Curik, group armament officer, conducted a "close inspection" of the 3rd Squadron. Ilefeldt wrote that "their helpful suggestions for the betterment in the efficiency of the squadron was [were] well received by all the departments."

Squadron planes flew one mission (#115) on April 24. Four crews were briefed on railroad tracks between Siaokan and Sinyang as target and took off at 1115. In the lead was Lt. Pulaski as pilot of A/C #715 (with MacNeil, Kilian, Barge, DeFabritis, and Rieks), followed by Lt. Yen P. S. in A/C #720 (with Chang C. L., Hsiao H. T., Ku C. C., Feng C. K., and Shu S. S.), Lt. In Y. S. in A/C #723 (with Tu N. L., Chow H., Chiu H. P., Lui C. C., and Li L.), and Lt. Greene in A/C #716 (with Banger, Trout, Magyar, and Mills). Greene's aircraft became lost in the thick cloud deck crossing the mountains and turned back so Banger could take a new heading. Passing over the airfield at Fanyang, it received meager, inaccurate gunfire before taking a heading to Ichang. Greene went in for a bombing run on oil storage south of Ichang and released two 250 lb. bombs that hit the middle tank. He released two more on a storehouse

Before MSgt. Hanrahan returned to "Uncle Sugar Able," Maj. Hamilton presented him with the Bronze Star in recognition of his exemplary service that included shooting down an enemy bomber. *R. N. Solyn collection, courtesy of Robert N. Solin*

Faherty captioned this one "Supply detail, China." When they were not permitted to go back to India, supply details typically flew to Kunming, the terminus for most Hump flights. These men are (*left to right, standing*) J. J. Ryan Jr., W. H. Whearty, G. J. Winter, J. A. Wadlow; (*kneeling*) J. F. Faherty, H. L. Chasse, and P. Piecuch. *J. F. Faherty collection, courtesy of Dennis Faherty*

on the second run. On the third run, he dropped the remaining four bombs on a hostel in the area, and then gunners strafed Japanese troops on the drill field. Six or eight were seen lying dead or wounded on the ground.

Hank was back on flying status and in his usual position as tail gunner on this raid. Sitting on a bicycle-type seat in a kneeling position with his knees on pads mounted on the deck to either side, he operated twin .50-caliber machine guns on flexible mounts in a cramped compartment encased by a Plexiglas canopy. Although protected by a fixed armor chest plate, his was one of the most exposed duty positions on the aircraft. It was the responsibility of the tail gunner to do the "cleanup" by strafing whatever enemy activity was observed after the target had been bombed.

Holding Chihkiang

The planes often dived down to within 50 feet above the ground on strafing runs—close enough to enemy soldiers that Hank could see their faces as he squeezed the triggers. He explained that on this mission, as the H model came in over the camp, some of the soldiers were doing calisthenics on the field. Lt. Greene came in low for the strafing pass. The soldiers immediately scattered and ran for cover under a clump of trees. From his position in the tail, Hank fired several bursts at them. Then he trained his guns on another of the fleeing men and was preparing to shoot again when he realized, "That wasn't a Japanese soldier. It was a Chinese civilian." Years later, he confided, "That really shook me. I knew how close I had come to shooting that man."

After Japan resumed the drive to overrun 14th Air Force bases, intelligence reported that some Japanese reinforcements were dressing in Chinese peasants' clothing in an effort to mislead American fliers as they strafed enemy columns. At the same time, "puppet troops" wearing Japanese uniforms were being forced out onto the roads as decoys to divert the attacks of American airmen from the main Japanese forces.[12] It is likely that the "Chinese civilian" Hank almost shot was, in fact, a Japanese soldier who had disguised himself as a poor farmer to avoid detection.

The other three aircraft maintained formation to the railroad south of Sinyangang, turned south, and dropped twenty-four 250-pounders along the track. A "good run" was impossible because the tracks were not straight and there were high embankments along each side. Crewmen reported six direct hits on the tracks, and In scored another direct hit with the cannon. Pulaski's lead aircraft was struck by small-arms fire that punctured its left tire. Three planes landed safely at Liangshan at 1540 and one at 1550.

Only one 3rd Squadron mission was off on April 25, and Hank volunteered to take part in it. Hamilton, pilot of A/C #720 (with MacNeil, Banger, Fox, Mills, and DeFabritis), was airborne at 0930 and formed up with two 2nd Squadron B-25s, whose target was in the same general vicinity. Two 7th Fighter Squadron P-51s flew escort. Capt. Wendell D. Lack was mission leader for the 2nd Squadron, with a second plane piloted by Lt. Joseph J. Walsh. The three Mitchells flew in "V" formation to the target area before hitting separate targets on the Ping-Han Railroad.

Hamilton's crew first dropped supplies to Chinese ground troops at a remote location (114°07' E, 31°24' N) north of Hankow. Airdrops of food and ammunition such as this contributed significantly toward maintaining the morale of Chinese soldiers who were now pushing back against their oppressors. Hank was in position as waist gunner on this mission, and his recollections included few specifics of the mission—"only that I was helping shove equipment out of a plane." He did recall, "Sometimes we'd fly over the lines back into occupied China, and I would see lines where soldiers were, just like they were during World War I—a big line on one side of Chinese[, and] Japanese on the other side. I'd always think how thankful I am I'm not down there on that ground with them."

After the supply drop, Hamilton flew on to the northeast to hit the railroad between Hwayuan and Sintien. Crew members sighted a locomotive 8 miles north of Wangkiaten. Hamilton made four bombing runs, releasing two 250 lb. GPs on each pass. Two were near misses with probable damage to the locomotive, while two were direct hits on the tracks. Gunners strafed the locomotive and observed steam coming from the boiler. Then they strafed about twenty railroad cars spotted 3 miles south of Wangkiaten. One car exploded with bright-orange flame, and another burned with thick black smoke. It was another satisfying mission for Hank, who explained, "The Japanese would always run a train in a place between two mountains. I don't know why, but they were like shooting ducks on a pond. I don't know what they thought. We could fly right over them and couldn't miss them."

The final mission of the month was on April 26. It was a joint mission that took off at 1100, with two 3rd Squadron planes in the lead element and two from the 2nd Squadron following. Eight 3rd Fighter Group P-51s escorted the bombers. Railroad bridge #113 on the Ping-Han Railroad, located 9.9 miles north of the mouth of the Han River at Hankow, was the target. Each of the four Mitchells approached the bridge at minimum altitude and made individual bombing runs from north-northwest to south-southeast along the length of the bridge. Although it was noted that the bridge had already been knocked out, Hamilton's lead plane, A/C #715 (with Greene, Edgerton, Cantor, Schlicher, Peters, and Schroeder), dropped four 1,000 lb. GPs that caused additional damage to its southern portion. Lt. Yen P. S. flew the wing plane, A/C #723 (with Chow H., Ku C. C., Ho W. C., and Lei M.), and dropped four bombs that inflicted further damage to the bridge and caused part of it to fall into the water. Bombs scored near misses "on the right side going south."

Antiaircraft fire damaged Hamilton's aircraft, which "received a hit from a 20 mm explosive shell in the trailing edge of the left wing, also a hit in the tail section back of the camera hatch from a 12.07 mm shell." The trailing plane received a hit from a shell "larger than a 40 mm, probably a 75 mm[,] hitting bottom of fuselage at rear of nose wheel door passing through the lower left side of fuselage." Most of the bombs released by all four B-25s fell to the west of the bridge, and no direct hits resulted. As 2nd Squadron planes (with Lt. L. G. Bains and Lt. R. H. Frost as their pilots) made their run against the target, an explosion was observed about a mile southeast of the bridge. The mission's duration was four hours and fifty minutes, Edgerton recorded in his flight log.

As April drew to a close, the 3rd Bomb Squadron was assigned, along with the 1st and 2nd Squadrons, to attacking rail traffic, and their Mitchells were successful in holding the enemy's transportation of supplies to a minimum. Ilefeldt reported that the squadron's greatest amount of activity had been on the Ping-Han Railroad. "We have hit it constantly, knocking out bridges, tearing up the tracks, and generally disrupting communications along the very important avenue that the enemy uses to carry its supplies from the north to Hankow in Central China. We knocked out a very important bridge in the very hot Hankow area."

Observers noted large concentrations of enemy troops in the Kingman area. "It is expected that a drive will stem from that area of the Yangtze River. This drive is expected because the Yangtze is the one avenue of approach that leads to the very heart of China from the area around Kingman and Ichang," according to Ilefeldt. "The terrain surrounding the river is very rugged country and would make operations on the ground difficult. We bombed Ichang attempting to slow up concentrations in the town, which may very well be the enemy's jumping[-]off place, from the expected drive up the river." While the squadron waited for the enemy's next move, rain set in once again.

As Chinese and American air strikes continued to neutralize the threat to the Chihkiang base, revitalized and reinforced Chinese ground troops moved into positions farther north and south, in a maneuver to outflank the enemy. The 74th Army, defending the Chinese center on a 50-mile front, put up a stout resistance and successfully slowed the advance. Gradually, and at high cost to the Chinese in men and materiel, each of the offensive's four prongs was thrown back. Enemy losses were equally heavy, not only because of the intense fighting but also because, as the effort lost momentum and direction, many Japanese troops were cut off, surrounded, and liquidated.

Even as life-or-death operations were being conducted, the daily business of the squadron went on. Capt. Kelso, who had spent a week at rest camp, returned at the end of the month. It was the adjutant's first R&R in twenty-three months of service. Ilefeldt noted that during the recent period of inactivity, Capt. Hamilton had instigated a procedure that was well received by everyone in the squadron. "All the men who have been overseas for a rather long time, or those who seem to need a little diversion and rest are being sent to Chengtu, several at a time, to enjoy the 'almost stateside' atmosphere, the good 'American' food, and the almost white creatures of feminine pulchritude. Everyone comes back to the squadron greatly benefited by their little vacation." TSgt. Jakubasz and Sgts. Allegretto, Jackson, Rickman, and Trout were the next to be sent, off April 26 and returning on May 5.

Jackson had been having some sort of health problems that were still unresolved. Aimee Millican, a Presbyterian missionary from Seattle who had first come to China with her husband, Frank, in 1907, managed the facility at Kwan-sien. Mr. Millican had been imprisoned by the Japanese in 1941 and was detained in a POW camp near Shanghai until Japan's surrender. Their daughter Edith, a medical missionary who had been working at a hospital in Kweichow Province, arrived for a visit during the same period that 3rd Squadron guests were enjoying their time there. She wrote to friends, "I found [Mother] very busy in the hospitality work of our servicemen.

Maj. Hamilton's new policy of sending small groups of men to rest camp was well received by all who were its beneficiaries. Here Frank T. Jakubasz (flight chief) and Jack A. Trout (A/P engineer-mechanic) enjoy a trip into Chengtu. *A. R. Allegretto collection, courtesy of Mary Allegretto Henry*

Lloyd E. Jackson Jr. (instrument specialist), Andrew R. Allegretto (armorer-gunner), and Stanley B. Rickman (engineer-mechanic) completed the party. *A. R. Allegretto collection, courtesy of Mary Allegretto Henry*

Trout, Allegretto, and Jakubasz escape military life at Kwan-sien Rest Camp. *F. T. Jakubasz collection, courtesy of Robert Jakubasz*

She had a beautiful location for it in a fine big residence with a lovely lawn and garden." Mrs. Millican wrote a letter to Eleanor Jackson, offering assurance that her husband was well and in good hands. Jackson and his companions spent a leisurely week enjoying the accommodations before returning to Liangshan. After the war, the Millicans remained in China until 1950, when they were forced to leave when the Communists assumed control.[13]

Cpl. Albert J. Keller was attached as a radio mechanic during the third week of April. From North Dakota, Keller stated in a postwar interview that he had been trained in the maintenance, testing, and repair of radio transmitting and receiving equipment but had flown about twenty missions as a B-25 radio operator. He had been "pressed into flight duty with the 14th Air Force—the world[-]famous 'Flying Tigers'—because of a shortage of trained men," he explained. He told a story of once being asked if he knew how to drive. Keller, who had driven only passenger autos up to that time, answered in the affirmative. "Early the next morning, they woke me up and put me behind the wheel of a double-tandem cargo truck and I wound up leading a convoy up the Burma Road," he said. "It was rough, but we lost only two trucks along the way." Records of the 3rd Squadron unfortunately do not include reference to Keller's prior service, and his name does not appear in its mission reports.[14]

Maj. Clarence H. Drake joined the squadron and briefly served as a pilot on China missions before moving on to his next assignment as commanding officer of the 4th Bomb Squadron. *C. H. Drake collection, courtesy of Dennis Drake*

Maj. Clarence H. ("Hank") Drake was attached as a B-25 pilot in late April and flew missions with the 3rd Squadron into June. Raised by his widowed mother in Ohio, he had enlisted in the Air Corps as an aviation cadet in March 1941. Drake summarized his early career in a brief autobiographical sketch for the USAF's Air War College at Montgomery, Alabama. "After graduating from pilot training in Class 41-H [in 1941, but before the US entered the war], I was assigned to an observation squadron by choice (my third choice, the

Holding Chihkiang

Drake flew with his blood chit stitched inside his jacket, as did all flight crew members when they went out on missions in China. Its purpose was to identify him as a "friendly" to any locals who might find him in the event he had to vacate a stricken plane, and to provide instructions for returning him to his unit. *C. H. Drake collection, courtesy of Dennis Drake*

Air Corps' first choice). From spotting artillery fire and throwing flour sack bombs at tanks from liaison aircraft, I graduated to anti-submarine patrol in B-25s; to instructing in a B-25 OTU; and then to China."[15]

While flying observation planes to patrol for German submarines in the Atlantic early in the war, Drake had been awarded the Air Medal with Oak Leaf Cluster. He served in North Africa from March 1944. One of his later assignments had been to train elements of the 332nd Fighter Group—the now-famous "Tuskegee Airmen"—at Fort Knox, Kentucky. He was promoted to major in March 1945, at about the time he moved to China. A welcome addition, Drake had logged almost two thousand hours in flight by the time he joined Hamilton's squadron.

Pfc. Outen transferred from the 3rd Bomb Squadron back to the 1st. Lt. Fuller, on detached service to 1st Bomb Group Headquarters, was released and returned to Liangshan. This was the same time that Maj. William L. Curik came to the 3rd from Group on detached service. Formerly All Conference right tackle for Texas Christian University, Curik joined the Air Corps in February 1941 and had been in the CBI since August 1943. He was one of the original members of the 2nd Bomb Squadron. Unable to become a pilot because he failed the vision exam, he had served as the 1st Bomb Group's armament officer, administrative inspector, technical inspector, transportation officer, and coordination and compliance officer earlier in the year.[16]

SSgt. Walter E. Hartung, who had also enlisted before the Pearl Harbor attack, joined the squadron as quartermaster supply technician. Basic training was interrupted when he underwent an appendectomy in November 1941 at Fort Francis in Wyoming. Following completion of training at Perrin Field at Sherman, Texas, and Officer's Training School at Camp Lee, Virginia, Hartung entered basic flying school at Garden City Air Base in Kansas. An accident requiring surgery to repair torn cartilage in his left knee in April 1944 ended Hartung's hopes of becoming a pilot, however, and his military service took a different direction.

During the month, several current and former members of the squadron received awards for outstanding service: Capt. Simpson, the Silver Star; Maj. Hodges, the Distinguished Flying Cross; Capt. MacNeil, 1Lt. Edgerton, MSgt. Grant, TSgt. Shock, SSgt. Hoyle, and Sgts. Allegretto and Peters, the Air Medal; and Maj. Seacrest, the Oak Leaf Cluster to his DFC.

The citation that accompanied Simpson's award summarized his courageous actions on the previous July 4 and stated, "Captain Simpson's calmness and great courage reflect honor upon himself and are in keeping with the finest traditions of the Army Air Forces." It was signed by Maj. Gen. Chennault.

Throughout the month, the squadron flew sixty-two sorties against the enemy. Seven were on daytime medium-altitude missions, and sixteen were executed at low level. Squadron Mitchells dropped 710 bombs (186 tons) that comprised 216 500 lb. demos, forty 250 lb. GPs, 700 300 lb. GPs, twenty-two 300 lb. RDX, 100 100 lb. GPs, 168 100 lb. frag clusters, twenty-four napalm clusters, and twenty-four thermite clusters on enemy installations and activities. Personnel consisted of twenty-two American officers, forty-nine American enlisted men, eighty-two Chinese officers, and 130 Chinese enlisted men. Their B-25s included five H and five J models. One B-25J had been lost.

CHAPTER FIFTEEN
Turning the Tide

On May 1, Gen. Wedemeyer selected Lt. Gen. George E. Stratemeyer to command the newly formed Army Air Forces, China theater, with both the 14th Air Force and the 10th Air Force from India under his command. This consolidation was made to facilitate the planned amphibious landing on the China coast. Wedemeyer, who had recently returned from a meeting with Roosevelt and other officials and top-ranking officers, had presented the problems and plans of the China theater shortly before the president's death. Now he offered this message of encouragement to those men serving under his command: "Perhaps there have been times in the past when we in this part of the world have felt that ours is the forgotten front. I can assure you that there is no occasion for such a feeling."

It had previously been necessary to focus the greater part of the military might of the United Nations on the defeat of Germany and on "the task of reaching the outer ring of the Japanese bastions" in the Pacific, he explained. "But now great battles have been won. Our armies and those of our gallant allies have swept like roaring torrents through the heart of Germany. Japan hears the thunder of doom approaching crescendo; now our turn is coming." Despite his reassurances that those in Washington had "a consciousness of our problems and a firm purpose to give us assistance and material support," the deprivations experienced at bases across China went unabated.[1]

Cpl. Russell J. Armbruster joined Hamilton's squadron on the same date. Known back home in Cleveland as "the Itaska street electrical wiz ... who spends hours rigging up contrivances with which to shock his friends" when he was younger, his hope was to become a pilot when he enlisted soon after hearing the news of Pearl Harbor. However, vision testing

A relative latecomer to the squadron, Cpl. Russell J. Armbruster had completed six months of military police training after he finished basic training, despite his occupation in civilian life as a policeman. He was a graduate of bombardier school as a bombsight mechanic following an eighteen-month course of study, and he qualified as an airplane instrument mechanic after an additional four months of training. His separation documents specified that he was in foreign service for one year, two months, and seven days, but gave no indication as to where he served for the six months prior to his transfer to the 3rd Bomb Squadron. R. J. Armbruster collection, courtesy of Christine Armbruster Moore revealed that he was color blind, disqualifying him from training as an aviation cadet. A traffic patrolman before enlistment, he was initially assigned to the military police before receiving training in maintenance of Norden equipment in summer of 1943. Armbruster, who had been in the CBI since early October 1944, was attached to the 3rd Squadron as a bombsight mechanic, later reclassified as an A/P instrument mechanic. Although he had not been granted his wings, his duties nevertheless allowed him to fly the planes on test hops to check out repairs.[2]

Originally in the Signal Corps, Jim Ryan had trained as a B-24 mechanic before transitioning to B-25s and had served in the 3rd Squadron as an A/P mechanic–gunner–flight engineer since mid-October. He wrote, in a letter dated May 1 to his father, in Wisconsin, "It is raining out now and has been for too long to suit me. Naturally, I can do no flying, but then again, neither can they."[3] Bad weather had set in again, keeping the squadron's planes grounded for about a week. Airmen were always frustrated by their inability to strike the enemy during periods of operational inactivity, and Ryan wanted to be back in the fight.

The squadron's first mission for the month was off at 0935 on May 4, when two B-25s with two P-51s from the 3rd Fighter Group took a heading to Kaifeng and once again hit the railroad yards (section 15 this time). Ilefeldt, flying A/C #719 (with Drake, Banger, Schlicher, DeFabritis, Hugel, SSgt. George W. Allnoch of the 28th Fighter Squadron, and Schroeder), led the formation, with #722 (with Chiang T., Meng C. M., Young C. H., Ku C. C., Kao C. K., and Feng C. K.) following, and 1Lts. Jean P. Doar and Joe L. Page flew the fighter planes. Heavy ground haze severely restricted visibility throughout the mission. Aircraft hammered the railroad 5 miles east of Kaifeng with seven direct hits and seven near misses, and crewmen reported two misses on the tracks between Kaifeng and Lanfen. Leaflets were dropped. Gunners strafed three boxcars sighted 10 miles west of Lanfen.

It was Maj. Drake's first bombing mission, and he described it years later to his son. As he told the story, the Mitchell was approaching the target and flying up against some high mountains to the right when it encountered heavy flak. They could not fly any higher, and they dared not fly lower. If they maneuvered left, away from the mountain, they would be off target. The situation seemed impossible to the rookie copilot, whose past flying experience had not prepared him for combat conditions such as these.

Drake asked the pilot, "What do we do now?"

"Why, we just fly on through," Ilefeldt replied. They flew on through, completed their mission, and returned safely to base. It was a lesson Drake remembered for long afterward. "Fly on through" became a guiding principle as he dealt with difficulties later in life.[4]

Two planes took off on another mission to Kaifeng the following day at 0945, but Lt. In Y. S., flying the wing aircraft, #724 (with Chang L. T., Chow H., Chen Y. L., Chung C., and Chang T. H.), reported trouble in the right engine about an hour and ten minutes out and returned to base. When engineering later examined it, no malfunction could be found. Senecal (with Wherritt, Kilian, Koss, Magyar, Ryan, Fox, and Schroeder) proceeded to the target flying the lead plane, A/C #719. Kilian dropped bombsight and three 500 lb. aimable incendiary clusters at medium altitude on warehouses at Kaifeng rail yards, all entering the target area. Definite hits were reported on three buildings, although crewmen observed no fires on the second run.

Throughout the past several months, American airmen had gradually begun to realize that their counterparts were no longer providing the same level of support that they had in the past. Chinese pilots frequently developed "mechanical problems" and turned back before reaching the target. Chinese commanders began to protest against targets that they considered to be too well defended. When the Americans insisted on attacking these targets, the Chinese would "run out of gas," leaving the planes on the ground and the missions canceled. The Chinese remained friendly and courteous, but they controlled if and when their missions took place. The sense of brotherhood initially enjoyed by the Americans and Chinese gradually diminished, and the two national groups began to more frequently operate independently of each other, although officially nothing had changed.[5]

Lt. Tu provided insight regarding the situation from the Chinese point of view. Because American airmen could apply for return to the US after completing fifty missions, they often requested assignment to more-frequent missions to reach that goal. Their Chinese counterparts wanted to fly more missions as well, not only to build up their personal flight records but also because they were fighting for liberation of their own country. Many of them believed that only the Americans' needs were being considered, and the situation adversely affected the morale of the squadron's Chinese members. As a result, competition developed between the two nationalities over who would fly missions that were necessarily limited by fuel and ammunition shortages, although the Chinese preferred to avoid direct confrontation to make their point.[6]

In the mornings, the B-25 mechanics often found that the batteries had been drained, and could not determine a reason for it. Hank recounted this story that explained it: "One night I went out to the revetments where the planes were kept. I heard a noise, so I went to see what it was. Those planes had a letdown ladder, and one of them had been pulled down. I climbed up that ladder." Inside he found two Chinese officers huddled together, listening to a radio that they had connected to the battery. "I walked up behind them. They couldn't hear me because they had on headphones, so I—POW—I knocked their heads together."

They jumped up and shouted, "You can't do that! We're officers."

"You can't do what you're doing," he shouted in reply. Then he turned and left. The Americans had strict rules against touching the Chinese or doing anything that might cause them to "lose face," and Hank's actions most certainly violated those restrictions.

"I laid low for a few days. I knew if they said anything they would have my stripes." Although they outranked him and he could have been court-martialed for what he had done, Hank's confrontation with the officers was never reported. Nothing came of the incident, so his activities soon returned to normal—and the batteries no longer lost their charge overnight.

Hank explained his opinion regarding this change: "The Chinese really weren't too worried about that war—about that World War II. They were concerned with the revolution that was coming. They stole ammunition, bombs, and even airplanes and hid them in caves for the coming revolution." In one example of many, a cache of fifty US field guns and 50,000 rounds of shells was afterward discovered at Doyun, near Kunming, stashed away by the Nationalists in preparation for the anticipated civil war.[7] When that revolution later came, "the Nationalists—the people that I was with—they lost."

Perhaps in an attempt to counter the negative direction that relationships were taking, "fast-talking, go-getter" Col. Bennett praised the CACW for its achievements that had been attained in spite of its binational character: "The statistical record, made in less than 2 years after activation, includes more than 5,000 sorties, which brought down or wrecked on the ground 878 Japanese planes, 431 locomotives, 1,675 railroad cars, 4,000 trucks, 600 steamboats, 3 gunboats, 3,874 other watercraft, 141 bridges, 11,062 enemy troops killed and 3,887 horses killed." He gave particular credit to those units that had participated in the defense of Chihkiang: "The 'Flying Skunk,' the 'Flying Hatchet,' 'Lady Luck,' and 'Exterminator' [7th Fighter Squadron] outfits killed plenty of Japs and destroyed their installations."

He commented on the difficulties caused by barriers of language that resulted in formation of one-nation crews, and explained, "On a typical mission eight Chinese and two American craft participate. Chinese fliers are 'hot' in that they take chances our fliers are not allowed to take. This caused considerable worry on the part of American airmen, who want to save every pilot and plane possible in this theater where scarcity of everything prevails."

Bennett commended the wing's "brilliant work" in supporting Chinese ground troops, bombing Japanese airfields to keep them out of efficient operation, and attacking communications, transportation, and supplies, even during "filthy flying weather." He termed the use of Chinese pilots a success that had resulted in requiring fewer Americans in China, at the same time giving the Chinese experience in defending their own country in the air. "For what we had, we have accomplished more than expected. It has been a successful experiment, though at times we had our troubles."[8]

By this time, the bomber squadrons were receiving more B-25Js to replace their older, battle-worn H models. On May 7, Capt. Hamilton and Lts. Wood, Ilefeldt, and Edgerton, along with Sgts. Duffin and Wilkerson, left Liangshan en route to Ondal to pick up another new J model, returning the squadron's line to its usual allotment of eleven. Ilefeldt commented, "This trip was indeed a surprise to all concerned, for during the past few months all trips to India by personnel of this group have been denied them." Capt. MacNeil, serving as operations officer, was appointed acting CO in Capt. Hamilton's absence. Lts. Faherty and Winter, FO Wherritt, TSgt. Libolt, and SSgt. Mier were sent to Kunming on a supply run. SSgts. Haines and Thomas and Sgts. Burton and Peters left for Chengtu, and a week of R&R. TSgt. Shock was promoted to master sergeant.

Two planes from the 3rd Squadron and a second element of three planes from the 2nd Squadron, along with two 32nd Fighter Squadron P-51s, took off at 0910 on the eighth. They separated at Hsiangchang, south of Chenghsien, and flew to separate targets. Led by Capt. Lack, the second element turned north to target the Yu Feng Spinning Mill at Chenghsien, reported to be serving as a gas and ammo dump. The two 3rd Squadron Mitchells flew on to hit section 13A of the railroad, about 4 miles west of Kaifeng. This was the 3rd Squadron's mission #120. Greene flew the lead plane, A/C #719 (with Pulaski, Banger, Jakubasz, England, Hoyle, and Schroeder), and dropped 250 lb. bombs. Six of them bounced off the tracks; four of the six were near misses that caused damage, and one was a direct hit. Capt. Cheng Y. K., pilot of the trailing plane, A/C #724 (with Chang L. T., Liu P. C., Chen Y. C., Li L., and Kao C. K.), claimed to have trouble dropping bombs. However, when the bombs were jettisoned, six of them hit the tracks.

A mission off at 0905 on May 9 targeted section 12 of the railroad between Hokiatsi and Sinkow (Xingou), about 20 miles northwest of Hankow. Two B-25s and three 3rd Fighter Group P-51s flew from Liangshan to the railroad 4 miles south of Hokiatsi and then headed up the tracks. The fighter pilots were 1Lts. Myers and Doer and 2Lt. Coale. In the lead of the bombers, MacNeil was pilot of A/C #714, the squadron's new J model (with Drake, Koss, Holmes, Trout, Magyar, and Schroeder as his aircrew). He made four bombing runs but was unable to release. After the fourth pass, he salvoed near the town of Siszepa. Lt. Chiang T., pilot of the second aircraft, #718 (with Meng C. M., Ting C. L., Ku C. C., Chow K. Y., and Feng C. K.), then made four bombing passes. All three 250 lb. GPs dropped on the first run hit the tracks. One bomb missed on the second run, and one was a near miss that caused some damage on the third pass. The single bomb dropped on the fourth run was a direct hit.

Turning the Tide

The flight crew spotted fifteen to twenty boxcars and a locomotive in the rail yards at Kioshan, so the B-25s and the fighters riddled them with machine gun fire. Before the Mitchells returned to base, MacNeil and Chiang flew low over the Yangtze at Ichang to allow gunners to strafe three 40-to-60-foot powerboats, as well as a large barge on the south bank of the river. It was an exceptionally long mission. Cpl. Schroeder's log noted the target as Pengpu and the mission duration as seven hours and thirty minutes.

The same two pilots flew the squadron's next mission three days later, off at 0840. They proceeded to the Yangtze River south of Ichang, where gunners strafed three powerboats. Members of the flight crew observed prior damage to two of the boats and one large barge, likely victims of the May 9 raid. The Mitchells encountered small-arms fire from the tops of all the minor hills in the area, and MacNeil's A/C #713 (with Banger as navigator and Fuller, Mier, Ryan, and DeFabritis all listed as gunners) was hit, puncturing the feed line from the right-wing tank. MacNeil salvoed all bombs and was able to return to base, in spite of damage. Lt. Chiang, flying A/C #716 (with Chang L. T., Liu P. C., Chang T. M., Li L., and Feng C. K.), completed the mission. He flew on to the railroad between Chowchihtien and Sinyang and dropped ten 250 lb. bombs, four of them scoring direct hits on the tracks. Spikes were used on three of the bombs to prevent skipping. Chiang expressed his opinion that if all the bombs had been equipped with spikes, more hits would have been probable.

The second mission of the day took off at 0850. Lt. Col. Bill Dick, recently promoted and transferred from the 4th Squadron to group HQ as operations officer, flew the 3rd Squadron's lead plane. The Mitchells picked up two P-51s at Ankang. Twenty minutes out of Ankang, 2Lt. Liu P. C. turned the wing plane, A/C #720 (with Sung S. C., Chow H., Chang F. C., Mao C. H., and Shu S. S.), back to base. Col. Dick proceeded to the target aboard A/C #719 (with Wherritt, Koss, Gaffney, Allegretto, Cantor, Hugel, and an OWI observer whose name is not legible). Dick flew around Chenghsien to the tracks north of the town and then turned to make a bombing run toward the south. He released eight 250 lb. GP bombs, scoring one direct hit and two near misses. He then circled Chenghsien and made another run south on the tracks, but no explosions resulted. Strafing followed up on the railroad and the town. Gunners attacked twelve to fifteen boxcars and one flatcar with two sedan autos, scoring definite hits on the autos and two boxcars.

On the first of two missions on May 13, six B-25s took off at 1100 to again hit railroad bridge #113 near Hankow. Four planes from the 2nd Squadron and two from the 3rd took part in this joint mission, and eight 3rd Fighter Group P-51s provided escort. The 2nd Squadron's Capt. Lack again led the formation. Aircraft flew in two elements of three planes each to the target area and then broke into three elements of two planes each for bombing. As the first element approached the target and the lead plane opened its bomb bay doors, Lack's wing plane dropped two bombs. Fortunately, both scored direct hits on a large factory and caused significant damage, although the element's remaining bombs fell short of the bridge. Led over the target by Lt. Bains, the second element scored at least two direct hits on the south end of the bridge and destroyed trackage.

Aircraft of the 3rd Squadron formed the final element and dropped eight 1,000 lb. GPs at 7,300 feet. Flying the lead plane, #719, Greene (with Senecal, Koss, Rieks, Magyar, Whearty, and Fox) scored two hits on the southern portion of the bridge, knocking out the third span from the south end. After dropping their bombs, the two aircraft turned to do strafing in the Sinyang area. West of Ying-ch'-eng, gunners of both planes attacked about a hundred horses and a bivouac area on two runs and claimed thirty to thirty-five horses and twelve to fifteen men as killed. The wing aircraft, #724 (Cheng Y. H., Meng C. M., Shen M. C., Liu T. C., Tung

N. C., and Yuan C. F.), hit three times by small-arms fire, flew back to home base. A/C #719 proceeded to the Han River, 10 miles north of Shayang, where gunners hit ten to twelve sampans. Then they strafed two 100-foot riverboats sighted 20 miles west of Ichang.

Railroad bridge #103 (31º30' N, 113º52' E), near Hwayuan, was the target of two planes that took off at 1120 for a low-level mission. Eight 100 lb. GPs were dropped from 75 feet by pilot release. One bomb from MacNeil's lead plane, #720 (with Pulaski, Banger, Mills, Barge, England, and Schroeder), damaged the southeast span of the bridge. Small-arms fire hit the aircraft, leaving two holes, one of them in the wing tank. It then turned to strafe in the Kingman area, although no enemy activity was noted. Hank flew as top-turret gunner rather than as tail gunner on this mission. In Y. S., pilot of A/C #718 (with Lee K. A., Hsiao H. T., Chen Y. L., Kao C. K., and Chow K. P.), flew in wing position. Small-arms fire hit Lt. In and fractured his leg, and he flew no other 3rd Squadron missions. His copilot, Lt. Lee, flew back to base. Greene turned to strafe in the Kingman area, where crewmen spotted a Chinese flag outside a building but observed no activity.

Squadron planes flew three missions on the following morning. The target of two planes that were airborne at 0700 was railroad bridge #102 (31º28' N, 114º02' E), near Chowshihtien. Drake flew A/C #721 (with MacNeil noted as copilot, Banger as navigator, Allegretto as armorer-gunner, Holmes as engineer-gunner, DeFabritis as radio-gunner, and Gaffney as photo-gunner), followed by Lt. Teng C. C. as pilot of #719 (with Sung S. C., Chow H., Chen Y. C., Lu H. W., and Ho W. C.). Eight 1,000 lb. GP bombs were dropped by pilot release at 400 feet. Two hit the bridge, bounced off, and exploded. One bomb hit a gun position, but the others overshot the bridge. The aircraft flew on to Kingman, where their gunners made three strafing runs on the town. Despite damage reported to Drake's plane, both were back down at 1210.

A second mission that took off on the fourteenth at 0820 targeted a stretch of railroad (section #7) between Sinyang and Kioshan. Two P-51s flew escort for two B-25s, A/C #714 (Greene, Pulaski, Koss, Schlicher, Hugel, Cantor, and Ryan) and #718 (Chang K. L., Chen C. S., Lee C. C., Liu H. T., Chung C., and Chang C. Y.). The planes intersected the tracks 4 miles north of Sinyang and then turned to the north. When aircrewmen sighted two locomotives and fifteen cars near Changtukwan, Greene and Chang released eighteen 250 lb. bombs at 400 feet in two passes, scoring five hits and four near misses. Both the bombers and fighters strafed and damaged the cars and the locomotive. The leader then dropped two bombs on the tracks 4 miles south of Mingkiang, situated 120 miles north of Hankow on the Peiping-Hankow Railroad. When fifty rail cars were sighted at Sinantien, no visible damage resulted from two strafing passes.

The day's final mission was by a single plane, A/C #722 (Senecal, Chang L. T., Kao W. C., Whearty, Magyar, and Schroeder), which took off at 1155. Its target was the railroad between Hwayuan and Sinyang. Senecal made two bombing runs on a locomotive sighted between Hwayuan and Wankiatien. Three 250 lb. GPs fell short but hit the tracks on the first pass. Three more bombs that he released on the second run overshot the locomotive, although one bomb was a direct hit on the track and another a near miss. Strafing caused damage to the locomotive, which could not be moved until tracks were repaired. When he dropped the remaining four bombs, one was a direct hit on the tracks. Meager, inaccurate ground fire came up from the vicinity of bridge #103. About 10 miles west of Anlu, crew members spotted a crashed Japanese Lily. It appeared that parts were being salvaged, so gunners inflicted further damage by strafing. On the return to base, they shot up a radio station at Shayang and a truck 2 miles west of Tsaoshih. Schroeder's log noted the target as Siaopan and the flight duration as five hours and thirty minutes.

By this time, 14th Air Force personnel stationed at bases across China had received news of the Allied victory in Europe on May 8, most viewing it as simply one step closer to going home. Lt. Eisner noted in that month's bomb group historical report, "V-E Day came as an anti-climax to what had been anticipated for a month. For us in this theater of operations it meant no slackening in our efforts, but we look forward to the time when the mass of power in Europe is transferred to the Pacific to press greater blows against the Japanese. We did not celebrate this victory but took it just as another day."

Recently promoted Col. McGehee, wing adjutant, wrote another letter to his hometown newspaper soon after the Axis defeat. "I've been away from home too long to suit me, but I haven't any idea when I will be getting back," he wrote. "My two years are almost over but with VE-Day all rotation was cancelled. So, the prospects aren't very bright right now." He concluded that he was "still hoping hard" to be "back home this fall."[9]

The men at Liangshan had felt confident that Europe would soon be freed from the Axis grip, and Lt. Pulaski had set up a pool to guess the date. On April 23, he typed up a grid consisting of five columns, with this explanation: "Pool for the end of the war in Europe - (End of organized resistance as announced by the War Department. [Hand-printed after: "Ike's word."] If no official date is announced, the date we hear about it will be used.)" The price for entry was fifty cents per chance. Across the top was the hand-printed title "WINNER or WINNERS TAKE ALL." At the bottom, following the names of squadron officers: "You may take as many chances as you wish. May the best man win." About half of the officers participated. Those who splurged with five chances were Hamilton, MacNeil, Banger, Edgerton, Greene, Jeffries, Pulaski, and Fuller. Wood purchased two, and Davis and Winter took only one chance each. The earliest, proposed by Edgerton, was April 28. MacNeil thought it might go as late as July 1, but all were confident that it would end no later than that. Banger's guess of May 8 made him the winner of the $22.00 pot.[10]

Squadron personnel received this surprising message from Gen. Wedemeyer soon afterward: "Instructions have been issued, establishing a curfew for all United States military personnel in the China Theater at 2400 hours on Saturday and holiday nights and 2300

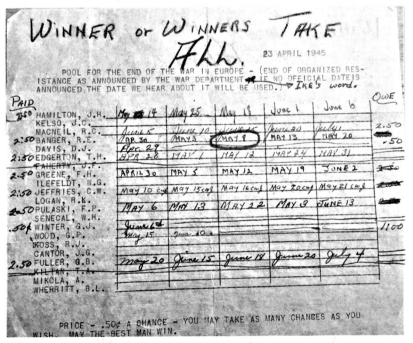

Lt. Pulaski conducted a "pool" to guess the date of VE-day and included the names of twenty-one officers as potential participants. Lt. Banger's guess made him the big winner. *R. E. Banger collection, courtesy of Beth Banger Meehan*

hours on all other nights effective 15 May 1945." Similar instructions were issued by Generalissimo Chiang Kai-shek through Free China, applying to all Chinese military personnel. Curfews had been enforced in the Pacific, in Britain, and in the Service Commands within the United States but had not yet been ordered in China. "The purpose of the curfew is to assist in the maintenance of good health and maximum efficiency in furtherance of the war effort. After the defeat of Germany, the center of gravity of the war will shift to the far east. It is the recognized duty of every American to maintain himself at the peak of efficiency in order to meet increased responsibilities." Wedemeyer expressed his belief that the curfew would not "impose a hardship," and gave the assurance "The inauguration of the curfew does not mean that we must or should curtail our plans for recreation and entertainment. It simply means that we must start earlier, come home earlier, get a good night's rest, and be in better shape for the following day's work."[11]

Only one mission was off on May 15, when four planes led by Lt. Greene were airborne at 0925 with a section of railroad between Hsuchang and Chenghsien as their target. Participating in this mission were Greene's A/C #721 (with Pulaski, Koss, Jakubasz, DeFabritis, Fox, and Schlicher), #714 (Chaing T., Chang L. T., Yang C. H., Pai J. H., Chang Y. H., Wang M. T., and Chow K. P.), #719 (Wherritt, Davis, Faherty, Hugel, Holmes, Gaffney, and Ryan), and #722 (Wang Y. S., Meng C. M., Kao W. C., Wang C. H., Liu T. C., and Shu S. S.). They intersected the track 12 miles south of Hsuchang and made two bombing runs, dropping by pilot release. The first was at 1,000 feet, using the Norden sight, but no bombs hit the tracks. Dropping down to 200 feet, the Chinese crews scored eight hits on the tracks and one hit on a string of boxcars that damaged five or six. One of the American crews scored two hits on the tracks south of Chenghsien. At 3 miles south of Hoshawkiao, crewmen sighted and strafed a locomotive, hitting the engine. Pilots of the Mitchells dropped forty 250 lb. GP bombs; eleven were hits, with one that damaged the engine. One aircraft received five holes from small-arms fire, one of them to the gas tank. All planes returned safely to base.

For five of these men, it was their final return.

May 16 began as many other days, but its events lived on in the memories of 3rd Bomb Squadron members for many years afterward. In the early-morning hours, six crews were briefed at Liangshan on separate targets in the Ichang, Chingmen, and Shashih triangle in western Hubei Province on mission #130, for the purpose of hitting enemy troops and supplies on low-level raids. They flew without escort, as had become common practice in this phase of the war. All aircraft carried M1A1 fragmentation bombs (twenty on two Mitchells and seventeen on four), all instantaneous fuse and dropped by pilot release. Three bombers were sent out with American aircrews and three with all-Chinese crews: A/C #721 (MacNeil, Senecal, Banger, Jakubasz, England, Cantor, and Schroeder), #714 (Liu P. C., Chen S. C., Huang C., Li L., Cheng F. C., and Yuan C. F.), #722 (Davis, Wherritt, Koss, Ryan, Wadlow, and Fox), #720 (Sung S. C., Tu N. L., Chow H., Lu H. W., Tung N. T., and Ho W. C.), #725 (Drake, Pulaski, Whearty, Gaffney, DeFabritis, and Hugel), and #726 (Teng C. C., Lee K. A., Ting C. L., Mao C. H., and Chang Y.), as specified in the mission report's "crew list" section. The uncharacteristic lack of clarity in details suggests the heavy emotional toll that this mission took on those affected by it.

The first plane listed in the report's narrative was off at 0530 and bombed a supply dump in the Chengyangi (Xiangyang) area, about 100 miles east-northeast of Ichang on the Han River, a tributary of the Yangtze. Although not specified, A/C number was likely #714. On the first run, three bombs fell short of the target; on the second run, three dropped from 1,200 feet scored hits on the supply dump. Next, gunners strafed and damaged three trucks found west of Chengyangi on four passes. Machine gun fire from the ground knocked out the plane's hydraulic system and hit the left engine. Its aircrew counted a total of ten hits. The bombs could not be released due to damage to mechanism, so three were pushed out and the remaining eight were brought back to base. The aircraft landed at 0930.

The second listed for takeoff in the report was a B-25 (A/C number again not specified but likely #720) off at 0950 (error?), which dropped twenty bombs on the barracks area at Chingmen on the Han River. About half hit the target. Strafing produced unobservable results. The explosion of one of the plane's own bombs caused some damage to the aircraft, but it was able to return to base.

Time of takeoff was recorded as 0550 for the next three planes. A/C #726 proceeded to the Chingmen barracks area (perhaps accompanying #720), and Lt. Teng dropped all seventeen bombs, nine of them hitting in the target area and eight missing the target but falling into the edge of town. Results of a strafing run on Tanyung were unobservable. Sgt. Mao C. H. (X-2116), waist gunner, received two hits from small-arms fire to his right leg near the knee, believed to be flesh wounds. It was this aircraft's first 3rd Squadron mission.

The crew of A/C #725, which took a heading toward the same vicinity, sighted a Sally in the revetment area at Chingmen. Drake dropped five bombs, but all missed the enemy bomber. He released ten bombs on the barracks area in Shihchiaoi and then dropped the remaining five on boats near Ichang, missing them but burning a house on the riverbank. When he dropped in to enable his gunners to strafe the boats, a small explosion on one of them resulted. He concluded with another strafing pass on the barracks area in Shihchiaoi, where crewmen sighted five horses tied outside a building. Small-arms fire shattered the plane's right waist Plexiglas window, inflicting slight cuts to the chin and hand of Cpl. DeFabritis, waist gunner. No serious damage was done to the aircraft, which returned to base at 1010. Maj. Drake, for whom this was his second mission as pilot, later revealed that aircrews were always administered pharmaceuticals to prepare them for early-morning raids such as this: sedatives on the night before and amphetamines on mission mornings to ensure that aircrews performed at peak efficiency.

One of the planes (A/C number not specified but likely #721), flying to the same vicinity as #722, released its seventeen bombs over barracks on the outskirts of Ichang. All hit in the target area, but crewmen observed no damage. It then made a strafing pass on the city, firing 13,000 rounds. Encountering no ground fire, this Mitchell returned to base at 0940.

Capt. MacNeil's target was Sha-Shih (Shashih), according to Schroeder's combat mission's certification. Shashih (30°18'58" N, 112°15'07" E), located on the northern bank of the Yangtze, about 70 air miles downriver from Ichang, was an important port city used by the Japanese for shipment of supplies. Schroeder noted the mission's duration as four hours and fifteen minutes. His details are consistent with the operational intelligence report for A/C #721.

Modified to carry eighteen Browning M2 .50-caliber machine guns, a B-25J-2, serial #44-30656, A/C #722, took off from Liangshan with seventeen frags to bomb and strafe the Japanese-held airfield at Ichang. Red letters spelled out "BIG DAVE" on the aircraft's nose. Although the mission report listed time of takeoff as 0545, Lt. Mikola later wrote that it was fifth on the runway in order of takeoff. The pilot on this mission was 1Lt. Davis, with FO Wherritt as copilot, 1Lt. Koss as navigator-bombardier, Cpl. Ryan as radio-gunner, recently promoted Sgt. Wadlow as engineer-gunner, and Sgt. Fox as armorer-gunner in the tail compartment. After taking off in good weather, the bomber made no further radio contact with

the tower. Visibility en route and at the target was poor, and A/C #722 became separated from its wing plane, A/C #721, soon after takeoff. At the target, Davis made several bombing and strafing passes. A Chinese observer estimated that between two hundred and three hundred enemy soldiers were killed, and large quantities of stores were destroyed. Chinese authorities at Enshih reported that the aircraft was hit by ground fire and crashed almost immediately on the field, burning as it went down. One unidentified man was said to have bailed out, although other observers believed that all of them had parachuted from the plane.

When A/C #722 failed to return, three 3rd Squadron aircraft took off to search the Ichang area for the missing plane and crew, accompanied by a single B-25 from the 2nd Squadron. Greene, pilot of A/C #726 (with MacNeil, Banger, Holmes, Magyar, Hugel, and Reynard), was in the air at 1600, followed by Pulaski in #714 (with Senecal, Faherty, Schlicher, Gaffney, and Cantor) and 2Lt. Chiang T. in #725 (with Chang L. T., Liu P. C., Ku C. C., Kao C. K, and Wang M. T.). Chiang's Mitchell had engine trouble caused by a faulty carburetor and turned back after about ten minutes, while Greene and Pulaski spent twenty to twenty-five minutes searching the area without locating any wreckage or evidence of the crew. They flew on to the railroad in the vicinity of Siaping, where aircrews sighted two locomotives 20 miles north of Sinyang. Two strafing passes by each aircraft scored eight hundred to a thousand hits and inflicted severe damage to the engines. The planes flew on to Mingkiang. About 35 miles west of Kioshan, one turned up the road leading to Hiyang, and the other turned down. Faherty specified #714's destination as Tangyang in his combat mission certifications. Aircrews of both planes reported good dispersal of bombs along the roadway.

Assigned to the squadron on the previous day, TSgt. Harley D. Reynard regularly flew as aerial photographer on 3rd Squadron missions from this time forward, also taking his turn as a gunner whenever necessary. He had previously served a tour of duty in Europe and sent home boxes of war souvenirs that included German Lugers, many of them received in trade for chocolate bars. His travels gave him an opportunity to indulge his love of music by buying and selling violins at pawn shops around the world.[12]

Although he took no part in this mission, May 16 was also significant for MSgt. Hoyle, who began his journey bound for "Uncle Sugar." His final mission had been on the eighth, when he flew as tail gunner on the Kaifeng mission.

Capt. MacNeil reported on the following day that aircraft of the 2nd and 3rd Bomb Squadrons were again searching the vicinity of Ichang and Shashih for wreckage, and Chinese ground parties were searching the area as well. The next week, a follow-up report of "downed Baker Two Five" stated that one crew member had been seriously

TSgt. Harley D. Reynard joined the squadron as an aerial photographer but filled in as a gunner as needed. Here ready for a mission, he is surrounded by his photographic equipment. *H. D. Reynard collection, courtesy of David Reynard*

injured and was captured by the Japanese, while the other five had been killed in the crash. Another notification stated that one pilot was killed, and others had been captured.

"This reported loss of a crew comes as somewhat a shock to the squadron, for although we have had quite a number of our American crewmen walk-out [sic] from enemy territory, this is the first time an American of our squadron has been reported killed since the squadron has been activated," Ilefeldt wrote. Conflicting intelligence reports continued to come in throughout the following weeks. On the basis of a recently received report, he still held out hope for survivors: "The other crew members were not mentioned on the report, and it is assumed that they evaded capture and regressed through the enemy lines. If they evaded capture, we feel sure that they will be 'walking out,' for Ichang is close to friendly territory."

When no reports came in providing confirmation of their survival, all were officially listed as missing in action and presumed dead.[13] Their fate was not confirmed until after the war had ended. It is ironic that the first of all the reports received was the most accurate. Sgt. Fox's date of death was recorded in official documents as July 5, 1945. Although hit by the plane's propeller as he jumped, he survived the crash and was hospitalized by his captors. He was later reported to have died as the result of his injuries—inevitable, considering the brutality consistently inflicted upon their captives by the Japanese.[14] All the others died in the crash.

Fred Greene and Bob Koss had become close friends before they were transferred together from the 17th Fighter Squadron as replacements to the 3rd Bomb Squadron in January. Greene had the responsibility of assigning crews for the May 16 missions. On that morning, Koss said he did not want to fly and asked Greene to replace him. Perhaps he had a premonition. Regardless of their friendship, Greene replied that he had no one else who could fill in as navigator on the raid, and the assignment stood. When word came in that Koss was one of the missing flight crew, he felt responsible, although he knew that he had no other choice in making the call. Greene carried the sense of guilt for the rest of his life.[15]

On May 17, two planes took off at 1105 to Silipou, where Drake, flying A/C #725 (the lead aircraft, with Greene, Faherty, DeFabritis, Schlicher, Trout, and Schroeder), dropped three 500 lb. M29 butterfly bombs on the barracks area and supply dump. The wing plane, #714 (carrying the same Chinese aircrew that flew aboard A/C #725 on the previous day), dropped twelve 100 lb. GPs and ten napalm bombs. Twenty hit the target and started fires. When Drake sighted a small compound 25 miles south of Chingmen, he released three 500 lb. M29 bombs that covered the entire compound.

An early-morning raid, off at 0515 on the following day by the same two aircraft, was directed against bridge #103. It was a target of prime importance. Because there was no alternate road, destroying the bridge would significantly impede the movement of supplies from the north. MacNeil, flying A/C #725 (with Pulaski, Banger, Magyar, Gaffney, and Reynard), led the attack, and Lt. Chang K. L., in #714 (with Chiang J. M., Lee C. C., Liu T. C., Chung C., and Chen Y. C.), followed. Each plane dropped eight 500 lb. GPs, all completely missing their target. It was a disappointing performance for all those involved.

Lt. Ilefeldt wrote that a great many of the squadron's planes came back "rather shot up from ground fire" during the increased operational activity around the middle of the month. "At one time we had eight planes in the service group in need of repairs due to enemy action," he reported. "However hazardous the increased defense the enemy is putting up against us, it proves that we have been hurting them for we have run many missions in the past on large, important undefended bridges without any trouble at all. We no longer go out on any 'milk runs.' Our squadron motto 'Spray and Pray' is an apt one."

As the Japanese advance bore down on them in early May, the 4th Bomb Squadron detachment had implemented plans to abandon their threatened base. A convoy that consisted of a 6×6 and four jeeps and trailers loaded with supplies and equipment left on the third. A day out of Peishiyi they received word that the Chinese counteroffensive, supported by CACW fighters and bombers, was gaining momentum, so they turned around and headed back to Chihkiang to continue the fight.

It became obvious by mid-May that the defense of Chihkiang had held. Col. Dunning, in command of the 5th Fighter Group, was given credit for much of the success in resisting the Japanese advance. In spite of its being on the verge of evacuation, Col. Dunning's determination to stay until the last possible moment saved the airfield, and the Japanese were driven back. The enemy advance was stopped 65 miles away. It was the first time since the beginning of the Second Sino-Japanese War in 1937 that any of Japan's seriously sought objectives had been denied.

A war correspondent praised Dunning and his "midget air force operating on a shoestring—a small part of the small 14th," which "played the odd role of both causing and helping to stop the recent abortive Japanese effort against the base." He wrote, "Dunning's tactics undoubtedly helped precipitate the recent Japanese offensive against the air base at Chihkiang, but a few days later it became apparent that if 'Dunning's Demons' were strong enough to convince the Japanese of the necessity of knocking out the air base they also were strong enough to knock the enemy back on his heels when he tried it." The inevitable results: "The fliers, collaborating with attack-minded Chinese troops, did just that."[16]

Dunning, from San Antonio, Texas, went on to fly more than a hundred missions from Chihkiang. He destroyed two Japanese planes in the air, damaged three, destroyed one on the ground, damaged eight, and probably destroyed three more. He was later awarded the Legion of Merit, the DFC with OLC, and Air Medal with OLC.

The 4th Squadron's Sgt. Weinert later told his family that the Japanese would drive them off a base and later they got it back. He described long lines of Chinese carrying yo-yo baskets full of rocks to fill bomb craters on the runway. The women brought eggs for the men stationed there as well, sharing what little they had to show their appreciation.[17] The 4th Squadron's detachment remained there until the end of the war, often flying missions in cooperation with 3rd Squadron detachments operating out of the same base.

An unnamed 14th Air Force colonel (perhaps Dunning) was quoted in a service publication at about this time: "One of the best indications that the threat has at least temporarily subsided is that Chinese villagers and peasants who had fled westward in long lines during the early stages of the Jap advance are now trickling back to their homes in increasing numbers." He offered his opinion that "when the reserved, practical Chinese peasant decides the danger is past for the time being, it usually is." Informational leaflets dropped from the planes had informed the Chinese civilian population of the dangers of remaining, so very few, if any, had stayed. The anonymous colonel observed that civilians were returning eastward to their homes around the Chinese defense perimeter of Chihkiang "in a fairly steady trickle now," though not in sufficient numbers to interfere with Chinese military traffic. "Most residents are returning home with their household effects suspended from sticks across their shoulders; however, they also use wheelbarrows and carts where the few roads permit."[18]

"In the only battle of its kind in any war, young men of two nations of different languages, customs and cultures fight side by side," wrote a war correspondent soon after the battle's successful conclusion. "The Chinese-American Composite Wing of the fabulous 14th Air Force, the one that has done mostest with the leastest," was praised for its part in driving back the enemy. "The Japs were soundly whipped in seven weeks. Thousands never got back to their starting point along what was then a completely Jap-held inland corridor from the Chengsha Lake district south via Hengyang, Kweilin, Liuchow and Nanning to Hanoi in French Indo-China," he stated. "Units had to retreat in little groups of stragglers, infiltrating back through encircling Chinese lines. All were given rough handling. The Japs are today the same distance from the air base as when they started." Parts of three Japanese divisions totaling 45,000 men were committed to battle. One-third of them—an entire division—were killed.[19]

The Battle of Chihkiang proved to be the turning point of the war in China. Following their defeat, the Japanese made the decision to relinquish their Greater East Asia Corridor and withdraw from South China to positions north of the Yellow River. Imperial headquarters ordered the evacuation of the southern rail line extending to Kweilin and Liuchow, a branch of the main Hankow–Canton railway. Within a few days of the end of the Chihkiang campaign, units began to move from South China to be redeployed into northern and central China.

By the third week of May, revitalized Chinese troops, still in close coordination with air support, were reported to be so definitely masters of the situation that the Japanese were in full retreat along the Hsiang valley. Within a few days it became evident, too, that the enemy was moving back toward the Indochina border and that preparations were being made to abandon Liuchow. Rather than decreasing efforts in response to the retreat, the 14th Air Force accelerated the air campaign, with the aim of disrupting the imminent withdrawal of the enemy. Attacks from the air were concentrated on rail and road movements and river shipping, critically reducing the enemy's mobility and supply lines. Bombing missions throughout South and East China concentrated on attacks against communications targets and supply lines, as well as a large variety of targets of opportunity.[20]

Destroying bridges and burning supplies remained priorities of the 1st Bomb Group and the 3rd Fighter Group. The 3rd Squadron's specific focus continued to be along the Ping-Han Railroad, on which it "relentlessly inflicted enough damage to cause the enemy to remove railroads from Southern China to replace the bridges and tracks that we have knocked out," wrote Ilefeldt. "It is gratifying to know that we are hurting them in our zone of operations." Severe fighting was reported in the Ichang area through the month, with many Japanese officers being captured or killed.

When Gen. Chennault was interviewed at about this time, he stated, "I don't believe that the Japs can point to a single outstanding achievement as a result of having opened the corridor. The enemy threw troops away when they were desperately needed elsewhere—the Japanese divisions employed in the east China campaign, if they were thrown into the Philippines, might have altered the military picture considerably." With the severing of their land link with Southeast Asia, the entire Japanese effort over the past year to forge a landline of communication and supply across East China, joining the Yangtze and French Indochina, had proved an almost total failure.[21]

Capt. Hamilton and a crew that included Lts. Edgerton, Ilefeldt, and Wood, as well as TSgt. Wilkerson and SSgt. Duffin, returned from India in midmonth with another new B-25J "heavily loaded down with morale in the form of rations that are so scarce in China." As on past ferrying missions, this one was used to replenish stocks of food, liquor, coffee, and PX items, which aided in relieving the squadron's sense of deprivation. Especially welcome were the barracks bags filled with canned foods: fruits that included pineapple, peaches, pears, and cherries, and meats such as chicken, turkey, sardines, salmon, Vienna sausage, and Spam that provided a break from the incessant chewy water buffalo. TSgts. Gruber and Meikle, SSgts. Evitts and Holmes, and Cpl. Piecuch were ordered to rest camp at Chengtu to enjoy its luxuries.

Two B-25s were off on May 21 at 1335, with an ammunition dump at Kioshan as primary target. Unable to find the ammo dump, they flew on to their secondary target, railroad bridge #102 at Chowshihtien. Each carried eight 500 lb. RDX bombs. Greene, in the lead aboard A/C #725 (with Senecal, Banger, Cantor, Trout, England, and Stearns), dropped his bombs at 6,000 feet, but all missed the target. Lt. Wang Y. S., following with #714 (with Meng C. M., Chow H., Chang T. H., Chow K. Y., and Shu S. S.), dropped his bombs 6 miles south of the bridge. When the bombs exploded, the plane left the formation, although Wang did not inform the leader regarding any difficulty. Greene's aircrew reported meager, inaccurate gunfire. On the way home, they reported two locomotives, camouflaged and in yards, and twelve flatcars loaded with trucks along the tracks, as well as fifteen trucks on the road. The lead aircraft returned to base at 1855, but the wing plane was still missing, last sighted 6 miles south of Chowshihtien. Of the aircrew of #714, only Sgt. Shu, tail gunner, has been found on any later mission, but the aircraft was back in service from early June.

TSgt. Fred S. Stearns, placed on detached service on the eighteenth, flew this as his first 3rd Squadron mission. According to a newspaper article from his hometown in South Texas, he joined the army with his brother Cullen at Kelly Field in August 1939. Attached since before the war to the Antilles Air Command, Stearns was stationed in San Juan, Puerto Rico, one of the West Indies air bases guarding the vital approaches to the Caribbean area. "Planes of the Antilles Air Command, of which Sergeant Stearns is a member, fly daily patrols over an area seven times that of Texas, extending from the western tip of Cuba to the sweltering equatorial belt of South America. Palm-fringed AAC air bases are strategically located on small volcanic islands and in the midst of lush tropical jungles, forming a protective barrier for the gateways to the three Americas." Stearns told his family that he had photographed the entire coast of South America twice, and he related many stories involving perilous landing on all kinds of airstrips on those missions, especially along the Amazon. He had taken part in thirty combat missions on B-24s and B-25s in Burma and India, often filling in as a gunner in addition to his duties as photographer.²²

TSgt. Fred S. Stearns, another photographer who joined during this time, aided in documenting missions and tracking enemy movement. *Courtesy of Duane Kimbrow*

A mission off at 1210 on the twenty-second was only marginally more successful than the previous raid. Three 3rd Squadron planes flew a joint mission with three from the 2nd Squadron. Maj. S. T. Smith led the formation, with 1Lt. C. V. Brown and Kan Y. C. as pilots in the first element. Six P-51s flew escort (pilots Hundley, Scott, Laurence Kelly, Charles H. Freeburn, Wednell, and Combs). Their target was again bridge #103, which had been targeted unsuccessfully on the eighteenth. Hamilton flew A/C #725 (with Ilefeldt, Edgerton, Whearty, England, and Mier) in the lead of the 3rd Squadron's bombers, followed by #722 (Yen P. S., Chen Y. P., Lee C. C., Lu H. W., Wei C. S., and Kao C. K.) and #724 (Lui P. C., Hsiao H. T., Chang F. C., Li L., and Chow K. P.). Aboard Hamilton's bomber as an observer was Lt. J. E. Claringbould, identified as "S.G., R.N.N.K." He served as secretary general of the Dutch National Committee on Trade and later as secretary of Rotary International and the Dutch National Committee,

International Chamber of Commerce. Smith's element made the first bombing run. Hamilton's trailing element then dropped twenty-three 500 lb. RDX bombs at 7,000 feet. Although Edgerton relied on the Norden bombsight, all fell short of the bridge by 500 to 1,000 yards, yet destroying about 300 feet of trackage. Meager, inaccurate ground fire caused no damage.

On May 23, a three-plane formation took off at 1200, intersected the railroad 5 miles north of Siokan, and turned north to the target—once again bridge #103—but because of "faulty identification" hit bridge #105 instead. The plan was to first disable gun positions at each end of the bridge before attacking the main structure. While MacNeil in #725 (with Drake, Banger, Jakubasz, Peters, Mier, and Reynard) and Ilefeldt in #722 (with Pulaski, Edgerton, Gaffney, DeFabritis, Hugel, and Schroeder) dropped seventeen M1A1 frags on two runs, a third plane, #724 (Teng C. C., Yang P. C., Chen Y. K., Wang M. T., Liu T. C., and Chen Y. C.), strafed gun positions. Each of the aircraft dropped four 1,000 lb. bombs on a third pass. Three hit the tracks, and one in the center of the bridge ignited a fire. Four were near misses. One span of the bridge was shifted, according to reports. When the planes made their strafing runs, gunners caused "meager inaccurate A/W fire to cease on bridge." Schroeder gave the target location as Hwayuan.

As on many other missions during this period, this one was in cooperation with the 2nd Squadron, with four B-25s that took off at 1220 to hit bridge #102 in the same vicinity. Capt. Leslie L. Mondelli, who joined the 3rd Squadron soon afterward, flew one of the 2nd Squadron Mitchells. Two 3rd Fighter Group P-51s (pilots Freeburn and Kelly) flew escort.

Lt. Edgerton was transferred the following day from group HQ to the 4th Squadron. He had taken part in twenty-eight combat missions, including eighteen while serving with Task Force 34. His transfer was well received by the 4th Squadron's "old hands," whose respect he had earned while flying earlier missions out of Chihkiang.

Capt. Hamilton briefed three crews on a section of railroad track between Sinyang and Saiping and took off from Liangshan at 1030 on May 25 aboard A/C #725 (with Ilefeldt, Faherty, Allegretto, Peters, Whearty, and Schroeder). Lts. Men T. C. in #722 (Tsuei W. P., Yang C., Chen Y. L., Chang Y., and Tung N. T.) and Yen P. S. in #726 (with Chang L. T., Yang C. H., Ku C. T., Chung C., and Kuo H. Y.) took wing positions. The pilot of each plane dropped ten 250 lb. GPs along the track. Thirteen were direct hits that ruptured the tracks, and one destroyed a small bridge 15 miles north of Kioshan. Five were near misses that produced some damage to the tracks, and twelve were misses. When fifteen boxcars were sighted at Sinantien, gunners strafed, and about half were hits on the cars. Crewmen sighted three dummy aircraft in a field near Mingkiang but lacked ordnance to strike. This mission was coordinated with that of a single 2nd Squadron B-25 (time of takeoff 1035) piloted by Col. Russell that hit targets of opportunity along the rails in the same vicinity.

Lts. Greene and Senecal and Sgt. Mills returned with a new J model near the end of the month. Hank said that they went back to India for it, and recalled details about their return: "There were three men in our squadron—one was named Fox, and one was Ryan, and another had been there in the squadron for a while, name of Wadlow. We came back from a mission, and they just weren't there." He expected them to have returned by that time after being reported missing. Instead, their belongings had been cleared out of their quarters, without explanation. Because he had worked closely with the three gunners, he felt their loss most keenly and always wondered through the years that followed what had become of his friends. "I always thought I knew what happened to them, but I never did *know*." He remembered Wadlow, who had arrived with him at Karachi, as a good-natured, friendly fellow, and Fox usually had a smile and a humorous comment. Ryan was an often-serious young man who "always looked like he was fixin' to cry."

On the day of Hank's return, TSgt. Libolt began his return to the ZI. TSgt. Barge, who had been appointed airplane inspector to fill the vacancy created by his departure, assumed responsibility for making inspections to determine the planes' airworthiness and quality of the work performed by maintenance and repair crews. His approval was required for repairs made to grounded airplanes before they were restored to flying status, and he ordered additional work on any found to be questionable. It seems that Hank took over this important duty at some later date. He recalled being responsible for determining whether the bombers were "fit to fly," and his was the final word for whether they took part in a mission. "I was in charge of all the maintenance," he said.

The combined mission off on May 26 was unsuccessful from the beginning. Six aircraft of the 2nd Squadron and six of the 3rd, all carrying firebombs, were off at 0715, with bridge #113 once again as the target. The Mitchells flew in box formation of four elements of three planes each. Six 3rd Fighter Group P-51s were to fly escort, but Capt. Freeburn's Mustang lost its coolant on takeoff, so he turned back immediately. It crashed on the runway, but no one was injured. Pilots of the other fighters were Thomas J. Cribbs, Dallas S. Cone, Hundley, Chung, and Tung (no given names found for the last three). The twelve B-25s and the remaining five P-51s took a heading that brought them to the Ping-Han Railroad at Sioakan, where they turned south. Without explanation, the 2nd Squadron leader, Maj. Smith, headed for bridge #115 instead of bridge #113. A 2nd Squadron mission report later stated that his navigator could not locate the targeted bridge, in part because of scattered clouds at 6,000 feet. Pilots of the other 2nd Squadron Mitchells were 1Lt. A. A. Frost, Capt. L. L. Mondelli, and Yang S. W., Tsai T. C., and Chang H. H. (no ranks given for the Chinese pilots).

Maj. Smith's element made the first run, and five out of six planes dropped their bombs. All fell at the approach span on the south end of the bridge, and aircrews reported a large volume of explosive smoke. The 3rd Squadron planes separated into two echelons. Leading the 3rd Squadron Mitchells, Hamilton was pilot of A/C #725 (Pulaski, Banger, Barge, England, Trout, and Reynard as his aircrew), with #722 (Chiang T., Tu N. L., Lee C. C., Ku C. T., Wei C. S., and Li L.) and #723 (Liu P. C., Shen S., Chen Y. K., Chang F. C., Wang M. T., and Kao C. K.) flying on his wings. Trailing behind Hamilton's element, Drake flew #726 (with MacNeil, Faherty, Cantor, Long, Wilkerson, and Stearns), leading #715 (Teng C. C., Chen K. C., Ting C. L., Chen Y. L., Liu H. T., and Chow K. P.) and #716 (Chen C. S., Chang C. C., Chen Y. C., Liu T. C., and Yuan C. F.). The bombload for 3rd Squadron planes was eight 500 lb. RDX per aircraft.

Capt. Hamilton's element dropped no bombs on its first run. On the second pass, all twenty-four bombs splashed into the water 150 to 300 feet west of the bridge, near its south end. Two of the P-51s, each carrying two M64 500 lb. demos, dive-bombed and released at 4,000 feet. All fell to the east at the extreme north end. The sixth plane of Maj. Smith's element, unable to release because of a rack malfunction, salvoed 50 miles northwest of Hankow as it returned home. Although aircraft encountered enemy AA from the north end of the bridge and over Hankow Airdrome, all landed safely.

Ironically, orders came through for Flight Officer Wherritt's commission to second lieutenant on the twenty-sixth, when his fate (and that of the other missing crew members) was still unconfirmed. Lt. Ilefeldt, in his May historical report, remarked that ever since Wherritt had joined the squadron, he and others had wondered why Wherritt was made a flight officer instead of a second lieutenant when he received his wings. "Those of us who have flown with him and associated with him in daily contact appreciated his proficiency as a pilot and his good judgement, common sense, and other attributes for the makings of a good officer." Ilefeldt speculated that Wherritt's extreme youth may have been the determining factor. "In spite of his age (21), his actions, decisions, and military bearing were those of an older man. However, Wherritt must execute an oath of office before he can be put down in the morning report as a 2Lt. as he may be dead, or at best, a prisoner of the Jap. This predicament calls for the decision of a Solomon as to what course of action to take in Wherritt's behalf."

Four crews that took off at 1745 on the following day went after targets of opportunity along the Ping-Han Railroad in the Ichang-Sinyang area. Lt. Greene was in the lead of the second element with a B-25J, A/C #722 (Senecal, Banger, Whearty, Peters, Hugel, and Reynard as his aircrew). According to Greene's postmission report, they were about 30 miles west of Sinyang when his left engine began to smoke. "It was evident that there was a heavy oil leak behind the inboard cowl flaps. Shortly afterward the left engine cut out momentarily and backfired several times. I salvoed the bombs (10 × 250 G.P.) over occupied territory and decided to land at Valley Field. Flying time from that point to Liangshan was 1:45." Recognizing the hazards inherent in attempting to return directly to base, he rejected that option. "It would have been necessary to maintain 9,000 to 10,000 feet over the mountains during the last hour of the trip. Had the engine failed during that time, it would have been impossible to maintain that altitude for a protracted period on one engine. The nearest friendly territory was east of the Ping-Han Railroad."

Greene called on VHF and notified Lt. Pulaski, flight leader, of his intentions to head for Valley Field in "the pocket." This was a secret base that had recently been established in a Chinese-controlled area that was completely surrounded by enemy territory. Since the loss of Laohokow, its purpose was to provide a safe place to land for aircraft that were in trouble, and it was there that Greene attempted to reach. He left the formation and passed around Sinyang at 10,000 feet. The engine was still running, and he had plenty of altitude. Darkness fell fifteen minutes later. Under Banger's direction, the pilot took up a direct heading for Kushih (Gushi) as the first checkpoint of the route to Valley Field, but ground haze obscured the area. Unable to find Kushih, Greene flew east to Si Lake, clearly visible in the light of the full moon. "From Si Lake we took up a heading west to Kushih. Again, we were unable to see Kushih but made a timed turn to a heading of 175' mag., flew 50 miles to Lihuang, were unable to see the city and made a timed turn to a heading of 212'. We flew this heading for 17 miles as briefed and at that time circled, fired a red flare, and keyed all recognition lights."

From the vicinity of Kushih, Senecal and Peters began a series of attempts to make radio contact but received no reply on any of the authorized frequencies. "We then observed mountainous terrain to the southeast and circled about 10 miles to the southeast, again firing a flare. We later learned that this flare was seen by personnel at Valley and that we were at that time very near the Valley Field. Ground haze still obscured the terrain, and we could see nothing but numerous small fires scattered over the entire area." Greene turned to the southwest and flew for about six minutes. "This placed us definitely beyond Valley by direct, so we turned northeast and again circled the mountainous area where we suspected the field lay." They fired another flare, also seen from the field, "but observing no lights and receiving no radio reply we continued north to ensure that we were well within the pocket before being required to bail out." The left engine was still operating but cutting out sporadically and still leaking oil.

Oil temperature rose to 95 degrees despite the automatic temperature regulator, so finding a place to put down became increasingly urgent, particularly before they might be out of the "free pocket." Greene wrote, "At 2120 we flew over a river, one of several in the immediate area, and from an altitude of 8,500 feet saw a prominent sand bar in the riverbed. We descended to the river valley, dragged the area several times and landed wheels up to the south." Aided by the bright moonlight, he was able to put the plane down with relatively little damage. It slid 700 feet in the soft sand before coming to a stop. Extending about 1,500 feet in length, the sandbar was located on the west side of the Kwan River, they later learned.[23]

All the men were astonished to discover that no one was injured. Reynard later related that they all just sat there, looking at each other in stunned silence for a few moments. "We're not dead" was their relieved conclusion. After recovering from the initial shock, they climbed out of the plane and prepared to make their escape.[24] A/C #722 was the fourth of the squadron's planes bearing that number to go down, and the second of them piloted by Lt. Greene.

They removed maps, canteens, and radio facilities and detonated the IFF, according to Greene's report. Then they took cover along the bank of the river and made a hasty reconnaissance of the immediate area. There seemed to be no activity, although they had noticed several nearby fires from the air. "There was a hill approximately 800 feet high, covered with rocks and scrub trees near our position[,] and we decided to take cover on or behind it until daybreak," he later reported. "We were not at the time absolutely certain that we were in friendly territory, although we felt sure enough to leave the plane intact."

A well-traveled foot path extended between the river and the hill, and a house stood at the foot of the hill. Since it would have been difficult to cross the road unobserved from the house in the moonlight, they crossed individually and at intervals, assembling in a small draw on the hillside. They observed two men in light-colored clothing running "in a crouched attitude" through the scrub about 20 yards higher up the slope, but were unable to recognize the uniform or determine whether they were armed. "Once assembled we proceeded to the top of the hill but encountered more men near rocks on the summit," Greene wrote. "We then withdrew below the crest and flanked the slope to the right. We reached an area of large rocks on the north side and affording good cover and spent the night there with local security posted." From their concealed position, they observed several people inspecting the airplane during the night.

At 0430 the next morning—daybreak—a squad of soldiers climbed to the summit of the hill and began searching the area. After quickly identifying them in the early-morning light by their uniforms as Chinese Nationalist troops, the

Cpl. Robert G. Hugel, attached as an armorer-gunner, participated in this mission as its tail gunner. R. G. Hugel collection, courtesy of Robert G. Hugel

Hugel's diary, written in pencil, provides a detailed account of events following the emergency landing of A/C #722 on a sandbar in the river. R. G. Hugel collection, courtesy of Robert G. Hugel

Hugel captioned this photo "Crash landing behind the lines 27 May 1945." R. G. Hugel collection, courtesy of Robert G. Hugel

crew made contact. The Chinese recognized them immediately. They set a guard on the plane and its contents while others took the Americans into the nearby town of Tang Chuan, district of Shang Cheng, Honan (Tangzhuang, Ziangcheng District, Henan Province on current maps).

Cpl. Hugel was tail gunner on this mission, and he recorded his experiences in a diary. On Sunday, May 27, he wrote: "Crash land at 2130 hours on sand bar dried up river beside the small town of Tung Chuan. Doubtful of locality. Hide on top of nearby mountain for that night. Slept in bushes and posted guards. No alarm during night although we know we are being watched by anonymous eyes."[25]

Lt. Senecal related his own recollections of going down behind enemy lines. This mission was his thirty-seventh, and he flew as Greene's copilot. He later told his family that he and the crew were discovered by a group of people whom they were unable to immediately identify as friend or foe. Senecal waved a white flag but told another of the men who was "a pretty good shot" to be ready in case they had to defend themselves. Peters, whom Hank described as "a little ol' skinny fella" who had arrived with him at Karachi, was from a rural area of North Texas, making him likely the man called upon to be ready with his gun. The strangers turned out to be friendly Chinese, who took them to "the underground," a network of villagers who fed and sheltered them and helped them return to their base.[26]

The day following the crash was a busy one, according to Hugel: "Confident we were in Chinese pocket after being discovered by Chinese patrol at 0445 hours. Patrol leader led us into the town of Tung Chuan approximately ½ mile from where we had spent the night. Introduced to the town magistrate[,] who spoke broken English and [was] a army captain." An English-speaking school teacher translated. They were served a breakfast of hard-boiled eggs and tea at a nearby shop. Greene relayed messages to the American commanding officer at Lihuang describing the condition of the aircraft and crew.

After daylight, crew members returned to the plane and assessed the damage. Then they prepared the parachutes, bombsight, and camera for transport and removed rations. "Returned to village and bathed in a natural hot spring. Refreshed, we were put on the road in the direction of Valley Field by the Chinese," Hugel wrote. "A Chinese patrol consisting of five soldiers and the captain together with a score of coolies carrying our equipment accompanied us. The terrain was fairly rough and the day warm with a cool breeze." They left the village at 0900 hours. Served hot water and "weak tea" at various small shops en route, the crew walked to the city of Shang Cheng (32°53' N, 115°21' E), 12 miles north.

The party arrived at a Chinese regimental headquarters 3 miles outside the city, where they met Col. Lee, secretary to the general of the 51st Army, and other officers. Hugel noted, "Col. Lee speaks broken English." The 51st Army, which had suffered heavy losses earlier in the war in Shandong Province over control of this vital piece of real estate located between the Japanese-occupied north of China and the Shanghai and Nanking areas, was reduced to division strength.

Very active in the Dabie Mountain area (a central China mountain range that constitutes the boundary between Hubei Province and Honan Province to the north and Anhui Province to the east), it operated as an effective guerrilla force inside occupied territory. Guerrilla forces at that time were generally far more effective than Chinese regular troops. Led by their own, they had an intimate knowledge of the countryside and knew how to live off the land. Guerrillas seldom engaged in actual combat against the enemy. Instead, they hurt the Japanese as much as possible by engaging in acts of sabotage and assisting downed airmen to return to their bases.[27]

Members of the crew were served a light lunch and then continued along their way on horseback. At the outskirts of the city, they were met by Lt. Gen. Chow (Zhou) Yu-ying, commanding general of the 51st Army, and his staff. They all dismounted, and Col. Lee made introductions. After remounting, the processional entered the city. These were the first Caucasians ever to enter Shang Cheng, a city with a population of ten thousand, and multitudes of the city's civilian population turned out to see them. "People line the streets by the score. Every pair of eyes are on us. The air is filled with the smoke of firecrackers. It is a terrific ovation. A candidate for president at a convention couldn't have received a better welcome than we," wrote Hugel. In passing an officers training school, they discovered that the entire school was out in full dress. The visitors reviewed them with proper military respect. Their welcome march lasted about a half hour. Afterward they were led to an exclusive hotel where they met Dr. Liu, Chinese government entomologist of the district, who was "English spoken and a post-grad of Harvard University (Boxer Indemnity)." They were then introduced to Magistrate Koo and "other army wheels." After being served refreshments and allowed time to bathe, "we hit the sack for several hours. At 2000 hours we are given a dinner. Our host for this meal was General Yu, a representative of the Chinese National army from Chungking. The meal consists of approximately twenty to twenty-five courses."

Earlier in the day, each of the Americans had received a formal invitation to the dinner. Bob Banger's invitation, now in the possession of his daughter, reads: "Lt. General Y. Y. Chow, Commander of the 51 Army, requests the honor of Lt. Robert E. Banger's company at dinner at 6:30 on the afternoon of May 29 at the Headquarters of the Army."[28]

Lt. Robert E. Banger, navigator on this mission, kept the formal invitation to a dinner hosted by Lt. Gen. Y. Y. Chou, commander of the 51st Army. R. E. Banger collection, courtesy of Beth Banger Meehan

The following morning, the men had a late breakfast with Dr. Liu and Mr. Young of the army. "That morning we meet more wheels representing city schools, chamber of commerce, etc. Our noon meal was served with Magistrate Koo acting as host. Strictly Chinese menu with about fifteen courses. The afternoon is spent soaking up the hospitality of our host."

That evening, the commanding general and staff of the 51st Army invited them to dine at army headquarters. During dinner, Lt. W. G. Miller and Fisk, his Chinese interpreter of the Army Ground Aid Station (AGAS), arrived from Lihuang to take charge of the downed flight crew and assist them in returning to their base. After dinner, a Chinese drama was presented for their entertainment. Hugel wrote, "Pay off of the drama is when one of the characters sings Old Black Joe in English and does the Fox Trot across the stage. Following the drama, we thank the general for his kindness and return to our hotel."

After their B-25J went down in "the pocket" near Sinyang on May 28, members of its aircrew were taken in and lavishly feted by their rescuers. Seated here near an ancient pagoda, the Americans are (*left to right*) Lt. W. G. Miller (Army Ground Aid Station at Lihuang), Sgt. E. W. Peters (radio), TSgt. H. D. Reynard (photographer), Capt. F. H. Greene Jr. (pilot), 1Lt. R. E. Banger (navigator), SSgt. W. H. Whearty (engineer / top-turret gunner), Cpl. R. G. Hugel (tail gunner), and 1Lt. W. H. Senecal (copilot). The Chinese notables, *standing*, are not individually identified but include Dr. Liu, Mr. Lee, Lt. Gen. Chow (Zhou) Yu-ying, commanding general of the 51st Army, and his staff; the tall man wearing a dark traditional robe is Magistrate Koos. *F. H. Greene Jr. collection, courtesy of Sibyl Greene Cryer*

On Wednesday after breakfast, they assembled to have their photograph taken with Dr. Liu, Mr. Lee, Magistrate Koo, and the general and his staff in front of a 1,400-year-old pagoda. Each member of the party was presented a copy, while the civilian photographer retained the negatives. During the morning, Greene made a speech to school children. It was one of about a dozen speeches that he was called upon to make while they were in the area. An article that listed the names of the city's foreign visitors appeared in the local newspaper.

That afternoon, Greene, Miller, Fisk, Peters, and Whearty traveled by horseback back to the plane to salvage whatever they could, including bombsight, radio equipment, and other miscellaneous equipment that could be removed with few tools and transported by coolies. The CAF's Commission on Aeronautical Affairs (COAA) later salvaged the remainder of the aircraft, since it was impractical to repair and fly it out. Banger, Senecal, Reynard, and Hugel took advantage of the free time to "hit the horizontal." Later that afternoon, Dr. Liu took the four of them swimming in a nearby pond. Returning after the swim to the hotel, they met an eleven-year-old Russian American boy—a refugee who was attempting to get to the States. The boy had been turned over to guerrilla representatives by Communist troops in the southwest. AGAS took control of the situation. They also met a P-51 pilot, Lt. Chen, who had bailed out of his stricken ship and was trying to get back to his base at Hanchung. "Greene and party return laden with radio equipment. Wash up, eat, and hit the sack."

Hugel's Thursday entry: "Prepare for departure. Receive many gifts from everyone." They were each presented with souvenirs that included silk handkerchiefs inscribed "Shang Cheng" and their names, as well as autograph books signed by Chinese personnel present, both military and civilians. At 0900 the party (with the addition of Lt. Miller, Fisk, and Lt. Chen) got underway for the American base at Lihuang. "We are told that it is a two-day journey and that we must be constantly on our guard from enemy assassins that have infiltrated into the area." Greene recorded the distance as 40 miles. The "convoy" consisted of ten sedan chairs, one hundred coolies to carry the men and their equipment, and a detachment of twelve soldiers. "Travel all day in beautiful country. At noon we stop at a small village for food. Continue traveling until 1700 hrs[,] when we stop for the night at a small village deep in the heart of the mountains. Bathe in nearby stream. Eat and hit the sack. Straw mattresses have plenty of bed bugs. Senecal and I are their victims."

On Friday, June 1, they were on the road by 0700 hours. "Rough going along steep mountain foot paths. Forced to leave sedan chairs several times to climb steep grades," Hugel wrote. They stopped in the afternoon to bathe in a mountain stream before resuming their journey, arriving at Lihuang at 1800 hours. Hugel described it as a small American base only recently established. "Bathe and shave. (First shave in five days.) Resort to the horizontal."

Greene wrote that after arriving at Lihuang they reported to Lt. Vernon Hill, commanding officer, AGAS Station. The men were warned that Japanese agents and assassins were active in the area, so Chinese troops escorted them during all of their movements outside the hostel area.

They all slept late the following morning, according to Hugel. They decided to remain where they were for the day before pushing on to Valley Field, 30 miles from Lihuang. "Lay around all morning and afternoon. Late afternoon we walk through the town for a looksee. One of the cleanest villages I've got to see in China. Chow at 1900 hrs and hit the sack."

After an early breakfast on Sunday, they proceeded to Valley Field on horseback. "Travel through mountains on small paths. Horses gave us all a rough time. We forge small streams and rivers. Noon we stop, eat and bathe in stream. Continue journey[,] stopping a lot to rest horses. Arrive at Valley Field 1830 hours. We all have plenty of saddle sores. Eat and sack up." On Monday the tired men slept late and waited for a B-25 or C-47 to pick them up. No transport appeared. They filled the time as they waited by swimming. At noon on Tuesday, a C-47 flown by Lt. Col. D. E. Coster and escorted by two P-51s finally arrived to take them back to base. The return was uneventful except for some light flak in flight. The men landed at Liangshan on the afternoon of June 5, none the worse for wear and with stories to tell.

Greene wrote in his report dated June 7, "Chinese civilian and military personnel displayed great hospitality to our party and made every effort to cooperate. A.G.A.S. personnel also were extremely cooperative and rendered aid and comfort in every way possible." Lt. Banger, as squadron security officer, came under censure for allowing the group photograph to be taken at Shang Cheng, although Lt. Miller, as AGAS representative, had offered no objection. Their souvenirs, including copies of the photograph, were confiscated after their return and held as classified material. Seventy years later, Hugel still remembered his adventures in vivid detail.

As Lt. Greene and his crew began their adventure, the remaining three planes went on to complete the mission. Flying A/C #715, Pulaski (with Drake, Faherty, Cantor, Jakubasz, DeFabritis, and Stearns) led, with A/C #721 (Cheng Y. K., Chen Y. P., Ting C. L., Chang Y., Liu T. C., and Wang M. T.) and #725 (Chang K. L., Chang L. T., Lee C. C., Chen Y. C., Tung N. T., and Chung C.) in wing positions, to scout for targets of opportunity. At 5 miles south of Sinyang, they sighted a locomotive and twenty cars. Two planes dropped ten 250 lb. GPs by pilot release that scored one direct hit on the cars, four reported as destroyed and four others as probables. Six bombs hit and destroyed sections of track, but three fell farther to the right. One plane dropped seventeen M1A1 bombs. Three hit the tracks about 100 yards from the train, and the other fourteen hit to the side. Definite damage was inflicted on the locomotive by strafing, the hits estimated as seven hundred. One plane dropped ten M1A1 frags on railroad yards at Sinyang, scoring five hits and five misses. Although a convoy of trucks was sighted near Anlu, the remaining bombs were not released because all switched off their lights. Seven M1A1s were returned to base.

Lt. Kilian, who had been sent on detached service to the 2nd Bomb Squadron on May 12, was transferred to that squadron on the twenty-fourth. The following week, Lts. Ilefeldt and Fuller returned to Liangshan with "some Air Corps supply equipment," at the same time bringing back with them TSgts. Gruber and Meikle, SSgts. Holmes and Evitts, and Cpl. Piecuch, who had spent a week at rest camp. Cpl. Morris returned with them after being released from the hospital, where he had been recovering from a broken ankle. "Morris walks with a limp with the aid of a cane, which he will discard in a month or so," wrote Ilefeldt.

Uncertainty persisted regarding the crew reported as shot down on the sixteenth. Another intelligence report with an authenticity rating of "reliable" came in through Communications. It claimed that two of the men were dead, one seriously injured and hospitalized, and the rest taken prisoner.

Word circulated through base personnel that 1Lt. Lois G. Bains, who had served briefly with the 3rd Squadron the previous autumn, had failed to return from a 2nd Bomb Squadron low-level mission on May 26. As pilot of a B-25H, he was off Liangshan at 0500 with a crew that consisted of Lt. Kuo C. (navigator), Cpls. Charles B. Knight (engineer-turret gunner) and William C. Hawks (radio-waist gunner), and Sgt. Lo L. J. (tail gunner), in search of targets of opportunity. Contact was last made after takeoff, when the wing plane turned back because of engine trouble. The bomber proceeded to section 7 of the Ping-Han Railroad (between Chenghsien and Sinyang) in the Lohochai sector, known to be well protected by small arms and automatic weapons. Subsequent searches of the area produced no results, and crew members were reported as MIA and presumed dead.

Cpl. Johnson, attached to the same squadron, wrote in his memoirs that the Mitchell had attacked a Japanese railroad train that had been sighted by Chinese intelligence Johnson was originally scheduled to fly the mission, but Bill Hawks, who had recently completed his required fifty missions and was waiting for orders to go home, volunteered to fly one more mission if he was permitted to fly on the train-strafing mission. Johnson revealed that Charlie Knight, usually an optimist, had a premonition of his own death and said on the previous evening that this would be his last flight.

"No one really knew what had happened to Charlie's B-25 that day," Johnson wrote. "It took off before dawn, and when I returned from our mission to Hankow, it hadn't returned. My friends and I stood on a hill overlooking our airfield all day, watching and waiting for word." Nothing was ever heard from them. For several days, 2nd Squadron planes searched the area where the train had been destroyed, but no sign of them or their B-25 was found. About two weeks later, Chinese intelligence reported that the B-25 had crashed, leaving no survivors. Their airplane went down in a populated farm area, and local Chinese buried the crew's bodies and notified the Chinese authorities as to the location of their graves.

"We wondered what had happened to Charlie's airplane to cause it to crash. In strafing ground targets, the B-25 pilot aimed the cannon and machine guns in the nose of the airplane through an optical gun sight located on the instrument panel in front of him. A pilot might become so intent on looking through the gun sight at what he was shooting that he might forget that he was flying only a few feet above the ground and could crash into it at 250 miles per hour." He revealed that Bains was not considered to be a very competent pilot, so they suspected that was what had happened. "Alternatively, the B-25 might have been hit by ground fire and the pilot either lost control or the airplane might have been damaged and became uncontrollable. We would never know what caused the airplane to crash. All we knew was that there were no survivors, and our friends were dead."[29]

When their bodies were recovered from their common grave near the crash site at Chuchou in Anhwei Province (Chuzhou, Anhui Province) and moved to Mausoleum No. 2 in the Hawaiian Islands, authorities were unable to individually identify the bodies of Bains and Hawks. Their remains were shipped to the US and buried together at Little Rock National Cemetery, Little Rock, Arkansas.

On the day following the 2nd Squadron crew's disappearance, Lts. Ilefeldt and Fuller left for Chengtu, taking with them Sgt. England, who was to be hospitalized there. TSgt. Rieks, SSgt. McCann, and Sgt. Trout left for Kunming to begin their return to the ZI. Rieks's final mission had been against bridge #113 on May 13, and Trout had participated in his last mission against the same target on May 26.

The last mission on which McCann was listed as a crew member had been on February 11. Suffering from malarial relapses for some time, he was very sick and weighed only about 130 pounds when he returned home. He was hospitalized and then entered the convalescent hospital at Greensboro in August. After being released the following month, he was discharged from military service for disability.[30]

In addition to being hit in the head by a fire ax, he had at some time (date undetermined) been wounded by shrapnel, although no mention of it has been found in records for the 3rd Bomb Squadron, Task Force 34, or the 1st Bomb Group. Doc Yeoh removed the shrapnel by using acupuncture. McCann told his family that he felt no pain during the procedure. He continued to correspond with the Chinese doctor, who spoke and wrote English, for years afterward. According to McCann's postwar registration with the local draft board, he had a 4-inch "Service Scar on right side." He admitted to being afraid on missions and told his family, "I knew I would never live through that war." Regardless of his earlier pessimism, he was always good natured and positive where his family was concerned, and told them that every laugh he had after he returned home was "icing on the cake."[31]

The final mission of the month off on the morning of May 29 once again had bridge #102 as the target of four B-25s. Takeoff was at 0945. Five P-51s provided escort. The 3rd Fighter Group pilots were 1Lts. Thomas J. Cribbs, Charles H. Freeburn, and Laurence Kelly and 2Lts. Dallas S. Cone and Mitchell W. Beardsley. Hamilton led, piloting A/C #721 (with Drake, Gaffney, Magyar, Mier, and Schroeder), and #722 (Teng C. C., Yang P. C., Shen M. C., Li L., Kuo H. Y., and Wei C. S.), #716 (MacNeil, Pulaski, Schlicher, DeFabritis, Cantor, and Stearns), and #725 (Chang C. L., Yen P. S., Kao W. C., Liu H. T., Kao C. K., and Chow K. P.) followed. Destroying the bridge was considered crucial to disruption of the enemy's supply line between north and south.

Capt. Hamilton first made a bombing pass to hit gun positions at each end of the bridge. Eleven of the plane's seventeen M1A1 frags, released at 1,500 feet, fell along the edges of the bridge, but six failed to release and were brought back. Lt. Teng and Capt. MacNeil took their Mitchells down to 100 feet to strafe the gun positions, and then Lt Chang dropped eight 500 lb. GPs at 600 feet. Two spans on the southern end of the bridge fell into the water. The bombers circled and made a second run using the same tactics—one plane fragged, two strafed, and the trailing plane dropped GPs. This time, definite damage was reported to the north portion of the bridge. Ground fire began to be received after the first pass, but no damage was reported.

Because bridge #102 had been knocked out, the planes flew on to bridge #101, 5 miles farther north. The same strategy of fragging, strafing, and bombing that had proved successful on bridge #102 was again used on three runs, but only one of the 500 lb. bombs hit the bridge's railing. Three of the bombers and three fighters proceeded back to base. Schroeder's log gave the mission's target as Wangkiahie, and the duration as three hours and fifteen minutes. Capt. Hamilton and two of the fighters took a heading to Valley Field to contact the crew reported

Turning the Tide

to have landed there. Finding no evidence of the plane or crew, they took off again and returned to Liangshan, logged as an administrative mission.

Through the month of May, life for the men stationed at Liangshan proceeded in a way they had come to consider as normal. Lt. Eisner, bomb group historical officer, lamented that Liangshan's mess was not as good as at Peishiyi, although the same provisions were available to cooks at both bases. His proposed solution was the appointment of a mess officer. There were still movies three times a week. "In the barracks, bull sessions abound, with card games and an occasional 'Gambey' party to liven up otherwise dull evenings," he added. "Hunting around for a unique form of relaxation, the officers came up with the idea of having picnics on afternoons off. Three have been held to date, with great success." Their favorite outing spot was a mountain stream and waterfall on the road to Wanhsien.

Hank recalled, "For fun, there was a river that, in summertime, we'd go to it, swim in it. That was about the only fun we had, I guess. I don't know how many times we went there, but someone discovered a dead Chinese." He did not recall whether it was upstream or down, "but we never went there again. It was warm weather, and it was a time when we weren't having enough gas to fly."

The men occasionally visited the "Cockeye Restaurant" or the "Friends of the Allies Club" (recommended for its "good Chinese food") in Liangshan village, and some of them visited the brothel that had recently opened.

The 2nd Squadron's Cpl. Johnson described an event that occurred at about this time, likely involving the "Friends of the Allies Club" mentioned by Eisner. In the early spring of 1945, Chinese authorities built a recreational facility in Liangshan called "the Chinese American Friendship Club," he wrote in his memoirs. "A banquet hall, game room and meeting rooms were set in a pleasant park-like surrounding, and to kick off the friendship theme, American and Chinese enlisted men were invited to a banquet one evening." The American GIs were warned to behave and not drink too much or otherwise cause problems that might offend the Chinese.

At the banquet, Chinese officials gave speeches praising the friendship between the two countries with their diverse cultures. An English-speaking Chinese interpreter was assigned to each table. "We were served a delicious Chinese dinner and one of the items was dumplings filled with a spicy meat," Johnson recalled. "The interpreter was reluctant to tell us what was in the dumplings that made them so tasty. Eventually, he admitted they contained dog meat, but by then we all had drunk enough wine that it didn't matter—we just enjoyed."

Each Chinese speaker paused frequently and held up a tiny cup of warm rice wine as a toast, each time calling out "Gambay" (bottoms up). The guests then raised their cups and repeated "Gambay," suggesting that they agreed with what he had said. "The evening went smoothly, and no one became obnoxiously drunk, which was a wonder after many toasts of the warm wine."

The banquet held for the officers on the following evening was not as successful. Some of the American officers became quite drunk and "rudely responded to the Chinese speeches by saying that China was a dirty, smelly place with a corrupt government that did nothing for its citizens." They added that the Chinese were "lousy fighters" and it was up to the Americans to save China, which in their opinion wasn't worth saving. The Chinese were, of course, insulted, and lost face, Johnson related. "No friendship was built that night, and the friendship club never opened for business after that disaster."[32]

As May came to a close, the squadron's statistical report showed twenty-nine American officers, forty-nine American enlisted men, seventy-nine Chinese officers, and 131 Chinese enlisted men. Of the eleven B-25s assigned, four were H models and seven were Js. All the recently assigned aircraft were J models. The old Hs would continue to be used "until claimed by attrition," according to Ilefeldt. Two aircraft were in the service group for repairs: one H and one J. During the month, Hamilton's squadron had completed sixty-four sorties against the enemy, nine of them on medium-altitude and fifteen on low-level missions. Bombs dropped by squadron aircraft on enemy installations totaled 583 (89 tons). These included three 500 lb. demos, 100 250 lb. RDX, thirty-two 1,000 lb. demos, twelve 100 lb. demos, 202 frags, ten napalm, six butterfly, and twelve incendiaries.

The Japanese, after withdrawing forces following the Chihkiang campaign, were making progress toward concentrating troops along the East China Sea to protect their coastal cities against the anticipated Allied invasion. With the full expectation that the home islands would soon be overrun, imperial forces continued their preparations to make their final stand in China. Troops were digging in and reinforcing their garrisons in the vicinities of Canton and Shanghai. Additional troops were sent to the Swatow and Amoy coastal areas between the Canton–Hong Kong area and Foochow. Chinese troops reoccupied former 14th Air Force bases along the escape corridor as the Japanese pulled out.

As the Chinese trailed the retreating enemy, preparations were, in fact, underway for a plan of attack named "CARBANADO" to be launched in August. It called for a rapid advance by Chinese ground forces to the coast to seize Fort Bayard on the Liuchow Peninsula, about 250 miles southwest of Canton, followed by a push from the Kweilin-Liuchow area on September 1, with a final assault on Canton on November 1. Wedemeyer continued moving forward with his plan until the war's end appeared inevitable.

The Allies had additionally begun making plans for an offensive to be launched in its first phase against the southernmost main Japanese island of Kyushu. Under code name "OPERATION DOWNFALL," preparations had begun in early 1945 for the invasion that was scheduled to take place on November 1 (designated "X-Day"), to be coordinated with the attack on Canton for maximum intimidation value, although no details were made public until after the war ended. Casualty predictions on both sides varied according to the source but were consistently estimated as extremely high. Maynard Rieks recalled that the men of the 3rd Squadron had heard rumors and were expecting to provide air support for the invasion of Japan, but it was a venture that few of them expected to survive.[33]

In response to Allied advances in the Pacific, the Japanese persisted in preparations for the anticipated invasion of their home islands as well as port cities along the China coast. Tokyo recalled some of its Manchurian troops to Japan and issued warning orders to prepare for concentrating forces in the Yangtze River valley between Shanghai and Hankow; around the main ports of China, such as Shanghai and Canton; and across northern China, joining with the remaining units of the Manchurian Kwangtung Army. Newly mobilized units from Japan were to be sent as reinforcements. Redeployment of forces in China was intended to guard against not only the anticipated American amphibious landings along the coast, but also a possible Soviet attack from the north. Japanese leaders hoped not only to deny the Allies staging areas from which they could support the coastal attacks, but additionally to protect Chinese mines and factories, which could still supply Japan's military forces.[34]

All four of the 1st Bomb Group squadrons maintained their focus on destroying bridges and burning supplies as the Japanese withdrew. The 4th Bomb Squadron, operating out of Chihkiang, received credit for the majority of the group's total for the month, and the 3rd Squadron soon began making plans to join the 4th in the heavy action there.

Turning the Tide

CHAPTER SIXTEEN
End in Sight

Days in early June dawned sunny and warm. Lt. Pulaski and Sgts. Schlicher and Supsic left for Kunming to pick up yet another new B-25J. Lt. Mikola transferred to the 2nd Squadron, and 1Sgt. Earley and SSgts. Dunlap and Mier left to take their turn at rest camp. Squadron personnel began to receive their mail via a new address during this period. Still APO 627 after the move from Peishiyi to Liangshan, it was changed to APO 271.

Another report came in concerning the squadron's missing aircrew, stating that five of the men had been killed in action and one who had been injured was captured by the enemy. Although still officially MIA, FO Wherritt's promotion to second lieutenant was confirmed. Capt. Hamilton was promoted to major and 1Lt. Greene to captain. Other promotions were SSgts. Holmes and Mier to technical sergeants, Sgts. Long (noted as radio chief) and Whearty to staff sergeants, and Cpls. Magyar, Supsic, and Schlicher to sergeants. Schlicher, who began preflight training in April 1943 at Kansas State College, Fort Hays, which was intended to prepare him to become an aviation cadet, had nevertheless proved his capability in aerial combat. He was awarded the Air Medal for completion of more than one hundred hours of combat flying as a B-25 engineer-gunner, according to a newspaper write-up at his hometown in South Louisiana.[1]

At the same time, TSgt. Barge joined the "Zebra Club" with his promotion to master sergeant—"three stripes up and three down." His high school friend who served as wing A-1, Col. McGehee, sent another status report to their hometown newspaper that included news of John Barge's promotion. In it, he included excerpts from a letter that he had recently received from Barge: "A few days ago a Chinese peddler came around selling sets

Sgt. Robert E. Schlicher Jr. joined the squadron as an A/P mechanic–gunner–flight engineer and works here with a pipe-smoking Chinese mechanic to keep this B-25 in top condition for operations. *R. E. Schlicher Jr. collection, courtesy of Charles Schlicher*

of Chinese stamps. They aren't much, but I thought some of the kids back home might like to have them. So, I'm enclosing three sets of them and I would appreciate it if you would give them to some of the younger generation of collectors."

McGehee wrote that Barge was an airplane maintenance technician and line chief. "He has really done a wonderful job with us," he stated. "We all wish we had more like him." The editor of the newspaper promised to pass along the stamps to the local scoutmaster for use by boys who were working on a merit badge in collecting.

In his letter, McGee provided a lengthy description of the war situation from his personal point of view, told in a way the folks back home could not read about it in their local newspapers:

> Everything has been going along pretty well over here. It's still the forgotten theater so far as men and supplies go, but we have all learned to do pretty well with practically nothing. I'm enclosing a clipping of the activities of one of our groups in repelling the recent Jap offensive against Chihkiang. You people back there probably heard very little about it, but we over here all are very proud of it. It was truly a glorious victory for the US and China and was the first time the long line of Jap conquests in China was broken and the enemy utterly defeated. This, of course, is the spectacular part of what we do over here, but day in and day out the Japs know we are around. . . .
>
> You probably wonder what brought on the above paragraph and here is the answer. We get pretty fed up with the question "What do you people do in China? We never get any news back here." That is what we always hear from home and from the people who are new arrivals over here. So maybe the above and the clipping will give you an idea of our part in what is going on over here.[2]

Capt. Joseph A. Langridge joined from the 2nd Bomb Squadron as assistant intelligence officer. Born in Cordova, Mexico, about 80 miles inland from Veracruz, his early childhood had acquainted him with danger. In 1914, as "gringos" were being rounded up and shot during the Mexican Revolution, he and his family took refuge in the British embassy at Veracruz before escaping by Marine gunboat to Corpus Christi, Texas. Later they evacuated from a category 4 hurricane that hit their home in 1916. Although married and holding a responsible position with a financial institution, he had volunteered for service soon after hearing news of the attack on Pearl Harbor. Langridge was determined to get into the military, despite a detached retina that resulted in extremely limited vision in one eye, so he "cheated" on the eye exam and passed.

Capt. Joseph A. Langridge, the squadron's new assistant intelligence officer, is shown here in the obligatory rickshaw photo. *J. A. Langridge collection, courtesy of Susan Langridge Rees*

A favorite story that he later told his children involved traveling by ship up a large river as he arrived in India (probably at Calcutta). The area was densely populated, and hundreds of locals came out in canoes, begging for handouts of either money or food. One of the Americans had a Baby Ruth candy bar and tossed it out to one of them, thinking that it would be a special treat. The day was warm, and the chocolate was soft. Never having seen a Baby Ruth before, the man thought it was "poop," so he threw it into the river and angrily shook his fist at the soldiers. They, of course, thought it was hilarious. Like many others, Langridge caught a bad case of dysentery while he was in China, and endured its effects for long afterward.[3]

Maj. Drake, who had been flying missions as an operational officer with 3rd Squadron bombers, received orders for transfer to the 4th Squadron. Effective June 5, he replaced Capt. Henry A. Stanley, who was moving to Group Operations, as the "Lucky Lady" squadron's commanding officer.

Lt. Francis H. Bowen proved his value by flying eleven 3rd Bomb Squadron missions as a navigator-bombardier before hostilities ended. *Courtesy of Steve Bowen*

Transferred in on the ninth was 1Lt. Francis H. Bowen, navigator-bombardier, who had served with the 11th Bomb Squadron, 341st Bomb Group of the 69th Composite Wing, since October 1944. Bowen had originally enlisted as a diesel mechanic in the tank corps but later transferred to the Air Corps. According to unconfirmed family stories, he was shot down twice. On the first occasion, he was picked up by Chinese pirates, who stole everything except a small compass kept hidden by one of the crew members, and then turned them loose naked on the beach. The second time, Bowen was captured by a Japanese patrol and spent some time in a POW camp. Awarded the Purple Heart, he had only recently been released when he was attached to the 3rd Squadron, in which he proved to be a valuable asset.[4]

The squadron's Chinese received more personnel during this period, when three additions to the Armament section were attached: Sgts. Chen Shu-yi (X-2283), Ho Yang-king (X-1712), and Yun Chang-chen (X-1715). A few days later, 1Lt. Ting Cheng-liang was ordered to travel by first available aircraft for temporary duty at Peishiyi, his purpose not stated, and 1Lt. Wang Kuan-che (X-958) was ordered to the hospital at Chengtu for observation and treatment.

The squadron's historical report for June, but dated August 3, stated that early that month, "Chinese Air Force Wings were officially awarded to Major Hamilton, Capt. Greene, 1Lt. Davis, and F/O Wherritt. Lt. Davis and F/O Wherritt may never receive the wings, for a third and probably final intelligence report

Lt. Donald J. Davis sent this photo home to his wife, Jeanette. It seems to prove that he was awarded Chinese Air Force Wings sometime before his death at Ichang. *D. J. Davis collection, courtesy of Jarrett McConnell*

Chapter Sixteen

F/O Barton L. Wherritt sent a similar photo home to his family. *Courtesy of Terry Godfrey Healy*

Lt. Willard G. Ilefeldt was part of the group who received their Chinese wings from Lt. Col. Hsu Huan-sheng. *Courtesy of Christine Ilefeldt Hance*

Lt. Wayne H. Senecal sent this photo home to his family. *Courtesy of Kevin Senecal*

Lt. Robert L. Logan seems to have received his wings at the same time as the others. *R. L. Logan Collection, courtesy of Katherine A. Logan*

came the first week of June concerning the ill-fated crew." According to the report, five of the men had died in the crash and a sixth was taken captive by the enemy. Confusion arises from the fact that Davis and Wherritt had sent home photographs of themselves receiving their wings, presented by Lt. Col. Hsu Huan-sheng, Chinese deputy commander of the CACW, so obviously before the May 16 mission. Lts. Ilefeldt, Logan, Senecal, and Hamilton sent home similar photos of themselves, but the dates the wings were awarded remains a mystery.

When Hamilton's proud mother received a letter from him soon afterward, she contacted the Houston newspaper to spread the news about her son's most recent accomplishments. The article stated, "A veteran pilot with 60 hard-earned missions . . . to his credit, Maj. Jack M. Hamilton went all the way to China to receive a pair of wings. He has been overseas for a second tour of duty since January of this year." It went on to briefly explain the CACW's cooperative efforts with the Chinese air force, which had presented him the wings. "Jack doesn't write much about what he's doing because he's afraid I might worry," Mrs. Hamilton was quoted as saying. "He has complained about the food though."[5]

End in Sight

Group historian Lt. Eisner wrote as the month began that "the outlook for June seems to be very poor[,] with current schedules giving us very little in the way of gasoline. Such a situation is beyond anything we can do, so we shall sit tight awaiting such a time as the high command deems our operations important enough to warrant giving us the necessary supplies." The chronically short supply of gasoline limited the 3rd Squadron to only four missions during the month.

Two Mitchells took off at 1525 on June 3 to search once again for targets of opportunity along the Ping-Han Railroad, with Maj. Hamilton leading. Each carried ten M57 250 lb. demos. Hamilton flew A/C #718 (Ilefeldt, Yang C. H., Cantor, Holmes, and DeFabritis as his aircrew), and Capt. Lo S. S. followed in #719 (Chang L. T., Kao W. C., Chang C., Chen Y. C., and Yuan C. F.). They proceeded directly to the railroad 5 miles north of Sinyang and then turned north along the tracks. At the railroad bridge at Mingkiang, Lo dropped all of his bombs, which fell short and to the east. Maj. Hamilton dropped his bombs on trackage between Sinyang (Xinyang) and Lohochai. Tracks were twisted and turned up. Two bombs were duds that bounced off the tracks and into rice paddies. Hamilton's gunners strafed a previously damaged locomotive, as well as what he believed to be another locomotive camouflaged under natural foliage in a small siding. Crewmen reported that it may have been a booby trap because it was "in a position that was easy to see yet camouflaged in an obvious way with tree boughs," and the plane that made the strafing run over the locomotive was holed by five hits from small-arms fire.

Four planes took off at 0515 on the fifth, Hamilton leading the first echelon with a mixed crew aboard A/C #714 (with Tsuei W. P., Yang C., Barge, DeFabritis, Wilkerson, and Stearns), and A/C #719 (Chow K. C., Chiang T., Liu C. C., Ku C. T., Kao C. H., and Wei C. S.) flew on his wing. MacNeil, pilot of A/C #721 (with Ilefeldt, Holmes, Long, Allegretto, and Schroeder) led the second echelon, with #722 (Chen S. C., Chang Y. K., Chang Y. C., Liu H. T., Wang M. T., and Chang Y.) as his wing plane. They were searching for any activity along the roads northeast of the city of Nanyang to Hsiang-Chengyang and vicinity. MacNeil's gunners first strafed trucks on the outskirts of the village of Sanehihlitien, 2 miles south of Nanyang, and more sighted northeast of Nanyang between Poyang and Chaohochen. Flying on, he dropped nine M1A1 frag clusters in the northeast quadrant of Nanyang. Lt. Chen's gunners strafed two barracks and an estimated 150 enemy soldiers about a mile north of the village of Chaohochen before bombing Nanyang. Then Maj. Hamilton's and Lt. Chow's gunners strafed trucks northeast of Nanyang before the pilots dropped their bombs on the city. Coming across two field guns on the road, A/C #719 strafed those before taking a heading for home.

An article dated June 7 in the *China Lantern* quoted a statement from HQ US Chinese Combat Command that described the action in China during this first week of June:

> As the week ended, the Japanese, after having given up the relatively important Nanning-Liuchow corridor town south of Pinyang and Tsinkong, had reached the area of Tatang, less than 35 miles from Liuchow. Though closely followed by the Chinese forces and subjected to harassing rear guard actions, there were no indications that the enemy withdrawal was not according to plan, thus strengthening the Allied belief that a change in overall Japanese strategy for the interior of South China has occurred, the full implications of which can only be surmised.
>
> Planned or otherwise, however, the fact remains that each day of the past seven found more hundreds of square miles of formerly Jap[-]occupied Chinese

territory in Chinese hands and more tens of thousands of Chinese civilians liberated from enemy domination. The Chinese advance northeastward from Nanning through Pinyang and Tsinkong to the Tatang area represents a gain of 115 air miles since the reoccupation of Nanning on May 27[,] indicating the scope of the enemy withdrawal.

Little ground action was reported elsewhere in the China theater. East-northeast of Liuchow, in the area of Ishan, Japanese forces had stopped their retreat from the former Hochih salient. Southwest of Nanning, the Chinese reoccupied Sohu and had reached the area of Suilu, near the French Indochina border in the Paoching area. In western Hunan, combat lines were drawn in essentially the same positions as those from which the Japanese launched their abortive offensive toward Chihkiang in early April.[6]

Chinese ground forces retook Liuchow on June 6 as the Japanese in Kwangsi Province continued their steady withdrawal from the Nanning area. Liuchow's airfield, overrun by enemy troops seven months earlier, was the first of nine in southern China to be recaptured within a period of weeks as the Chinese trailed the retreating enemy. It became obvious that the Japanese would not try to redeploy troops south of the Yellow River, and before the end of the month, coastal positions below Shanghai that had previously been strongly held were being evacuated. There were even signs that the estimated 100,000 troops in the Canton region would be moved out.[7]

Four planes were off in two echelons at 0900 on the seventh and proceeded to Kuanshuishih to hit railroad bridge #277 (31°37′ N, 113°55′ E). Capt. MacNeil was leader of the first flight, and Lt. Teng C. C. was his wingman. Lt. Ilefeldt led the second element, and Lt. Yen flew on his wing. A/C #717 (Yen P. S., Kuo Y. H., Lai H. L., Chow K. P., and Chen K. Y.) turned back between Ichang and the target due to an "alleged" mechanical problem involving its right engine (oil leak, smoke, and uneven performance), although subsequent examination and testing determined that the engine was operative. On his way back to Liangshan, Lt. Teng dropped his eight 500 lb. GP bombs along the road 5 to 10 miles southeast of Ichang. Three were direct hits that fell in an unidentified village, from which black smoke rose to 500 feet, and two were near misses.

The other three Mitchells proceeded to the target. In an effort to reduce the amount of damage being caused to the planes by ground fire, a strategy similar to that tried in late May was used. On approach, Lt. Ilefeldt, flying A/C #724 (Lowy R. L., Lee C. C., Barge, DeFabritis, Jakubasz, and Stearns as his crew), pulled away from the formation and "surprised the target" by coming in low from behind a mountain in the vicinity of the bridge. He made seven strafing passes that started fires and destroyed two flak towers and machine gun positions near the bridge, as well as machine gun nests along the ridge. On the first two passes, his gunners hit the flak towers and the first machine gun pits with eleven M1A1 frag clusters and ten 100 lb. demolition bombs. On the next three passes, gunners covered gun positions along the ridge and near the bridge with a hail of machine gun fire. The final two passes were coordinated with the other planes.

Capt. MacNeil's A/C #725 (with Yang P. C., Ting C. L., Holmes, Magyar, Mills, and Schroeder), made a strafing pass with A/C #724 over the bridge and approaches before following up with bombing. The pilot released eight 300 lb. GP bombs. Four were direct hits: one each on the roadbed, north approach, south approach, and first span from the south bank. The span collapsed and the ends were detached from the piling.

End in Sight

Lt. Teng C. C., in A/C #726 (with Chen Y. S., Hsiao N. T., Shu S. S., Chang F. C., and Tung N. T.), made two runs to strafe the bridge and approaches and then, led in by #725, dropped eight 500 lb. GP bombs. Two were direct hits on the bridge, landing in the vicinity of the second and third concrete piers. The other six were near misses that fell into the river and near the north abutment. The third pier from the south bank was demolished, and the north end of the third span and south end of the fourth span sagged to the riverbed. Leaflets were distributed. Teng made three strafing runs on a machine gun emplacement east of the bridge, along the north–south ridge of the mountains. The strategy was a success. All planes returned without damage. After the bombers turned toward home, crews spotted wreckage of an unidentified aircraft that appeared to be a P-51, wheels up in a field. The planes landed back at Liangshan undamaged.

On earlier missions to Burma, the squadron's Americans and Chinese often flew with mixed crews, but the practice was discontinued soon after the move to China because of mishaps caused by difficulties in communication. Now, late in the war, it was resumed. Although Hank had become friends with some of the Chinese mechanics, he was never well acquainted with any of the aircrews. "There were different Chinese that flew with us, but not always the same ones." Chinese fliers were generally assigned to specific crews that "stuck together and flew together," he said. The names of flight crew members were posted each morning on the bulletin board for the following day's missions. "Well, the next day would be different people altogether. We wouldn't fly with the same people. It was different every day."

SSgts. Lawrence J. Benedict (A/P maintenance technician), Bernard J. Czerniak, Dave H. Ewell Jr., Andrew Foorman, and Otto W. Hutchinson (all A/P mechanics) and Pfc. Richard Calloway (A/P armorer) joined the 3rd Squadron from CACW HQ in early June. SSgt. Hutchinson (and likely the others) had recently arrived aboard USS *General Robert E. Callan* (AP-139), which departed terminal 230E, Terminal Island, Los Angeles Port of Embarkation at San Pedro, California, on March 23 with 3,072 Army enlisted men, officers, and nurses, Red Cross officials (male and female), Chinese army air force personnel, and several Chinese diplomats. Bound first for Australia, the ship crossed the equator on April 1 (necessitating King Neptune to hold court and deal fittingly with the initiates) and then crossed the international date line on April 4. The ship's crew held gunnery practice on April 9 before arrival in Melbourne, mooring port side at Princes Pier at 1457.

After through passengers returned from shore leave, *Callan* continued the voyage on the thirteenth. Soon after departure, colors were half-masted when news of President Roosevelt's death was received. Steaming on to Calcutta, the vessel passed through the Australian Bight, rounded the point of Australia, and headed north through the Indian Ocean, accompanied by USS *General LeRoy Eltinge* (AP-154), 1,500 yards astern in column open order. When passing through the Bay of Bengal, one of the passengers died from heat prostration. Funeral services were held that same day, followed by burial at sea according to long-established naval custom. Approaching Calcutta on April 27 through Hoogley River's narrow channels and shallow water, *Callan* moored to buoys off Outran Ghat because it was unable to dock at a pier. Troops were offloaded by barge to shore, about 100 feet distant.[8] Hutchinson completed the journey to Liangshan by air transport. His daughter now has his Shellback Certificate, which by definition recorded latitude as 0.00'00" but longitude as "censored," as well as other documents relating to his service.[9]

SSgt. Ewell's family remembered him as a funny Cajun guy who "made friends easily and had a phenomenal memory for those he met" and liked to "show off," drink, have a good time, and make others laugh. An auto mechanic before entering service, he had enlisted in the regular army in June 1941 and been chosen to attend the auto mechanics course, Armored Force School, at Fort Knox, Kentucky. Assigned in September 1941 to a tank training unit— Company G, 33rd Armored Regiment (L), a part of the Third Armored ("Bayou Blitz") Division, stationed at Camp Polk, Louisiana—his reply when questioned about his impressions of the camp were printed in his hometown Baton Rouge newspaper. "I am thrilled to death to be sent to Camp Polk, because I am close to home." He said that he liked Fort Knox and its people, but they could not compare with the home folks. "The boys in this camp are swell—those that I have met. Most of them don't like my state. Well, anyway, I like it, and that counts." He was certain he would be "one of the most contented soldiers in the outfit" if allowed to stay. "I love Louisiana because I am near my folks, and also my girl. That's plenty." He had attended LSU before enlistment and was looking forward to seeing some of the football games when he had weekends off. "I have never been away from home before without seeing my Dad and Mother—but I am looking forward to seeing them this weekend because they are coming up to get me."[10]

According to a story that Ewell recalled and was related by his daughter, General Patton came one day to give the men a pep talk. "He encouraged them to work hard at learning how to drive and repair tanks because, he apparently said, 'We can always get more men, but we can't get more tanks.' Or something to that effect. In any event, my dad said that he turned to his buddy . . . and said, 'We gotta get outta this unit!' And so, he applied to the new Army Air Force and was accepted—and went off to become a pilot." Approved as an aviation cadet, Ewell received preflight training at San Antonio, Texas, followed by preliminary flight training at Grider Field in Arkansas. That, however, did not work out for him. "He said he should have passed the flight training, but he evidently smarted off to the instructor and washed out." His future wife, Ruth, who met him on a blind date at about that time, confided that she thought he was "cute and a good dancer, but a

SSgt. Otto W. Hutchinson joined as an airplane mechanic and meticulously documented his time in the 3rd Bomb Squadron. *Otto W. Hutchinson collection, courtesy of Jackie Hutchinson Pitts*

SSgt. Dave H. Ewell Jr., who joined at the same time as Hutchinson, added levity while working on the planes, as well as proving as his capabilities as an airplane mechanic. *Courtesy of Barbara Ewell*

End in Sight

terrible smart aleck and just too full of himself."[11] Ewell's training veered to a different path, and he became an airplane mechanic. Stationed at Altus, Oklahoma, in early 1945, he soon found himself on his way to China, as far away from home and family as conceivable.

SSgt. Foorman's family in a Sacramento suburb received a letter from him in late June reassuring them that he had arrived safely in China and was assigned to the CACW as an airplane mechanic. He had graduated from aviation mechanics school at Sheppard Field, followed by an aviation mechanics course at the North American Aircraft Factory School in Inglewood, California. Assigned to the 1st Emergency Rescue Squadron, the then Sgt. Foorman was transferred to the 40th Technical School Training Squadron in late January 1944. Both outfits were at Boca Raton, Florida, where the AAF not only provided technical training but also operated Overseas Replacement Depot #4, from which he was sent soon afterward as an airplane and engine mechanic to the China theater.[12]

"All I know is that my dad was a mechanic," remarked a daughter of SSgt. Czerniak, who shared very little about his service with his family. After graduating as a machinist from a technical school on Chicago's North Side, he enlisted in the Air Corps in 1940, with his civilian occupation specified as motor vehicle mechanic/repairman. He received training in airplane mechanics at Chanute Field near Rantoul, Illinois, graduating in December 1941. Czerniak's family remembered his admonitions to always wash their dishes thoroughly to prevent sickness—likely a result of measures against dysentery learned in the military. He remembered sleeping in a tent with a knife on his chest because Japanese infiltrators occasionally slipped in and slit the throats of the somnolent soldiers. Morning reports reveal that during the war's final days, he was on detached duty at Chihkiang, where acts of sabotage were relatively common.[13]

At about the same time that these replacements arrived, the Chinese received three radio operators: SLts. Teng Chun-chen (X-5110) and Chow Shao-nan (X-5111), as well as Sgt. Wang Fu-ying (X-1867). Lt. Pulaski and company returned soon afterward.

Three Mitchells took off at 0915 on June 9 (mission #144) escorted by four 3rd Fighter Group P-51s, their target railroad bridge #281 (31°15' N, 113°52' E), north of Hwayuan, to disrupt rail traffic. Lt. Pulaski was flight leader. Capt. W. Storms, 1Lt. R. Cook, and 2Lts. M. W. Beardsley and C. W. Sharp flew the fighter planes. Two of the P-51s carried two 500 lb. RDX bombs, and two carried cameras. The two bomb-carrying P-51s initiated the run by dropping their bombs on the bridge terminals. The B-25s, each carrying eight 500 lb. GPs, followed and made three passes, dropping at 400 feet by pilot release. Bombs of Pulaski's A/C #725 (with Ilefeldt, Liu P. C., Cantor, DeFabritis, Wilkerson, and Schroeder) all hit 100 yards to the left of the bridge. When bombs of the second Mitchell, A/C #726 (Chen C. S., Tsuei W. P., Huang C., Chui H. P., Chung C., and Chen Y. C.), were dropped, one hit the third span from the west end and five hit to the right of the tracks. All bombs of A/C #719 (Lo S. S., Sheng C. J., Chen Y. K., Yuan C. F., Kao C. K., and Wei C. S.) drifted to the right of the east end of the bridge, where aircrews observed meager, inaccurate AA. Bombers and fighters also strafed on each run, but damage was minimal. Schroeder took photos and Liu dropped leaflets.

The crew of downed A/C #722 returned from Valley Field by air transport on the same day. After a forced landing in "the pocket," they had taken about a week to walk out and returned to Liangshan "in perfect health and in the best of spirits." However, their return through enemy territory presented a dilemma. Ilefeldt wrote, "In that they walked-out [sic] in territory that is right in the middle of enemy[-]occupied territory—territory that contains many secret aids to the evasion and escape of our airmen fortunate enough to make their way there, it has been deemed that they know too much, and they may never fly combat again." If they were captured by the Japanese, they would undoubtedly be subjected to extreme torture in an attempt to extract information concerning their previous evasion and escape, and "consequently, that secret information could be drawn out of them, and the position of many men and women, who risk their lives to get our downed airmen out and back to safety, would be surely jeopardized." This was particularly true of the crew that had bellied in on May 27, because they had been photographed with some of their Chinese rescuers. Ilefeldt speculated that the six of them would either be transferred to transport units to fly supplies and personnel or, in some cases, be sent home. In the meantime, they were allowed to fly administrative missions as necessary.

Lt. Cantor's expertise as an aerial gunner led group headquarters to place him in charge of training several classes of Chinese gunners, but he lamented that the interpreters did not adequately translate his instructions. J. G. Cantor collection, courtesy of Ronnie Cantor

Lt. Cantor received orders for transfer to 1st Bomb Group HQ for special duty as group gunnery instructor in mid-June. Capt. Yang Lu-shiang (X-927) was transferred from the 4th to the 3rd Squadron. Lt. Banger, MSgt. Shock, and Sgt. Peters received orders to fly to Chihkiang for temporary duty. TSgt. Solyn was treated at the dispensary, the nature of his illness not specified. Sgt. England was released from the hospital at Chengtu and sent to rest camp. Lt. Logan returned from the hospital at Kunming, where he had been "laid up" since April 20 with dysentery, which had plagued him since March. Although not yet fully recovered, he expected to be back on flying status soon. Missing members of the May 16 mission were officially dropped from 3rd Bomb Squadron rosters.

End in Sight

Capt. Leslie L. Mondelli joined from the 2nd Squadron as operations officer on the sixteenth in anticipation of MacNeil's departure. He had participated in several joint missions with the 3rd Squadron during the previous few weeks. Exactly a month before, Mondelli was copilot of a B-25J that took off from Liangshan with bridge #113, on the Ping-Han Railroad north of Hankow, as target. The airplane lost an engine in the vicinity of Wanhsien (30°51' N, 108°26' E), salvoed its bombs, and bellied in on a sandbar in the Yangtze River 1 mile south of the town. Two were able to parachute out, but the other four went down with the plane. Miraculously, there were no injuries to any of the crew, which included former 3rd Squadron navigator 1Lt. T. A. Kilian.

This was not Mondelli's first crash landing. He related a story about bellying in earlier in the war aboard a B-25C, which was equipped with a retractable ventral turret. Although the belly turret's twin .50-caliber guns were operated remotely, the gunner who controlled them occupied a vulnerable position. Mondelli later told his family that as the plane was going down, crew members frantically screamed at the gunner to get back up into the plane. The man was able to climb to safety with little time to spare.[14]

Mondelli had enlisted in the Air Corps in July 1941 and demonstrated his audacity when he buzzed his parents' house and a nearby baseball field at Scranton, Pennsylvania, soon after receiving his wings. Before his assignment to the 1st Bomb Group, Mondelli completed nearly fifty missions in the South Pacific with the 405th ("Green Dragons") Bomb Squadron, 38th Bomb Group, 5th Air Force, which was stationed in Queensland, Australia, while operating in New Guinea, and in Port Moseby, New Guinea, attacking in the Bismarck Archipelago. Mondelli earned a reputation as a flying ace in December 1942, when a hometown newspaper reported that he had "played a leading role in an attack of two formations of Japanese planes in which twenty-one Jap planes, including six medium bombers, five dive bombers, eight Zeros and two unidentified planes were bagged."

The same source quoted from a dispatch dated January 12: "With Lieut. Leslie Mondelli . . . leading the way, United States Mitchell Bombers (B-25s) continued today to soften up the dwindling Japanese positions in the Sanananda sector of Papua." Reportedly carrying nearly 5,000 pounds of bombs, "Mondelli's fliers roared over the big enemy supply dumps in the area and started a number of huge fires in many of the key dumps. Said Mondelli: 'Where there's smoke there ought to be plenty of fire[,] and we saw enough today to know we'd burned up a lotta stuff the Japs were counting on.'"[15]

On March 3, 1943, Mondelli again garnered praise, this time taking part in a successful attack against Japanese shipping in the Battle of the Bismarck Sea. In a combined mission that included Liberators and Fortresses, the attackers sank a thirty-three-ship convoy with ships "loaded to the decks with soldiers" intended to reinforce Japanese troops on New Guinea. The bombers "swept down to 50 feet above the ships and invoked the skip-bomb that struck ships at the water line," destroying them all. The raid was so successful that it was described as "the turning point of the Southwest Pacific campaign." Mondelli was awarded the Air Medal with OLC in May.[16]

SSgt. Richard C. Wellman (administrative NCO) and Sgt. Arnold H. Ryave (A/P armorer) were other replacements attached in mid-June, as the war was drawing to a close. Wellman, from Cincinnati, later recalled his arrival at Calcutta, where one of his earliest impressions was of the extreme heat. He told his family that while he was here, he was assigned to a detail that was given the task of opening up and unloading boxes of rifles packed in animal grease in temperatures that topped 100 degrees.[17] The city's daytime summer temperatures routinely reach 100 to 110 degrees, although its proximity to the Indian Ocean generally brings down the heat to more-tolerable levels at night.

On the day after Mondelli's arrival, Capt. MacNeil and Lt. Senecal left for Peishiyi on temporary duty. MSgt. Shock, TSgts. Chasse and Reynard, SSgt. Hoke, Sgt. Peters, and Cpl. Hugel constituted the next group bound for rest camp at Chengtu. Lts. Senecal and Banger and Sgt. Jackson went to Chihkiang and returned a few days later. TSgt. Jakubasz began his return to the ZI. SSgt. Whearty and Sgt. England, who had been recuperating at rest camp, returned to duty. Capt. MacNeil and Lt. Wood returned at the end of the month.

Conflicting reports were still trickling in from the vicinity of Ichang regarding members of the aircrew missing since the previous month, but none gave any indication that the missing men were being kept safe by the local Chinese. Next of kin had received notification from Adjutant General J. A. Ulio by telegram on June 5, stating that the men were missing in action and presumed to be dead, followed up the next day by letters that included his condolences and the promise to provide more details as they became known.

As hope turned to dread, Jeanette Davis received this letter from 14th Air Force Headquarters dated June 18:

My dear Mrs. Davis,

It is with deep regret that I must inform you that your husband, First Lieutenant Donald J. Davis, has been missing in action since May 16, 1945. No doubt you have already been notified by the War Department.

Lieutenant Davis was pilot of an airplane which set out on an important combat mission to the area of Ichang, Hupeh Province, China. No word has been heard from the crew since the take-off. Every possible effort has been and will continue to be made to locate your husband. However, while the complete facts are not available, his disappearance for over a month without word from any of our sources of information, viewed in the light of our experience in this area, leaves little basis for optimism.

There are times when words are particularly futile, but you should know of the respect and admiration which was felt for your husband by his many friends and comrades among both officers and men. He was in every respect a fine officer and true American, able at his appointed task and devoted to his duty. We will always cherish his memory.

On behalf of the officers and men of the Fourteenth Air Force, I extend my heartfelt sympathy.

Sincerely yours,
[signed] C. L. Chennault
Major General, USA,
Commanding[18]

Since the end of the war in Europe, supplies of gas, ammunition, food, and other necessities coming into China had undergone some improvement, and opening of the land route from Ledo to Kunming had contributed toward making equipment and supplies less scarce. However, fueling the heavy bombers in the Pacific was now the Army's priority, so little had changed at China's gasoline-starved bases. "Operations of this group were at a minimum this month due to an almost negative supply of gasoline. The lack of gas gave us

```
HEADQUARTERS FOURTEENTH AIR FORCE
     A.P.O. 627, C/O POSTMASTER
       NEW YORK CITY, NEW YORK
```

June 18, 1945

My dear Mrs. Davis,

    It is with deep regret that I must inform you that your husband, First Lieutenant Donald J. Davis, has been missing in action since May 16, 1945. No doubt you have already been notified by the War Department.

    Lieutenant Davis was Pilot of an airplane which set out on an important combat mission to the area of Ichang, Hupeh Province, China. No word has been heard from the crew since the take-off. Every possible effort has been and will continue to be made to locate your husband. However, while the complete facts are not available, his disappearance for over a month without word from any of our sources of information, viewed in the light of our experience in this area, leaves little basis for optimism.

    There are times when words are particularly futile, but you should know of the respect and admiration which was felt for your husband by his many friends and comrades among both officers and men. He was in every respect a fine officer and true American, able at his appointed task and devoted to his duty. We will always cherish his memory.

    On behalf of the officers and men of the Fourteenth Air Force, I extend my heartfelt sympathy.

                                                Sincerely yours,

                                                C. L. CHENNAULT,
                                                Major General, U.S.A.,
                                                Commanding.

Mrs. Donald J. Davis,
Rt. 4, Box 354,
Anaheim, California.

Following the disappearance of the six-man flight crew of A/C #722 on May 16, families of the missing men were notified through official channels that their loved ones were missing as the result of enemy action and presumed dead. Gen. Chennault wrote this letter to Jeanette Davis, whose husband was the pilot on the ill-fated mission. *D. J. Davis collection, courtesy of Jarrett McConnell* anxious moments as to whether the planes could be flown sufficiently to maintain them," according to the bomb group's monthly historical report. Flying personnel feared that if they could not get in their required missions, many of them would be unable to return home for six months or more later than they anticipated.

Distribution of supplies during this time was unevenly experienced by the four squadrons of the 1st Bomb Group. The inequity in the supply of gas was largely the result of the command decision to concentrate gas supplies to bases farther south for use by units that could strike against the main Japanese retreat. The 1st Bomb Group flew 108 sorties and dropped 160.3 tons of bombs through the month of June, according to statistical reports. Most of these were run by the 4th Squadron—the only squadron whose gas supply was sufficient to take out "fat targets of large convoys" on night missions from Chihkiang. Hanchung, where the 1st Squadron was based to the north, had only a fair supply during this period and flew eight missions in June.

The 2nd and 3rd Squadrons operating out of Liangshan were the hardest hit. Their base saw what was likely the least activity of all the CACW airfields through the month, and neither squadron was able to get much flying time. It was still necessary to fly in the little gas that was allotted over the Hump to Luhsien (Luzhou) on the Yangtze River. From there it was floated on barges about 300 miles to Wanhsien and then carried in drums by truck for another two hours over the mountains along winding, switchback roads to Liangshan. Rain that fell day and night began on the tenth and continued through the twenty-third, further limiting operational activity. Even after the weather cleared, 3rd Squadron bombers remained grounded because of the chronic shortage of gas through the end of the month.

The 2nd Squadron flew only two missions during that period, on June 24 and 25. Delayed-action (from two to 144 hours) 500 lb. demos fell across Railroad Yards #288 at Siaokan on the Ping-Han Railroad (30°55' N, 113°53' E) on both dates "to make it impossible for the Japs to repair the yards without considerable damage." By the end of the war the two squadrons began to "take turns," flying missions on alternate weeks to allow both to get some flying time.

With little operational activity possible, innovative personnel at Liangshan set up a local broadcasting station, commercially known as PBS (for "Paddy Broadcasting System"). Volunteer DJs played record requests during the evening hours, as well as "a fine variety of recorded programs from the states." Because of the station's location on the field, reception was exceptionally clear, often bringing in broadcasts from as far away as San Francisco.

When reception was bad, they listened to phonograph records or read from the wide variety of books shared among base personnel. Capt. MacNeil recalled that he read "everything from *Buck Rogers* to Plato's *Republic* (twice)." Card games such as poker and hearts continued to provide a diversion during leisure hours. MacNeil once won $36,000 CN from the house boys playing poker. Later he calculated that his winnings amounted to about nine dollars in US currency at the then-current rate of inflation.[19]

The bomb squadrons had recently begun to receive greater numbers of aircraft designated as B-25J-2s and configured more like the older H models, with the solid-metal "strafer nose," while retaining the copilot's seat, dual controls, and elongated nose of the J. Some were modified to include eight underwing-mounted, 5-inch (130 mm), high-velocity aircraft rockets (HVAR) as a means of attack and carried twenty-four rounds of 75 mm ammunition. All were equipped with a minimum of eighteen .50 in. (12.7 mm) light-barrel AN/M2 Browning machine guns.

End in Sight

Capt. Joseph Adlestein, group ordnance officer, and Capt. Henry A. Stanley, formerly 4th Bomb Squadron CO and now 1st Bomb Group operations officer, along with armament and operations officers of the 2nd and 3rd Bomb Squadrons, flew down to Kunming to attend a conference at 14th Air Force HQ with Maj. Fruehaun, an expert on rocket installations. Attending from the 3rd Squadron between June 27 and July 8 were Maj. Curik, Capt. Mondelli, and 1Lts. Cantor, Banger, and Senecal. "Much valuable information was obtained," with the expectation that it would be put to use as soon as factory-provided modification kits could be installed and operations permitted, Ilefeldt wrote.

The squadrons' mechanics received additional training during this period of limited activity. Maj. Michael P. Henneck, group engineering officer as well as technical and administrative inspector, had his staff of specialists conduct classes in the maintenance and repair of the various parts of the B-25 and its accessories. Already on Henneck's staff was a representative from North American Aviation, and two more technical representatives—one for Wright engines and another for Holley carburetors—were brought in as instructors. Engineering further utilized their expertise to troubleshoot particularly tough maintenance work. Afterward, Maj. Henneck conducted a thorough administrative and technical inspection of the 3rd Squadron for the purpose of instructing personnel in the preparation of required reports on aircraft, equipment, personnel, and operations. Ilefeldt noted that he came "to give us a thorough going over, inspecting our files, our organization and efficiency," although Henneck's appraisal was not included in the squadron history.

"Part of the mission of this Group has always been to train the Chinese in combat techniques and to improve their performance as crews. One of the phases of this training is accomplished by the Group Gunnery School under the direction of 1Lt. Jerome G. Cantor, Gunnery Officer, and Sgt. Manuel C. Smith, Gunnery Instructor," wrote Lt. Eisner, group historian. "The Chinese commanding officers have been very enthusiastic about this program" and presented Sgt. Smith with Chinese aviator wings in appreciation for the fine work he had done as gunnery instructor for Chinese airmen since the program's inception at Peishiyi. Smith, formerly attached to the 3rd Squadron, had the previous August been assigned the task of training the Chinese in nomenclature, function, operation, and adjustment of the B-25s' .50-caliber machine guns, as well as maintenance and manipulation of turrets, sighting and position firing, and aircraft identification. To date he had conducted seven classes composed of about 120 officers and enlisted men.

Japanese premier Suzuki had announced on June 9 that Japan would fight to the finish rather than accept unconditional surrender to the Allies. The Chinese army continued to push forward through June, retaking Nanning and thereby splitting the Japanese corridor that extended from the Tungting Lake region to Canton. After retaking Liuchow, they had advanced to within 10 miles of Kweilin by the end of the month. Chinese troops now occupied many villages and towns in the Hunan campaign.

Successful interdiction from the air forced the retreating enemy to abandon rail transportation altogether. Japanese in the Sinyang area were withdrawing on foot, proving the effectiveness of attacks on the Ping-Han Railroad, which had inflicted such heavy damage as to render it inoperative. At one time for a period of weeks, intelligence reports stated that the Ping-Han Railroad from Hankow to Chengshien had only one operational locomotive. Certain vital bridges along the line were kept bombed out and impassable. The Chinese were within 150 miles south of Shanghai and had opened more than 365 miles along the China coast.

The men grounded at Liangshan wanted to be back in the fray. "The outlook for operations in July is very dark, with a consequent decline in the morale of all personnel due to the lack of activity," wrote the 1st Bomb Group's historical officer.

Squadron personnel at the end of June comprised nineteen American officers, fifty American enlisted men, seventy-eight Chinese officers, and 126 Chinese enlisted men. There were fourteen B-25s: five H models and nine Js. Also assigned was one BT-14A (a North American Yale basic trainer aircraft) to facilitate training of recent arrivals. Never had the squadron been assigned so many aircraft, yet with so little gas with which to operate them. They flew thirteen sorties in four missions (all low level) and dropped eighty-nine bombs totaling 12½ tons: 400 500 lb. demos, eleven frags, twenty 250 lb. RDX demos, and ten 100 lb. demos.

CHAPTER SEVENTEEN
Victory in China

As days grew longer and temperatures soared, men stationed at Liangshan eagerly awaited the end of each working day. They rushed to the mess hall "to gulp down the chow, get out of the steaming building, and thence to the barracks to tear off wet uniforms," according to Eisner. Escaping the heat was a priority for most of them as summer got underway.

Capt. Wu, returning to the 2nd Squadron, was replaced by Mao Shang-chien as 3rd Squadron cocommander. The squadron historical report for July was not submitted until late September, after the end of hostilities, so its account of events is largely incomplete. "Nothing of real importance happened" during the month, the writer stated in retrospect, although he did mention some occurrences of interest.

After twenty-four months overseas, Capt. MacNeil began his journey back to the US in early July. With the squadron since soon after its activation, he was the last of the original pilots to leave for home. He had flown forty-six combat missions and had been awarded the Air Medal and the Distinguished Flying Cross. According to the squadron's final historical report, Capt. MacNeil's absence would be keenly felt when he left, "for no one in all of the CACW was more adamant in spreading good will between the Chinese and the Americans." If there was ever any friction arising, it was MacNeil who straightened things out. "The Chinese lost a good friend, and so did we, but more important, he was an exceptionally good pilot, engineering officer and later Operations officer, and he left with one of the best combat records in the theater."

Before his departure, Chinese officers hosted a typical "gambay party" for MacNeil at which he was encouraged to drink to seventy toasts. To show their appreciation for his efforts on behalf of the Chinese members of the squadron, the officers with whom he flew presented MacNeil with a red silk banner featuring the "Spray and Pray" insignia on the front (but more nearly resembling a ferret than a skunk), with embroidered characters

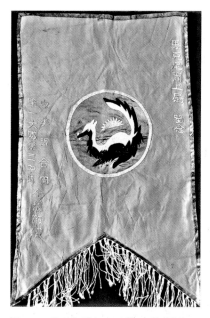

The squadron's Chinese officers held Capt. Robert C. MacNeil in such high regard that they presented him with an embroidered silk banner featuring the "Spray and Pray" insignia before his return to the US. *Courtesy of Szu-ming (James) Peng, from his extensive collection of WWII memorabilia*

transcribed "Captain Robert C. MacNeil (馬克尼爾上尉) from the Chinese pilots of the 3rd BS of the 1st BG, CACW (中美混合團. 第一大隊 第三中隊)." Thirty-two officers signed their names in Mandarin and in English.[1]

After arriving at Calcutta and finding dozens of priorities over him waiting to be transported by air, MacNeil determined that traveling by ship by way of the Suez Canal would probably be the quickest way to go home. He was back with his wife, Barbara, and their three-year-old son after a grueling thirty days and wanting little other than to be left alone with his family, according to a Minneapolis newspaper interview published soon after his return.[2]

Morning reports from this period provide greater detail than was included in the monthly historical report. MSgt. Shock; TSgts. Chasse, Reynard, and Solyn; SSgt. Hoke; and Cpl. Hugel returned from rest camp at Chengtu, and MSgt. Barge, TSgt. Wilkerson, SSgts. Mills and Long, Sgt. Learn, and Cpl. Armbruster left for the same destination. SSgt. Thomas returned from the hospital at Chengtu, where he had been treated for acute bronchitis. Sgt. Jackson checked in and remained there for about a week. Cpl. Piecuch was treated at the dispensary for diarrhea.

Officers present at the gambay party held in his honor added their signatures in English and in Mandarin on the reverse. *Courtesy of Szu-ming (James) Peng*

Men stationed at 14th Air Force bases in China received this message of encouragement from Gen. Chennault on Independence Day:

> Today, July 4, 1945, we celebrate three important occasions—the 169th anniversary of the Declaration of Independence, the third anniversary of the establishment of the American Army Air Forces in China, and the third anniversary of the activation of the Twenty-third fighter group. These three anniversaries mark days of adversity for people struggling for independence and to throw off the yoke of oppression. They also make days of hope and determination for victory.

TSgt. Wilkerson and MSgt. Barge smile for the camera as Hank records their second visit to Kwan-sien Rest Camp. *J. H. Mills collection*

SSgt. Mills (soon to receive an additional stripe) poses in front of the stately residence cum rest camp. *J. H. Mills collection*

Victory in China

On July 4, 1942, the Japanese air force was still very strong in China although the gallant pilots of the American Volunteer Group had destroyed many of their planes and had forced them to respect the ability of American airmen. Since July 4, 1942, the China Air Task Force and later the Fourteenth Air Force with the 23rd fighter group spearheading the attack, have shown the world and particularly the Japanese what a small, well-trained, and determined air force can accomplish with the help of our Chinese Allies. We have demonstrated that a few Americans with their native initiative, ingenuity, courage, and leadership, and with a minimum of combat airplanes, could defeat the Japanese air force in China with its initial huge numerical superiority, unlimited facilities, and supplies.

Our job is not finished, however, and will not be finished until all Japanese dreams of conquest have been shattered. At every opportunity we must strike the enemy with every weapon at hand until with our Allies the final complete defeat of Japan is accomplished.

On this historic day, remembering the ideals of our forefathers who fought in the War of Independence, I charge you, the officers and enlisted men of the Fourteenth Air Force, to rededicate yourselves to the principles of freedom and the determination that will end this war in early victory. I join you in the hope that we may be able to celebrate final victory and the next Fourth of July at home.[3]

As the war in China was winding down, Maj. Gen. Wedemeyer received orders from Washington for the reorganization of the air forces for the primary purpose of liberating a port on the China coast. The plan called for moving the 10th Air Force, under the command of Maj. Gen. George E. Stratemeyer, from now-liberated Burma to China to replace the existing 14th Air Force, commanded by Maj. Gen. Chennault. According to the plan that was eventually approved, Stratemeyer would command the "China Theater Air Forces," and under him Chennault would command the "Strategical Air Force" and Maj. Gen. Davidson the "Tactical Air Force." The 10th Air Force would be based south and west of Chihkiang for direct support of Chinese ground forces, while the 14th Air Force and its unconventional and outspoken commander would be banished to areas north of the Yangtze River, where significant targets and needed supplies were sparse. The 10th Air Force would extract from the 14th the crack veteran 23rd and 51st Fighter Groups, along with the two best B-25 squadrons, and then make "a dash to final victory" with the Chinese armies. The 14th would be left "to die on the vine" after it had been whittled down to the size of a normal wing. "This was the fate of the Fourteenth Air Force—the air force that Chennault had nurtured from its meager beginning of 250 men and a hundred planes to twenty thousand men and a thousand planes and a record of air victories unsurpassed in the Air Annals of World War II."[4]

Chennault had little intention of being put out to pasture and entered a vigorous protest against the entire plan. Six days later, on July 6, Stratemeyer officially assumed command as commanding general, AAF China theater. Chennault's request for retirement, handed in on the same date, was promptly approved. "This came as a shock to us all," wrote the squadron historian with regard to their beloved commander. "General Chennault claimed that his reason for resignation was due to the fact that the China skies have been cleared of enemy aircraft, which of course, is true; and he, if anyone, is responsible. Since 1938, General Chennault, guiding his AVG's and later the Americans and Chinese Air men, had fought hard to drive the Japs out of China, and this was done on the proverbial shoe-string." Voicing the sentiment of the entire squadron, he concluded, "We all join in saluting a superb commander, and one who has inspired his ill-equipped, but courageous and resourceful Air Force."

As these high-level changes were being implemented and the war in China neared an end, the 3rd Squadron received another replacement pilot: 1Lt. John A. Trumm, who transferred in from the 322nd Troop Carrier Squadron in mid-July. From Oregon, he had earned his wings at Stockton, California, and received B-25 transition training at Mather Field, California, and C-47 transition training at Malden, Missouri. He had been flying C-47s that transported troops and supplies over the Hump since his transfer into the theater in late 1944. Recently awarded Chinese Air Force Wings, Trumm had additionally received the Air Medal for completion of 150 hours of flight over China in transport-type aircraft.

Capt. Greene, Lt. Pulaski, and Cpl. DeFabritis returned from India with yet another new plane. Sgt. Burton was released from the 3rd Squadron and attached to Replacement Depot No. 3 at Kanchrapara, located about 35 miles north of Calcutta. In anticipation of the Japanese surrender and the return of the thousands of China-Burma-India veterans back to the US, the camp featured movie theaters and stage shows, clubs, chapels, libraries, athletic facilities for sports of almost every description, tailor shops, shoe shops, barbershops, PXs, and educational and informational facilities to provide aid to those who were returning soon to civilian life back home.

As the month progressed, only the 4th Squadron, operating out of Chihkiang, had supplies sufficient to allow almost-daily operations, although three of its B-25Js had been sent to India for modifications to increase their firepower. Its Mitchells incessantly pounded convoys carrying supplies and troops as they moved back up the Hsiang River corridor through Kweilin and Hengyang, heading east toward Shanghai, where they were either transported back to the home islands or repositioned to defend Shanghai and Manchuria from Allied landings. Truck convoys remained the 4th Squadron's primary targets. Clear, moonless nights created perfect hunting conditions for the Mitchells prowling along the valley, so most of the missions were night raids. So successful were these missions—often wiping out four to six or even more convoys on each raid—that both the 2nd and 3rd Squadrons sent detachments to join in the extermination. Lt. Eisner aptly called these enemy convoys "the Sitting Duck parade" in his group historical report.

In addition to having a better supply of gas, bombs, and ammunition, Chihkiang was closer to the enemy retreat. To supplement the 4th Squadron's operational aircraft, Maj. Stanley (recently promoted) and one plane and crew each from the 2nd and 3rd Squadrons moved to Chihkiang to take part in operations in early July. Stanley had participated in many missions while in command of the 4th Squadron in the Battle of Chihkiang and knew the hunting grounds well. After being grounded for a few days by bad weather, the 3rd Squadron detachment flew missions for the duration of about a week to attack enemy supply movements, operating much as it did with Task Force 34.

Maj. Stanley was listed as the pilot on four missions in "Detachment 4th Bombardment Squadron" operational reports during this period. On July 11, he was off from Chihkiang at 2045 and flew a moonless night mission with a single Mitchell that carried seventeen M1A1 frag clusters and five M50A2 incendiaries, considered to be the ideal bombload to hit enemy supply movements. Maj. Hamilton was his copilot; all others were 4th Squadron personnel.

Victory in China

Their objective was to alert and harass enemy supply movements in the Hsiang valley. The 4th Squadron bombardier released five frags and one incendiary on a convoy of more than ten vehicles sighted north of Changsha. The hits produced a large explosion, and crewmen noted one truck wheels up on the road. Construction work to repair the Kweiyi Bridge was interdicted with two frags that probably caused casualties. Farther south, the bombardier hit a fifteen-vehicle westbound convoy with five frags and two incendiaries. A large fire, possibly fueled by oil or gas, was the result. Strafing followed. Gunners strafed several more trucks near Siangtan. The bombardier then attacked a row of bright lights with four bombs. A large fire that spread rapidly revealed buildings and revetments that may have been a motor pool and repair area. He dropped the remaining three bombs on Siangyin, resulting in two small fires. On the return route, crewmen spotted a fifty-vehicle convoy at Siangtan but could not attack it because all bombs had been expended and ammunition was low. Leaflets, printed both in Japanese and Chinese, were dropped.

The following night, Maj. Drake was off at 2000 in another B-25J carrying the same bombload as on the previous mission. His crew included Lt. Cantor, duty position designated as "AO" (aerial observer), and five 4th Squadron crewmen. The bombardier released five frags and one incendiary (individually for range and deflection by select) on a convoy of five to seven trucks sighted 8 miles north of Siangtan. Due east of Siangtan, he dropped three frags and one incendiary on a northbound convoy of about fifteen vehicles, causing a secondary explosion and burning several vehicles. One incendiary and one frag were toggled on a light 4 miles east of Kweiyi. In the northern section of Siangtan, many secondary explosions resulted when eight frags and ten incendiaries were dropped on target. Japanese-language leaflets were dropped.

Five B-25Js and one B-25H were off from Chihkiang at 1320 on July 13, Maj. Drake leading. Four 5th Fighter Group P-51s provided escort. Lts. Pulaski as copilot and Cantor as top-turret gunner were part of an otherwise 4th Squadron crew. Carrying an aggregate load of eighteen 2,000 lb. GPs, their objective was to attack the Puchi Railroad Bridge (no. 24). Crewmen sighted a number of small boats in coves along the south side of Tungting Lake (114 counted, mostly one-mast sampans) and a large two-stack steamer thought to be a tanker between Yochow and Pailochi. They spotted a convoy of several trucks on the road south of Yunglowtung, dispersed at the side of the road, headed south.

Visibility was good at the target. Cloud cover was about three-tenths, with considerable turbulence. Drake initiated one run on a heading of 60 degrees at 1510, and bombs were released from 4,100 feet. His bombardier, Lt. Doran, sighted for range and deflection, and the bombardier in the second flight, Lt. Kilian, sighted for range only. Photographs revealed an excellent pattern but with a range error of 1,200 feet and a deflection error of 800 feet left. The escorting fighters, exhibiting their usual efficiency, "smothered whatever A/A positions there may have been," and the Mitchells encountered no opposition.

Stanley flew another night mission on the fifteenth. With Lt. Kilian as navigator-bombardier, Sgts. Gaffney and Schlicher as waist and tail gunners, and Lt. Cantor again as aerial observer, the Mitchell took off at 2050 with eight M57 parademos to destroy the pontoon bridge reported to be in operation at the Isuho ferry crossing. "Parachute bombs" had first been tried by the "Burma Banshees" (80th Fighter Group) in late 1944 and were by this time in common use throughout the theater. Parademos were simply demolition bombs to which parachutes were attached to slow their rate of descent before hitting the target. Their purpose was to allow planes to come in low to increase accuracy in dropping their bombs, while the loss of acceleration gave the bombers time to escape the bomb blast.

Because the bridge was not in position where it had been indicated, Stanley began a sweep for convoys in the area. When crewmen sighted ten vehicles 2 miles east of Siangtan, Kilian released three bombs. He dropped three more on thirty trucks in a vehicle storage area spotted immediately west of Siangtan airfield. The final two were hits on the ferry crossing. All bombs were dropped from 250 feet true, because a trajectory test that morning had indicated this to be the best altitude for accuracy and nonskip results, slowing descent to about one-third. When crewmen spotted a "possible convoy" crossing the bridge 1 mile north of Changsha, the pilot dropped down for strafing. No results from bombing or strafing were observed because of darkness.

Truck convoys in the Hsiang valley were again Maj. Stanley's target in the early morning of July 16, flying 3rd Squadron A/C #725. This time Schlicher flew as turret gunner, with Gaffney once again as waist gunner and Cantor as AO. Off at 0300, the Mitchell carried the same bombload as on July 11. The main purpose of this mission was to locate and attack the huge northbound convoys reported to be evacuating Kweilin, thereby keeping them alerted and immobile until P-51s could catch them on the roads at dawn. Heavy cumulus buildup in the area that reduced visibility to 2–3 miles prevented the mission from accomplishing its goal. A forty-to-fifty-vehicle convoy was the only one that was spotted. Due to the rugged terrain in the area, Kilian dropped all bombs from 3,000 feet, and strafing was deemed inadvisable because of poor visibility.

Stanley led a two-plane formation that was off at 1250 on July 19. No 3rd Bomb Squadron personnel were listed among crews of either aircraft. The lead plane carried four 500 lb. M64 parademos and one 1,000 lb. M65 parademo, and the wing plane carried nineteen 100 lb. M30 parademos. Their target was bridge #45 if the fighter escort of two P-51s missed it, and then the railroad track south with the M30s as alternate. The fighters damaged the south end, so Maj. Stanley made a low-level pass at 100 feet and his bombardier dropped three 500-pounders. The first two missed, and the third caused minor track damage. On the second run, the M65 hung up on the bridge by the parachute, destroying a third of the structure.

The trailing plane scored four direct hits and eleven near misses that caused multiple breaks in the track by M30s released at 150 feet. Both planes returned to base, in spite of a burst of automatic-weapon fire that severed an oil line in the right wing of Stanley's plane on its second pass over the bridge. Experience gained by this mission determined the best altitude for dropping parademos to be from 75 to 150 feet because they were less likely to skip or drift from that range. Stanley's name does not appear in reports of mission out of Chihkiang for the month after the nineteenth.

It wasn't until after mid-July, when Lt. Gen. Wedemeyer made a visit to Liangshan and learned of the extreme deprivation at that base, that the gas situation began to improve. The group historian wrote that the situation was "bad to the point of negligence on the part of higher headquarters." There was insufficient gas to preflight the planes daily and fly them once a week, let alone fly any missions. Later that month, when gas in quantities to fly missions was received, it became a usual occurrence for planes to return with only one engine, and this was not a result of enemy action. Due to the shortages of gasoline and defective reconditioned spark plugs, the 2nd and the 3rd Squadrons had six abortive missions because of mechanical failures.

With this increase in gas supply, the 3rd Squadron was able to complete a few missions from Liangshan near the end of the month to the Wuhan vicinity. The squadron's historical report for the month noted that it flew missions on successive days between July 20 and 27. A report signed by Maj. Hamilton stated that twenty enlisted personnel were on flying status, and Hank was one of those flying missions from July into August.

Mission #145 was a two-plane night mission from Liangshan on July 20. Both aircraft were rocket-equipped B-25J-2s. Their target was a spinning mill (14th Air Force photo grid no. 26, J.5-5.8) used as a warehouse in Wuchang, on the east bank of the Yangtze River opposite the mouth of the Han River, and their objective was to destroy it. Maj. Hamilton was pilot of A/C #715 (with Trumm, Faherty, Mier, England, and Mills), off at 1920. Arriving in the target area at 2125, Hamilton went in on the Hankow (enemy) homing beam, which cut off about five minutes from the target. His approach was northward along the west bank of the Yangtze, to avoid anti-aircraft fire in the vicinity of the Wuchang Airdrome. At the confluence of the Han and Yangtze Rivers, the pilot turned east and crossed the river at 250 feet in true altitude. Faherty was bombardier on this mission—his first in almost two months. After he lined up the target, Hamilton released all twenty-two 100 lb. M47-A1 napalm bombs fused instantaneous at 250 feet, in train, at 50-foot intervals. Huge fires that could be seen from 50 miles away engulfed the target.

Six or eight enemy searchlights, all of them powerful and illuminated simultaneously, flashed on as the aircraft made its bombing run. Two of them flicked and held the plane in their powerful beam for about fifteen seconds. There was no evidence of spread beam technique for low-level searchlight interception. From the haphazard sweeping of individual beams and the scattered searching, it appeared that no radar control was involved. Diving slightly at the critical moment allowed Hamilton to escape the blinding beams. AA fire was meager and inaccurate; crewmen observed three or four A/W bursts, scattered behind and above.

"We went on a mission way up north of us. It was a night mission, and those big ol' spotlights were on the ground," Hank related. "They'd track us in the air, and that antiaircraft fire was popping all around us." Locked in the bright, white beam and surrounded by a barrage of flak, he felt totally helpless and vulnerable. Each second seemed an eternity. "I was thinking, I hope none of that stuff hits me." Once again, he made it back unharmed. He clearly remembered this mission, which he described as identical to those for which Allegretto and Peters had been recognized for their participation the previous year.

As the invaders withdrew to defensive positions, 1Lt. John A. Trumm joined the squadron as a pilot to hasten their departure from China. *J. A. Trumm collection, courtesy of Robert Trumm*

After circling the area several times, Hamilton proceeded to the secondary target (14th Air Force photo grid no. 26, K.1-6.4). This warehouse was about 120 yards north of the primary target on a small island. The pilot fired eight RM8 rockets, but no explosions resulted. On the return flight, they came across a fifteen-truck convoy near Ichang at the western end of Hubei Province. Gunners strafed heavily, expending 2,300 rounds, but ground haze obscured results. They spotted another convoy of twenty-five trucks moving north on the road near Chiangsien but did not attack. A/C #715 was back down safely at Liangshan at 0030. Hank recalled, "It took a long time. We used nearly all of our gas to get there and back." Trumm recorded this, his first mission with the 3rd Bomb Squadron, as five hours and thirty minutes, in agreement with Faherty's combat missions' certificate.[5]

A/C #718 (Yen P. S., Sheng S., Yang C. H., Chang C., Cheng Y., and Lee L.) was off at 2117. It followed the same course and employed the same tactics. Lt. Yen dropped all twenty-two bombs on the primary target. Fires from the previous attack were still visible but had diminished considerably. The second attack rekindled flames that were still

Lt. Trumm's flight log documents squadron missions during the last days of the war as the enemy's military rampage was forced to an end. J. A. Trumm collection, courtesy of Robert Trumm

visible twenty-five minutes later. Secondary explosions, numbered at six or seven and pale green in color, burst at the north end of the target. Six searchlights were active, three flicking the aircraft momentarily. Crewmen observed several AA flashes on the ground in the Hankow area and two or three from the east bank of the Yangtze River, 150 feet north of the primary target. On the return flight, they sighted a ten-truck convoy moving north. Yen's plane was down at 0130. Leaflets dropped by both planes in the Ichang area totaled 503,040 CM-122 and 51,120 JM-131. OWI representatives supplied many thousands more leaflets printed in Chinese and Japanese that were scattered from combat cargo aircraft during the same period.

On the following day, 2nd Squadron B-25s flew a follow-up raid (its mission #312) against enemy warehouses and stores in the Hankow/Wuchang area. Two B-25s with crews that included that squadron's Cpl. Johnson completed the mission, while a third plane, with a Chinese crew, flew in the wrong direction and was lost in the darkness. The target was Japanese Military Headquarters (Installation #121 on 3rd Phase PI report number 57) at Wuchang, but a nearby "light industry building" (a cotton-spinning mill, Installation #150 on the 3rd Phase PI report) formerly used as a gasoline storage point was hit instead. In a supplementary report of 2nd Squadron mission #312, a similarity in roof design of the two buildings (both with "saw-toothed rooves") was given as a contributing factor for the pilot's mistake. Intense searchlight activity in the area further contributed to the misidentification.

Johnson described the experience in his memoirs, closely mirroring Hank's account of the previous day:

> Standing in the waist window, I held my .50-caliber machine gun ready to shoot. As we came within range and began our dive toward the target, the searchlights were turned on. It seemed like dozens of lights were shining on us from all directions, lighting up the sky like high noon. In movies I had seen, searchlights sweep across the sky to locate their target, but the instant these lights were turned on, they locked right on us. We were nearly blinded by their intensity.
>
> The lights shining in my window lit the interior of the airplane brighter than day. I felt naked except for the flak helmet I wore on my head. "If they can find us so easily in their lights, how can they miss us with their bullets," I thought. I heard the rattle of flak hitting the metal of our airplane and I watched the red lines of tracer bullets zip by. I fired a long burst from my machine gun into the source of the light and the tracer bullets.[6]

Victory in China

On the same date as this 2nd Squadron mission, three 4th Squadron Mitchells were off Chihkiang at 1010 with two 5th Fighter Group P-51s to destroy the Puchi Bridge (railroad bridge #24), about midway between Tungting Lake and Wuchang. The bridge, located near the village of Puchi, crossed a small river near where it entered the Yangtze northeast of Tungting Lake, and destroying the bridge would stop all rail traffic in that area south of Hankow. About 200 yards in length, it was of steel truss construction set on concrete piers, with open spaces between the trusses.

The lead plane dropped three M65 parademos by pilot release—one reported as a near miss because the chute failed to open, although causing probable damage to the west approach and the other two over. The second aircraft, piloted by Lt. J. H. Rich, with the 3rd Squadron's Lt. Bowen as navigator, dropped M57 parademos on tracks from Puchi north to Sienning with five direct hits, causing severe damage to the track and roadbed. Three were near misses; one struck and blew up a truck along the railroad. Three M57 GPs were misses. One of the planes, a B-25J-2 strafer, made a pass over the bridge to put out any AA positions still in operation. All three aircraft then made a sweep of the entire railroad from Puchi north to Sienning, heavily damaging three locomotives at a town believed to be Shishihpu. Three large fires were ignited in camouflaged warehouses. Gunners intensely strafed many villages and camouflaged areas presumably holding supplies.

Bowen was navigator-bombardier for a second 4th Squadron mission (Lt. McCullar as pilot) that same evening. Off at 1850, the plane carried seventeen M1A1 frag clusters and five M50A2 incendiaries to harass enemy supply movements in the Hsiang valley. About 10 miles north of Kweiyi, Bowen dropped eight frags and two incendiaries on a twenty-seven-to-thirty-vehicle convoy, igniting multiple small fires. When a twenty-truck convoy was sighted 15 miles south of Isuho, he released three frags and one incendiary, followed by six frags and two incendiaries on Siangyin that started ten small fires.

Off again at 2345, Bowen participated in a third mission (with 1Lt. W. R. Laederlich, pilot) on the twenty-first. Carrying the same bombload as on the previous mission, a single Mitchell hit three convoys, all observed heading north. Bowen dropped three frags and one incendiary on two trucks spotted 3 miles south of Kiyang. When a second convoy of five trucks was sighted 17 miles farther south, the pilot made six strafing passes, and Bowen released six frags and two incendiaries about 73 feet from the road. Finally, when crewmen spotted a convoy of over forty-five trucks extending for about 1.5 miles south from the ferry crossing at Lingling, he attacked it with eight frags and two incendiaries, and gunners followed up with two strafing passes.

A cooperative mission from Liangshan on July 22 included a 2nd Squadron B-25H and a J (its mission #318) that took off at 1100 and two 3rd Squadron Js (mission #146) off at 1115. Participating 3rd Squadron airmen were Capt. Mondelli, flying A/C #714, with Ilefeldt, Faherty, Holmes, Morris, Gaffney, and Schroeder, and Capt. Lo S. S., in #721, with Chen Y. P., Ting C. L., Wang M. T., Tung N. T., and Kao H. Y. as his aircrew. Recovered sufficiently to be back on flying status, Cpl. Morris was in position as Mondelli's waist gunner. Four 5th Fighter Group P-51s (pilots Wagner, Spurgeon, Cotton, and Lee) accompanied them to provide increased firepower.

The 2nd Squadron's Col. Smith led the four-plane box formation. Planes of Smith's element each carried eight 500 lb. M64 RDX fused instantaneous at the nose and 0.025-second delay at the tail, and 3rd Squadron bombers each carried six GP 500 lb. M64 RDX fused instantaneous and four GP 500 lb. M64A1 RDX fused to 12-to-144-hour delay. Their target was the Siaokan railroad yards, Ping-Han Railroad installation #288; the objective was to destroy them in continuation of the policy of neutralizing railroad yards on the Ping-Han Railroad south of Sinyang. The use of delayed-action bombs effectively prevented repair or any other use of the yards during the period it took for all of them to detonate.

The 2nd Squadron's H model developed engine trouble before reaching the target, jettisoned its bombs, and returned to base. The two 3rd Squadron planes took up positions #2 and #3 in a "V" behind the leader, and the formation continued to the target, over the yards at 1315. All bombs were released at 3,500 feet, in train on the lead bombardier. All fell in the target area. Smith's bombardier dropped bombs that fell directly down the center of the yards, destroying five railroad cars and damaging five more, as well as ripping up sufficient trackage to prevent through service.

Both wing planes dropped late. Faherty's bombs started at the center on the southwestern side and extended to the end of the yards, while those that Ting released started at the end and north of the yards and fell harmlessly to the side the tracks. Smoke rose to 200 feet, with no secondary explosions or fires. Cpl. Schroeder took photos. A/C #721's Chinese crew reported two trains of about twenty cars each, two locomotives, and about fifteen more cars in the yards. They saw no activity in the vicinity of the airdrome or barracks, which seemed deserted, and observed no truck convoys. At 4 miles north of the railroad yards, crewmen sighted one locomotive and one car, but producing no smoke or steam. Leaflets were released over Hankow. Aircraft returned individually on separate headings in search of the 2nd Squadron B-25 missing near Hankow since the previous day, as well as a missing fighter plane, but no evidence of either was discovered. Schroeder and Faherty both recorded duration as four hours in their logs of combat missions.

As 3rd Squadron Mitchells were again engaging in operations from Liangshan, Lt. Bowen remained at Chihkiang with the 4th Bomb Squadron detachment until early August. Off at 1830 on July 22, and again flying as Lt. Laederlich's navigator-bombardier, he attacked an estimated thirty sampans found 10 miles north of Changsha with M1A1 frags and M50A2 incendiaries, damaging seven. He next delivered direct hits with nine frags and three incendiaries on a convoy of thirty to thirty-five trucks, igniting one large and several small fires that were visible at a distance of 35 miles. Finally, he bombed the town of Henguyang from north to south with frags and incendiaries, resulting in several small fires that burned for about ten minutes. Gunners finished up by heavily strafing a convoy of about thirty-five trucks sighted east of the river at Henguyang.

Lt. Faherty kept photos of the successful mission against Ping-Han Railroad installation #288, the railroad yards at Siaokan in Hupeh Province. *J. F. Faherty collection, courtesy of Dennis Faherty*

At 0800 on July 23, Col. Smith was off Liangshan in the lead of a four-plane 2nd Squadron formation. Four 3rd Squadron planes were off at 0812 and joined Smith's element, along with four P-51s from the 3rd Fighter Group (pilots Spurgin, Lee, Wagner, and Cotton) as escort on a mission to bomb and strafe the railroad yards (Ping-Han installation #263 and #264) at Sinyang. When an engine of Smith's plane started cutting out, he broke away from the formation and 1Lt. Marvin Borodkin took his place. The three-plane formation then proceeded to the railroad yards and dropped 500 lb. RDX M64A1 bombs from 5,000 feet, released on the lead bombardier. All bombs hit in the target area. Those of the lead plane walked up the middle of the yards, 1,200 feet from the southeast corner. The bombs of Borodkin's left and right wingmen fell on the tracks parallel to those of the lead plane. Two of the fighters dropped single 500 lb. RDX bombs in formation with the bombers, destroying about 900 feet of track and fifteen cars.

Bombing by fighter planes was an innovation that had only recently been implemented in the 3rd Fighter Group, calling for bomb-carrying P-51s to pull in close behind the B-25s and synchronize their releases with the bombers. Used on short missions when the Mustangs could carry one or two 500 lb. bombs on their wing racks, the technique was made feasible because Japanese aerial opposition had been completely eliminated from the skies of the CACW's hunting grounds.

Hamilton led the 3rd Squadron formation (three B-25Js and one B-25J-2) as pilot of A/C #714 (Trumm, Faherty, Wilkerson, Morris, Holmes, and Stearns comprising his aircrew). Lt. Chen Y. P., in #721 (with Yang P. C., Yang C., Yuan C. F., Chow S. N., and Fang C. K.), and Lt. Ilefeldt, in #719 (with Pulaski, Cantor, Jackson, England, and Schlicher), took wing positions, and Lt. Chiang D., in #718 (with Tu N. L., Ching K. L., Lai H. L., Lu H. W., and Chang Y.), completed the box. Following the 2nd Squadron, the Mitchells made their first run at 1030, and two of the bombardiers dropped on the lead plane. On the second pass, bombardiers released the remaining bombs on the leader. From details provided by interrogation and bomb strike photos, several hits registered on tracks at the west end of yards. The remaining bombs fell along the east side of the yard, probably hitting spur tracks. Crewmen observed hits by 2nd Squadron bombs in yard #264, several boxcars appearing to be derailed and trackage damaged. Fifty to sixty railroad cars were in the yards, and the car count between Sinyang and Chowshihtien was another 130. No activity of any kind was evident.

At Anlu the formation discontinued, and aircraft returned to Liangshan individually, covering the east–west road network toward Ichang. Flight crews reported truck revetments but no movement, and two dummy A/C were in two of the three revetments at the Sinyang airfield. Most of the buildings were burned out in the barracks area, and all was quiet. Crews reported that Ping-Han Railroad bridge #265 was intact. Trumm and Faherty noted the mission's duration as 5:30.

On July 24, four 3rd Squadron B-25s took off at 0613 from Liangshan and flew to Wuchang. Their primary target was the spinning mill / warehouse (30°34' N, 114°29' E), 14th Air Force photo grid #26 (J.5-5.8), with the objective of destroying the warehouse and enemy stores. It was designated as mission #148. This was another cooperative mission with the 2nd Squadron (its mission #320), with four B-25s. Col. Smith led the formation to the target area. The 2nd Squadron's target was again the Japanese Military Headquarters Building (installation #121). It had conducted a raid to destroy the same target on the twenty-first; however, because of poor visibility and intense searchlight activity at the target, the cotton-spinning mill was hit instead. The intended target was considered important enough that this follow-up mission was scheduled. Aircrews of the two bomb squadrons were briefed to fly to the target together and then separate into two elements to make their bomb runs. Their route took them to Siaokan and then on to Wuchang. Circling north of Hankow, the aircraft passed beyond the twin cities in order to approach Wuchang from the west.

Four 3rd Fighter Group P-51s (pilots Sturgis, Cotton, Porter, and Wong) flew escort. Each fighter plane carried one 500 lb. M64 RDX on one wing and a gas tank on the other. Two of the Mustangs were directed to fall into formation with each of the two echelons of bombers, with their pilots dropping their single bombs when they saw the bombs falling from the Mitchells.

Maj. Hamilton led the 3rd Squadron bombers, flying A/C #714 (with Ilefeldt, Faherty, Wilkerson, Morris, Allegretto, and Stearns), and Lt. Chang K. L. as pilot of #724 (Lee C. C., Chung C., Ho W. C., and Kao C. K.), Mondelli flying #719 (with Pulaski, Cantor, Holmes, England, and Mills), and Lt. Hu T. C. in A/C #718 (with Chang L. T., Huang C., Chiu H. P., Tai P. S., and Tuan T. P.) followed. They circled to the west and north of Wuchang, coming in toward the south for the attack. The B-25s included three J models, each carrying eight 500 lb. GP M64 RDX, and one H (#724) that carried seven, all fused instantaneous. Over the target at 0830, Faherty, Lee, and Cantor, bombardiers of the first three planes, released twenty-three bombs at 100-foot intervals from 5,000 feet. They scored hits diagonally from the northeast to the southwest corner of the target area, and black smoke and some white smoke immediately columned to 1,000 feet.

A/C #718's bombardier, Lt. Huang C., dropped late, and his bombs fell in the dock area on the Hankow side of the Yangtze, just south of the mouth of the Han. Crewmen reported moderate and accurate enemy antiaircraft fire, estimated as forty to fifty black bursts, with several white bursts below the aircraft at 2,000 feet. Many bursts occurred within the formation, and one of the fighters was hit. "I dreaded night-bombing runs and those big spotlights the Japanese had," Hank confided many years later. "They'd flash on us—lock onto our plane—and I could see ack-ack all around us," he recalled. "The sky was full of those little black puffs, and they were trying to shoot us down. You couldn't see how you'd get through it—but we did, always." No strafing was done because of the AA, and no leaflets were dropped because of depleted supply. All four planes were back down at 1045.

One of the 2nd Squadron Mitchells developed engine trouble about thirty minutes out and returned to Liangshan. The remaining three flew on in "V" formation to complete the mission and were over their target at 0840. Each carried eight 500 lb. GP M64 RDX bombs. As the bombers approached Wuchang, they made several course changes to avoid ground fire. "Only one bomber in the formation of eight was hit[,] and the hit did not penetrate the skin," according to Capt. William C. Rittman, the 2nd Squadron's intelligence officer. "The fire was apparently from 75 mm because it broke with black bursts, and it broke in groups from four to six. They were sufficiently large to be from a shell of that size." Reported as intense and accurate, it was close enough to be heard and to "bounce" the airplanes. One crewman reported seeing automatic weapons time-fused, breaking 3,000 feet below the formation, and others reported small-arms fire.

Bombs were dropped on Smith's lead bombardier, successfully hammering the target. One string of bombs ran from the northeast to the southwest corner of the large area. Each of the other planes cut the northwest and southeast corners. Smoke billowed to 4,000 feet. Leaflets were dropped. After completing the bomb run, bombers went into a diving turn and missed a heavy barrage put up from Hankow Airdrome. As with the 3rd Squadron, no strafing followed. Planes returned to base at 1155.

The 2nd Squadron report of the mission noted, "Crewmen did not have much to offer concerning the Hankow-Wuchang area. They all were watching the flak." Hank, who was also watching the flak, experienced a fortunate near miss. In his position as tail gunner "right on the end of the plane," he felt a sudden impact to the front of his lower leg from ground fire. "I had always heard that you don't feel any pain when you first get shot, so I was afraid to even try to find out how bad it was." Because of his kneeling position in the cramped compartment, it was impossible to look down at his leg to determine the extent of injury.

"When I got shot—I thought, here I am shot—shot in the leg. And when the plane pulled up, I decided, well, I've got to feel back there to know how bad it is. I ran my hand down my leg—felt around—pulled my hand back. There was no blood. I couldn't understand that. I took my hand down there again—still no blood." Later he checked the deck. "There that shell was, the spent bullet that hit me." Although it had maintained sufficient momentum to penetrate the B-25's fuselage, it only "gouged a place" in his boot but did not even break the skin. "I never did even report that. Nobody ever knew it." He kept the spent bullet as a souvenir and as a reminder of his good fortune, and he kept his eligibility to the "Close Shavers Club" to himself.

Off Chihkiang at 1000, Bowen flew with the 4th Squadron's Capt. H. L. Knoll (pilot) and Col. Russell (copilot) in the lead of a four-plane formation to again hit the Puchi Bridge with parademos. Bowen dropped three bombs, but parachutes failed to open. The bombs landed on the bridge and slid harmlessly along the tracks before exploding, causing absolutely no damage. Bombing by the following three planes was equally unsuccessful. The Mitchells encountered some ground fire near the bridge and on the return to base but landed safely.

The following day, Capt. Mondelli led a formation of four B-25s (three J and one H model) that took off at 0900 with two 3rd Fighter Group P-51s. The mission's objective was "to damage enemy R. R. yards and deny enemy use of communication lines." A 2nd Squadron plane had taken off at 0640 to hit the same target but had not yet returned to report results. Over the target at 1205, Mondelli's formation bombed the Kwanshuishih railroad yards #275 (31°37' N, 113°55' E), registering hits in the southwest-central section of the target. This was the mission's secondary target, chosen in preference to the primary target of the Hwayuan railroad yards because more rail activity was observed there. All carried a mixed load of 500 lb. GP M64 RDX and 500 lb. GP M64A1 RDX, released at 4,000 feet. Eight of the M64A1 bombs were fused with delays of two, four, six, twelve (two bombs), twenty-four, thirty-six, and 144 hours; the others were fused instantaneous.

Mondelli, flying A/C #714 (with Trumm, Faherty, Wilkerson, DeFabritis, Mier, Schroeder, and Maj. Kelly, flight surgeon), Tu K. M. as pilot of the H, #716 (with Liu P. C., Chow K. P., Tung H. T., and Lee L.), and Pulaski, in #721 (with Ilefeldt, Cantor, Holmes, Magyar, Jackson, Stearns, and M. Bakalar, observer), arrived over the yards and Faherty, Liu, and Cantor released on two 175-foot buildings. Capt. Lo S. S., in A/C #715 (with Yu Y. T., Ting C. L., Wang M. T., Kuo H. Y., and Lai F. L.), moved on to the southeast-central part of the yards, near the sidings, where Lt. Ting dropped his bombs. Antiaircraft fire was meager and automatic-weapons fire was far below the formation.

Northwest of Sinyang, the two fighters left the formation and returned to bomb railroad yard #263 at Sinyang. They released four 500 lb. GPs in a diving pass, two hitting north of the target and two farther east. Pilots of the fighters were 1st Lt. Martin C. Cotton of the 8th Fighter Squadron and Lt. Hwang C. C. of the 32nd Fighter Squadron. As the bombers returned to base, Lt. Tu made an emergency landing at Ankang for refueling before proceeding to Liangshan. Faherty noted duration as 5:10, and Trumm recorded 2:35 as pilot and 2:35 as copilot.

Lt. Tu, back on flying status despite his walkout, commented that by this time, "when going out on missions, we rarely saw Japanese aircraft attempting to intercept us, no matter we had fighter escorts or not. Even when we encountered the Japanese aircraft, they would immediately lower the altitude and escape us." He credited the 312th Fighter Wing of the 14th Air Force, also stationed at Liangshan, in addition to the CACW's bombers and fighters, for providing increased firepower necessary for repelling enemy aircraft. "Even the B-24 heavy bombers originally stationed in Chengdu came to support us," he said.[7]

On July 26, the Lohochai railroad yards (Ping-Han installation #234) were the target of four B-25s that took off at 0930 with two 3rd Fighter Group P-51s. Four 2nd Squadron B-25s had taken off at 0700 to attack the same target (33°32' N, 114°03' E). This was the 3rd Squadron's 150th numbered mission. The planes (two J models, one J-2, and one H) carried the same bombload as on the previous day's mission: twenty-three fused instantaneous and eight with delays of between one and forty-eight hours. Col. Russell led the raid as pilot of A/C #719 (Trumm, Faherty, Wilkerson, Morris, Mills, and Schroeder as his aircrew). Lt. Yen P. S. flew A/C #718, the J-2 (Tsuei W. P., Yang S. H., Chow S. H., Ho W. C., and Feng C. K.), Mondelli flew #721 (with Pulaski, Fuller, Holmes, Magyar, Allegretto, DeFabritis, and Sgt. E. J. Reddish, the last two as photographers), and Lt. Chen C. S. flew #724, the H (with Kuo Y. H., Yuan C. F., Lu H. W., and Chang Y.). Pilots of the fighters were 1Lt. Charles Wagner and Capt. Willard Lee, 7th Fighter Squadron.

Planes were over the target at 1050. Both fighters and bombers released 500 lb. bombs from 5,780 feet, all registering hits in the central portion of the yards on the first pass. Two fires, one large and one small, with bright-red flames and columns of black smoke visible to 30 miles, were ignited in the east-central side of the yards, and an estimated 25 percent of the fifty or more boxcars were derailed. After the bomb run, fighter A/C #675 strafed a locomotive between the yards and the bridge, resulting in direct hits and possible damage to a second locomotive. Crewmen observed four or five flashes at the south end of the yards but encountered no other enemy AA. Other than ten or twelve Japanese soldiers near a small hut on the western side of Nanyang, they observed no enemy activity. The bomber formation searched the roads from Lohochai to Nanyang and strafed eighty to a hundred two-wheeled carts loaded with sacks and supplies just west of Fangchang. Gunners then strafed a group of about twenty enemy soldiers spotted in the same vicinity, but most escaped into a clump of trees. Mission duration was 4:55, according to Trumm and Faherty.

At 0800 on July 27, four B-25s (two J models, a J-2, and an H) took off from Liangshan with two 3rd Fighter Group P-51s. The bombers again carried a mixed load of GP 500 lb. M64A1 RDX and GP 500 lb. M64 RDX fused instantaneous and with from 1-to-144-hour delay. The H model, A/C #716 (Hu Y. C., Shen W. C., Wang H. T., Kuo H. Y., and Lee L.), immediately returned because of gasoline leaking from the tank cap. Its ground crew quickly determined that the transfer pump was on and gasoline was being pumped from the auxiliary tank to the main tank and then escaping through the cap because of a slightly worn rubber seal. The malfunction was remedied, and the plane took off alone at 0920 to bomb the mission's secondary target, the warehouse area at Ichang (30°40' N, 111°15' E). Lt. Shen released 500 lb. bombs at 1030; three of seven were direct hits in the southwest section. The remaining four bombs fell on the waterfront in the central section of town.

The three remaining B-25s flew on after takeoff to the primary target, Ping-Han installation #288: the railroad yards at Siaokan. Hamilton was in the lead with A/C #714 (Pulaski, Faherty, Gaffney, Morris, Mier, and Stearns as his aircrew), with Lt. Chang C. K. as pilot of the J-2, #715 (with Chen K. C., Huang T. H., Chiu H. P., Tuan T. P., and Tai P. S.), and Ilefeldt as pilot of #726 (with Trumm, Cantor, Wilkerson, DeFabritis, Schlicher, and Magyar) following. They were over the target at 1205, and bombardiers Huang and Cantor dropped on Faherty's lead at 5,200 feet. All fell in the target area and scored hits on the north half of the yards. A secondary explosion that produced bright-red and orange flames to 600 feet and dense black smoke erupted. No AA came up from the target, although crewmen noticed two or three white bursts at 2,000 feet at Hwayuan and Kwanshuishih. No strafing was done. Trumm and Faherty, flying separately, both noted duration as 5:10.

The two fighter planes failed to reach the primary target because of low fuel levels, having turned back at Shayang. Their pilots were Capt. Willard Lee of the 7th Fighter Squadron and 1Lt. Hwang C. C. of the 32nd Fighter Squadron (both Chinese). The fighters flew to Ichang and dropped their four bombs on warehouse offices and other targets on the bank of the river.

Still with the 4th Squadron at Chihkiang, Lt. Bowen was off at 2315 on July 27 aboard a Mitchell piloted by Lt. McCullar, and dropped three M1A1 frags and one M50A2 incendiary on the northeast section of the town of Wung Le Tung. Scouting afterward for targets of opportunity, they found them to be typically plentiful. When McCullar spotted a train of undetermined size north of bridge #45, Bowen dropped three frags and one incendiary, followed by five frags and one incendiary on a twenty-vehicle convoy 2 miles south of the bridge, starting one large fire visible for fifteen minutes from the target. He released four frags and two incendiaries over a convoy about 13 miles farther south of the bridge and then two frags over the island opposite Changsha before McCullar turned for home.

Two 4th Squadron B-25Js were off at 1300 on July 28 to attack enemy troop concentrations on the riverbank at Kian, and Bowen was bombardier of the wing plane. Four 5th Fighter Group P-51s flew escort. The leader dropped nineteen M1A1 frags, all short. Bowen's bombs fell into the river. Both planes then heavily strafed the entire area until gunners had expended all ammunition, giving special attention to the numerous sampans on the river. Fires that were still burning as the aircraft left the target area were the result of strafing by the bombers and fighters.

Bowen was off on another 4th Squadron raid to the Hsiang valley at 1820 on the thirtieth, aboard a B-25J piloted by Maj. Drake. He dropped nine M1A1 frags and three M6 incendiaries on a small village 8 miles west of Yochow, followed by eight frags and two incendiaries on a group of lights 10 miles west of Yochow. Gunners strafed twenty to twenty-five sampans spotted 30 miles north of Changsha.

Chinese ground forces retook Kweilin on July 27 as Japanese troops continued their withdrawal. By this time in the war, 3rd Squadron operations along rivers, roads, and rails were primarily for the purpose of "mopping up," since very little enemy activity was evident on any of these missions. Farmers in the vicinity began to harvest their crops. "We used to fly over Chinese farmers, and they would be threshing their grain in the fields," Hank recalled. "I would think, they're doing that just like they did back thousands of years ago, just like they did in the Bible." It was a reassuring sign that life was returning to normal in war-weary China.

On the same day, Maj. Hamilton completed the sad task of signing letters of condolence addressed to next of kin of the six men still listed as MIA. Although family members of all of them had received the dreaded news soon after A/C #722 was lost, he confirmed that each man had "failed to return" from the mission on May 16 and was "missing as a result of enemy action" and presumed to be dead. Hamilton wrote about each of them, "It may comfort you to know that he died a hero's death, carrying his battle to the enemy." He gave assurances that each had been an excellent soldier and that "before the plane was shot down, extensive damage was done over the target." The letters were sent to CACW headquarters to be forwarded to their intended recipients through military channels.

In spite of having received official notification that their son was missing, the parents of Cpl. Ryan still held out hope that there was some mistake—that he had bailed out or he had not been on the flight—"anything that would make him live." They began a letter-writing campaign to learn more about what had happened to their son. If he was dead, how did he die? They wrote to the War Department and to Jim's buddies, desperately searching for answers.

Frank Jakubasz replied, "Yes, I knew your son, Jim, Mr. Ryan. He joined my squadron in China in November, I believe, and since then Jim and I had much fun joking and laughing." Jakubasz had participated in the same mission from which Ryan failed to return, but as part of a different aircrew. He wrote that Jim often spoke of "the very fine people he had and of the girl he loved," his fiancée, Audrey. "He was just a boy, Mr. Ryan, as jolly as could be."

Al Magyar sent a letter written on Red Cross stationery. He was with the crew that had searched for the missing plane when it failed to return from its mission. "I had gotten to know Jim well," he wrote. "We lived, trained, and fought together. I am proud to be a member of that crew and to have flown with Jimmy. He became one of my best friends and I shan't forget him, ever." He wrote again after he had learned more, providing the few additional details that had been discovered about the crash since his earlier letter. Magyar wrote a third time to offer his condolences.

The wife of one of the other missing crewmen (whether Jeanette Davis or Clovis Wadlow is not stated) wrote, "I'm afraid they were all killed. It's a horrible thing to think about let alone say, but it is something we have to face."

In July came a letter from a Catholic chaplain: "You may be pleased to know that on the preceding Sunday, your boy went to confession and received Holy Communion. So, no matter what happened, spiritually, he was prepared for it."[8]

Lt. Greene corresponded with two of Lt. Koss's sisters. He later wrote in a letter to Koss's mother, "I took the liberty of reading portions of those letters to a few of Bob's closest friends in our squadron[,] and I think they appreciate them too and were very glad to hear from members of Bob's family." With the fate of the crew still unconfirmed, Greene offered this assurance: "But at least we know that we will all be 'home' someday, whether in China, America, or elsewhere."[9]

By the end of July, central China and the China coast were nearly free of Japanese domination. No enemy fighters had appeared in the skies for the previous nine months, so the CACW flew exclusively bombing and strafing missions. Hank commented that he never saw an enemy plane in the air on any of his missions. There remained the possibility of a tedious fight along the southern boundary of Manchuria, but another two weeks brought about the enemy's surrender.[10]

The July 31 morning report indicated nineteen American officers and forty-eight enlisted men on the roster; no corresponding statistics of the squadron's Chinese contingent have been found.

At about this time, a new base was being prepared at Hsupu (Xupu), about 70 miles northeast of Chihkiang. To be in position to support the planned amphibious landing, plans were being developed for the 1st Bomb Group, 3rd Fighter Group, 14th Air Service Group, and other service groups to move up to the new facility. This would be the first time it was possible for 1st Bomb Group headquarters and all four of its squadrons to operate out of the same base. Even if the landing proved unnecessary or inadvisable, they would provide air support if the invasion of Japan became a necessity.

Maj. Curik made a trip to the new base on August 3. The headquarters contingent at Liangshan spent early August packing, and then it boarded transports bound for Hsupu on August 10 to begin moving equipment, supplies, and records. Lt. Wood logged a two-hour mission that day, as well as four others through that week, to facilitate setting up headquarters. He made the move to join Maj. Curik with 1Sgt. Earley and SSgt. Wellman on the eleventh. A series of conflicting orders came in during the next few weeks as brass tried to decide how to proceed as the war drew to an end. The bomb squadrons remained behind at their bases at Liangshan, Hanchung, and Chihkiang, and the 3rd and 5th Fighter Groups' squadrons were still at Ankang and Chihkiang.

Still at Liangshan were Capts. Greene, Kelso, and Langridge; 1Lts. Banger, Logan, and Winter; 2Lt. Fuller; MSgt. Barge; TSgts. Gruber, Reynard, Solyn, and Summerville; SSgts. Czerniak, Dunlap, Ewell, Evitts, Foorman, Haines, Hartung, Hutchinson, Hoke, Long, Thomas, and Whearty; Sgts. Learn, Peters, and Supsic; Cpls. Delahoyde, Hugel, Keller, Ryave, and Armbruster; and Pvt. Calloway—all noted as there on detached service according to the morning report of August 11 signed by Greene.

In spite of the official change of station, bombers and fighters flying out of Chihkiang against the Japanese withdrawal were unrelenting. The 4th Bomb Squadron and the 5th Fighter Group flew raids to pound the Japanese retreat until the very last. Missions recorded for the fighters alone totaled 101 during the first fourteen days of August.[11]

The 3rd Squadron detachment at Chihkiang had been recalled to Liangshan during the third week of July in anticipation of the move to Hsupu, but Maj. Hamilton returned there on August 4 with a detachment of four B-25s with crews as others were packing equipment and supplies for transport. With him went Capt. Mondelli; 1Lts. Bowen, Cantor, Faherty, Ilefeldt, Jeffries, and Trumm; TSgts. Holmes, Mier, Stearns, and Wilkerson; SSgts. Benedict and Mills; Sgts. Allegretto, England, Gaffney, Jackson, Magyar, Rickman, and Schlicher; and Cpls. DeFabritis, Morris, and Schroeder. Four days later, 1Lt. Pulaski followed in a fifth bomber with TSgts. Chasse and Meikle, SSgt. Duffin, and Cpl. Piecuch, all ground personnel. Bad weather prevented operations for a few days, and then aircrews ran five missions that included "three missions in a row," according to the 3rd Squadron's historical report.

Listed as 4th Squadron mission #420 but including mixed crews both of 3rd and 4th Squadron personnel, reminiscent of Task Force 34, six B-25Js were off Chihkiang on August 8 at 1545. The mission report included only serial numbers and no "Chinese numbers" that identified the planes by squadron, although the 3rd Squadron's aircraft numbers can be determined by comparison with other records. Mondelli led with A/C #720 (with Maj. Lucien C. Proby, Bowen, Morris, Mier, Holmes, Schroeder, and Maj. E. A. Kelly, observer), followed by Ilefeldt in A/C #722 (with Capt. G. A. Barber, Faherty, Wilkerson, Allegretto, Stearns, and Magyar), Pulaski in A/C #723 (with 1Lt. J. A. Truman, Cantor, Mills, Jackson, and England), the 3rd Squadron's Lt. Chang K. L. in A/C #724 (with 1Lt. Sheng M. C. and Sgts. Ho W. C., Feng C. K., and Li L.), the 4th Squadron's Capt. Yang L. H. in #44-30666 (with Capt. Chen

W. C., 2nd Lts. Chen Y. K. and Chow S. N., and Sgts. Tung H. C. and Chang Y.), and the 3rd Squadron's 2Lt. Yen P. S. in #43-28165 (with 2Lt. Tu N. L., 1Lt. Liu P. C., and Sgts. Yuan C. F., Lai H. L., and Tai P. S.). Planes were airborne at 1545. Four 27th Fighter Squadron P-51s joined them. Their objective was to destroy the warehouses on the island opposite Changsha. Four of the bombers carried twenty-two 100 lb. M30 demos, and one carried twenty-two 100 lb. M47A2 white phosphorus bombs.

One aircraft (its identity not noted) was unable to retract landing gear and aborted, down ten minutes after takeoff. The five remaining planes proceeded on course, arriving over the target area at 1645. One A/C broke off formation to drop smoke bombs. Its bombardier released eighteen M47A2 white phosphorus bombs on the south end of town from 5,000 feet. Then pilots of the remaining four entered a bombing run from north to south, starting at 7,000 feet in a slow dive and reducing elevation to 5,000 feet. Leveling out to 4,500 feet, each bombardier dropped his GP bombs by select. Bowen's bombs hit in the center of the island, igniting a fire. The bombs of two aircraft hit on the southern one-third of the island, each causing a secondary explosion and starting a fire. Forty to fifty bursts of heavy AA came up as aircraft were leaving, but all were misses. Three fires were raging on the island as planes turned for home. Faherty recorded it as a three-hour mission.

Hamilton was in the lead of six B-25s that took off from Chihkiang at 0945 on August 9. Four 27th Fighter Squadron aircraft flew escort. Each of the B-25s carried three 1,000 lb. M65 demos. Their objective was to destroy the Puchi Bridge. Although it had been hit repeatedly in the past, little damage had ever been inflicted to the Puchi Bridge because of its steel truss construction on concrete piers and open spaces between the trusses.

Mondelli's A/C #720 (with Pulaski, Schlicher, Gaffney, Morris, and Schroeder) developed engine trouble and turned back fifteen minutes after takeoff. The remaining five arrived over the target area at 1145: Hamilton, flying A/C #722 (with the 4th Squadron's Maj. Proby, Bowen, DeFabritis, Holmes, Wilkerson, and Stearns), Ilefeldt in A/C #723 (with Trumm, Jackson, Magyar, and Allegretto), 1Lt. Teng C. C. in A/C #721 (with 1Lts. Chen K. C. and Ting C. L. and Sgts. Wang M. T., Thiou H. P., and Kou C. K.), A/C #724 (an H model with the same aircrew as the previous day on #43-28165), and #43-28165 (the same crew as on the previous day's mission aboard #44-30666). The fifth plane was a 4th Squadron Mitchell; the mission was recorded as that squadron's 423rd. Fighters went in first to strafe gun positions, reducing AA to meager, inaccurate automatic-weapons fire.

"Glip bombing" was then employed over the target. Using this technique, the aircraft came in at a 30-to-35-degree glide, decreased to 15 to 20 degrees, and then skip-bombed along the length of the bridge before leveling off. The bombing run started from 1,200 feet in a slow dive from west to east. Bombardiers released fifteen 1,000 lb. M65 GPs by select at 400 feet. Two bombs hit near the center of the bridge but went on through, and one fell farther north. Three bombs hit the bridge's east end, causing minor damage. Six detonated on tracks at the east end, gouging two large craters on the tracks and tearing up an estimated 400 feet of trackage. This was Bowen's third failed attempt to destroy the bridge. The minor amount of damage inflicted led to the assessment "This mission gave further conclusive evidence to the accepted theory that this bridge cannot be heavily damaged from 1,000[-pound] direct hits."

After bombing, the B-25s and P-51s scouted rail yards, track, and highways north of Sinsiangin for strafing targets. When flight crews sighted two boxcars near Huangshachien, one aircraft strafed, causing explosions that demolished both cars. The 3rd Squadron's B-25H strafed and fired two rounds of 75 mm HE at a truck sighted near Siansiang, destroying it completely, but aircrews observed no river traffic. Trumm logged two hours as pilot and two hours as copilot aboard A/C #723.

Aircrews were off at 0845 on August 10 for another cooperative mission, this one a river sweep from Hengyang to Changsha. Maj. Hamilton was pilot of a rocket-equipped B-25J-32, A/C #715 (with Lt. Col. P. D. Wynn, Cantor, Holmes, Magyar, and Allegretto), and 2Lt. Yen P. S. flew a 4th Squadron H model, #43-4925 (with 1Lt. Liu P. C. and Sgts. Yuan C. F., Lai H. L., and Tai P. S.). Each carried twelve M4 parafrag clusters. When crewmen sighted an estimated one hundred sampans and junks along the river north of Hengyang, Cantor and Liu released their bombs by select. Bombing scored twelve direct hits, ten near misses, and two complete misses. Eight thousand rounds of .50-caliber, about 40 percent of them hits, peppered thirty to forty sampans. One of the sampans exploded. Machine gunners then attacked what appeared to be storage houses 5 miles north of Hengshan and then a small convoy of twelve trucks about 5 miles farther northwest. On record as 4th Bomb Squadron detachment mission #428, the report was signed by the 3rd Squadron's 1Lt. Jeffries as detachment intelligence officer.

Lt. Charles W. Jeffries, 3rd Bomb Squadron intelligence officer since early March, served as the 4th Bomb Squadron Detachment's intelligence officer during the war's final few weeks. *J. H. Mills collection*

On mission #152, two Js and a J2 were off Liangshan at 0930 on the tenth with 3rd Squadron all-Chinese crews. In the lead was A/C #725 (Yu Y. T., Sheng C. J., Yang C. H., Hoi W. C., Kuo C. C., and Wang S. C.); wing planes were A/C #721 (Chen Y. H, Tsui W. P., Hsieh W. W., Yang Y. H., Chow K. Y., and Yang S. L.) and #715 (Chang C. K., Kaing J. M., Kuo Y. W., Liu H. T., Chung C., and Fun C. K.). They proceeded on a direct course toward Nanking, each carrying four 500 lb. GP M64 bombs. After crossing the pocket, Lt. Yu decided that gas supply was not sufficient to reach the primary target (rolling stock on the Tientsien-Pukow railroad), so he selected a secondary target: the Hwainan railroad in the vicinity of Kiulungkang (32°25' N, 117°08' E). When crewmen sighted a locomotive, Yu attacked, first toggling two bombs at 500 feet before dropping in for strafing. White and yellow smoke was the result. He then dropped two bombs on a nearby wooden trestle. Because crewmen observed splintered lumber flying into the air, they claimed it as probably destroyed. "Due to alleged malfunction of release mechanism," Lt. Chen was unable to drop bombs but strafed three trucks on the road adjacent to the railroad in the same vicinity. Some smoke arose. These two Mitchells returned to home base at 1635. Lt. Chang, pilot of the B-25J-2 (A/C #715), proceeded to hit the primary target in the vicinity of Pengpu. Although the aircraft failed to return to home base when expected, information came in stating that it had made an emergency landing at Valley Field. This report was the last signed by Capt. Langridge as squadron intelligence officer.

The final recorded 3rd Bomb Squadron mission was another joint operation with the 4th Squadron. Capt. Mondelli took off from Chihkiang at 1000 on August 10 in the lead of a three-plane formation. Each of the B-25Js carried six M69 incendiary clusters nicknamed "Tokyo calling cards." Weighing about 6 pounds each and usually dropped in clusters of thirty-six to forty, each bomb consisted of a plain steel pipe with a hexagonal cross section that was 3 inches in diameter and 20 inches long. Filled with napalm as incendiary filler, the bombs were fused to ignite after hitting a target or the ground, producing multiple intense fires. "On one mission at the end of the war, we dropped incendiary bombs," Hank still recalled, although he could remember few other details after the passing of so many years.

The mission's objective was to destroy storage areas at Nanchang. Mondelli flew A/C #721 (with the 4th Squadron's Capt. Barber as copilot, Bowen, Wilkerson, DeFabritis, Mills, and Schroeder), 2Lt. Chang K. L. as pilot of A/C #722 (with Tu N. L., Sheng M. C., Ho W. C., Feng C. K., and Li L.), and Pulaski as pilot of #43-36069, a veteran 4th Squadron B-25J that saw service with Task Force 34 (with Trumm, Faherty, Gaffney, England, Schlicher, and Pfc. Edward Reddish, 16th Combat Camera Unit). A fourth plane, A/C #724, with an all-Chinese crew, had been unable to take off because of mechanical issues.

Sheng and Faherty dropped their bombs on Bowen's lead at 5,200 feet. Crews believed that they missed the target, although they could not agree upon exactly where the bombs hit. On the course home, the Mitchells encountered moderate, accurate small-arms and machine gun fire. Mondelli reported a hole in his right aileron trim tab, as well as Plexiglas of the aircraft's nose "holed" by machine gun fire. Lt. Bowen was cut slightly by flying Plexiglas shards and later received an OLC to his previously awarded Purple Heart. Schroeder again flew as photographer, taking "K-20" photos (using a Fairchild K-20 aerial photography camera) on this final mission.

On the course home, gunners strafed the town of Lingling, which appeared to be burned out. Then they strafed a bridge in the town, hitting two of its towers. Finishing up, they fired on a compound 10 miles north of Nanchang. All aircraft returned to Chihkiang at 1515. Aboard the 4th Squadron J, Trumm recorded 2:50 as copilot (twenty minutes on instruments) and 2:30 as pilot. No leaflets were dropped because of a special mission soon to follow. Lt. Jeffries, 3rd Squadron S-2, signed this final operational intelligence report, designated as the 4th Bomb Squadron's mission #429.

This was Hank's thirteenth verified combat mission in China, and he participated in his usual position as tail gunner. "I didn't know the names of most of the places that we bombed—just that it was another mission in China," he remarked many years later. Although he heard the target designations at premission briefings, his focus was on aiming and shooting as instructed rather than on geography. If his estimate of fifteen missions from India to Burma was correct, he qualified to receive the Air Medal. However, with the degree of carelessness in record keeping that developed as the war ended, he did not receive it.

Maj. Drake took off at 1310 in a 4th Squadron B-25H (no crew listed) to saturate the areas from Kiyang to Siangtan with "morale and news leaflets" dropped on connecting roads and railways. He carried no bombs and expended no ammunition. The leaflets, with versions printed both in Chinese and Japanese, were "carried in boxes shackled to the bomb bay in such a manner as to cause the box to tip and spill its contents when the toggle button was pushed." Included were leaflets #JM-145, JP-1, JN-105, CP-40, CP-112, and CN-119. Released by select by the pilot were 71,760 on Kiyang, 89,160 on Hengshan, 71,760 on Hengyang, 78,980 on

Siangtan, 18,950 on Kiyang (repeated but correct according to the report), 41,080 on the road and railroad from Kiyang to Hengyang, and 36,000 on the road and railroad from Hengyang to Siangtan. Encountering no opposition, he was back down at Chihkiang at 1720.

Drake told his family about a remarkable sequence of events that culminated at about this time. It began on July 28, when 1Lt. Wu J. W. was off from Chihkiang with an all-Chinese crew on a typical night mission (the 4th Squadron's #399) to bomb and strafe enemy convoys but ran into trouble. "King Able" tower first notified 4th Bomb Operations at 0150 that A/C B-25J call sign "Snow Baby" was coming in on one engine. Wu, one of many Chinese pilots trained by Drake, notified the tower that he was just west of Paoching at 4,000 feet. His plane, hit by flak resulting in a dead left engine and the other cutting out and beginning to sprout flames, was incapable of gaining any more altitude. The pilot wanted to know what to do. Maj. Drake, notified of the situation at 0200, gave the pilot orders to bail the crew out. All cleared the plane about 25 miles west of Paoching at 0250.

Word that came in subsequently from Chinese sources reported that 1Lt. Wu, along with 2Lt. Lu F. Y. (copilot), 1Lt. Chu C. L. (navigator), and Sgt. Sha P. C. (top-turret gunner), were recovered safely. Landing at Lungwei, they were immediately sent on their way by a combination of sedan chair, horseback, and transport plane back to Chihkiang, where they arrived on August 2. The whereabouts of Sgts. Chiang L. Y. (waist gunner) and Lee C. S. (tail gunner), who had been the first two to jump, remained uncertain; they were reported as "missing, believed safe."

On August 8, Lt. Laederlich (in the pilot's seat) and Maj. Drake, as his copilot, were flying up the valley in a rocket-equipped, Plexiglas-nosed B-25J-32 on a similar mission. The moon was full and very bright 7 miles north of Kiatow when Drake spotted a train flying two big flags with red "meatballs" on the steam engine. All six frags and two incendiaries missed the locomotive. They made six strafing passes "which caused probably heavy damage," according to the mission report. Coming in low, Laederlich lined up the nose and Drake fired a rocket (remarking when he later told the story that the recoil caused the plane to "jump backward"). "Just like in the movies," the locomotive blew up and the train derailed.

The war was nearing its end when one of the missing gunners came walking into camp. Taken prisoner by the enemy following the bailout, he had been on the train when it was blown up. He made a dash for freedom and escaped his captors during the confusion, eventually finding his way back to Chihkiang. The grateful man forever afterward believed that he owed his life to Drake and that mission.[12]

Lts. Wu and Lu were back in action and taking part in the 4th Squadron's mission #431 to attack enemy supply movement in the Hsiang valley on the evening of August 10—Wu again flying as pilot and Lu as copilot. No further reference to other crew members of the downed plane has been found.

The 2nd Squadron was still operating out of Liangshan in early August and continued to target primarily the Ping-Han Railroad. Its final two mission reports were also dated August 10, the first of these in coordination with Maj. Hamilton's river sweep. Four 2nd Squadron B-25s led by Maj. Lack, accompanied by two P-51s, bombed and strafed river traffic along the Yangtze east of Hankow. The 2nd Squadron's final reported mission, its #330, took off at 0755 with three Mitchells led by Col. Smith that hit the railroad yards at Sinyang.

Strategic bombing of the Japanese home islands had failed to bring about capitulation, so President Truman made the difficult decision to escalate the effort. On August 6, an atomic bomb hit Hiroshima, at that time a regional hub that served as an important military communications center, storage depot, and troop-gathering area, but Japanese authorities, steeped in the Bushido tradition, continued their refusal to surrender. Another fell on the ninth, this time about 185 miles farther southwest on Nagasaki, site of a major Imperial Japanese Navy base situated on a large natural harbor on the island of Kyushu. Devastation from the second blast finally led Emperor Hirohito and Premier Suzuki to consider the wisdom of accepting Allied terms. Forward bases had not received news of the bombings, nor of the negotiations to end the war, so life proceeded as usual for American airmen stationed across China.

Maj. Gen. Charles B. Stone III assumed command of the 14th Air Force on August 10, now with Chennault out of the equation. Headquarters of the 14th Air Force had been moved only days before from Kunming to Peishiyi. The 10th Air Force, under the command of Maj. Gen. Albert F. Hegenberger, was in the process of moving from India to Kunming, but the deployment of 10th Air Force units to China was not completed by the end of the war. Its proposed role was to act as the tactical air force giving direct support and providing air supply to Chinese ground forces operating south of the twenty-seventh parallel north. By the time the air forces of China were undergoing reorganization, victory had been achieved against the Axis powers in Europe, and the Allies had made a number of major advancements against the Japanese in the Pacific, capturing many of their island strongholds that were being used to take the war to the emperor's doorstep.

It was Saturday, August 11, 1945. Assigned code name "Butcher," this early-morning mission was to include all four squadrons of the 1st Bomb Group, as well as several of the wing's fighter squadrons. The Yellow River Bridge was once again the target. This 2-mile-long, 10-foot-wide bridge had been bombed repeatedly in the past, but the Japanese had always been able to repair it quickly and resume rail traffic on the vital Peiping–Hankow line within a matter of days. This was to be a final assault on the bridge, to destroy it "once and for all." The raid had been planned by Col. John S. ("Jack") Chennault, commander of the 311th ("Flying Comanches") Fighter Group, stationed at Hsian. Col. Chennault, eldest son of Gen. Chennault, would personally oversee the strike, circling high above the bridge in his P-51 and "directing traffic." Hank remembered it as a very important target, with the bridge stretching across "a big lake," and there were "some bridges between islands that went across that lake."

The Japanese had covered the bridge deck with 1.25-inch boilerplate steel and installed antiaircraft guns on the flats on the north bank of the river, as well as on the mesa on the south bank, several hundred feet above the river. Caves dug into the bluffs were equipped with antiaircraft and large-caliber machine guns so that any low-level bombing attempt would surely be a suicide mission. Hank explained that the thing that made the target so dangerous was that "there were mountains on both sides that had gun emplacements, and all they had to do was fire and you had to fly through that fire to get to the target." There was little hope that they would all come back alive. "I figured if we didn't make it, that was my time to go."

In this proposed combined strike, B-24s and B-29s were assigned to first conduct high-level saturation bombing to knock out the antiaircraft guns both on the north and south banks of the river. Next, the fighters would create a smoke screen in front of the machine gun emplacements on the south bank, refreshing the smoke screens every five minutes to reduce visibility from the caves. Then the 1st Bomb Group's four B-25 squadrons, using twelve planes each, would come in from the north and fly south along the length of the bridge at fifteen- or twenty-second intervals, two on each side. Attacking in units of four, they would release their bombs, armed with fusing set to four-to-five-second delay, on the best angle possible. If the first four destroyed the south end, the next four would go no farther south than necessary to hit the next portion of the bridge. If the assigned section was not destroyed, the next four would go in to hit the undamaged section, and others would proceed in the same way until all forty-eight aircraft had dropped their bombs. By utilizing this strategy, mission planners believed there was good probability that the entire bridge could be wiped out at once.[13]

Sgt. Daniels and others of his 1st Bomb Squadron, along with aircrews from the other three CACW bomb squadrons and the fighter squadrons chosen to participate, had attended a briefing at Liangshan on the tenth. Many years later he described his reaction to the planned strike: "My hair stood on end when I heard what was being proposed. . . . I wasn't anxious to go back to that bridge again with the war so near its end, especially on such a nightmarish mission as this." Daniels was doubtful of any chance of success:

> This operation didn't sound good to me on paper, and its successful execution seemed unworkable. The fighters laying smoke screens would be crossing our flight path at ninety degrees—in smoke? It was my understanding that any object, like a B-25, would trigger the proximity fuses when they came within the range they were set for. What if some B-24s were late to arrive and dropped those proximity[-]fused bombs over us? How were two B-25s supposed to hit the bridge flying parallel beside it?

In spite of his skepticism, Daniels concluded, "Mine was not to reason why, mine was but to do, or possibly die."[14]

Weather conditions must be perfect, and there had been several delays. On this morning the radio message "Butcher on green" came in at 0400. Aircrews were briefed at 0500. The first elements were off an hour later and had been in the air for about twenty minutes. The 1st Bomb Squadron's Mitchells had just fired up their engines for departure, according to Daniels. Aircraft of the 3rd Bomb Squadron were loaded, and preflight checklists completed. They were in position and ready to roll. "We were on the end of the runway, fixing to take off," Hank recalled. He was in his usual position as tail gunner. Before the bomber was airborne, the pilot received a radio message from the tower instructing him, in Hank's words, "Don't take off. The flight's been canceled." The pilot turned the plane around and taxied back in. Someone ran out onto the runway shouting, "The Japs have surrendered!" That was when Hank and his crew learned that for them, the war was over.

He said the same thing had happened two days before that: "We were on the end of the runway, and we were ordered to come back. We didn't know that there were any negotiations going on to end the war." Although Japan had not yet officially surrendered, discussions had begun and a ceasefire issued that stopped "Butcher" in its tracks.

No crew lists have been discovered for this aborted mission. The 3rd Squadron's morning report for August 11 listed Capts. Greene, Kelso, and Langridge; 1Lts. Banger, Logan, and Winter; 2Lt. Fuller; MSgt. Barge; TSgts. Gruber, Reynard, Solyn, and Summerville; SSgts. Czerniak, Dunlap, Ewell, Evitts, Foorman, Haines, Hartung, Hutchinson, Hoke, Long, Thomas, and Whearty; Sgts. Learn, Peters, and Supsic; Cpls. Delahoyde, Hugel, Keller, Ryave, and

Armbruster; and Pvt. Calloway as on detached service at Liangshan. Some of these may have participated, although most were ground personnel. Hank and others on detached service at Chihkiang were to rendezvous with the other participants to take part in what proved to be the CACW's final scheduled combat mission.

The 4th Squadron recorded one last mission out of Chihkiang, its #433. Lt. McCullar took off at 1235 on August 12 aboard an unescorted B-25H and flew to the Nangyang-Yochow-Siangying delta area to scatter hundreds of thousands of informational leaflets printed both in the Japanese and Chinese languages. The pilot released those loaded in the bomb bay, and waist gunners heaved out others loaded in that compartment.

CM-129, which bears that date, announced to the people of China the joyous news that "JAPAN HAS SURRENDERED! WAR IS COMPLETELY OVER!" The leaflet, which featured the flags of the United States and China, read in part: "Chinese friends, Japan has surrendered! She has accepted the surrender terms imposed by the United States, Great Britain, China, and the Soviet Union. The hostilities will cease at once. The gloomy and painful days you suffered for eight painful years are over and the dawn glows now. . . . Thus, Chinese friends, the final victory is here. You are happy. We are happy too."[15]

Although the plane encountered some ground fire at Yochow, it returned undamaged. Lt. Edgerton, copilot, included this mission in his log and noted that the plane was down after four hours and forty minutes in the air. None of the other three 1st Bomb Group squadrons recorded missions to drop leaflets.

Hirohito, known to his subjects as Emperor Showa, made a somewhat ambiguous public announcement on August 15, stating that he intended to accept the Allied terms of surrender although without actually admitting defeat. He gave as his reason for capitulation a desire to protect his people from "a new and most cruel bomb" while denying that Japan's attack on America and Britain was motivated by "territorial aggrandizement" but "out of our sincere desire to insure [sic] Japan's self-preservation and the stabilization of East Asia."[16]

Fierce opposition to his decision that went as far as an attempted coup to prevent broadcast of the announcement persisted within his own ranks. Nevertheless, the celebrations across China began. "When we heard the news regarding the unconditional surrender of Japan on the evening of Aug. 15, 1945, we all went crazy to celebrate the day of victory," Tu Kai-mu recalled. "For the Americans of my squadron, it meant that they could finally go home."[17] He described the joyous celebration: "The whole airbase fell into a state of jubilation. Chinese and American members were ecstatic and hugged each other. I did not drink much up to then, but I drank myself into a drunken stupor that day. I also fired my pistol into the sky until all the bullets were spent. The base and the city were filled with the sounds of fireworks, until all the fireworks at Liangshan had been used up."[18]

If Japan's surrender was not sufficient reason to celebrate, Hank had another. That was the day he learned of his promotion to technical sergeant, effective from August 1.

It was not until more than two weeks had passed that the formal document of Japan's unconditional capitulation was signed. Regardless of the delay, arrangements began for the positioning of CACW personnel to allow them to begin the journey home as soon as the surrender became official.

Even after the ceasefire, squadron mechanics were expected to maintain their planes and keep them ready to fly, just as they had previously during times of bad weather or gas shortage. Although preparations had begun for transporting the men back to the States, Allied high command did not trust the Japanese to follow through with their surrender.

As late as August 17, plans were being carried forward for the CACW to support an amphibious landing on the China coast, where Allied troops would stage the planned invasion in the event Japan continued its aggression.

Meanwhile, bomb group HQ at Hsupu received a radiogram asking for volunteers to participate in a postwar air mission to the Chinese air force. No further details were provided. "In all truthfulness, it can be said that the radiogram was passed around the orderly room strictly for laughs," wrote Capt. Richard T. Mallon, 1st Bomb Group adjutant and historian. "The general derision at the prospect of spending an indefinite period in China was silenced to a great extent when we received rumors that anyone who volunteered would be on a per diem status, his base pay would be matched by the Chinese Air Force, that wives could be brought over to China in the near future, etc., etc."

The bomb squadrons finally received their orders to move to the new base at Hsupu. According to the 3rd Squadron's historical report, its personnel made the move on August 16 and 17, just before word came that the CACW was to be deactivated within the next thirty days and its members sent home. However, morning reports provided more-accurate details, indicating that Maj. Curik was still at Hsupu, and 1Lt. Wood, 1Sgt. Earley, and SSgt. Wellman had moved there on August 11, when Hsupu became the squadron's permanent station. Others trickled in through the following week. Sgt. Peters moved from Liangshan, and TSgts. Chasse and Meikle, SSgt. Duffin, and Cpl. Piecuch from Chihkiang, followed by Capt. Langridge; TSgts. Gruber, Reynard, Solyn, and Summerville; SSgts. Evitts, Hoke, Czerniak, Whearty, Hartung, and Thomas; Sgt. Supsic; and Cpl. Keller. Capt. Kelso and 1Lt. Winter made the move on August 15.

The list of men who moved from Liangshan on the sixteenth included 1Lts. Banger and Senecal; 2Lt. Fuller; SSgts. Dunlap, Ewell, Foorman, Haines, and Hutchinson; Sgt. Learn; Cpls. Armbruster, Delahoyde, Hugel, and Ryave; and Pfc. Calloway (promoted on August 1), while Maj. Hamilton; 1Lts. Cantor, Ilefeldt, Pulaski, and Faherty; TSgts. Holmes, Mills, and Wilkerson; Sgts. Gaffney and Schlicher; and Cpl. Shroeder arrived from Chihkiang. Maj. Curik was transferred from the 3rd Squadron to 1st Bomb Group HQ on the same date.

Capt. Greene, 1Lts. Jeffries and Logan, MSgt. Barge, and SSgt. Long arrived from Liangshan, and 1Lt. Trumm; TSgt. Stearns; Sgts. Allegretto, England, Magyar, and Rickman; and Cpl. DeFabritis from Chihkiang on the following day. It was during this period that Allegretto was treated at the dispensary for cellulitis, a painful bacterial skin infection that affected his buttock and hip, according to medical records. Cpl. Morris, still at Chihkiang, was hospitalized once again.

Capt. Mondelli, 1Lt. Bowen, TSgt. Mier, SSgt. Benedict, and Sgt. Jackson arrived from Chihkiang, and 1Lt. Senecal from detached duty at Peishiyi during the next several days. As plans were being implemented to send most of them home, Maj. Hamilton, Lts. Pulaski and Winter, and Sgts. Chasse, Long, Benedict, Mier, and Duffin volunteered to remain behind for a brief time to facilitate the final transfer of the squadron to the Chinese.

In a letter dated August 18, 1945, Col. Bennett expressed his appreciation to those who had served under his command:

SUBJECT: Farewell Message.

TO: All Personnel of all units of the Chinese American Composite Wing.

1. On the eve of the inactivation of the Chinese American Composite Wing, I want to take this means of expressing my appreciation to all of you for your loyalty, courage, devotion to duty, and efficiency. The achievements of the Chinese American Composite Wing are a tribute to each individual and we can all look with justifiable pride on the record we have made.

2. The difficulties encountered have been many and I know that all of you have been discouraged at times. Yet, in the finest American tradition, you have had the perseverance and plain guts to stick to a tough job and see it through to a glorious finish.

3. Although we have been few in number, we can all enjoy a feeling of deep gratification in the knowledge that in the achievement of final victory, the Chinese American Composite Wing contributed in full measure to the defeat of the enemy. The record of the Chinese American Composite Wing is written in large letters in the blood and supplies of Japan.

4. Many of you will soon be leaving for home. Others will remain here for a short period of time. But, to all I want to wish you good luck and Godspeed and to say a simple and sincere "thank you" for a good job well done.

[signed] T. Alan Bennett, Colonel, Air Corps,
Commanding

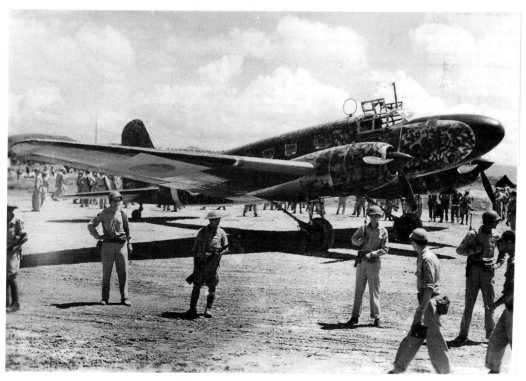

Armed guards surround the Japanese Topsy transport that brought Maj. Gen. Takeo Imai to Chihkiang for the purpose of formally surrendering all Japanese forces in China. R. L. Logan collection, courtesy of Katherine A. Logan

The Japanese emissary travels by jeep to meet with Gen. Hsiao Yi-shu and accept the terms of surrender as hundreds of onlookers observe the proceedings. *R. L. Logan collection, courtesy of Katherine A. Logan*

Chinese and American personnel still stationed at Chihkiang witnessed the arrival on August 21 of Japanese dignitaries, when a Japanese Ki-57 Topsy transport, escorted by three P-51s of the 5th Fighter Group, landed for a preliminary surrender conference. Maj. Gen. Takeo Imai, vice chief of the general staff of the China Expeditionary Army (acting for Lt. Gen. Yasuji Okamura, commander of all Japanese forces in China), landed at Chihkiang Air Base, accompanied by two staff officers, an interpreter, and the pilot. The Japanese emissary was received by Gen. Hsiao Yi-shu, chief of staff of the Republic of China Army Headquarters (acting for Gen. Ho Ying-chin, supreme commander of the ROC Army).

In an audience attended by more than one hundred Chinese and American officers the following day, the Japanese general received instructions for the formal surrender of military forces in China, set to take place in Nanking, accepted the terms of surrender, and signed the documents, officially ending hostilities between Japan and China. Imai stated in a press conference that the Japanese army of three million was well able to continue the war if it had not been affected by destruction of the Japanese air force and navy, and that the airdromes at Shanghai and Nanking were intact but had little remaining gasoline with which to operate.[19]

Lt. Logan had not yet made the move from Chihkiang and kept photos of some of the proceedings. It is probable that Cpl. Morris also witnessed at least some of the official activities. He remained on detached service at Chihkiang until August 28, returning at that time to duty with what remained of the 3rd Squadron at Hsupu.

American military advisors and technicians who had worked to build a more effective Chinese military force had completed their task. The China theater suspended all training under US supervision on August 22. This marked the beginning of the end for the elaborate system of American liaison, air and logistical support, and advice, and the armies of Chiang Kai-shek were on their own to face the Communists soon afterward.[20]

"Through the C.A.C.W., a handful of Americans were carrying out Claire Chennault's ideas. General Chennault was one of the greatest men I ever met," Jim McCann commented when summarizing his service in a postwar interview. "A handful of Americans trained and built a powerful offensive weapon from personnel of the Chinese Air Force. We taught them how to fly and how to skip[-]bomb. We fought beside them and they beside us. We were members of a great team."[21]

With the planned invasion of the China coast no longer necessary, Gen. Stratemeyer, commanding the Army Air Force, China theater, offered his congratulations and assurances. "We want to get every man in the AAF back to his home and his family as soon as we possibly can. But the occupational requirements, plus the assistance which we still shall have to give to the Chinese Air Force, will keep some of us here for some time," he announced. "We are taking a personal interest in every individual of the AAF in the China Theater[,] and our personnel experts are working night and day to get the most deserving—those deserving members—those who have been out here the longest—back to the United States as expeditiously as possible."[22]

Following the Allied victory in Europe, the War Department had devised a system of "discharge points" that was used to determine the order in which veterans were sent home. Officially termed "Adjusted Service Rating Credits," points were assigned on the basis of length of total service, overseas service, combat stars and decorations, and children under eighteen years of age (up to a total of three children). As demobilization began, the first group included those who had been overseas for at least twenty-four months or who had eighty-five points toward rotation. Of those who did not have the requisite service, some were transferred to units in which their skills could be utilized, while others were assigned to "class 4" units that were scheduled to be sent back to the States over the next few months.

In the 2008 interview, Tu Kai-mu recalled those last few weeks as the Americans were taking their departure. "Before the Americans left, we held a farewell party for those American comrades who once risked their lives to fight side by side with us. During the party, American and Chinese members shared their farewells and best wishes." Just ten days after the preliminary Japanese surrender at Chihkiang, American airmen and ground crews began their journey back home. According to Tu, "We all hugged each other before they departed, and it was indeed a very sad moment for all of us. . . . During the war against Japan, we lived and fought together against a common enemy, and that made us even closer than real brothers."

Tu was still affected by the emotions he had experienced so many years earlier. Although sixty years had passed, he still wondered whatever happened to those friends. "It would be very difficult for an individual who has not been through life-and-death situations to understand why it felt like departing from my family when I said goodbye to my American friends," he said. "At that time, I was so sad that my eyes were red for a long time. Even as I think back on those memories today, I still could not refrain from shedding tears."[23]

Twenty-three men were released from the 3rd Squadron on August 27. Capt. Kelso was transferred to Yangkai, located 33 miles northeast of Kunming and home of the 341st Bomb Group, and Capt. Langridge was sent to Peishiyi on detached service. Off on the first leg of their journey back to "Uncle Sugar" via Replacement Depot #3 at Karachi were Capt. Greene, 1Lts. Banger and Senecal, TSgt. Reynard, SSgt. Whearty, Sgt. Peters, and Cpl. Hugel (all members of the aircrew that bellied in on May 27), while 1Sgt. Earley; TSgts. Gruber, Holmes, Meikle, Stearns, Summerville, and Wilkerson; SSgts. Duffin, Evitts, Haines, Hoke, and Thomas; Sgt. Rickman; and Cpl. Delahoyde were assigned and transferred to Yangkai. The American component of the 3rd Bomb Squadron was reduced to fourteen officers and thirty enlisted men.

The official instrument of surrender that acknowledged Japan's complete capitulation to the Allies was signed by envoys acting for the emperor on September 2 aboard USS *Missouri* in Tokyo Bay. "VJ-Day" was a reality at last.

The month of September marked the final period of the existence of the 1st Bomb Group. "Almost two years of operations were climaxed in August by the sudden ending of the war, thus bringing about the disbanding of the Chinese American Composite Wing. This unique unit was formed with the intention of having Americans in it who would work in close cooperation with the Chinese members of the organization and who would train them in all phases of operations," wrote the group adjutant (acting as historical officer). "That we were successful in welding together a striking force that wreaked havoc with Japanese supply lines, personnel, and military installations is self-evident—our record speaks for itself."

During the last two years of the war, pilots and crews of the CACW battered the Japanese from one end of occupied China to the other. Their mission was to paralyze the infrastructure of the Japanese war machine and to inhibit Japanese troop movements by destroying cargo caravans, troop transports, railroads, tunnels, and bridges. Efforts by Chennault's fliers to harass the Japanese and prevent their complete control of China were unquestionably successful.

After the war ended, Lt. Gen. Gaku Takahashi, commander of Japanese forces in central China, surmised that 60 to 75 percent of the effective opposition his forces faced in China during the war was due to the 14th Air Force. "Without the air force we could have gone anywhere we wished," he concluded.[24]

In three years of combat, Chennault's airmen destroyed at least 2,600 Japanese aircraft while losing five hundred from all combat causes. They sank or damaged 2,230,000 tons of Japanese merchant vessels and forty-four naval ships, and it was estimated that they killed more than 66,000 Japanese soldiers, airmen, and sailors.[25]

The 3rd Bomb Squadron officially flew 155 combat missions, according to the squadron's final historical report, but the actual number, which included squadron aircrew members, was considerably greater than that. Many missions were undertaken as part of detachments in cooperation with other units and were not credited to the 3rd Squadron or detailed in its numbered operational intelligence reports. Fourteen B-25s were lost because of enemy action and mishaps on administrative flights. Although, nearly every airman had at least one bailout or crash landing and consequent walkout only one American crew had been lost. At the end of the war, their deaths were yet to be confirmed.

"All in all, that is not such a bad record considering the composite nature of the outfit. We all feel that the squadron has enjoyed good fortune. May good fortune continue to smile on all members of this squadron," the writer expressed. "We say adieu to China and go our individual ways, scattering to the four corners of the good old USA, content and satisfied with the knowledge that we are forever bound together with the ties of friendship and mutual admiration for each man's 'job well done.'"

CHAPTER EIGHTEEN
Back to the ZI

It was a time of transition. After the formal surrender was signed in early September, men of the 3rd Bombardment Squadron were officially assigned to other units in preparation for their return to the Zone of the Interior. MSgt. Barge; TSgt. Mills; SSgts. Ewell, Foorman, and Hutchinson; Sgt. Jackson; and Cpl. Piecuch were transferred to the 26th Fighter Squadron, 51st Fighter Group, 69th Composite Wing, stationed at Kunming, and Lt. Jeffries, SSgt. Wellman, Sgts. Learn and Allegretto, Cpl. Ryave, and Pfc. Calloway to the 23rd Fighter Group, 68th Composite Wing, at Liuchow. They all remained temporarily attached to the 3rd Squadron as of September 1 and were released on the fifth. TSgt. Hartung, SSgt. Czerniak, and Sgts. Gaffney and Schlicher were transferred to Detachment HQ & HQ Sqdn., 14th Air Force, and SSgt. Dunlap to Yangkai Army Air Base on the fifth. On the same date, Cpl. Schroeder was attached to the 311th Fighter Group, which was tasked to ferry P-51s to locations in China as needed to equip the Chinese air force, before he returned to the US in December 1945.

The morning report for September 5 suggested a change of station from Hsupu back to Liangshan, as more and more squadron personnel were being released. Sgt. Daniels reported similar indecisiveness regarding his 1st Bomb Squadron, which had been ordered to move to the "large new base," he wrote. "We hastily gathered things up for the move," including the squadron's semisedated mascot, Vic, by that time a fully grown Himalayan sun bear. "The evening I arrived at rain[-]soaked Hsupu it was a desolate[-]looking place, covered knee deep in mud. It seemed as though I was destined to spend the rest of my life at some miserable muddy base in China. The next day we were told the Chinese American Composite Wing had

It was during the brief period that 1st Bomb Group personnel were straggling into the new base at Hsupu that Lt. Greene met Vic, a Himalayan sun bear that served as the 1st Bomb Squadron's mascot. *F. H. Greene Jr. collection, courtesy of Sibyl Greene Cryer* been disbanded and we were returning to Hanchung. We had experienced a one-day permanent change of station without regret."[1] With the relaxed attitude toward record keeping that developed late in the war, it is probable but unconfirmed that the 3rd Bomb Squadron had likewise officially returned to its home turf.

Maj. Mondelli, whose promotion was effective August 16, left for Yangkai to begin his return home on September 5. With him went Lts. Bowen, Cantor, Faherty, Ilefeldt, and Logan; Sgt. Magyar; and Cpl. Morris. Lts. Fuller and Wood and Sgt. England arrived at the same base during the following few days. Capt. Kelso, accompanied by 1Sgt. Earley; TSgts. Gruber, Holmes, Meikle, Stearns, Summerville, and Wilkerson; SSgts. Duffin, Evitts, Haines, Hoke, and Thomas; Sgt. Rickman; and Cpl. Delahoyde, arrived on the fifteenth. Their departure left five officers and nine enlisted men remaining in the squadron at Liangshan. All of those sent to Yangkai were assigned to the 341st Bomb Group, and the majority were attached to the 22nd Bomb Squadron. In mid-September, 22nd Squadron personnel moved to Camp Kanchrapara, the replacement center near Calcutta used to process troops returning to the US, where they stayed for about two weeks before departure.[2]

Lt. Trumm and Cpl. DeFabritis were transferred to the 10th Air Force to facilitate the transfer of Chinese Nationalist troops to northern coastal cities formerly controlled by the Japanese. Trumm recorded in his flight log that he was transferred to the 4th Combat Cargo Group and traveled aboard a Curtiss C-46D Commando as copilot on September 17, the flight's duration two hours and forty minutes.

Orders to disband the Chinese-American Composite Wing were issued on September 19. On the same date, 1Lts. Pulaski and Winter, TSgt. Mier, Sgt. Supsic, and Cpl. Armbruster left for Liuliang, where they were attached to the 36th Fighter Control Squadron, 51st Fighter Group, for transport home. Capt. Langridge went to Yangkai for temporary duty, and TSgt. Chasse and SSgt. Benedict were sent on their way home via the India-Burma Replacement Center at Karachi. Maj. Mondelli received orders on September 25 to report to the CO of "POD (point of departure) Air Gateway" for further orders. He and Maj. Hamilton were later transferred to the China Air Mission, continuing the objective of training airmen for the Republic of China.

Maj. Hamilton, Capt. Langridge, TSgt. Long (promoted on September 1), SSgt. Hartung, and Cpl. Keller, as well as Sgt. Paul R. Johnson, who had been transferred in from the bomb group on September 7 as others were departing, were the squadron's final members. They were transferred to the Air Force Liaison Detachment at Chihkiang when it was activated on September 27.

This team was intended to help with setting up systems of operations, maintenance, and supply so the Chinese could utilize all the American equipment that was being turned over to them. The liaison team was kept until the air mission to the CAF took over, although there was little they needed to do, since duplicate commands were already in place. Most of these men remained in China until January 1946.

Sgt. Johnson later told his family that his decision to take typing in high school had probably saved his life. "I would most likely have gone into the infantry and gone into France, where chances of being killed were very high." After basic training at Fort Dix in New Jersey, he was shipped to Greensboro, North Carolina, where he received the rest of basic training and more testing. On the basis of those test results, he was informed that he would be sent to a school for radio-gunnery on airplanes. Then someone noticed that he had taken typing classes in high school, and the plan was revised. He was sent instead

Back to the ZI

to MacDill Field, where he was assigned to an office and taught about payrolls, typing special orders, and other administrative duties. Johnson was eventually sent to Liangshan in early 1945 and attached to 1st Bomb Group headquarters.[3]

The squadron's acting historical officer wrote, "From the 18 August 1945 to the date of disbandment, the ranks of the 3rd Bombardment Squadron have been decimated, day by day." Capt. Mallon, in his final historical report, probably best expressed the sentiments of others of the group:

> In conclusion, let it be said that while most of the personnel who have served in the 1st Bomb Group are not exactly anxious to return to China by the first boat, they have definitely had experiences which will be good for numerous drinks in their neighborhood saloons and with which they can regale their grandchildren for years to come. The air raids, lost comrades in arms who went down fighting, rice wine, water buffalo meat with rice and vice versa, lack of mail and Post Exchange supplies, and lack of sufficient supplies with which to conduct the war will not be easily forgotten.
>
> GOOMBAY!!

All equipment and aircraft having been transferred to the Chinese and all personnel relieved from assignment, "the famous Spray and Pray Squadron ceased to exist as a potent and powerful factor of the Chinese-American Composite Wing and the 14th Air Force," according to the 3rd Squadron's final historical report. "In retrospect, as we depart from the Squadron, we cherish all the friendships established, take pride in the work accomplished and give thanks that we were under sterling leadership of men that proved their worth in battle." The author of this final report is uncertain, since Lt. Ilefeldt had departed in early September, although it may have been compiled by Maj. Hamilton, who signed it. It was likely typed by Sgt. Johnson, who kept a carbon copy of it with his military memorabilia.

At the end of the war in Europe, there had begun a reshuffling of personnel, and replacements were being received in this still-active theater while others were reassigned elsewhere. Released from the 3rd Squadron on July 23 and bound for the ZI, MSgt. Ned Shock had boarded USS *General Edgar T. Collins* (AP-157), which embarked 379 Army officers, ninety-five Army nurses, 2,620 Army enlisted men, six Army civilians, seven Navy officers, one Marine officer, fifty Navy enlisted men, and four Marine enlisted men at Prinsep Ghat, Calcutta, India, on August 5. With its primary purpose to deliver replacement troops where they were required, it made stops that included Colombo, Ceylon; Freemantle, Western Australia; Hollandia, New Guinea; Leyte Gulf, Philippine Islands; Lingayen Gulf, Philippine Islands; and Hagushi, Okinawa Shima, Nansei Shoto. Steaming from Colombo to Freemantle, *Collins* crossed the equator on August 13 and was still en route when Hirohito announced his intention to surrender on the fifteenth (the fourteenth west of the international date line). The ship was at anchor at Hollandia when word came that the official surrender had been signed. Army and Navy personnel were offloaded in the Philippines and at Okinawa and others boarded. Originally bound for San Francisco, *Collins* arrived at San Pedro, California, at 0747 on October 6, 1945.[4] Shock, who had not crossed the equator when he arrived in the CBI two years earlier, proudly displayed his Shellback Certificate through the years that followed.[5]

With the war officially over, many hundreds of thousands of the victors needed to be restored to their homes and loved ones. Although some returned by transport plane, the greatest number of these war-weary veterans came home by way of "Magic Carpet cruises," generally aboard US Navy ships used to transport the great throngs who were returning after the war. Maj. Curik, 1Sgt. Earley, and TSgt. Gruber, all "high pointers," got underway from Karachi aboard USS *General James H. McRae* (AP-149) on September 24. This was the first of many ships to depart from Karachi over the next several months. Because enemy planes, ships, and submarines no longer posed a threat to Allied shipping, *McRae* passed through the Suez Canal and the Strait of Gibraltar and then steamed directly west. These three 3rd Bomb Squadron men were among two hundred Army officers and 2,658 enlisted personnel who passed through customs at New York on October 15. Earley and Gruber were attached to a group of China theater veterans who went to the processing center at Ft. Dix to be discharged, and Curik was sent on his way to Fort Sam Houston at San Antonio, Texas.[6]

Other members of the squadron traveled back to the US aboard USS *General C. G. Morton* (AP-138), which steamed from Karachi on September 30 and traveled through the Suez Canal and on to New York, arriving on October 22. The ship carried 261 returning US Army officers and 2,655 enlisted personnel, including Army nurses who received the doting attention of soldiers who had in many cases not enjoyed the company of an American female for a year or more. Equally notable among the passengers disembarking at Pier 88, Hudson River at 48th Street, were sixteen "war dogs" accompanied by their soldier handlers. Trained to track down Japanese in the dense jungles of Burma, they additionally acted as sentries at ammunition dumps when not in combat. Occupying individual kennels on the top deck, they were joined by six "stow-away dogs of doubtful ancestry, all pets of soldiers" soon after leaving India. Capt. Kelso, scheduled for readjustment at Port Devers, Massachusetts, was one of *Morton*'s passengers listed as returning home from China, along with TSgt. Stearns.[7]

As 3rd Bomb Squadron personnel made their way back home, the largest group of them traveled aboard USS *General Charles H. Muir* to New York. US Navy photo

Back to the ZI

The greatest number from the 3rd Squadron traveled home aboard USS *General Charles H. Muir* (AP-142). Navy records reported that 423 Army officers and 2,650 enlisted men boarded *Muir* at Prinsep Ghat, Calcutta, on October 3 and got underway the following day at 1503 "down Hoogley River." Among the ship's civilian passengers were famed cultural anthropologist Dr. Margaret Mead Bates and her husband. *Muir* made stops for refueling at Columbo, Ceylon, and at Port Said, Egypt, before steaming west and arriving at Pier 88, New York, at 0721 on November 1. Streamers with the legend "China, Burma, India" flapped in the breeze as *Muir* pulled into position, and crowds waving "Welcome Home" banners greeted passengers at the pier. Hundreds of soldiers lined the rails and tossed Chinese, Indian, and Japanese money to those waiting below.[8] Lts. Cantor, Edgerton, Faherty, Ilefeldt, Kilian, Logan, and Wood; TSgts. Holmes, Meikle, Summerville, and Wilkerson; SSgts. Duffin, Evitts, Thomas, Haines, and Hoke; Sgt. Magyar; Cpls. Delahoyde, Morris, Richards, and Rickman; and Pfc. Outen were listed among veterans of the China theater who passed through customs that day.[9]

Al Magyar was one of four "North Jersey airmen" interviewed as they disembarked. "In contrast to the usual quiet composure of C-B-I veterans homeward bound, the *Muir's* passengers cheered and cat-called as the navy transport was warped in to Pier 88, North River, shortly after 7:00 a.m. With flying caps askew and brown leather jackets covered with multicolored squadron's insignia, North Jersey pilots told of their experiences with the Chinese American Composite Wing." Although not a pilot, Magyar described the March 30 mission on which his plane "had its left engine shot out 200 feet over the bridge" before the crew bailed out and "were nine days on the way back to their base."[10]

A week after departure of *Muir*, 1Lts. Pulaski and Winter, TSgt. Mier, Sgt. Supsic, and Cpl. Armbruster were among the 348 officers and 2,447 enlisted personnel (Army and Navy) who steamed out of Calcutta aboard USS *General Charles C. Ballou* (AP-157) on October 10. The passenger list included 245 US Army patients, forty-five female US Army nurses, and twenty-seven WACs. *Ballou* followed the same route and arrived in New York on November 6.[11]

Hank's return home was less straightforward. His ASR point score, calculated at 77, had not allowed him to go home along with the squadron's "old China hands." He was issued a lapel button that indicated his status on September 2. As of early October, the reduction of the critical point score for enlisted male personnel was dropped to 70 and was scheduled to be further reduced to 60 on November 1, the War Department announced.

After the cessation of hostilities, Hank had few duties to occupy his time as he waited for his turn to be on his way, so he spent some of it exploring the countryside. Buddhism, Taoism, and Confucianism formed the belief systems of the local population, and evidence from the distant past could be found throughout the area. A giant Buddha housed in a dilapidated wooden building stood at the eastern end of Liangshan valley, and the village of Dazu, beyond the mountains to the west, featured more than a thousand Buddha likenesses. "I was out, away from the orderly room, away from everything. I was just out. There was an old ruin where there had been a temple, and I found a brass coin about that big [indicating about 1.5 inches in diameter]. No telling how many thousand years old it was, and I had it. I don't know whatever happened to it." The coin's importance faded to insignificance by events that followed its discovery.

"I was out there, and someone from the orderly room came and found me and told me that the war is over, and you have enough points to go home. You can wait and you'll be transferred to a fighter squadron that is gonna be sent back to the States as a unit in about three months, or you can strike out on your own." Hank immediately returned to base and went to Maj. Hamilton's office. "I told him, 'Cut me some orders. I'm going home right now, one way or another.'" The papers were issued, and Hank took the first flight out that had space for him. Classified as a "casual," he made his way across China and then across India, a process that took about two weeks.

He remembered seeing a stockpile of vehicles that were being transferred to the Chinese at one of the stops along his route: "Right at the end of the war I came across a place as far as you could see was brand-new cars and trucks, and all that was left for them." The Moran Vehicle Control Depot was used as the gathering point for all ordnance vehicles to be relinquished to the Chinese. Included were not only new vehicles but also combat vehicles used in the North and Central Burma campaigns, as well as veteran equipment recently retired from hard duty on the Stilwell Road. Official control of 14th Air Force planes and vehicles was turned over to the Chinese air force, although the aircraft and other equipment had actually been owned by the CAF all along because it was purchased with money loaned to Chiang Kai-shek's Nationalist government under Lend-Lease.

GIs were warned against confiscating American goods and equipment from soldiers of the Chinese army "unless specifically assigned to such detail." Under the terms of Lend-Lease, the Chinese were entitled to items such as wristwatches, pocket watches, binoculars, compasses, flashlights, goggles, flexible-nozzle tubes for filling gasoline cans, and 5-gallon drums for inflammable liquids, a statement from headquarters announced. "The American Army is in China to forge bonds of friendship," it declared. "This is being done. Don't destroy those bonds!"[12]

Hank clearly remembered his journey and described it in an interview many years later:

> The transport plane that I was on—I had just got into India—the plane had something wrong with the engine. We stopped at a little camp—a little air base a couple of hundred miles north of Calcutta, so I caught that flight out. And when I got to Calcutta, they told me, "You've made a mistake. There are twelve hundred men here that have got to get out before you do." Well, I got out on the flight line. Didn't even spend the night there, and I caught a—a Yankee pilot was flying a transport back to India. That plane had nothing but engine mounts on it. An engine mount was a frame that they fastened a new engine—an aircraft engine onto to ship it. So, I spent the night in the back end of that plane with those engine mounts. Took off—another cold trip—*cold* at night.

He continued to "hitchhike," taking any flight that conveyed him closer to home. He made his way to Karachi, where he checked into Camp Malir, then known as Replacement Depot No. 1. He was one of thousands of GIs coming in from China, Burma, and India by plane and train to be staged and processed prior to their return to the US. "Men arriving as casuals are handled differently from those coming in as members of Category IV Units (units declared surplus and being returned to the States for deactivation and in which personnel will either be discharged or reassigned after receiving furlough)." Casuals were processed almost immediately upon arrival. They were taken to a station where a thorough check was made of clothing and equipment to discover shortages. Their orders were checked, and points were verified. After filling in a simple form and being provided a PX card, the GIs were issued replacements for any missing items, "much the same as they were upon induction, except that an effort is made to give the men the size they indicate."

Details were kept to a minimum for their brief stay, although casuals were asked to help out in guard duty. Activities available to fill the time as they waited were ping-pong; miniature golf; beach picnics; wienie roasts; shopping tours; use of the library, canteen, and lounge; trivia quizzes; bingo, cards; and the company of Red Cross girls. "As ships arrive, GIs are alerted and made ready for the trip to the docks and their last glimpse of India. Everything is being done to keep the men only three or four days at Malir before embarking for home."[13]

On October 12, Hank was among servicemen crowded into trucks that took them to the docks, where they boarded USS *General George O. Squier* (AP-130), moored port side to berth #2, Upper Harbor. One of the other passengers heading home as a casual that day was TSgt. Bob Solyn, who had also traveled with Hank to Karachi aboard *Mission Bay*. Released from the 3rd Squadron on September 12, Solyn had been transferred to the Replacement Depot at Karachi to await transportation.

The ship got underway the following morning with 331 Army officers, 2,992 Army enlisted men, one Navy enlisted man, and nineteen civilians. Among its passengers were aerial photographers / photo processors of the 2nd Photo Procurement Detachment, as well as seventeen Office of War Information personnel. The greatest number were "muleskinners" of the 31st, 33rd, 37th, 252nd, and 253rd Pack Troops, assigned to Mars Task Force. These were men in charge of the animals that provided a lifeline to troops fighting in Burma by packing in supplies.[14]

It was "just a troop transport is all I know about it," Hank admitted. He did not recall the name of the ship or its stops along the way, but Navy records report that *Squier* traversed the Suez Canal on October 20 and moored overnight at Port Said. The ship passed through the Strait of Gibraltar on the evening of October 25 and headed west. Steaming past the Statue of Liberty as joyful GIs crowded the decks for their first glimpse of America in many months, it arrived at the Port of New York on November 2 and moored on the starboard side of Pier 88. Debarkation of all passengers was completed by 2005.[15]

Discovery of stowaways both of the two- and four-legged varieties smuggled aboard by returning GIs was a relatively common occurrence, and this voyage was no exception. Arriving aboard *Squier* was "Susie," a six-month-old monkey brought back from Burma by SSgt. Carl E. Mauldin, an A/F control tower operator. When interviewed, he explained that he had been tiger hunting when he heard a rustle

Cheers erupted from the men lining the rails aboard USS *General George O. Squier* as the Statue of Liberty came into view. J. H. Mills collection

in the brush and fired his rifle. The shot killed a pregnant monkey, and he performed a Caesarian operation with his jack knife to deliver the 8-pound infant. Mauldin said that he was taking the animal home as a pet for his eleven-year-old son.[16]

Men who intended to remain in the Army were routed to a reception center, where they were processed to continue their military careers. Those who did not were ordered to a separation center. Hank was sent for processing to Ft. Dix and then on to Camp Chaffee, where he was honorably discharged on November 13, 1945.

He had been recommended for promotion to master sergeant, but the war ended before the paperwork came through. Many of the veterans entered the reserves after their return, but Hank did not. "The day I got discharged, I had to go into one office, and somebody, I think it was a staff sergeant, tried to talk me into getting in the reserve. I said, 'Nooo.'"

The sergeant reacted, "Man, if I had the kind of rating you've got—no way I'd not agree to go into the reserves."

"I'm gonna tell you why," Hank replied. "The reserves is a force of men that, any time this country wants you, they can reach out and get you. Is that right?"

"That's right. I don't blame you."

Hank was back home in time to celebrate Thanksgiving with his family, and he arrived before the fighter squadron to which he had been assigned. After his return, he saw in the newspaper an announcement that the fighter squadron had arrived in the US, "and there I was, already home ahead of them."

SSgt. Otto Hutchinson, attached to the 26th Fighter Squadron of the 51st Fighter Group (the same outfit to which Hank had been assigned for transport home), kept an "Enlisted Man's Pass" issued to him at Camp Kanchrapara on November 6, 1945, when he was authorized to visit the city between 0800 and 2130. He could take one of the buses scheduled to leave Kanchrapara between 0800 and 0830, and he could return to camp on any of them, leaving Calcutta hourly between 1600 and 1900 (five buses on each of those runs) or at 2130 (ten on the final run). Printed on it additionally was the acknowledgment "I understand that all brothels are off limits, and it is my responsibility to remain out of all 'off limit' areas." There were, however, a variety of approved activities about which the men were informed, including shopping for souvenirs at the city's numerous bazaars, enjoying good food at low prices from approved eating and drinking establishments, and joining sightseeing tours sponsored and conducted daily by the Red Cross to the many religious temples and burning ghats, the Black Hole of Calcutta, Maharajah's Palace, the beautiful Maidan and Victoria Memorial, and other must-see-before-you-leave attractions.

Along with others attached to the same squadron, Hutchinson had been sent to Barrackpore Field near Calcutta before moving to Camp Kanchrapara, one of the processing centers for troops heading home. Then the men spent a few days at Camp Hialeah, a staging area near Princep Ghat for troops awaiting departure, before boarding SS *Marine Angel* on November 16. Hutchinson kept copies of the ship's newspaper, *Angel's Harp*, which featured an unofficial ship's log. After weighing anchor at 1200 the following day and then completing the time-consuming process of refueling, the ship got underway down Hoogley River and headed south to the open sea. The pilot dropped off, and the log showed progress of 323 miles from Calcutta at 1200 on the twentieth. Radar pinged floating objects suspected of being mines in the Bay of Bengal on the next day, but the captain maneuvered to avoid them. On the twenty-second, ship's log recorded position as off the Andaman Islands. Moving through the Malacca Straits on the following day,

Marine Angel passed Singapore in the distance at 1800 and then veered north, entering the South China Sea on the twenty-fourth and "in dead calm sea" on the twenty-fifth. The ship was in the Luzon Straits between Formosa and the Philippines on November 27 and proceeded toward Japan; position was recorded as 130 miles southwest of Okinawa at 1200 on the following day.

Thanksgiving was observed on November 29 with a short program presented by the transport commander and various chaplains, followed by a holiday feast served from 1300 to 1600 about 140 miles off the coast of Japan. The menu featured roast Vermont turkey accompanied by savory dressing, cranberry sauce, mashed potatoes, giblet gravy, string beans, dill pickles, and green olives. Dessert consisted of assorted cookies, fruit salad, and ice cream, served with coffee. Entertainment was provided afterward. "This afternoon at 4:30 the 'Jolly Jokers' hillbilly orchestra and Eddie Bonnemere's 8-piece swing band will perform on Hatch 3." Other excitement during that afternoon was the result of the ship's collision with a whale. When a Japanese fishing boat was spotted the following day, the ship reduced speed and circled to determine if any assistance was needed. It then proceeded by a great circle route toward Seattle. The vessel was 130 miles south of Yokohama in early evening.

On December 1, as it steamed through choppy seas against a strong wind, scuppers overflowed, and C-4 compartment was partially flooded. Lowering temperatures prevailed on the second as the ship passed the 5,000-mile mark. Passengers began wearing their ODs on the fourth. Scuppers overflowed again on the next day, this time into the troop mess hall. The ship rolled in choppy seas, and ten men were injured in falls, although none seriously. *Angel* passed the international date line at 0930 and was positioned 140 miles south of the Aleutians at 2000 on December 6. "Second Thursday" (the sixth again) was observed on the following day, when the log noted "heavy ground swells and stiff head winds." Wind abated but heavy swells persisted on the next day. Here ends the ship's unofficial log, with *Marine Angel*'s distance to port noted as 1,747 miles and official ETA as 2:00 p.m. on December 12. Arriving on that date at Pier 2 in Tacoma, Washington, ship records indicate that 2,511 returning troops were disembarked.[17]

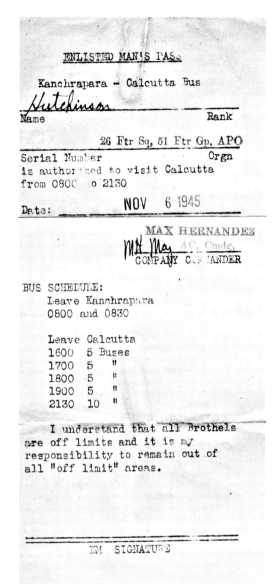

Billeted briefly at Camp Kanchrapara before steaming to Tacoma, Sgt. Hutchinson kept his pass to Calcutta among his military memorabilia. O. W. Hutchinson collection, courtesy of Jackie Hutchinson Pitts

SSgt. Dave Ewell, transferred to the 3rd Squadron with Hutchinson and Foorman in June, was another of the passengers who returned home aboard *Marine Angel*. Assigned to the 26th Fighter Squadron at the same time as Hank and others, Ewell later told his family that the ship on which he returned had docked at nearby Seattle. Records state that the 26th Fighter Squadron, 36th Fighter Control Squadron, and others of the 51st Fighter Group left in November and were inactivated on December 12, 1945, the same date that *Marine Angel* returned to the US. Sgt. Lloyd Jackson's return to the US on December 12 also places him aboard *Marine Angel*.[18]

SSgt. Richard Wellman remembered a ship's newspaper, too, and told his family that he was in charge of its publication, although he did not mention the title. He recalled that it took thirty-five days to cross the Pacific on his return home, most of that time spent waiting in line for breakfast, lunch, and dinner. "As soon as you were finished with breakfast, you got in line for lunch." Conditions were extremely crowded, with returning veterans sleeping in bunk beds stacked six high. One of his most vivid memories was of a stowaway who was discovered on board before the ship's arrival at Seattle.

Wellman had joined the 3rd Squadron in July along with Cpl. Ryave, and he was transferred on September 1 to the 23rd Fighter Group ("Chennault's Sharks"), 68th Composite Wing, with Lt. Jeffries, Sgts. Learn and Allegretto, Cpl. Ryave, and Pfc. Calloway. The fighter group boasted a proud history. Composed of the 74th ("Guerrilla"), the 75th ("Flying Shark"), and the 76th ("Vanguard") Squadrons, it had been formed from Chennault's original "Flying Tigers" when the AVG was disbanded on July 4, 1942.

The war diary of USS *Alderamin* (AK-116) reported it to be moored port side of dock #4, Hongkew Wharf, Shanghai, China, on Saturday, December 8, 1945. Passengers, mail, and troops began loading at 1115 the following day and continued into the evening. *Alderamin* anchored overnight in Quarantine Anchorage berth 24-29 at Hongkew River entrance and then got underway the following morning at 0604 en route to Seattle. On the thirteenth, it passed Uji Island abeam to port at 1739, Kusakaki Jima abeam to port at 1739, and Take Shima, 019° (Rel.) at 42,000 yards, at 2038. All are small islands or island chains off the western end of southern Kyushu. Passing below Japan, the ship continued on a course that took it almost due east.

A Chinese stowaway was discovered in the #2 hold on December 19. He identified himself as Stephen Chin from Kweilin, China, age eight, formerly mascot for the 23rd Fighter Group. He was an orphan whose parents had been killed by Japanese invasion troops. Chin Ta-bin, called "Stevie" by his unofficial foster fathers, who had provided him with a cut-down-to-size uniform complete with first sergeant's stripes, had been brought aboard and kept hidden by Cpl. Louis Jew of the 74th Fighter Squadron. An American citizen of Chinese descent, Jew planned to adopt the boy if immigration authorities granted their approval. *Alderamin* crossed the international date line on Sunday, December 23, and steamed nonstop by the most direct route before docking at Tacoma on January 3, 1946.[19]

Conditions that Wellman described were confirmed by an American Broadcasting Company China correspondent and fellow passenger, Ed Souder Jr., who alleged that the converted Liberty ship crowded with homeward-bound veterans had lifeboats and quarters adequate to handle only 150 men. "When we left Shanghai almost 1,100 men were stuffed into every square inch, and I exaggerate very little when I say there was barely room to turn around." Cargo holds used to house the men were "such tremendous, closely packed affairs, and had such few and narrow exits that a hasty yet orderly emptying of those areas was a practical impossibility." He further charged that "the safety problem was largely ignored" and that no emergency drills were ever held, even as *Alderamin* passed through waters where the danger of mines was always present. "No one went very hungry during the trip, but the *Alderamin*'s cold storage locker was designed for five-day short inter-island runs[,] and long before our arrival in Tacoma we were either out or almost out of salt, sugar, milk, fruit and fresh vegetables."[20]

Wellman told his family that as he was leaving the ship, he passed a sidewalk stand selling Washington State apples. They were expensive—twenty-five cents each—but he couldn't resist. He didn't care about the inflated price because he just had to have one of the gleaming, red beauties![21]

Sgt. Learn, attached to the 23rd Fighter Group at the same time as the others, seems to have made his way home as a casual, on the basis of his return to domestic service on November 30, 1945. Although no passenger list has been found to verify it, recently promoted TSgt. Hartung, with the Liaison Detachment at Hankow, likely did return with them, on the basis of his release date of January 14, 1946.

Sgt. Schlicher was released from service on the same date as Hartung and may have traveled home with Wellman aboard *Alderamin*. He, along with SSgt. Czerniak and Sgt. Gaffney, had been transferred to Detachment HQ & HQ Squadron 14th Air Force at Peishiyi in early September. A historical report for the month of October provided some details of the final period in that organization's existence that included an afternoon tea party hosted by Generalissimo and Madame Chiang Kai-shek at their summer home. "The occasion was a farewell party, or I should say a garden tea" that was moved indoors because of showers. "Tea was served with very enjoyable assorted cookies, roasted peanuts, Chinese enchiladas (bean sprouts and meat rolled in a crisp cover), Chinese hot dogs, and assorted Chinese nuts."

Enlisted men and officers introduced themselves and shook hands with the generalissimo and the madame. Speeches followed. The generalissimo welcomed and thanked the men in Mandarin, which was translated into English. Madame Chiang gave a talk on the problems of China and the necessity of continuing the struggle to win peace. General Stone, as spokesman, thanked the Chiangs for their hospitality. All those present, officers and enlisted, received an autographed photo of the generalissimo, as well as a "metal good-luck souvenir" inscribed with his seal on one side and the phrase "Victorious Allies" in Chinese on the other.

The detachment left Peishiyi on October 20 and moved to Lunghwa, near Shanghai. Enlisted men occupied the fourth floor of the Rockefeller Institute, and officers resided in the Fourteenth Compound (formerly the Japanese Technology Institute). "The enlisted men's morale was very high with their new comforts of Beer Parlor, Barber Shop, PX, Tailor Shop, and Sandwich Shop on the main floor of their barracks. Dishes, Plates, and silverware replaced the meat cans in the chow line[,] which no longer existed. The men sat down at the tables and awaited the Chinese K.P.s to bring on the Chow."

With their task completed, the final members were allowed to go home. "Now that all had seen the Great and Famous City of Shanghai[,] everyone with only few exceptions (of which we knew none) awaited the wonderful and glorious day of the inactivation of Hq and Hq Squadron and the return of the men to the United States and their loved ones."

Gen. Stratemeyer announced on December 3 that both the 10th and 14th Air Forces were nonoperational and all except three squadrons of low-point men and volunteers were being processed to return home. The few remaining members of HQ & HQ Squadron Detachment of the renowned "Fighting Fourteenth" left on December 15. It was inactivated at Fort Lawton, Washington, on January 6, 1946.

CHAPTER NINETEEN
Aftermath of War

As veterans of the China theater returned by the thousands, an intensive search began for those who were not going home with their comrades. At the conclusion of hostilities, about seven hundred US airmen were still listed as missing in action. In an effort to learn the fate of as many of them as possible, the China Theater Search Detachment was organized under the command of Col. David B. Barrett, a veteran of sixteen years with the Army in China who wrote Mandarin and spoke four dialects. The detachment was made up of fifty-eight officers and sixty-one enlisted men whose duty it was to comb the vast Asiatic mainland, islands, and coastal areas. Using radio broadcasts and leaflets, they requested Chinese citizens to come forward with any information that they had about the MIAs. Generalissimo Chiang issued orders calling for full cooperation by all military and civil officials throughout China. Even defeated Japanese soldiers occasionally reported locations of the American dead. The investigators, in teams of four officers and four enlisted men each, painstakingly followed up the leads, often traveling by mule or on foot into isolated or desolate regions, packing in their own rations and equipment.[1]

Anna Wherritt, Lt. Wherritt's mother, kept a newspaper clipping that included the results of one such search: "The end of the trail may be a lonely grave on a bare hill, or a memorial erected by humble villagers. Sometimes the Chinese build elaborate arches or tombs in honor of the brave men who came from far off to help drive the Japanese away," it stated. "Such an arch is at Ichang, at the mouth of the Yangtze gorges, which honors 'six brave soldiers.' The bodies are usually removed to Shanghai but in this case Ichang hopes the six Americans will be allowed to rest in the soil of China."[2]

In early June 1945, all those listed as next of kin had received official notification that the aircraft had failed to return from the May 16 mission, and neither it nor any of its crew had been located. In a letter dated July 5 to Jeanette Davis, whose husband was the pilot of the missing plane, Maj. Wm. D. Sanders of the Air Corps' Office of Personnel wrote, "Please be assured that a continuing search by land, sea, and air is being made to discover the whereabouts of our missing personnel. As our armies advance over enemy[-]occupied territory, special troops are assigned to this task, and agencies of our government and allies frequently send in details which aid us in bringing additional information to you."[3]

Further details were provided to the families as they became available. Lt. Mikola spoke to Mr. and Mrs. Wherritt by telephone on November 9, 1945, and he sent a letter to them the following day providing additional information that had recently been discovered about their son's death. He wrote that "by accident," he had met a Chinese officer stationed at Ichang who told the story through an interpreter. The six men, including Wherritt, were buried side by side outside the city of Ichang. "We never had any information before I met this Chinese officer." Mikola assured the Wherritts, "You can well be proud of Pete, but as a man and as a pilot. On many missions he flew he had a Captain flying copilot with him. There are not very many flight officers whose ability and general character are such that an Operational Officer will fly copilot for them."[4]

Gen. Chennault had offered his condolences and reassurance in a letter to the mother of Bob Koss as the war drew to a close. "The many friends and comrades of your son share your sense of loss, for they, too, have lost a loyal friend. They are proud of his fine record and the splendid way he obeyed the command of duty and conscience," he wrote. "His fine personal traits made him a favorite among all who knew him. It is the men of his type who are carrying forward the finest traditions of the army air forces and whose bravery, determination and sacrifice are hastening the day of ultimate victory."

Next of kin all received official notifications in February 1946 of the deaths of the six men, previously listed as missing in action. Mrs. Koss received a final letter from the adjutant general of the army stating that her son was killed in action and his body had been recovered. "I realize the anxiety you have suffered since he was first reported missing in action[,] and deeply regret the sorrow this later report brings you. May the knowledge that he made the supreme sacrifice for his country be a source of sustaining comfort. My sympathy is with you in this time of great sorrow."[5]

By late 1948, the story of that doomed mission could be considered complete. For the families of the six missing men, the months of agonizing suspense finally came to an end. A letter from Maj. James F. Smith of the Memorial Division to Mrs. Davis confirmed:

> Our records reveal that your husband was one of the six crew members manifested aboard Aircraft Number 44-30656 which departed from Liangshan on 16 May on a bombing mission to Ichang, China. The plane crashed at Ichang, resulting in the death of five of the crew. Through investigation, it was learned that their remains were buried by the enemy in a common grave at Ichang, China. The sixth crew member died later as a result of wounds and his remains were also buried in the grave with those of his comrades. The remains of these honored dead were recovered by our American Graves Registration Personnel and buried in the American Military Section, Hungjao Road Cemetery, Shanghai, China.

There they were reinterred with full military honors on January 24, 1946. Chaplain Otis W. Garland offered his condolences to Davis's widow and informed her that he and two other chaplains had conducted the funeral services at Hungjao Cemetery, "a beautiful cemetery under perpetual care." He wrote, "You can feel proud of the fact that he gave his life in helping to save his Country and the rest of the world from the horrors of Japanese domination."

The letter from Maj. Smith contained further details: "Later these remains were taken to Hawaii, where qualified technicians conducted a detailed examination and based upon their findings, individual identification was established." The remains of the six were identified using the best investigative methods available at the time by age and physical characteristics, including height and dental records. They were casketed and held at United States Army Mausoleum #2 at Schofield Barracks, Territory of Hawaii, under protection of the American Graves Registration Service pending disposition instructions from the next of kin, either for return by ship to the United States or for permanent burial in an overseas cemetery.[6]

Letters almost identical to these were addressed to Mrs. Anna Koss, but she did not live to see her son's return. She died in early 1947 of a broken heart, according to her family.

Remains of four crew members were returned by ship and then by train to their hometowns in the summer of 1949. Graveside services for Lt. Don Davis were held at Sunnyside Memorial Park in Long Beach, California, on July 13, 1949. VFW Golden State Post 279 conducted the services, which were attended by friends and family, which included his parents and two-year-old son.[7]

Bart and Anna Wherritt reburied their son's remains at Fairview Cemetery in Montezuma, Kansas, on Saturday, July 16. The funeral was attended by family members from as far away as Oklahoma.[8] His fiancée, Coleen Stanley, had married in 1946.

On the following day, services for Sgt. Jim Wadlow were held at the Baptist church in Hobart, Oklahoma, followed by reinterment at the Rose Cemetery with full military honors provided by the Hobart post of the American Legion. In attendance were his parents, brothers, sisters, and their families, as well as his widow and friends who had known him since childhood.[9] By this time, Jeanette Davis and Clovis Wadlow had moved on past the tragedy and remarried. When Clovis bore her first son soon afterward, she and her husband named him Alton; it was Jim Wadlow's middle name.

Jim Wadlow's family members treasure this photo, taken six days before his death. J. A. Wadlow collection, courtesy of Stephen Jackson

Reinterment with full military honors were held for Sgt. Wadlow on July 17, 1949, at the Hobart Rose Cemetery. J. A. Wadlow collection, courtesy of Stephen Jackson

All who attended reburial ceremonies for Lt. Koss received a copy of this prayer card. R. J. Koss collection, courtesy of Barbara Hughes

Later that month, a Roman Catholic funeral mass for Lt. Bob Koss, followed by reinterment at Grandview Cemetery, Johnstown, Pennsylvania, was attended by his siblings and their families.[10]

Remains of Sgt. Fox and Cpl. Ryan were reinterred at the National Memorial Cemetery of the Pacific at Honolulu on December 1, 1949. Family friends who lived nearby placed flowers on Jimmy Ryan's grave every birthday, Christmas, Easter, and Memorial Day. Audrey June Skoien, Ryan's fiancée, whom he called "Aud," never married but focused her life on a career as an accountant that took her first to California, then to New York, and finally back to Wisconsin. She was employed until retirement by the State of Wisconsin's Department of Conservation. His younger sister, Mary Lucille, recalls going with her family on a kind of "pilgrimage" to Hawaii during summer vacations. After visiting the grave of her brother at the "Punchbowl," they always walked the few steps to pay their respects at the grave of Loyal Fox.[11] When Jimmy Ryan's father died in 1961, he left a bequest of $1,000 to the Pacific War Memorial Commission at Honolulu in memory of his only son.

After the CACW was disbanded and the organization was transferred to the Chinese, headquarters of the 1st Bomb Group was moved to Hankow, where the 1st and 4th Squadrons were also stationed. The 2nd Squadron moved to Shanghai, and the 3rd Squadron to Nanyuan Airfield in Beijing and later to Hankow.

Ting Cheng-liang later described to his son a humorous incident that occurred during this period. As the squadron's planes were on the runway ready to take off, their Chinese pilots received orders to stop. While preparing to serve the next meal, the mess hall cooks discovered that a special delicacy had vanished, and they suspected the departing pilots of stealing it. An inspection of the bombers confirmed their suspicions. Several buckets of ice cream were discovered hidden away in the bomb bay of one of the B-25s. The ice cream was retrieved, and the bombers were allowed to go on their way.[12]

Paul Johnson, who had remained with the liaison detachment, wrote the following in his memoirs: "At the end of the war, when Japan had surrendered, we moved up to a bigger city, Hankow, that was on the Yangtze River." He recalled that Japanese soldiers were still there, and the Americans

Among his memorabilia, Johnson kept this pass granting him permission to visit Hankow. *Paul R. Johnson collection, courtesy of Daniel P. Johnson*

SSgt. Paul R. Johnson joined the 3rd Bomb Squadron as others were departing. His task was to type orders and perform other clerical services necessary for transferring the squadron organization and all equipment and supplies to the Chinese air force. *Paul R. Johnson collection, courtesy of Daniel P. Johnson*

Johnson stands beside Cpl. Albert J. Keller, attached to the squadron as a radio mechanic. Both men served with the Air Force Liaison Detachment after the CACW was disbanded. *Paul R. Johnson collection, courtesy of Daniel P. Johnson*

played a game similar to baseball with them. "I can't remember who won, but the ball was made of hard rubber, bigger than a golf ball, but smaller than a baseball that we were used to playing with in the States," he wrote. "We lived on a former British compound, and we had servants to fix our meals and clean the house. That was a big change for us[,] and we certainly didn't mind getting seven[-]course meals for supper."

Johnson was issued a pass to visit the city ordinarily viewed by Americans during the past decade only from above. Signed by Capt. Roland G. Lyman, it read: "SSgt. Paul R. Johnson 42026160 is assigned to Hq AAF China Theater (on TDY at Hankow, China) and is authorized to visit the city of Hankow, China[,] when not on duty, conforming with applicable regulations." He bought a camera for $25,000.00 CN on one of his trips to town and kept the receipt as a souvenir.

Sometime after his return home in June 1946, Johnson received an "Army Air Forces Certificate of Appreciation for War Service":

> I cannot meet you personally to thank you for a job well done; nor can I hope to put in written words the great hope I have for your success in future life.
>
> Together we built the striking force that swept the Luftwaffe from the skies and broke the German power to resist. The total might of that striking force was then unleashed upon the Japanese. Although you no longer play an active military part, the contribution you made to the Air Forces was essential in making us the greatest team in the world.
>
> The ties that bound us under stress of combat must not be broken in peacetime. Together we share the responsibility for guarding our country in the air. We who stay will never forget the part you have played while in uniform. We know you will continue to play a comparable role as a civilian. As our ways part, let me wish you God speed and the best of luck on your road in life. Our gratitude and respect go with you.

It was signed by Henry H. ("Hap") Arnold, commanding general of the Army Air Forces.[13]

SSgt. Otto Hutchinson received an identical certificate at about the same time. Both are now treasured mementos kept by their families.[14]

The struggle for power between Chiang Kai-shek's nominally democratic Nationalists and Mao Tse-tung's Communists had been temporarily abated, but the Japanese surrender set the stage for the resurgence of civil war. Conflict that began in the 1920s soon intensified between the two parties over who would have political control of China. The Nationalist government continued to receive support from the US after the end of World War II, both as its former war ally and ideologically as the only option against Communist control of China.

Following the departure of the US military in 1945, Chiang and Mao engaged in a series of talks regarding the formation of a postwar government. Both agreed on the importance of democracy, a unified military, and equality for all Chinese political parties, although the truce broke down before any resolution could be reached. Despite efforts by US general George Marshall to broker an agreement, the two factions were fighting a full-scale civil war by 1946. The Communists possessed superior military organization and morale, large stocks of weapons left behind by the Japanese in Manchuria, and the popular support of the Chinese people, while years of corruption and mismanagement led to distrust for the Nationalists.

Financial aid from the US continued, although officials of the Truman administration grew increasingly doubtful of the strategic value of maintaining relations with Nationalist China. While Chiang received aid from the US, Mao had the support of the Soviet Union. Even as hostilities drew to a close, the Soviet Union had declared war on Japan as Soviet troops invaded and held Manchuria until Chinese Communist forces were in place to claim the territory. After years of conflict, a series of military victories by the Communists led Mao to declare the creation of the People's Republic of China (PRC) on October 1, 1949. Chiang and his forces fled to Taiwan (formerly Formosa), off the coast of Fukian Province, to regroup and plan their strategy for retaking the mainland, but their hopes were eventually abandoned.[15]

Although American training of ROC airmen had been halted in China at the end of the war, the mentor relationship continued in support of the Nationalist government. In the spring of 1946, a special military program was instituted to train Chinese fliers as troop carrier pilots and crews. Five hundred Chinese officers and enlisted men, making up more than one hundred complete air crews, were moved to Bergstrom Field, near Austin, Texas, where they were trained to fly Curtiss Commando planes to be used for transporting troops. In charge of this detachment were Maj. Chester M. Conrad and his cocommander, Maj. Ku C. C., both 14th Air Force veterans. Many of the trainees were decorated combat veterans who had served in the CACW. Graduation ceremonies were held on July 13.[16]

One of these graduates was Lt. Tu Kai-mu. Afterward, he was relieved from the frontline unit and flew cargo aircraft for the ROC Air Force. When the Communist Party of China gained control over the mainland in 1949, he retreated to Taiwan with the Nationalist government. Tu related that family members of those who remained loyal to the generalissimo were gathered in Hankow before being transported to Taiwan by air:

> The policy of sending our family members to Taiwan in advance was to ensure high morale. Once we knew that our family members were safe in Taiwan, we who fought on the frontlines would have nothing to worry about. At that time, several large air force bases in mainland China, such as Hengyang, Dinghai, and Shanghai, were still controlled by the Nationalists. After the 1st Group arrived in Taichung, we were still going back and forth between those bases. While my wife and children were sent to Taichung, my parents, younger brother, and two younger sisters were

still in Shanghai, a city already in chaos. As I was worrying over how to send them to Taiwan, there happened to be a B-25 going to Shanghai, and it stayed at Shanghai's Dachang Airport for maintenance because of mechanical problems. The pilot of this aircraft happened to be my ROCAFA classmate. I tried and succeeded in contacting him, and my family members were ultimately able to take this B-25 "private plane" to Taiwan.[17]

When the US resumed military aid and provided the ROC with C-119 transport aircraft, Tu began his service with the 6th Airlift Wing in Pingtung in southern Taiwan, which spanned the next fourteen years. During his career, Tu continued to work with the United States Air Force. He became commander of the 6th Airlift Wing and later retired with the rank of major general in 1980. In 2015, an interview that included his wartime recollections appeared in an animated documentary film titled *Rocking Sky*, about young men who served in the Second Sino-Japanese War. As this squadron history neared completion came notification of Mr. Tu's death on January 30, 2021, in Taipei, Taiwan, at the age of ninety-nine.[18]

Yen Pao-shen (or Pao-san) and Cheng Yung-koen were, along with Tu, among the Chinese pilots reassigned from the 4th to the 3rd Squadron on March 13, 1944. The three of them, all sublieutenants at that time, went on to fly many successful missions from those early days through the eventual expulsion of the Japanese from China. "Paul" Yen ("Paul Pao-shen Yen," born October 13, 1919; died December 11, 2018) and "Peter" Cheng ("Yungkoen P. Cheng," born February 18, 1920; died July 6, 2016) later made their homes in the San Francisco Bay area.[19]

Tu Kai-mu, one of the original Chinese pilots attached to the 3rd Bomb Squadron, continued to share the story of his service in the Chinese-American Composite Wing for many years after the end of World War II. He retained fond memories of that period in his life and of the Americans with whom he served. In this photo, taken on September 21, 2018, Mr. Tu examines photos of James H. Mills, as well as documents relating to the squadron in which they served together. His death on January 30, 2021, coincided with what would have been Hank's ninety-ninth birthday. *Courtesy of Szu-ming Peng*

Ting Cheng-liang, former 3rd Squadron navigator who had also remained loyal to the Kuomintang, was another who fled with his family to Taiwan after Chiang Kai-shek's defeat. He took a keen interest in the escalation of conflict between the Democratic People's Republic of Korea (North Korea) and the Republic of Korea (South Korea) and placed a map on his dining room wall that allowed him to visualize the movements of the war's combatants. In about 1952 he was sent for more training to the US, where he took part in a program that prepared him to be an air traffic controller. When he returned to Taiwan in 1953, he brought with him a gift for his wife, Lucy: a personalized brooch that spelled out her name in English.[20]

Bob MacNeil wrote, in a letter to Jim McCann in 1982, "Most of the CAF, with wives, kids etc made it out of the mainland in CAF planes—they are happy but would be more so if back. Our better pilots fly for CATA [China Air Transport Association] & few went over to the commies." He had met with many of the squadron's Chinese members in Taiwan and Hong Kong during later years.

As the squadron was being deactivated and its members were sent on their way, either back home or to other military units, they exchanged addresses and promised to write, and many of them did remain in contact. Hank and Wilkie corresponded for a number of years. "I would send him a letter, and then after a while he would send one to me, and then I would send one to him." Sometimes weeks or even months separated their correspondence, but they stayed in touch. "Then it was his turn to write, and he didn't."

George Wood, whose duty required him to compile a list of squadron personnel and their addresses at the close of the war, made an effort to maintain contact with as many as possible and visited with Hank in El Dorado in the early 1950s. Howard Goeller and Tom Simpson corresponded and visited in each other's homes when they could. Tom Edgerton and Wayne Senecal remained friends. With their families, they met for weekend visits whenever possible. Tom Simpson, George Cunningham, and Gene Dorr also stayed in touch. For many years they marked the anniversary of their July 4 forced landing in Burma with a telephone call. When Lou Graves took his family to Colorado on vacation, they stopped in Denver for a visit with the Dorrs.

Thirty-five years after the CACW was disbanded, Jim McCann began compiling a history of the 3rd Bomb Squadron, and he wrote to as many of its former members as he was able to locate. Graves, who met with John Hanrahan in the fall of 1980, wrote to McCann that they had "a delightful visit," and added, "We stayed sober and recalled lots of times in China. The Hanrahans are wonderful, as you know." Grady Fuller, who had retired from the Air Force in 1972, wrote that he too had been in touch with Hanrahan, as well as Ray Hodges. Hodges had remained in communication with Tu Kai-mu and took his family to visit with the Cunninghams. John Hinrichs wrote that he was in contact with Lou Graves, as well as Tom Simpson, Gene Dorr, and Bob MacNeil, but had lost contact with several others. Dorr provided addresses for Graves, Simpson, and MacNeil, as well as George Cunningham, Paul Young, and Dr. S. T. Yoeh. Doc Yeoh had visited with several American friends, including Jerry Cantor in Clifton, New Jersey, during an around-the-world tour that he took in 1965.[21]

MacNeil wrote that he and Graves had corresponded and that they had visited a couple of times. MacNeil often called some of his old buddies whenever he was feeling reminiscent. Living in a cabin on Lake Alice in northern Minnesota, he urged McCann to "come up for a summer any time you can & pass the word to anyone from the 3rd B. We can sit on the dock, fish, drink beer, & tell big lies."[22]

After defeat of the Japanese, the majority of the squadron's veterans, including Hank, just wanted to go home and resume their lives. "I was *sooo* glad that war was over," he confided many years afterward. A meat cutter before enlistment, he returned to that trade and worked for a short time at the meat market of a local grocery store in El Dorado, Arkansas, where he had been employed before signing up. Former employers were required by law to offer returning veterans their previous jobs, but not all complied willingly. When the store owner handed Hank his first postwar paycheck, he remarked, "If you are half the man I think you are, you'll give that back to me." Hank did not, knowing that he had earned it and he had a family to support. Soon afterward he went to work for Safeway, followed by Model Grocery, another locally owned food store. Distinguishing himself from a butcher, he explained, "I didn't kill the animals. I cut the meat up and put it out for sale." He took a job in 1948 with Lion Oil Co.'s refinery, where he remained for nine years, despite frequent labor disputes that resulted in layoffs and strikes. In 1957, he moved his family to Orange, Texas, where he was employed by Firestone Tire and Rubber Co. as a production operator, then as production foreman, and finally as maintenance foreman until his retirement in 1985. He credited his experience in the Air Force for his abilities as a supervisor: "It taught me to be a leader of men." Among his responsibilities was participating in the opening or expansion of several foreign Firestone/Bridgestone facilities. How strange it must have seemed when he spent several months in 1964 as a consultant for Bridgestone's recently opened Tokyo plant.

Bill Daniels received his orders to return to the States in November 1944 and was sent to Long Beach, California. From May until October 1945, he was at Homestead Field in Florida, followed by Charleston, South Carolina, and was then transferred to Shanghai after the war, all while assigned to air traffic control. In October 1946, Bill went to Philippine Airlines in Manila before being discharged as a major in November. In the early 1970s, he recognized the need for an updated system of providing aviation maintenance publications and regulatory updates and developed a system for transferring them to microfiche to replace the reams of paper documents previously used. In 1973, he became the founder of Aircraft Technical Publishers, providing maintenance technical library services to the aviation industry. Now relying on the latest in technology, ATP still operates under the direction of Bill's daughter.[23]

Reuben Ragland related that as he was in the process of being discharged from the service, "they asked me when we docked if I wanted to get out of the service, and I said, 'Heck yeah; I want to get out.'" He joined the Florida Air National Guard's 159th Fighter Squadron, 125th Fighter Wing, back home in Jacksonville. He became a plant manager at Sinclair Refining (later known as Atlantic Richfield) and continued flying for the National Guard. Ragland took early retirement in 1973, when the oil industry fell on hard times. Unfortunate investments in the stock market led to financial loss. For a time, he earned a living by selling cemetery plots and later worked as a night watchman before establishing a successful lawn maintenance business. When he sold it ten years later, it gave him and his wife, "PG," the financial security to finally enjoy retirement.[24]

After his return home, Maynard Rieks went back to his family's farm in Iowa. In time he farmed his own land near Iowa Falls, later in life with the assistance of one of his sons. Elmer Thompson went home to Caddo, Texas, and raised cattle, sheep, and goats on his family's ranch. Arnold Ryave returned to Pittsburgh and worked with his father in the family-operated funeral business serving the Jewish community, eventually becoming its director. It continues to be operated by his daughter.

Dave Ewell joined his father's business as an earthmoving contractor in Baton Rouge, leveling lots and building streets and levees. He became an early environmentalist in 1969, filing suit against fourteen of Louisiana's biggest chemical companies (including Dow, Exxon, and Ethyl) for polluting the land and waters that overflowed onto his family's farm with industrial waste, killing cattle and destroying swampland and wildlife. It was a battle he fought for the next thirty years. *Ewell v. Petro-Processors* was finally resolved in 2003, four years after his death.[25]

Jack Hinrichs renewed his association with Mack Trucks, later as president of Norwesco Machinery Distributors, Inc. (Mack distributor for northwestern Connecticut), and Equipment Lease and Sales Corporation. After floodwaters destroyed his business in 1955, he found employment at several corporations as a leasing and sales engineer and consultant.[26]

Howard Goeller was sales manager at the Molton Hotel in Birmingham in 1953 before moving soon afterward to Huntsville, Alabama. He purchased the Columbus Vulcanizing Co. with a partner in 1959. In addition, he continued operation of the St. Denis Hotel in Columbus, Indiana, until he sold it, along with the vulcanizing business, in 1961. Goeller later operated and eventually retired from the air-conditioning business.[27]

Bill Duffin went back to New York Central Railroad (later Penn Central / Conrail Railroad), where he was employed as paymaster for forty-two years. Richard Wellman returned to the teaching profession, conducting classes in business education in high school and college as well as becoming a high school principal. Joe Langridge returned to banking and became vice president of San Antonio Savings in 1960. Russ Armbruster, a police officer before enlisting, returned to his position with the St. Louis Metropolitan Police Department. Bill Meikle went back to Otis Elevator Co. in Yonkers, New York, eventually retiring as head of its printing department.

Stan Rickman returned to his job as a building superintendent in Seattle, Washington. Bob Schlicher went back to Louisiana State Rice Milling (later known as Riviana), became a rice buyer, and managed its Kinder plant for twenty-five years. After the plant closed, he worked for Kinder Bean Elevator and Liquid Fertilizer until he retired. Wendell Peters continued working in housing construction in North Texas. Walter Hartung returned to Illinois, where he became an operating engineer for Shell Oil Company at its Roxana refinery and later at Wood River. Phil Piecuch worked for various shoe manufacturers and later became a machine operator for Coca Cola in Nashua, New Hampshire.

Some former squadron members relied upon their wartime training when they sought employment after returning home. Charlie Miles had a long career with Boeing Aircraft and retired as a senior aircraft supervisor. Ray Hodges operated a business that conducted aerial inspection of pipelines for oil companies in Alaska. Trained by the military as a welder and flame cutter, Loren Gaffney was employed for many years by the Morton Salt Co. on its production line as a welder and machine operator in Hutchinson, Kansas. Ed Schroeder found his photography experience to be useful during his twenty-five-year career as a sales representative for Arkin Media, and Harley Reynard became vice president and director of the Jack Lacey Advertising Agency. Both Fred Libolt and Frank Hoke found employment as automobile mechanics. Norm Long worked in the shipping department at General Motors for thirty years, until his retirement in 1974. Ned Shock retired from Machinery Supply in 1991.

Wayne Senecal considered a career in the military but rejected the notion because he disliked all the record keeping and other paperwork that were required. He returned to Michigan and became a steward of the Muskegon Yacht Club, worked at Garden Center Nursery & Market, and managed Glen Aire Trailer Park in Benton Harbor. He was later president of Senecal's Imports in Muskegon. Still later he oversaw leasing shopping-center space for the Fairplain Development Co., and he was in partnership with his brother Ralph in Key Largo, Florida, for several years.[28]

Rae Delahoyde became an entrepreneur as well and operated several businesses in Ukiah, California, and Yuma, Arizona, that included a service station, drive-in theater, delicatessen, pizzeria, and wholesale automobile sales lot, as well as selling fire equipment and paint and art supplies. He was very active in Junior Achievement, a program that promotes principles of successful entrepreneurship to young people.[29]

Frasier Wilkerson, who had studied horticulture before enlistment, opened Frasier's Nursery soon after his return to Biloxi, Mississippi. His children continue to operate the business begun by "Wilkie" and his wife, Aileen, still offering gardening supplies and landscaping services to their customers. John Barge established a heating and air-conditioning business back home in Cordele, Georgia, that was operated by his son, John Jr., until his recent death. Andy Allegretto worked for several plumbing businesses before starting his own, Allegretto Plumbing and Heating in Ocean City, New Jersey. It is still in operation by his family. John Hanrahan was involved in operation of Hanrahan's City Line Tap, a family-owned bar in Providence, Rhode Island, before becoming a clerk with the US Postal Service.

Jerry Winter was proprietor of Woolen Fashion Wagon in Wausau, Wisconsin, and later became Wisconsin district director of sales for Woolen Mills in Duluth. Bud Keller owned and operated a dry-cleaning business in Las Vegas, Nevada, and Fred Stearns operated a drapery and dry-cleaning business in San Jose, California, in the 1970s. Joe Supsic returned to Pennsylvania and became a buyer for Allen Clark Poultry Co. until his retirement in 1993. Allan Mikola was a certified public accountant with the partnership of Mikola, Fierstein & Malkin in Paterson, New Jersey, and he taught courses in local property taxation at Rutgers University in Newark.

Fred Greene was employed by Corning Glass, the Massachusetts Institute of Technology (MIT), Norton Corp., and Nuclear Energy Institute as director. He became vice president of National Research Corp., specializing in the technology of high vacuums and exploring ways to store and convert energy to be used for space travel. Jim Kelso was employed by the State Department as well as the Department of Defense on the munitions board and was instrumental in setting up NATO. He later served as executive secretary of the New York Armed Forces Regional Council and worked as an accountant for the State of Connecticut Labor Department. Bill Earley moved to Daytona Beach, Florida, and became a manager with the Howard Johnson chain of motels.

Mannie Smith worked in construction as a pipe fitter. Budd Evitts, an employee of Frane Construction Co., was shoveling crushed stone in the street as part of a sewer construction project at the time of his death in 1963. Herman Burton had a number of jobs that included working as a salesclerk at Sears, Roebuck and Co.; as a janitor at the American Legion Hall; and as a driver for Yellow Cab. Before the war, he had worked in a shoe factory and been a bartender. A lifelong bachelor, he had promised his mother before she died in 1943 to always take care of his disabled sister, Bessie, and just never got around to marriage, according to family members.

Mark Seacrest worked with his family's newspaper in Lincoln, Nebraska, before eventually taking over the publishing company. In 1955, he accepted an invitation from the Crusade for Freedom to make an overseas inspection tour of the facilities of Free Europe and Free Europe Press.[30] Also a newspaperman, Lou Graves was sports editor and city editor of the *Texarkana Gazette* before purchasing the *Nashville News* in Nashville, Arkansas, in 1950. As the *Nashville News-Leader*, it is still operated by his son, Lou III.[31] Frank Jakubasz was a linotype operator for the *Boston Globe* for twenty-three years until his retirement, and Paul Johnson had a long career as an offset pressman working primarily for Journal Press, Inc., in Jamestown, New York.

Because their education had been interrupted by the war, others who had served with the 3rd Squadron chose to continue it after they went home. Making this option even more enticing were benefits offered to veterans under the Servicemen's Readjustment Act of 1944 (more commonly called the GI Bill of Rights). John Trumm received his bachelor's degree in mechanical engineering from Oregon State University and worked as a processing engineer at the Avon Petroleum Refinery in Martinez, California, for thirty-five years. Al Magyar graduated from the University of Michigan and became the chief planning officer for GPU Energy Corp. at Convent Station, New Jersey.

Lloyd Jackson graduated from Tulsa University with a BA in engineering in 1949 and later received his MS in engineering from Oklahoma State University. He spent thirty-six years as an aerospace engineer and engineering executive, primarily with Douglas Aircraft, North American Aviation, and Rockwell International. His accomplishments included working on several high-profile programs such as Apollo and the space shuttle.[32]

Bob Hugel graduated from Rider College at Trenton, New Jersey, in 1949. He spent his early career with Sentinel Insurance, his family's insurance agency in New York City. He was later employed by the insurance department of General Telephone before moving to Connecticut in 1964, when he started as insurance manager for Pratt & Whitney Aircraft. He retired as assistant treasurer / risk manager from United Technologies Corp. in 1988.[33]

Frank Pulaski graduated with a bachelor of science degree from the School of Business Administration at the University of Connecticut in 1950. He was employed first as an engineer and later as assistant plant manager for Plastic Wire and Cable Corp. in Jewett City, Connecticut. He was granted a patent in June 1961 for a "Core Wrapping Apparatus" used for "folding and forming an insulated tape shield or wrapper longitudinally around an elongate continuous electrical cable core."[34]

Willard Ilefeldt studied for the ministry and was ordained an Episcopal priest in 1961. He served as rector for parishes in Orange County, California, before earning a doctorate in pastoral counseling in 1969. He practiced in Orange County until his retirement to Sky Ranch in Carmel Valley, where he raised sheep. During this period, he wrote a memoir called *Thoughts While Tending Sheep* that was published in 1988.[35]

Tom Kilian attended Pennsylvania State College of Optometry and opened his practice in Charleston, South Carolina. Paul Haines, from Pennsylvania, graduated from the Progressive School of Photography in New Haven, Connecticut, and was afterward employed by a commercial photography company in Philadelphia. He retired from Kaiser Aluminum and later worked part-time for the South Carolina Criminal Justice Academy, although he retained his interest in photography, as well as singing in barber shop quartets and acting in Little Theater. Bert Thomas graduated from the University of Missouri with a bachelor of science degree in business administration and became an accountant, later employed by Missouri Farmers Association Oil Co. in Columbia, Missouri.

Les Mondelli was at Eglin Field, assigned to the 611th Air Force Base Unit, Air Proving Ground Command, in the summer of 1946 but left the military soon afterward. He received his law degree from Vanderbilt Law School in 1951 and worked as an insurance claims adjuster before joining the law practice of Lester, Loser, Hildebrand, Nolan, Lane & Mondelli. He later served as a judge in Nashville, Tennessee, for nineteen years. Paul Young attended the University of California at Berkeley, where he received his bachelor of arts degree in 1947 and master of arts degree with a major in history and minor in Oriental languages in 1948. He became a junior college teacher and was later employed as an engineer with Sirocco, Inc., in Fremont, California.

A number of former 3rd Squadron members chose to make their careers in the Air Force after it was established on September 18, 1947, while others were recalled from the reserves for the Korean War in the early 1950s and some for the Vietnam War in the mid-1960s. After his return to the US in late 1944, Gene Dorr was processed through Atlantic City and assigned to the 3rd Air Force. He was sent to Morse Field, North Carolina, where he was appointed armament officer and later assistant ground safety officer. He was sent for training to Chanute Field, Illinois, where he was appointed base ground safety officer, and finally to Mitchell Field, New York, to be assistant ground safety officer for HQ 1st Air Force. Plagued throughout this period by repeated bouts of malaria that eventually damaged his spleen, Dorr was retired with disability on September 19, 1945, and returned to Boston. In an effort to alleviate his asthma, Dorr then moved to the Denver area with his family, because of Colorado's dry climate. He initially went back to teaching before becoming an elementary school principal and later a junior high school and then high school principal.[36]

Bob MacNeil wrote to Jim McCann that when he was called up in 1950, he was first assigned to SAC headquarters and was then sent to the Military Assistance Advisory Group (MAAG) at Formosa for two years. There he met many former Chinese squadron members from the mainland. "I got stopped many times on the street by our old Chinese airmen[,] which resulted in a few parties. I also met a few in Hong Kong who were civilians. The last one year I was out there I maintained the Madame's C-47 & the General's C-54. . . . There were a few trips to Clark Field, which was a pleasant change."[37]

Leo Baker, who retired from the Air Force as a major in August 1963, owned and operated Leo's Phillip's 66 service station in Pima, Arizona, soon afterward, later moving to Fort Smith, Arkansas. Frank Bowen was stationed in Japan and later at Harlingen AFB in Texas. He was sent to Clark Air Base in the Philippines, where he served in the 5th Tactical Control Group. While at Clark, he was voted outstanding Air Force supply officer in 1963. Bowen, too, retired as a major. Attaining that rank was so important to Bob Logan that he never took vacations but instead went for two weeks every year to reserve officers' training so he could make the grade of major, according to his daughter. He was so proud of having achieved his goal that he had it engraved on his gravestone: "Robert L. Logan, USAF Major, ret."

George Cunningham served in the Air Force Reserve before taking a regular commission. He transitioned from bombers to fighters, flying F-100s. In 1961 he retired as a colonel and went on to work at Pan Am as an engineer, then became a bank vice president, and finally worked for the State Department before retiring in the early 1980s. As was the case with so many others whose military experience included combat, he was uncomfortable talking about it with his family. Attempts by his eldest son, George Jr., to learn about his service were rebuffed until a fishing trip they took together after he retired. Sitting in a boat in the middle of a lake, George Sr. finally gave a thirty-minute "condensed" version that included his memories of the July 4 Burma mission, and then he never consented to discuss it again.[38]

Tom Simpson remained in the military and was offered a brigadier general's star in 1962 but turned it down when a visit to Strategic Air Command headquarters revealed that he would be required to stop flying. He retired as a colonel with a total of six thousand in-flight hours.[39]

Jack Hamilton served both in the Korean War and the Vietnam War. He was awarded the Distinguished Flying Cross and other decorations for his World War II service in the Mediterranean and China-Burma-India theaters and for NATO duty in Turkey. In 1960, he was commander of the 12th Bomb Squadron, 341st Bomb Wing, 15th Air Force, at Dyess Air Force Base, Abilene, Texas. He enrolled at Texas Tech under the USAF Institute of Technology program to study engineering as part of a program to educate experienced officers to fill critical duty assignments, and he received a bachelor of science degree in industrial engineering. Hamilton was awarded the Air Force Commendation Medal in 1961, cited for his direction of planning and briefing of the B-47 Unit Simulated Combat Mission, for which the wing received the highest score ever made in the Strategic Air Command by a B-47 unit. Hamilton received a master of science degree in industrial engineering (in absentia) at Texas Tech in May 1964. His thesis was titled "An Approximation of the Cumulative Binomial Probability Distribution." He retired with the rank of colonel.[40]

Chester Conrad, another career officer, was stationed in Karachi in the late 1940s and early 1950s and in Japan, with the rank of lieutenant colonel at the time of his death in 1955 at the age of thirty-eight.[41] Grady Fuller became warehouse section chief at Tinker Air Force Base at Oklahoma City after the war and continued training Chinese students. While there, he received the Nationalist Chinese government's Breast Order of Jun Hui for his service as an aircraft maintenance instructor in China. He later served in Tokyo, Japan, and at Rhein-Main Air Base in Germany, where he was commanding officer of the 7310th Material Squadron.[42] Willie Curik, who retired from the Air Force in 1961, returned to Denison, Texas, where he had established Denison Frozen Food Lockers while still in college and continued to operate it through the years that followed his retirement. Fuller, Curik, and Hank Drake, whose military career included commanding the nation's first operational ICBM missile wing during the Cold War, all retired with the rank of lieutenant colonel.

Lou Graves, whose military service had started in the Naval Reserve, was called up and served in the Marine Corps Reserve during the Korean War. Jack Hinrichs, promoted to lieutenant colonel, served as commanding officer of the 309th Transportation Truck Squadron, USA Reserves. Wilbur Dunlap also served in Korea and Vietnam, retiring after a total of thirty years in the military.

Pete Chasse was in the Air Force for twenty-four years and with the US State Department for seven years. Bob Solyn was called up in 1954 and served in the Air Force as a policeman, retiring in 1961. He, Dunlap, and Chasse all ended their military careers with the rank of master sergeant. Allen Malone retired from the Air Force as a senior master sergeant in 1972 after serving thirty-one years. Don Grant reenlisted as a private in February 1946 and remained with the Air Force after its activation, attaining the rank of staff sergeant by 1950. He was released from service in about 1953 and became a patrolman with the North Sacramento Police Department, later serving as chief of police of the Folsom Police Department.

Jack Trout enlisted in the Air Force Reserve in January 1946. He was stationed in Germany in 1948 and was at Lajes AFB in the Azores, serving in cooperation with the Portuguese air force in 1953. Jack Holmes reenlisted in May 1946 and was stationed at Hill Air Force Base in northern Utah, playing baseball during that time on the base team. Otto Hutchinson enlisted in the Air Force Reserve in September 1946 and served a three-year tour of duty. Afterward he was employed in civilian life as an airplane mechanic and later as a mechanic for Mack Trucks.[43]

Bernard Czerniak's postwar service was with the 66th Fighter Wing of the Chicago Air National Guard, which had built an efficient "M-day" (mobilization day) organization at Douglas Field in the event its services should be required.[44] Bud Keller joined the 9524th Air Force Reserve Recovery Squadron at Bismarck, North Dakota, in 1962 and was assigned to its personnel section. The unit's purpose was to serve at the Bismarck Municipal Airport to assist US strike forces in accomplishing their mission in the event of a national emergency.[45]

Many of the squadron's former members joined veterans' associations, at least in part to maintain a sense of connection to their comrades in arms. Most common of these were the American Legion and Veterans of Foreign Wars. Members attended meetings at local "posts" with other veterans whose experiences were similar to their own, and who understood the horror that is war in a way the folks at home could never comprehend. Their official goals included encouraging patriotism in their communities, promoting strong national security, and providing support to fellow veterans, but their primary motivation was to spend time with others who had "been there."

Les Mondelli was cofounder and first commander of American Legion Post 920 in Scranton, Pennsylvania. Dr. Lloyd Smith was an active member of Post 277 at Lampasas, Texas, and served as its historian and chaplain. Maynard Rieks was a member of Post 188 in Iowa Falls, Iowa; Clyde Learn of Post 141 in Indiana, Pennsylvania; Phil Piecuch of the James E. Coffey Post 3 in Nashua, New Hampshire; and Bud Keller of Post #8 in Las Vegas, Nevada.

Pete Chasse was a longtime member of the VFW and was very active in its Post 1845 at Simpsonville, South Carolina, as well as the Disabled American Veterans. Andrew Foorman was a member of VFW Post 9498 in Bryte, California.

In the China-Burma-India Veterans Association, members met at local "bashas," and annual conventions, attended by veterans and their families, were additionally held. Bob Schlicher and his wife, Rose, attended a few of these CBI reunions later in life. Parker Collins, a member of the Washington State Dhobi Wallah Basha, was elected its commander in July 1962. George Cunningham was active in the Valley of the Sun Basha in Sun City, Arizona. Gene Dorr was a member of the Colorado Basha. He and his wife, Sonny, attended its conventions and the husband-and-wife affairs held every other month, he wrote in a letter to Jim McCann.

The 14th Air Force Association, organized like the others soon after the war, established chapters in major cities. Many of these veterans attended conventions that were held annually.

Leo Baker was a faithful member who eagerly looked forward to the conventions, where he was able to "relive his days as a Flying Tiger." He commented in an interview, "The only sad part about going to a reunion is you see these people that used to look so young, and you think, my Lord, how they've set over there and aged. But you forget to look in the mirror at yourself." Leo was one of the "Flying Tigers" awarded the China War Memorial Medal, called the "lost decoration of World War II" for good reason. He knew the medal was authorized before he left China, but "I'd quit wondering about it until about two years ago." It had been authorized by the Nationalist Chinese government on September 29, 1945, as many of the Americans were going home. However, the medal was never distributed among its intended recipients after the war.

"Circular No. 166 that authorized the medal was lost amid the quick demobilization of soldiers and the growing struggle between the Nationalists and Communist for control over China," according to a newspaper article. It was finally discovered after twenty-nine years of searching by Graham Kidd, from Florida. The 14th Air Force Association notified the Chinese embassy through Anna Chennault, widow of Gen. Chennault. "The Chinese Nationalist Government on Taiwan then authenticated the award and announced that members of the 14th Air Force Association would receive the K'ang Chan-Nien Chang, as the medal was known in China." Baker and other members of "the American Flying Tigers" were awarded their medals by Taiwan's former ambassador to the United States in the summer of 1975 at Kansas City. Gen. Chennault's award was presented posthumously.[46]

Dorr was a member of this organization, as well as of the CBI Association. In 1980 he attended a convention in Reno where he met with Paul Young and "three replacements that joined the 3rd Bomb after I left": Tom Edgerton, Robert Logan, and Wayne Senecal. Also present was Alan Bennett, according to a letter that Dorr wrote to McCann.

Grady Fuller attended the three-day reunion in July 1982 at the Westin Hotel in Seattle. He kept a letter of invitation for a special gathering of 1st Bomb Group officers hosted by the 4th Squadron's Bill Dick, who booked a suite for use as a hospitality room for the event. Tom Edgerton, Gene Dorr, and Bob Logan were other 3rd Squadron veterans who had committed to attend, and Dick was contacting as many others as he could reach.[47]

To celebrate the fortieth anniversary of the end of the war, the 14th Air Force Association held its annual convention in Taipei, Taiwan. More than three hundred American veterans—all members of the famed Flying Tigers, who attended with more than 350 family members—met at the Grand Hotel for ceremonies and festivities during the last week of May 1985. In attendance were many former members of the Chinese air force who had served with the American airmen to drive out the Japanese.

George Cunningham, who had retired from the Air Force with the rank of colonel and later worked in the private sector, attended with his wife and younger daughter. It was the highlight of his retirement years. The group attended a commemorative rally at which a bronze plaque was dedicated to the Chinese and Americans who gave their lives in the war. A memorial service was then held at the site of a statue of Gen. Chennault, who had died in 1958. Then they paid their respects to the late generalissimo at the Chung Cheng Memorial Hall. Madame Chiang attended and presented Cunningham with a belt buckle of carved green jade.[48]

George Wood, another active member, kept a collection of the association's newsletters, *Hoo Bao Hoo*. Diminishing membership eventually led to the cessation of these gatherings. The 14th Air Force Association's final reunion took place in May 2007, in Washington, DC, and Wood's daughter and son-in-law attended. In an emotional closing ceremony at Arlington National Cemetery, a bugle played "Taps" for the final time. A moving tribute honored Wood as one of the fallen members to be remembered. After the ceremony, many of those present walked to Lt. Gen. Claire Chennault's grave, located nearby, placed wreaths around his gravestone, and paid their respects.[49]

Ceremonies held in 2015 marked seven decades since World War II ended with Japan's surrender. To commemorate this historic anniversary, China made elaborate preparations to celebrate as never before. Officially called the "70th Anniversary of Chinese People's Anti-Japanese War and World Anti-Fascist War Victory Commemoration Day," this nationally observed holiday culminated a weeklong celebration with an enormous military parade on September 3—the day after the date of the Japanese surrender to Allied forces in 1945. As part of the imposing spectacle, which included dozens of amphibious armored fighting vehicles, battle tanks, trucks bearing antitank guided missiles, and other military vehicles, as well as flyovers by two hundred fighter jets and military helicopters, some 12,000 troops marched along Beijing's Changan Avenue up to Tiananmen for inspection by Communist leader Xi Jinping.

Leading the parade were surviving soldiers from the war in China, riding in open-top buses and escorted by armed motorcycle police. The veterans, most of them over ninety years old, had fought under various commands, including the New Fourth Army, the National Revolutionary Army, and the Eighth Route Army. Widows of some of the deceased veterans participated in their honor. Besides the Chinese soldiers, some still-living airmen of the United States Air Forces who had fought alongside Chinese forces joined the veterans' column. All wearing commemorative medals presented to them by President Xi, the participants included ninety-five-year-old Li Chan-jui, who had taken part in 3rd Squadron missions in 1944 and remained in China with his family following the war. Because of his Nationalist service, he had not been permitted to keep any of his wartime mementos, even his medals, after the PRC assumed control.[50]

As one of the relative handful of remaining veterans who took part in the air war in China, Hank Mills was invited to join the celebration, which included not only the parade but also receptions, banquets, guided tours, and other events intended to express China's gratitude for the service he and others had rendered in the fight to defeat the foreign invaders. Regrettably, his health had begun to fail, and he feared that the long flight and demanding schedule would be too difficult for him, so he declined the invitation. He died peacefully in his sleep a few months afterward.

For a little over a year and a half, American and Chinese members of the 3rd Bombardment Squadron had lived, worked, and fought side by side as part of Chennault's grand experiment to revitalize the Chinese army and enable it to drive the Japanese from their homeland. As brothers in arms, these men shared a bond that could not be broken by distance or the passage of time.

Almost eighty years have now passed since those courageous airmen flew the skies over China. Few of them remain to tell the story, and no Americans of the 3rd Squadron are left among the ever-diminishing number of those who still survive. Like those old H-model B-25s, they have been "claimed by attrition."

Their dedication in driving back the forces of tyranny cannot be overestimated. To those brave men of the Spray and Pray Squadron, we owe our deepest gratitude and respect.

APPENDIXES

APPENDIX A
B-25s Assigned to 3rd Bomb Squadron

Note: Operational intelligence reports for missions from India to Burma (June 25–August 1944) and out of Kweilin, China, prior to evacuation (mid-September 1944) did not include serial numbers, "Chinese" airplane numbers, or aircrews.

"Chinese" A/C Number	Serial Number	Serial Number	Serial Number	Serial Number
	India/Burma	China	China	China
	May–Aug. 1944	Sep. 1944–Jan. 1945	Feb.–May 1945	June–Aug. 1945
713	43-4123 (H)	43-4351 (H)	43-4351 (H)	Not found
	Forced landing, mechanical failure, R. L. Hodges, June 4, near Moran (Photos)			
714	43-4114 (H)	43-27809 (J)	43-27809 (J)	44-30867 (J)
	(photos, Moran) Landing accident, Hsu T. C., July 10, Barrackpore (repaired) Bailout, ground fire, M. T. Seacrest, Aug. 14, Yunnan Prov., China	(also 43-2709) Assigned to Task Force 34 in Nov. 1944 (photos)	In background of squadron photo, Mar. 1, Liangshan Landing accident, Apr. 16, Liangshan missions 44-30867 (J) Acquired in early May	Missing after leaving formation at Chowshihtien, cause not known, Wang Y. S., May 21, not found on later 44-311114 (J)

715	Unknown (H)	43-4122 (J)	43-27938 (J)	44-31075 (J-32)
	(photos, Moran)	Wheels-up landing at Chiuling-po, C. M. Conrad, Sep. 16; bailout, weather/gas depletion, R. C. MacNeil, Oct. 22, near Kweintown 60 mi. SE of Chungking 43-27938 (J)	Damage to vertical stabilizer, rudder, wingtip, and propeller as pilot pulled up from bombing bridge but returned to base, W. H. Senecal, Mar. 8, Hsiangcheng (photo)	Assigned to 4th Bomb Squadron Detachment at Chihkiang
716	Unknown	43-4116 (H)	43-4116 (H)	43-4116 (H)
			(photo, April)	
717	43-4124 (H)	43-4124 (H)	43-4124 (H)	43-4124 (H)
	Landing accident, In Y. S. July 10, Barrackpore, India (repaired)	(photo)		
718	Unknown (H)	43-5051 (H)	43-5051 (H)	44-30862 (J-2)
	(photos, Moran)	Assigned to Task Force 34, Dec. 1944–Jan. 45	Assigned to Nimrod Detachment in Feb. 1945 Bailout, lost in darkness/depleted gas, Teng C. C., Mar. 30, 38 mi. WNW of Liangshan (Ouyang C., navigator, and Lui H. L., waist gunner, not found in later records)	(photo, probably Chihkiang)
719	43-4183 (H)	43-4183 (H)	43-4183 (H)	44-30840 (J)
	(photo, Moran)	Personalized for Lt. R. L. Logan with "MY FRISCO JOE!"	Bailout, ground fire, Tu K. M., Mar. 26, near Chingmen	
720	Unknown	43-4184 (H)	44-30671 (J)	44-30671 (J)
		Bailout, weather/gas depleted, In Y. S., Dec. 18, near Chiangcheng, 20 mi. W of Peishiyi (Sgt. Yao S. C. killed)		Assigned to 4th Bomb Squadron Detachment in Aug.

721	43-4285 (H)	Not found	43-3449 (J)	44-31137 (J)
	Forced landing, ground fire, T. S. Simpson, July 4, Ledo Rd. near Mogaung, Burma		44-31137 (J)	Assigned to 4th Bomb Squadron Detachment in Aug.
722	43-4286 (H)	43-3939 (J)	43-4093 (J)	44-31126 (J)
	Forced landing, enemy fire, Liu P. C., Aug. 14, W bank of Salween River, Burma	Assigned to Task Force 34, Nov. 1944–Jan. 1945	(photo, Hanchung) Bailout, ground fire, F. H. Greene, Mar. 30, Han River 35 mi. E of Ankang 44-30656 (J) Crash landing, ground fire, D. J. Davis, May 16, Ichang Airdrome (D. J. Davis, B. L. Wherritt, R. J. Koss, J. J. Ryan Jr., and J. A. Wadlow KIA, L. L. Fox died from wounds) 44-31126 (J) Bellied in, mechanical failure, F. H. Greene Jr., May 27, in "free pocket" near Valley Field; returned to service	Assigned to 4th Bomb Squadron Detachment in Aug.
723	Not found	43-4289 (H)	43-4289 (H)	Not found
			43-4399 (unknown model) Bailout, ground fire, Chang C. K., Mar. 26, near Kunhsien (Lee C. C. injured and later died)	
724	Not found (H)	43-4296 (H)	43-4296 (H)	43-4296 (H)
	(photos, Moran)			Assigned to 4th Bomb Squadron Detachment in Aug.

725	Not assigned	Not assigned	44-31121 (J)	44-31121 (J)
			Acquired in early May	Assigned briefly to 4th Bomb Squadron Detachment in July
726	Not assigned	Not assigned	44-31124 (J)	44-31124 (J)
			Acquired in early May	
Unknown	41-29909 (D)			
	Training accident, pilot SLts. Shiong S. K., Mar. 22, Arabian Sea near Malir (he and Lin Y. C., 3BS; 1Lt. Lt. C. F. Yunghans, 91FS, 81FG; Sgt. C. Alton Jr., 375BS, 308BG, died; 2Lt. Webster Smith, injured)			
Unknown	43-3897			
	(unknown model) July 8, Ragland mission to Burma			
Unknown	43-3888 (J)			
	July 10, R. L. Hodges, admin mission to Barrackpore			
Unknown		43-28164 (J)		
		Bailout, lost in darkness/gas depleted, Jan. 15, L. C. Baker, near Kweiyang, (Task Force 34 out of Chihkiang)		

Appendix A

APPENDIX B
Chinese Air Force Personnel Listed in Movement Orders

Special Orders No. 100, May 26, 1944, CBI HQ, Armed Forces Training Command (Prov.), movement from Malir to Moran, India, to travel by air transport:

Capts. Lee Yu-hwa (X-288) and Tsuei Shiang-cheng (X-222); 1Lts. Ouyang Chu (X-277) and Huang Chi (X-124); 2Lts. Hsiao Han-ting (X-281), Liu Ping-chuen (X-282), Chow Jen-mein (X-242), Hsu Hung-wu (X-287), and Tsai Chang-an (X-280); SLts. Chang Yi-sheng (X-735), Cheng Shih-chin (X-748), Cheng Shih-chin (X-748), Chao Chan-fu (X-284), Chang Chih-yung (X-818), Chen Chang-shiang (X-820), Kuo Tung-teh (X-828), Wang Chih-lin (X-814), Chiu Kwang-shih (X-827), Wu Pao-yi (X-835), Tu Hsiang (X-892), Liang Kwan-yuing (X-141), and Kuo Chun (X-135); and Sgts. Chung Hsiu-han (X-2135), Jen Fu-sheng (X-2122), Chang Tou-yin (X-2137), Ku Wen-sheng (X-2138), Chao Lien-hwa (X-2142), Tai Pin-san (X-2123), Lai Hui-liang (X-2124), Tung Nien-chih (X-2125), Liu Ho-te (X-2126), Chang Yang (X-2127), Yang Hsiao-li (X-2128), Chiu Hsien-pin (X-2115), Kan Kwei-ming (X-2118), Pai Yun-ting (X-2119), Kuan Hsien-chien (X-2120), Wang Hsueh-ting (X-2121), Chang Chin-hua (X-2173), Tsai Kao-ling (X-2174), Ching Chuo-shu (X-2178), Tung Chih-kuang (X-2179), Hsiao Tsu-p'ei (X-2180), Chao Kuo-pin (X-2184), Kao Chen-k'ai (X-1316), Liu Kwan-ping (X-1318), Li Chan-jui (X-1317), Feng Cheng-k'wen (X-1323), Kuo Feng (X-1324), Cheng Kuo-wei (X-1326), Wang Chun-sheng (X-1327), Liang Yun-tien (X-1334), Tso Jui-heng (X-1339), Ma Lung (X-1340), Mai Pei-chen (X-1345), Liu Chung-chieh (X-1346), Chow Kwan-yuan (X-1347), and Wang Yin-ch'ing (X-1350)

By same orders, to travel by military transport (the squadron's B-25s):
Capts. Sung S. C. (X-221) and Wu C. C. (X-510); 1Lts. Cheng Y. K. (X-271), Lee C. C. (X-272), Sheng C. J. (X-225), Chow H. (X-276), Shen M. C. (X-130), Ting C. L. (X-275), Chang H. H. (X-226), and Hwang T. P. (X-273); 2Lts. Feng M. T. (X-823), Hsu I. K. (X-824), Yu Y. T. (X-837), Hsu C. H. (X-132), Liu P. C. (X-830), Wang Y. S. (X-834), Hu T. C. (X-825), Hsieh W. W. (X-278), Chang C. C. (X-137), Cheng Y. K. (X-821), Teng C. C. (X-734; should be 374), Tu K. M. (X-832), Chang H. L. (X-819), Yang C. H. (X-279), Fan W. S. (X-286), Lu H. C. (X-285), In Y. S. (X-286), Chang O. K. (X-817), Tung S. L. (X-833), and Chiang T. (X-822); and Sgts. Chow H. C. (X-1349), Li L. (X-1319), Shieh H. J. (X-2175), Shu S. S. (X-2117), Haiso Y. T. (X-1312), Li S. L. (X-1314), Yang S. F. (X-2177), Ho W. C. (X-1315), Li C. S. (X-1313), Chen Y. O. (X-2176), Ho W. C. (X-1337), Chang T. H. (X-2183), Wu K. Y. (X-1338), Taun T. P. (X-1321), Mao C. F. (X-2116), Kuo H. Y. (X-1322), Wang C. C. (X-1320), Nieh L. Y. (X-1332), Chang F. T. (X-2182), Yao S. C. (X-1330), Huang T. S. (X-1328), Hu Y. F. (X-2181), and Wei C. S. (X-1335)

Special Orders No. 89, August 20, 1944, 1st Bombardment Group, movement from "Deragon," India, to Kweilin, China:
Maj. Wu C. C. (X-510); Capt. Tsuei H. C. (X-222); 1Lts. Cheng H. H. (X-226), Hwang T. P. (X-273), Pai J. H. (X-274), Chen Y. K. (X-271), Ou-young C. (X-277), Hwang C. (X-124),

Lee Y. H. (X-288), Lee C. C. (X-272), Fan C. Y. (X-286), and Chu S. C. (no #); 2Lts. Chen S. C. (X-748), Chang C. K. (X-817), Tu K. M. (X-832), Hsiao H. T. (X-281), Chao C. F. (X-284), Hsu H. Y. (X-287), Chang C. C. (X-137), Cheng Y. K. (X-821), Wang Y. S. (X-834), Yang C. H. (X-279), Tsao C. M. (X-242), Teng C. C. (X-374), Yu Y. T. (X-837), In Y. S. (X-286), Hsu C. H. (X-132), and Lu H. C. (X-285); SLts. Chieng T. (X-522), Wang C. L. (X-814), Chang C. L. (X-818), Hsu J. K. (X-824), Chen C. S. (X-820), and Kuo T. T. (X-828); Warrant Officer Fan W. H. (X-286); and Sgts. Sung H. H. (X-2146), Liao K. T. (X-2149), Lee E. H. (X-2152), Kwang T. (X-2287), Yang C. L. (X-2145), Wang M. T. (X-2156), Ma T. Y. (X-2204), Chang C. H. (X-2173), Wang Y. P. (X-2141), Yu Y. P. (X-2156), Liu Y. C. (X-2290), Chang T. H. (X-2183), Hsiao T. P. (X-2180), Fang C. K. (X-1403), Chow K. Y. (X-1418), Wang C. C. (X-1400), Liu K. P. (X-1397), Shu S. S. (X-2117), Li C. J. (X-1317), Yao S. C. (X-1410), Wang Y. C. (X-1420), Hsiao Y. T. (X-1392), Chiu H. P. (X-2115), Tsai K. L. (X-2174), Chen Y. C. (X-2175), Chiang C. S. (X-2178), Chao K. P. (X-2184), Wang C. S. (X-1406), Nieh L. Y. (X-1409), Chao L. H. (X-2142), Chiu C. L. (X-2141), Chow J. S. (X-2298), Huang Y. M. (X-2151), Lee P. L. (X-2206), Chang T. L. (X-2301), Chu Y. S. (X-2139), Chu C. H. (X-2300), Chang K. Y. (X-2297), Liang M. H. (X-2288), Tung N. C. (X-2125), Liu T. W. (X-2131), Chang Y. (X-2127), Tai P. S. (X-2123), Lai H. L. (X-2124), Fang C. H. (X-2143), Chu T. C. (X-2148), Wang Y. T. (X-2159), Wang S. L. (X-2202), Wang T. H. (# illegible), Kwan C. C. (X-2303), Su C. Y. (X-2305), Wang L. S. (X-2140), Chin P. M. (X-2154), Tsai L. T. (X-2160), Wang T. F. (X-2295), Mao C. H. (X-2116), Li L. (X-1319), Liang Y. T. (X-1411), Kuo H. Y. (X-1402), Wu K. Y. (X-1421), Liu C. C. (X-1416), Kan K. M. (X-2118), Kwan H. C. (X-2120), Chang K. W. (X-1405), Li S. L. (X-1393), Pai Y. T. (X-2119), Shieh Y. J. (X-2175), Hu Y. F. (X-2131), Chang F. T. (X-2182), Kao C. K. (X-1396), Chung C. (X-1408), Ku W. S. (X-2138), Chang T. Y. (X-2137), Chi C. C. (X-2153), Chang H. S. (X-2157), Huang Y. (X-2289), Wei C. S. (X-2291), Lee S. C. (X-2302), Lu C. P. (X-2203), Lee J. S. (X-2296), Pao T. (X-2286), Wang S. C. (X-2134), Yang H. L. (X-2128), Wang M. T. (X-2129), Chi M. (X-2130), Teng C. S. (X-2133), Liu H. T. (X-2126), Kao C. C. (X-2136), Chang K. H. (X-2150), Chang C. L. (X-2207), Xiang Y. (X-2144), Chen S. Y. (X-2293), Hu C. S. (X-2304), You K. C. (X-2306), Yang C. C. (X-2201), Lee Y. C. (X-2155), and Yuan H. S. (X-2292)

Special Orders No. 81, September 20, 1944, 1st Bombardment Group, movement from Kweilin to Peishiyi:

Maj. Wu C. C. (X-510); Capt. Tsuei H. C. (X-222); 1Lts. Lee Y. H. (X-288), Cheng H. H. (X-225), Chen Y. K. (X-271), Lee C. C. (X-272), Hwang T. P. (X-273), Ou-young C. (X-277), Fan C. Y. (X-229), Pai J. H. (X-274), Hwang C. (X-123), and Chu S. C. (no #); 2Lts. Chen S. C. (X-748), Chang C. C. (X-137), Teng C. C. (X-374), Chang C. K. (X-817), Cheng Y. K. (X-821), Yu Y. T. (X-837), Tu K. M. (X-832), Wang Y. S. (X-831), In Y. S. (X-826), Hsiao H. T. (X-281), Yang C. H. (X-279), Hsu C. H. (X-132), Chao C. F. (X-284), Tsao C. M. (X-242), Lu H. C. (X-285), and Hsu H. Y (X-287); SLts. Chang C. L. (X-818), Chen C. S. (X-820), Chieng T. (X-822), Hsu J. K. (X-824), Kuo T. T. (X-828), and Wang C. L. (X-814); W/O Fan W. H. (X-286); and Sgts. Sung H. H. (X-2146), Yang C. L. (X-2145), Wang Y. F. (X-2147), Liao K. T. (X-2149), Wang M. T. (X-2156), Yu Y. P. (X-2156; duplicate), Lee E. H. (X-2152), Ma T. Y. (X-2204), Liu Y. C. (X-2290), Kwang T. (X-2287), Chang C. H. (X-2173), Chang T. H. (X-2183), Hsiao T. P. (X-2180), Mao C. H. (X-2116), Fong C. K. (X-1403), Li L. (X-1319), Chow K. Y. (X-1418), Liang Y. T. (X 1411), Wang C. C. (X-1400), Kuo H. Y. (X-1402), Liu K. P. (X-1318), Wu K. Y. (X-1421), Shu S. S. (X-2117), Liu C. C. (X-1416), Li C. J. (X-1317), Kan K. M. (X-2118), Yao S. C. (X-1410), Kuan H. C. (X-2120), Wang Y. C. (X-1420),

Chang K. W. (X-1405), Haiso Y. T. (X-1392), Li S. L. (X-1393), Chiu H. P. (X-2115), Pai Y. T. (X-2119), Tsai K. L. (X-2174), Shieh Y. J. (X-2175), Chen Y. C. (X-2176), Hu Y. F. (X-2131), Chiang C. S. (X-2178), Chang F. T. (X-2182), Chao K. P. (X-2184), Kao C. K. (X-1396), Wang C. S. (X-1406), Chung C. (X-1408), Nieh L. Y. (X-1409), Ku W. S. (X-2138), Chao L. H. (X-2142), Chang T. Y. (X-2137), Chiu C. L. (X-2141), Chi C. C. (X-2153), Chow J. S. (X-2298), Chang H. S. (X-2157), Huang Y. M. (X-2151), Huang Y. (X-2289), Lee P. L. (X-2205), Wei C. S. (X-2291), Cheng T. L. (X-2301), Lee S. C. (X-2302), Chu Y. S. (X-2139), Lu C. P. (X-2203), Chu C. H. (X-2300), Lee J. S. (X-2296), Chang K. Y. (X-2297), Pao T. (X-2286), Liang M. H. (X-2288), Wang S. C. (X-2134), Tung N. C. (X-2125), Yang H. L. (X-2128), Liu T. W. (X-2131), Wang M. T. (X-2129), Chang Y. (X-2127), Lei M. (X-2130), Tai P. S. (X-2123), Teng C. S. (X-2133), Lai H. L. (X-2124), Liu H. T. (X-2126), Fang C. H. (X-2142), Kao C. C. (X-2136), Chu T. C. (X-2148), Chang K. H. (X-2150), Wang Y. T. (X-2159), Chang C. L. (X-2207), Wang S. L. (X-2202), Kiang Y. (X-2144), Wang T. C. (X-2294), Chen S. Y. (X-2293), Kwan C. C. (X-2303), Hu C. C. (X-2304), Su C. Y. (X-2305), You K. C. (X-2306), Wang Y. S. (X-2140), Yang C. C. (X-2201), Chen P. M. (X-2154), Lee Y. C. (X-2155), Tsai M. T. (X-2160), Yuan H. S. (X-2292), and Wang T. Y. (X-2295)

Other orders for change of station from Moran to Dergaon, India, and from Peishiyi to Liangshan, China, have not been found.

APPENDIX C
Biographical Sketches

American members of the 3rd Bombardment Squadron generally numbered between fifty-five and seventy at any given time. During the squadron's tenure with the CACW, some of them were transferred to other units, rotated home, or lost in combat. To keep the number relatively constant, replacements were transferred in from other units or sent directly from the US.

In common with all American servicemen, each was identified by a serial number (also called a service number) in which each digit or group of digits had significance. The initial digit provided enlistment information. For example, "0" indicated that the soldier served before America entered the war, "1" that he volunteered for service, "2" that he joined from a recognized National Guard unit, and "3" that he was drafted. The letter "O" followed by a dash was used to identify officers; it was changed to "0" (zero) in 1942. The next number group was a code that indicated the geographical area where he enlisted, and the final group was his individual number.

Although there were undoubtedly others, since unidentified personnel appear in early squadron photos, these are names and biographical sketches of 120 members taken from Chinese-American Composite Wing, 1st Bombardment Group, and 3rd Bombardment Squadron morning reports, monthly historical reports, operational intelligence reports, special and general orders, and other documents:

ALLEGRETTO, Andrew Ralph ("Swifty," "Andy"), Sgt. (serial #32750955)
Born December 18, 1924, in Ocean City, NJ. Son of Michele (Michael, "Mike") Alfredo and Condita (Iacona) Allegretto, Italian immigrants. In 1930 census, enumerated with parents and four siblings, address 933 Simpson Ave., Ocean City, student. In 1940, with parents, three sisters, and two brothers, same address, completed seven years of school and still attending school. Registered for the draft on December 29, 1942, same address, employer W. Bartholomew, 9th & Asbury Ave., Ocean City (brown eyes, brown hair, ruddy complexion, 5'3", 140#). Enlisted on February 13, 1943, in Camden, NJ, as a private (completed two years of high school, occupation gas station attendant, 5'5", 138#). Arrived at Karachi aboard USS *Mission Bay* on March 29, 1944. Assigned to 3rd Squadron as an airplane armorer. Promoted to corporal on June 1. Assigned to detached service with Task Force 34 at Chihkiang. Treated with penicillin for undisclosed ailment in October and December. Promoted to sergeant on April 1, 1945. Awarded Air Medal on April 9; later received the American Service Medal, Asiatic-Pacific Service Medal, Good Conduct Medal, and World War II Victory Medal. Assigned to 4th Bomb Squadron detachment at Chihkiang in August. Treated for cellulitis of buttock and hip during same month. Transferred to 23rd Fighter Group, 68th Composite Wing, for transport home. Wood's address list at end of the war: "933 Simpson Ave., Ocean City, New Jersey." Released from service December 24, 1945. Married Madeleine ("Maddy") Sannino in 1946; parents of ten sons and two daughters. Had tattoo of a nude woman on his arm; later added shorts and a top at insistence of wife and mother. In 1950, with wife, three sons, and a daughter, address 1008 __ (street illegible). Ocean City, occupation plumber's helper. Worked for various plumbing companies before establishing Allegretto Plumbing and Heating in Ocean City; still in operation by his family. Died February 10, 2006; cause, cancer. Buried at Cape May County Veterans Cemetery, Cape May Court House, NJ.

ARMBRUSTER, Russell John ("Russ"), Cpl. (serial #37131258)

Born February 19, 1917, in St. Louis, MO. Son of John Henry and Isabelle (Pohlmann) Armbruster. In 1930, enumerated with parents and maternal grandmother, address 2422 Lemp St., St. Louis, attending school. Married Melberne Edna May Steeger in St. Louis, date undetermined but engagement announced in February 1936; divorced in June 1938. In 1940, lived with parents, sister, maternal grandmother, and aunt, 5841 Itaska, St. Louis, completed eighth grade, occupation policeman, civil government. Completed eleven years and six months of school per discharge documents. Registered for the draft on October 16, 1940, same address as census, employer Metropolitan Police (blue eyes, brown hair, light complexion, 6'2", 180#). Enlisted January 14, 1942, at Jefferson Barracks, MO, as a private (6'1", 168#). Married Ida Mary Dierkes on November 2, 1942, at San Angelo, TX; parents of three sons and three daughters. Assigned to 1043rd Guard Squadron, San Angelo, graduated from Air Forces Technical School as a bombsight mechanic on July 31, 1943; later completed training as airplane instrument mechanic. Promoted to corporal in February 1944. Departed US on August 30; arrived in CBI on October 8. Transferred from 1st Bomb Group to 3rd Squadron on May 1, 1945, as bombsight mechanic. Reclassified as airplane instrument mechanic. Sent to rest camp at Chengtu on July 2. Transferred to 36th Fighter Control Squadron at Luliang on September 19, for transport home (ASR score 78). Arrived in New York aboard USS *General C. C. Ballou* on November 6, 1945. Wood's list: "4406 Shrewsbury Ave., Shrewsbury, Mo." Released from service November 11, 1945, at Jefferson Barracks. Awarded two Bronze Stars, China War Memorial Badge with Ribbon, and Good Conduct Medal; entitled to wear Asiatic-Pacific Theatre Campaign Ribbon, American Theatre Campaign Ribbon, two overseas bars, and Victory Ribbon. Also awarded Purple Heart per obituary. In 1950, with parents, sister, wife, son, and daughter, address 4016 Flora Place, St. Louis, occupation police sergeant, city police. Retired in 1976 as a sergeant, St. Louis Metropolitan Police. Died June 12, 1985, at St. Louis; cause, cancer. Buried at Sunset Cemetery, St. Louis.

ARMSTRONG, William LeRoy ("Shorty," "Bill"), TSgt. (serial #39197335)

Born October 19, 1919, in Brownlee, Saskatchewan, Canada. Son of Louis Everett and Catherine (Thomas) Armstrong, homesteaders born in Michigan and Minnesota, respectively. Lived in Eyebrow Municipality, Swift Current District, Saskatchewan, in 1921. Moved to US when parents returned in 1922. In 1930, enumerated with parents, nine brothers, three sisters, a brother-in-law, and a niece, no address but not a farm, Wallace, Shoshone County, ID, attending school. Completed four years of high school. Married Jean McNeil on February 18, 1938, at Coeur d'Alene, ID; divorced soon after. In 1940, enumerated on April 13 at San Bruno, CA, address Barn 12, #3, Tanforan Racetrack, occupation groom. Married Ollie Rose Cosby on April 27, 1940, in Virginia City, Montana; residence of both, Wallace, ID; divorced soon after. Registered for the draft July 1, 1941, address 1260 Mirmar St., Apt. 38, Los Angeles, CA, occupation mechanic, employed by Howard Automobile Co., Figueroa; "person who will always know your address: no-one" (blue eyes, brown hair, light complexion, 5'5", 148#). Enlisted in Air Corps on December 28, 1942. Arrived at Karachi on July 30, 1943. Attached to USAAF OTU at Malir on August 1, 1943. Placed on flying status September 1 and October 1, 1943. Attached to 2nd Bomb Squadron on October 9. On January 25, 1944, as turret gunner, was knocked unconscious and received a 1-inch cut on his brow when Plexiglas dome of the turret was struck by antiaircraft fire. Joined 3rd Squadron on March 4, 1944, as AAF radio operator. Promoted to staff sergeant on April 1.

Promoted to technical sergeant on September 1. May have been the "mechanical sergeant" in altercation with Chinese pilot. Completed twenty-nine combat missions as aerial gunner. Ordered to Kunming to begin transfer to US on November 30, 1944. Wood's list: "Nampa, Idaho." Married Ruth Matthews on January 18, 1945, at Bremerton, WA; his address 315 16th Ave. N, Nampa, ID; parents of a son (?); divorced ca. 1948. In convalescent hospital at Santa Ana, CA, from February to June 1945 for chronic tonsillitis and "internal derangement of knee, old"; treatment included tonsillectomy. Discharged after four years of service and reenlisted in regular army at Fort George Wright, Spokane, WA, for three years on November 7, 1945, for the Hawaiian Department. Residence given as Spokane; occupation doorman; height and weight transcribed as "86, 066." Awarded Air Medal in December 1944 and Purple Heart in February 1946 at Fort Wright. That spring, placed in charge of "tighten-the-belt garden" on unused parade grounds in effort to increase domestic crop production to allow commercially grown food products to be shipped to starving people overseas. Also kept a 1-acre garden at his home, 3025 Dick St., Route 9, Spokane. Married Lillian Mae Farmer (a nurse), date undetermined. In 1950, with wife, son (age three), and five foster children (ages one to fourteen), address E7715 Marietta, Spokane, occupation "flier, plane mechanic," US Air Force. Divorced October 30, 1956. Married Whilden Alois (Walker) Corey on December 20, 1957, in Spokane (his residence Geiger Air Base, Spokane); divorced May 12, 1962. Released from service May 30, 1962; lived in Moses Lake, WA. Pleaded guilty to an aggravated assault charge in November 1963; residence Rathdrum, ID. Filed for bankruptcy in July 1966. Married Florence Ann (Gavalin) Puryear on February 4, 1967, at Coeur d'Alene, residence of both Moses Lake. Died January 23, 1987, in Las Vegas, NV. (Sometimes listed in civil records as William LeRoy Peters Armstrong.)

BAINS, Lois Garland, 1Lt. (serial #18076152; later #0-748888)

Born March 24, 1918, in Oplin, TX. Son of Wiley Otto and Emma Beulah (Needham) Bains. In 1930, lived on a farm with parents, three brothers, and a sister, address 161 Goldsboro & Tokeen Rd., Precinct 4, Coleman County, TX, occupation farm laborer. "Garland Bains" listed in Company D, First Platoon, ROTC, at John Tarleton Agricultural College, Stephenville, TX, in 1939–40. Graduated from JTAC with degree in agriculture in 1940. Not found in 1940 census. Registered for the draft as "Garland Lois Bains" on October 16, 1940, student at Texas A&M (blue eyes, brown hair, ruddy complexion, 6', 152#). Married Jeanne Elizabeth Draper. Enlisted in Air Corps as a private at Lubbock, TX, on May 27, 1942 (residence Ector County, TX, completed four years of college, occupation teacher, 6', 142#). At Sheppard Field, TX, in June 1942. Graduated from advanced flying school and commissioned 2nd lieutenant at Williams Field, AZ, in June 1943. Attached and joined 3rd Squadron on September 28, 1944; released on October 16 and transferred to 1st Bomb Group. Later attached to 2nd Bomb Squadron and flew several missions in cooperation with 3rd Squadron. On May 26, 1945, reported as MIA while searching for targets of opportunity in the Lohochai section of the Ping-Han Railroad. Buried by Chinese near crash site at Chuzhou, Chuxian, Anhui Province, China; moved to US Mausoleum No. 2, Scofield Barracks, HI, and reburied. Remains "not individually identified" and not turned over to family for final reburial but reinterred with those of Cpl. William C. Hawks, radio-gunner, on December 15, 1949, at Little Rock National Cemetery, Little Rock, AR.

BAKER, Leo Clayton ("Lee"), 1Lt. (serial #15060357; later #0-689115)

Born October 1, 1921, in Bedford, IN. Son of Clayton Lester and Roseanna Katherine (Wires) Baker. Completed two years at Shawswick High School. Employed by Sherwood-Chastain Auto Co. (Ford agency), Bedford, and then Frank Hatfield Motor Co., Indianapolis, IN. Married Doris Ilene Huff on October 21, 1937, in Bedford; divorced about June 1938. In 1940, enumerated with parents, address 46 West 21st St., Center Twp., Indianapolis, divorced, occupation mechanic and repairman of motor vehicles. Enlisted in Air Corps on November 1, 1940, at Fort Benjamin Harris, IN, as a private for the Panama Canal Department, address 2264 North Illinois St., Indianapolis (5'8", 117#). Stationed at France Field, Canal Zone, in early 1942. Began training as an aviation cadet at Brooks Field, TX, in early 1943. Married Kathryn Louise Buster on April 20, 1943, in Tulsa, OK; parents of a daughter; later divorced. Completed basic flight training at Majors Field, Greenville, TX. Graduated from advanced flight training school of the Central Flying Training Command, Randolph Field, TX, and commissioned 2nd lieutenant on July 24, 1943. Moved to Brooks Field, San Antonio, TX. Departed US for CBI on March 4, 1944. Attached to the 22nd Bomb Squadron, 341st Bomb Group, at Yangkai. Promoted to 1st lieutenant on September 1, 1944; joined 3rd Squadron on September 28 (order dated September 6), as a B-25 pilot. Served in Task Force 34 at Chihkiang. Reported as MIA on January 15, 1945; returned to duty. Promoted to captain and transferred to 1st Bomb Group HQ in February as assistant operations officer. Awarded Distinguished Flying Cross and Purple Heart. Awarded the Air Medal on March 24, 1945, for flying more than 100 hours in combat. Transferred to 4th Squadron in May 1945. Transferred to 22nd Bomb Squadron, 341st Bomb Group, as pilot for transport home. Not included on Wood's list. Registered for military service on November 15, 1945, "recently discharged" (gray eyes, brown hair, light complexion, 5'9", 132#). In 1950, with wife and daughter, address 133 Rodeo, Contra Costa, CA, occupation Armed Forces. Served as a major in Korean War. Married Laura Jane (Goodwin) Calloway on December 21, 1952, Los Angeles, CA; divorced in October 1957 in Tucson, AZ. Married Bexta Jean Callan, on October 8, 1958, Contra Costa, CA. Base project manager at Larson AFB, Spokane, WA, in early 1960. Retired from Air Force on August 1, 1963. Owned and operated Leo's Phillips 66 service station in Pima, AZ, in mid-1960s. Moved to Branch, AR, in early 1970s. Awarded the K'ang Chan-Nien Chang (the China War Memorial Medal) in summer of 1975. Died June 14, 1998. Buried at Ft. Smith National Cemetery, Ft. Smith, AR.

BANGER, Robert E. ("Bob"), 1Lt. (serial #16058631; later #0-667229)

Born April 22, 1916, in Bismarck, ND. Son of Robert Elmer and Irene Mary (Cox) Banger. Enumerated with parents and paternal grandparents at Big Creek Twp., Blackhawk County, IA, in 1920. In 1930, lived with parents and younger sister and brother, address 11453 Longwood Dr., Chicago, IL, attending school. Graduated from Morgan Park High School, Chicago, in 1934 and from University of Iowa, Iowa City, IA, with a bachelor of arts degree in 1938. Attended Medical College at University of Chicago. In 1940, lived with mother, brother, and sister, 10342 Wood St., Chicago, occupation time study, manufacturing. Registered for the draft as "Robert E. (initial only) Banger" on October 20, 1940, at Chicago, employer Johnson & Johnson, Chicago (hazel eyes, brown hair, light complexion, 6'2½", 180#). Enlisted in Air Corps on March 18, 1942, in Chicago as a private, occupation industrial engineer, (6', 159#). Trained as a bombardier and commissioned 2nd lieutenant at Midland, TX, on November 25, 1942; graduated from navigator school on March 11, 1943, at Hondo Field,

TX. Advanced flying school at Carlsbad, NM, in March 1943. Married Glyn Etta Gilpin of San Antonio on February 11, 1944, at post chapel, Roswell, NM, where he was an instructor. Joined 3rd Squadron on January 3, 1945. Assigned to Nimrod Detachment at Laohokow in March. Reported as MIA on May 27; returned to duty. Released from 3rd Squadron on August 27; sent to Karachi for transport home. Wood's list: "10342 South Wood Street, Chicago, Illinois, Beverly 8-3068." Released from service November 12, 1945. Married Elaine Ethel Werninghaus about July 1946; parents of two daughters and two sons. In 1950, with wife and sons, address 314 Lathrop Ave., River Forest, IL, occupation superintendent at a cotton mill, surgical needs factory. Lived in Forest Park, IL; Fort Worth, TX; and Spokane, Centralia, and Clarkston, WA. Employed by Chicago and Northwestern Railroad. Died April 29, 1981, at Clarkston. (Civilian sources sometimes refer to him as Robert E. Banger Jr.)

BARGE, John Powell ("Johnny"), MSgt. (serial #34267064)
Born May 7, 1915, in Monterey, AL. Son of Daniel Blythewood and Frances ("Frankie") Atkins (Yeldell) Barge. In 1930, enumerated with parents, two brothers, a sister, and maternal grandmother on a farm, "Forest House & Monterey Rd.," Monterey, AL, attending school. After graduating from Greenville High School, Greenville, AL, moved to Baxley, GA. In 1940, "Johnny Barge" was enumerated as lodger at a private residence on Swift St., Perry, GA, occupation appliance repairman, electric utility. Registered for the draft on October 16, 1940, at Perry, employer Georgia Power Co., (brown eyes, black hair, ruddy complexion, 5'9", 170#). Married Ada M. Williams on May 3, 1941, Cordele, GA; parents of a daughter and two sons. Employed by Georgia Power Co. in Zebulon and Milledgeville, GA. Enlisted as a private on April 6, 1942, at Fort McPherson, Atlanta, GA (occupation skilled mechanic and repairman, 5'8", 175#). Joined 3rd Squadron on March 4, 1944, as A/P and engine mechanic. Reclassified to crew chief on March 21. Promoted to sergeant on April 1, 1944, and to staff sergeant on August 1. On detached service to Wenkiang / rest camp on December 12. Promoted to technical sergeant on April 1; appointed squadron A/P inspector. Promoted to master sergeant on June 1, 1945. Sent to rest camp on July 2. Released from 3rd Squadron on September 1; transferred to 51st Fighter Group for transport home. Likely arrived aboard SS *Marine Angel* at Tacoma, WA, on December 12, 1945. Wood's list: "209 13th Ave., Cordele, Georgia." In 1946, owned and operated Barge Air Conditioning Co.; business continued until recently by his son, John Jr. In 1950, with wife, a son, and a daughter, address 811 20th Ave., Cordele, occupation refrigeration, appliance company. Vice president of Cordele Kiwanis Club in 1950s. Died March 31, 1995. Buried at Sunnyside Cemetery, Cordele.

BENEDICT, Lawrence James, SSgt. (serial #17025420)
Born May 27, 1919, in Redwood, MN. Son of John James and Elizabeth Catherine (Rinke) Benedict. In 1930, enumerated with parents and two younger siblings on a farm near Charleston, MN. In 1940, with parents, two brothers, and a hired man, address Route 1, Charleston, MN, completed four years of high school, no occupation. Occupation later mechanic/repairman of motor vehicles. Registered for the draft on October 16, 1940, address RFD#1, Lamberton, MN (marked out), 413 So. 35th St., Omaha, Neb. (written beside), self-employed (blue eyes, brown hair, ruddy complexion, 5'7", 170#). Enlisted in Air Corps on April 1, 1941, at Fort Snelling, MN (occupation semiskilled mechanic and repairman, 5'1", 199#). Stationed at Maxwell Field, AL, as a "grease monkey" in 1942. Married Hester King Stradtner on November 17, 1943, in Indiana; parents of five sons and two daughters. Likely arrived at Calcutta aboard

USS *General Robert E. Callan* on April 27, 1945. Transferred to 1st Bomb Group as A/P mechanic in May 1945 and to 3rd Squadron on June 7. Assigned to 4th Bomb Squadron detachment at Chihkiang in August. Remained with Liaison Detachment to facilitate transfer to the Chinese. Released from 3rd Squadron on September 22; transferred to India-Burma replacement center, Karachi, for transport home. Wood's list: "Route #1, Lamberton, Minnesota." In 1950, with wife and three sons, no address, Osakis, MN, occupation plumber for a plumbing shop. Member of VFW in Osakis in early 1950s. Died December 21, 2006, in Winter Haven, FL; cause, heart disease. Buried at Calvary Cemetery, Osakis.

BOWEN, Francis Harold ("Frank"), 1Lt. (serial #12172730; later #0-711322)

Born June 4, 1917, in Cooperstown, NY. Son of Samuel Adams and Maude Ann (Palmer) Bowen. Lived in Syracuse, NY. In 1930, enumerated with parents and two sisters, 168 Cliford Rd., Menands, NY, attending school. Completed four years of high school; occupation auto mechanic. In 1940 census, listed with parents at Colonie, NY, with notation "Enumerated on boat Socony [Standard Oil Company New York]." Enumerated separately as head of household, occupation "oiler" in oil transportation, address 239 Chico Rd., East Greenbush, NY, residence in 1935 Menands, Albany. Registered for the draft on October 16, 1940, at East Greenbush, address Couse, East Greenbush (marked out), 50 West Elizabeth St., Waterloo, N.Y. (written above), employer Montgomery Ward, North Broadway, Albany, NY (gray eyes, brown hair, ruddy complexion, 6'5½", 194#; "Tattoo Mark on Right Arm"). Married Daisy Jane Crider on March 27, 1942, in Albany; parents of two daughters and two sons. Enlisted in US Army on November 20, 1942, in Albany as a private, occupation skilled mechanic (6'4", 170#); inducted the following day. Initially assigned as diesel mechanic in tank corps but transferred to the USAAF on March 27, 1943. Received commission as 2nd lieutenant in 1944. Attached to 11th Bomb Squadron, 341st Bomb Group, 69th Composite Wing, in October 1944; transported to Asiatic-Pacific theater on December 23. Flew forty-nine aerial missions with 210 combat hours. Shot down twice and spent some time in POW camp according to family stories (unconfirmed). Transferred to 3rd Squadron as navigator-bombardier on June 9, 1945. Assigned to 4th Bomb Squadron detachment at Chihkiang in July/August. Slightly injured by Plexiglas on final mission on August 10, 1945. Awarded Purple Heart with OLC. Released from 3rd Squadron on September 5 and sent to Yangkai; transferred to 22nd Bomb Squadron, 341st Bomb Group, for transport home. Wood's list: "RD #1, Box 647, West Albany, New York." Released from service March 5, 1946. In 1950, with wife, two daughters, and a son, address "9-D," Oswego, occupation fireman, Sheldon Hall. Graduated from Oswego State University in 1951; president of Alpha Phi Omega fraternity, member Kappa Delta Pi international honor society in education, and editor in chief of *Ontarian*. Graduated from Cornell University with a degree in music education and published *A Guide for Making and Using Miniature (2" × 2") Instructional Slides* in 1952. Reenlisted on February 15, 1953; stationed in Japan as navigator of 36th Sqdn. at Johnson Air Base. Returned to US on June 7, 1956; stationed at Harlingen AFB, Harlingen, TX. Divorced ca. 1960. With 5th Tactical Control Group at Clark Air Base, Philippines, voted outstanding Air Force supply officer in March 1963. In San Francisco, CA, in August 1963. Promoted to major and released November 20, 1965. Member of Mt. Vernon Lodge No. 3, Free and Accepted Masons, Albany; San Antonio Consistory Scottish Rite of Texas; and San Benito Commandery No. 62, Knights Templar of Texas and Islam Temple of the Shrine. Died on December 14, 1978, in San Francisco. Buried at Blooming Grove Cemetery, Defreestville, NY; grave marker shared with sister Leah A. (Bowen) Hepinstall.

BURTON, Herman Luther, Sgt. (serial #35133117)

Born July 3, 1905, in Vanceburg, KY. Son of General Jack and Susanna ("Anna") (Hackworth) Burton. Completed one year of high school. Lived in Vanceburg in 1920. In 1930, enumerated with parents and two sisters, 1102 Findlay St., Portsmouth, OH, occupation odd jobs at a shoe factory. In 1940, lived with parents and younger sister, occupation "buttoning" in a shoe factory, address 1108 Gay St., Portsmouth. Registered for the draft October 16, 1940, same address as census, employer Elden Stroud, 1231 Kinney Ln., Portsmouth (brown eyes, brown hair, ruddy complexion, 5'8", 130#, "Scar on right cheek"). Worked as a bartender in 1941. Enlisted on March 2, 1942, at Fort Thomas, Newport, KY, as a private (5'8", 116#). At Duncan Field, TX, for basic training in March 1942. Sent to CBI and attached to 4th Bomb Squadron. Joined 3rd Squadron on March 12, 1944, as A/P and engine mechanic. Promoted to corporal on June 1. Reclassified to crew chief in late July. Assigned to Task Force 34 at Chihkiang in late October. Promoted to sergeant on December 1. Released from 3rd Squadron on July 20, 1945, and attached to Replacement Depot No. 3 at Camp Kanchrapara for transport home. Wood's list: "1102 Findley Street, Portsmouth, Ohio." Released from service on October 12, 1945. In 1950, with father and sister, address 2213 Vinton Ave., Portsmouth, occupation warehouse man, general retail store. Worked as a salesclerk at Sears, Roebuck and Co. about 1950, a janitor at American Legion in 1956, a driver for Yellow Cab from about 1957. Never married. Died May 10, 1979, in Portsmouth. Buried at Woodlawn Cemetery, Vanceburg.

CALLOWAY, Richard (NMI) ("Swimmer"), Pfc. (serial #06925689)

Born February 24, 1916, in Rock View, NC. Son of Fred A. and Mary Christine ("Christie") (Blankenship) Calloway. Name on birth record "Joseph Richard Calloway." In 1930, lived with parents and four siblings on a farm on North Fork Road, Ivy Township, NC, attending school. Completed four years of high school. Departed from Fort Bragg, NC, on September 27, 1937, aboard USS *Chateau Thierry*; arrived in Panama same date, unit Engineers. Enlisted in US Army on October 21, 1939. Enumerated as a soldier with US Army at Maxwell Field, Kendall, AL, in April 1940. With "Dortha" Hensley, issued marriage license in June 1941 at Greenville, SC; both residents of Bernardsville, NC; no marriage date found. Likely arrived at Calcutta aboard USS *General Robert E. Callan* on April 27, 1945. Transferred to 1st Bomb Group as A/P armorer in May and to 3rd Squadron June 7. Promoted to private first class on August 1. Released from 3rd Squadron on September 1; transferred to 23rd Fighter Group, 68th Composite Wing, for transport home. Wood's list: "Barnardsville, North Carolina." Released from service on December 15, 1945; in foreign service nine months and four days. Registered with Buncombe County, NC, Local Board Group H, on December 26, 1945 (blue eyes, brown hair, ruddy complexion, 5'7", 150#), "Just Honorably Discharged from Army." Entitled to wear American Defense Service Medal, American Theater Campaign Medal, Asiatic-Pacific Theater Campaign Medal with one Bronze Service Star, and WWII Victory Medal. Reenlisted in Air Force on February 9, 1946, at Ft. Bragg, NC (civilian occupation lab technician/assistant); released from service March 30, 1947. Served in 11th Engineers of US Army, according to obituary. Highest grade or rating held noted as sergeant, according to discharge documents. Divorced in April 1949 after two years of separation. Married Margaret __. In 1950, with wife, address 26 Jefferson Dr., Asheville, NC, no occupation. Married Bertha Lorraine Hensley on April 28, 1959, at Burnsville, NC; parents of a son; divorced August 13, 1963. In November 1962, shot a man in the thigh with a 12-gauge shotgun; indicted for assault with a deadly weapon with intent to kill. In June 1970, hospitalized for a gunshot wound in the back; treated and released. Employed as a rock mason. Died December 24, 1982, in Buncombe County, NC. Buried at Calloway Cemetery behind parents' former home on North Fork Road, Barnardsville. (Listed in civil sources as Joseph Calloway, Richard Joseph Calloway, or Joseph Richard Calloway.)

CANTOR, Jerome Gerald ("Jerry"), 1Lt. (serial #32237636; later #0-1321609)

Born August 17, 1914, in Clifton, NJ. Son of Morris and Rebecca ("Ray") (Horowitz) Cantor; father Polish and mother Russian immigrant. In 1930, enumerated with parents and two younger brothers, address 318 Lexington Ave., Clifton, NJ, attending school; parents spoke Yiddish. Graduated from Clifton High School. Completed one year of college. Occupation salesman at Sears Roebuck & Co. in 1937. Not found in 1940 census. Registered for the draft on October 16, 1940, at Passaic, NJ, same address as census, employer Jewel Products, NY, NY (brown eyes, brown hair, ruddy complexion, 5'8½", 162#). Employed by Arrow Electrical Corporation. Enlisted on February 16, 1942, at Fort Dix, NJ, as a private (5'5", 158#). Originally assigned to an infantry unit. Transferred to USAAF. Graduated from aerial gunner school at Harlingen, TX, in September 1942 and received gunner's wings. Commissioned 2nd lieutenant on June 28, 1943. Gunnery instructor at Yuma Army Air Field, Yuma, AZ, in 1944. Married Lillian Prail, WAVES yeoman 2nd class, in March 1944, in Irvington, NJ; parents of a son and a daughter. Joined 3rd Squadron on November 13, 1944, classified as aerial gunnery instructor, appointed assistant gunnery officer. On detached service to Task Force 34 at Chihkiang from December 4, 1944, to January 14, 1945. Promoted to 1st lieutenant on April 1, 1945. On special duty at 1st Bomb Group HQ as group aerial gunnery instructor from June 11, 1945; returned to 3rd Squadron at Liangshan in July. Assigned to 4th Bomb Squadron detachment at Chihkiang in August; sometimes listed on aircrews as aerial observer. Flew forty-two combat missions. Released from 3rd Squadron on September 5 and sent to Yangkai; transferred to 341st Bomb Group for transport home. Arrived in New York aboard USS *General Charles H. Muir* on November 1, 1945. Wood's list: "13 Wheeler Street, West Orange, New Jersey." Released from service December 16, 1945. In 1950, with wife, a daughter, and a son, address 22 Martha Ave., Clifton, occupation salesman, wholesale television distributor. Later lived at 5 Grant Ave., Clifton. Active in United Jewish Appeal. Employed as sales manager for Ral Plumbing Supply in Fairfield, NJ. Died May 25, 1986.

CHASSE, Homer Leo ("Pete"), TSgt. (serial #11015482)

Born August 6, 1919, at Fall River, MA. Son of Louis Honore and Anna Elizabeth (Deschenes) Chasse, both French Canadian. In 1930, enumerated with parents, three sisters, and five brothers, 172 Earle St., Fall River, attending school. Moved to Somersworth, NH. Member of 1101st Co., Civilian Conservation Corps (CCC), at White Mountain National Forest, Compton, NH, in 1939. Entered Catholic seminary but then "discovered women." In 1940, with parents, two sisters, and two brothers, 1426 Pleasant Street, Fall River, completed two years of high school, occupation mechanic's helper at a garage. Registered for the draft on October 16, 1940, Fall River, same address as census, employer C.C.C., War Department, 1101 Co., West Compton, NH (brown eyes, brown hair, ruddy complexion, 5'4", 122#); notation "Ret Det Macon Ga. 1st Inf R-O Recruiting Officer." Enlisted on February 27, 1941, as a private. At Air Corps Basic Flying School, Shaw Field, SC; promoted to corporal in January 1942. Arrived at Karachi on July 29, 1943. Attached to USAAF OTU at Malir on August 1. Attached to 2nd Bomb Squadron on October 9. Joined 3rd Squadron on March

3, 1944, as AAF supply technician. Promoted to technical sergeant on December 1. Sent to rest camp at Chengtu on July 1, 1945. Assigned to 4th Bomb Squadron detachment at Chihkiang in August. Released from 3rd Squadron on September 22 and transferred to India-Burma Replacement Center, Karachi, for transport home. Wood's list: "1426 Pleasant Street, Fall River, Mass." Released from service on December 1, 1945. Reenlisted on December 18, 1945, at Fort Devens, MA, as technical sergeant for the Hawaiian Department; residence Bristol, MA (four years high school, single, with dependents; height and weight "08', 260#"). Married Louise Ferraro on August 30, 1947, in Bristol, MA; parents of two sons. Released from service December 17, 1948. In 1950, with wife and two sons, 107 Cliff Ave., Sayville, MA, occupation Armed Forces. Reenlisted June 30, 1954. Divorced May 3, 1959, Chaves County, NM; sent to Keflavik, Iceland. Married Virginia Dare (Rogers) Tutt Bullock about 1959 in Roswell, NM; parents of three daughters. Released from service June 29, 1962. Moved to Greenville, SC, and worked for Lockheed Martin out of Donaldson AFB. Divorced on August 25, 1969, in Wayne County, NC. Spent twenty-four years in the Air Force and seven years with US State Department before retiring as a master sergeant. In Vietnam in early 1970s. Married Khiem M. Nguyen in 1972; divorced in November 1975 in Los Angeles, CA. In Honolulu, HI, in mid- to late 1970s. Lived in Fall River and Holyoke, MA; Greenville, SC; Richmond, VA; and Miami, FL. Lifetime member of VFW and DAV. Died on September 7, 1995, in Austin, TX; cause, lung, heart, and kidney disease. Buried at Ft. Sam Houston National Cemetery, San Antonio, TX. (First name sometimes "Omer" in civil records.)

COLLINS, Parker Pratt, Cpl. (serial #39183547)

Born October 8, 1902, in Kansas City, MO. Son of John Davison and Catherine Helen (Pratt) Collins. Attended New Mexico Military Institute, Roswell, NM, from September 1918. Transferred to Queen Anne High School, Seattle, WA, in September 1920; graduated in 1922. Graduated from University of Washington; served as assistant to the dean of men in 1928. Resigned and went to New York and then to Europe to study and write. Returned through the Port of New York aboard *Samaria* on August 10, 1930, from Belfast, Northern Ireland. In 1930, enumerated with parents and younger brother, address Perkins Rd. (no house number), Richmond, WA, no occupation. Wrote a series of newspaper articles about the Seattle Symphony Orchestra in 1933. In 1940, with parents at 19316 8th Ave. NW, in Richmond; completed five years of college; employed as a social worker, "welfare service." Registered for the draft on February 15, 1942, in Seattle, same address as census, employer King County Welfare Dept., Seattle (brown eyes, brown hair, ruddy complexion, 5'10", 155#, "Z— Fraternity brand on left ear"). Enlisted on July 19, 1942, as a private at Tacoma, WA; employed as a social worker on the staff of the King County Welfare Department (5'9", 155#). Arrived in CBI about February 1943. Joined the 3rd Squadron on detached service from 10th Air Force headquarters on August 12, 1944. Not included in orders for move to Kweilin. Returned to Seattle on February 17, 1945, after twenty-four months in Burma and India. Sent to California for reassignment. Awarded Bronze Star. In 1950, with parents, address 845 E. 88th, Seattle, occupation interviewer for the Red Cross. Made repeated voyages to Japan and Korea and returning to Seattle and San Francisco as an employee aboard US Navy ships between 1947 and about 1956. Position specified as "Jr. S/T/clerk," junior administrative clerk, and "Yeoman Engine," Engine Department, on various trips. Joined Washington State Dhobi Wallah Basha, China-Burma-India Veterans Association; installed as commander in September 1962. Presented slide show of "recent visit to Asia" in March 1971. Seems to have never married. Died August 22, 1983, in Seattle. Buried at Evergreen Washelli Memorial Park, Seattle.

CONRAD, Chester Melvin ("Chet," "Coondog"), Maj. (serial #0-45623; later #7888A)

Born July 3, 1917, at Cape Girardeau, MO. Son of Oscar Clarence and Cora Elizabeth (Ervin) Conrad. In 1930, enumerated with mother and sister on Kathleen Ave., Sikestown, MO, attending school. Enlisted in the Missouri National Guard on February 6, 1933; gave his date of birth as July 3, 1914. On football team as left tackle at Sikeston High School and graduated ca. 1935. Served in Missouri National Guard from July 3, 1935, to May 10, 1938. Not found in 1940 census. Graduated in May 1940 from Southeast Missouri State Teachers College, Cape Girardeau, MO; All-Star lineman on football team; later assistant athletic coach. Registered for the draft on October 16, 1940, address 336 N. Park, Cape Girardeau; employer Southeast Missouri Telephone Co. (hazel eyes, brown hair, light-brown complexion, 6', 200#). Enlisted in Air Corps as an aviation cadet on March 15, 1941, at Jefferson Barracks, MO (5'11", 181#). Primary flight training at the Missouri Institute of Aeronautics in Sikeston. Assigned to Goodfellow Field, San Angelo, TX, on Memorial Day 1941. Completed advanced flight training and commissioned 2nd lieutenant, Air Reserve, October 31 at Turner Field, Albany, GA. Became an instructor in aerial combat tactics at Gunter Field at Greenville, SC, in December. Transferred as instructor to base at AAF Advanced Twin Engine Flying School, Blytheville, AR. Promoted to 1st lieutenant June 1, 1942, and assigned as instructor to Columbia Army Air Base, Columbia, SC, in December. Promoted to captain on July 20, 1943. Reported for duty at HQ 2nd Staging Squadron, Floridian Hotel, Miami Beach, FL, on July 21 and attached to 1st Bomb Group. Attached to USAAF OTU at Malir on August 3. Attached to 2nd Bomb Squadron; moved to China in October. Served as 1st Bomb Group assistant operations and training officer. Transferred to 3rd Squadron, promoted to major, and appointed commanding officer on March 1, 1944. Ordered back to US in early February 1945. Wood's list: "336 North Park, Cape Girardeau, Missouri." Visited family in San Antonio, TX, in March 1945. Married Barbara ("Bobby") Ann McConnell on May 1, 1945, in Los Angeles, CA; parents of a daughter and two sons. Reported for duty at Santa Ana, CA, after a brief honeymoon. Assigned to Army Air Base in Greenville, SC, in May. Moved to Columbia, SC, and continued training Chinese airmen. Trained CAF pilots and other trainees at Bergstrom Field, Austin, TX, in mid-1946. Became professor of military science and air tactics at Kansas State College in Manhattan, KS, in 1946, and later had command of the Reserve Officers Training Corps (ROTC) of St. Louis University. Stationed at Karachi in late '40s and early '50s. Not found in 1950 census. Served in Korean War from December 14, 1950, assigned to 5th Air Force HQ. Promoted to lieutenant colonel on February 20, 1951. Died October 29, 1955, due to heart attack at age 38 while stationed at Tokyo, Japan. Buried at San Francisco National Cemetery, San Francisco, CA.

COURY, Thomas Vincent, Sgt. (serial #32338103)

Born January 8, 1918, in Cranford, NJ. Son of Abdoo (or Abdul) and Sadda ("Sadie") Coury, Syrian immigrants; father died in 1928. In 1930, enumerated with widowed mother, two sisters, and three brothers, address 313 Hicks St., 1st Assembly Dist., Tract 7, Brooklyn, NY, attending school; parents spoke Arabic. Graduated from Brooklyn Technical High School. Lived with cousin Edward Coury, mother, and siblings in 1940, address 772 46th St., New York, NY, no occupation but seeking work. Registered for the draft on October 16, 1940, residence 99 State St., Brooklyn, unemployed (brown eyes, brown hair, dark complexion, 5'8", 155#). Enlisted as a private on May 15, 1942, at Fort Jay, Governor's Island, NY, occupation shipping and receiving clerk, single, no dependents (5'7", 148#). Promoted to private first class at AAF Basic Flying School, Bainbridge, GA, in October 1942. Promoted to corporal in October 1942 and to sergeant in February 1943, still at Bainbridge. Departed US for China November 1, 1944. Attached and joined 3rd Squadron from 1st Bomb Group as clerk non-typist on April 6, 1945; released and transferred to 1st Bomb Group HQ on April 18. Treated at dispensary with penicillin for chronic frontal sinusitis. Not included in Wood's list. Reenlisted July 2, 1945; released October 16, 1945, as staff sergeant. Married Frances De Domenico, an Italian immigrant, on October 20, 1946, in Brooklyn; parents of two sons. In 1950, with wife and infant son, address 172 Dean St., Brooklyn, no occupation. Died February 25, 1967. Buried at Long Island National Cemetery, East Farmington, NY.

CUNNINGHAM, George Chancellor, Capt. (serial #13042404; later #0-731033; later #12135A; later #O40947)

Born March 13, 1920, in Shelbyville, KY. Son of Elijah Washington (III) and Mary Lucinda (Yager) Cunningham. In 1930, enumerated with parents and older brother on a farm on Ward Avenue (no house number) in rural Jefferson County, KY, attending school. In 1940, with parents and brother, 298 Ward Ave., Magisterial District #1 Rural, Jefferson County, no occupation. Also enumerated with cousin, Lady C. (Cunningham) Steele, and her daughter, Sally, address 138 Euclid Street NW, Washington, DC, one year of college, no occupation. Prelaw student at George Washington University, Washington, DC. Registered for the draft on July 1, 1941, residence Ward Ave, Anchorage, KY; mailing address 1460 Euclid St. NW, Apt. #7, occupation "Bookkeeping operator," Dept. of Agriculture, Washington, DC (brown eyes, brown hair, light complexion, 5'9½", 150#). Enlisted in Air Corps as a private on September 9, 1941, at Washington, DC, one year of college, occupation bookkeeper/cashier (5'9", 146#). Following primary flight training as aviation cadet, transferred to bombardier training; graduated from Advanced Bombardier School and commissioned 2nd lieutenant at Kirtland Field, Albuquerque, NM, on September 26, 1942. Transferred to Columbia, SC. Married Laura Marie Gilley on November 14, 1942, at her home in Southland; parents of a son and two daughters (the first born while he was overseas). Promoted to 1st lieutenant January 29, 1943. Reported for duty at HQ 2nd Staging Squadron, Floridian Hotel, Miami Beach, FL, on July 21, 1943, and attached to 1st Bomb Group. Attached to USAAF OTU at Malir on August 3, 1943. Served in 1st Bomb Group as assistant operations and training officer and as PX officer. Attached to 2nd Bomb Squadron; arrived at Kunming on October 19, 1943. Joined 3rd Squadron as bombardier and promoted to captain on March 1, 1944. Reported as MIA on July 4; returned to duty. On detached duty to Task Force 34. Completed forty-seven missions; awarded the Air Medal. Returned to US in late January 1945 by ATC after serving thirteen months as bombardier. Wood's list: "Anchorage, KY." Remained in military service. In Big Spring, TX, in April 1945. Promoted to 1st lieutenant, Air Reserve, on September 26, 1945. Took a regular commission on January 27, 1947. Stationed at San Angelo, TX, in 1948. In 1950, with wife, two daughters, and a son, address 206 LaSalle, San Angelo, TX, occupation Armed Forces. Promoted to major on February 15, 1951. In London, England, 1950 to 1953; in Amarillo, TX, in 1956. Promoted to lieutenant colonel on September 26, 1956. Transitioned from bombers to fighters. Trained as squadron commander flying F-100s, said to be one of the fastest and most dangerous planes ever made, but he thought more about wife and children than about the plane's capabilities. Retired on December 31, 1961, as a colonel. Employed by Pan Am as an engineer for about seven years, then at a bank as vice president of operations, and with the State Department, Library and Archives. In Las

Vegas, NV, in 1968, and Phoenix, AZ, in 1974. Moved to Sun City, AZ, in 1979. Retired in the early 1980s. Address at that time 9520 Brokenstone Drive, Sun City, AZ 85351, according to letter written by Gene Dorr. Elected vice commander of Valley of the Sun China-Burma-India (CBI) Veterans Association in November 1985. Died May 1, 1986, in Sun City; cause, cancer. Described in obituary as a "planning analyst" and "civic activist" who served on numerous planning and zoning councils in Phoenix; recently honored by the People's Republic of China. Buried with full military honors at Grove Hill Cemetery, Shelbyville, KY. (Obituary gives his name as Lt. Col. George Chancellor Yager Cunningham.)

CURIK, William Louis ("Willie"), Maj. (serial #38039260; later #0-432605)
Born July 19, 1914, in Corsicana, TX. Son of Louis J. and Bettie (Schlovacek) Curik. In 1930, enumerated with parents and younger brother on a farm on "Taylor to Coupland Road," attending school. Graduated from Taylor High School in May 1933. Attended North Texas Agricultural College, Arlington, TX. Played varsity football, right tackle, for Southern Methodist University, Dallas, in 1938 and 1939 (praised as a "One-Man Gang" by sports writers); member of Alpha Tau Omega fraternity; graduated in February 1940. In 1940, lived with parents and younger brother on a farm, address RFD #1, Williamson County, occupation unpaid farm laborer. Registered for the draft on October 16, 1940, address 530 W. Chestnut, Denison, TX; self-employed, Denison Frozen foods (brown eyes, black hair, dark complexion, 6', 175#). Family story says he was drafted by the New York Giants but entered military service instead. Inducted into US Army on February 26, 1941, in Dallas (6', 169#); transferred to Air Corps as aviation cadet at Camp Hulen, TX, on April 24, 1941. Attended armament school at Lowry Field, Denver, CO; graduated and commissioned 2nd lieutenant in December 1941. Later stationed at Buckley Field, Denver. Married Angie Lou Waters on July 3, 1942, in Denison; parents of a son and a daughter (both adopted). Sent to CBI in July 1943 and assigned to CACW. Transferred from 3rd Fighter Group to 1st Bomb Group on August 9. Attached to 2nd Bomb Squadron on October 9; arrived at Kunming on October 16. Promoted to major about December 1944. Served as 1st Bomb Group armament officer in early 1945. On temporary duty to 3rd Squadron from April 29, 1945. Returned to US aboard USS *General J. H. McRae*; arrived in New York on October 15, 1945. Sent to processing center at Ft. Sam Houston, San Antonio, TX. Wood's list: "904 West Sears Street, Denison, Texas." Stationed at Reese AFB, Lubbock, TX, in 1949. In 1950, with wife, address 2012 Ave. L, Lubbock, teaching armament at ROTC, US Air Forces. At Wright-Patterson AFB, Dayton, OH, in 1957, and in Baltimore, MD, as executive officer of Air Research and Development Commission, same year. Retired as lieutenant colonel on August 31, 1961. Manager and president of Denison Frozen Food Lockers, Inc. Later lived in Taylor, TX. Died February 14, 1997. Buried at Taylor City Cemetery, Taylor, TX.

CZERNIAK, Bernard Joseph ("Ben"), SSgt. (serial #16001031)
Born February 25, 1918, in Rhinelander, WI. Son of Frank and Agnieszka (Agnes) (Dwornik) Czerniak, naturalized Polish immigrants. Moved to Chicago, IL, before 1920. In 1930, enumerated with parents, four brothers, and a sister, 2915 Spaulding Ave., Chicago, attending school. Studied to be a machinist and graduated from Lane Technical High School in 1937. In 1940, with widowed mother and siblings, same address, occupation "assembler" in lamp manufacturing. Enlisted in the Air Corps on August 19, 1940, in Chicago, as a private (occupation semiskilled mechanic/repairman of motor vehicles, 5'9", 148#). Graduated from Air Corps technical schools as airplane mechanic at Chanute Field in early December 1941;

transferred to 424th School Squadron, Barksdale Field. In July and again in August 1942, admitted to 5th General Hospital for strain of sacroiliac caused by lifting and twisting. Promoted to staff sergeant at Blytheville (AR) Army Air Base in February 1943. Likely arrived at Calcutta aboard USS *General Robert E. Callan* on April 27, 1945. Attached to 1st Bomb Group as airplane mechanic in May and to 3rd Squadron on June 7, 1945. Released from 3rd Squadron; transferred to Detachment HQ and HQ Squadron, 14th Air Force, on September 5. Wood's list: "2919 North Spaulding Ave., Chicago, Ill." Released from service December 23, 1945. Joined the 66th Fighter Wing of the National Guard at Douglas Airport in preparation for "M-day" (mobilization day). Married Eleonore Bernadette Bartoszek; parents of two daughters and three sons. In 1950, with wife and a daughter, address same as Wood's list, occupation airplane mechanic, US National Guard. Lived in Round Lake, Palatine, and Chicago, IL, and El Cajon, CA. Died November 27, 2000.

DANIELS, William ("Bill") Lee, 1Lt. (serial #0-351056)

Born January 31, 1916, in Saint Paul, MN. Son of Henry Carl and Gladys Mildred (Heimbach) Daniels. Lived in Duluth, MN, and Edmonton, Alberta, Canada. His father, a German immigrant and building contractor, changed surname from Damkroeger in 1920, when they moved to West Palm Beach, FL. In 1930, enumerated with parents, a sister, and three servants, 635 Palmetto, West Palm Beach, attending school. Graduated from Riverside Military Academy, Gainesville, GA, in 1934. Worked as helper in a bakery in 1935. Attended University of Alabama and studied aeronautical engineering; member of Delta Sigma Phi Fraternity, and 2nd lieutenant in ROTC. Lived with his mother in 1940; address 5801 Parker St., West Palm Beach, completed first year of college. Employed by Eastern Air Lines as a pilot. Married Elise Phalen on May 17, 1940, at Stuart, FL. Enlisted in US Army on August 12, 1940. At Ft. Benning, GA, attached to the 2nd Armored Division, rank 2nd lieutenant. Transferred to Air Corps in late 1941. Completed primary training at Pine Bluff, AR, and basic at Randolph Field, TX. Graduated with Class 42G from Advanced Flight Training and commissioned 2nd lieutenant at Kelly Field, TX, in August 1942. Completed postgraduate training at Ellington Field, south of Houston, TX. Had B-25 OTU at Greenville, SC, from September 1942 to July 1943. Reported for duty at HQ 2nd Staging Squadron, Floridian Hotel, Miami Beach, FL, on July 21, 1943, and attached to 1st Bomb Group. Attached to 2nd Bomb Squadron on October 9. Joined 3rd Squadron as B-25 pilot and promoted to 1st lieutenant on March 4, 1944. Transferred to 5390th Gunnery School on April 5. Promoted to captain in late April. Awarded Air Medal by Gen. Chennault for missions in China. Returned to US on November 2, 1944, after seventeen months in CBI. Wood's list: "25 East 73rd Street, New York City, N.Y." Address given in citation for Air Medal: 215 South County Road, Palm Beach, Florida. Made a "brief stop" at Miami before joining his wife in New York, where she resided. Stationed at Long Beach, CA, assigned to air traffic control. Transferred to Homestead, FL, in mid-April 1945 for special duty and then to Charleston, SC. Divorced in June 1945 in Palm Beach. Stationed at Hamilton Field, San Francisco, CA. Stationed in Shanghai from about April 1946. Went to Philippine Airlines in Manila in October 1946. Discharged November 20, 1946, as a major. Married Gladys Mary ("Hap" or "Happy") Eustis on January 31, 1948, in San Francisco; parents of five daughters and two sons. In 1950, with wife, a daughter, and a son, address 603 Capistrano, San Mateo, CA, occupation salesman, contracting company. In 1973, established Aircraft Technical Publishers, providing maintenance technical library services to the aviation industry; still operated by his daughter. Divorced April 6, 1981. Died February 20, 1986, in San Mateo.

DAVIS, Donald John ("Don"), 1Lt. (serial #19081971; later #0-739740)
Born March 4, 1916, in Red Oak, Lincoln Township, IA. Son of John William and Frances Luella (Conger) Davis. In January 1920, family enumerated in Eagle Precinct, Cheyenne County, NE, where his father owned a farm. Moved later that year to Long Beach, CA. In 1930, enumerated with parents, three sisters, and six brothers, no address but not a farm in Gurley Village, NE, attending school; father did odd jobs. Moved to rural Noble County, OK, before 1935. Completed four years of high school. In 1940, lived on a farm with parents and five younger siblings, address West 8th St., West Palisade, CO; occupation day laborer. Registered for the draft on October 16, 1940; residence Enid, Oklahoma (light complexion, blue eyes, blonde hair, 6', 192#); specified his mother as contact person, her residence Palisade, CO. Married Anna Jeanette Hastings on March 21, 1942, in Las Vegas, NV; parents of a son born in 1943. Lived in Anaheim, CA. Enlisted in Air Corps in Los Angeles, CA, on March 30, 1942, as a private, occupation store clerk (6'4", 185#). Stationed at Minter Field, Shafter, CA, assigned to headquarters squadron in early 1942. Graduated with Class WC 43-C from AAF West Coast Training Center, Santa Ana, CA, on March 10, 1943; commissioned 2nd lieutenant. Served a tour of duty in New Guinea; completed forty-four missions. Requested service in China and transferred to 3rd Squadron in about mid-March 1945 as a B-25 pilot. Killed in action on May 16, 1945. Awarded Chinese Air Force Wings; date uncertain but early June 1945 according to squadron history. Not included in Wood's list; address for next of kin (wife) Route Four, Box 354, Humboldt, California. Posthumously awarded Purple Heart. Remains returned to US in June 1949; buried at Sunnyside Memorial Park, Long Beach, CA, on July 13, 1949.

DEFABRITIS, John Julius, Cpl. (serial #32984256)
Born April 11, 1925, in Mt. Vernon, NY. Son of Pasquale ("Patsy") and Mary (Chianise) DeFabritis, Italian immigrants. In 1930, lived with parents and five older siblings, address 4531 Mundy Lane, Bronx, NY, not in school. In 1940, lived with parents and a sister, address 158 South Second Ave., Mount Vernon, completed one year of high school, no occupation noted for any family member. Registered for the draft on April 12, 1943, at Mt. Vernon, address 12 Beekman Ave., listed as "Employer" (1) Student Edison H.S., (2) Bon Ton Dairy, Mt. Vernon (brown eyes, black hair, dark complexion, 5'6", 130#, "birthmark on nose"). Graduated from Edison High School, Mount Vernon, in 1943. Later worked at a laundry. Enlisted August 4, 1943, in New York, NY, as a private; inducted into service same date. Joined 3rd Squadron as radio operator–mechanic–gunner on December 28, 1944. Assigned to Nimrod Detachment at Laohokow in March 1945. Assigned to 4th Bomb Squadron Detachment at Chihkiang in August. Transferred to 10th Air Force on August 30. Wood's list: "111 Crary Ave., Mt. Vernon, N.Y." Released from service January 3, 1946. Awarded Purple Heart and Flying Cross, according to obituary. In 1950, with brother-in-law, sister, niece, and parents, address same as Wood's list, occupation fur dresser, fur business. Married Anne Theresa Andrea on July 27, 1955, in Alexandria, VA; his occupation fur shearer, residence 39 Glen Ave., Mt. Vernon. Had no children. Employed as a furrier, preparing skins to be made into coats, for 32 years. Moved to Hartsdale, NY, in about 1965. Lived at 33 Fieldstone Drive, Apt. C2, Hartsdale, in 1980s. Director of shipping department, R. L. Albert & Son, a candy company in Greenwich, CT; retired in early 1988. Died September 27, 1988, at home in Hartsdale; cause, cancer. ("John DeFabritis," with no middle name, on "New York State Birth Index, 1880–1942.")

DELAHOYDE, Rae Marvin, Cpl. (serial #36569405)

Born December 5, 1922, in Hills City, SD. Son of Rae Orville and Vera Mae (Burleson) Delahoyde. In 1930, enumerated with parents, address 10156 Nottingham Rd., Detroit, MI, attending school. In 1940, enumerated in household of William Liebelt as a lodger, address 1173 Longview Ave., Detroit, completed three years of high school, attending school, worked forty-six hours/week in 1939, income $200; parents divorced in June of that year. Attended Edwin Denby Technical and Preparatory High School, Detroit, in 1940; graduated from Cannon High School, Kannapolis, NC, in 1941. Married Marjorie Evelyn Fuller on April 6, 1942, in Detroit; later divorced. Registered for the draft on June 30, 1942, at Creston, IA, residence 17111 Second St., unemployed (brown eyes, brown hair, dark complexion, 6', 165#). Enlistment not found. Inducted at Jefferson Ave., Center, Detroit, in February 1943, residence 17111 2nd Blvd., Detroit. Departed US on September 24, 1943. Attached to 1st Bomb Group HQ on January 3, 1944. Hospitalized for malaria in August and October to November for "disease of teeth." Joined 3rd Squadron from 4th Bomb Squadron as clerk nontypist on April 18, 1945. Released from 3rd Squadron on August 27 and sent to Yangkai; transferred as intelligence NCO to 22nd Bomb Squadron, 341st Bomb Group, for transport home. Arrived in New York aboard USS *Charles H. Muir* on November 1, 1945. Wood's list: "17111 Second Blvd., Apt. 305, Detroit, Michigan." In 1950, with mother (both lodgers in household of Elsie Hutchinson), 620 Joseph, Ukiah, CA, occupation garage attendant. Married June Elluese Zimmerman on February 23, 1951, in Santa Rosa, CA; parents of a son. Lived at Ukiah, CA, and Yuma, AZ. Owned and operated several businesses, including a service station, drive-in theater, delicatessen, pizzeria, and wholesale auto sales; also sold fire equipment and paint and art supplies. Active in Junior Achievement and served as executive director, 1964–69. Died May 22, 1990, in Yuma. Buried at Ukiah Cemetery, Ukiah, CA.

DORR, Eugene Henry ("Gene"), Jr., 1Lt. (serial #11024666; later #0-430700)

Born November 5, 1916, in Boston, MA. Son of Eugene H. and Flora E. (Cameron) Dorr; mother died in 1919. Graduated from St. Michael's College, Boston Latin School, in 1934. Graduated with master of education from Boston State College in 1939. Captain of the Rifle Team, official of the Military Club, and trooper in the National Guard. In 1940, enumerated with father, stepmother, and younger brother, address 151 Newbury St., Boston, completed five years of college, "new worker." Registered for the draft on December 19, 1940, at West Roxbury, MA, address same as census, unemployed (brown eyes, brown hair, dark complexion, 6'0", 170#); notation "Discharged from Bat E 180 Field Artillery 12/12/40." Enlisted in Air Corps on February 11, 1941, in Boston as an aviation cadet (6'1", 173#) but "washed out" and trained in armaments and bombsight maintenance in Midland, TX, and then at Lowry Field, Denver, CO; graduated on December 5, 1941 (two days before Pearl Harbor attack). Entered active duty from the Air Reserve on December 8 and commissioned 2nd lieutenant on December 15, 1941. Moved to Kelly Field, TX, in January 1942. Married Opal Elizabeth ("Sonny") Sontag, a 2nd lieutenant and Army nurse, in 1942; parents of two sons (the first born while he was overseas) and three daughters. Spent "a long stretch" in the training command at West Texas bombardier training schools; at bombardier school at Big Spring, TX, in spring 1943. Reported for duty at HQ 2nd Staging Squadron, Floridian Hotel, Miami Beach, FL, and attached to 1st Bomb Group on August 26, 1943. Attached to 2nd Bomb Squadron; arrived at Kunming on October 18, 1943. Served in 1st Bomb Group as armament and materiel officer and fire marshal. Suffered from asthma throughout service. Joined 3rd

Squadron as armament officer on March 2, 1944, at about the time first son was born. Reported as MIA on July 4; returned to duty. Sent to 111th Hospital for malaria on July 21. Remained behind at hospital at Chabua when squadron moved to China. Released from 3rd Squadron and transferred in grade to Detachment of Patients, 95th Station Hospital, Kunming, for malaria relapse on October 21 and received orders for return to US. Wood's list: "Stroud, Oklahoma." Awarded Purple Heart for gash in groin during bailout. Processed through Atlantic City to 3rd Air Force; reported at MacDill and assigned as armament officer at Morse Field in Charlotte, NC. Reassigned as assistant ground safety officer under post engineer. Later sent for training at Chanute Field and came down again with malaria, so again in hospital (hospitalized eleven times before he finally recovered). After return, appointed base ground safety officer. Took a physical when base was transferred to the 1st Air Force and was permanently grounded because of hearing loss. Transferred to Mitchell Field to be assistant ground safety officer for HQ 1st Air Force. Another physical revealed damage to spleen because of repeated bouts of malaria. Retired with disability as 1st lieutenant, September 19, 1945. Released from service December 18, 1945. Returned to Boston but moved to Lakewood, CO, for its dry climate, thought to be beneficial to his asthma. In 1950s, with wife, a son, and two daughters, address 2170 Cody, North Lakewood, CO, occupation science teacher. At same address in early 1980s, according to letter written by John Hinrichs. Employed as a teacher and then in reservations for Western Airlines. Went back to teaching; became a principal at an elementary school, then at a junior high school, and finally at a high school. Active in 14th Air Force Association. Contributed to Carl Molesworth's *Wing to Wing: Air Combat in China, 1943–45* (history of the CACW). Died May 4, 1994, in Wheat Ridge, CO; buried at Ft. Logan National Cemetery, Denver, CO.

DRAKE, Clarence Henry ("Hank"), Maj. (serial #15018290; later #0-429622)
Born on June 21, 1920, in Zanesville, OH. Son of John Frederick and Lena A. (Devore) Drake; father died in 1924. In 1930, enumerated with widowed mother, a brother, and a sister, 671 Convers, Zanesville, attending school; mother worked at a laundry. Graduated from Lash High School, Zanesville, in 1938. Employed by T. D. Bridges Novelty Company. Studied journalism at Ohio State University, Columbus, OH, for two years. Occupation general office clerk. In 1940, lived with mother and sister, 1129 Convers, Zanesville; employed by the National Youth Administration (NYA). Enlisted as an aviation cadet in Air Corps on March 15, 1941, at Fort Hayes, Columbus, OH, residence Muskingum County, OH (5'9", 147#); assigned to Spartan School of Aeronautics, Muskogee Field, OK, for primary training. Completed basic training at Brady Field, TX; graduated from advanced flying school at Brooks Field, TX (class 41-H) and commissioned 2nd lieutenant on October 31, 1941. Married Theresa Adel ("Terri") Kilbourne at Randolph AFB Chapel on December 11, 1941 (four days after Pearl Harbor attack); parents of two sons. From June 1942 to October 1943, flew observation planes to patrol for submarines in the Atlantic. Supervised flying training of the only then-activated Negro medium bomb group in the US at Godman Field, Ft. Knox, KY. Promoted to 1st lieutenant in April 1942 and to captain in October 1942. Awarded Air Medal in May 1943 and OLC in December 1943, stationed in Miami, FL. In foreign service from March 1944. In North Africa in early 1945. Logged almost 2,000 flying hours. Promoted to major on March 24, 1945. Departed US for China on March 26. Attached to 3rd Squadron on April 27. Transferred to 4th Squadron on May 31 and appointed CO on June 5. Not included in Wood's list. Served as director of instrument flying training at Enid, OK. Released from service December 24, 1946. Became a building contractor in San Antonio, TX. In 1950, with wife and three sons in

household of brother-in-law, sister, and her mother-in-law, 215 Carnahan, occupation contracting, home office. Lieutenant colonel in XXI Air Force Service Command, Air Force Reserve, at Kelly Field. Recalled to active duty April 5, 1951, in the Office of Readiness Inspection, Deputy Inspector General, USAF, at Kelly AFB; later moved to Norton AFB, CA. Attended Command and Staff College in 1954. Served in South Korea as detachment commander and advisor to the Republic of Korea pilot-training base, where Korean cadets completed primary, basic, and advanced training in L-19, T-6, and F-51 aircraft. In 1955, stationed at Lackland AFB as assistant director of operations (wing) and as deputy commander of the Basic Training Group. In 1958 at Vandenberg AFB, assigned as deputy commander of the first operational Atlas ICBM Squadron in SAC and USAF history. Selected to attend War College, Class of 1961. At Randolph AFB as head of Ballistic Missiles Training Div., Air Training Command. In August 1964, assigned to 38th Tactical Missile Wing in Germany. Retired as lieutenant colonel; released from service December 31, 1967. Lived in San Antonio, TX. Died April 27, 2001. Buried at Ft. Sam Houston National Cemetery, San Antonio.

DUFFIN, William George ("Bill"), SSgt. (serial #35313732)
Born February 20, 1921, in Cleveland, OH. Son of Leo Charles and Elizabeth M. (Ott) Duffin. In 1930, enumerated with parents and two sisters, 18706 Cherokee Ave., Cleveland, attending school. Pitcher for high school baseball team, which won the Ohio State Championship. Graduated from Collingswood High School, Cleveland, in 1939. In 1940, lived with parents and two sisters (one of them his twin), same address; occupation "R. clerk Food Store." Later worked as a railroad clerk; played semipro baseball. Registered for the draft on February 15, 1942, address same as census, employed by New York Central Railroad, 577 E. 152, Cleveland (hazel eyes, brown hair, light complexion, 6'2", 175#). Enlisted on July 11, 1942, at Cleveland as a private (6', 161#). Basic training in New Jersey. Arrived at Karachi on July 28, 1943. Attached to USAAF OTU at Malir on August 1. Attached to 2nd Bomb Squadron on October 9; arrived at Kunming on October 23. Joined 3rd Squadron on March 2, 1944, as administrative and technical clerk. Reclassified as personnel NCO on March 21. Promoted to sergeant on April 1 and to staff sergeant on August 1. Appointed squadron mail orderly on November 29. Hospitalized several times for malaria. Awarded Bronze Star. Released from 3rd Squadron on August 27 and sent to Yangkai; transferred to 22nd Bomb Squadron, 341st Bomb Group, as administrative NCO for transport home. Arrived in New York aboard USS *Charles H. Muir* on November 1, 1945. Wood's list: "18706 Cherokee Ave., Cleveland 19, Ohio." In 1950, with parents and a sister, same address, occupation timekeeper, railroad. Married Marianne Jeanette Sullivan in Euclid, OH; parents of two sons; later divorced. Worked for the New York Central / Penn Central / Conrail Railroad for forty-two years; retired as paymaster in 1981. Died April 10, 2004. Buried at All Souls Cemetery, Chardon Twp., OH.

DUNLAP, Wilbur Carlos, Sgt. (serial #06988462)
Born August 7, 1917, in Summit, WV. Son of Percy Elsworth and Georgia A. (Kendrick) Dunlap; mother died perhaps in childbirth. Lived in Washington, WV, with father and stepmother in 1920. In 1930, "Carlos W. Dunlap" was enumerated with father, stepmother, four brothers, and two sisters, no address; at Ivaton Village, Lincoln County, WV, in 1935. Graduated from Scott High School, Madison, WV, in 1936; completed one year of college. Enlisted on January 9, 1940, for the Puerto Rican Department as a private. In 1940 census, listed as a soldier at Maxwell Field, Montgomery, AL. Attended Air Corps Technical School, Scott Field, IL, in June 1940; returned to Maxwell Field after completion. With 24th Bombardment

Squadron, 23rd Composite Air Group, Orlando, FL, in late 1940. Promoted to sergeant at Southeast Air Corps Training Center, Maxwell Field, in January 1942. Moved to Southwestern Proving Grounds, Hope, AR, in early 1943 and later to Air Corps Proving Grounds, Eglin Field, FL. Married Allie Meade ("Polly") Palmer in about 1942; parents of three children. Arrived at Karachi aboard USS *Mission Bay* on March 29, 1944, and assigned to 27th Fighter Squadron as a crew chief. Transferred to the 3rd Squadron as bombsight maintenance technician on April 15, 1944. At 95th Sta. Hosp., Kunming, December 21–26, 1944, and again for observation and treatment on January 3, 1945. Assigned to 4th Bomb Squadron detachment at Chihkiang in August 1945. Released from 3rd Squadron on September 5; transferred to AAB at Yangkai. Wood's list: "19 Pinehurst Dr., Charleston, West Va." Discharged on October 20, 1945, at Fort Meade, MD. Registered with Kanawha County, WV, Local Board on November 1, 1945; address same as Wood's list (brown eyes, black hair, light complexion, 5'10", 165#). Reenlisted June 26, 1946. In Lakenheath, England, in late 1940s. In 1950, with wife, a daughter, and two sons, address 16 Elder, Pomonkey, MD, occupation Armed Forces, Andrews AFB. In Fairbanks, AK, in early 1950s. Served in Korea and Vietnam; total of thirty years' military service. In Victorville, CA, in 1960s. Retired as master sergeant; released from service on November 30, 1970. In Walla Walla, WA, in 1974; later in Salinas, CA, and Mesa, AZ. Died on March 6, 2005, in Mesa. Buried with military honors at Arlington National Cemetery, Richmond, VA.

EARLEY, William Thomas ("Bill"), Jr., 1Sgt. (serial #32460092)

Born December 16, 1920, in Clifton, NJ. Son of William Lyle and Jessie M. (Wright) Earley. In 1930, with parents and two sisters, 1095 Van Houten Ave., Clifton. Lived in Wyckoff, NJ, in 1935. Graduated from Ramsey High School, Ramsey, NJ. In 1940, lived with parents and a sister, 74 Park Ave., Allendale, NJ, occupation clerk in a grocery store. Registered for the draft on February 15, 1942, at Ramsey, residence 32 New Street, Allendale, employer Atlantic & Pacific Tea Co., Fairlawn, NJ (brown eyes, brown hair, ruddy complexion, 5'9", 150#, "Birthmark on Rt. Shoulder). Enlisted on August 15, 1942, at Newark, NJ, occupation salesclerk (5'8", 144#). Married Myra Ackerman on August 19, 1942, in Park Ridge, NJ; parents of a son born while he was overseas. Basic training at Atlantic City; assigned to the Permanent Party at General Headquarters. Ordered to Ft. Logan, CO, for further training; promoted to corporal. Achieved high academic standing and received two letters of commendation from post commanding officer. Promoted to sergeant and arrived at Karachi on July 29, 1943. Attached to USAAF OTU at Malir on August 1. On Seacrest's plane that turned back for engine change on the way to China on October 25; arrived in Kunming on October 26. Joined 3rd Squadron from 2nd Bomb Squadron on March 1, 1944, as personnel NCO; appointed first sergeant same date. Awarded Bronze Star for supervising security detail during evacuation from Kweilin by train. Released from 3rd Squadron on September 15 and sent to Yangkai; transferred to 341st Bomb Group for transport home. Arrived at New York aboard USS *General J. H. McRae* on October 15, 1945. Wood's list: "5 Park Ave., Park Ridge, New Jersey." Released from service October 20, 1945. In 1950, with wife and son, address 23 North Maple Ave., Park Ridge, occupation assistant manager, retail food market. Married Adele L. (Chudzik) Vancheri in February 1961, Ridgewood, NJ; parents of a son and a daughter. Lived in Park Ridge, Hawthorne, and Wyckoff, NJ; moved to Daytona Beach, FL, in about 1983. Occupation manager for Howard Johnson chain of motels. Died November 17, 2003, at Daytona Beach. Cremated and ashes scattered in the ocean at Flagler Beach, FL. (Name consistently recorded as "William Thomas Earley Jr.," although his father's middle name was "Lyle.")

EDGERTON, Thomas Hugh ("Tom"), 1Lt. (serial #39242841; later #0-766230)

Born January 6, 1918, in Richmond, IN. Son of Chauncey W. and Rhea M. (Turner) Edgerton, Quakers. In 1930, enumerated with maternal grandparents, parents, and sister, 117 South Fourth, Richmond, attending school. Family moved to Fullerton, CA, after 1935. Worked as a waiter at the Brown Mug, Anaheim, in 1939. In 1940, with parents at 124½ Ellis Pl., Fullerton, a student, completed two years of college. Registered for the draft on October 16, 1940, same address; occupation fry cook and fountain man, Wilkinson Drug Store (gray eyes, brown hair, light complexion, 5'8", 135#; "mole on left arm"). Enlisted June 1, 1942, at Los Angeles, CA, as a private (5'6", 138#). (1940 census states he completed two years of college; enlistment shows four years of high school.) Married Edna Beatrice Grimes on March 18, 1944; daughter born while he was overseas. Joined squadron on September 28, 1944, as a navigator. On detached duty with Task Force 34 at Chihkiang. Reported as MIA on January 15, 1945; returned to duty. Member of the Caterpillar Club. Awarded Air Medal on April 18, 1945. Transferred to 4th Bomb Squadron on May 24, 1945. Arrived in New York aboard USS *General Charles H. Muir* on November 1, 1945. Wood's list: "515 South Spadra Road, Fullerton, Calif." In 1950, with wife and two sons, address 5892 Indiana, Anaheim, CA, occupation oil field sales, oil field supply. Manager at Republic Supply Company of California in 1950s and 1960s; residence Buena Park. Died October 18, 1990, in San Bernardino, CA. Buried at Ft. Rosecrans National Cemetery, San Diego, CA.

EGDORF, Walter Charles, SSgt. (serial #37656693)

Born September 29, 1923, in Archer, IA. Son of Charles August ("Charley") and Stella Grace Edgdorf. In 1930, enumerated with parents and three sisters on a farm in rural Baker Twp. In 1940, lived with parents, two sisters, and a brother, same location, completed three years of high school, attending school. Graduated from Archer Community School in 1941. Registered for the draft June 30, 1942, address 253 Clark St., Bellflower, Los Angeles, CA; employer Douglas Aircraft Corp., Long Beach, CA (blue eyes, red hair, light complexion, 5'11", 150#). Enlisted as a private on January 19, 1943, at Camp Dodge, Herrold, IA (occupation metal worker; 5'10", 147#); inducted January 26, 1943. Departed US for CBI on August 2, 1943. Transferred from 4th to 3rd Squadron on February 28, 1944; order rescinded on March 18. Served as B-25 power plant mechanic and gunner. Awarded Air Medal on April 18, 1945. Not included on Wood's list. Returned to US on July 12, 1945; discharged October 18, 1945. Married Josena Cornelia Brouwer on April 10, 1947; parents of four sons and two daughters. In 1949, veteran's compensation approved for $350.00 (35 months of domestic service) plus $57.50 (23 months of foreign service) for total of $407.50; residence Primghar, IA. In 1950, with wife and infant son, address "Darby & Rowan's," Primghar, occupation laborer, Primghar Lumber Co. Worked at Associated Milk Producers, Inc. (AMPI), before retiring in 1988. Died April 24, 2015, in Sanborn. Buried at Pleasant Hill Cemetery near Pringhar.

ENGLAND, John Warren, Sgt. (serial #11116639)

Born March 27, 1914, in San Francisco, CA. Son of George McClellen and Mary Ann (Burke) England (mother was born in England, emigrated from Ireland, naturalized in 1910). Moved with family to Salt Lake City, UT, in about 1915 and with mother and siblings to Boston, MA, about 1919, after death of his father (a railroad switchman) in 1918. In 1920, "Warren England" was enumerated with widowed mother, three brothers, and a sister, 236 Silver St., Boston. In 1930, lived with mother, same siblings, same address, attending school. Completed one year of high school. In 1936, arrested for stealing a car from a parking garage and wrecking it while attempting to evade authorities. Not found in 1940 census. Registered for draft on October 16, 1940, in South Boston, address same as 1930 census, employer Gillette Safety Razor Co., 15 W. First St., S. Boston (blue eyes, blonde hair, light complexion, 5'10", 155#). Enlisted November 12, 1942, in Boston as a private (occupation "unskilled construction occupations," 5'8", 147#). Married Alice Bertha (Erley) Buskey (Canadian citizen) on November 25, 1943, in Leominster, MA; parents of a daughter and a son. Arrived at Karachi aboard USS *Mission Bay* on March 29, 1944. Attached to 3rd Squadron on April 3 as A/F radio operator. Promoted to corporal on July 1 and to sergeant on September 1. On detached service to Kunming in October, attending VHF radio school. On detached service to Task Force 34 at Chihkiang in November. Ordered to 95th Sta. Hosp., Kunming, for observation and treatment on January 3, 1945. Hospitalized at Chengtu on May 27. Sent to rest camp at Chengtu on June 24. Assigned to 4th Bomb Squadron detachment at Chihkiang in August. Released from 3rd Squadron on September 10 and sent to Yangkai; transferred to 341st Bomb Group for transport home. Arrived in New York aboard USS *General Charles H. Muir* on November 1, 1945. Wood's list: "117 Second Street, Leominster, Mass." Released from service November 12, 1945. In 1950, with wife and daughter, address 3286 Soutel, Duval, FL, occupation radio technician, National Guard. In Bridgeport, CT, employed by Aviation Corp. (Avco). in early 1960s to early 1970s. Divorced on July 16, 1975, Stratford, CT; his residence Boston. Died November 17, 1986, in South Boston. Buried with military honors at Massachusetts National Cemetery, Bourne, MA. (Often appears in civil records as "Warren England.")

EVITTS, Budd William, SSgt. (serial #13046390)

Born September 1, 1919, in Llewellyn, PA. Son of Edwin Clair (or Clare) and Orpha (Clark) Evitts. In 1930, enumerated with parents, two brothers, and a sister, no address but not a farm, Willing Street, Branch Township, Schuylkill County, PA, attending school. Graduated from Branch Twp. High School in 1937. With parents and sister in 1940, address "Wheeling St. Llewellyn S side moving W," "new worker." Registered for the draft on October 16, 1940, address "Llewellyn, Schuylkill, Penna."; employer Reininger Brothers, Zerbe, PA (brown eyes and hair, dark complexion, 5'5½", 140#). Enlisted in Air Corps on January 7, 1942, in Philadelphia as a private (5'4", 140#). Stationed at Westover Field, MA; transferred to Seymour Johnson Airfield about August 1943; shipped overseas about October 1943. Attached to 1st Bomb Group HQ on January 3, 1944. Joined 3rd Squadron from 4th Bomb Squadron on March 12, 1944, as administrative NCO. Promoted to staff sergeant on January 1, 1945. Released from 3rd Squadron on August 27 and sent to Yangkai; transferred to 341st Bomb Group. Arrived in New York aboard USS *General Charles H. Muir* on November 1, 1945. Wood's list: "Llewellyn, Pa." Discharged November 5, 1945, at Indiantown Gap Military Reservation, PA. In 1950 census, with father, no address, Branch, PA, occupation gas station attendant, retail gasoline. In June 1950, veteran's compensation approved by the Commonwealth of Pennsylvania for $210 for twenty-one months of active domestic service and $290 for twenty-five months of foreign service during WWII. Married Margaret Minnier in 1959; had no children. Employed by Frane Construction Co. Died March 21, 1963; cause, coronary occlusion due to arteriosclerotic heart disease while shoveling crushed stone in the street for sewer construction (Upper Southampton Twp., Bucks County, PA). Buried at Llewellyn Cemetery, Branch. (Serial number occasionally typed as 13046590 in squadron records. Sometimes referenced in civil sources as "Bud.")

EWELL, Dave Haas, Jr., SSgt. (serial #34078809)

Born July 15, 1918, in Mamou, LA. Son of Dave Haas and Rosa Dennis (Robin) Ewell. In 1930, enumerated with parents, three sisters, two brothers, two boarders, and a servant on a farm, Westdale Rd., E. Baton Rouge, LA, attending school. Graduated from Baton Rouge High School. Attended Louisiana State University, School of Agriculture; pledged to Kappa Sigma Fraternity. In 1940, with parents, five sisters, and a brother on a farm on College Dr., East Baton Rouge, completed one year of college, occupation unpaid farm laborer. Registered for the draft on October 16, 1940, student at LSU (brown eyes and hair, light complexion, 5'10", 165#). Operated a used-car business with a friend until he was drafted. Enlisted on June 26, 1941, at Jacksonville Army Airfield, Jacksonville, FL, as a private, occupation automotive mechanic (5'9", 171#). Attended the auto mechanics course, armored force school, at Fort Knox, KY. Assigned to Company G, 33rd Armored Regiment (L), Camp Polk, LA, a part of the Third Armored ("Bayou Blitz") Division. As an aviation cadet, received preflight training at San Antonio, TX; preliminary flight training at Grider Field, Pine Bluff, AR, in early 1943. Treated in August 1944 for stricture of the urethra (postgonorrheal). Stationed at Altus, OK, in February 1945. Likely arrived at Calcutta aboard USS *General Robert E. Callan* on April 27, 1945. Attached to 1st Bomb Group as airplane mechanic in May and to 3rd Squadron on June 7, 1945. Released from 3rd Squadron on September 1; transferred to 26th Fighter Squadron, 51st Fighter Group, for transport home. Arrived at Tacoma, WA, aboard SS *Marine Angel* on December 12, 1945. Wood's list: "Baton Rouge, Louisiana." Married Ruth Chloe Guidry, a former WAVE, on July 5, 1946, in Brusly, LA; parents of six daughters. Not found in 1950 census. Operated Ewell Real Estate as a broker in the mid-1950s. Worked as heavy-equipment operator and dirt contractor. Filed lawsuits in 1975 against thirteen of Louisiana's biggest petrochemical companies for dumping toxic materials near his 545-acre farm, Fairview Ranch, causing death to his cattle and local wildlife when pits overflowed and wastes drained onto his property. Died June 15, 1999, at Baker, LA. Buried at Green Oaks Memorial Park, Baton Rouge.

FAHERTY, John Francis, 1Lt. (serial #16033371; later #0-743770)

Born October 26, 1919, in Cuba City, WI. Son of Basil James and Ester Mary or Marie (Gierens) Faherty. In 1925, with parents and a sister at Valley Junction, IA. In 1930, enumerated with parents and three younger sisters, no address but not a farm, N. Clay, Smelser Twp., Cuba City. Completed two years at Wisconsin Institute of Technology at Platteville, WI. Employed by Chicago and Northwestern Railroad as a track laborer. In 1940, lived with parents and four sisters, address 1262 Clay, Smelser Twp., Cuba City, no occupation listed. Registered for the draft on July 1, 1941, in Platteville, residence Cuba City but mailing address 1617 W. National Ave., Milwaukee, WI, employer Cutler-Hammer Mfg. Co., 3019 S. 20th St., Milwaukee (blue eyes, brown hair, ruddy complexion, 5'10", 150#). Enlisted in Air Corps on April 7, 1942, at Camp Grant, IL, as a private, occupation manufacturing of electrical machinery and accessories (5'9", 143#). Completed flight course at Santa Ana Army Air Base, Santa Ana, CA. Graduated from bombardier school and commissioned 2nd lieutenant at Deming Army Airfield, Deming, NM, on April 17, 1943. Assigned to Carlsbad, NM, air training field for advanced training. Joined 3rd Squadron from CACW HQ on April 15, 1944, as bombardier and appointed assistant operations officer. First mission as lead bombardier on July 23 against Wanting supply area along border of Burma/Yunnan. Reported as MIA on August 14, 1944; returned to duty. In charge of squadron personnel evacuated by train from Kweilin in mid-September. Promoted to 1st lieutenant on October 10. Appointed armament officer October 24, and as fire marshal on November 30. Assigned to 4th Bomb Squadron detachment at Chihkiang in August 1945. Released from 3rd Squadron on September 5 and sent to Yangkai; transferred to 341st Bomb Group for transport home. Arrived in New York aboard USS *General Charles H. Muir* on November 1, 1945. Wood's list: "Cuba City, Wisconsin." Discharged January 2, 1946. Married Verena Marie Cahill on August 20, 1946, in Iowa City, IA; parents of four sons and two daughters. In 1950, with wife and two daughters, address Box 16C, N. Cape Rd., Franklin, WI, occupation "assembly man," construction machines. At Hales Corners near Milwaukee in early '50s. Died February 17, 1984, in Milwaukee. Buried at St. Martin de Tours Cemetery, Franklin, WI.

FOORMAN, Andrew (NMI), SSgt. (serial #39838192)
Born May 22, 1920, in Kerman, CA. Son of Frederick Gabrealoff (Gabriel) and Mary (Bercheque or Berchuck) Foorman, immigrants from Kiev, Ukraine. In 1930, enumerated with parents and ten siblings at 108 Water Street, Riverbank Town (later renamed Bryte), Washington Twp., Yolo County, CA, attending school. Completed grammar school. Not found in 1940 census. Worked in processing of dairy products. Registered for the draft on July 1, 1941, same address, occupation laborer, Anson Casselman Ranch, Elkhorn Dist., Yolo County (blue eyes, blonde hair, light complexion, 5'8", 145#, "Birth-mark on inner side of right forearm"). Enlisted on May 1, 1942, at San Francisco, CA, as a private (occupation decorator and window dresser, 5'7", 133#); residence 1830 Golden Gate Ave., San Francisco. Completed courses in aviation mechanics at Sheppard Field, Wichita Falls, TX, in February 1943 and at North American Aircraft Factory School, Inglewood, CA, in March 1943. In early 1944, transferred from 1st Emergency Rescue Squadron to 40th Technical School Squadron at HQ Technical School, AAF Technical Training Command, AAF Overseas Replacement Depot #4, Boca Raton, FL. Treated in September for migraine headaches. Likely arrived at Calcutta aboard USS *General Robert E. Callan* on April 27, 1945. Assigned to 1st Bomb Group as airplane mechanic in May 1945 and to 3rd Squadron on June 7. Released from 3rd Squadron on September 5 and sent to Yangkai; transferred to 26th Fighter Squadron, 51st Fighter Group, for transport home. Arrived in Tacoma, WA, aboard SS *Marine Angel* on December 12, 1945. Wood's list: "108 Water Street, Bryte, California." Discharged January 11, 1946. Charter member of Bryte VFW Post 9498 from 1947. In 1950, with partner, Albert L. Dupree, address 3R, street not named but described as "1st street on left of Hwy 101 starting at the Murry Garage," South Beach, OR, occupation night watchman, mill planning. Later lived in Valdez-Cordova and Chenega Bay, AK. Died June 27, 1992, in Cordova.

FOX, Loyal Leonard, Sgt. (serial #36815490)
Born June 12, 1924, in Amery, WI. Only child of Hugh Leonard and Evelyn Violet (Sommers) Fox. Lived with parents in Ida, IA, in 1925, per state census. In 1930, enumerated with parents, no address but not a farm, Amery, not attending school. In 1940, lived with parents, address C. H. Johnson Addition, Block 2, Lincoln Twp., Amery, WI, attending school, completed seven years. Graduated from Amery High School in June 1941. Registered for the draft on June 30, 1942, at Balsam Lake, WI, residence Lincoln Township, mailing address Amery, Route 3, employer Lakeside Packing Company (blue eyes, brown hair, light complexion, 5'11", 175#, "Scar on left hand on index finger"). Submitted employment application to Northern Pacific Railroad in August 1942, address 1735 S. Roberts, St. Paul, MN (blue eyes, brown hair, 5'6", 165#). Recommended for employment as third cook in dining car, St. Paul Station, effective September 1, 1942, at $100.80 per month. Resigned September 7, 1942. Enlistment and training

not found. Assigned to the 3rd Squadron on October 19, 1944, as A/P armorer-gunner. Reported as MIA on a bombing mission against enemy-held airfield at Ichang on May 16, 1945. Critically wounded when hit by a propeller as he parachuted out. Captured by Japanese and reported to have died in the hospital on July 5, 1945, as result of injuries. Posthumously awarded Air Medal and Purple Heart. Not included in Wood's list; address of next of kin (his mother) "Amery, Wisconsin." Buried at National Memorial Cemetery of the Pacific, Honolulu, HI, on December 1, 1949. Memorial marker also at Fox Family Cemetery, Amery, WI.

FULLER, Grady Barron, 2Lt. (serial #07000940; later #0-889942; later #042868; #O50145)
Born September 20, 1919, at Reynolds, GA. Son of Henry Grady and Ila Louise (Barron) Fuller. In 1930, enumerated with parents, a brother, and a sister on a farm, address 118 Carsonville Road, Panhandle, GA. Graduated from Reynolds High School ca. 1937. Attended Abraham Baldwin Jr. College; graduated from the University of Georgia. Enlisted October 8, 1939, for the Philippine Department (birth year transcribed as "1859," nativity "not yet a citizen," education "post-graduate," occupation lithographer, widower without dependents, height and weight "98, 666"). Inducted into Air Corps on October 9. Attended the Air Corps technical schools of airplane mechanics at Chanute Field and Scott Field, IL. In 1940, enumerated as a soldier at Maxwell Field, Kendall, AL. Married Maxine Elizabeth Guss on December 14, 1941, Lake, FL; parents of a son and a daughter. Promoted to staff sergeant in February 1942 and to technical sergeant in August 1942. In early 1943, promoted to master sergeant and held position of crew chief in the engineering division of Air Force unit stationed at Westover Field near Springfield, MA. Arrived at Karachi on July 29, 1943. Attached to USAAF OTU at Malir on August 1. Attached to 2nd Bomb Squadron on October 9. Joined 3rd Squadron on March 4, 1944. Appointed squadron line chief. Ordered to 95th Sta. Hosp. at Kunming for physical examination on October 1; on detached service to 95th Station Hospital October 4–17. Received direct field commission to 2nd lieutenant on March 17, 1945. Returned from temporary duty at 1st Bomb Group in April. Released from 3rd Squadron on September 8 and sent to Yangkai; transferred to 341st Bomb Group for transport home. Returned to US aboard USS *General C. G. Morton* on October 22, 1945. Wood's list: "Route #1, Reynolds, Georgia." Promoted to 1st lieutenant on July 13, 1946. Warehouse section chief at Tinker Field, Oklahoma City, OK, training Chinese students in mid-1947; awarded Breast Order of Jun Hui for service as an aircraft maintenance instructor in China. In 1950, with wife, a son, and a daughter, address 414 Babb Dr., Midwest City, OK, occupation Armed Forces. Stationed in Tokyo in mid-1950s. In late 1950s, rank major, assigned to KC-135 branch, B-52 & Missiles Div., at Tinker Air Base. In command of 7310th Material Sq. at Rhein-Main, Germany, Air Base in mid-1960s. Retired in January 1973 as a lieutenant colonel after thirty-three years and twenty-two days of military service. Member of Medinah Shriners. Died October 26, 2010, in McLean, VA. Buried with military honors at Arlington National Cemetery.

GAFFNEY, Loren Earl, Sgt. (serial #37511079)
Born July 20, 1923, in Bazaar, KS. Son of Albert Louis and Roanna Eulala (Gaddie) Gaffney. In 1930, enumerated with parents and younger sister on a farm in Janesville Twp., KS, attending school. Moved to Burrton, KS, between 1935 and 1940. In 1940, lived with parents and a sister on a farm, address Lincoln St., Burrton, completed one year of high school, attending school. Registered for the draft on June 30, 1942, completed four years of high school, employed by National Youth Administration, Hutchinson, KS (blue eyes, brown hair, ruddy

complexion, 5'10", 149#). In August 1942, sent to Cessna facility at "secret location for war industry job" as a welder trainee. Enlisted on February 25, 1943, at Ft. Leavenworth, KS, as a private, occupation welder and flame cutter (5'8", 156#). Joined 3rd Squadron on December 28, 1944, as A/P mechanic–gunner–flight engineer. On detached service with Task Force 34 at Chihkiang in January, with Nimrod Detachment at Laohokow in March, and with 4th Bomb Squadron detachment at Chihkiang in August 1945. Released from 3rd Squadron on September 5; transferred to Detachment HQ & HQ Squadron, 14th Air Force. Wood's list: "Burrton, Kansas." Address in 1949 114 W. Bigger, Hutchinson, KS; arrested and fined $103 for "drunk driving" in February. In 1950, with parents, same address, occupation general laborer, salt mine. In 1955, with his parents, same address, occupation "loader" at Morton Salt Co. Married Alberta May Williams on November 3, 1955, in Albuquerque, NM; had no children. In 1956, lived with wife, address 1503 E. 5th, Hutchinson, occupation "plant worker," Morton Salt. Occupation shown in directories as "welder" and "machine operator" at various times during this period. Retired from Morton Salt Co. Died August 12, 2002. Buried at Memorial Park Cemetery, Hutchinson.

GOELLER, Howard Marshall ("Pop"), Capt. (serial #0-909502)
Born October 20, 1909, in Columbus, IN; name on birth register "Marshall Goeller." Son of Harold ("Harry") Leander and Ida Grace (Huff) Goeller. Ran away from home several times; shot himself in the abdomen with .22 rifle in apparent suicide attempt in March 1916 (per newspaper reports). Graduated from Columbus High School in May 1926. Completed one year of college at Depauw University, Greencastle, IN. In 1930, enumerated with parents and two brothers, 603 Maple Ave., Columbus, occupation accountant at a lumber company. On July 10, 1930, signed on as deck boy aboard *Edgehill*, sailing from Galveston, TX; gave year of birth as 1908 and address same as census. On Application for Seaman's Protection Certificate, gave age as 21 (blue eyes, black hair, fair complexion, 5'10", 135#). Married Louise Suhre on October 15, 1932, in Columbus; parents of a son. Longtime member of the Toastmasters Club. With brother Wallace Goeller, co-owned the St. Denis Hotel at Fifth and Washington and the St. Denis laundry on Maple Street. In June 1935, hospitalized following automobile accident that caused severe bruising and a broken nose. Registered for the draft on October 16, 1940, at Columbus, address RR #5, Columbus, self-employed at St. Denis Hotel (blue eyes, black hair, light-brown complexion, 5'10½", 175#). In 1940, lived with wife, son, and mother-in-law on a farm, address 215 Rocky Point Rd., Columbus, occupation farmer. Accepted a direct commission as 1st lieutenant in army on July 1, 1942; reported to officer's training school, Miami Beach, FL. Sent to Salt Lake City, UT, to complete training and then to Pendleton, OR, in August 1942. Served as administrative inspector at Great Falls Army Air Base before appointment to commanding officer at air base in Glasgow, MT, in May 1943. Arrived at Karachi aboard USS *Mission Bay* on March 29, 1944. Attached to 3rd Squadron and appointed adjutant on April 3, 1944. Accused of kicking a Chinese sergeant in mid-July 1944 and placed under house arrest in his tent. Appointed to Summary Court-Martial on August 1, 1944. Released from squadron August 16, 1944, and transferred to the 10th Air Force as assistant air inspector. Promoted to major, date undetermined. Returned to US in late March 1945 after serving fourteen months' overseas duty in the CBI. Wood's list: "Columbus, Indiana." Awarded Bronze Star for meritorious service in India. Arrived in early May 1945 at Army Air Forces Redistribution Station No. 2 in Miami Beach for reassignment processing.

Stationed at the Boston port of embarkation, serving as an orientation officer for redeployed Air Force personnel returning to the US. Processed at Camp Atterbury and placed on terminal leave in late August; discharged on October 29, 1945, as a lieutenant colonel. In 1950, with wife and son, address "off 46—North Road 3 miles from city limits," occupation farmer. Divorced in about January 1952. Occupation sales manager at Molton Hotel, Birmingham, AL, in early 1953; moved to Huntsville, AL. Married Lamar A. __ in about November 1953; divorced in May 1954. Address in mid-1950s was 2908 10th Court S, Birmingham. Hospitalized in July 1956 due to three self-inflicted bullet wounds by an army automatic; address 2320 Highland Ave., Birmingham. Purchased Columbus Vulcanizing Co. with a partner in 1959. Sold it and St. Denis Hotel in 1961. Later operated an air-conditioning business until retirement. Died December 23, 1974, in Huntsville, AL. Buried at Garland Brook Cemetery, Columbus.

GRANT, Donald Wycoff ("Don"), MSgt. (serial #06560440)

Born September 9, 1916, in San Francisco, CA. Son of Harry Morton and Laura M. (Lyman) Grant; mother died in early 1920. In 1930, enumerated as inmate of Salvation Army Boys' and Girls' Industrial Home and Farm, Healdsburg, CA. Completed four years of high school. In 1935, lived with his father at 411 Ellis, San Francisco; occupation doorman. Original enlistment not found but probably about 1934. In 1940, enumerated as a sergeant in US Regular Army at France Field, Cristobal, Panama Canal Zone. Reenlisted December 16, 1942, in Air Corps. Arrived at Karachi on July 30, 1943. Attached to USAAF OTU at Malir on August 1. Attached to 2nd Bomb Squadron on October 9. Joined 3rd Bomb Squadron on March 2, 1944, as A/P flight chief. Awarded Purple Heart after being wounded when Plexiglas of a B-25 turret was shattered while test-firing a machine gun. Transferred to CACW HQ on October 20, 1944. Accompanied Brig. Gen. Morse to Europe as his crew chief. Awarded Air Medal on April 18, 1945. Returned to US at about the same time. Wood's list: "Jones Street, San Francisco, CA." (Harry M. Grant lived at Layne Hotel, 345 Jones St., San Francisco.) Registered with Local Board No. 1, Seattle, WA, on September 6, 1945, address 3250 29th West, Seattle, living with his brother Harold L. Grant, no employer (blue eyes, brown hair, ruddy complexion, 5'8", 193#). Reenlisted on February 26, 1946, in San Francisco as a private for the Hawaiian Department (height and weight "27, 505"). Married Diane Shaffer in March 1946, in San Francisco. Not found in 1950 census. Attained rank of technical sergeant by 1950. In 1953, still in USAF, lived with wife, address 5338 Folsom Blvd., Sacramento. In 1954, retired from USAF after twenty years' service and employed as patrolman with Folsom Police Department; left Folsom in July after three weeks to join California State Police at Davis. In early 1955, patrolman with North Sacramento Police Dept. Estranged from his wife, who remained in Sacramento. Returned to Folsom and served as chief of police from June 7, 1955, to May 15, 1956. Remained in Folsom after resigning to work in the private police force at University of California at Davis. Graduated from fingerprint school of the California branch of criminal identification and investigation. Married Mabel Emily (Francis) Rugani on February 20, 1960, in Minden, NV. Arrested on March 30 and charged with bigamy. Beginning April 29, served seven months in the county jail as part of a two-year probation sentence. Annulment granted to second wife on May 5, 1960. Residence Sacramento, CA, in 1967. Died February 23, 1970, in Sacramento. Buried at Sacramento County Veterans Memorial Cemetery, Sacramento; rank on grave marker specified as master sergeant, veteran of WWII and Korean War.

GRAVES, Louis Francis ("Lou," "Swampy"), Jr., Capt. (serial #38044788; later #0-793240, #049708)

Born April 7, 1914, in Texarkana, AR. Son of Louis F. and Agnes Julia (Fant) Graves. In 1930, enumerated with parents, two sisters, and two brothers, 2103 State Line, Texarkana, TX, attending school. Moved with family to nearby Bowie, TX, in 1930s. Graduated with a bachelor of arts degree from St. Edward's University, Austin, TX, in 1937; received award as the graduate of the College of Arts and Letters with the highest general average in the four-year course at the university. In 1940, with parents and four siblings, address 3107 Hazel St., Bowie, occupation newspaper reporter. Registered for the draft March 12, 1941, address 3107 Walnut St., Texarkana; employer *Texarkana Gazette and Daily News* (blue eyes, blonde hair, light complexion, 6', 160#). Enlisted in Air Corps from US Naval Reserve on August 15, 1941, in Dallas, TX, as a private (occupation photographer, 5'11", 156#). Married Frances Wilton Clement about 1942; parents of ten children, the first a son born while he was overseas. Stationed at Columbia Army Air Base in November 1942. Flight instructor for Chinese at Luke and Thunderbird Air Bases. Arrived at USAAF OTU at Malir on August 3, 1943. Attached to 2nd Bomb Squadron; arrived in Kunming on October 27. On November 16, 1943, as navigator on a low-level mission against a Japanese freighter, received a slight wound to his forehead when nose of B-25 was shattered by enemy fire. Served in 1st Bomb Group as assistant operations and training officer and historical officer. Awarded Purple Heart at Kweilin on January 10, 1944. Transferred to 3rd Squadron on March 1, 1944, as navigator; promoted to captain on March 4, 1944. Appointed squadron historian, censor, and publications and schools officer. Ordered to rest camp near Kunming on October 5, 1944. Transferred to 1st Bomb Group HQ on October 3, 1944. Returned to US in November 1944. Wood's list: "Texarkana, Texas [marked out]; Nashville, Ark [written after in pencil]." Called up for active duty on July 31, 1950, in the Marine Corps Reserve; sent to training camp at Oceanside, CA. In command of Battery C, 2nd 155 mm. Howitzer Battalion, Texarkana, which won the William McK. Fleming Award for 84.1% drill attendance in 1949. Sports editor and city editor of the *Texarkana Gazette* before purchasing the *Nashville News* in 1950. (*Nashville News-Leader* now operated by Louis F. Graves III.) Served as captain in the US Marine Corps Reserve during the Korean War. In 1950, with wife and four sons, address 59 College, Nashville, occupation editor of paper, newspaper business. In July 1950, at Marine Corps Air Station (MCAS) with HQSq at AirFMFPac (Fleet Marine Force, Pacific) at El Toro, CA. In February 1951, completed a nine-week school at US Naval Intelligence School at Washington, DC. In Officers Volunteer Reserve, 8th MCRD, New Orleans, until July 17; returned to El Toro. Awarded the Distinguished Flying Cross and other military decorations. Retired in 1979. Died June 1, 2001, in Texarkana. Buried at Restland Memorial Park, Nashville, AR, with Marine Corps military honors.

GREENE, Frederick Hartwell ("Fred"), Jr., Capt. (serial #32029966; later #0-792584)

Born April 22, 1918, in Woburn County, MA. Son of Frederick Hartwell and Ruth (Silver) Greene. In 1930, enumerated with parents, sister, nurse, lodger, and servant, 130 March St., Belmont, MA, attending school. Graduated from Belmont Hill School in 1935. Graduated cum laude from Brown University in 1939; member of Alpha Delta Phi and Sigma Xi fraternities. In 1940, lived with parents, sister, and brother, same address, completed four years of college, occupation apprentice in glass manufacturing. Moved to Steuben County, NY, occupation statistical clerk. Registered for the draft on October 16,

1940, at Corning, NY, address 247 Pine St., Corning, employer Corning Glass Works (blue eyes, blonde and brown hair [both checked], ruddy complexion, 6'3", 170#). Enlisted on January 16, 1941, in Buffalo, NY, as a private, residence Steuben, NY (6'4", 170#). At Maxwell Field, AL, in early 1942; graduated from Army Basic Flying School at Shaw Field, SC, mid-1942; at Columbia Army Air Base in late 1942. Married Helen Scott Hoffman on June 29, 1943, at Rosemont, PA (rank given as lieutenant); parents of a son and three daughters. Joined 3rd Squadron from 17th Fighter Squadron on January 16, 1945, as B-25 pilot, rank 1st lieutenant. Reported as MIA on March 30 and May 27, 1945; returned to duty after both. Promoted to captain on June 1. Flew twenty-six combat missions. Released from 3rd Squadron on August 27 and sent to Replacement Depot at Karachi for transport home. Wood's list: "Radnor Road, Radnor, Pa." Employed by Corning Glass and at MIT as assistant director of the flight control lab. In 1950, with wife, two daughters, a son, and a maid, no address, Lincoln, MA, occupation administrative, engineering college. Vice president and general manager of Vacuum Equipment Division, National Research Corp., Cambridge, MA, in late 1950s; specialized in technology of high vacuums, exploring ways to store and convert energy "to enable space travel to become a reality." Director of marketing and development at Norton Research Corp., Cambridge. Moved to Cape Elizabeth, ME, in early 1970s. Joined management consulting firm of Technical Marketing Associates, Inc., Concord, in March 1971. On Brunswick Board of Assessment Review and on board of Topsham-Brunswick Land Trust. Director of the New Enterprise Institute at the University of Southern Maine. After retirement, volunteered as delivery driver for Meals on Wheels. Died May 8, 2007, in Bath, ME. Memorial service held July 7 at St. Paul's Episcopal Church, Brunswick.

GRUBER, George (NMI) ("Joey"), TSgt. (serial #32343506)
Born March 2, 1920, in Brooklyn, NY. Son of Samuel and Fannie (Gettinger) Gruber, Jewish Austro-Polish immigrants. In 1930, enumerated with parents, two brothers, and a sister, 1805 Pitkin Ave., Brooklyn, parents spoke Yiddish. In 1940, lived with his parents, a brother, and a sister, address 220 Bristol St., Brooklyn, completed four years of high school, occupation "General." Member of the Eleventh Ward Democratic Club. Registered for the draft on July 1, 1941, in Brooklyn, address 339 Legion St., occupation factory helper, employed by Jay Hawk Manufacturing Co., 79 Pearl Street (brown eyes, brown hair, ruddy complexion, 5'11", 156#). Enlisted May 26, 1942, at Fort Jay, Governor's Island, NY, as a private, completed one year of college, occupation shipping and receiving clerk (5'9", 154#). Married Harriet Rosenstein in September 1942, Brooklyn; parents of a son. Arrived at Karachi on July 24, 1943. Attached to USAAF OTU at Malir on August 1. Attached to 2nd Bomb Squadron. Placed on flight status September 17. Arrived at Kunming on October 14. Joined 3rd Squadron on March 1, 1944, as AAF radio mechanic. Reclassified as squadron supply sergeant. Promoted to technical sergeant on January 1, 1945. Released from 3rd Squadron on August 27 and sent to Yangkai; transferred to 22nd Bomb Squadron, 341st Bomb Group, as quartermaster for transport home. Returned to New York aboard USS *General J. H. McRae* on October 15, 1945; sent to Ft. Dix, NJ, for processing. Wood's list: "390 Sutter Ave., Brooklyn, New York." Released from service October 20, 1945. In 1950, with wife and son, Apt. 5 at same address, occupation supply clerk, US Veterans Administration. Divorced in 1953, Volusia, FL. Married __ in Daytona Beach, FL; had no children. Died February 8, 1975, in New York. Buried at Long Island National Cemetery, Farmingdale, NY.

HAINES, Paul Earnest, SSgt. (serial #33186123)

Born January 18, 1915, in Philadelphia, PA. Son of Adam F. and Sarah ("Sadie") Halsey (Kilpatrick) Haines. Moved to Norristown, PA, before 1920. In 1920, enumerated with parents, three brothers, and two sisters, address 153 Elm St., Norristown. Completed one year of college. Worked for a utilities provider. Married Frances Mildred Heist about 1939; residence Norristown. In 1940, lived with wife and mother-in-law, address 930 (no street name), Norristown, four years of high school, occupation "magnisa." Registered for the draft on October 16, 1940, address 568 Noble St., Norristown; employed by Philip Carey Manufacturing Co., Plymouth Meeting, PA (gray eyes, brown hair, light complexion, 6'1", 140#). Enlisted on July 14, 1942, at Allentown, PA, as a private (marital status separated, 6', 144#). Inducted on July 29, 1942; address 806 W. Lafayette St., Norristown. At Greenville (SC) Army Air Base in early 1943. Arrived at Karachi on July 28. Attached to USAAF OTU at Malir on August 1. Placed on flying status September 1 and October 1. Attached to 2nd Bomb Squadron on October 9. Arrived at Kunming on October 16. Joined 3rd Squadron as A/P armorer in March 1944. Reclassified to power turret specialist on March 21. Promoted to staff sergeant on April 1. Hospitalized for enteritis in July and for malaria in October 1944. Released from 3rd Squadron on August 27, 1945, and sent to Yangkai; transferred to 341st Bomb Group for transport home. Arrived in New York aboard USS *General Charles H. Muir* on November 1. Wood's list: "657 Kohn Street, Norristown, Pa." Released from service November 5, 1945, at Indiantown Gap Military Reservation, PA. Graduated from the Progressive School of Photography, New Haven, CT. Married Celestine Woodson on July 12, 1947, in Norristown; had no children. In 1950 census, with wife, address 207 Potts Road, W. Norristown, occupation commercial photographer, Philadelphia. In February 1950, veteran's compensation by Commonwealth of Pennsylvania approved for $120 for domestic service and $380 for foreign service during WWII. Later lived in Ambler, PA, and Columbia, SC. Retired from Kaiser Aluminum; later employed part-time by the South Carolina Criminal Justice Academy. Sang tenor with barbershop quartets; active in Little Theater. Died September 20, 1991. Buried at Greenlawn Memorial Park, Columbia.

HALL, Alvin Alfred, SSgt. (serial #37212021)

Born September 10, 1920, in Devon, KS. Son of William Chester and Elsie Mae (Harper) Hall. Lived on family farm at Mill Creek in 1925. In 1930, enumerated with parents and three brothers on a farm at Pawnee Twp., KS, attending school. In 1940, lived with parents and four siblings on a farm in Mill Creek Twp., occupation unpaid farm laborer. Registered for the draft on February 14, 1942, employed by Civilian Conservation Corps, Co. 4702, Burlington, KS (blue eyes, blonde hair, ruddy complexion, 6', 160#). With Etta Henthorn, also of Devon, issued marriage license in June 1942 in Nevada, MO; no information found regarding marriage. Enlisted July 31, 1942. Original unit, which later fought in the Battle of the Bulge, shipped out while he was hospitalized in New York. Reassigned and sent to North Africa and later to Sicily and Italy, then shipped to the CBI. Joined 3rd Squadron on July 3, 1944, as a cook (perhaps from one of the squadrons of the 12th Bomb Group also stationed at Moran). Listed with squadron personnel on move from "Deragon" to Kweilin. On detached service to Luliang on September 10, 1944. Transferred to 1st Bomb Squadron on September 30. Hospitalized for malaria in October 1944. No further military record found. Told his family that he did preflight checks for Gen. Chennault's planes, and he also ran mule trains into Burma and India. Not included in Wood's list. Released from service January 17, 1946.

Employed in 1948 by St. Louis–San Francisco Railway at Fort Scott, KS, as "B & B Helper." Married Dorothy Fern Crane on April 12, 1948, at Mound City, KS; parents of three sons and two daughters. In 1950, with wife and a son, no address, Mill Creek, occupation carpenter for railroad. Later lived in Uniontown and Eudora, KS. Died on July 12, 1976. Buried at Eudora City Cemetery, Eudora.

HAMILTON, Jack Murval, Maj. (serial #18061493; later #0-664583)

Born November 13, 1921, in DeSoto Parish, LA. Son of John Preston and Clara Myrtle (Stephens) Hamilton. Lived in Shreveport in 1924. Moved to Houston, TX, before 1930. Graduated from Reagan High School. Completed one year at Rice University, Houston. In 1940, enumerated with widowed mother, brother, two sisters, brother-in-law, and nephew, address 114 Fairview, Houston, attending college, completed one year. Employed by Humble Oil and Refining Co. in California. Enlisted in Air Corps as an aviation cadet on January 5, 1942, in Houston, occupation salesman (5'9", 146#). Received primary flight instruction at Oklahoma City, OK. Completed advanced training with Class 42-H at Foster Field, Victoria, TX, in September 1942, commissioned 2nd lieutenant. Flew sixty combat missions as a B-25 pilot in North Africa and Europe with the 489th Bomb Squadron, 340th Bomb Group, 57th Bomb Wing of the 9th and later 12th Air Force. Awarded Air Medal for missions in Sicily and later six OLCs. Returned from Casablanca to LaGuardia, New York City, by ATC on March 21, 1944; rank captain. At Baltimore, MD, and Columbia, SC, in 1944. Arrived in China on December 2. Joined 3rd Squadron on January 3, 1945, as a B-25 pilot / flight leader. Appointed commanding officer in February. B-25J A/C #714 personalized for him with "Smilin' Jack" below pilot-side window. Promoted to major on June 1. Assigned to 4th Bomb Squadron Detachment at Chihkiang in August 1945. Released from 3rd Squadron on September 27; transferred to Air Force Liaison Detachment. Signed the squadron's final morning report same date, as well as final historical report. Later assigned to China Air Mission after war ended to continue training China's airmen. Wood's list: "442 West 23rd Street, Houston, Texas." Married Lillian Lee Bragg on June 10, 1946, in Houston; his address same as Wood's list and hers 136 Tillman Cir., Goldsville, SC; parents of a daughter born while he was in China; divorced soon afterward. In 1950, enumerated on April 19 with Joyce M. Blackwell, "lodger," address 507½ S. 2nd St., #3, Las Vegas, NV, his occupation dealer, gambling club. She was granted divorce from E. W. Blackwell on April 18; granted marriage license on same date as census. Married Joyce Melvin (Ward) Blackwell soon afterward (date not found) in Las Vegas, NV; parents of three sons and a daughter. Reenlisted on March 25, 1951, for Korean War. In Roswell, NM, in 1951; Tucson, AZ, in mid-1950s; Izmir, Turkey, in 1958; and Rhein Main AFB, Germany, in 1959. Commander of 12th Bomb Squadron, 341st Bomb Wing, 15th Air Force, at Dyess Air Force Base, Abilene, in 1960; rank lieutenant colonel. Enrolled in Texas Tech under the USAF Institute of Technology program to study engineering as part of a program to educate experienced officers to fill critical duty assignment. Received bachelor of science degree in industrial engineering; also majored in mathematics with emphasis on statistics. Awarded Air Force Commendation Medal in 1961; cited for direction of planning and briefing of the B-47 Unit Simulated Combat Mission for which the wing received the highest score ever made in the Strategic Air Command by a B-47 unit. Received master of science degree in industrial engineering (in absentia) at Texas Tech in May 1964 (home address "Houston"); thesis titled "An Approximation of the Cumulative Binomial Probability Distribution." Served in Vietnam War; retired as a colonel. Awarded the Distinguished Flying Cross, the Air Medal with eight OLCs, six battle stars, a Presidential Citation, two Air Force Commendation Medals, and several other decorations. Credited with 400 aerial combat hours at retirement. Lived in Houston, TX; Mesa, AZ; and Cañon City and Colorado Springs, CO. In 1976, address shown as 2503 Fairmount St., Colorado Springs, per city directory. Died September 13, 1979, in Colorado Springs. Buried at Ft. Logan National Cemetery, Denver, CO.

HANRAHAN, John Patrick, MSgt. (serial #31119067)

Born May 1, 1912, in Providence, RI. Son of Patrick Egan and Mary (O'Reilly) Hanrahan, immigrants from County Clare, Ireland. In 1930, enumerated with parents, a brother, two sisters, and a brother-in-law, 43 Lincoln St., Cranston, RI, attending school. Graduated from Cranston High School in 1930 and from Providence College in 1934. Employed in 1935 as a stockman in a department store, same address. In 1940, with parents, two sisters, and a brother, same address, completed four years of college, occupation civil engineer. Registered for the draft on October 16, 1940, in Cranston, same address, employer Midair Construction Co. (blue eyes, brown hair, light complexion, 6'1", 165#). Married Mabelle G. Perry about 1942; parents of a son and a daughter. Their address 95 Daboll, Providence, his occupation chauffeur for Crahan Engraving Co. Enlisted May 5, 1942, in Boston, MA, as a private, occupation salesman (6', 135#). Arrived at Karachi on July 24, 1943. Attached to USAAF OTU at Malir on August 1. Placed on flying status September 1 and October 1. Attached to 2nd Bomb Squadron on October 9; arrived at Kunming on October 18. Credited with shooting down a Japanese bomber in January 1944. Transferred to 3rd Squadron on March 2, as AAF radio operator. Reclassified to communications chief on March 21. Promoted to master sergeant on November 1. Interviewed at Christmas 1944 on NBC's *Coast to Coast Army Hour*. Flew forty-two combat missions. Awarded Distinguished Flying Cross, Air Medal with OLC, and Bronze Star. Received orders to return to US on April 24, 1945. Wood's list: "124 A. Street, Lowell, Mass. [marked out]; 31 Ausdale Rd., Cranston 10 R.I. [written above]." Released from service October 21, 1945. In 1945–46, lived with parents and three siblings, address 1234 Elmwood Ave., Providence, RI, single, employer US Air Corps. In 1950, with wife and a son, same address as Wood's list, occupation bartender. Worked at Hanrahan's City Line Tap (family owned and operated). Member of 14th Air Force Assoc., VFW, and DAV. Resident of Providence, RI, for forty-five years. Employed as a clerk for US Postal service for twenty years, the last five at Brown University. Contributed to Carl Molesworth's *Wing to Wing: Air Combat in China, 1943–45* (history of the CACW). Died January 13, 1993. Buried at Saint Ann's Cemetery, Cranston.

HARTUNG, Walter Edward ("Wally"), TSgt. (serial #36049962)

Born October 8, 1913, in Edwardsville, IL. Son of Louis Herman and Caroline ("Lena") B. (Wiegers) Hartung. In 1930, enumerated with parents, two brothers, and a sister, 119 South Main, Edwardsville, attending school. In 1940, lived with parents, three brothers, and a sister, address 419 Center St., Edwardsville, completed four years of high school, occupation machinist for a petroleum company (another source says boiler operator at a petroleum refinery). Registered for the draft on October 16, 1940, at Edwardsville, same address as census, employer Shell Oil Co., Roxana, IL (blue eyes, blonde hair, light complexion, 5'10½", 157#). Enlisted September 25, 1941, at Chicago, IL, as a private, unskilled occupation in refining petroleum (5'10", 155#); inducted following day. Stationed at Fort Francis, E. Warren, WY;

Perrin Field, Sherman, TX; Camp Lee, VA; Camp Grant, IL; and Garden City, KS. Had appendectomy at Fort Francis in November 1941. At Garden City, attended basic flying school in July 1943; hospitalized for injured knee in late January 1944; had surgery to repair torn cartilage in left knee in April 1944. Transferred to 1st Bomb Group in March 1945 and to 3rd Squadron as a quartermaster supply technician on April 30, 1945 (effective April 1). Released from 3rd Squadron on September 27; transferred to 1st Bomb Group, Air Force Liaison Detachment, Det. Hq. Sqdn., 14th Air Force. Promoted to technical sergeant in October. Arrived in Tacoma, WA, aboard SS *Alderamin* on January 3, 1946. Released from service January 14, 1946, at Jefferson Barracks, MO; in service four years and three months. Wood's list: "419 Center Street, Edwardsville, Illinois." Received three Bronze Stars and the China Defensive and China Offensive campaign ribbons. In 1950, with parents and two brothers, same address, occupation operating engineer, oil refinery. Employed as operating engineer for Shell Oil Co. in Roxana, later Wood River. Married Helen Augusta Erbacher on May 6, 1956, in Manhattan, KS; parents of a daughter and a son. Their address 235 Crane, Edwardsville, IL. Later lived in Granite City, IL, and St. Louis, MO. Died May 20, 1973, in Granite City. Buried at Jefferson Barracks National Cemetery, Oakville, MO.

HINRICHS, John Christoph Ehringhaus ("Jack"), Jr., Capt. (serial #0-908135)

Born September 6, 1907, in Brooklyn, NY. Son of John C. E. and Isabelle (Erenburg) Hinrichs. Moved to Davenport, IA, about 1920. Graduated from Brown University, Providence, RI, in 1929. Member of Beta Theta Pi fraternity. Married Grace Olla Gamber in about 1929; parents of two sons. In 1930, enumerated with wife, address 640 Williams S., New London, CT, occupation salesman for a motor truck company. Not found in 1940 census. Registered for the draft on October 16, 1940, at Waterford, CT, address 2 Quaker Ln., Quaker Hill, Box 151, CT, employer Mack Motor Truck Co., Hartford (hazel eyes, brown hair, ruddy complexion, 5'11½", 235#). Served in Connecticut State Guard in May 1941. Promoted to captain of State Guard, Company I, at activation and appointed officer-in-charge of the New London State Armory. Occupation zone manager for Mack Motor Truck Company at Hartford, Connecticut branch. Resigned from the Connecticut Guard; accepted a direct commission as 1st lieutenant in the Air Forces in April 1941 and stationed at Chanute Field. Transferred to basic training center at St. Petersburg, FL; promoted to captain. Reported for duty at HQ 2nd Staging Squadron, Floridian Hotel, Miami Beach, FL, and attached to 1st Bomb Group on July 21, 1943. Attached to USAAF OTU at Malir on August 3, 1943. Attached to 2nd Bomb Squadron; arrived at Kunming on October 14. Served as 1st Bomb Group materiel, utilities, transportation, and mess officer in late 1943; later as engineering and technical inspector. Joined 3rd Squadron on March 1, 1944, from 2nd Bomb Squadron as supply officer. Designed the 3rd Squadron's "Spray and Pray" insignia. Transferred to CACW HQ on October 18. Ordered to Yangkai on August 24, 1945, for transport home. Wood's list: "Quaker Hill, Conn." Not found in 1950 census. Promoted to lieutenant colonel in Air Force Reserve during Korean War. Commanding officer of the 309th Transportation Truck Battalion, USA Reserves, in 1951. President of both Norwesco Machinery Distributors, Inc. (Mack distributor for northwestern Connecticut), and Equipment Lease and Sales Corporation; lived in Middlebury, CT. Business destroyed in 1955 flood; later employed by several corporations as leasing and sales engineer and consultant. Died December 11, 1967, in Waterbury, CT; residence Bristol Estates, Middlebury. (Military records list him as "Jr.," but he was actually III.)

HODGES, Raymond Lafayette ("Junior," "Ray," "Ponza," "Hodge"), Jr., Capt. (serial #14024149; later #0-433197)

Born May 3, 1919, in Randolph County, AL. Only child of Raymond L. and Evie Lee (Green) Hodges. In 1930, enumerated with parents, 114 LaFayette St., Roanoke, AL, attending school. Graduated from Handley High School, Roanoke. In 1940, "Junior" Hodges lived with parents, address 315 N. Main St., Roanoke, completed two years of college, occupation bookkeeper for Standard Oil Co. Graduated from Georgia Military College, Milledgeville, GA. Enlisted in Air Corps on September 19, 1940, at Fort McPherson, Atlanta, GA, as a private (5'7", 152#); in mechanical department at Maxwell Field, Montgomery, AL. Began preflight training as member of Class 42-A at Mississippi Institute of Aeronautics at Jackson, MS, on June 4, 1941. Completed Basic Flying School at Gunter Field, Montgomery, AL, on August 17, 1941, followed by advanced training in bombardment flying at Barksdale Field, Shreveport, LA, where he graduated and was commissioned 2nd lieutenant in January 1942. Called to active duty on January 2, 1942. Served as a test pilot at AAF Proving Grounds, Eglin Field, FL; worked on development of the P-61 Black Widow night fighter and over fifty other new aircraft, including Navy and foreign planes. Promoted to 1st lieutenant in June 1942. Arrived at Karachi aboard USS *Mission Bay* on March 29, 1944. Assigned to 3rd Squadron as a B-25 pilot / flight leader on April 4. Survived a crash during a test flight on June 4. Released from 3rd Squadron on September 6 and transferred to 1st Bomb Squadron. In November 1944, awarded Air Medal for combat missions flown earlier in Burma and the Southwest Pacific; also awarded the Distinguished Flying Cross for a mission against the Yellow River Bridge in late October. Promoted to major and given command of 1st Bomb Squadron on December 29, 1944. Wood's list: "315 North Main Street, Roanoke, Alabama." Awarded two more DFCs, another Air Medal, the Silver Star, and the Chiang Kai-shek Medal, per obituary. Returned to US before end of the war and reported to Greensboro, NC, in about July 1945 for reassignment. Released from service on December 30, 1945. Married Eleanor Manley on November 22, 1947, in Decatur, GA; parents of two sons and two daughters. Registered for Selective Service with Local Draft Board No. 56, Randolph, AL, in July 1948. Became chairman of local draft board in August 1948. In 1950, with parents, wife, and infant daughter, no address, West Point St., Roanoke, occupation assistant agent, oil company. Operated a business that conducted aerial inspection of pipelines for oil companies in Alaska. Maintained contact with Tu Kai-mu for a number of years. Contributed to Ken Daniels's *China Bombers: The Chinese-American Composite Wing in WWII* (history of the 1st Bomb Squadron). Died November 6, 2008, in Randolph County, AL. Buried at Cedarwood Cemetery, Roanoke.

HOKE, Isadore Franklin ("Frank"), SSgt. (serial #33014179)

Born August 25, 1918, Lewistown, PA. Son of Franklin and Della Grace (Reisinger) Hoke; father was Jewish German immigrant. In 1930, enumerated with parents and five brothers, no address but not a farm, Sugar Run Valley Road, Tuscarora, PA, attending school. In 1940, lived with parents and four brothers on Buckwheat Road, Tuscarora, completed one year of high school, occupation laborer on family farm. Registered for the draft on October 16, 1940, residence RD1, Millerstown, PA; unemployed (blue eyes, brown hair, ruddy complexion, 5'11", 156#). Sent with brother Wayne to Pennsylvania Industrial Reformatory at Huntingdon, PA, in February 1941 for stealing equipment and machinery from the Susquehanna River Coal Company and selling it to scrap-iron dealers. Enlisted on April 10, 1942, at Harrisburg,

PA, as a private (blue eyes, brown hair, ruddy complexion, 5'11", 145#); inducted same date at New Cumberland, PA. Received basic training at Keesler Field, Biloxi, MS; transferred to Lowry Field, Denver, in June 1942. Received additional training at Bendix Air Line School, South Bend, IN; graduated with the second-highest honor in his class. In "a bomb training squad" at Roswell, NM, in May 1943. At Kearns, UT, in June to receive overseas training and await orders. Attached to 853rd Engineering Battalion, Aviation Corps of Engineering; departed US for North Africa on October 2, 1943. Wounded (contusions of thorax) but survived sinking of HMS *Rohna* by Luftwaffe on November 26, 1943; welfare inquiry by National Jewish Welfare Board, Bureau of War Records, on January 24, 1944; awarded Purple Heart. After recovery, again sent on his way to CBI. Date he joined 3rd Squadron undetermined, but before move to Moran. Promoted to sergeant on June 1 and to staff sergeant on November 1. Noted as gun turret specialist and aerial gunner in April 1945, although he was not listed on aircrews. Sent to rest camp at Chengtu on July 1. Released from 3rd Squadron on August 27 and sent to Yangkai; transferred to 22nd Bomb Squadron, 341st Bomb Group, as turret gun specialist for transport home. Arrived in New York aboard USS *General Charles H. Muir* on November 1. Released from service on November 5, 1945, at Indiantown Gap, PA. Wood's list: "RD #2, Newport, Pa." Married Bertha Mae Gipe on December 31, 1945; residence of both recorded as East Newport, PA; parents of a daughter. In February 1950, compensation approved by Commonwealth of Pennsylvania for $180 for eighteen months of active domestic service and $320 for twenty-five months of active foreign service; address 506 S. 3rd St., Newport, PA. In 1950 census, enumerated in April with wife and daughter, no address, Oliver, PA, occupation machine operator, SnapOn Tools. Employed as an auto mechanic by State Garage, Newport, in early 1960s. Died on November 5, 1965; cause, coronary occlusion. Buried at Newport Cemetery, Newport.

HOLMES, Jack (NMI), TSgt. (serial #39682273)

Born August 22, 1919, at Hocking, IA. Son of John George and Elsie (Harwood) Holmes, English immigrants. In 1930, enumerated with parents, a brother, and a sister, 48 Consolidated Coal Camp, Williamson, IA, attending school. Graduated from Clariton High School, Williamson, in 1937. Moved with parents to Kenilworth, UT, soon afterward. In 1940, lived with parents and younger brother, address "31, Row 2 south of school," Kenilworth, occupation "bony picker" in a coal mine (a *boney* picker separated out bits of slate, rock, etc. from coal before it was weighed). Completed one year at Price Junior College. Registered for the draft on October 16, 1940, occupation Slack Plant Operator, Independent Coal & Coke Co., Ft. Douglas, UT (blue eyes, brown hair, light complexion, 5'11" 145#, "small finger on left hand has been broken"). Inducted on February 19, 1942, as a private. At USAAF technical training command, Atlantic City, NJ; promoted to sergeant in late January 1943. Awarded Good Conduct Medal in June. Departed US on July 19, 1943; arrived at Karachi on July 29. Attached to USAAF OTU at Malir on August 1. Attached to 2nd Bomb Squadron on October 9; arrived at Kunming on October 18. Joined 3rd Squadron on March 1, 1944, as supply NCO. Reclassified to crew chief on March 21. Promoted to technical sergeant on June 1, 1945. Assigned to 4th Bomb Squadron detachment at Chihkiang in August. Awarded Air Medal on September 19. Released from 3rd Squadron on August 27 and sent to Yangkai; transferred to 22nd Bomb Squadron, 341st Bomb Group, for transport home. Arrived in New York aboard USS *General Charles H. Muir* on November 1, 1945. Wood's list: "Kenilworth, Utah." Released from service November 9, 1945. Reenlisted on

May 21, 1946, as staff sergeant at Salt Lake City. Married Ann E. King on February 15, 1947, in Reno, NV; parents of two sons. Employed at Hill Air Force Base as a clerk; played on baseball and basketball teams. Played in semipros for Pinney Beverage in 1948. In 1950, with wife and son, address 477 3rd South, Salt Lake City, occupation parts man, automotive supply. At Hill AFB in mid-1970s. Died June 29, 1990, in Salt Lake City; residence 344 Garfield Ave.; cause, pulmonary emphysema and atheroschlerotic cardiovascular disease. Buried at Mountain View Memorial Estates, Salt Lake City.

HOYLE, Charlie Halson, Jr., TSgt. (serial #34263920)
Born October 5, 1919, in Elmore, AL. Son of Charlie H. and Martha ("Mattie") E. (Macon) Hoyle. In 1930, enumerated with parents, a brother, three sisters, and a brother-in-law, no house number, Dubois St., Tallassee, AL. Completed four years of high school. In 1940, lived with parents and a younger brother, address 10 Jones St., Tallassee, completed eleven years of school, occupation laborer in a cotton mill. Registered for the draft on October 16, 1940, employer Tallassee Mills, Tallassee (gray eyes, black hair, ruddy complexion, 6'2", 150#). Date of enlistment not determined. At Fort Benning, GA, in 1943. Arrived at Karachi on July 28, 1943. Attached to USAAF OTU at Malir on August 1, 1943. Placed on flying status September 1 and October 1. Promoted to sergeant on October 1. Attached to 2nd Bomb Squadron on October 9. Arrived at Kunming on October 18. Joined 3rd Squadron on March 2, 1944, as A/P armorer. Reclassified to armament chief on March 21. Promoted to staff sergeant on April 1 and to technical sergeant on August 1. Hospitalized for corneal ulcer in September. Detached to Task Force 34 from December 4, 1944, to January 14, 1945. On detached service to Chihkiang in February. Awarded Bronze Star and Air Medal on April 18, 1945, for flying twenty-nine combat missions; also awarded Asiatic-Pacific ribbon with one battle star. Began his return to US on May 16. Wood's list: "1 James Street, Tallassee, Alabama." Promoted to master sergeant, date undetermined. Married Nellie Mae Anderson on January 18, 1946, at Elmore, AL; parents of three sons and one daughter. In 1950, with wife and a son, address 123 First Ave., Lee, AL, occupation "loom fixer," textile mill. In Marietta, GA, in 1960s. Died May 16, 1985, in Opelika, AL. Buried at Rose Hill Cemetery, Tallassee.

HUGEL, Robert George ("Bob"), Cpl. (serial #32979860)
Born April 8, 1925, in Bronx, NY. Son of George A. and Mable E. (Larsen) Hugel. In 1930, enumerated with parents and younger brother, A.D. 2, Block No. E, Bronx, not attending school. In 1940, lived with parents and two younger brothers, 231 East 435 St., Bronx, attending school, completed two years of high school. Enlisted in Co. C, 5th Regiment, New York Guard, on December 4, 1942; dropped on September 2, 1943, because of failure to attend drills. Registered for the draft on April 8, 1943 (his eighteenth birthday), Bronx, address same as census, "employer" Evander Childs H.S. (blue eyes, brown hair, light complexion, 5'11", 150#). Enlistment and training records not found. Joined 3rd Squadron on December 28, 1944, as A/P armorer-gunner. On detached service to Nimrod Detachment at Laohokow in March 1945. Reported as MIA on May 27; returned to duty. Kept a diary of experiences during walkout. Sent to rest camp at Chengtu on July 1. Released from 3rd Squadron on August 27 and sent to Yangkai for transport home. Wood's list: "231 East 235 Street, New York City, N.Y." Graduated from Rider College, Trenton, NJ, in 1949 with bachelor of science degree in business administration. Worked with his family's insurance agency, Sentinel Insurance Agency, in NYC. Married Audrey Bell on August 27, 1949; parents of two sons

and a daughter. In 1950, with wife, address same as 1940 census, occupation underwriter, insurance company. Later employed by the insurance department of General Telephone before moving to Connecticut in 1964; became insurance manager for Pratt & Whitney Aircraft. Retired as assistant treasurer / risk manager from United Technologies in 1988. Lived in New York City, Southampton, and Chrystal Lake, NY, and Simsbury and Avon, CT. Contributed to this squadron history. Died October 19, 2016. Buried at Evergreen Cemetery, Avon. (Name often appears as "George Robert Hugel" in civil records.)

HUTCHINSON, Otto Wilson, SSgt. (serial #14054272)
Born May 23, 1918, in Collins, AR. Son of Allen Sylvester and Willie Ivy (Newton) Hutchinson. Lived in Tallahatchie, MS, in 1920. In 1930, enumerated with parents, a brother, and two sisters on a cotton farm, Smith Road, Beat 4, Bolivar County, MS. In 1940, lived with parents and younger sister on family farm in rural Sunflower, MS, completed four years of high school, occupation unpaid farm laborer. Registered for the draft on October 19, 1940, address RFD Drew, MS, self-employed (dark-brown eyes, black hair, ruddy complexion, 5'9", 140#). Enlisted in Air Corps on July 8, 1941, at Jackson, MS, as a private, residence Tallahatchie, occupation farm hand (5'10", 134#). Stationed at Columbus, MS, and Blytheville, AR. Married Joy Alice Smith at Blytheville; parents of a son and a daughter. Arrived at Calcutta aboard USS *Robert E. Callan* on April 27, 1945. Attached to 1st Bomb Group as A/P mechanic in May and to 3rd Squadron on June 7, 1945. Released from 3rd Squadron on September 1; transferred to 26th Fighter Squadron, 51st Fighter Group, for transport home. Arrived in Tacoma, WA, aboard SS *Marine Angel* on December 12, 1945. Wood's list: "220 North Long Street, Aberdeen, Miss." Reenlisted in Air Force Reserve and served September 16, 1946, to September 15, 1949. In 1950, with wife and daughter, no address, Monroe, MS, occupation carpenter, building industry. Later lived in Mission, TX, employed at McAllen AFB as an A/P mechanic, and in Birmingham, AL, as a mechanic at Hayes Aircraft. Worked on transmissions for Mack Truck until retirement. Member of Dolcita Masonic Lodge. Died September 22, 1993. Buried at Center Hill Baptist Church Cemetery, Hamilton, MS.

ILEFELDT, Willard Garcia ("Tex"), Capt. (serial #31032361; later #0-1295220)
Born February 22, 1917, in Cooper, TX. Son of George Herman and Grace Helen Victoria (Schlichting) Ilefeldt; father was a German immigrant. In 1920, "Willard Ihlefeldt" was enumerated with parents and younger sister at State Orphan's Home, Navarro County, TX, where his father was a mechanical engineer who also sang opera. After death of his father from diabetes in Corsicana later that year, moved with family to Boston, MA. In 1930, "Willard Schlichting" lived with maternal grandmother and mother (both widowed), address 125 Fisher Ave., Boston, attending school. Received specialized training to overcome dyslexia at prompting of his grandmother. Graduated from Boston High School of Commerce in June 1935. Later attended New England Conservatory of Music and Leland Powers Acting School for four years. Sang with dance bands, played in summer stock, and wrote plays. Not found in 1940 census. Registered for the draft on October 16, 1940, in Boston, address 501 Beacon St., occupation playwright (blue eyes, brown hair, light-brown complexion, 6', 150#). Enlisted on March 21, 1941, in Boston as a private, completed four years college, occupation actor (6', 143#). Served in the 26th Infantry Division, Massachusetts National Guard; transferred to Air Corps and trained as a pilot. Married Ellen Martha Clancy (a film actress; screen name Janet Shaw) on April 19, 1944, in Beverly Vista (Los Angeles), CA. Joined 3rd Squadron on

November 21, 1944, as a B-25 pilot. Appointed flight leader on November 29. On detached service to Wenkiang / rest camp on December 12. Appointed squadron historical officer on January 1, 1945. Promoted to captain. Assigned to 4th Bomb Squadron detachment at Chihkiang in August. Flew thirty-six combat missions. Released from 3rd Squadron on September 5 and sent to Yangkai; transferred to 341st Bomb Group for transport home. Arrived in New York aboard USS *General Charles H. Muir* on November 1, 1945. Wood's list: "141 South Oakhurst Drive, Beverly Hills, California." Divorced in early 1946; address 501 Beacon, Boston (his mother's address). Married Louise Syminton in Los Angeles on May 30, 1947 (both members of "Nine O'Clock Players" little theater group); parents of a son and a daughter. In 1950, with wife, a son, and a daughter, address 1212 Orange Grove Ave., South Pasadena, CA, occupation plastic salesman, plastic novelties. Studied for the ministry and ordained an Episcopal priest in 1961, residence La Mirada, CA. Earned a doctorate in pastoral counseling at Claremont School of Theology in 1969; thesis and dissertation "The Absent Father." Practiced in Orange County until retirement to Sky Ranch in Carmel Valley. Raised sheep and wrote memoir, *Thoughts While Tending Sheep*, published in 1988. Moved to Hacienda Carmel in 1991. Died May 23, 2010. Buried at San Gabriel Cemetery, San Gabriel, California. (Surname sometimes appears as "Ilefeld" in early records.)

JACKSON, Lloyd Earl, Jr., Sgt. (serial #18160468)

Born September 21, 1923, in Pittsburgh, PA. Son of Lloyd E. and Hazel M. (Day) Jackson (later divorced). In 1930, enumerated with parents, older brother, and three lodgers, Haddon Hall Hotel, Centre Avenue, Pittsburgh. Parents divorced in 1934. Moved to Tulsa, OK, between 1935 and 1940. In 1940, lived with mother and brother, address 232 W. 9th St., Tulsa, completed three years of high school, attending school. Graduated from Central High School, Tulsa. Registered for the draft on June 29, 1942; address 912 South Denver, Tulsa; employed by Student Window Cleaners, Tulsa Loan Bldg. (brown eyes, brown hair, ruddy complexion, 5'8½", 135#, "Scar on calf of left leg"). Attended University of Tulsa. Enlisted in Air Corps in Tulsa on September 1, 1942, as a private, completed one year of college, occupation general office clerk (5'9", 128#). Stationed at Sheppard Field, Wichita Falls, TX. Married Eleanor Beatrice Bacon in Wichita Falls on November 29, 1942; parents of a daughter and a son. Later stationed at Tampa, FL; Bossier City, LA; and Goldsboro, NC. Arrived at Karachi aboard USS *Mission Bay* on March 29, 1944. Assigned to 3rd Squadron as instrument specialist on April 3. Promoted to corporal on June 1. On detached service with Task Force 34 at Chihkiang. Promoted to sergeant on December 1. Mentioned as crew chief in January 1945. At rest camp at Chengtu April 26–May 5. On detached service to Chihkiang June 18–21. In hospital at Chengtu July 4–9. Assigned to 4th Bomb Squadron detachment at Chihkiang in August 1945. Released from 3rd Squadron on September 1; transferred to 26th Fighter Squadron, 51st Fighter Group, for transport home. Arrived in Tacoma, WA, aboard SS *Marine Angel* on December 12, 1945. Wood's list: "1615 South Florence Place, Tulsa, Okla. [crossed out], 1406 NE 38 79673 [written beside]." Discharged November 10, 1945. Graduated May 30, 1949, from Tulsa University with a bachelor of science degree in aeronautical engineering. In 1950, with wife and daughter, address 114 NW 14th St., Grand Prairie, TX, occupation aerodynacist engineer, airplane factory. Later received a master of science degree in engineering from Oklahoma State University. Joined North American Rockwell's Tulsa Division in 1962; played key roles in design development of the Apollo 11 Lunar Module Adapter, C-5A, and Boeing 747 as director of commercial programs. Named director of engineering in 1972 and contributed to development of the B-1 bomber and space shuttle. Retired in 1986 after a thirty-six-year career as an aerospace engineer and engineering executive, primarily with Douglas Aircraft, North American Aviation, and Rockwell International. Contributed to this squadron history. Died on November 7, 2014, in Tulsa as the result of leukemia and congestive heart failure. Buried at Memorial Park Cemetery, Tulsa.

JAKUBASZ, Frank Thomas, TSgt. (serial #31096395)

Born January 25, 1912, at Holyoke, MA. (Recorded as "Francis Jakubasz" in birth register.) Son of Thomas (Tomasz) and Mary (Marya) (Dominik) Jakubasz, Austro-Polish immigrants; mother died in 1923. In 1930, enumerated with widowed father, 120 Lyman St., Holyoke, laborer at a cloth mill. In 1940, with father and a sister at 22 Elm St., Holyoke, completed four years of high school, occupation weaver, textile manufacturing. Later became an inspector. Registered for the draft on October 16, 1940, at Holyoke, residence same as census [marked out], 68 Newton St. [written above], employer Livingston Worsted Mills, Race and South Streets (brown eyes, black hair, light-brown complexion, 5'9", 160#). Enlisted on April 6, 1942, at Springfield, MA, as a private, occupation cook (5'8", 100#). One of first to receive basic training at Miami Beach, FL. Mechanic at Gunter Field, AL, from mid-May 1942. Promoted to corporal on October 1, 1942. Arrived at Karachi on July 29, 1943. Attached to USAAF OTU at Malir on August 1. Placed on flying status September 1 and October 1. Attached to 2nd Bomb Squadron on October 9. Arrived at Kunming on October 16. Joined 3rd Squadron as A/P crew chief on March 4, 1944. Reclassified to flight chief on March 21. Promoted to staff sergeant on April 1 and to technical sergeant on September 1, 1944. At Chengtu rest camp April 26–May 5, 1945. Departed for US on June 22, 1945. Wood's list: "68 Newton Street, Holyoke, Mass." Discharged October 2, 1945. Awarded Bronze Star. Married Alice E. Bonney in 1948 at Metheun, MA; parents of a son and two daughters. At same address, occupation "sampler" at LWM, Inc., in early 1950. In April 1950, with wife, address 152 Merrimac, Methuen, MA, occupation weaver, woolen mill. Worked as linotype operator for the *Boston Globe* for twenty-three years until retirement. Died October 21, 2007; cause, "heart failure." Buried at Atkinson New Cemetery, Atkinson, NH.

JEFFRIES, Charles Webb, 1Lt. (serial #0-493372)

Born October 27, 1915, in Purdy, MO. Son of Norris Chester and Effie H. (Adams) Jeffries; mother died in 1917 and father enlisted in US Navy. In 1920, enumerated with paternal grandparents, Charles B. and Ida (Tucker) Jeffries, on a farm near Butterfield, MO. In 1930, "Webb Jeffries" lived with grandparents, 1001 W. Moses, Cushing, OK, attending school. Later lived in Nowata, OK, working in grandfather's grocery store. In 1935, listed as "student," lived with father and stepmother, 409 SE 54th St., Oklahoma City, OK, per city directory. Graduated from Oklahoma State University, Stillwater, OK, in about 1936. Married Donna Aldeena Rankin on March 17, 1937, in Neosho, MO; no children. In 1940, lived with his wife, address Ramsey St. (no house number), Stillwater, completed three years of college, employed by Shell Oil Co. refinery. Completed summer course at Reserve Officers training camp at Camp Bullis, San Antonio, TX, in July 1941. Registered for the draft on September 2, 1941; attending Oklahoma A&M College, agriculture major, Stillwater (brown eyes, brown hair, ruddy complexion, 5'9", 160#), signed as "Webb C. Jeffries." Graduated from Oklahoma A&M, School of Agriculture, on July 31, 1942; lieutenant in the infantry reserve. Enlisted on September 26, 1943. Attached to 3rd Squadron and served as intelligence officer from early March 1945. Assigned to 4th

Bomb Squadron Detachment as intelligence officer in August 1945. Released from 3rd Squadron on September 1; transferred to 23rd Fighter Group, 68th Composite Wing, for transport home. Arrived at Tacoma, WA, aboard SS *Alderamin* on January 3, 1946. Wood's list: "Route #2, Stillwater, Oklahoma." Not found in 1950 census. Served in Korean War; promoted to captain. Lived in Bryan, TX, and on faculty at Texas A&M College in mid-1950s. Retired from USAF on January 12, 1963, as a major. Lived in Kilgore, TX, in 1985. Died on April 13, 2002, in Denison, TX. Buried at Dallas–Ft. Worth National Cemetery, Dallas, TX.

JOHNSON, Paul Raymond, SSgt. (serial #42026160)

Born August 21, 1925, in Jamestown, NY. Son of Johan (John) Albert and Anne Andersdotter (Berg) Johnson (Johanson), Swedish immigrants. Baptized on January 5, 1927, at First Covenant (Swedish Mission) Church, Jamestown. In 1930, enumerated with parents and an older brother and sister, 236 Clyde Ave., Jamestown, not attending school. In 1940, at same address with widowed mother, completed one year of high school. Graduated from Jamestown High School in 1943. Employed by Lafayette Press, Inc., as an administrative clerk. Enlisted in Co. E, 74th Regiment, New York Guard, on June 28, 1943; address 1117 Newland Ave., Jamestown. Registered for the draft on August 21, 1943 (his eighteenth birthday), at Jamestown, same address, employer Lafayette Press (blue eyes, blonde hair, light complexion, 5'8", 123#). Enlisted in Air Corps on December 19, 1943, at Fort Dix, as a private (height and weight "00, 606"); inducted on February 3, 1944. Stationed at MacDill Field before being sent to CBI; departed US on December 19, 1944; arrived January 23, 1945. Promoted to corporal in May 1945; at 1st Bomb Group HQ as "understudy typist." ASR score 40 on September 2, 1945. Transferred to 3rd Squadron on September 7 as clerk typist. Not included in Wood's list but mentioned as sergeant in July/August squadron historical report (perhaps its typist). Released from 3rd Squadron on September 27; transferred to Air Force Liaison Detachment. Reclassified as administrative specialist. Departed for US May 17, 1946; arrived May 30. Discharged as staff sergeant on June 8, 1946, at Fort Dix, NJ; blue eyes, blonde hair, 5'8", 140#). Awarded the Marksmanship Medal, Good Conduct Medal, Asiatic-Pacific Theater Ribbon, two Bronze Battle Stars, American Theater Ribbon, WWII Victory Medal, and Distinguished Unit Badge. Married Betty Marie Lundin on October 15, 1949, in Jamestown; parents of three sons and two daughters. In 1950, with wife, address 869 Spring St. ("1 floor R"), Jamestown, occupation pressman, commercial printing. Employed as an offset pressman, primarily for Journal Press, Inc., in Jamestown. Moved to Lynchburg, VA, in about 2001. Died there April 4, 2014. Buried at Sunset Hill Cemetery, Lakewood, NY.

KELLER, Albert John ("Bud"), Cpl. (#37578875)

Born July 7, 1925, in Amidon, ND. Son of Johannes (John) Christ and Josephine Matilda (Koffler) Keller, Russian immigrants (mother tongue German). In 1930, enumerated with parents and three older brothers, 136 1st Avenue S. West, Dickinson, ND, not attending school. In 1940, with parents and five siblings, 304 East Broadway, Dickinson. Graduated from Dickinson High School in 1943. Registered for the draft on July 7, 1943 (his eighteenth birthday), residence 1304 N. Blissfield Rd., Palmyra, MI, "person who will always know your address" George A. Keller, employer Bohn Alum. & Brass, Adrian, MI (blue eyes, black hair, light complexion, 5'7", 124#). Enlisted October 20, 1943; original records not found. Original assignment in CBI not found. Flew twenty missions as a B-25 radio-gunner; led a truck convoy "up the Burma Road," per a postwar interview. Transferred to 3rd Squadron from

1st Bomb Group HQ as a radio mechanic on April 23, 1945. Wood's list: "327 1st Street, Dickinson, North Dakota." Released from 3rd Squadron on September 27; transferred to Air Force Liaison Detachment. Released from service May 14, 1946. Married Constance ("Connie") Eckroth on September 2, 1946, in Dickinson; parents of a daughter and two sons. In 1950, with wife and son, address 808 2nd St., Apt. 10, Bismarck, ND, occupation presser, dry-cleaning plant. Owned and operated a dry-cleaning business. Member of the American Legion. Joined the 9524th Air Force Reserve Recovery Squadron in personnel section at Bismarck, in 1962; residence Dickinson. Lived in Las Vegas, NV. Died December 21, 2002, in Pahrump, NV. Buried at St. Joseph's Catholic Cemetery, Dickinson.

KELSO, James Campbell ("Jim," "Jimmy"), Jr., Capt. (serial #11032215; later #0-559992)
Born May 21, 1917, in Stoneham, MA. Son of James C. and Jane E. (Taggart) Kelso. In 1930, enumerated with parents and older brother, 21 Parker Rd., Wakefield, MA, attending school. Graduated from Wakefield High School in 1935 and from Dartmouth College in 1939; member of Gamma Delta Chi. In 1940, lived with parents and older brother, same address, occupation salesman at a meatpacking company. Registered for the draft (no date on form), address 152 Dover Rd., W. Hartford, CT, occupation United Aircraft, Pratt and Whitney Div. (brown eyes, brown hair, sallow complexion, 5'8", 140#). Enlisted in Air Corps on April 1, 1942, as a private (occupation general office clerk, 5'8", 142#). Joined 3rd Squadron on August 16, 1944, and appointed adjutant. Ordered to rest camp at Chengtu on April 21, 1945. Released from 3rd Squadron on August 27 and sent to Yangkai; transferred to 341st Bomb Group. Returned to New York from Karachi aboard USS *General C. G. Morton* on October 22, 1945. Wood's list: "42 Emerson Street, Wakefield, Mass." Departed Westover AFB via MATS (Military Air Transport Service) on March 20, 1950, bound for London, England. Not found in 1950 census. Married Elise Marie Free on August 2, 1952, in Chevy Chase, Washington, DC; residence White Plains, NY. Employed by the State Department and Department of Defense on the munitions board, instrumental in setting up NATO. Later served as executive secretary of the New York Armed Forces Regional Council. Employed by Nationwide Insurance and Phoenix Insurance Company in 1960s. Occupation accountant, State of Connecticut Labor Dept., before retiring in 1986. Died July 25, 1998, at Hamden, CT. Cremated and ashes entombed at Dunbar United Church of Christ, Hamden.

KILIAN, Thomas Alexander ("Tom," "Alec"), 1Lt. (serial #11099006; later #0-708482)
Born December 20, 1921, at Pittsfield, MA. Son of Ernest Edward and Elizabeth Patterson (Grey) Kilian; mother a Scottish immigrant. In 1930, lived with parents and sister, 63 Taylor St., Pittsfield, attending school. Graduated from Pittsfield High School in 1939. In 1940, enumerated with parents, 88 Church St., Pittsfield, completed four years of high school, occupation "new worker." On the production staff of the tank shop at General Electric. Registered for the draft on February 16, 1942, at Pittsfield, residence 29 Meadow Ln., employer G.E. Co. (brown eyes, black hair, light complexion, 6'2", 190#, "3 Scars on Face"). Sworn in to Air Reserve on August 8, 1942. Enlisted in Air Corps from the Air Reserve on January 28, 1943, at Springfield, MA, as a private (completed four years of college, occupation clerk, 6'1", 180#). Received preflight training at Syracuse University, Syracuse, NY; basic training at Atlantic City, NJ, and North Carolina. Graduated from flight school and commissioned 2nd lieutenant at San Marcos, TX, in May 1943; received advanced training at San Antonio. Married Frances E. ("Fran") Wev on July 15, 1944, at

Columbia, SC; parents of two sons. Received navigator training at San Marcos (TX) AAF training school and bombardier training at Roswell (NM) Army Airfield. At Savannah, GA, in September 1944. Sent to the CBI in November 1944. Suffered a broken leg and was one of two survivors of a plane crash on the runway at Chihkiang on January 18, 1945; reported as KIA in his hometown newspaper. Joined 3rd Squadron from 11th Bomb Squadron on March 23 as navigator. On detached service to 2nd Bomb Squadron in early May; transferred to 2nd Bomb Squadron on May 24. Crash-landed again on May 21 near Wanhsien but was unhurt. Arrived in New York aboard USS *General Charles H. Muir* on November 1, 1945. Not included in Wood's list but resided at 29 Meadow Ln., Pittsfield (his parents' address) per newspaper article. Awarded Distinguished Flying Cross with OLC, Air Medal, Purple Heart, Asiatic Pacific Theater Ribbon with two battle stars, American Theater Ribbon, Victory Medal, Distinguished Unit Citation with OLC, and the Chinese Star of Honor awarded by the Chinese government. Promoted to 1st lieutenant; assigned to 157th Fighter Squadron in National Guard at Columbia, SC, in June 1947. In 1950, with wife and a son, address 13 Luther St., Warminster, PA, occupation student (marked out), no occupation (written beside). Attended University of South Carolina, Columbia, and Pennsylvania State College of Optometry, Philadelphia, PA. Lived in Charleston, SC; occupation optometrist. Died on September 5, 1975, from a massive hemorrhage during attempted aortocoronary artery bypass surgery at St. Luke's Hospital, Houston, TX. Buried at Live Oak Memorial Gardens, Charleston, SC.

KING, James Lyon ("Jim," "Doc"), Capt. (serial #0-485752)
Born May 23, 1916, in Troy, SC. Son of Samuel Jones and Maud (Lyon) King. In 1930, with parents and sister on a farm, Plum Branch, SC, attending school. Graduated from University of South Carolina; graduated from the Medical College of South Carolina, Charleston, in May 1939. Interned at Baker Sanitorium, Charleston. In 1940, enumerated as intern at Columbia Hospital at Columbia, SC. Married Helen Morrow on August 27, 1940, in Columbia; parents of a son. Registered for the draft on October 16, 1940, in Florence, SC, address Saunders Memorial Hospital, Florence (marked out), Manning, SC (written above), employer Dr. J. D. Smyser, Saunders Memorial Hospital (brown eyes, brown hair, dark complexion, 5'11½", 157#, "Has a moustache"). Enlisted in US Army in August 1942. Served with the Army Transport Command in Alaska before beginning tour of duty in CBI. Arrived at Karachi aboard USS *Mission Bay* on March 29, 1944. Attached to 1st Bomb Group HQ on April 3 as flight surgeon. Attached from 5th Fighter Group to 3rd Squadron in early July. Released from 3rd Squadron on August 22; transferred back to 5th Fighter Group HQ. Ordered to Yangkai on August 24, 1945, for transport home. Arrived in New York aboard USS *General Tasker H. Bliss* on October 23. Wood's list: "Plum Branch, South Carolina." In 1950, with wife and son, address 39 Earlwood, Eau Claire, SC, occupation physician, medical practice. Married Flora ("Flo") May (Boyle) Swinford from Townsville, Queensland, Australia, mother of two sons and two daughters. In private practice at Columbia for forty-five years; continued practice from home, 213 Old Edgefield Road, Plum Branch, until his death. Died June 27, 2002, at home in Plum Branch. Buried at Troy Cemetery, Troy, SC.

KOSS, Robert James ("Bob"), 1Lt. (serial #36018082; later #0-733202)
Born March 26, 1919, in Tire Hill, PA. Son of George and Anna E. (Gracner) Koss, Slovenian immigrants to US in 1904. Youngest of ten children; father died in February before he was

born. In 1920, enumerated with mother (naturalized in 1915), five brothers, and four sisters in Conemaugh, PA. Moved to Chicago, IL, after family farm and store were lost during the Depression. Attended Warren grade school; graduated from Bowen High School on Chicago's South Side. In 1938, address 9037 Kingston Ave., Chicago; president of the Alumni Club. In 1940, enumerated in household of brother Louis, with mother and brother Joseph, same address as previous, no occupation. Graduated from Woodrow Wilson Junior College in June 1940. Registered for the draft on October 16, 1940, in Chicago, address 1615 E. 85th St., employer Carnegie Illinois Steel Co., Chicago (gray eyes, brown hair, light-brown complexion, 5'10", 180#). Employed as "personnel man" at Carnegie's South Works. Completed three years of college and worked as an office clerk. Enlisted April 9, 1941, in Chicago as a private (5'9", 183#). Served in infantry for a year; accepted as aviation cadet in Air Corps and began training at Santa Ana, CA. Received navigator's wings at Roswell, NM. Attached to the 378th Bombardment Squadron (Medium), 309th Bombardment Group, at Columbia Army Air Base in early 1944 to train B-25 pilots and aircrews prior to their assignment to combat units overseas. When offered another US training assignment in May 1944, declined because he wanted to be in the action. Sent to the CBI and trained Chinese airmen at Karachi. Received orders to China in late December 1944. Joined 3rd Squadron from 17th Fighter Squadron on January 17, 1945, as a navigator. Led a detail for change of station from Peishiyi to Liangshan. On mission that clipped a building at Hsiangcheng on March 8, 1945. Crash-landed near Valley Field on March 30 but returned safely. Completed twenty-six missions. Killed in action on May 16, 1945. Not included in Wood's list; next of kin (his mother) 1625 N. 29th Street, Chicago, IL. Posthumously awarded Purple Heart. Buried at Grandview Cemetery, Johnstown, PA, in 1949. (Surname appears as *Koss* in military records, sometimes *Kos* in civil records. His parents added second "S" because people often mispronounced the name.)

LANGRIDGE, Joseph Antonio ("Joe"), Capt. (serial #0-314586)
Born October 22, 1911, in Córdoba, Veracruz, Mexico. Son of William Thomas and Mary Leonora (Antonio) Langridge; father was a law clerk working in Mexico. Evacuated during the Mexican Revolution with his family by Marine gunboat in 1914 to Corpus Christi, TX. Evacuated again because of category 4 "Hurricane 6" that hit the coast on August 18, 1916. Moved to San Antonio; lived with family at historic Menger Hotel near the Alamo in 1920. In 1930, enumerated with parents, no address, San Antonio, attending school. Attended Louisiana State University, Baton Rouge. With Co. D, Cadet Corps, received "President's Medal" in 1931 "for general excellence in military science"; 2nd lieutenant in Co. I, Cadet Corps, in October 1933. Earned bachelor's degree at LSU in 1934 and later a master's degree. In 1940, lived with parents, address 111 E. Dewey Place, San Antonio, completed four years of college, occupation "credit man" at a finance corporation. Registered for the draft on October 16, 1940, address same as census (marked out), 1822 Schley Ave. (written above), San Antonio; employer General Motors Acceptance Corp, San Antonio (brown eyes, brown hair, ruddy complexion, 6'1", 150#). Married Margaret Ellouise Carnes in San Antonio on June 28, 1941. Enlisted on July 15, 1942, from the ROTC. Had a detached retina but "cheated" on eye exam. Promoted to captain on April 6, 1944. Transferred from 2nd Bomb Squadron to 3rd Squadron on June 2, 1945, as intelligence officer. Released from 3rd Squadron on September 27; transferred to Air Force Liaison Detachment. Wood's list: "111 East Dewey Place, San Antonio, Texas." Released from service February 16, 1946. Married Minnie Nelwyn Rogers on September 17, 1947; parents of two daughters. Manager of US Department of Commerce business reference and advisory division designed to

stimulate trade with Mexico out of Corpus Christi. In September 1949, reported to Lackland AFB for duty in connection with the mobilization and training of officers; rank major. In 1950, with wife and daughter, address 1047 Alexander Hamilton, San Antonio, occupation office manager, real estate, and loan office. Employed by San Antonio Savings; elected vice president in 1960. Died October 21, 1996, at Diamond L Ranch, Comfort, Kerr County, TX. Buried at Langridge Family Cemetery, Boerne, TX.

LEARN, Clyde Leroy ("Pop"), SSgt. (serial #13048431)
Born October 27, 1916, in Indiana, PA. Son of David Earl and Effie Della (Kring) Learn. In 1930, enumerated with parents and sister, 436 Public Road 4, Chevy Chase, PA, attending school. Graduated from Indiana High School in 1935. In 1940, lived with parents, address R#1, Chevy Chase; occupation laborer for a junk dealer. Registered for the draft on October 16, 1940, address R.D. #1, Indiana, PA; employer Kovalchick Salvage Co., Indiana (blue eyes, blonde hair, light complexion, 5'6", 130#). Enlisted on January 22, 1942, at Harrisburg, PA, as a private; residence N. Cumberland, PA; occupation carpenter (5'6", 123#). Arrived at Karachi aboard USS *Mission Bay* on March 29, 1944. Assigned to 3rd Squadron as A/P armorer; later noted as cannon specialist. Promoted to corporal on June 1 and to sergeant on November 1, 1944. Sent to rest camp at Chengtu on July 2, 1945. Released from 3rd Squadron on September 1; transferred to 23rd Fighter Group, 68th Composite Wing, for transport home. Returned to US on November 30, 1945, likely as a casual. Wood's list: "RD #3, Indiana, Pa." Discharged at Indiantown Gap, PA, December 12, 1945. Married Helen Danko on November 4, 1947, in Winchester, VA; parents of four daughters. Member of American Legion Post 141 in Indiana from January 4, 1946. Compensation approved in 1950 for $260 for domestic service and $240 foreign service by Commonwealth of Pennsylvania. In 1950 census, enumerated in April with wife and two daughters, 291 Hill Crest, Indiana, occupation carpenter's helper, salvage, and real estate company. Lived in Shelocta, PA, in 2008. Died April 3, 2010. Buried at Mount Airy Cemetery, Natrona Heights, PA. (Obituary stated that he flew missions over China but not verified by operational reports.)

LIBOLT, Frederick Christian ("Fred"), TSgt. (serial #06669203)
Born May 12, 1916, in Newark, NJ. Son of Christian Frederick (Jr.) and Ada Margaret (Riley) Paul. In 1920, father deserted family and returned to Austin, TX, where he was a chemical engineer in the oil industry. In 1920, "Frederick J. Paul" lived with mother (born in England of Irish parents; naturalized) and younger brother in New Haven, CT. She married William Richard Libolt in 1924 in Queens County, NY, and Fred and brother took stepfather's surname. In 1930, enumerated with mother, stepfather, brother, and sister at 105 Fiske St., Waterbury, CT, attending school. Worked for stepfather at Fernwood Farms Dairy, Inc., in 1937. Family moved to Ft. Wayne, IN, in 1939. Enlisted May 14, 1940, as a private (completed two years of high school, height and weight "05', 002#"). Enumerated in 1940 census as patient at US Sta. Hosp., Fairfield Village, OH; mechanic helper. Married Pauline Amelia Schroer on May 17, 1941, in Camden, NC; parents of two daughters. Reported for duty at HQ 2nd Staging Squadron, Floridian Hotel, Miami Beach, FL, and attached to 3rd Fighter Group. Transferred to 1st Bomb Group on September 3, 1943. Attached to 2nd Bomb Squadron on October 9; arrived at Kunming on October 15. Joined the 3rd Squadron on March 2, 1944, as airplane instrument specialist. Appointed A/P inspector on March 21. Treated at dispensary for nasopharyngitis in February 1945. Released from 3rd Squadron

and departed for return to US on May 25, 1945. Admitted in July to convalescent hospital, Miami Beach, for dermatophytosis ("ringworm") of the foot. Released from service September 21, 1945. Wood's list: "2315 Curdes Ave., Ft. Wayne, Indiana." Registered for military service on September 26, 1945, at Ft. Wayne, IN, same address, unemployed (blue eyes, brown hair, light complexion, 5'10", 164#). In 1949, employed by Fort Wayne YMCA. In 1950, with wife and two daughters, address 1501 Sinclair, Fort Wayne, occupation tester, refrigeration manufacturing. Lived in Pomoma, CA, in early 1950s, occupation mechanic; in Baldwin Park, CA, in mid-1950s, mechanic; in Los Angeles in 1960; and later Whittier, CA. Died September 11, 2002. Buried at Rose Hills Memorial Park, Whittier.

LOGAN, Robert Lee ("Bob"), 1Lt. (serial #39125749; later #0-773178)
Born March 27, 1916, in San Francisco, CA. Son of (Dr.) Roscoe Lee and Evelyn Susan (Wyatt) Logan. In 1920, not enumerated with parents (father, a physician/surgeon, died in 1926) and not found. In 1930, with widowed mother and older brother, 128 Hugo St., San Francisco, attending school (mother died in 1931). Attended Polytechnic High School; member of ROTC. Completed two years at the University of California; occupation bookkeeper and "credit man." Not found in 1940 census. Married Barbara Mae Johnsen on April 6, 1940; parents of a son and a daughter. Registered for the draft on October 16, 1940, address 2110 32nd Ave., San Francisco; employed by Bank of California NA, San Francisco, contact person George C. Sampson, his great-uncle (blue eyes, black hair, dark complexion, 6'1", 160#). Enlisted February 27, 1943, as a private (6', 160#). Received preflight training with AAF Technical Training Command at Kearns, UT, from June 1943. Completed advanced aviation training at La Junta Army Airfield, CO, and commissioned 2nd lieutenant in April 1944. Joined 3rd Squadron on November 21, 1944, as B-25 pilot. Appointed flight leader on November 29. On detached service to Task Force 34 at Chihkiang in January 1945. Sent to hospital in Kunming for amoebic dysentery April 19 to June 1945. Released from 3rd Squadron on September 5 and sent to Yangkai; transferred to 341st Bomb Group for transport home. Arrived in New York aboard USS *General Charles H. Muir* on November 1, 1945. Wood's list: "1950 12th Ave., San Francisco, California." In Danville, CA, in 1949. In 1950, with wife, a son, and a daughter, address 37 Gil Blass Rd., Contra Costa, CA, occupation head of sales order department, Ford Manufacturing Co. Divorced in February 1976. Lived in E. Tustin, CA, for eight years from mid-1960s; Danville, CA, in early 1980s; Orinda, CA; and Napa, CA, in early 1990s. Spent two weeks of annual vacations serving in the reserves and retired as a major. Employed as a salesman for thirty years with Transport Supply Co., a trucking equipment firm. Died on May 15, 2001, in Vallejo, CA. Buried in family plot at Saint Helena Public Cemetery, St. Helena, CA.

LONG, Norman Lavern, TSgt. (serial #35360182)
Born May 22, 1918, in Middle Twp., Hendricks County, IN (Pittsburgh, IN, per draft registration). Son of Hollis Erbin and America Elizabeth (Long) Long. Enumerated with family in Washington Twp., IN, in 1920. In 1930, with parents, a brother, and a sister, 4923 Baltimore Ave., Indianapolis, IN, attending school. In 1940, lived with parents, younger brother, and paternal grandfather, address 1056½ West 28th St., Center Twp., Indianapolis; completed one year of high school, occupation laborer, car manufacturing. Registered for the draft on October 16, 1940, at Indianapolis, address 1058 W. 28th, Indianapolis, employer Chevrolet Body Co. (brown eyes, brown hair, ruddy complexion, 6'2", 175#). Enlisted July 25, 1942, as

a private. Married Lena May Soots in October 1943 in Charleson, SC; residence of both Indianapolis; parents of a son. Arrived at Karachi aboard USS *Mission Bay* on March 29, 1944. Assigned to 3rd Squadron as A/F radio mechanic on April 3. Promoted to corporal on July 1 and to sergeant on September 1. Sent to VHF school in Kunming on October 9. On detached service to Wenkiang / rest camp on December 12. On detached service to Nimrod Detachment at Laohokow in March 1945. Promoted to staff sergeant on June 1, 1945; noted as radio chief. Sent to rest camp at Chengtu on July 2. Promoted to technical sergeant September 1. Released from 3rd Squadron on September 27, 1945; transferred to Air Force Liaison Detachment. Wood's list: "608 Middle Dr., Woodruff Place, Indianapolis 1, Indiana." Released from service January 13, 1946. In 1950, with wife and son, address 243 Trowbridge, Indianapolis, occupation foreman, Chevrolet body. Employed by General Motors Corp. for thirty years, Truck and Bus Operations in shipping department; retired in 1974. Died October 9, 1990, in Indianapolis; cause, lung cancer. Buried at Fairview Cemetery, North Salem, IN. (Middle name "Luvern" on birth certificate.)

MACNEIL, Robert Cornell ("Bob," "Mac"), Capt. (serial #0-662961)

Born May 16, 1919, in Minneapolis, MN. Son of (Dr.) Walter Hill and Harriett B. (Cornell) MacNeil; father was a dentist and mother an opera singer. In 1920, enumerated with family in Minneapolis Ward 13. In 1930, with parents and two brothers, 58 Normandale Rd., Edina, MN, attending school. Graduated from West High School, Minneapolis, in 1938. In 1940, lived with parents, younger brother, paternal grandfather, and a cousin, address 1417 Texas Ave., St. Louis Park, MN, no occupation, and no income. Registered for the draft on October 16, 1940, address Route 1, Hopkins, MN, student, Northwest Military & Naval Academy, 2763 E. Lake St., Minneapolis (gray eyes, brown hair, light complexion, 5'11", 154#, "scar on left hand"). Enlisted in Air Corps as air cadet in November 1941 at Kelly Field, San Antonio, TX. Attended flight school at Foster Field, Victoria, TX; graduated and received commission as 2nd lieutenant on July 5, 1942. Married Barbara Jane Dunn on August 7, 1942, in Edina, MN; parents of a son and two daughters. Reported to Columbia Air Base, Columbia, SC, in December 1942 for advanced flight training. Arrived at Karachi about October 1943. Stationed at Kweilin in late December 1943; unit undetermined. Joined 3rd Squadron in early April 1944 as B-25 pilot / flight leader and appointed engineering officer. Received a "Dear John letter" according to Hank. Promoted to captain on October 1. On detached service to Wenkiang / rest camp on December 12. Awarded Air Medal on April 18, 1945. Left for US on July 3; the last of the original pilots to leave for home. Traveled by ship from Calcutta. Wood's list: "4009 Xerxes Ave. South, Minneapolis, Minn." Discharged on January 19, 1946. Not found in 1950 census. Reenlisted as a major on August 7, 1950, Korean War. Lived in Rapid City, SD, in 1951. Released from service in 1955. Employed as mortgage loan officer in a bank. Went into land development and home building. Operated Dade Marine on the South Dixie Highway, Miami, FL, in the early 1960s. Moved back to Park Rapids area in Minnesota. Divorced March 4, 1976, Hennepin County, MN. Married Ellen Arlene (Frahm) Collier, a widow with six children, on September 3, 1976, in Brookings, SD. Moved to Lake Alice in northern Minnesota in 1978 and bought a resort. Address in early 1980s was Star Route, Box 74, LaPorte, Minn. 56461, according to letter written by Gene Dorr. Contributed to Carl Molesworth's *Wing to Wing: Air Combat in China, 1943–45* (history of the CACW). Died January 24, 1997, at Saint Cloud, MN; cause, heart disease. Buried at Fort Snelling National Cemetery, Minneapolis, MN.

MAGYAR, Alfred John ("Al"), Sgt. (serial #32911797)
Born May 25, 1924, in Maplewood, NJ. Son of Janos (John) and Rozsa (Rose) (Haydu) Magyar, Hungarian immigrants. In 1930, enumerated with parents and a sister, 87 Rutgers St., Maplewood, attending school. In 1940, lived with parents, same address, completed one year of high school, attending school. Graduated from Columbia High School at Maplewood in 1942. Registered for the draft on June 30, 1942, same address as census, no employer (hazel eyes, brown hair, ruddy complexion, 5'10½", 164#). Enlisted on April 5, 1943, at Newark as a private (occupation "machine shop and related professions," height "36," weight 132#). Graduated from flexible gunnery school at Yuma Army Airfield, Yuma, AZ, on January 24, 1944. Assigned to 3rd Squadron on October 19, 1944, as radio operator–mechanic–gunner. On detached service to Task Force 34 at Chihkiang on November 25. Reported as MIA on March 30, 1945; returned to duty. Promoted to sergeant on June 1. Assigned to 4th Bomb Squadron Detachment at Chihkiang in August. Completed fifty missions and 200 flying hours. Released from 3rd Squadron on September 5 and sent to Yangkai; transferred to 22nd Bomb Squadron, 341st Bomb Group, as a radio-gunner for transport home. Arrived in New York aboard USS *General Charles H. Muir* on November 1, 1945. Released from service November 5, 1945. Wood's list: "98 Rutgers Street, Maplewood, New Jersey." Awarded Distinguished Flying Cross and Air Medal with OLC, as well as State of New Jersey's Distinguished Service Medal for Distinguished Meritorious Service in air combat in the Asiatic Pacific theater. Member of the Caterpillar Club. Graduated from the University of Michigan with a bachelor of science degree in mathematics and electrical engineering. In 1950, with mother and sister, 87 Rutgers St., Maplewood, occupation electrical engineer. Married Laura Kathryn Windon on September 29, 1951, in Maplewood; parents of two daughters. In early 1950s, in South Orange, NJ, employed as electrical engineer at Ebasco Service, Inc. Moved to Whippany, NJ, in 1957. Assistant planning engineer for Jersey Central Power and Light Co. in early 1960s; later senior engineering consultant / chief planning officer for General Public Utilities Energy Corp. in Convent Station. Died December 5, 2002. Buried at Hollywood Cemetery, Union, NJ.

MALONE, Allen Brooks ("Pat," "Bud"), Jr., Sgt. (serial #35383369)
Born June 2, 1919, in Murray, WV. Son of Allen Brooks and Pearle Ellen Virginia (DeVault) Malone. In 1930, enumerated with parents, two sisters, and a brother, no address but not a farm, Winfield, WV, attending school. Attended East High School. In 1940, lived with parents, a sister, and a brother, address Meadowdale Rd., Route 73, Winfield District, Marion County, WV, completed two years of high school, laborer for a coal company. Registered for the draft on October 16, 1940, address Route 3, Fairmont, WV; employer Consolidation Coal Co., Inc., Mine 36, Fairmont (brown eyes, brown hair, light complexion, 5'10", 132#). Enlisted in 1942 as a private. Married Eva Virginia Constable on September 15, 1943, in Oakland, MD; stationed at Camp Sibert, AL. Hospitalized in February 1944 for streptococcal throat infection and in June for peritonsillar abscess. Previous unit undetermined. Transferred to 3rd Squadron on July 3, 1944, as a cook. On detached service to 2nd Bomb Squadron from September 30. On detached service to Luliang from October 22. Transferred to 2nd Squadron at Liangshan on October 30. Not included in Wood's list. In 1950, stationed at Eielson AFB, Fairbanks, AK. Later served in the Korean War and Vietnam War. Retired from USAF as senior master sergeant in 1972 after thirty-one years in the military. Member of Disabled American Veterans. Died June 25, 2010, at Meadowdale Community, WV; cremated.

McCANN, James Earl ("Dingie," "Jim"), SSgt. (serial #15073288)

Born June 2, 1921, in New Martinsville, WV. Son of James and Mabel Grace (Burch) McCann. In 1930, enumerated as "Dingie Masters," with stepfather Hulbert I. Masters, mother, sister, and maternal grandmother, 210 Jefferson St., Mannington, WV, attending school. (Nickname "Ding" or "Dingie" was given by an aunt who sang "Ding Bat the Acrobat" to him when he was a child.) In 1940, "James E. Masters" lived with mother and stepfather, brother, and sister, same address, completed four years of high school, attending school. Completed two years at University of West Virginia, Morgantown, WV; served in the ROTC (2nd Battalion, Company E in 1940; Company F, 2nd Platoon, in 1941) listed as "Dingie B. McCann." Married Helen Ruth Dawson in Kentucky about 1941; parents of a son and a daughter. Enlisted in Air Corps on January 2, 1942, at Fort Hayes, Columbus, OH, as a private (completed two years of college, occupation photographic processor, 5'6", 166#). Assigned as drill sergeant at Atlantic City base and trained soldiers on the boardwalk. Reported for duty at HQ 2nd Staging Squadron, Floridian Hotel, Miami Beach, FL, and attached to OTU on August 16, 1943. Sent to Karachi and assigned to 1st Bomb Group. Attached to 2nd Bomb Squadron September 6, 1943. Hospitalized for yellow fever. Transferred to 1st Bomb Squadron. Placed on flying status October 1 and November 16, 1943. Transferred to CACW HQ on November 20, 1943. On special duty with OTU on December 1, 1943, to provide gunnery training to Chinese soldiers. Hit in the forehead with fire ax on one mission and wounded by shrapnel on another (dates undetermined). Joined 3rd Squadron from 1st Bomb Squadron on March 5, 1944, as section leader. Reclassified to A/P armorer on May 1. On detached duty with Task Force 34 at Chihkiang from November 1944 to January 1945 as turret gunner. Hospitalized multiple times for malaria. Received orders home on May 28. Wood's list: "Box 163, Mannington, West Virginia." Entered convalescent hospital at Greensboro, NC, in August; discharged in September. Released from service on September 28, 1945. Registered for military recall October 4, 1945, residence Mannington, WV; employer Hope Gas Co., Hastings, WV (his stepfather was plant manager) (gray eyes, brown hair, ruddy complexion, 5'6½", 166#; "Service Scar on right side 4" [inches]"). Moved to Charleston, WV, in about 1947; employed by O. R. Lawson (Helen's uncle) as an insurance adjuster. In 1950, with wife, son, and daughter, address 317 Laidley, Apt. #3, Charleston, occupation adjuster for insurance company. Later moved to Ft. Lauderdale, FL. Began compiling a history of the 3rd Squadron in the 1980s but was unable to complete it. Contributed to Malcolm Rosholt's *Flight in the China Air Space, 1910–1950*. Died February 7, 1995; cause, non-Hodgkin's lymphoma.

MEIKLE, William (NMI) ("Bill"), TSgt. (serial #32632312)

Born July 26, 1922, in Kilbarchan, Renfrewshire, Scotland. Son of Alexander and Isabelle ("Sybil") (Gray) Meikle. Immigrated at eight months (blue eyes, brown hair, "fresh" complexion) with mother and sister aboard SS *Columbia* from Glasgow to Boston; arrived July 1, 1923, to join father, address 325 Walnut St., Yonkers, NY. Father and both children naturalized before 1930. In 1930, enumerated with parents, a brother, and a sister, 84 Saratoga Ave., Yonkers, attending school. In 1940, lived with parents, brother, and sister, address 87 N. Broadway, Yonkers, completed three years of high school, attending school. Graduated from Gorton High School same year. Registered for the draft on June 30, 1942, in Yonkers, address 64 Locust Hill Ave. (marked out), 78 Onondaga St. (written above), employer Otis Elevator (hazel eyes, brown hair, light complexion, 5'11", 158#, "appendix scar"). Enlisted November 16, 1942, in New York City (occupation office machine operator, residence Westchester County, NY, 5'6", 151#). Attached to 1st Bomb Group on August 14, 1943, and then to 2nd Bomb Squadron; arrived at Kunming on October 24. Joined 3rd Squadron on March 4, 1944, as administrative and technical clerk. Reclassified to intelligence NCO on March 21. Promoted to technical sergeant on August 1. Assigned to 4th Bomb Squadron detachment at Chihkiang in August 1945. Released from 3rd Squadron on August 27 and sent to Yangkai; transferred to 22nd Bomb Squadron, 341st Bomb Group, for transport home. Arrived in New York aboard USS *General Charles H. Muir* on November 1, 1945. Wood's list: "78 Onondaga Street, Yonkers, New York." Married Beatrice Anita Petrash on November 9, 1947. Not found in 1950 census. Employed his entire career by Otis Elevator Co.; retired as head of the printing department. Later lived in Fort Myers, FL. Died December 6, 2006, in Fort Myers; cause, "massive heart attack."

MIER, Isabel Gil ("Izzy"), TSgt. (serial #38092809)

Born on November 17, 1916, in Gonzales, TX. Son of Sebastian and Conception (Gil) Mier; father was a Mexican immigrant. In 1930, enumerated with widowed father, three older brothers, and three younger sisters on a farm, address "Country Road," Justice Pct. #3, Gonzales County, TX, attending school, father spoke Spanish. In 1940, "Escaville" Mier lived with his brother Vivian Mier and family, as well as three boarders, address 701½ East Ninth Street, B rear, Austin. Registered for the draft on October 16, 1940, address 701½ East 9th, Austin (marked out), Rt. 1, Box 150, Waelder, Texas (written above); employer Mr. Monroe Linder, contractor, Austin, Texas (brown eyes, black hair, dark complexion, 5'4", 116#). Enlisted on March 3, 1942, at Ft. Sam Houston, San Antonio, TX, as a private (completed one year of college, occupation farm hand, 5'3", 115#). Attended gunnery school at Page Field, Ft. Myers, FL, in summer of 1942. Arrived at Karachi aboard USS *Mission Bay* on March 29, 1944. Assigned to 3rd Squadron as A/P armorer on April 3. On detached service to Wenkiang / rest camp on December 12. Promoted to technical sergeant on June 1, 1945. Assigned to 4th Bomb Squadron Detachment at Chihkiang in August. Assigned to 36th Fighter Control Squadron at Luliang on September 19 for transport home. Arrived in New York aboard USS *General C. C. Ballou* on November 6, 1945. Wood's list: "Box 382, Waelder, TX." Released from service November 14, 1945. Married Velia Gandara on December 9, 1945, both residing at Rt. 4, Box 575, Houston, TX; parents of two sons and two daughters. In 1950, with wife, a daughter, and a son, address Rice Rd. (no house #), Houston, occupation helper, greenhouses. Died April 3, 1984. Buried at Houston National Cemetery, Houston, TX.

MIKOLA, Allan (NMI), 2Lt. (serial #32609529; later #0-2065174)

Born June 6, 1921, in Paterson, NJ. Son of Jacob ("Jack") and Sophie (Einhorn) Mikola. In 1930, enumerated with parents, address 271 19th Ave., Paterson, attending school. Bar mitzvah / confirmation at Bernert Memorial Temple, Paterson, on May 20, 1934. Graduated from Eastside High School, Paterson. In 1940, lived with his parents, address 316 17th Ave., Paterson, no occupation. As student at Indiana University, selected as one of fifteen outstanding senior accounting majors granted leave of absence from school to accept a position with a public accounting firm in Chicago. Registered for the draft on February 16, 1942, at Paterson, residence same as census, mailing address 30 W. Chicago, Chicago, IL, employer Wolf and Co. (Student), 7 South Dearborn, Chicago (hazel eyes, brown hair, ruddy complexion, 5'9", 175#). Graduated with bachelor of science degree in business administration from Indiana University, Bloomington, IN, on May 10, 1942; employed as an accountant at Ashton and Thieberg. Enlisted on January 23, 1943, at Newark, NJ, as a private (5'7",

183#). Arrived in February at Finance Replacement Training Center, Fort Benjamin Harris, IN, to begin training. Transferred to Army Air Forces as aviation cadet in September 1943. Received training at Miami Beach, FL, and Tulsa, OK. Completed navigator training and commissioned 2nd lieutenant on July 22, 1944, at Columbia, SC. Joined 3rd Squadron from 2nd Bomb Squadron on December 28 as squadron navigator. On April 1, 1945, sent to USAAF Station Hospital at Chengtu for observation and treatment; returned to hospital on April 16. Transferred back to 2nd Bomb Squadron on June 1. Arrived in New York aboard USS *General C. C. Ballou* on November 6, 1945. Released from service on February 12, 1946. Not included in Wood's list. Reached the rank of captain, according to obituary. Passed Certified Public Accounting examinations administered by New Jersey State Board of Public Accountants in February 1948. In 1950, with parents, address 340 E. 38th St., Paterson, occupation certified public accountant, auditing company. Served as Paterson city comptroller and Paterson Housing Authority comptroller in late 1950s and early 1960s. Taught courses in local property taxation at Rutgers University in Newark. Member and president of the Passaic County Board of Taxation and served as comptroller for the City of Paterson from 1957. Certified public accountant and a senior partner at Mikola, Fierstein & Malkin in Paterson from 1952 until retirement in 1985. Founding member of the board of directors of Paterson Boys and Girls Club in 1960s. Auditor for Passaic County Democratic Party in mid-1970s. Lived in Ocean City and Paterson, NJ, and Palm Beach Gardens, FL. Seems to have never married. Died October 15, 1990, in Ridgewood Village, NJ; cause, cancer. Entombed at Mount Nebo Cemetery, Totowa, NJ.

MILES, Charles Dempsey ("Charlie," "Howie"), 1Lt. (serial #17061092; later #0-732046) Born July 2, 1921, in St. Aimé, Algeria. Son of Frank Ottley and Maria (Llabres) Miles; father was an American oil rig builder, born in Iowa, and mother was Spanish, from Majorca. Emigrated with parents aboard SS *Paris*; arrived in New York from LaHavre, France, on June 10, 1922; mother naturalized in 1922. In 1930, enumerated with parents and younger sister on a farm in Spring Twp., Butler County, KS, attending school. In 1940, lived with parents and two sisters on a farm in Spring Twp., completed four years of high school, occupation farmer. Enlisted in Air Corps on January 29, 1942, at Wichita, KS, as a private (residence Butler County, completed one year of college, occupation airplane mechanic and repairman, 5'11", 182#); inducted on January 30 as aviation cadet. Preflight training at Bakersfield, CA. Reported for duty at HQ 2nd Staging Squadron, Floridian Hotel, Miami Beach, FL, and attached to 1st Bomb Group on August 16, 1943. Attached to 2nd Bomb Squadron on October 9; arrived at Kunming on October 16. Joined 3rd Squadron on March 2, 1944, as flight leader and engineering officer. Transferred to 5390th Gunnery School at Karachi on April 5. Attached to 1st Bomb Group HQ on May 28 and later reassigned to the 2nd Bomb Squadron. Returned to US before end of the war. Wood's list: "Route #2, Augusta, KS." Married Maude Eleanor McLain about 1944; parents of two daughters and five sons. Released from service January 15, 1947. In 1950, with wife and a daughter, address 4189 Fitzgerald Ct., Sedgwick, KS, occupation aircraft structural mechanic, aircraft company. Recalled for Korean War. Address in late 1950s was 1224 Starkey, El Dorado, KS. Retired from US Air Force as a major. Lived in Wichita, KS; Sweet Home, OR; Keechi, KS; and Augusta, KS. Lived in Towanda, KS, in 1983. Employed until retirement by Boeing Aircraft as a senior aircraft supervisor. Died April 8, 2001. Buried at Brownlow Cemetery, Latham, KS.

MILLS, James Henry ("Hank"), TSgt. (serial #18165393)

Born January 30, 1922, in Traskwood, AR. Son of James Emmett and Hazel Verne (Henry) Mills. Moved to El Dorado, AR, before 1930. In 1930, enumerated with parents and two younger brothers, no address but not a farm, El Dorado, attending school (family was enumerated twice). In 1940, lived with parents and two brothers, no address, El Dorado, completed two years of high school, attending school. Graduated from El Dorado High School in 1941. Address 1411 W. Hillsboro, El Dorado. Enlisted in Air Corps on September 2, 1942, at Little Rock, AR, as a private, occupation skilled meatcutter, 5'10", 143#); inducted next day at Fort Smith. Basic training at Keesler Field, MS. Married Nancy Mae Risinger on October 18, 1942, in El Dorado; parents of a daughter (born while he was overseas) and two sons. Completed A/P crew chief training at Sheppard Field, Wichita Falls, TX, in mid-January 1943; certified as B-26 airplane mechanics specialist at Glenn L. Martin Co., Middle River, MD, in late February; graduated from advanced electrical-systems training at Rome Air Depot, Rome, NY, in late March; promoted to corporal and assigned duty as a B-26 crew chief at McDill Air Base, Tampa, FL; moved to Barksdale Field, Bossier City, LA; moved to Provisional Overseas Replacement Training Center, Seymour Johnson Field, Goldsboro, NC, and transitioned to B-25 repair and maintenance; transported by train to Fort Hamilton, New York. Arrived at Karachi aboard USS *Mission Bay* on March 29, 1944. Attached to 3rd Squadron as A/P crew chief on April 3, 1944. Promoted to sergeant on June 1, 1944. On detached service to Comilla, India, July 2–4. Placed on flying status about mid-July 1944 and flew combat missions as an aerial gunner until the end of the war. On detached service to Wenkiang / rest camp on December 12, 1944. Likely assigned to Nimrod Detachment. Hospitalized twice in China for dysentery. Promoted to staff sergeant on April 1, 1945. Assigned duties as airplane inspector, date undetermined. Sent to rest camp at Chengtu on July 2. Promoted to technical sergeant on August 1 but not notified until August 15. Assigned to 4th Bomb Squadron Detachment at Chihkiang in August 1945. Released from 3rd Squadron on September 1; transferred to 51st Fighter Group for transport to US but "hitchhiked" home as a casual. Arrived in New York aboard USS *General George O. Squier* on November 2, 1945. Wood's list: "403 Southwest Ave. [marked out], 1113 Coy Dumas [written above], El Dorado, Arkansas." Released from service November 13, 1945, at Fort Smith. Received American Theater Ribbon, Asiatic Pacific Theater Ribbon, WWII Victory Ribbon, Good Conduct Medal, and two Bronze Service Stars. Employed as a meatcutter after return and then for nine years at Lion Oil Refinery. In 1950, with wife, a daughter, and a son, address 1417 Hwy. 82 (south side, west of El Dorado city limits, adjacent to his parents), occupation operator helper, fertilizer plant. Worked for two months for Dow Chemical Co. in Freeport, TX, in 1956 during labor disputes at Lion. Moved to West Orange, TX, address 703 Sherril, in summer of 1957; employed as production operator, then production foreman, and later as maintenance foreman for Firestone's butadiene plant. Credited his experiences in the military for teaching him to be "a leader of men." Traveled to Japan in 1964 as a consultant with Bridgestone's Tokyo's plant. Later consulted for Firestone in Edinburgh, Scotland, and Nairobi, Kenya. Retired on July 1, 1985. Moved to a small apartment on property of his youngest son after home was flooded by Hurricane Ike in September 2008. Died April 15, 2016, in Beaumont, TX. Buried at Antioch Cemetery, Spearsville, LA.

MONDELLI, Leslie Louis ("Les"), Maj. (serial #13028374; later #0-436527)
Born June 25, 1919, in Scranton, PA. Son of Vincent J. and Amelia (Ciongoli) Mondelli, Italian immigrants. In 1930, enumerated with parents, two sisters, two brothers, and uncle, 1100 Watson St., Scranton, attending school. Quarterback on football team; graduated from Central High School, Scranton, in 1937. Received football scholarship and attended University of Pittsburgh. In 1940, lived with parents, sister, brother, and uncle, address 1100 Watson Ave., Scranton, completed two years of college, attending school. Registered for the draft on October 16, 1940, a student at University of Scranton (brown eyes, brown hair, dark complexion, 5'6", 155#). Completed an aeronautical course at Scranton Airport, Schultzville, PA, and qualified to begin pilot training. Enlisted in Air Corps on July 11, 1941, in Philadelphia, PA, as an aviation cadet (completed three years of college, occupation actor, 5'6", 155#); began preflight school at Muscogee, OK. Completed basic training at Randolph Field, TX, on December 7, 1941. Graduated from Air Cadet Class 42-B and commissioned 2nd lieutenant in Air Corps Reserve at Randolph Field in February 1942. Had appendectomy at Jackson Air Base Hospital, Jackson, MS, in May 1942. At Patterson Field, Dayton, OH, in mid-1942 as flying instructor. In June 1942, both reprimanded and praised for buzzing his parents' home and a baseball field in West Scranton and then buzzing Scranton Airport. Promoted to 1st lieutenant in July 1942. Sent to the South Pacific on August 2, 1942, to defend against Japanese advance on Australia; attached to 405th ("Green Dragons") Bomb Squadron, 38th Bomb Group, 5th Air Force. Stationed at Townsville, Australia, and Port Moresby, New Guinea. Flew almost fifty missions, many against the Japanese bases of Buna and Lae. Returned to US on December 30, 1943. Stationed at Army training center at Atlantic City, NJ. Promoted to captain and transferred to the CACW on March 20, 1945. Joined 3rd Squadron from 2nd Bomb Squadron as a B-25 pilot / flight leader and appointed operations officer on June 16, 1945. Assigned to 4th Bomb Squadron detachment at Chihkiang in August 1945. Promoted to major on August 16, 1945. Flew seventy missions as a B-25 pilot. Released from 3rd Squadron on September 5 and sent to Yangkai. On September 25, order revised to transfer and report to "CO POD Air Gateway" for further orders; assigned to training Chinese pilots. Wood's list: "1100 Watson Ave., Scranton, PA." Assigned to 611th Air Force Base Unit, Air Proving Ground Command, at Eglin Field. Married Lt. Frances Leon Kelso, a US Army nurse, on October 4, 1945, at hospital where she worked in Memphis, TN; parents of six sons (one of them stillborn). Stationed at Greensboro, NC. Released from service March 2, 1946, at Eglin Field. Cofounder and first commander of American Legion Post 920 in Scranton. In 1950, with wife and two sons, address 2112 Dellwood Dr., Nashville, TN, occupation inspector, insurance company. In January 1951, veteran's compensation from the Commonwealth of Pennsylvania approved for $500 (fifty months of combined domestic and foreign service, maximum allowable). Received his law degree from Vanderbilt Law School in 1951. Employed as senior claims adjuster for the American Insurance Company. Later practiced law with the firm of Lester, Loser, Hildebrand, Nolan, Lane & Mondelli. Served as a judge in Nashville with General Sessions Court Division VI for nineteen years. Retired in 1990 when his son Les Jr. was elected to the position. Died March 21, 2000, in Nashville; buried at Calvary Cemetery, Nashville.

MORRIS, James Joseph ("Joe"), Jr., Cpl. (serial #31311141)

Born November 9, 1924, in Cambridge, MA. Son of James J. and Sarah ("Sadie") Lucille (Mack) Morris. In 1930, enumerated with parents, three sisters, two brothers, and an aunt, 349 Broadway, Cambridge, attending school. In 1940, lived with parents, five siblings, and paternal grandmother, same address, completed one year of high school, attending school. Graduated from Boston College High School on June 10, 1942. Registered for the draft on December 29, 1942, in Cambridge, address 1 Leonard Ave., a student at Boston College (blue eyes, brown hair, light complexion, 5'9", 170#). Enlisted on April 16, 1943, at Boston, MA (completed one year of college, occupation actor, height and weight "46," 115#); inducted April 23. Joined 3rd Squadron from 4th Bomb Squadron as radio operator–mechanic–gunner on December 14, 1944. Broke his ankle on a mission on March 24, 1945, and hospitalized for two months. Assigned to 4th Bomb Squadron Detachment at Chihkiang in August 1945. Released from 3rd Squadron on September 5 and sent to Yangkai; transferred to 22nd Bomb Squadron, 341st Bomb Group, as radio-gunner for transport home. Arrived in New York aboard USS *General Charles H. Muir* on November 1, 1945. Wood's list: "1 Leonard Avenue, Cambridge, Mass." Discharged January 10, 1946. Attended Boston College in 1946. Married Dolores Mary Fogerty at Belmont, MA, in 1947; parents of three sons and two daughters. In 1950, with wife and a daughter, address 77-773 Washington, Cambridge, occupation accountant, vending machine company. Address 90 Hammond, Marlborough, MA, in mid-1950s. Died on July 26, 1967, in Marlborough, address 56 Clinton St. Buried at Evergreen Cemetery, Marlborough.

MROSKEY, Joseph Walter, Sgt. (serial #13145486)

Born October 10, 1923, in Cleveland, OH. Son of Joseph and Caroline (Student) Mroskey. In 1930, enumerated as "Joseph Student, cousin," with mother ("adopted daughter"), in household of maternal grandparents, no address but not a farm, Glen Campbell, PA, not attending school. In 1940, "Joseph Student," with maternal grandfather and mother, address Route 80, Borough Twp., Glen Campbell, completed one year of high school, attending school. Graduated from Glen Campbell High School. Registered for the draft on June 30, 1942, address 884½ Market St., Glen Campbell; employer Fraser Brace, Geneva, PA (brown eyes, red hair, complexion freckled, 5'9", 145#, "mole on left cheek"). Enlisted in Air Corps as a private on October 10, 1942, at Altoona, PA (completed one year of high school, occupation "production of clay products," 5'9", 150#); inducted on October 26, 1942, at New Cumberland, WV. Graduated from flexible gunnery school at Kingsman, AZ, in about June 1943. In foreign service from September 7, 1943. Attached to 1st Bomb Group HQ on January 4, 1944. Transferred from 4th to 3rd Squadron on March 12, as A/P and engine mechanic; order rescinded on March 18, and attached to 4th Squadron. On same date, reduced in grade from sergeant to private "with cause." Assigned to 326th Airborne Squadron. Arrived in New York aboard USS *General H. F. Hodges* on November 1, 1945. Not included in Wood's list. Discharged on January 9, 1946, at Greensboro, NC. On February 26, 1949, married Margaret Ann Yanoski; parents of eleven children. In 1950, enumerated with wife and son, address First St. ("3 house on R"), Glen Campbell, occupation "oiler & pitter on shovel," strip coal mine. In April 1950, veteran's compensation from Commonwealth of Pennsylvania approved for $500 ($130 for thirteen months of domestic service and $370 for twenty-six months of foreign service). Member of Glen Campbell American Legion Post #435 and Barnsboro VFW post. Worked as a bricklayer for thirty-five years. Died December 25, 2003, in Glen Campbell. Buried at Church of the Resurrection Cemetery, Banks Twp., PA, with military honors by his American Legion post.

OUTEN, Raymond Lee, Jr., Pfc. (serial #33566156)

Born July 25, 1924, in Baltimore, MD. Son of Raymond L. and Myrtle Marie (Bell) Outen (later divorced). Employed by Consolidated Gas Electric Light and Power Co, Baltimore. In 1940, enumerated with stepfather Robert B. Scott Jr., mother, and brother, address 2308 Garrett Ave., Baltimore. Registered for the draft on December 12, 1942, residence 3523 Ailsa Ave., Baltimore, employer "Gas & Electric Co." (blue eyes, blonde hair, ruddy complexion, 6'2", 180#). Enlisted March 21, 1943, Baltimore (residence "US at Large," completed four years of high school, occupation athletes, sports instructors or officials, height and weight transcribed as "54, 139#"); inducted March 22. Treated in August 1944 for urethritis (non-gonococcal). Served for a year in India before moving to China about March 1945. Attached from 1st Bomb Group to 3rd Squadron as a bombsight maintenance specialist on April 12, 1945; returned to 1st Bomb Group on April 27; attached to 1st Bomb Squadron. Arrived in New York aboard USS *General Charles H. Muir* on November 1, 1945. Not included in Wood's list. Released from service January 10, 1946. Married Betty Lee Woolston on September 6, 1947, in Baltimore; parents of a son and a daughter. Graduated with bachelor of science degree in engineering from Johns Hopkins University on June 8, 1948. In 1950, with wife and son, address 30 Ridge Rd. ("2nd fl"), Baltimore, occupation electrical engineer, utility gas company. Retired as an electrical engineer from Baltimore Gas and Electric Co. Afterward taught adult literacy classes and cared for elderly who had no family. Died September 23, 1998, in Baltimore. Buried at Parkwood Cemetery, Baltimore.

PETERS, Eril Wendell, Sgt. (serial #38279857)

Born January 31, 1922, in Nocona, TX. Son of Frederick Clifford and Stella (Simpson) Peters. In 1930, enumerated with parents and younger sister, 832 Ash Street, Nacoma, attending school. In 1940, lived with parents, sister, and brother, same address, completed three years of high school, occupation "cement man" for his father's concrete business. Registered for the draft on June 30, 1942, residence 1516 Weaver St., Gainesville, TX, employer Robert E. McKee (blue eyes, blonde hair, light complexion, 5'8", 130#). Enlisted on September 26, 1942, in Dallas, TX, as a private (completed three years of high school, occupation carpenter, 5'7", 113#). Arrived at Karachi aboard USS *Mission Bay* on March 29, 1944. Assigned to 3rd Squadron as A/F radio operator on April 3, 1944. Promoted to corporal on July 1 and to sergeant on September 1. Sent to hospital for malaria on October 2. On detached duty to 2nd Bomb Squadron at Liangshan on October 17 and on detached service with Task Force 34 to Chihkiang on November 21. Awarded Air Medal on April 9, 1945; later awarded two OLCs. Reported as MIA on May 27; returned to duty. Released from 3rd Squadron on August 27 and sent to Karachi for transport home. Wood's list: "Boyd, Texas." Promoted to staff sergeant and attached to 18th Fighter Communication Squadron, according to tombstone inscription (likely 18th Communications Squadron, 18th Fighter Wing, USAF). Married Dorothy Mae Wolfe on March 31, 1946, in Wise County, TX; parents of a son and two daughters. In 1950, with wife, a daughter, and a son, address #2 Tourist courts at Azle, Parker County, TX, occupation carpenter, building trade. Later lived in Sansom Park, TX. Died in a fire in a house under construction on June 13, 1965, near Possum Kingdom Lake, Palo Pinto County, TX, after falling asleep with a lighted cigarette; cause of death, suffocation from smoke and heat. Buried at Pleasant Grove Cemetery #2 in Boyd.

PIECUCH, Philip ("Phil"), Cpl. (serial #31268975)

Born March 19, 1921, in Manchester, NH. Son of Walter (Edward per some sources) and Caroline (Kramasz or Kramos) Piecuch, Polish immigrants (father returned to Poland). In 1940, enumerated with his mother, two sisters, and a brother-in-law, address 308 Rhode Island Ave, Manchester, completed two years of high school, occupation "tacking shanks" in a shoe shop. Registered for the draft on February 14, 1942, at Manchester, address 308 Rhode Island (marked out) #2 Box 21, Reed's Ferry N.H. (written above), employer Fletcher's Shoe, Goff Falls, NH (brown eyes, brown hair, light complexion, 5'4", 130#). Married Marjorie Alice Ricker on April 4, 1942, in Nashua, NH; parents of a daughter; divorced in April 1946. Enlisted on April 13, 1943, in Manchester as a private (occupation "unskilled manufacture of textiles," height and weight "05," 108#); inducted on April 20. Hospitalized April–May for acute tonsillitis and again May–June; tonsillectomy in June. Joined 3rd Squadron on July 3, 1944, as a cook. Treated same month at the dispensary for diarrhea. Promoted to private first class on September 1. On detached service to 2nd Bomb Squadron at Liangshan on October 17; returned to duty November 14. Released from 3rd Squadron; transferred to CACW HQ on November 21. Promoted to corporal, date undetermined. Returned to 3rd Squadron on February 26, 1945, and assigned to duty as mess sergeant effective March 4. Assigned to 4th Bomb Squadron detachment at Chihkiang in August 1945. Wood's list: "Route #2, Box 21, Reeds Ferry, N.H." Released from service December 24, 1945. Awarded Distinguished Unit Badge, Good Conduct Medal, Asiatic Pacific Theater Campaign Ribbon, China War Memorial Ribbon, and Victory Medal. Married Phyllis Edith Jackson on May 25, 1946, in Nashua; parents of two sons (one stillborn). In 1950, with wife, address 3 Ash Court, Nashua, occupation stapler, shoe factory. Employed as a supervisor at various shoe manufacturers and later as a machine operator at Coca Cola. Played with, coached, and managed several amateur and semipro softball teams, including the Bronze Craft New Hampshire State Champions in 1967. Member of the James E. Coffey American Legion Post #3, Nashua. Died September 1, 2000, at Chelmsford, MA. Buried at St. Stanislaus Cemetery, Nashua.

PULASKI, Frank Paul, 1Lt. (serial #11072641; later #0-758061)

Born September 13, 1920, in Norwich, CT. Son of Ludwik (Louis) and Maryann (Dryzba) Pulaski (Pawlowski), Polish immigrants. In 1930, enumerated as "Frank Pawlowski," with his parents, three brothers, and a sister, 27 Garfield Ave., Norwich, attending school. In 1940, lived with his brother-in-law, two sisters, and a brother, same address, occupation bookkeeper at a woolen mill. Norwich city directory for 1939–44 listed "Frank Pawlowski," a clerk at SW Corp., same home address. Registered for the draft February 16, 1942, same address as census; employer L. Henry and Charles Saxton, the Saxton Woolen Corp., Norwich (brown eyes, brown hair, dark complexion, 5'6", 160#). Enlisted in Air Corps as an aviation cadet on January 15, 1943, at Hartford, CT (completed four years of high school, occupation general office clerk, height and weight "98," 906#"). Married Elldina Christine ("Sis") Quinn on August 17, 1943, in Los Angeles, CA; parents of two daughters. Joined 3rd Squadron on September 28, 1944, as a B-25 pilot. On detached duty to Task Force 34 at Chihkiang in December. Promoted to 1st lieutenant in early March 1945. Reported as MIA on March 30; returned to duty. Assigned to 4th Bomb Squadron detachment at Chihkiang in August 1945. Assigned to Liaison Team at end of the war. Assigned to 36th Fighter Control Squadron at Luliang on September 19 for transport home. Arrived in New York aboard USS *General C. C. Ballou* on November 6, 1945. Wood's list: "27 Garfield Ave., Norwich, Conn." In 1950 census, with wife and a daughter, same address ("left"), occupation student. Graduated with bachelor of science degree, School of Business Administration, University of Connecticut, on June 11, 1950. Employed as an engineer and later assistant plant manager, Plastic Wire and Cable Corp., Jewett City. On June 20, 1961, granted patent for "Core Wrapping Apparatus" used for folding and forming an insulated tape shield or wrapper longitudinally around an elongate continuous electrical cable core. Lived on Ross Hill Road in Bradford, CT; moved to Rhode Island. Died in May 1984 at Charlestown, RI. Buried at Divine Providence Cemetery, Uncasville, CT. (First name appears as "Francis" in some civil records.)

RAGLAND, Reuben (NMI), ("Rags"), Jr., Capt. (serial #0-377592)

Born June 19, 1917, in Jacksonville, FL. Son of Reuben and Anna (Hodgson) Ragland, formerly of Petersburg, VA. In 1930, enumerated with parents and younger brother, address 1271 Edgewood Ave., Jacksonville, not attending school. Attended John Gorrie High School, Jacksonville; graduated from Robert E. Lee High School, Jacksonville. Graduated from Virginia Military Institute, Lexington, VA, and commissioned 2nd lieutenant on June 1, 1939, in Field Artillery Reserve; received bachelor of science degree in electrical engineering. Employed by US Steel in Pittsburgh. Joined the Pennsylvania National Guard; assigned to Battery B, 176th Field Artillery, at Fort Meade; promoted to 1st lieutenant on March 18, 1940. In 1940, enumerated as a lodger in the household of __ (illegible) Lawson, address East Adams Ave. (no house number), Vandergrift, PA, occupation industrial engineer at a steel mill. Called up on December 7, 1941; entered active service on February 3, 1941, at Logan Armory, Pittsburgh, PA. In service at Jacksonville, FL, 1942–44. Arrived at Karachi aboard USS *Mission Bay* on March 29, 1944. Assigned to 3rd Squadron as a B-25 pilot/flight commander on April 3, 1944. Participated as pilot in the squadron's first combat mission on June 25. Promoted to captain on October 10. On detached service with Task Force 34 at Chihkiang as operations officer. In charge of a detail moving from Peishiyi to Liangshan in January 1945. Received orders home on April 11; arrived back in US by ship on June 28. Discharged on November 4, 1945, at Fort McPherson, GA. Wood's list: "1271 Edgewood Ave., Jacksonville, Florida." Married Pearl (McLeod) Genovar (known as "PG"), 1st lieutenant and US Army nurse, on August 4, 1946; parents of a son. Joined Florida Air National Guard's 159th Fighter Squadron, 125th Fighter Wing, Jacksonville Airport. Member of Veterans Businessmen's Club. Employed in 1948 as salesman for Sinclair Refining, address 1518 Willow Branch Ave., Jacksonville. Compensation approved in 1950 for $300 for domestic service and $200 foreign service by Commonwealth of Pennsylvania. In 1950, with wife and son, address 270 Boyleton, Daytona Beach, FL, occupation branch manager, gasoline refining company. Employed as a plant manager at Sinclair Refining in Daytona Beach, FL, and Savannah, GA. Retired from Atlantic Richfield in 1973. Sold cemetery lots and worked as night watchman before establishing successful lawn maintenance business. Died August 5, 2002, in Birmingham, Alabama. Buried at Evergreen Cemetery, Jacksonville, FL.

REYNARD, Harley David, TSgt. (serial #06999651)

Born November 2, 1917, in St. Paul, MN. Son of Harley Ames and Minnie I. (Fischer) Reynard. In 1930, enumerated with parents, a brother, and a sister, 817 West Third Street, Erie, PA, attending school. Played violin in school orchestra. Graduated from Strong Vincent High School in 1936. Enlisted in regular Army from reserve on November 17, 1939, at Pope

Field, Ft. Bragg, NC, for the Panama Canal Dept., completed two years of college (height and weight "88, 684"). In 1940, enumerated as airplane mechanic at Langley Field, Elizabeth City, VA; also listed with household of parents and two sisters, address 935 West Ninth, Erie, occupation newspaper pressman. Received training as a bombardier and photographer. In foreign service (theater undetermined) from December 7, 1941, to October 1, 1943; in US to December 20, 1943; again, in foreign service (likely Europe) to March 2, 1944. Returned to US and sent to CBI on February 6, 1945. Joined 3rd Squadron on May 15, 1945, as aerial combat photographer. Listed as MIA on May 27, 1945; returned to duty but prohibited from flying further combat missions. Sent to rest camp at Chengtu on July 1. Released from 3rd Squadron and sent to Karachi for transport home. Sent back to US September 13, 1945. Wood's list: "4117 Pine Ave., Erie, Pa." Released from service November 6, 1945, at Greensboro, NC. Registered for military service on January 9, 1946, as "Harlie David Reynard," address 200 S. Chester Rd., Swarthmore, PA; employer John Middleton Tobacco Co. (brown eyes, brown hair, light complexion, 5'11", 175#, "single, will be married 2-16-1946"). Married Marjorie Jean (Tomlinson) Bird on February 16, 1946, at Swarthmore; parents of a son. In 1950, with wife and son, address 190 Dogwood St., Park Forest (Chicago Heights), IL, occupation Armed Forces. In same year, veteran's compensation approved for $500 ($160 for sixteen months of domestic service and $340 for thirty-two months of foreign service) by Commonwealth of Pennsylvania. Moved to Tampa, FL, in 1956 and built an 18-foot fishing boat. Moved to southern Pinellas County in 1961. Employed at Jack Lacey Advertising Agency as director and vice president. In about 1972, completed construction of a Pazmany PL-1 airplane (a low-wing, two-seat trainer) at his home in St. Petersburg, FL, after seven years of work. In charge of proposals group for Raytheon Co. Hobbies included photography, art, and handcrafting violins. Awarded patents for several devices, including male sexual-performance aids. Died September 12, 2006. (Harley often spelled in civil records as "Harlie" and middle name as "Davidson.")

RICHARDS, Charles William, Sgt. (serial #33401801)

Born August 17, 1919, in Pittsburgh, PA. Son of Thomas Henry and Agnes W. (DeLong) Richards. In 1930, enumerated with parents, a brother, and a sister, 523 Burgess St., Pittsburgh. Completed one year of college. In 1940, lived with parents, sister, and brother, address 411 Burgess St., Pittsburgh, occupation stenographer, "wire rope." Registered for the draft on October 16, 1940, address 56 Kenwood Ave., Pittsburgh; employer John A. Boebling's Sons Co., Pittsburgh (blue eyes, brown hair, light complexion, 5'10½", 130#). Enlisted November 20, 1942, in Pittsburgh, residence Alaska (5'10", 126#); inducted December 5, 1942, at Fort Meade, MD. Arrived in CBI on September 23, 1943. Joined 3rd Squadron from CACW HQ on February 22, 1944, as administrative and technical clerk, rank corporal. Released on March 1, 1944, and returned to CACW HQ; promoted to sergeant same date. Hospitalized for acute appendicitis in December 1944. Ordered to Yangkai on August 24, 1945, for transport home. Arrived in New York aboard USS *Charles H. Muir* on November 1, 1945. Not included in Wood's list. Reenlisted on November 4, 1945. Married Grace Jean Davidson on November 16, 1945, in Allegheny County, PA; parents of a son and a daughter. Released from service November 3, 1948. Not found in 1950 census. Veteran's compensation approved in 1950 for $475 ($100 for ten months of domestic service and $375 for twenty-five months of foreign service) by Commonwealth of Pennsylvania, residence 303 Englewood Rd., Middlesboro, KY. Died September 9, 2009, Union Lake, MI.

RICKMAN, Stanley Burton ("Stan," "Rick"), Sgt. (serial #39197319)
Born September 10, 1911, in Chicago, IL. Son of Peder (Peter) and Leah M. (Peterson) Rickman, both Norwegian immigrants. His father was naturalized and changed surname from Reinertaen in 1916; died in 1917. In 1920, enumerated with sister Vivian at Evangelical Lutheran Home Finding Society of Illinois, address 4834 Byron St., Chicago. In 1930, both lived with mother and stepfather, address 2419 Kedzic Blvd., Chicago; occupation "embosser of tinfoil." Moved with mother to King County, WA. Employed as assistant building superintendent on night shift at "MBCo," 411 North 63rd, Seattle (resident of Apt. 6), in 1938. In 1940, same address and occupation, completed one year of high school. Registered for the draft on October 16, 1940, at Seattle, same address, employer Metropolitan Bldg. Co (blue eyes, brown hair, light-brown complexion, 5'9½", 157#). Enlisted December 21, 1942, at Tacoma, WA, as a private (5'9", 158#). Attached to 1st Bomb Group HQ on January 4, 1944. Transferred to 4th Bomb Squadron on January 25, 1944. Hospitalized in February for "atrophy or paralysis of muscle." Joined 3rd Squadron as A/P and engine mechanic on March 12, 1944. Promoted to corporal on June 1 and to sergeant on November 1. Assigned to 4th Bomb Squadron detachment at Chihkiang in August 1945. Released from 3rd Squadron on August 27 and sent to Yangkai; transferred to 22nd Bomb Squadron, 341st Bomb Group, as aircraft maintenance technician for transport home. Arrived in New York aboard USS *Charles H. Muir* on November 1, 1945. Wood's list: "6026 6th Ave., N.E. Seattle, Washington." Released from service November 10, 1945. Married Irene Lenora Anderson on May 17, 1946, in Seattle, his occupation assistant night superintendent, Metro Bldg. Co.; no children. In 1950, with wife, address 411 N. 63rd, Apt. 2, Seattle, occupation night superintendent, building management. Died February 16, 1972.

RIEKS, Maynard Walter, TSgt. (serial #37192431)
Born July 7, 1917, in Hubbard, IA. Son of Chris and Esther (Tintjer) Rieks; father was a German immigrant. In 1930, enumerated with parents and two younger brothers on a farm, Alden Twp., IA, attending school. In 1940, lived with parents and two younger brothers on family farm, Alden Twp., completed eight years of school, occupation unpaid farm laborer. Registered for the draft on October 16, 1940, at Alden, address RR2, Alden, employer Chris Rieks (blue eyes, brown hair, light complexion, 5'10", 150#). Reported for physical at Iowa Falls, IA, on December 12, 1941. Original enlistment not found; inducted April 24, 1942, at Iowa Falls. Departed US on July 21, 1943; arrived in Karachi on July 29. Attached to USAAF OTU at Malir on August 1. Placed on flying status September 1 and October 1. Attached to 2nd Bomb Squadron on October 9; arrived at Kunming on October 16. Joined 3rd Squadron in early March 1944, as A/P crew chief. Promoted to staff sergeant on April 1, 1944. Reclassified to propeller specialist on April 12 but continued duties as crew chief. Promoted to technical sergeant on September 1. Ordered to return to US on May 28, 1945; arrived July 2. Discharged October 19, 1945. Wood's list: "Route #2, Alden, Iowa." Married Doris Klein on September 22, 1948, in Iowa Falls; parents of two sons. In 1949, veteran's compensation by State of Iowa approved for $477.50 ($420 for forty-two months of domestic service and $57.50 for twenty-three months of foreign service). In 1950, with wife on a farm (no address), Alden, occupation farmer. Continued farming north of Alden until 1956. Moved to a farm east of Owasa, where he retired. Fell and broke his hip at age ninety-six and did not recover from replacement surgery. Died September 23, 2013; buried at Northlawn Memory Gardens Cemetery, Iowa Falls, with full military honors.

RYAN, James Joseph ("Jim," "Jimmy"), Jr., Cpl. (serial #16156129)
Born February 27, 1924, in Chicago, IL. Son of James J. and Florence Marie (Prager) Ryan. In 1930, enumerated with parents in Chicago, address 5105 Augusta St. In 1940, with parents and younger brother and sister in Madison, WI, address 422 N. Ingersoll St. Completed three years of high school. Registered for the draft on June 30, 1942, address same as census, employer James Joseph Ryan Sr., Pyramid Motors, Inc. (brown eyes, brown hair, light complexion, 5'9", 115#). Enlisted in Milwaukee on December 4, 1942, in Signal Corps as a private (5'8", 114#). Stationed at Fort Monmouth, NJ. In November 1943, graduated from B-24 Liberator bomber mechanics school at Keesler Field, MS. Engaged to Audrey June Skoien, his high school sweetheart. Assigned to 3rd Squadron on October 19, 1944, as mechanic-gunner-engineer; placed on flying status in November. Crash-landed March 30, 1945; returned to duty. Killed in action on May 16, 1945. Not included in Wood's list; next of kin (his mother) 2700 Waunona Way, Madison, WI. Posthumously awarded Purple Heart. Parents preferred that he remain where he was buried at Ichang, but US government moved his body to Hawaii. Burial at National Memorial Cemetery of the Pacific, Honolulu, HI, on June 15, 1949.

RYAVE, Arnold Henry, Sgt. (serial #33424919)
Born February 9, 1924, in Pittsburgh, PA. Son of Jacob ("Jack") E. and Ethel (Shapiro) Ryave; father was a Russian immigrant and mother was daughter of Russian immigrant. In 1930, enumerated with parents, two sisters, and a brother, 764 Cherokee St., Pittsburgh, attending school. In 1940, lived with parents, a brother, and a sister, address 200 Craft Ave., Pittsburgh, completed two years of high school, attending school. Graduated from Schenley High School, Oakland, PA. Registered for the draft on June 30, 1942, address same as census, employed at Valley Dairy Co., E. Pittsburgh (blue eyes, brown hair, ruddy complexion, 5'10½", #148, "mole on right ear"). Enlisted February 8, 1943, at Pittsburgh as a private ("semiskilled routeman," 5'8", 144#); inducted February 15. Promoted to corporal at Greensboro, NC, in September 1943. Graduated from Armament School, Lowry Field, in May 1944. Sent to CBI March 23, 1945. Assigned to 3rd Squadron as A/P armorer on June 20, 1945. Released from 3rd Squadron on September 1; transferred to 23rd Fighter Group, 68th Composite Wing, at Liuchow. Returned to US on March 2, 1946. Wood's list: "200 Craft Ave., Pittsburgh, Pa." Released from service April 14, 1946, at Camp Allerbury, IN. Married Lillian Wanger on June 20, 1947, in Atlantic City, NJ; divorced June 29, 1977; parents of two daughters and two sons. Graduated from Pittsburgh Institute of Mortuary on September 25, 1949, with faculty award for outstanding achievement. In 1950, with wife and two daughters in household of in-laws, Morris and Dora Wanger, 5519 Stanton Ave. (2nd fl), Pittsburgh, no occupation. Veteran's compensation approved in 1950 for $430 ($250 for twenty-five months of domestic service and $180 for twelve months of foreign service) by Commonwealth of Pennsylvania. In 1953, employed at Taylor's Bar & Grill. Served as president of Shadyside Chamber of Commerce in 1960s. Married Gail Ann (Perlut) Lockhart about 1970; mother of a daughter and a son. After death of his father in 1978, took over as funeral director at Ralph Schugar Chapel, serving the Jewish community in Pittsburgh (now operated by his daughter). Died on October 26, 1985, cause, heart attack; residence given as Squirrel Hill. Buried at Beth Shalom Cemetery, Pittsburgh.

SARVER, Harold Gibb, Cpl. (serial #39850769)
Born February 9, 1899, in Canton, OH. Son of Harry D. and Ida (Gibb) Sarver. Lived in Kingsbury, NY, in 1910. Attended New York State Military Training Camp at Peekskill, NY,

in summer of 1917. Enlisted in Company K, 2nd Infantry, New York Guard, on August 13, 1917; discharged December 23, 1918, "removal from district." Registered for WWI draft on September 12, 1918, a student, address 28 Sherman Ave., Glen Falls, NY (brown eyes, brown hair, medium height, slender build). Employed as a sales rep for Victor X-Ray Corp. of Chicago, Erie, PA, in 1919; by Imperial Paper Co., Glen Falls, 1920–22; by Glen Falls Insurance Co., 1922–24; and as an insurance broker in Chicago, 1924–26. Married Marion Tarr on June 13, 1927, in Chicago; parents of a son. In 1930, enumerated with wife and son in Alameda, CA, occupation x-ray technician. In 1940, lived with widowed father and a sister, address 1127 North Shere Ave., Chicago, IL, divorced, completed two years of college, occupation specialty salesman of wholesale medical supplies. Moved to Pima, AZ, about 1941; occupation salesman. Enlisted October 7, 1942, at Selman Field, Monroe, LA, from National Guard, divorced without dependents (5'8", 140#). Aboard *Rohna* when it was hit by German bombs in November 1943, recovered from burns and sent to Karachi. Transferred from 4th to 3rd Squadron on February 28, 1944; order rescinded March 18, 1944. On May 12, 1944, as tail gunner on a two-plane sea sweep near Hong Kong, when plane either hit the mast of an enemy ship (gunboat or destroyer) or was hit by antiaircraft fire on a strafing run; exploded in the air and burned. All crew listed as MIA and presumed to be dead; posthumously awarded Purple Heart. Not included in Wood's list. Remains deemed unrecoverable; memorial at West Lawn Cemetery, Canton, OH, and Fort William McKinley, Manila, the Philippines.

SCHLICHER, Robert Edward ("Dizzy," "Bob"), Jr., Sgt. (serial #18171056)

Born December 10, 1922, in Crowley, LA. Son of Robert Edward and Daisy Louise (Weekly) Schlicher. In 1930, enumerated with parents, a brother, and paternal grandfather, address 404 Fifteenth Street, Crowley, attending school. In 1940, with parents and younger brother, 226 13th St., Crowley, attending school. Graduated from Crowley High School later that year. Employed by Louisiana State Rice Milling Co. (his father was plant manager) before entering service. Enlisted in Air Corps Reserves on October 27, 1942, Lafayette, LA, occupation "weigher"; inducted January 30, 1943, in Lafayette. In April 1943, at Fort Hays State University, Hays, KS, for preflight training as aviation cadet; address 13th Street and Avenue E, Crowley. Sent to Kelly Aviation Center, San Antonio, TX, in August 1943; promoted to corporal. At Sheppard Field, Wichita Falls, TX, in late 1943. In CBI from October 1944. Joined 3rd Squadron on November 21, 1944, as A/P mechanic–gunner–flight engineer. On detached service to Nimrod Detachment at Laohokow in early March 1945. Promoted to sergeant on June 1, 1945; assigned duties as crew chief. In about July 1945, awarded Air Medal for 100+ hours of combat flying. Assigned to 4th Bomb Squadron detachment at Chihkiang in August 1945. Released from 3rd Squadron on September 5; transferred to Detachment HQ & HQ Squadron, 14th Air Force. Wood's list: "Box 375, Crowley, Louisiana." Released from service January 14, 1946. Married Rose Mary Fremaux in Rayne, LA, on June 20, 1946; parents of three sons and two daughters. Not found in 1950 census. Lived in Welsh, LA. Worked for Louisiana State Rice Milling (later Riviana) as a rice buyer. Managed Riviana's Kinder plant for twenty-five years. Worked for Kinder Bean Elevator and Liquid Fertilizer until retirement in 1991. With Rose, attended CBI Association reunions in later years. Member of American Legion and VFW. Died November 15, 2002, in Lake Charles, LA. Buried with full military honors rendered by honor guard of VFW Post No. 9046 at Our Lady of Dolors Catholic Mausoleum, Welsh, LA. (Search results for Schlicher's name and serial number in *WWII US Enlistments* database show errors in transcription: birth date 1882, birthplace Puerto Rico, nationality Negro, education one year of high school, skilled occupations in manufacturing of knit goods, marital status widower. Fold3 records contain fewer errors.)

SCHROEDER, Edmund (NMI) ("Ed"), Cpl. (serial #32806023)
Born March 9, 1920, in Bronx, NY. Son of Frederick N. and Anna M. (Fredenberg) Schroeder. In 1930, enumerated with parents and three brothers, 777 East 225 Street, Bronx, attending school. In 1940, lived with parents, two brothers, and a sister, address 4208 Wilder Ave., Bronx, completed eight years of school, employed as a delivery boy for a fruit store. Registered for the draft on July 1, 1941, Bronx, address same as census, occupation shipping clerk, employer Medo Photo Supply Corp., 15 W. 47th St., New York, NY (gray eyes, brown hair, light complexion, 5'11", 145#, "Protruding Bone left leg-knee)." Enlisted in Company C, 8th Regiment, New York State Guard, on October 1, 1942; dropped January 4, 1943, because of failure to attend drills. Enlisted on February 15, 1943, in New York City as a private, completed two years of high school, occupation shipping and receiving clerk (5'11", 134#). Graduated from Photography Class 43C at Lowry Field, CO, in July 1943. Attached to 2nd Squadron in late March 1945; flew three missions as aerial photographer / gunner. Transferred to 3rd Squadron on April 14 as photo lab technician; flew twenty-five additional combat missions (total hours 138:20). Assigned to 4th Bomb Squadron detachment at Chihkiang in August 1945. Released from 3rd Squadron on September 5; transferred to 311th Fighter Group; moved from Hsian to Shanghai in November and back to the US in December 1945. Wood's list: "4208 Wilder Ave., Bronx, New York." Married Genevieve Elizabeth Wesolowski ca. 1945; parents of two sons. In 1950, with wife and son, address 2461 Elm Place, 4C, Bronx, occupation office clerk, photography studio. Continued career in photography; employed at Arkin Media as a sales representative for over twenty-five years. Lived in Floral Park, Elmont, and Ridge, NY, and Downingtown, PA. Died July 18, 2015, in Coatesville, PA. Buried at Calverton National Cemetery, Calverton, NY.

SEACREST, Mark Tilton, Maj. (serial #18047181; later #0-662499)
Born April 20, 1920, in Lincoln, NE. Son of Frederick Snivley and Dorris (Tilton) Seacrest (divorced in 1930). In 1930, not enumerated with either parent and not found. Attended Lincoln High School. Graduated from Fort Collins High School, Fort Collins, CO, in 1938. Attended New Mexico Military Institute in 1939. In 1940, "Mark T. Chapin" was with stepfather Don A. Chapin and mother, 1304 S. College Ave., Fort Collins, CO, no occupation. Attended Colorado State University in Fort Collins in 1940; pledged to Sigma Phi Epsilon. Registered for the draft on July 1, 1941, student, same address as census (blue eyes, blonde hair, light complexion, 6'½", 190#, "appendicitis scar, hernia scar." Received orders on December 17, 1941, and left immediately from Lincoln to report to Kelly Field, TX, as an aviation cadet. Enlisted in Air Corps on December 18, occupation actor (6', 187#). Basic training at Cristman Field, Lehighton, PA. Married Margaret Lowe on July 30, 1942, in Houston, TX; parents of three children. Completed advanced training and commissioned 2nd lieutenant at Ellington Field south of Houston on August 5, 1942. Promoted to 1st lieutenant at Greenville, SC, in December 1942; aviation instructor in early 1943. Classified as a B-25 pilot from July 22, 1943. Attached to USAAF OTU at Malir on August 1, 1943. Attached to 2nd Bomb Squadron on October 9. Turned back for engine change on way to China on October 25; arrived in Kunming October 26. Joined 3rd Squadron on March 4, 1944, as B-25 pilot / flight leader. Hospitalized for "yellow jaundice" in May. Appointed squadron operations officer on July 15. Reported as MIA on August 14; hospitalized briefly for injuries to his hands and returned to duty. Awarded Air Medal with OLC and Purple Heart on October 8. Promoted to major on December 1 and appointed

commanding officer on December 8. Received orders back home on February 26, 1945; released from squadron effective March 1. Awarded OLC to Distinguished Flying Cross on April 10 and OLC to Air Medal on April 18. Stationed at March Field, Riverside, CA, as civilian personnel officer, in charge of the central post fund, a member of the board of property survey, and other functions. Discharged at Fort Logan separation center in mid-September 1945. In service for two years and flew about seventy missions. Wood's list: "1304 South College Ave., Fort Collins, Colorado." Returned to Lincoln in 1948 and worked with his family's newspaper publishing company in circulation department. In 1950, with wife, a daughter, and a son, address 2039 S. 23, Lincoln, occupation circulation manager, newspaper. In October 1955, served on Crusade for Freedom committee to inspect facilities of Radio Free Europe and Free Europe Press and promote freedom of information. Became vice president of Journal-Star Publishing Co. in 1960 and became president after retirement of his father and uncle in 1971. Elected chairman of board of directors in 1982; retired in 1985. Died December 2, 1999, at Lincoln, NE; cause, "heart failure." Buried at Wynka Cemetery, Lincoln.

SENECAL, Wayne Herbert, 1Lt. (serial #16167462; later #0-822114)
Born May 8, 1923, in Racine, MI. Son of Wilfred H. and Hannah (Johnson) Senecal. In 1930, enumerated with parents, brother, sister, and grandmother at 2194 Cottage Grove Ave., Muskegon, MI, attending school. In 1940, lived with parents, brother, and sister, address 1838 Sherry, Muskegon, completed two years of high school, occupation ice salesman. Attended Hackley Manual Training School, Muskegon; completed three years. Registered for the draft on June 30, 1942, at Muskegon, residence 2194 Cottage Grove Ave., employer Mart on Mart Street (brown eyes, brown hair, dark complexion, 6', 200#). Enlisted November 24, 1942, as a private in Muskegon from National Guard for Medical Administrative Corps; birth year given as 1922. Married Shirley Marion Jesson on February 10, 1944; parents of two sons and a daughter; later divorced. Joined 3rd Squadron on October 19, 1944, as B-25 pilot. Assigned to Task Force 34 at Chihkiang in late October. "Clipped a building of rock construction" on a mission to Hsiangchen on March 8, 1945. Reported as MIA on May 27, 1945; returned to duty but no longer allowed to fly in combat. Flew total of thirty-seven missions. Released from 3rd Squadron on August 27 and sent to Karachi for transport home. Wood's list: "2194 Cottage Grove Ave., Muskegon, Michigan." Listed as "station attendant" in Muskegon in 1949, per city directory. Not found in 1950 census. Steward of Muskegon Yacht Club in early 1950s; employed at Garden Center Nursery & Market, at Gray Trailer Sales, Benton Harbor lot, and managed Glen Aire Trailer Park, Benton Harbor, St. Joseph, MI, in late 1950s; president of Senecal's Import, Inc., Muskegon, in early 1960s. Married Gloria (Jensen) Fortenbacher in 1966; parents of a son. Owned and operated a wig shop in early 1970s. Became a commercial real estate developer. Address 2806 Lakeside Dr. in early 1970s. Partner in Fairplain Development Co., in charge of leasing shopping-center space at Fairplain Plaza in mid-1970s. Founded the St. Joseph Rocket Football Association for eight-to-thirteen-year-olds in 1978 and contributed to support its programs. Co-owner of Henry's Hamburgers in the 1980s. Address 2714 Sunnydale Ct., St. Joseph, MI, in 1980s. In partnership with his brother, Ralph, for several years in Key Largo, FL; residence West Palm Beach in mid-1990s. Contributed to Carl Molesworth's *Wing to Wing: Air Combat in China, 1943–45* (history of the CACW). Moved back to St. Joseph, MI, in late 1990s. Died there April 4, 2015.

SENKBEIL, Edwin Arthur, 1Lt. (serial #16057104; later #37133)

Born October 12, 1921, in Cleveland, OH. Son of Erwin and Bernice Senkbeil. In 1930, enumerated with parents, nine brothers, and a sister, 5922 Schady Way, Garfield Heights, OH, attending school. In 1940, lived with parents, a brother, and a sister, no street address, Midland County, MI, completed four years of high school, occupation usher in a theater. Enlisted in Air Corps as a private on January 27, 1942, in Saginaw, MI, residence Midland, MI, occupation salesman (5'9", 142#). Married Dorothy O. Blosing same year. Lived in Ann Arbor, MI. Graduated from training center with HQ at Randolph Field near San Antonio, TX, in about October 1942. Served as a B-25 pilot with the 22nd Bomb Squadron, 341st Bomb Group, stationed at Chakulia, India, in March 1943 to January 1944. Assigned temporarily to 3rd Squadron in March 1944 to assist in training Chinese pilots; not listed for transfer to Moran. Returned to 22nd Bomb Squadron. Registered for military service on October 22, 1945, Midland, MI, address RFD2, unemployed (hazel eyes, brown hair, light complexion, 5'8", 142#). Promoted to captain December 30, 1946. At Ann Arbor, MI, in 1947; a student at University of Michigan. Graduated from the University of Michigan in 1949 with bachelor of science degree in aeronautical engineering. Not found in 1950 census. At Barksdale Field, Shreveport, LA, in 1955. Promoted to major on April 18, 1956; promoted to lieutenant colonel (date undetermined). Assigned as chief of Aerospace Ground Equipment Division, USAF, effective June 18, 1965. Retired as lieutenant colonel in July 1966. Divorced in June 1967, Los Angeles, CA. Married Joanne Rae (Marquette) Blaty on November 15, 1968, in Orange County, CA. Lived at El Conquistador Resort, Tucson, AZ. Died October 10, 2017, in Tucson.

SHEPARD, Lyle Lewis, Maj. (serial #O-902980)

Born April 12, 1904, in Norwood, NY. Son of George Langdon and Bertha Florrie (Lewis) Shepard. Graduated from Pennsylvania State University, in 1926, member of Alpha Sigma Phi fraternity, Omicron Chapter. Married Helen Margaret Burr on May 4, 1929, in White Plains, NY. In 1930, enumerated with wife, address 9 Greenridge Ave., White Plains, occupation stockbroker. Employed by Dominick and Dominick investment firm. In 1940, enumerated with his wife in White Plains, 20 North Broadway (a large apartment building), occupation security broker for a brokerage corporation. Registered for the draft on February 16, 1942, residence Round Hill Rd., Greenwich, CT (hazel eyes, brown hair, ruddy complexion, 6'1", 127#, "scar on index finger left hand." Enlisted April 25, 1942. Given command of 3rd Squadron at activation on February 22, 1944; relieved March 1, 1944, and promoted to lieutenant colonel on April 1, 1944. Awarded Bronze Star and four battle stars. Not included in Wood's list. Processed through separation center at Ft. Dix, NJ, in November 1945. Released from service March 6, 1946. Reenlisted on June 4, 1946. Appointed head of New York City office, Ketchum, Inc. (fundraising and public-relations firm), in late 1946. Retired as a colonel. In 1950, with wife and mother-in-law, Wire Mill Rd. (no house #), Stamford, CT, occupation executive carbon company. Joined the Columbian Carbon Co. as treasurer in 1950; named president and a director in 1959. Lived on Westover Rd., Stamford. Named executive vice president of Cities Service, a petroleum company, after merger with Columbian Carbon in 1964. Active in charitable organizations; on the board of West Side YMCA in New York City and a member of the advisory board of the Salvation Army in Stamford and New York. Moved to New Canaan, CT, in about 1976. Died June 4, 1983, in New Canaan.

SHOCK, Joseph Ned, MSgt. (serial #17008506)

Born June 14, 1920, in Mt. Vernon, AR. Son of Joseph Benton and Lois Agnes Othelia (Setzler) Shock; mother died in 1924. In 1930, enumerated with father, stepmother, a sister, and a brother, 901 Cypress, North Little Rock, attending school. Graduated from North Little Rock High School. In 1940, lived with father, stepmother, and brother, address 809 West 22nd St., North Little Rock, occupation pipe fitter for steam railroad. Enlisted as a private in Air Corps on July 1, 1940, for the Panama Canal Department, occupation airplane mechanic and repairman (5'6", 129#). Noted as sheet metal worker before enlistment. Promoted to staff sergeant in August 1942; member of the 11th Air Base Group at Randolph Field, TX. Completed a course in A/P mechanics at Air Corps technical school at Chanute Field, IL. Arrived at Karachi on July 29, 1943. Attached to USAAF OTU at Malir on August. Placed on flying status September 1 and October 1. Attached to 2nd Bomb Squadron on October 9. Arrived at Kunming on October 16. Joined 3rd Squadron on March 2, 1944, as AAF radio mechanic. Promoted to technical sergeant on April 1, 1944. Survived crash during test flight on October 22. On detached service to 1st Bomb Squadron at Hanchung on November 16, 1944. Awarded Air Medal on April 18, 1945. Promoted to master sergeant on May 10. Sent to rest camp at Chengtu on July 1. Arrived in San Pedro, CA, aboard USS *General Edgar T. Collins* on October 6, 1945. Wood's list: "4218½ Clay Street [marked out], 4909 Valorie [written beside original], Houston, TX." Discharged October 18, 1945. Registered for military service on October 19, 1945, address 601 Willow, N. Little Rock, AR; "person who will always know your address," Mr. Hassell F. Shock (his uncle), same address (gray eyes, brown hair, light complexion, 5'6," 140#). Married Margaret Hargis on October 2, 1949, in Nacogdoches, TX; parents of a daughter. In 1950, with wife, address 4408 Bell, Houston, occupation laborer, water department. Moved from Houston to Longview, TX, in 1971; address 1000 Eagle Hill Trail. Retired from Machinery Supply in 1991. Died August 30, 1997, in Longview. Buried at Forest Park Westheimer Cemetery, Houston. (Generally found as "Ned Shock" in civilian sources.)

SIMPSON, Thomas Samuel ("Tom," "Tommy"), Capt. (serial #19066281; later #0-663101; later 03636456)

Born April 2, 1921, in Fayetteville, AR. Son of Odis Reavely and Evilee Emily (Pankey) Simpson. In 1930, enumerated with parents and a brother on a farm in Wynne Twp., Cross County, AR, attending school. Moved to Los Angeles, CA, about 1935, address 3120 Sanford Ave. Graduated from Santa Monica High School in 1939. In 1940, lived with parents and two brothers, address 505 W. Elm St., Inglewood, CA, completed one year of college, attending school. Attended University of California at Los Angeles for two years, member of the ROTC Rifle Team. Married Marjorie Jane ("Marge") Bouffard on November 12, 1941, in Santa Monica; parents of three sons (the first born while he was overseas). Enlisted in Air Corps on December 20, 1941, Los Angeles, CA, as an aviation cadet, occupation semiskilled photographic processing (5'7", 142#). Graduated with Class 42-G in March 1942 at Corsicana, TX, earned outstanding cadet award, and commissioned 2nd lieutenant. Joined Air Reserve on July 30, 1942; promoted to 1st lieutenant January 14, 1943. Attached to USAAF OTU at Malir on August 3, 1943. Assigned to 1st Bomb Group and then to 2nd Bomb Squadron as operations officer. Transferred to 1st Bomb Squadron as operations officer on October 25, 1943. Appointed recorder for A/C accident classification committee on November 1. Promoted to captain February 1, 1944. Presented carved jade dragon with monkey by Madame Chiang Kai-shek on February 17. Joined 3rd Squadron from 1st Bomb Squadron on March 1 as B-25 pilot / flight leader. Kept a diary from February to November 1944 in which he recorded events and listed many men of this group. Appointed assistant operations officer and then operations officer. Led the 3rd Squadron's first mission on June 25, 1944. Reported as MIA on July 4; returned to duty. Hospitalized repeatedly for malaria. Released from 3rd Squadron on September 28; transferred to 1st Bomb Group HQ. Sent to Calcutta and then left from Karachi on November 11, 1944, for return to US. Wood's list: 364 21st Place, Santa Monica, California. Appointed CO of Squadron "N," Air Training Command, at Douglas Field, Douglas, AZ. Awarded Silver Star on April 9, 1945. Appointed 1st lieutenant, Air Reserve, August 5, 1945. Awarded Hau Chow Medal in September 1945 and Breast Order of Yun Hui with Ribbon on January 21, 1946. In 1950, with wife and three sons, address 705 Hallwood St., Providence, VA, occupation Armed Forces. Promoted to major on December 14, 1950. Divorced in 1953. Promoted to lieutenant colonel on October 4, 1958. Graduated from the Air War College at Maxwell AFB on June 18, 1954. Promoted to full colonel at Hickam AFB, Oahu, HI, in 1960. Served as director of nuclear operations for US Navy's 7th Fleet at CINCPAC between 1959 to 1962. Recommended for transfer to Strategic Air Command and promotion in September 1962 while stationed at Wheeler AFB, Oahu, but turned down brigadier general star when told he must stop flying. Flew a total of more than 6,000 hours. Retired as colonel on January 1, 1963. Married Esther Rubenstein. Became a successful stock market investor. Address in early 1980s was Rt. #1, Box 269A, Everton, Arkansas 72633, according to letter written by Gene Dorr. Lived in Castroville, Rancho Murieta, and Salinas, CA; resided in Monterey County for thirty years. Died February 17, 2011, in Salinas. Buried with full military honors at San Joaquin Valley National Cemetery, Gustine, CA.

SMITH, Lloyd Sidney, Maj. (serial #0-368841; later #043182)

Born November 8, 1915, in Grundyville, TX. Son of William Walter and Alta Eula (Carpenter) Smith. In 1930, enumerated with parents, 853 Spring St., Lampasas, TX, attending school. Married Margaret Jeanette Wooten on December 25, 1935, at Lampasas; parents of four sons. Attended Howard Payne College, Brownwood; Southwest Texas State Teachers College, San Marcos; and Texas Dental College, Houston, where he received DDS in 1938. From June 6, 1938, 1st lieutenant and district dental officer for Civilian Conservation Corps. Enlisted in US Army in October 1939. In 1940, lived with wife and infant son, address 863 W. Kirk, Houston, completed four years of college, occupation dentist, US Army Dental Corps. Dental surgeon at Kelly Field in 1940–41. Promoted to captain November 1, 1941, at Kelly Field, TX, and moved to Lake Charles, LA, as chief of dental service at Army Flying School. Still as chief of dental service, promoted to major November 21, 1942, at Tarrant Field, Fort Worth, TX. Assigned to 1st Bomb Group as dental surgeon on August 2, 1943. Temporarily attached to 3rd Squadron in mid-July 1944 at Dergaon. Served twenty-seven months in the CBI. Released from service February 3, 1946. Lieutenant colonel in the reserve from July 22, 1946. Professor of military science and tactics at New York University Medical and Dental College. Installed as historian at American Legion Post 277, Lampasas, in September 1946 and as chaplain in July 1947. Reenlisted in November 1946 and returned to active service during Korean War. Promoted to lieutenant colonel in regular Army in June 1947. Not found in 1950 census. Elected to American College of Dentists in 1955. Served as base dental surgeon at Carswell AFB in Ft. Worth, TX; at Dyess AFB, Abilene, TX, from January 1957; at Ramey AFB, Puerto Rico, in July 1957. Retired from USAF as a colonel after twenty-six years in military service. Employed as a dentist for the State of Texas. Died December 21, 1988. Buried at Smith Cemetery, School Creek Community, Lampasas County.

SMITH, Manuel Cecil ("Mannie"), TSgt. (serial #38018627)

Born June 28, 1917, in Sapulpa, OK. Son of Samuel Cecil and Laura Ellen (Davis) Smith. In 1930, enumerated with parents, three brothers, and three sisters, no street address but not a farm, Justice Pct. #2, Pampa, TX, attending school. In 1940, enumerated as "M. L. Smith," roomer in household of Henry Hugo, address 302 W. 3rd, Block 39, Centralia, IL, occupation oil field driller. Registered for the draft in October 1940; address 517 Hodge St., Sapulpa Creek; employer Parker Drilling Co., Salem, IL (blue eyes, black hair, light complexion, 5'11½", 165#). Enlisted in Air Corps on September 13, 1941, at Camp Barkeley near Abilene, TX, as a private, residence Creek County, OK, completed four years of high school, employed in production of petroleum (5'10", 168#). Married Marjorie Faye Baker on September 24, 1942, in Florida; parents of four children. Departed US for CBI on October 5, 1943. Attached to the 1st Bomb Group. Transferred to 4th Bomb Squadron on December 23, 1943. Transferred to 3rd Squadron as intelligence specialist, date undetermined. Moved with squadron from Malir to Moran but not from Dergaon to Kweilin. Detached for special service from 4th to 2nd Bomb Squadron on August 8. Reduced in grade to private "with cause" on August 11. Treated in September 1944 for prostatitis (nongonococcal). Transferred to 1st Bomb Group HQ as gunnery instructor. Awarded CAF wings in June 1945 to express appreciation for his training of Chinese gunners. Awarded Purple Heart. Not included in Wood's list. Not found in 1950 census. Employed as a pipe fitter. Divorced August 10, 1971. Died December 26, 1993; apparent cause, heart attack. Buried with military honors at Springfield National Cemetery, Springfield, MO.

SOLYN, Robert Nelse ("Bob"), TSgt. (serial #20135483)

Born April 30, 1913, in Meriden, CT. Son of Robert A. and Lillie (Pauline) Solyn; mother was a Swedish immigrant and father was a son of Swedish immigrants. Baptized on September 17, 1913, at Bethesda Lutheran Church, New Haven, CT. In 1930, enumerated with parents and a sister, 75 Bradley Ave., Meriden, attending school. Occupation usher in 1936; employed by ISCo and lived with parents in 1937. Married Hope Mildred Freitag on January 1, 1938, in Brewster, NY; parents of two sons and a daughter. Member of 118th Observation Squadron of 43rd Division, Connecticut Air National Guard, at Brainard Field. In 1940, lived with wife, address 127 Ann St., Meriden, occupation parachute rigger for US government (National Guard). Enlisted in Air Corps on February 24, 1941, from National Guard at Hartford, CT, as a sergeant, completed four years of high school, occupation office clerk (5'11", 140#). Stationed at Jacksonville, FL, in 1942; at Fort Myers, FL, in late 1943. Arrived at Karachi aboard USS *Mission Bay* on March 29, 1944. Assigned to 3rd Squadron as operations NCO on April 3, 1944. Promoted to technical sergeant in about May. Reclassified to intelligence specialist mid-July 1944. Ordered to USAAF Sta. Hosp. at Chengtu for "dental treatment" on October 13, 1944, although hospital records indicated cause as "Male Genital Organs, disease of (nonvenereal)." At hospital in Kunming, December 21–26, for treatment with penicillin for pharyngitis. Treated in June 1945 for unspecified ailment and sent to rest camp at Chengtu on July 1, 1945. Released from 3rd Bomb Squadron on September 12 and sent to Karachi for transport home. Returned to New York as a casual aboard USS *General George O. Squier* on November 2, 1945. Wood's list: "133 West 4th Street, Jacksonville, Fla." In 1950, with wife and a son, address Apt. 15N, Crabtree Corners, Jacksonville, occupation Armed Forces. Released from service on September 2, 1953, at Camp Blanding, FL, classified as intelligence NCO. Reenlisted February 25, 1954. Retired as US Air Force policeman / master sergeant; released from service August 31, 1961. Member of Freemason Social Harmony Lodge in Wareham, MA, 1958–1973; residence Falmouth, MA. Died September 23, 1987, at New Haven, CT. Buried at Monroe Center Cemetery, Monroe, CT. (Surname sometimes appears as *Solin* in civil sources, and some family members use that spelling.)

STEARNS, Fred Samuel, TSgt. (serial #06293506)

Born October 20, 1920, at Burkburnett, TX. Son of Clayton Phelps and Effie Elizabeth (Ray) Stearns. In 1930, enumerated with parents, three sisters, and two brothers, no address but not a farm, Benavides, TX. Completed two years at Rio Grande City High School, McAllen, TX. Worked with Civilian Conservation Corps and as an oil field worker. Enlisted August 13, 1939, at Findlay, OH ("enlistment for Alaska," residence Starr, TX); inducted into service following day. In 1940, at Kelly Field near San Antonio, TX, with brother Cullen P. Stearns, both listed as "soldier." Also enumerated with his parents at Starr, listed as "soldier"; marked out with notation "entered by mistake." Sailed from Charleston, SC, to Puerto Rico aboard troop transport USS *Hunter Liggett* on October 28, 1940; rank private. Assigned to Antilles Air Command as aerial photographer in April 1941. Married Carmen Lopez about 1941; parents of a daughter. Still in Puerto Rico in 1943; promoted to technical sergeant in about June. In foreign service with Air Forces from May 1944. Flew as aerial photographer on thirty missions, often serving as a gunner on B-24s and B-25s. On temporary duty to 3rd Squadron from May 15, 1945; attached to same on June 8. Assigned to 4th Bomb Squadron detachment at Chihkiang in August 1945. Released from 3rd Squadron on August 27 and sent to Yangkai for transport home; transferred to 341st Bomb Group. Arrived in New York aboard USS *General C. G. Morton* on October 22, 1945. Sent to Ft. Sam Houston, San Antonio, TX, for processing; released from service October 28, 1945. Wood's list: "Box 736, McAllen, Texas." Registered for military service November 2, 1945, residence McAllen, TX, unemployed (brown eyes, brown hair, light complexion, 5'10", 154#). Not found in 1950 census. In Orange County, CA, from about 1952. Married Zula Margie (Harris) Henderson on May 9, 1958, in Orange County; divorced in November 1971 at Riverside. Lived in Corvallis, OR; Arcala, Santa Ana, and Concord, CA; and Jacksonville, FL. Moved from Benecia to Shasta County in 1985. Operated a drapery and dry-cleaning business at 522 Harbor Blvd., San Jose, CA, in 1972. Member of VFW. Died April 10, 1998, in Redding, CA.

SUMMERVILLE, James Roy, TSgt. (serial #35478106)

Born October 12, 1915, in McCameron Twp., Martin County, IN. Son of Calvin Everett and Nettie Lear (Newton) Summerville. In 1920, enumerated with parents, a sister, and an aunt on a farm, McCameron Twp. In 1930, enumerated with parents, two sisters, two brothers, and a sister-in-law, 202 Washington St., Bicknell, IN, attending school. Completed four years of high school. In 1940 lived with parents and five younger siblings, address 514 South Main, Vigo Twp., Bicknell, occupation mechanic at automobile garage. Registered for the draft on October 16, 1940, at Bicknell, same address as census, employer William Momady, mechanic (blue eyes, brown hair, light complexion, 5'9", 130#). Enlisted on April 29, 1942, at Evansville, IN, as a private, occupation semiskilled mechanic/repairman of motor vehicles (5'7", 134#). Attached to 2nd Bomb Squadron on October 9, 1943. Placed on flight status September 9. Arrived at Kunming on October 16. Joined 3rd Squadron on March 2, 1944, as an electrical specialist. Promoted to technical sergeant on September 1.

Released from 3rd Squadron on August 27 and sent to Yangkai; transferred to 22nd Bomb Squadron, 341st Bomb Group, as an electrical mechanic for transport home. Arrived in New York aboard USS *General Charles H. Muir* on November 1, 1945. Wood's list: "309 West York Street, Rockville, Indiana." Married Eva Gale Robertson on September 2, 1948, at Montezuma, IN; parents of a son (died in infancy) and a daughter. Lived on a farm south of Rockville. In 1950, lived with wife and infant son, address (no house #) Madison, Montezuma, occupation automotive mechanic. Lived in Marion, IN; Carrabelle and Leesville, FL; Arlington, Locust Grove, and McDonough, GA. Died August 6, 2006, at McDonough; cremated. (Often "Roy Summerville" in civil sources.)

SUPSIC, Joseph Paul ("Joe"), Sgt. (serial #33508108)
Born March 16, 1919, in Shamokin, PA. Son of Joseph J. and Feodora ("Dora") (Smalletz or Smaletts) Supsic (Zupecick, Zubejick, and other variants); father born in Pennsylvania of Austro-Polish parents, and mother born in Florynka in present-day Poland. In 1920, enumerated as "Joe Zuberzick Jr." with his parents in Shamokin Twp., Northumberland County, PA. In 1930, "Joe Zubecick" lived with parents, three sisters, and four brothers on a farm in Shamokin Twp., attending school. Not found in 1940 census. Registered for the draft on October 16, 1940, address RFD1, Paxinos, PA, completed one year of high school (brown eyes, brown hair, light complexion, 5'9", 168#, "little finger on left hand crippled"). Married Emily Kathryn Drumheller on August 8, 1942, in Shamokin; parents of a son and two daughters. Worked in "fabrication of metal products." Enlisted April 26, 1943, at Harrisburg, PA, as a private (height and weight "88," 098#"). Inducted May 9, 1943, at New Cumberland, PA. Received basic training in Atlantic City, NJ; graduated from Armament Department, AAF Technical Training Command, Lowry Field, CO, in September 1943, and from Flexible Gunnery School at Buckingham Field near Fort Myers, FL, in March 1944. Left for CBI on October 21, 1944. Joined 3rd Squadron on December 14 as A/P armorer-gunner; flew his only combat mission on January 15, 1945, against Hankow docks as waist gunner. Received notification that brother Peter had been KIA in Luxembourg on January 13, 1945, during Battle of the Bulge; flew no more combat missions. Promoted to sergeant on June 1. Released from 3rd Squadron on September 19; transferred to 36th Fighter Control Squadron, 51st Fighter Group, at Luliang on September 19, 1945, for transport home. Arrived at New York aboard USS *General C. C. Ballou* on November 6; released from service November 10, 1945, at Indiantown Gap, PA. Wood's list: "1750 West Pine Street, Shamokin, Pa." Lived in Coal Twp., PA. Address 1748 Wood St., Shamokin, in 1949. Not found in 1950 census but city directory lists him with wife, 1748 Wood, occupation truck driver. Veteran's compensation approved in 1950 for $375 ($180 for eighteen months of domestic service and $195 for thirteen months of foreign service) by Commonwealth of Pennsylvania. Occupation buyer for Allen Clark Poultry; retired in 1993. Died September 22, 1994, after an eight-month illness. Buried at Northumberland Memorial Park, Stonington, PA.

THOMAS, B. F., Jr., SSgt. (serial #37227183)
Born June 21, 1921, in Linn County, MO. Son of Bert Franklin and Emma Geneva (McLees) Thomas. In 1930, enumerated with parents and two sisters on a farm, rural Clay Twp., MO. In 1940, lived with parents, a sister, and a niece on family farm, Clay Twp., occupation "farmer's helper." Registered for the draft on February 15, 1942, "student at night, and work in the daytime," address RFD #1, Linneus, MO, completed four years of high school, employed

by Daniel Boon Hotel, Columbia, MO (blue eyes, blonde hair, light complexion, 5'7", 140#). Enlisted on October 10, 1942, as a private. Attached to 2nd Bomb Squadron. Placed on flight status September 9, 1943. Arrived at Kunming on October 18, 1943. Transferred to 4th Bomb Squadron. Reclassified from teletypewriter operator to radio mechanic on December 20, 1943. Treated for influenza January–February 1944. Completed a course in radar in September at Kunming. Treated for acute nasopharyngitis same month. Joined 3rd Squadron on December 30, 1944, as a radar specialist from Group Communication Section. On detached service to the 4th Squadron on May 18, 1945. Sent to hospital at Chengtu on May 24 for chronic bronchitis; discharged in early June. Released from 3rd Squadron on August 27 and sent to Yangkai; transferred to 22nd Bomb Squadron, 341st Bomb Group, for transport home. Arrived in New York aboard USS *General Charles H. Muir* on November 1, 1945. Released from service on November 6, 1945. Wood's list: "Linneus, Missouri." Attended University of Missouri, Columbia, MO, in 1946; graduated on June 7, 1949, with bachelor of science degree in business administration. Married Nealia Blanche ("Bea") Morris in July 1947; parents of six sons and five daughters. In 1950, with wife, address 1309 E. 71st St., Fry, OK, occupation statistician, accident insurance. Later worked as an accountant at Missouri Farmers Association Oil Co., Columbia. Died March 7, 1988. Buried at Elmwood Cemetery, Linneus. (Listed in civil records as Bert Franklin Thomas Jr.)

THOMPSON, Elmer Jackson, Sgt. (serial #38229909)
Born December 17, 1917, in Caddo, TX. Son of Henry Calvin and Jessie Anna (Thompson) Thompson. In 1930, enumerated with parents and older brother on a farm, Hwy. 1A, Caddo, attending school. In 1940, lived with parents and older brother on a farm located on Highway 80A "East to Fort Worth," Stephens County, TX; completed four years of high school, occupation "unpaid family worker." Registered for the draft on October 16, 1940, address General Delivery, Caddo, TX, "works for Himself—Farmer and Rancher" (gray eyes, brown hair, light complexion, 5'11", 125#, "two toes on each foot grown together"). Enlisted October 11, 1942, at Abilene, TX, as a private, occupation "farm hand, animal and livestock" (5'4", 127#). Departed US for CBI on March 23, 1944. Attached to 1st Bomb Group HQ and classified as switchboard operator. Attached to 3rd Squadron on July 3 as a cook. Transferred back to 1st Bomb Group HQ on September 30. Classified as finance clerk in November, as teletype/switchboard operator in May 1945, and as mess sergeant in June 1945. Not included in Wood's list. Returned to Caddo and operated family cattle ranch. In 1950, with parents and brother on family farm, address (no house #) Fort Worth Highway, occupation ranch hand. Married Minnie Elizabeth (Crowson) Green on October 8, 1983, in Parker County, TX; had no children of their own. Died July 8, 2013, in Breckenridge, TX. Buried in Caddo Cemetery, Stephens County, TX.

TROUT, Jack Andrew, Sgt. (serial #38332722)
Born April 21, 1920, in Gurdon, AR. Son of Andrew Redmon and Grace Elmira (Amy) Trout. In 1930, enumerated with parents, two sisters (one of them his twin), and a brother, address 705 South Third St., Mission Twp., Gurdon, AR, attending school. In 1940, lived with parents and younger brother on South 2nd St. (no house number), Missouri Twp., Gurdon, completed nine years of school, occupation attendant at a sandwich shop. Registered for the draft on July 1, 1941, address 506 S. 2nd St., Gurdon; completed grammar school, employer A. W. King's café (blue eyes, brown hair, ruddy complexion, 5'8", 138#). Original enlistment not

found. Joined 3rd Squadron from 4th Bomb Squadron on March 12, 1944, as A/P and engine mechanic. Hospitalized for appendicitis in May. Promoted to corporal on June 1 and to sergeant on November 1. Received orders back to US on May 28, 1945. Wood's list: "207-1/2 North Street, Gurdon, Arkansas." Reenlisted on January 18, 1946, in AAF at Little Rock, AR, as a sergeant for the Hawaiian Department; "single, with dependents." With Air Force Reserve, traveled by air transport from Westover AFB, Chicopee, MA, to Frankfurt, Germany, in September 1948. In 1950, stationed at Brookley AFB, Mobile, AL. Rank master sergeant, arrived at Chicopee, MA, on May 7, 1953, from Lajes AFB, Azores, where he served in co-operation with the Portuguese air force. Lived in Tulsa, OK, in mid-1950s. Helped raise nine nieces and nephews after the death of his older sister's husband in 1956. Married Goldie Irene Mattucks on August 22, 1958, in Tulsa; divorced the following month, decree signed on September 30. Never remarried. Lived in Phoenix, AZ, address 2832 Van Buren. Died June 2, 1994, in Phoenix; cremated.

TRUMM, John Aloysius, 1Lt. (serial #19122467; later #0-767688)
Born July 14, 1922, in Salem, OR. Son of William Henry and Rosalie Josefine ("Rose") (Mescher) Trumm. In 1930, enumerated with parents and two brothers, 662 North 14th, Salem, attending school. In 1940, with parents and older brother, same address, completed three years of high school, attending school. Graduated from Sacred Heart Academy and attended Mt. Angel and Oregon State Colleges. Registered for the draft on June 30, 1942; residence same as census; mailing address 245 Union; employer Paulus Bros. Cannery, S. High St. (blue eyes, brown hair, light-brown complexion, 5'9", 140#). Enlisted in Air Corps from National Guard on July 23, 1942, at Portland, OR, as a private. Joined the University of Nebraska College Training Detachment and went to Santa Anna, CA, for preflight training; primary training at King City, CA; basic training at Lemoore, CA; and advanced training at Stockton, CA. Commissioned 2nd lieutenant on February 8, 1944. Transition training at Mather Field, Stockton, and qualified to fly B-25s. Sent to Malden, MO, for C-47 transition training. In foreign service from October 1944. Flew C-47s to transport troops and supplies over the Hump. Assigned to CACW January 21, 1945. Promoted to 1st lieutenant in about June 1945; received Chinese Air Force Wings and the Air Medal for flying transport planes at about the same time. Transferred to 3rd Squadron on July 7, 1945; later received the Distinguished Flying Cross for flying B-25s. Assigned to 4th Bomb Squadron detachment at Chihkiang in August 1945. Released from 3rd Squadron on August 26; transferred to 4th Combat Cargo Group, 10th Air Force, at end of the war. Wood's list: "245 Union Street, Salem, Oregon." Released from service February 23, 1946, at Fort Lewis, WA. Married Germaine J. ("Geri") Godart on June 28, 1947, at Salem, OR; parents of nine children. Received bachelor's degree in mechanical engineering from Oregon State University, Corvallis, OR, about 1949. Moved to Concord, CA, in 1949. In 1950, with wife and two sons, address 2592 Park Ave., Concord, occupation mechanical engineer, oil refinery. Employed as a process engineer at the Avon Petroleum Refinery in Martinez for thirty-five years. Bought a small plane in 1980 and received much pleasure from its use. Address 2148 Frederick St., Concord, in mid-1990s. Died July 30, 2009, at Concord as result of Parkinson's disease. Buried at Queen of Heaven Cemetery at Lafayette, CA.

WADLOW, James Alton ("Jim," "Snooks," "Snookie"), Sgt. (serial #38181439)
Born February 15, 1921, in Hobart, OK. Son of George Washington and Ada Elizabeth (Simpson) Wadlow. In 1930, enumerated with parents, three sisters, and a brother on a cotton

farm, Hobart Twp., attending school. Attended at Koonkazachey until ninth grade; transferred to Hobart High School; sang in boys' glee club. In 1940, lived with parents, older brother, and younger sister on a farm in Otter Creek Twp., rural Kiowa County, completed three years of high school, attending school. Graduated from Hobart High School in 1940; planned to go to Randolph Field and train to be a pilot. Registered for the draft February 14, 1942, address RFD #3 "9 miles south of Hobart," unemployed (blue eyes, brown hair, light complexion, 6'1¼", 150#). Enlisted in Air Corps on August 5, 1942, at Oklahoma City, OK, as a private (occupation farmhand, 6'1", 138#). Trained in airplane mechanics at Sheppard Field, TX; at Eglin Field at Tampa, FL; Southwestern Proving Grounds at Hope, AR; and Johnson Field, Goldsboro, NC. Married Clovis Virginia Wheelis Hassell in November 1943 at Hope. Arrived at Karachi aboard USS *Mission Bay* on March 29, 1944. Assigned to 3rd Squadron as A/P crew chief on April 3. Promoted to corporal on October 1. On detached service to Task Force 34 at Chihkiang late 1944 to early 1945. On detached service to Nimrod Detachment in March 1945. Promoted to sergeant on April 1. Killed in action on May 16, 1945. Not included in Wood's list; next of kin (his wife), Box 424, 206 East 13th St., Hope, Arkansas. Posthumously awarded Purple Heart. Buried with full military honors at Rose Cemetery, Hobart, OK, on July 17, 1949.

WELLMAN, Richard Charles, SSgt. (serial #15200857)

Born May 6, 1913, in Cincinnati, OH. Son of Louis Charles and Emma Louise (Muller) Wellman. In 1930, enumerated with widowed mother (a public-school teacher) and older brother, 2008 Barrett Ave., Cincinnati, attending school. Graduated from University of Cincinnati in 1937. In 1940, lived with his mother, brother, sister, and niece, same address, employed as auditor for a grocery store chain. Registered for the draft on October 16, 1940, address same as census, student at University of Cincinnati, Clifton Ave. (brown eyes, brown hair, light complexion, 5'10", 140#). Enlisted in Air Corps on June 13, 1942, at Patterson Field, Fairfield, OH, as a private, occupation secondary school teacher (5'9", 124#). Promoted to corporal in May 1943. Married Florence Lenore Maxey on December 16, 1944, at Springdale, OH; parents of two sons and two daughters. Joined 3rd Squadron on June 19, 1945, as administrative NCO. Released from 3rd Squadron on September 1; transferred to 23rd Fighter Group for transport home. Arrived in Tacoma, WA, aboard SS *Alderamin* on January 3, 1946. Released from service January 17, 1946. Wood's list: "120 Farragut Rd., Greenhills, Ohio." In 1950, with wife and two sons, address 96 Farragut Place, Greenhills, occupation high school teacher, public school. Taught business education at Madeira, Glendale, Wyoming, and Greenhills High Schools and became an assistant principal at Greenhills High School. Later taught at the University of Cincinnati, Northern Kentucky University's Chase College of Law, and night school at Western Hills High School. Died May 15, 1991, in Hamilton County, OH; cause, pneumonia. Buried at Arlington Memorial Gardens, Cincinnati.

WHEARTY, William Henry ("Bill"), SSgt. (serial #31088418)

Born September 14, 1919, in Salem, MA. Son of William Francis and Mary I. Whearty. In 1930, enumerated with parents and younger brother, 69 Barstow St., Salem, MA, attending school. In 1940, lived with parents and a younger brother, same address, completed three years of high school, occupation milkman. Registered for the draft on October 16, 1940, in Salem, address same as census, employer Whiting Milk Co., 300 Lafayette St., Marblehead, MA (brown eyes, brown hair, light complexion, 6'1", 175#). In 1941, married Dorothy Marie Lyman in Salem;

parents of a son. Enlisted on March 28, 1942, in Boston, MA, as a private, completed three years of high school, occupation semiskilled routeman, (5'11", 163#). Completed a course at Technical Training Command School as an airplane mechanic at Kessler Field, MS, in August 1942. Hospitalized in January 1944 for treatment of phimosis and acute pharyngitis. Arrived at Karachi aboard USS *Mission Bay* on March 29, 1944. Attached to 3rd Squadron on April 3 as a crew chief. Ordered to 95th Sta. Hosp., Kunming, for observation and treatment of unspecified illness in early January 1945. Reported as MIA on May 27, 1945; returned to duty. Promoted to staff sergeant on June 1, 1945. Sent to rest camp at Chengtu on June 24. Released from 3rd Squadron on August 27 and sent to Karachi for transport home. Wood's list: "69 Barstow Street, Salem, Mass." Discharged November 9, 1945. Employed as a chauffeur in 1947. In 1950, with wife, address 4930 Southern, South Gate, CA, occupation salesman, Whole Beverage. Employed by Bob Harrell Oldsmobile and Advance Motors, Long Beach, in 1960s. Divorced May 1967 in Los Angeles, CA. Later lived in Wilmington, CA. Died December 25, 1978, in Los Angeles. Buried at Riverside National Cemetery, Riverside, CA.

WHERRITT, Barton Leroy ("Pete"), 2Lt. (serial #T-127895)

Born April 9, 1924, in Johnson, KS. Son of Barton William and Anna Mariah (Heck) Wherritt. Moved to Montezuma, KS, in 1927. In 1930, enumerated with parents, two sisters, and half brother, no address but not a farm, Montezuma, attending school. In 1940, lived with parents and two younger sisters, no address but not a farm, Montezuma Twp. (father was postmaster), completed one year of high school, attending school, paid laborer on a farm ($35 in 1939). Graduated from Montezuma High School in 1942. Registered for the draft as "Barton Wherritt" on June 30, 1942, mailing address 2314 Laura, Wichita, KS, but residence given as Montezuma, employer Aircraft Products & Supply Co., Wichita, KS (hazel eyes, brown hair, light complexion, 5'5½", 140#, "scar on small right finger"). Enlisted in the Air Corps in February 1943. Sent to Rockhurst College in Kansas City, MO, for preflight training; to San Antonio, TX, for primary; to Waco, TX, for basic; and back to San Antonio for advanced, graduating in June 1944 as a flight officer. Engaged to Coleen Stanley, his childhood sweetheart. Sent to China in November 1944. Joined 3rd Squadron on December 28, 1944. Led Nimrod Detachment at Laohokow in March 1945. Killed in action on May 16, 1945. Orders came through for commission to 2nd lieutenant on May 26, 1945. Awarded Chinese Air Force Wings (date uncertain but squadron history states early June 1945). Not included in Wood's list; address of next of kin (his father) Montezuma, Kansas. Posthumously awarded Purple Heart. Buried at Fairview Cemetery, Montezuma, KS, on July 16, 1949. (Sometimes called "Barton Wherritt Jr." in civil records.

WILKERSON, Ewell Frasier ("Wilkie"), TSgt. (serial #14095004)

Born January 31, 1920, in Agricola, MS. Son of Luther Franklin and Lillie Mae (West) Wilkerson. In 1930, enumerated as "Frasier E. Wilkerson," with parents, no address but not a farm, Dairy Vestry Road, attending school. Graduated from Ocean Springs High School in 1937. Attended Perkinston Junior College, Perkinston, MS. In 1940, lived with parents on a farm in Beat 4, Southwest Jackson County; completed two years of college, attending school, occupation salesman for a florist. Registered for the draft on July 1, 1941, at Pascagoula, MS, address Rt. 1, Biloxi, MS, occupation creosote plant laborer, L&NRR Co., Gautier, MS (blue eyes, brown hair, ruddy complexion, 5'9", 145#). Studied agriculture and graduated from Mississippi State University (bachelor of science degree in animal husbandry, Dept. of Horticulture) in 1942. Enlisted in Air Corps on February 4, 1942, at Jackson, MS, as a private, "professional occupations" (5'9", 138#). Graduated from Chanute Field AAF Technical Training Command ca. June 1942. Reported for duty at HQ 2nd Staging Squadron, Floridian Hotel, Miami Beach, FL, on July 21, 1943, and attached to 3rd Fighter Group. Transferred to 1st Bomb Group. Placed on flying status September 1. Attached to 2nd Bomb Squadron on October 9; arrived at Kunming on October 16. Transferred to 3rd Squadron on March 2, 1944, as A/P crew chief. Reclassified to flight chief on March 21. Promoted to staff sergeant on April 1 and to technical sergeant on September 1. On detached service to Wenkiang / rest camp on December 12, 1944. On detached service with Task Force 34 to Chihkiang. Reported as MIA on January 15, 1945; returned to duty. Sent to rest camp in Chengtu on July 2. Assigned to 4th Bomb Squadron Detachment at Chihkiang in August 1945. Released from 3rd Squadron on August 27 and sent to Yangkai; transferred to 22nd Bomb Squadron, 341st Bomb Group, as aircraft maintenance technician for transport home. Arrived in New York aboard USS *General Charles H. Muir* on November 1, 1945. Wood's list: "Route #2, Biloxi, Mississippi." Married Eileen Estelle Cox, a WAVE, on June 4, 1947, in Biloxi; parents of three sons and four daughters. In 1950 census, with wife and a son, address #11 on "road connecting Ridge Road and Old US 90," occupation crew leader, Census Bureau, Dept. of Commerce. Owned and operated Frasier's Nursery, established in 1950 in Biloxi; business still in operation by his children. Graduated from Mississippi Southern College with master of education on August 19, 1961. Died April 21, 1987. Buried at Pine Grove Cemetery, Jackson County, MS.

WINTER, Gerald James ("Jerry"), 1Lt. (serial # 0-475992)
Born July 20, 1921, in Marathon County, WI. Son of Charles Richard and Lillian M. (Swiggum) Winter. In 1930, enumerated with parents, a brother, and a sister, 504 Nina Ave., Wausau, WI, attending school. Attended St. John's Military Academy, Delafield, WI, from 1938. In 1940, with parents and younger sister, no address but not a farm on Old River Road, Rib Mountain, WI, a student, completed three years of high school. Played left tackle on football team. Graduated in 1941 and received certificate of eligibility from ROTC for commission as 2nd lieutenant in Officers Reserve Corps, US Army, upon reaching age twenty-one. Married Irene Delores Klos on January 2, 1942, at Pine City, MN; parents of two sons and a daughter. Registered for the draft on February 14, 1942, in Wausau, address 916½ So. Third St., employer Marathon Battery Company, Henrietta St. (blue eyes, black hair, light complexion, 5'8", 165#, "Mastoid—Rt ear"). Enlisted July 2, 1942. Joined 3rd Squadron as supply officer on December 18, 1944. Attached to 36th Fighter Control Squadron at Luliang on September 19, 1945, for transport home. Arrived in New York aboard USS *General C. C. Ballou* on November 6, 1945. Wood's list: "PO Box 13, Lake Wausau, Wisconsin." Released from service March 28, 1946. In 1950, with wife, a daughter, and a son, address 922 11th Ave., Wausau, occupation house-to-house clothing salesman, woolen company. Owned and operated Woolen Fashion Wagon, 922 South 11th Ave., Wausau, in 1950s and '60s; later Wisconsin district director of sales for Minnesota Woolen Mills in Duluth. Died June 2, 1982, in Wausau. Buried at Restlawn Cemetery, Wausau.

WOOD, George Porter ("Red," "Jack"), 1Lt. (serial #17029614; later # 0-579710)
Born January 5, 1923, in New London, MO. Son of Howard D. and Lucille Elizabeth (Porter) Wood. In 1930, enumerated with stepfather Charles H. Hall and mother, address 218 Main St., Hannibal, MO, attending school. Not found in 1940 census. Joined Civilian Conservation Corps at Wentzville, MO, on January 9, 1941. Enlisted in Air Corps on May 27, 1941, at

Jefferson Barracks, MO, as a private, completed four years of high school, occupation semi-skilled chauffeurs or drivers (6', 155#). Promoted to sergeant at Cochran Field, Macon, GA, on April 1, 1942. Promoted to staff sergeant, AAF Advanced Flying School, Stuttgart, AR, on October 1, 1942. Accepted to attend Air Forces Signal Corps, Maxwell Field, AL, as officer candidate student on January 6, 1943. Graduated from advanced training and commissioned 2nd lieutenant at Miami, FL, on April 16, 1943; assigned to Marianna Army Air Base, FL. Attached to 724th Training Group, Seymour Johnson Field, Greensboro, NC. Arrived at Karachi aboard USS *Mission Bay* on March 29, 1944. Attached to 3rd Squadron on April 4 as communications officer. Took part in squadron's first mission on June 25 Appointed acting supply officer from October 28. Appointed assistant operations officer on November 26. Flew eight combat missions. Awarded Bronze Star on May 26, 1945. Compiled a list that included the majority of former and current squadron members at end of the war; did not include himself. Released from 3rd Squadron on September 11 and transferred to 11th Bomb Squadron, 341st Bomb Group, for transport home. Arrived in New York aboard USS *General Charles H. Muir* on November 1, 1945. Appointed to Officers' Reserve Corps, Separation Center, Jefferson Barracks, MO, on November 6, 1945; promoted to 1st lieutenant. Released from service January 1, 1946. Received a private pilot's license in October 1948 at Hempel Airways Flight School in Warrenton, MO; a former medical student, employed at that time by the Katie Jane Memorial Home for the Aged in Warrenton and appointed assistant superintendent in 1949. In 1950 census for Liege, MO, name appears on list of "Persons Transcribed from J.C.R's Missed Persons Form," no address and no occupation specified but worked fifty hours during previous week. Member of the VFW. Married Catherine Geraldine ("Gerri") Hart on May 19, 1951, in Warrenton; parents of a son and a daughter (both adopted). Lived in Dallas, TX, in the early 1950s; in Atlanta, GA, in the late 1950s and early 1960s. Died December 29, 2005, at Indianapolis; cause, pancreatic cancer. Cremated; buried at Oaklawn Memorial Gardens, Fishers, IN.

YOUNG, Paul Lane, 1Lt. (serial #16003509; later #0-576792)

Born February 17, 1922, in Chicago, IL; American citizen of Chinese descent. Listed in Cook County, IL, birth records as "Paul Chung Young." Eldest child of Charles and Wong See (also Wung Shu, Wang Shee, "Mary") Young; father was an importer of Chinese merchandise, born in China, and mother was born in California of Chinese-immigrant parents. In 1930, enumerated with parents, four brothers, one sister, and two roomers, 2255 Wentworth Ave., Chicago, not attending school. In 1940, lived with parents, five sisters, and four brothers, same address, completed four years of high school, attending school. Enlisted in Air Corps on December 10, 1940, in Chicago, as a private for the Hawaiian Dept., completed one year of college, occupation messenger or errand boy (5'5", 121#). Inducted at Jefferson Barracks, MO, in December. Completed aircraft mechanic training at Chanute Field. Stationed at Wheeler Field in Honolulu, Hawaii, assigned to HI Interceptor Command, when Japanese bombed the field before attacking Pearl Harbor on December 7, 1941. Wounded while moving undamaged fighter planes away from others that were burning; the first American of Chinese descent awarded the Purple Heart in WWII. Attended Navigator School in San Marcos, TX. After spending twenty-two months with a heavy-bomb unit in the Southwest Pacific, returned to US for intelligence training. Attached to 3rd Squadron from 5th Fighter Group on April 5, 1944, as intelligence officer. Trained Chinese navigators. Appointed squadron historical officer in about August. Received a cut above right knee as he pulled a wounded Chinese gunner out of tail turret during an attack on Hsenwi Bridge on August 5. Appointed class "B" agent at Kunming as custodian for funds drawn for money belts on November 29. Appointed squadron security officer on November 30. Promoted to 1st lieutenant on December 1. Replaced as historical officer on January 1, 1945, by Lt. Ilefeldt. Hospitalized repeatedly for malaria. Dropped from squadron rosters on February 28 and ordered back to US on April 10, 1945. Wood's list: "225 Wentworth Ave., Chicago, Illinois." Moved to Oakland, CA, where his family had recently relocated. Released from service January 20, 1946. Attended University of California, Berkeley, and received bachelor of arts degree in 1947; graduated in 1948 from School of Education, curriculum for the training of junior college teachers, with master of arts degree (major: history, his thesis "The Japanese Industrialization of Manchuria"; minor: Oriental languages). Acquired a commercial pilot license and worked with Transocean Air Lines Flight School out of Oakland Municipal Airport. Traveled aboard SS *President Wilson* from Honolulu to Hong Kong in November 1949, with intention to remain abroad for two years. In 1950, with parents, four brothers, four sisters, and a cousin (from China), address 320 Newton Ave., Oakland, CA, no occupation specified for any other than head of household, Charles Young, proprietor, retail meat market and grocery store, and cousin, salesman, grocery store. Recalled for Korean War on July 10, 1950. Inducted on October 21, 1950; served in Europe. Retired as lieutenant colonel from Air Force; released from service July 31, 1952. Awarded Pre–Pearl Harbor and Pearl Harbor Commemorative Medals, Presidential Unit Citation, Asiatic-Pacific Medal with four Battle Stars, Air Medal, Victory Medal, American Campaign and China War Memorial Medals. Member of Pearl Harbor Survivors Association, Veterans of Foreign Wars, 14th Air Force Association, Retired Officers Association, and Military Order of Purple Heart. In May 1968, survived an automobile accident in San Francisco when a fleeing bank robber crashed broadside into his station wagon. Later employed by Sirocco, Inc., Fremont, CA, as an engineer. Married Suzie Law, date undetermined; later divorced. Died August 3, 2006, in Oakland; listed also in social security claims records as "Wong Paul Chung."

ENDNOTES

Preface

1. "Lt. Gen. Claire Lee Chennault," ID: 2334, Military Hall of Honor, https://militaryhallofhonor.com; and "Major General Claire Lee Chennault," Air Force, https://www.af.mil/About-Us/Biographies/Display/Article/107526/major-general-claire-lee-chennault/.

Chapter 1: Wars and Rumors of Wars

1. "Day of "Infamy," Mike Nichols Library, University of Missouri, Kansas City Libraries, https://info.umkc.edu/news/marr-archives-preserve-historic-day-of-infamy-audio/.

2. "James Henry Mills Collection," #AFC/2001/001/82472, Veterans History Project, American Folklife Center, Library of Congress, interview by Nell Calloway (granddaughter of Lt. Gen. Claire Lee Chennault), director, Chennault Aviation & Military Museum, Monroe, LA, July 5, 2011, CD-ROM. Other JHM comments cited are from informal interviews and private conversations.

3. "MacDill AFB History," *US Air Force Fact Sheet*, US Air Force, December 6, 2007, http://www.macdill.af.mil/library/factsheets/.

4. Nancy Jackson Yeager, daughter of Lloyd E. Jackson, email to author, March 19, 2014, and following.

5. C. E. Daniels, "SSgt. Glenn 'Red' Burnham," C. E. Daniels Collection, http://www.danielsww2.com/page25.html.

6. Penny L. Pool, "A Life That Could Have Been a Movie," *Randolph Leader* (Roanoke, AL), Nov. 9, 2005, https://www.therandolphleader.com/news/article_6e852950-7e6b-59dc-9377-db22376cb4e6.html.

7. USS *Mission Bay*: War Diary, 2/1/44 to 4/30/44, micro serial #71424, file #A16-3, serial #0010, reel #A937, *World War II War Diaries, 1941–1945*, Record Group #38, National Archives and Records Administration, catalog ID #4697018, http://www.fold3.com/; and USS *Wake Island*: War Diary, 2/1–29 and 3/1–31/45[44], micro serial #115003, file #A16-3, serial #055, reel #A1509, *World War II War Diaries, 1941–1945*, Record Group #38, National Archives and Records Administration, catalog ID #4697018, http://www.fold3.com/.

8. Ken Daniels, *China Bombers: The Chinese-American Composite Wing in World War II* (North Branch, MN: Specialty Press, 1998), 12.

Chapter 2: Scorching at Malir

1. Carl Molesworth and Steve Moseley, *Wing to Wing: Air Combat in China, 1943–45* (New York: Orion Books, 1990), 2; and Daniels, *China Bombers*, 9.

2. *Pilot's Handbook: Karachi to Chittagong*, CBI Order of Battle: Lineages and History, Gary Goldblatt, 70, http://www.cbi-history.com/cbi_airfields.html.

3. Charles F. Romanus and Riley Sunderland, "US Forces Organize and Prepare for New Tasks," in *US Army in WWII: Stillwell's [sic] Mission to China* (originally published by University Press of the Pacific, 2002), 24-5, https://www.ibiblio.org/hyperwar/USA/USA-CBI-Mission/index.html.

4. Daniels, *China Bombers*, 12, 107.

5. "Understanding the USA: The Flying Tigers," US embassy, Beijing, China, managed by US Department of State, December 6, 2007, http://beijing.usembassy-china.org.cn/flyingtigers.html.

6. John H. Yee, "Memories of the Jing Bao Days and the Coming of the A.V.G. to Kunming in 1941," *jing bao JOURNAL* 60, no. 366 (October–December 2006): 5–7.

7. Herbert Weaver, "Fourteenth Air Force Operations, January 1943–June 1944," in *The Army Air Forces in WWII*, vol. 4, *The Pacific: Guadalcanal to Saipan, August 1942 to July 1944; Part IV China-Burma-India*, ed. Wesley Frank Craven and James Lea Cate (originally published by the University of Chicago Press, 1950), 530, https://www.ibiblio.org/hyperwar/AAF/IV/AAF-IV-16.html.

8. Air Force Historical Research Agency (AFHRA), Maxwell Air Force Base, AL, microfilm reel #A8351, images #656–1375: historical records of the Chinese-American Composite Wing; microfilm reel #B0035, images #1–691 and #1465–1478: historical records of the 1st Bombardment Group (M) Provisional (the group as a whole and all four squadrons), and images #1479–1890: 2nd Bombardment Squadron; microfilm reel #A0535, images #5–646: additional 2nd Bombardment Squadron documents; images #962–2006: historical records of the 3rd Bombardment Squadron; and images #2007–2371: historical records of the 4th Bombardment Squadron; microfilm reel #B0036, images #12–276: historical records of Task Force 34; and images #278–526: all four squadrons during July and August 1945; all CD-ROM.

9. "Lend-Lease," *The Pacific War Online Encyclopedia*, http://pwencycl.kgbudge.com/L/e/Lend-Lease.htm.

10. Lt. Malcolm L. Rosholt, "Chinese-American Air Force Trains in India for Further Blows against the Japs," *Springfield Sunday Union and Republican* (Springfield, MA), November 21, 1943, 4E, 8E, https://www.cbi-theater.com/lantern/lantern042045.html.

11. Weaver, "Fourteenth Air Force Operations, January 1943–June 1944."

12. "Chinese-American Wing in Action with 14th AF," *CBI Roundup*, November 12, 1943, https://www.cbi-theater.com/ roundup/roundup111243.html.

13. "To Davy Jones' Locker: 195,000 Tons of Nip Ships Dispatched There by Two B-25 Squadrons," *CBI Roundup*, February 24, 1944, https://www.cbi-theater.com/roundup/roundup022444.html.

14. "Sgt. Bill Earley of Allendale in India with Chenault's [sic] Tigers," *Ridgewood Herald-News* (Ridgewood, NJ), March 30, 1944, https://www.newspapers.com/.

15. Ibid.

16. Larry Simpson, son of Thomas S. Simpson, email to author, July 26, 2013, and following.

17. "William L. Daniels" autobiographical sketch, original publication not specified, posted as "Bill Daniels Flying Tigers," Bob Jones, managing editor, Aircraft Technical Publishers (ATC), AskBob.aero forum for aircraft maintenance technicians, http://www.askbob.aero/special-stories/bill-daniels-flying-tigers.

18. Cheng (David) Ting, son of Ting Cheng-liang (Daniel), correspondence via Facebook Messenger, March 9, 2019, and following.

19. Samuel Hui, "A General's Wartime Memory of US-ROC Cooperation," *Want China Times*, April 7, 2014, http://www.wantchinatimes.com/; and "Tu Kai-mu," interview by Samuel Hui and Pan-I Jung, Taipei, Taiwan, December 2013.

20. Eric F. F. Huen, president of Society of Oral History on Modern China, email to author, December 18, 2014, and following.

Chapter 3: Training for Combat

1. James Duffin, son of William G. Duffin, telephone conversation, September 2, 2017.

2. Bill Coltrin, "Pinney vs. Brigham City Opens Semipro Season," *Salt Lake Telegram* (Salt Lake City, UT), May 8, 1948, https://www.newspapers.com/.

3. Richard Daniels, son of William L. Daniels, telephone conversation, October 15, 2015, and letter to author dated October 16, 2015.

4. "B-25J Mitchell 'Show Me,'" Commemorative Air Force: Missouri Wing, https://cafmo.org/index php?option=com_content&view=article&id=8&Itemid=32.

5. Simpson, email to author, July 26, 2013, and following.

6. Aircraft Accident Report #44-322-514, *USAAS-USAAC-USAAF-USAF Accident Reports, 1911–1955*, purchased from Craig Fuller, Aviation Archaeological Investigation & Research, and received by email, February 1, 2020.

7. "B-25J Mitchell 'Show Me.'"

8. "Sergeant in England [sic] Learns He's Father," *The Record* (Hackensack, NJ), March 29, 1944, 8, https://www.newspapers.com/.

9. "Goeller Will Enter Service," *Columbus Herald* (Columbus, IN), June 24, 1942, 1, https://www.newspapers.com/; and "Goeller Named Commander of Army Air Base at Glasgow," *Great Falls Tribune* (Great Falls, MT), May 15, 1943, 12.

10. Lt. Col. Kenneth Kay, USAF (retired), "Chinese-American Composite Wing," *Ex-CBI Roundup*, July 1976, reprint from *Air Force Magazine*, CBI Order of Battle: Lineages and History, Gary Goldblatt, September 7, 2010, https://www.cbi-history.com/part_vi_cacw.html.

11. Pool, "A Life That Could Have Been a Movie."

12. Kelly Lyon, daughter of Moncure N. Lyon, email to author, October 22, 2013, and following.

13. Kathy Bowers, "Reuben Ragland's Adventurous Spirit," *Senior Choices* (Baptist Health System and St. Vincent Hospital), Winter 1994, 4, contributed by John Ragland.

14. John Ragland, son of Reuben Ragland, email to author, March 27 and April 4, 2015.

15. Sgt. Ed Cunningham, "Teamwork in China," *Yank: The Army Weekly*, March 10, 1944, 9, https://www.cbitheater.com/yankcbi/yank_cbi_2.html.

16. *Guide to Karachi*, booklet originally published by US Army, http://cbi-theater.com/karachi/karachi.html.

17. "Interesting Letter Tells of Service in China and India," *Greenville Advocate* (Greenville, AL), March 2, 1944, 3, https://www.newspapers.com/.

18. Donald S. Lopez Sr., *Into the Teeth of the Tiger* (Washington, DC: Smithsonian Books, 1997), 52–53.

Chapter 4: Mildewing at Moran

1. Simpson, email to author, July 26, 2013.

2. R. Aubrey LaFoy, "Okoboji Stories," December 29, 2010, http://okobojistories.blogspot.com/2010_12_01_archive.atml; and R. Aubrey LaFoy, email to author, August 5, 2013.

3. Yeager, email to author, 2014; and Mary Allegretto Henry, daughter of Andrew R. Allegretto, email to author, January 10 and 21, 2014.

4. "Learn about the Rohna," Rohna Survivors Memorial Association, 2013, https://rohnasurvivors.org/; and US WWII Hospital Admission Card Files, 1942–1954, National Archives and Records Administration, NAI: 570973, Record Group Number: Records of the Office of the Surgeon General (Army), 1775–1994, Record Group Title: 112, https://www.ancestry.com/.

5. "Interesting Letter Tells of Service in China and India."

6. Lalit Pukhrambam, "Imphal and WW-II," *World War II: China-Burma-India (CBI) Theater—April 1942–January 1945, the Seige [sic] of Imphal-Kohima*, http://themanipurpage.tripod.com/history/wwII.html.

7. Sgt. Dave Richardson, "Earthquakers' Odyssey," *YANK: The Army Weekly*, China-Burma-India Edition, December 9, 1944, part 3, https://www.cbitheater.com/yankcbi/yank_cbi_3.html.

8. "12th Bombardment Group," Army Air Corps Library & Museum, 2013, data from *Air Force Combat Units of World War II* by Maurer Maurer, published in 1986, http://www.armyaircorpsmuseum.org/12th_Bombardment_Group.cfm.

9. Pool, "A Life That Could Have Been a Movie."

10. Aircraft Accident Report #44-64-524, "USAAF Incident & Accident Personnel List," Accident-Report.com, *Military Aviation Incident Reports*, purchased from Michael T. Stowe and received by email, October 9, 2013.

11. Daniels, *China Bombers*, 44, 57; and Edward Chen, from Mandarin Chinese *pangzi* [胖子], meaning "Fatty," post to author on "Remembering the CBI" group, Facebook, September 24, 2013.

12. Judy McCann Grimm, daughter of James E. McCann, telephone conversation, October 16, 2014, and following.

13. Robert H. Hinrichs, son of John C. Hinrichs, telephone conversation, June 13, 2016.

14. Steve Lin, squadron mascot "ferret" or "weasel," from Mandarin Chinese *yo shu* (鼬鼠), post on "Flying Tigers – AVG" group, Facebook, September 24, 2013.

15. Simpson, email to author, July 26, 2013.

16. Frederick M. Gruber, son of George Gruber, email to author, May 9, 2022.

17. "An Interview with Maj. Gen. Du Kai-mu," interview by Kuo Gwan-lin, translated by Kuo Gwan-lin and Wang Chien-chi, June 1, 2008, in *The Immortal Flying Tigers: An Oral History of the Chinese-American Composite Wing* (Taipei, Taiwan: Military History and Translation Office, Ministry of National Defense, ROC, 2009), 72–73.

18. Marc D. Bernstein, "Joseph Stilwell's Escape from Burma during World War II," Historynet.com, June 12, 2006, https://www.historynet.com/joseph-stilwells-escape-from-burma-during-world-war-ii.htm.

19. Robert E, Passanisi, "Merrill's Marauders, 5307 Composite Unit (Provisional) Unit History," Merrill's Marauders Association, http://www.marauder.org/marauder.htm.

20. Weaver, "Fourteenth Air Force Operations, January 1943–June 1944."

21. Lopez, *Into the Teeth of a Tiger*, 184.

22. "Chinese Take Base in Burma," *San Francisco Examiner*, June 18, 1944, 2, https://www.newspapers.com.

Chapter 5: Bombing in Burma

1. Glynis Marie Wood Jamora, daughter of George P. Wood, email to author, June 12 and July 21, 2014, and following.

2. Herbert Weaver, "The Pattern of India-Burma Operations, 1943," in *The Army Air Forces in World War II*, vol. 4, *The Pacific: Guadalcanal to Saipan, August 1942 to July 1944; Part IV—China-Burma-India*, ed. Wesley Frank Craven and James Lea Cate (originally published by the University of Chicago Press, 1950), 471, https://www.ibiblio.org/hyperwar/AAF/IV/AAF-IV-14.html.

3. "Missing Air Crew Report #6010," *Missing Air Crew Reports (MACRs) and Related Records at the US Army Air Forces, 1942–1947*, publication M1380, catalog ID 305256, Record Group 92, National Archives and Record Administration, https://www.fold3.com/.

4. Ray Panko, "Aerial Bomb Fuzes," Pacific Aviation Museum Pearl Harbor, https://www.pearlharboraviationmuseum.org/blog/aerial-bomb-fuzes/.

5. Bowers, "Reuben Ragland's Adventurous Spirit," 4.

6. Ting, correspondence via Facebook Messenger.

7. Thomas Earley, son of William T. Earley, email to author, March 20, 2015.

8. Daniels, *China Bombers*, 13.
9. Molesworth and Moseley, *Wing to Wing*, 68.
10. "Company Morning Report," July–December 1944 and April–September 1945, *Army Morning Reports and Unit Rosters*, National Personnel Records Center, National Archives and Records Administration, St. Louis, MO, acquired through services of Lori Berdak Miller, professional researcher, Redbird Research, April 8, 2019.
11. "The Story of Six Fliers and an Odd Jungle Epitaph," *Sunday Times Signal* (Zanesville, OH), December 31, 1944, 5, https://www.newspapers.com/.
12. Aircraft Accident Report #44-704-520, "USAAF Incident & Accident Personnel List," Accident-Report.com, *Military Aviation Incident Reports*, purchased from Michael T. Stowe and received by email, September 24, 2013.
13. "Roslindale Flyer Beats Air Crash, Japs, Jungles," *Boston Globe*, Jan. 1, 1945, https://www.newspapers.com/.
14. Dent, telephone conversation August 14, 2018, and email to author August 18, 2018, and following.
15. Brahos, email to author July 8, 2015.
16. Simpson, July 26 and September 8, 2013; and Farnsworth, "Wingless Victory," *Omaha World Herald*, Dec. 31, 1944, https://www.newspapers.com/.
17. "Simpson Killed Countless Japs as B-25 Burned," *Flight Pattern*, Oct. 26, 1945, contributed by Larry Simpson.
18. Aircraft Accident Report #44-0710-506, "USAAF Incident & Accident Personnel List," Accident-Report.com, *Military Aviation Incident Reports*, purchased from Michael T. Stowe and received by email, October 9, 2013.
19. George C. Cunningham Jr., son of George C. Cunningham, telephone conversation, July 7, 2015, and email to author, same date and following.
20. Letter from Headquarters Fourteenth Air Force, April 9, 1945, signed by Maj. Gen. C. L. Chennault.
21. Simpson, email to author, July 26, 2013.
22. Dennis Faherty, son of John F. Faherty, email to author, June 20, 2022.
23. SGM Herbert A. Friedman (Ret.), "OWI Leaflets for Burma," OWI Pacific PSYOP, Six Decades Ago: Principals [*sic*] of Propaganda, http://www.psywarrior.com/BurmaOWILeafs.html.
24. Robert N. Solin, son of Robert N. Solyn, email to author, June 27, 2016, and following.
25. Earley, email to author, March 10, 2015.

Chapter 6: Moving to Dergaon

1. "Word Received from Maj. Chester M. Conrad," *Sikeston Standard* (Sikeston, MO), July 11, 1944, 4, https://www.newspapers.com/.
2. Yeager, email to author, February 1, 2014.

3. US WWII Hospital Admission Card Files.

4. Lim, letter, June 16, 2016, and email to author, June 22, 2016, and following.

5. Grimm, telephone conversation, October 16, 2014, and following, and letter, July 11, 2015.

6. Malcolm Rosholt, *Flight in the China Air Space, 1910–1950* (Rosholt, WI: Rosholt House, 1984), 171–73; contributed by Mark E. McCann, message to author via Facebook Messenger, September 21, 2021.

7. Bernstein, "Joseph Stilwell's Escape."

8. "100 Men Brought Fall of Myitkyina," *CBI Roundup*, Aug. 10, 1944, https://cbi-theater-1.home.comcast.net/~cbi-theater-1/roundup/roundup081044.html.

9. "EAC's Support Aids in Victory at Myitkyina," *CBI Roundup*, August 20, 1944, https://cbi-theater-1.home.comcast.net/~cbi-theater-1/roundup/roundup082044.html.

10. "War and Remembrances: History Told by China's Flying Tigers Veteran," interview of Li Zhanrui by Wu Guoxiu, China Global Television Network, Beijing, China, July 6, 2015, https://www.youtube.com/watch?v=aMa0OBu-DAc.

11. Gerry Young Lim, sister of Paul L. Young, letter to author, June 16, 2016, and email to author, June 22, 2016, and following.

12. Faherty, email to author, June 20, 2022, and following.

13. Yeager, email to author, February 1 and 24, 2014, and following.

14. Earnest Dale Johnson, *A Long Journey Home: A Memoir of Life and War in Our Times* (Caldwell, ID: Caston, 2017).

15. Faherty, email to author, June 20, 2022, and following.

16. "Seattle Seems Unreal after India and Burma," *Seattle Daily Times*, February 18, 1945, 8, https://www.newspapers.com/.

17. "Missing Air Crew Report" for both B-25H aircraft submitted by Maj. Chester M. Conrad, contributed by William D. Grubbs, email to author June 19, 2013; and "Missing Air Crew Report," #7347 (also referenced as #7670) and #8442, *Missing Air Crew Reports (MACRs) and Related Records of the US Army Air Forces, 1942–1947*, publication M1380, catalog ID 3055256, Record Group 92, National Archives and Records Administration; "Supplementary Battle Casualty Report" to "Missing Crew Report No. 7670," letters submitted by Maj. Mark T. Seacrest, April 26, 1946, and John F. Faherty, n.d.; and "Individual Casualty Questionnaire" by Chang Huan-Hsin, Chu Shin-Chuan, Chiu Hsien-Pin, Hsu Hung-Yi, and Lt. Col. Sing, n.d., all https:// www.fold3.com/.

18. Millicent Faherty Kunesh, daughter of John F. Faherty, letter to author, November 3, 2015.

19. "Missing Flier Back at Base, Kin Informed," *Fort Collins Express-Courier* (Ft. Collins, CO), September 5, 1944, 1, 2, https://www.newspapers.com.

20. Ting, correspondence via Facebook Messenger, March 9, 2019, and following.

21. G. Cunningham, telephone conversation and email to author, July 7, 2015.

Chapter 7: Evacuating from Kweilin

1. Christopher Magoon, "Mining the 'Aluminum Trail': Search for Body of World War II Airman Continues in Southern China," TeaLeafNation, March 21, 2013, http://www.tealeafnation.com/2013/03/mining-the-aluminum-trail-search-for-body-of-world-war-ii-airman.
2. R. Daniels, telephone conversation, October 15, 2015, and letter to author dated October 16, 2015.
3. Lopez, *Into the Teeth of the Tiger*, 59, 60.
4. Lt. James R. Smith, "Kunming," in *Night Fighter: A Memoir of the China-Burma-India Theater*, published online by the family of James R. Smith, 2011, http://www.night-fighter.us/Chapter02.html.
5. Johnson, *A Long Journey Home*.
6. Daniels, *China Bombers*, 17, 44.
7. "World Battlefronts: Battle of China; Another Paris," *Time: The Weekly Newsmagazine* 44, no. 9 (August 28, 1944): 15.
8. "Pinyin Romanization: Chinese Writing System," *Britannica*, https://www.britannica.com/topic/Pinyin-romanization."
9. Lopez, *Into the Teeth of the Tiger*, 64.
10. Molesworth and Moseley, *Wing to Wing*, photo section following 48.
11. Sgt. Lou Stoumen, "Evacuation of Kweilin," *YANK: The Army Weekly*, November 24, 1944, https://www.cbi-theater.com/yankcbi/yank_cbi_3.html.
12. Ossie H. Weinert, son of Oswald Weinert, email to author, November 19, 2013, and following.
13. Theresa L. Kraus, "Strategic Setting," in *China Offensive: The US Army Campaigns of World War II*, US Army Center of Military History, 5, https://www.ibiblio.org/hyperwar/USA/USA-C-ChinaO/index.html.
14. Kunesh, letter to author dated November 3, 2015.
15. "World Battlefronts: Battle of China; Another Paris."
16. Virginia Safford, no title, *Star Tribune* (Minneapolis), October 7, 1945, 63, https://www.newspapers.com/.
17. Earley, email to author, March 10, 2015.
18. H. R. Isaacs, *Newsweek* correspondent, "Kweilin Destruction," *CBI Roundup*, September 28, 1944, 1, https://www.cbi-theater.com/roundup/ roundup092844.html.
19. Rosholt, *Flight in the China Air Space*.
20. "14th Air Force Pounds Enemy in Dark Hour," *CBI Roundup*, October 5, 1944, https://cbi-theater-home.comcast.net/~cbi-theater-1/roundup/roundup100544.html.
21. Spencer Moosa, "Jap Columns Enter Kweilin," *Altoona Tribune* (Altoona, PA), November 2, 1944, 2, https://www.newspapers.com/.

Chapter 8: Stagnating at Peishiyi

1. Aircraft Accident Report #45-1022-522, "USAAF Incident & Accident Personnel List," Accident-Report.com, *Military Aviation Incident Reports*, purchased from Michael T. Stowe and received by email, September 24, 2013.
2. Rosholt, *Flight in the China Air Space*, 173.
3. Sgt. Lou Stoumen, "What It's Like for Our China GIs," *YANK: The Army Weekly*, October 20, 1944, https://cbi-theater-2.home.comcast.net/~cbi-theater-2/yankcbi/yank_cbi.html.
4. Daniels, *China Bombers*, 44, 46, 48; and Pool, "A Life That Could Have Been a Movie."
5. Molesworth and Moseley, *Wing to Wing*, 110.
6. Grimm, telephone conversation, October 16, 2014, and following, and letter, July 11, 2015.
7. "Sophisticated Seniors," *Hobart Tribune* (Hobart, OK), April 15, 1940, 3, https://www.newspapers.com/.
8. "James Wadlow Treks across China in American Jeep," *Hobart Democrat-Chief* (Hobart, OK), October 6, 1944, https://www.newspapers.com/.
9. "T/Sgt. Robert N. Solyn with Bomber Squad in China," *The Journal* (Meriden, CT), April 11, 1945, 3, https://www.newspapers.com/.
10. Lim, letter to author, June 16, 2016, and email to author, June 22, 2016, and following.
11. Hinrichs, telephone conversation, June 6, 2016.
12. Solin, email to author, June 20, 2016, and following.
13. Alvin E. Hall, son of Alvin A. Hall, email to author, February 26, 2014, and following.
14. "Local GI Picks Tea in China," *Holyoke Daily Transcript and the Holyoke Telegram* (Holyoke, MA), October 21, 1944, https://www.newspapers.com/.
15. Elizabeth Fuller Zea, daughter of Grady B. Fuller, email to author, February 6, 2014, and following.
16. Daniels, *China Bombers*, 39, 42–43, 45.
17. Chasse, email to author June 16, 2017.
18. N. T. Steele, "Chronic Drizzle Chills U.S. Fliers at China Base," *Chicago Daily News*, December 14, 1944; reprinted in *Groop Poop* 1st Bomb Group HQQ, March 10, 1945, 2.
19. Pool, "A Life That Could Have Been a Movie."
20. Solin, email to author, June 20, 2016, and following.
21. Capt. Floyd Walter, "Myitkyina," *CBI Roundup*, September 7, 1944, https://www.cbi-theater.com/roundup/ roundup090744.html.
22. Capt. Kenneth P. Wilson, Hq CACW, APO 627 (Kunming), letter to his family dated October 11, 1944, "General Claire Lee Chennault (1890–1958)," China National Aviation Corp. (CNAC) Official Home Page, 2007, posted by Tom O. Moore Jr., https://cnac.org/chennault01.htm.

23. "Interesting Letter Tells of Service in China and India."
24. Stoumen, "What It's Like for Our China GIs."
25. US WWII Hospital Admission Card Files.
26. Aircraft Accident Report #45-1022-522.
27. "City Flier Tells of Close Call in Leap from Plane over China," *Minneapolis Star*, January 19, 1945, 13, https://www.newspapers.com/.
28. Susan L. Shock Garfield, daughter of Joseph N. Shock, telephone conversation, October 2, 2013, and email to author, same date, and following.
29. John T. Correll, "Chennault and Stilwell," *Air Force Magazine*, December 20, 2012, https://www.airforcemag.com/PDF/MagazineArchive/Magazine%20Documents/2015/December%202015/1215chennault.pdf.
30. Grimm, telephone conversation, October 16, 2014, and following, and letter, July 11, 2015.
31. US WWII Hospital Admission Card Files.
32. "War and Remembrances: History Told by China's Flying Tigers Veteran."
33. Simpson, email to author, July 26, 2013.

Chapter 9: Task Force 34 at Chihkiang

1. Lopez, *Into the Teeth of the Tiger*, 197–200.
2. Molesworth and Moseley, *Wing to Wing*, 67–70.
3. Safford, no title.
4. Richard Watts Jr., "New York Drama Critic Surveys the China Scene and Reports the GTravels of Pat, Jinx & Company," *CBI Roundup*, November 16, 1944, https://cbi-theater-1.home.comcast.net/~cbi-theater-1/roundup/roundup111644.html.
5. "While Family Thought Him in Safe Job, Lt. Cantor Flew 42 Missions in China," *Herald-News* (Passaic, NJ), November 15, 1944, https://www.newspapers.com/.
6. George H. Johnson, "Chungking," *China Lantern*, May 5, 1945, https://www.cbi-theater.com/lantern/lantern050445.html.
7. Lt. Lester H. Geiss, ed., "$2,500 (CN) for a Cat in Chungking," *China Command Post*, March 2, 1945, https://www.cbi-theater.com/china_ command_ post/command_post_030245.html.
8. Grimm, telephone conversation, October 16, 2014, and following, and letter, July 11, 2015.
9. "World War II Norden Bombsight," Factsheets, Hill Air Force Base, September 25, 2007, http://www.hill.af.mil/library/factsheets/factsheet.asp?id5664.
10. Debbie McCutcheon, email to author September 20, 2021, includes articles: James M. White, "Tiger Cubs," no title or publishing information, 9, 10; and Dave Hughes, "Flying Tigers Decorated," *Southwest Times Record* (Branch, AR), n.d. but probably 1976, 1A, 5A.

11. Rosholt, *Flight in the China Air Space, 1910–1950*, 173.

12. Oswald Weinert, letter to the Veterans' Administration; contributed by his son, Ossie H. Weinert, March 3, 2014.

13. "Resort Man in China Is Awarded Medal for Dangerous Volunteer Mission," *Sentinel-Ledger*, n.d. or page number, contributed by Mary Henry, email to author, June 22, 2014.

14. "Men in Uniform," *Times Record News* (Wichita Falls, TX), August 23, 1945, https://www.genealogybank.com/doc/newspapers/.

15. Yeager, email to author, February 24, 2014.

16. Weinert, email to author, November 19, 2013, and following.

17. 2nd Lt. James R. Smith, "Chengtu," in *Night Fighter: A Memoir of the China-Burma-India Theater*, published online by the family of James R. Smith, http://www.night-fighter.us/Chapter03.html.

18. "Kwan-Sien Rest Camp Opened near APO 210," *China Lantern*, Kunming and Calcutta, July 31, 1945, https://www.cbi-theater.com/lantern/lantern073145.html.

19. Joseph F. Baugher, "Operation Matterhorn," April 17, 2000, http://www.joebaugher.com/usaf_bombers/b29_9.html.

20. Lee Bowen, "Victory in China," in *HyperWar: The Army Air Forces in WWII*, vol. 5, *The Pacific: MATTERHORN to Nagasaki, June 1944 to August 1945; Part II—Aid to China; The Theater Air Forces in CBI*, ed. Wesley Frank Craven and James Lea Cate, 252, https://www.ibiblio.org/hyperwar/AAF/V/AAF-V-9.html; and Kraus, "Strategic Setting," 8–9.

21. US WWII Hospital Admission Card Files.

22. "Vet of 67 Missions Reenlists in Service," *Spokane Chronicle* (Spokane, WA), March 1, 1946, https://www.newspapers.com/; and "Hoe Replacing Sword at Fort," *Spokesman Review*, Apr. 7, 1945, ibid.

Chapter 10: Successes and Setbacks

1. Hughes, "Flying Tigers Decorated."

2. "While Family Thought Him in Safe Job, Lt. Cantor Flew 42 Missions in China."

3. Aircraft Accident Report #44-1218-519, "USAAF Incident & Accident Personnel List," Accident-Report.com, *Military Aviation Incident Reports*, purchased from Michael T. Stowe and received by email, October 9, 2013.

4. Ossie H. Weinert, email to author, November 19, 2013, and following.

5. Molesworth and Moseley, *Wing to Wing*, 115–16.

6. Daniels, *China Bombers*, 65.

7. Molesworth and Moseley, *Wing to Wing*, 125.

8. "Chinese Warned US Plans Attacks on Key Jap Ports" (quoting Maj. Gen. Robert B. McClure, US chief of staff, China theater, *Harrisburg Telegraph* (Harrisburg, PA), December 21, 1944, https://www.newspapers.com.

9. Kevin Senecal, son of Wayne H. Senecal, email to author, June 17, 2019, and following.
10. Lyon, email to author, October 23, 2013.
11. "College Graduate," *Morning Call* (Paterson, NJ), May 22, 1942, https://www.newspapers.com; and "Gets His Wings," *The News* (Paterson, NJ), July 27, 1944, Ibid.
12. US WWII Hospital Admission Card Files.

Chapter 11: Relocating to Liangshan

1. Christine Ilefeldt Hance, daughter of Willard G. Ilefeldt, email to author, February 3, 2014, and following.
2. Willard G. Ilefeldt, *Thoughts While Tending Sheep* (New York: Crown, 1988), 35, 111–16, 141, 180, 186, 220–21.
3. "Janet Shaw, 82; Actress Had Role in 'Jezebel,'" *Los Angeles Times*, October 23, 2001, B10, https://www.newspapers.com/.
4. Stoumen, "What It's Like for Our China GIs."
5. Wendi Borst, granddaughter of Thomas H. Edgerton, email to author, June 1, 2014, and following.
6. "Cessna Takes NYA Students," *Hutchinson News* (Hutchinson, KS), September 4, 1942, 12, https://www.newspapers.com/; and "Clyde Learn in China," *Indiana Gazette* (Indiana, PA), July 2, 1945, 10, Ibid.
7. Lyon, email to author, October 22 and December 8, 2013.
8. "Missing Air Crew Report No. 11885," *Missing Air Crew Reports (MACRs) and Related Records of the US Army Air Forces, 1942–1947*, publication M1380, catalog ID 3055256, Record Group 92, National Archives and Records Administration, https://www.fold3.com/.
9. Borst, email to author, May 20, 2014.
10. Kathy Koss Schaar, niece of Robert J. Koss, letter to author dated July 30, 2017.
11. Borst, email to author, May 20, 2014.
12. Johnson, *A Long Journey Home*.
13. Ibid.
14. R. Aubrey Lafoy, "Fragile," *Down Memory Lane Blog, Dickinson County News* (Spirit Lake, IA), July 12, 2013, http://www.dickinsoncountynews.com/blogs/1415/entry/53907/; and Lafoy, email to author August 5, 2013. (By this time, Lafoy had been transferred to the 2459th Quartermaster Truck Co. Avn., 12th Air Service Group).
15. Molesworth and Moseley, *Wing to Wing*, 50; and Daniels, *China Bombers*, 32, 60.
16. "An Interview with Maj. Gen. Du Kai-mu," 84.
17. Molesworth and Moseley, *Wing to Wing*, 163.
18. Kraus, "Strategic Setting," 12–13.

Chapter 12: Defending Laohokow

1. Daniels, *China Bombers*, 59–60.
2. Paige Conrad Boles, daughter of Chester M. Conrad, email to author, September 17, 2013, and following.
3. "Seacrest with Chinese Friend," *Nebraska State Journal* (Lincoln, NE), January 17, 1945, 1, https://www.newspapers.com/.
4. Johnson, *A Long Journey Home*.
5. Smith, "Laohokow," in *Night Fighter*.
6. Barbara Hughes, niece of Robert J. Koss, email to author, July 18, 2017, and following; Schaar, email to author, July 19, 2017, and Primozic, email to author, July 19, 2017, and following.
7. "Chinese Gain in Hankow Area," *China Command Post*, February 16, 1945, https://www.cbi-theater.com/china_command_post/command_post_021645.html.
8. "Japs Regain Pingshek on Canton-Hankow Railway," *Gazette and Daily* (York, PA), February 19, 1945, 24, https://www.newspapers.com/.
9. Daniels, *China Bombers*, 45.
10. Ibid., 65–66.
11. Ibid.
12. "War Diary of the 489th Bomb Squadron, February 1944," prepared by S-2 personnel under supervision of 1st Lt. Jack A. Casper, 57th Bomb Wing Association, 2008, http://57thbombwing.com/340th_History/489th_History/transcripts/7_Hist_Transcript_Feb_1944.pdf; and Daniel Setzer, 57th Bomb Wing historian, email to author, November 2, 2020.
13. Faherty, email to author, June 20, 2022, and following.
14. Daniel Thompson, "I grew up in Montezuma, KS and I remember . . ." group, Facebook, October 29, 2021, post describing Barton L. Wherritt's military service in honor of Memorial Day.

Chapter 13: Last Airfield Lost

1. Schaar, email to author, July 19, 2017, and following.
2. "An Interview with Maj. Gen. Du Kai-mu," 77.
3. "Lieutenant in Burma Area Reported Lost," *Long Beach Press-Telegram* (Long Beach, CA), June 15, 1945, https://www.newspapers.com/.
4. "More or Less Personal," *Bedford Daily-Times Mail* (Bedford, IN), May 7, 1945, https://www.newspapers.com/.
5. Johnson, *A Long Journey Home*.
6. Daniels, *China Bombers*, 75–6.
7. "An Interview with Maj. Gen. Du Kai-mu," 77–83; and Hui, "A General's Wartime Memory of US-ROC Cooperation."

8. "Chinese Open Counterblows against Six Jap Columns," *Salt Lake Tribune* (Salt Lake City, UT), March 28, 1945, 5, https://www.newspapers.com/.

9. Lopez, *Into the Teeth of the Tiger*, 124.

10. Sibyl Greene Cryer, daughter of Frederick H. Greene, email to author, September 9 and 10, 2015; and Elizabeth Greene Herrick, daughter of Frederick H. Greene, email to author, November 28 and December 1, 2015.

11. Barton Rieks, son of Maynard W. Rieks, telephone conversation, September 28, 2013.

12. Johnson, *A Long Journey Home*.

13. Molesworth and Moseley, *Wing to Wing*, 137.

14. "Chinese-American Composite Wing Hits Japs Hard in Sorties," *Brownsville Herald* (Brownsville, TX), August 5, 1945, 9, https://www.newspapers.com.

Chapter 14: Holding Chihkiang

1. Lynn Magyar Zwigard, daughter of Alfred J. Magyar, email to author, January 22, 2014, and following.

2. John Schroeder, son of Edmund Schroeder, email to author, September 22, 2015, and following.

3. Harry Grayson, "Yanks and Chinese Made Chihchiang Air Base Too Hot for Japanese to Hold," *Indiana Gazette* (Indiana, PA), July 25, 1945, 15, https://www.newspapers.com/.

4. "Chihkiang Loss Is Blow to Japanese Hopes," *Hump Express*, June 7, 1945, https://www.cbi-theater.com/hump_express/hump060745.html.

5. Molesworth and Moseley, *Wing to Wing*, 155–56; and Bowen, "Victory in China," 264, https://www.ibiblio.org/hyperwar/AAF/V/AAF-V-9.html.

6. Bowers, "Reuben Ragland's Adventurous Spirit," 10.

7. "Impressive Memorial Service for Roosevelt in Kunming," *China Lantern*, April 20, 1945, https://www.cbitheater.com/ lantern/lantern042045.html.

8. Molesworth and Moseley, *Wing to Wing*, 35–36, 103.

9. Schaar, email to author, July 19, 2017, and following.

10. Clyde A. Farnsworth, "Human Detonators Used by Japanese," *China Lantern*, May 18, 1945, https://www.cbi-theater.com/lantern/lantern051845.html.

11. John Hamilton and Michael Hamilton, sons of Jack M. Hamilton, emails to author July 26, 2016, and following.

12. Albert Ravenholt, "Japs Pour into Honan Sector," *China Lantern*, April 20, 1945, https://www.cbi-theater.com/lantern/lantern042045.html.

13. Yeager, email to author, February 1 and 24, 2014, and following; and "Papers of Edith Millican, M.D., 1943–1948: Edith Millican to Friends," item #a022_013, December 10, 1945, Archives and Special Collections, Drexel University, College of Medicine, http://xdl.drexelmed.edu/.

14. "Dickinson Reservist Finds Service Still Full of Forms," *Bismarck Tribune* (Bismarck, ND), April 25, 1962, 12, https://www.newspapers.com/.

15. Dennis K. Drake, son of Clarence H. Drake, telephone conversation, July 11, 2018, and email to author, July 6, 2018, and following.

16. Betsy Curik Ross, daughter of William L. Curik, email to author, July 9, 2016, and following.

Chapter 15: Turning the Tide

1. "China No Longer 'Forgotten Theater,'" *China Lantern*, May 4, 1945, https://www.cbi-theater.com/lantern/lantern050445.html.

2. Christine Armbruster Moore, daughter of Russell J. Armbruster, email to author, March 3, 2014.

3. Kenneth Lancaster, brother-in-law of James J. Ryan Jr., email to author, April 7 and 16, 2016.

4. Drake, telephone conversation, July 11, 2018, and email to author, July 6, 2018, and following.

5. Lt. Col. Kenneth Kay, USAF (retired), "Disturbing Events."

6. "An Interview with Maj. Gen. Du Kai-mu," 74.

7. Daniels, *China Bombers*, 32.

8. Cecil B. Dickson, "Chinese Fliers Successful, Colonel Says," *Ithaca Journal* (Ithaca, NY), June 25, 1945, 12, https://www.newspapers.com/.

9. "Col. McGehee Writes from China; Tells of Work of M/Sgt. John Barge," *Greenville Advocate* (Greenville, AL), June 28, 1945, 4, https://www.newspapers.com/.

10. Beth Banger Meehan, daughter of Robert E. Banger, email to author, October 29, 2015.

11. "Military Curfew Goes into Effect throughout China on May 15," *China Lantern*, May 4, 1945, http://www.cbi-theater.com/lantern/lantern050445.html.

12. "Harlie D. Reynard Sr., 88, St. Petersburg," *Tampa Bay Times* (St. Petersburg, FL), September 19, 2006, 9, https://www.newspapers.com/.

13. "Missing Air Crew Report #14442," *Missing Air Crew Reports (MACRs) and Related Records of the US Army Air Forces, 1942–1947*, publication M1380, catalog ID 3055256, Record Group 92, National Archives and Records Administration, https://www.fold3.com/.

14. "US Rosters of World War II Dead, 1939–1945," original data from United States Army, Quartermaster General's Office, Washington, DC, 2007, https://www.ancestry.com/.

15. Cryer, email to author, September 10, 2015, and following.

16. Farnsworth, "China Fliers Chastise Nips," *Arizona Republic* (Phoenix, AZ), May 20, 1945, 9, https://www.newspapers.com/.

17. O. H. Weinert, email to author, November 19, 2013, and following.

18. "Chinese Forces Gain Control on Hunan Front," *China Lantern*, May 18, 1945, https://www.cbi-theater.com/lantern/lantern051845.html.

19. Grayson, "Yanks and Chinese Made Chihchiang Air Base Too Hot for Japs to Hold."
20. Bowen, "Victory in China," 266.
21. "Tigers' Unspectacular Blow Neutralizes Japs' Advantages," *China Lantern*, June 8, 1945, https://www.cbi-theater.com/lantern/lantern060845.html.
22. "Stearns Promoted," *The Monitor* (McAllen, TX), July 4, 1943, 11, https://www.newspapers.com/; and Duane Kimbrow, nephew of Fred S. Stearns, email to author, March 1 and 2, 2014.
23. "Statement of Captain Frederick H. Greene Jr., Pilot A/C," contributed by Beth Meehan.
24. Dong-Phuong Nguyen, "Marked by WWII, Now Daily Loss," *Tampa Bay Times* (St. Petersburg, FL), September 6, 2006, https://www.tampabay.com/archive/2006/09/19/marked-by-wwii-now-daily-loss/; and David Reynard, son of Harley D. Reynard, email to author, June 6, 2016, and following.
25. Robert G. Hugel, letter and telephone conversation, June 27, 2014.
26. Gloria Senecal, wife of Wayne H. Senecal, telephone conversation, September 27, 2013.
27. Lopez, *Into the Teeth of the Tiger*, 125.
28. Meehan, telephone conversation, October 14, 2015, and email to author, October 29, 2015, and following.
29. "Missing Air Crew Report #14519," *Missing Air Crew Reports (MACRs) and Related Records of the US Army Air Forces, 1942–1947*, publication M1380, catalog ID 3055256, Record Group 92, National Archives and Records Administration, http://www.fold3.com/; and E. D. Johnson, *A Long Journey Home*.
30. US WWII Hospital Admission Card Files.
31. Grimm, telephone conversation, October 16, 2014, and following, and letter to author, July 11, 2015.
32. Johnson, *A Long Journey Home*.
33. Barton Rieks, telephone conversation, September 28, 2013.
34. Kraus, "Operations," 16.

Chapter 16: End in Sight

1. "With the Armed Forces," *Crowley Post-Signal* (Crowley, LA), August 3, 1945, 3, https://www.newspapers.com/.
2. "Col. McGehee Writes from China."
3. Susan Langridge Rees, daughter of Joseph A. Langridge, email to author, May 12, 2014, and following.
4. Steve Bowen, son of Francis H. Bowen, email to author, March 27, 2014.
5. "Veteran Houston War Flier Awarded Chinese Wings," *Houston Press* (Houston, TX), July 18, 1945, 12, clipping contributed by John Hamilton.

6. "Liuchow Threatened: Chinese Liberate Thousands as Jap Withdrawal Continues," *China Lantern*, June 6, 1945, https://www.cbi-theater.com/lantern/ lantern060845.html.

7. Bowen, "Victory in China," 266.

8. "Callan Cruises, August 1944–June 1946," in *USS R. E. Callan, WWII Navy Cruise Books*, 21, image 301673723 21, https://www.fold3.com/.

9. Jackie Hutchinson Pitts, daughter of Otto W. Hutchinson, email to author, June 28, 2018, and following, and telephone conversation, July 5, 2018.

10. "Dave Ewell Jr., Now at Camp Polk, Likes It," *State Times Advocate* (Baton Rouge, LA), September 17, 1941, 6, https://www.genealogybank.com/doc/newspapers/.

11. Barbara Ewell, daughter of Dave H. Ewell Jr., email to author, September 18, 2014, and following.

12. "Superior Californians Graduate as Mechanics," *Sacramento Bee* (Sacramento, CA), February 8, 1943, 15, https://www.genealogybank.com/doc/newspapers/; "In the Service: Graduations," *Sacramento Bee*, March 24, 1943, 2, https://www.newspapers.com/; and "In the Service: Overseas," *Sacramento Bee*, June 29, 1945, 3, https://www.newspapers.com/.

13. Cindy Czerniak Halsey, daughter of Bernard J. Czerniak, email to author, December 13, 2015.

14. Mark Mondelli, son of Leslie L. Mondelli, email to author, June 18, 2016, and following.

15. "Big Supply Dumps of Enemy in New Guinea Bombed by Local Flier," *Times-Tribune* (Scranton, PA), January 12, 1943, 12, https://www.newspapers.com/.

16. "Captain Mondelli Again Zooms over Home; Bids Adieu to Another Brother Entering Navy," *The Tribune* (Scranton, PA), March 27, 1944, 3, https://www.newspapers.com/; and "Promote Mondelli to Major; Serving with Flying Tigers," *The Tribune* (Scranton, PA), September 15, 1945, Ibid.

17. Stephen DiBartola, son of Richard C. Wellman, posts to author via Ancestry.com on July 30, 2018, and following.

18. Jarrett McConnell, son of Jeanette Davis McConnell (widow of Donald J. Davis) by second marriage, email to author, November 27, 2015, and following.

19. Safford, no title.

Chapter 17: Victory in China

1. John Gong, photos of banner posted on "The China Air War" Facebook group, April 9, 2018; and Szu-ming (James) Peng, owner of banner, email to author, April 9, 2018 (provided translation).

2. Safford, no title.

3. "Maj. Gen. Chennault's Order of the Day," *China Lantern*, USAAF in China Anniversary Edition, July 6, 1945, https://www.cbi-theater.com/lantern/lantern-aaf.html.

4. Wanda Cornelius and Thayne Short, *Ding Hao: America's Air War in China, 1937–1945* (Gretna, LA: Pelican, 2004), 468–69.

5. Robert Trumm, son of John A. Trumm, email to author, October 26, 2021, and following; and Faherty, email to author, June 20, 2022, and following.

6. Johnson, *A Long Journey Home.*

7. "An Interview with Maj. Gen. Du Kai-mu," 76.

8. Lancaster, email to author, April 7 and 16, 2016 (quotations from newspaper article referenced).

9. Hughes, email to author, July 18, 2017, and following.

10. Bowen, "Victory in China," 266.

11. Molesworth and Moseley, *Wing to Wing,* 175.

12. Drake, telephone conversation, July 11, 2018, and email to author, July 6, 2018.

13. Daniels, *China Bombers,* 94; and Molesworth and Moseley, *Wing to Wing,* 172–74.

14. Daniels, *China Bombers,* 94.

15. SGM Herbert A. Friedman (ret.), "Propaganda to the Occupied Nations."

16. Andrew Glass, "Hirohito Accepts Japan's Surrender Terms, August 14, 1945," *POLITICO Magazine,* August 14, 2008, https://www.politico.com/story/2018/08/14/hirohito-accepts-japanese-surrender-terms-aug-14-1945-771008.

17. Hui, "A General's Wartime Memory of US-ROC Cooperation."

18. "An Interview with Maj. Gen. Du Kai-mu," 86.

19. "Chinese Ready for Nip Chiefs," *Chico Record* (Chico, CA), August 23, 1945, 1, https://www.newspapers.com/; and "Japanese Envoys Reach Chihkiang," *The Gazette* (Montreal, Quebec, Canada), August 22, 1945, 21, Ibid.

20. Kraus, 19.

21. Rosholt, *Flight in the China Air Space,* 173.

22. "'Big Job' Still Ahead of CT Air Force Says 'Strat,'" *China Lantern,* August 23, 1945, https://www .cbi-theater.com/lantern/lantern082345.html.

23. "An Interview with Maj. Gen. Du Kai-mu," 86–87.

24. "14th Air Force in China: From Volunteers to Regulars," *US Air Force Fact Sheet,* Department of the Air Force, https://www.nationalmuseum.af.mil/Visit/Museum-Exhibits/Fact-Sheets/Display/Article/196212/14th-air-force-in-china-from-volunteers-to-regulars/.

25. "Accomplishments of the Fourteenth Air Force: March 10, 1943–August 1, 1945," *Fourteenth Air Force,* Sino-American Aviation Heritage Foundation, http://www.sinoam.com/photo_gallery_7-1.htm.

Chapter 18: Back to the ZI

1. Daniels, *China Bombers,* 94.

2. "22nd Bomb Squadron's Personnel Roster, May 42–Nov 45," source, *Eagles, Bulldogs and Tigers: History of the 22nd Bm Squadron in China-Burma-India,* no publishing information, http://www.usaaf-in-cbi.com/341st_web/intel/sqd_22/22nd_personnel.htm.

3. Daniel P. Johnson, son of Paul R. Johnson, email to author, October 26 and 30, 2017.

4. USS *General E. T. Collins*: War Diary, 8/31/45, micro serial #149845, serial #196, reel #A1953, from *World War II War Diaries, 1941–1945*, Record Group #38, National Archives and Records Administration, catalog ID #4697018, https://www.fold3.com/.

5. Garfield, telephone conversation, October 2, 2013, and email to author, October 2, 2013, and following.

6. USS *General J. H. McRae*, New York Passenger Lists, 1820–1957, https://www.ancestry.com/.

7. USS *General C. G. Morton*: War Diary, 10/1/45 to 10/30/45, micro serial #131751, reel #A1739, from *World War II War Diaries, 1941–1945*, Record Group #38, National Archives and Records Administration, catalog ID #4697018 https://www.fold3.com/; USS *General C. G. Morton*, New York Passenger Lists, 1820–1957, https://www.ancestry.com/; and "Hero Dogs, Too!," *Cincinnati Enquirer*, October 23, 1945, 10, https://www.newspapers.com/.

8. USS *General C. H. Muir*: War Diary, 11/1–30/45, micro serial #153739, serial #07017, reel #A1998, from *World War II War Diaries, 1941–1945*, Record Group #38, National Archives and Records Administration, catalog ID #4697018, https://www.fold3.com/; and "Prince Saved after Four Hours in Water," *Greenville News* (Greenville, SC), Nov. 2, 1945, 1, https://www.newspapers.com/.

9. USS *General Charles H. Muir*, New York, Passenger Lists, 1820–1957, https://www.ancestry.com/.

10. "Four Pilots Land in N. Y. From China," *Newark Star-Ledger*, Nov. 2, 1945, https://www.genealogybank.com/doc/newspapers/.

11. USS *General C. C. Ballou*, New York, Arriving Passenger and Crew Lists (including Castle Garden and Ellis Island), 1820–1957 (database) (Provo, UT: Ancestry.com Operations, 2010), original data: Passenger Lists of Vessels Arriving at New York, New York, 1820–1897, Microfilm Publication M237, 675 rolls, NAI: 6256867, Records of the US Customs Service, Record Group 36, National Archives at Washington, DC; and Passenger and Crew Lists of Vessels Arriving at New York, New York, 1897–1957, Microfilm Publication T715, 8,892 rolls, NAI: 300346, Records of the Immigration and Naturalization Service, National Archives at Washington, DC, https://www.ancestry.com/.

12. "Chinese Entitled to GI Equipment," *China Lantern*, August 23, 1945, https://www.cbi-theater.com/lantern/lantern082345.html.

13. "No 'Chicken' at Malir as G.I.'s Wait for Shangri-La Bound Vessels," *India-Burma Theater Roundup*, October 11, 1945, https://www.cbi-theater.com/roundup/roundup101145.html.

14. "19,000 Troops Due to Arrive in East Today," *St. Louis Globe-Democrat* (St. Louis, MO), November 2, 1945, 5, https://www.newspapers.com/.

15. USS *General George O. Squier*: War Diary, 10/1/45 to 10/31/45 and 11/1/45 to 1/30/45, micro serial #153742, serial #559, reel #A1998, from *World War II War Diaries, 1941–1945*, Record Group #38, National Archives and Records Administration, catalog ID #4697018, https://www.fold3.com/; and "USS *General George O. Squier*, New York, Passenger Lists, 1820–1957, https://www.ancestry.com/.

16. "Yank Brings Pet Monkey From Jungle," *Los Angeles Times*, November 4, 1944, 5, https://www.newspapers.com/.

17. Pitts, email to author, June 28, 2018, and following.

18. Ewell, email to author, September 18, 2014, and following.

19. USS *Alderamin*: War Diary, 12/1/45 to 12/31/45, micro serial #154474, serial #033, reel #A2004, from *World War II War Diaries, 1941–1945*, Record Group #38, National Archives and Records Administration, catalog ID #4697018, https://www.fold3.com/; and USS *General George O. Squier*, New York, Passenger Lists, 1820–1957, https://www.fold3.com/.

20. "Ship Jammed with Troops Writer Claims," *Great Falls Tribune* (Great Falls, MT), January 6, 1946, 3, https://www.newspapers.com/.

21. DiBartola.

Chapter 19: Aftermath of War

1. "Army Searches for 'Missing' in China," *Abilene Reporter* (Abilene, TX), January 30, 1946, 4, https://www.newspapers.com/.

2. "Indo-China Areas Are Being Scoured for Lost Airmen," *Kingston Daily Freeman* (Kingston, NY), February 12, 1946, 11, https://www.newspapers.com/.

3. McConnell, email to author, November 27, 2015, and following.

4. Terry Godfrey Healy, niece of Barton L. Wherritt, email to author, November 29, 2014, and following.

5. "Report 1st Lt. James Koss Killed in Action over China," *Daily Calumet* (Chicago), Feb. 25, 1946, 1, https://www.newspapers.com/.

6. McConnell, email to author, November 27, 2015, and following

7. "Memorial Set for War Hero," *Long Beach Independent* (Long Beach, CA), July 12, 1949, 10, https://www.newspapers.com/.

8. "Mrs. Peck Is Honored with Bridal Shower," *Leedey Star* (Leedey, OK), July 20, 1949, 4, https://www.newspapers.com/.

9. "James Wadlow's Funeral Sunday," *Daily Oklahoman* (Oklahoma City, OK), July 15, 1949, 36, https://www.newspapers.com/.

10. "Three More War Dead Are Coming to S.E. Chicago," *Daily Calumet* (Chicago), June 17, 1949, 1, https://www.newspapers.com/.

11. Lancaster, email to author, April 7 and 16, 2016.

12. Ting, correspondence via Facebook Messenger, March 9, 2019, and following.

13. Johnson, email to author, October 26, 30, and 31, 2017.

14. Pitts, email to author, June 28, 2018, and following.

15. "The Chinese Revolution of 1949," *Milestones: 1945–1952*, Office of the Historian, US Department of State, n.d., https://history.state.gov/milestones/1945–1952/chinese-rev#:~:text=The%20announcement %20ended%20the%20costly,two%20 sides%20since%20the%201920's.

16. "500 Chinese Are in Training at State Air Field," *Galveston Daily News* (Galveston, TX), July 19, 1946, 11, https://www.newspapers.com/.

17. "An Interview with Maj. Gen. Du Kai-mu," 87–88.

18. Hui, "A General's Wartime Memory of US-ROC Cooperation; and Peng, Facebook post, January 31, 2021.

19. Huen, email to author, December 14, 2014.

20. Ting, correspondence via Facebook Messenger, March 9, 2019, and following.

21. "20 Years Later," *Herald-News* (Passaic, NJ), July 13, 1965, 5, https://www.newspapers.com/; and Ronnie Cantor, daughter of Gerald J. Cantor, email to author, May 1, 2017, and following.

22. Grimm, telephone conversation, October 16, 2014, and following, and letter, July 11, 2015.

23. "William L. Daniels" autobiographical sketch.

24. Bowers, "Reuben Ragland's Adventurous Spirit."

25. Ewell, email to author, September 18, 2014, and following.

26. Hinrichs, telephone conversation, June 6, 2016.

27. "Howard Goeller Alabama," *Columbus Herald* (Columbus, IN), December 27, 1974, https://www.newspapers.com/.

28. K. Senecal, email to author, June 17, 2019, and following.

29. "Rae M. Delahoyde," *Ukiah Daily Journal* (Ukiah, UT), May 30, 1990, 14, https://www.newspapers.com/.

30. "Circulation Director Will Tour Europe," *Lincoln Journal Star* (Lincoln, NE), September 18, 1955, 8, https://www.newspapers.com/.

31. Alex H. Washburn, "Publisher Graves Leaves Nashville News for the War," *Hope Star* (Hope, AR), August 1, 1950, 1, https://www.newspapers.com/.

32. Yeager, email to author, February 1 and 24, 2014, and following.

33. "Hugel, Robert G.," *Hartford Courant* (Hartford, CT), October 23, 2016, B7, https://www.newspapers.com/.

34. "Core Wrapping Apparatus," US Patents, https://patents.google.com/patent/US2989430A/en.

35. Ilefeldt, *Thoughts While Tending Sheep*.

36. Grimm, telephone conversation, October 16, 202014, and following, and letter, July 11, 2015.

37. Ibid.

38. Cunningham, telephone conversation and email to author, July 7, 2015.

39. Simpson, email to author, July 26, 2013, and following.

40. J. Hamilton, email to author, July 26, 2016, and following.

41. Boles, email to author, September 17, 2013, and following.

42. "He Needs Help," *Daily Oklahoman* (Oklahoma City, OK), May 19, 1947, 3, https://www.newspapers.com/.

43. Pitts, email to author, June 28, 2018, and following.

44. "Guard Air Unit, Led by Heroes, Flexes Wings," *Chicago Tribune*, October 12, 1947, 48, https://www .newspapers.com/.

45. "Dickinson Reservist Finds Service Still Full of Forms."

46. Hughes, "Flying Tigers Decorated."

47. Zea, email to author, February 6, 2014, and following.

48. Cunningham, telephone conversation and email to author, July 7, 2015.

49. "Flying Tigers Hold Convention," *Taiwan Today*, Ministry of Foreign Affairs, Republic of China (Taiwan), originally published June 2, 1985, 2015, http://taiwaninfo.nat.gov.tw/fp.as;?xItem=113757&CtNode=103&mp=4; and Jamora, email to author, June 12 and July 21, 2014.

50. "War and Remembrances . . ."

BIBLIOGRAPHY

Unpublished histories

Air Force Historical Research Agency (AFHRA), Maxwell AFB, AL. Microfilm reel #A0535. Images #5–646. Historical records of the 2nd Bombardment Squadron (Provisional). Microfilmed November 14, 1973. CD-ROM.

———. Microfilm reel #A0535. Images #962–2006. Historical records of the 3rd Bombardment Squadron (Provisional). CD-ROM.

———. Microfilm reel #A0535. Images #2007–2371. Historical records of the 4th Bombardment Squadron (Provisional). CD-ROM.

———. Microfilm reel #A8351. Images #656–1375. Historical records of the Chinese-American Composite Wing (Provisional). Microfilmed September 20, 1976. CD-ROM.

———. Microfilm reel #B0035. Images #1–691. Historical records of the 1st Bombardment Group (M) (Provisional), Chinese-American Composite Wing. Microfilmed January 22, 1973. CD-ROM.

———. Microfilm reel #B0035. Images #1465–1890. Historical records of the 2nd Bombardment Squadron (Provisional). CD-ROM.

———. Microfilm reel #B0036. Images #12–276. Historical records of Task Force 34. Microfilmed January 22, 1973. CD-ROM.

———. Microfilm reel #B0036. Images #4–10 and #277–526. Historical records of the 1st Bomb Group (April 16–August 15, 1945). CD-ROM.

Interviews

"James Henry Mills Collection." #AFC/2001/001/82472. Veterans History Project, American Folklife Center, Library of Congress. Interview by Nell Calloway (granddaughter of Lt. Gen. Claire Lee Chennault), director, Chennault Aviation & Military Museum. Monroe, LA. July 5, 2011. CD-ROM.

"James Henry ('Hank') Mills." Interview by Eric F. F. Huen, president, Society of Oral History on Modern China. Orange, TX. January 24, 2015.

James H. Mills. Informal interviews by author. Orange, TX. January 17, 18, and 19, 2014; and July 25, 26, and 27, 2014.

Other JHM comments are from private conversations, various dates.

All details of events in this squadron history were taken from the above-referenced sources unless otherwise noted.

"Tu Kai-mu." Interview by Samuel Hui and Pan-I Jung. Taipei, Taiwan. December 2013.

"War and Remembrances: History Told by China's Flying Tigers Veteran." Interview of Li Zhanrui by Wu Guoxiu. China Global Television Network. Beijing, China. July 6, 2015. https://www.youtube.com/watch?v=aMa0OBu-DAc.

Articles

"12th Bombardment Group." Army Air Corps Library & Museum. 2013. Data from *Air Force Combat Units of World War II* by Maurer Maurer, published 1986. http://www.armyaircorpsmuseum.org/12th_Bombardment_Group.cfm.

"14th Air Force in China: From Volunteers to Regulars." *US Air Force Fact Sheet*. Department of the Air Force. https://www.nationalmuseum.af.mil/Visit/Museum-Exhibits/Fact-Sheets/Display/Article/196212/14th-air-force-in-china-from-volunteers-to-regulars/.

"14th Air Force Pounds Enemy in Dark Hour." *CBI Roundup*, October 5, 1944. Carl Warren Weidenburner, *China-Burma-India: Remembering the Forgotten Theater of World War II*, 2009 (hereafter cited as Weidenburner). https://cbi-theater-1.home.comcast.net/~cbi-theater-1/roundup/roundup100544.html.

"20 Years Later." *Herald-News* (Passaic, NJ), July 13, 1965, 5. https://www.newspapers.com/.

"22nd Bomb Squadron's Personnel Roster, May 42–Nov 45." Source, *Eagles, Bulldogs and Tigers: History of the 22nd Bm Sqdn in China-Burma-India*; no publishing information. http://www.usaaf-in-cbi.com/341st_web/intel/sqd_22/22nd_personnel.htm.

"100 Men Brought Fall of Myitkyina." *CBI Roundup*, August 10, 1944. Weidenburner 2006. https://cbi-theater-1.home.comcast.net/~cbi-theater-1/roundup/roundup081044.html.

"500 Chinese Are in Training at State Air Field." *Galveston Daily News* (Galveston, TX), July 19, 1946, 11. https://www.newspapers.com/.

"19,000 Troops Due to Arrive in East Today." *St. Louis Globe-Democrat* (St. Louis, MO), November 2,1945, 5. https://www.newspapers.com/.

"Accomplishments of the Fourteenth Air Force: March 10, 1943–August 1, 1945." *Fourteenth Air Force*. Sino-American Aviation Heritage Foundation. http://www.sinoam.com/photo_gallery_7-1.htm.

"Army Searches for 'Missing' in China." *Abilene Reporter* (Abilene, TX), January 30, 1946, 4. https://www.newspapers.com/.

"B-25J Mitchell 'Show Me.'" Commemorative Air Force: Missouri Wing. https://cafmo.org/index.php?option=com_content&view=article&id=8&Itemid=32.

Baugher, Joseph F. "Operation Matterhorn." April 17, 2000. http://www.joebaugher.com/usaf_bombers/b29_9.html.

Bernstein, Marc D. "Joseph Stilwell's Escape from Burma during World War II." Historynet.com, June 12, 2006. https://www.historynet.com/joseph-stilwells-escape-from-burma-during-world-war-ii.htm.

"'Big Job' Still Ahead of CT Air Force Says 'Strat.'" *China Lantern*, August 23, 1945. Weidenburner 2014. https://www.cbi-theater.com/lantern/lantern082345.html.

"Big Supply Dumps of Enemy in New Guinea Bombed by Local Flier." *Times-Tribune* (Scranton, PA), January 12, 1943, 12. https://www.newspapers.com/.

Bowers, Kathy. "Reuben Ragland's Adventurous Spirit." *Senior Choices* (Baptist Health System and St. Vincent Hospital), Winter 1994, 4. Contributed by John Ragland.

"Captain Mondelli Again Zooms over Home; Bids Adieu to Another Brother Entering Navy." *The Tribune* (Scranton, PA), March 27, 1944, 3. https://www.newspapers.com/.

Casper, 1st Lt. Jack A. "War Diary of the 489th Bomb Squadron, February 1944." 57th Bomb Wing Association: North Africa–Sicily–Corsica–Italy, 1942–1945. 2008. http://57thbombwing.com/340th_History/489th_History/transcripts/7_Hist_Transcript_Feb_1944.pdf.

"Cessna Takes NYA Students." *Hutchinson News* (Hutchinson, KS), September 4, 1942, 12. https://www.newspapers.com/.

"Chihkiang Loss Is Blow to Japanese Hopes." *Hump Express*, June 7, 1945. Weidenburner. https://www.cbi-theater.com/hump_express/hump060745.html.

"China No Longer 'Forgotten Theater.'" *China Lantern*, May 4, 1945. Weidenburner 2009. https://www.cbi-theater.com/lantern/lantern050445.html.

"Chinese-American Composite Wing Hits Japs Hard in Sorties." *Brownsville Herald* (Brownsville, TX), August 5, 1945, 9. https://www.newspapers.com/.

"Chinese-American Wing in Action with 14th AF." *CBI Roundup*, November 12, 1943. Weidenburner 2007. https://www.cbi-theater.com/roundup/ roundup111243.html.

"Chinese Entitled to GI Equipment." *China Lantern*, August 23, 1945. Weidenburner 2014. https://www.cbi-theater.com/lantern/lantern082345.html.

"Chinese Forces Gain Control on Hunan Front." *China Lantern*, May 18, 1945. Weidenburner 2008. https://www.cbi-theater.com/lantern/lantern051845.html.

"Chinese Gain in Hankow Area." *China Command Post*, February 16, 1945. Weidenburner 2009. https://www.cbi-theater.com/china_command_post/command_post_021645.html.

"Chinese Open Counterblows against Six Jap Columns." *Salt Lake Tribune* (Salt Lake City, UT), March 28, 1945, 5. https://www.newspapers.com/.

"Chinese Ready for Nip Chiefs." *Chico Record* (Chico, CA), August 23, 1945, 1. https://www.newspapers.com/.

"Chinese Revolution of 1949 (The)." *Milestones: 1945–1952*. Office of the Historian, US Department of State. n.d. https://history.state.gov/milestones/1945-1952/chinese-rev#:~:text=The%20announcement%20ended%20the%20costly,two%20sides%20since%20the%201920's.

"Chinese Take Base in Burma." *San Francisco Examiner*, June 18, 1944, 2. https://www.newspapers.com/.

"Chinese Warned US Plans Attacks on Key Jap Ports" (quoting Maj. Gen. Robert B. McClure, US chief of staff, China theater). *Harrisburg Telegraph* (Harrisburg, PA), December 21, 1944, 1. https://www.newspapers.com/.

"Circulation Director Will Tour Europe." *Lincoln Journal Star* (Lincoln, NE), September 18, 1955, 8. https://www.newspapers.com/.

"City Flier Tells of Close Call in Leap from Plane over China." *Minneapolis Star*, January 19, 1945, 13. https://www.newspapers.com/.

"Clyde Learn in China." *Indiana Gazette* (Indiana, PA), July 2, 1945, 10. https://www.newspapers.com/.

"Col. McGehee Writes from China; Tells of Work of M/Sgt. John Barge." *Greenville Advocate* (Greenville, AL), June 28, 1945, 4. https://www.newspapers.com/.

"College Graduate." *Morning Call* (Paterson, NJ), May 22, 1942, 12. https://www.newspapers.com/.

Coltrin, Bill. "Pinney vs. Brigham City Opens Semipro Season." *Salt Lake Telegram* (Salt Lake City, UT), May 8, 1948, 10. https://www.newspapers.com/.

Correll, John T. "Chennault and Stilwell." *Air Force Magazine*, December 20, 2012. https://www.airforcemag.com/PDF/MagazineArchive/Magazine%20Documents/2015/December%202015/1215chennault.pdf.

Cunningham, Sgt. Ed. "Teamwork in China." *Yank: The Army Weekly*. Branch Office, Information & Education Division, War Dept. (New York, NY), March 10, 1944, 9. https://www.cbitheater.com/yankcbi/yank_cbi_2.html.

Daniels, C. E. "SSgt. Glenn 'Red' Burnham." C. E. Daniel Collection. http://www.danielsww2.com/page25.html.

"Dave Ewell Jr., Now at Camp Polk, Likes It." *State Times Advocate* (Baton Rouge, LA), September 17, 1941, 6. https://www.genealogybank.com/doc/newspapers/.

"Day of Infamy." Miller Nichols Library, University of Missouri. Kansas City Libraries. https://info.umkc.edu/news/marr-archives-preserve-historic-day-of-infamy-audio/.

"Dickinson Reservist Finds Service Still Full of Forms." *Bismarck Tribune* (Bismarck, ND), April 25, 1962, 12. https://www.newspapers.com/.

Dickson, Cecil B. "Chinese Fliers Successful, Colonel Says." *Ithaca Journal* (Ithaca, NY), June 25, 1945, 12. https://www.newspapers.com/.

"EAC's Support Aids in Victory at Myitkyina." *CBI Roundup*, August 20, 1944. Weidenburner 2006. https://cbi-theater-1.home.comcast.net/~cbi-theater-1/roundup/roundup081044.html.

Farnsworth, Clyde A. "China Fliers Chastise Nips." *Arizona Republic* (Phoenix, AZ), May 20, 1945, 9. https://www.newspapers.com/.

———. "Human Detonators Used by Japanese." *China Lantern*, May 18, 1945. Weidenburner 2008. https://www.cbi-theater.com/lantern/lantern051845.html.

———. "Wingless Victory." *Omaha World Herald* (Omaha, NE), December 31, 1944, 16. https://www.genealogybank.com/doc/newspapers/.

"Flying Tigers Hold Convention." *Taiwan Today*. Ministry of Foreign Affairs, Republic of China (Taiwan). Originally published June 2, 1985. 2015. http://taiwaninfo.nat.gov.tw/fp.as;?xItem=113757&CtNode=103&mp=4.

"FOUR PILOTS Land in N.Y. from China: Jerseyites Taught Natives to Fly." *Newark Star-Ledger* (Newark, NJ), November 2, 1945, 5. https://www.genealogybank.com/doc/newspapers/.

Friedman, SGM Herbert A. (Ret.). "OWI Leaflets for Burma." OWI Pacific PSYOP, Six Decades Ago: Principals [sic] of Propaganda. January 22, 2005. http://www.psywarrior.com/BurmaOWILeafs.html.

Geiss, Lt. Lester H., ed. "$2,500 (CN) for a Cat in Chungking." *China Command Post*, March 2, 1945. Weidenburner 2009. https://www.cbi-theater.com/china_command_post/command_post_030245.html.

"Gets His Wings." *The News* (Paterson, NJ), July 27, 1944, 26. https://www.newspapers.com/.

Glass, Andrew. "Hirohito Accepts Japan's Surrender Terms, August 14, 1945." *POLITICO Magazine*, August 14, 2018. https://www.politico.com/story/2018/08/14/hirohito-accepts-japanese-surrender-terms-aug-14-1945-771008.

"Goeller Named Commander of Army Air Base at Glasgow." *Great Falls Tribune* (Great Falls, MT), May 15, 1943, 12. https://www.newspapers.com/.

"Goeller Will Enter Service." *Columbus Herald* (Columbus, IN), June 24, 1942, 1. https://www.newspapers.com/.

Grayson, Harry. "Yanks and Chinese Made Chihchiang Air Base Too Hot for Japs to Hold." *Indiana Gazette* (Indiana, PA), July 25, 1945, 15. https://www.newspapers.com/.

"Guard Air Unit, Led by Heroes, Flexes Wings." *Chicago Tribune*, October 12, 1947, 48. https://www.newspapers.com/.

"Harlie D. Reynard Sr., 88, St. Petersburg." *Tampa Bay Times* (St. Petersburg, FL), September 19, 2006, 9. https://www.newspapers.com/.

"He Needs Help." *Daily Oklahoman* (Oklahoma City, OK), May 19, 1947, 3. http://www.newspapers.com/.

"Hero Dogs, Too!" *Cincinnati Enquirer*, October 23, 1945, 10. http://www.newspapers.com/.

"Hoe Replacing Sword at Fort." *Spokane Chronicle* (Spokane, WA), April 7, 1946, 10. http://www.newspapers.com/.

"Howard Goeller Alabama." *Columbus Herald* (Columbus, IN), December 27, 1974. http://www.newspapers.com/.

"Hugel, Robert G." *Hartford Courant* (Hartford, CT), October 23, 2016, B7. http://newspapers.com/.

Hughes, Dave. "Flying Tigers Decorated." *Southwest Times Record* (Branch, AR), n.d., 1A, 5A. Contributed by Debbie McCutcheon.

Hui, Samuel. "A General's Wartime Memory of US-ROC Cooperation." *Want China Times*, April 7, 2014. http://www.wantchinatimes.com/.

"Impressive Memorial Service for Roosevelt in Kunming." *China Lantern*, April 20, 1945. Weidenburner 2007. https://www.cbi-theater.com/ lantern/lantern042045.html.

"In the Service: Graduations." *Sacramento Bee* (Sacramento, CA), March 24, 1943, 2. http://www .newspapers.com/.

"In the Service: Overseas." *Sacramento Bee* (Sacramento, CA), June 29, 1945, 3. http://www.newspapers.com/.

"Indianapolis Flyer Decorated by General." Public Relations Office, 14th Air Force, n.d. Contributed by Debbie McCutcheon.

"Indo-China Areas Are Being Scoured for Lost Airmen." *Kingston Daily Freeman* (Kingston, NY), February 12, 1946, 11. https://www.newspapers.com/.

"Interesting Letter Tells of Service in China and India." *Greenville* Advocate (Greenville, AL), March 2, 1944, 3. https://www.newspapers.com/.

Isaacs, H. R., *Newsweek* correspondent. "Kweilin Destruction." *CBI Roundup*, September 28, 1944, 1. Weidenburner 2007. https://www.cbi-theater.com/roundup/roundup092844.html.

"James Wadlow Treks across China in American Jeep." *Hobart Democrat-Chief* (Hobart, OK), October 6, 1944, 1. https://www.newspapers.com/.

"James Wadlow's Funeral Sunday." *Daily Oklahoman* (Oklahoma City, OK), July 15, 1949, 36. https://www.newspapers.com/.

"Japanese Envoys Reach Chihkiang." *The Gazette* (Montreal, Quebec, Canada), August 22, 1945, 21. https://www.newspapers.com/.

"Japs Regain Pingshek on Canton-Hankow Railway." *Gazette and Daily* (York, PA), February 19, 1945, 24. https://www.newspapers.com/.

"Janet Shaw, 82: Actress Had Role in 'Jezebel.'" *Los Angeles Times*, October 23, 2001, B10. https://www.newspapers.com/.

Johnson, George H. "Chungking." *China Lantern*, May 5, 1945. Weidenburner 2009. https://www.cbi-theater.com/lantern/lantern050445.html.

Kay, Lt. Col. Kenneth, USAF (retired). "Chinese-American Composite Wing." *Ex-CBI Roundup*, July 1976, reprint from *Air Force Magazine*. CBI Order of Battle: Lineages and History. Gary Goldblatt. September 7, 2010. https://www.cbi-history.com/part_vi_cacw.html.

Kraus, Theresa L. "Strategic Setting." *China Offensive: The U. S. Army Campaigns of World War II*. US Army Center of Military History. https://www.ibiblio.org/hyperwar/USA/USA-C- ChinaO/index.html.

"Kunming Airfield (Wujiaba)." PacificWrecks, January 2, 2013. http://www.pacificwrecks.com/airfields/china/kunming/index.html.

"Kwan-Sien Rest Camp Opened near APO 210." *China Lantern*, Kunming and Calcutta, July 31, 1945. Weidenburner 2014. https://www.cbi-theater.com/lantern/lantern073145.html.

LaFoy, R. Aubrey. "Fragile." *Down Memory Lane Blog. Dickinson County News* (Spirit Lake, IA), July 12, 2013. http://www.dickinsoncountynews.com/blogs/1415/entry/53907/.

———. "Okoboji Stories." December 29, 2010. http://okobojistories.blogspot.com/2010_12_01_archive.atml.

"Learn about the Rohna." Rohna Survivors Memorial Association, 2013. https://rohnasurvivors.org/.

"Lend-Lease." *The Pacific War Online Encyclopedia*. http://pwencycl.kgbudge.com/L/e/Lend-Lease.htm.

"Liuchow Threatened: Chinese Liberate Thousands as Jap Withdrawal Continues." *China Lantern*, June 6, 1945. Weidenburner 2007. https://www.cbi-theater.com/lantern/lantern060845.html.

"Lieutenant in Burma Area Reported Lost." *Long Beach Press-Telegram* (Long Beach, CA), June 15, 1945, 7. https://www.newspapers.com/.

"Local GI Picks Tea in China." *Holyoke Daily Transcript and the Holyoke Telegram* (Holyoke, MA), October 21, 1944. https://www.newspapers.com/.

"Lt. Gen. Claire Lee Chennault." ID: 2334. Military Hall of Honor. https://militaryhallofhonor.com.

"MacDill AFB History." *US Air Force Fact Sheet*. US Air Force. December 6, 2007. http://www.macdill.af.mil/library/factsheets/.

Magoon, Christopher. "Mining the 'Aluminum Trail': Search for Body of World War II Airman Continues in Southern China." TeaLeafNation, March 21, 2013. http://www.tealeafnation.com/2013/03/mining-the-aluminum-trail-search-for-body-of-world-war-ii-airman-continues-in-southern-china/.

"Maj. Gen. Chennault's Order of the Day." *China Lantern*, USAAF in China Anniversary Edition, July 6, 1945. Weidenburner 2007. https://www.cbi-theater.com/lantern/lantern-aaf.html.

"Major General Claire Lee Chennault." Air Force. https://www.af.mil/About-Us/Biographies/Display/Article/107526/Major-general-claire-lee-chennault/.

"Memorial Set for War Hero." *Long Beach Independent* (Long Beach, CA), July 12, 1949, 10. https://www.newspapers.com/.

"Men in Uniform." *Times Record News* (Wichita Falls, TX), August 23, 1945, 7. https://www.genealogybank.com/doc/newspapers/.

"Military Curfew Goes into Effect throughout China on May 15." *China Lantern*, May 4, 1945. Weidenburner 2009. https://www.cbi-theater.com/lantern/lantern050445.html.

"Missing Flier Back at Base, Kin Informed." *Fort Collins Express-Courier* (Fort Collins, CO), September 5, 1944, 1, 2. https://www.newspapers.com/.

Moosa, Spencer. "Jap Columns Enter Kweilin, Push South." *Altoona Tribune* (Altoona, PA), November 2, 1944, 2. https://www.newspapers.com/.

"More or Less Personal." *Bedford Daily-Times Mail* (Bedford, IN), May 7, 1945, 3. https:

"Mrs. Peck Is Honored with Bridal Shower." *Leedey Star* (Leedey, OK), July 20, 1949, 4. http://www.newspapers.com/.

Nguyen, Dong-Phuong. "Marked by WWII, Now Daily Loss." *Tampa Bay Times* (St. Petersburg, FL), September 19, 2006. https://www.tampabay.com/archive/2006/09/19/marked-by-wwii-now-daily-loss/.

"No 'Chicken' at Malir as G.I.'s Wait for Shangri-La Bound Vessels." *India-Burma Theater Roundup*, October 11, 1945. Weidenburner 2006. https://www.cbi-theater.com/roundup/roundup101145.html.

Panko, Ray. "Aerial Bomb Fuzes." Pacific Aviation Museum Pearl Harbor. https://www.pearlharboraviationmuseum.org/blog/aerial-bomb-fuzes/.

Passanisi, Robert E. "Merrill's Marauders, 5307 Composite Unit (Provisional) Unit History." Merrill's Marauders Association. http://www.marauder.org/marauder.htm.

"Pinyin Romanization: Chinese Writing System." *Britannica*. https://www.britannica.com/topic/Pinyin-romanization."

Pool, Penny L. "A Life That Could Have Been a Movie." *Randolph Leader* (Roanoke, AL), November 9, 2005. https://www.therandophleader.com/news/article_6e852950-7e6b-59dc-9377-db22376cb4e6.html.

"Prince Saved after Four Hours in Water." *Greenville News* (Greenville, SC), November 2, 1945, 1. https://www.newspapers.com/.

"Promote Mondelli to Major; Serving with Flying Tigers." *The Tribune* (Scranton, PA), September 15, 1945. https://www.newspapers.com/.

Pukhrambam, Lalit. "Imphal and WW-II." *World War II: China-Burma-India (CBI) Theater—April 1942–January 1945, the Seige [sic] of Imphal-Kohima*. https://themanipurpage.tripod.com/history/wwII.html.

"Rae M. Delahoyde." *Ukiah Daily Journal* (Ukiah, UT), May 30, 1990, 14. https://www.newspapers.com/.

Ravenholt, Albert. "Japs Pour into Honan Sector." *China Lantern*, April 20, 1945. Weidenburner 2007. http://www.cbi-theater.com/lantern/lantern042045.html.

"Report 1st Lt. James Koss Killed in Action over China." *Daily Calumet* (Chicago), February 25, 1946, 1. https://www.newspapers.com/.

Richardson, Sgt. Dave. "Earthquakers' Odyssey." *YANK: The Army Weekly*, China-Burma-India Edition, December 9, 1944, Part 3. Weidenburner 2006. https://www.cbitheater.com/yankcbi/yank_cbi_3.html.

Rosholt, Lt. Malcolm L. "Chinese-American Air Force Trains in India for Further Blows against the Japs." *Springfield Sunday Union and Republican* (Springfield, MA), November 21, 1943, 4E, 8E. https://www.genealogybank.com/doc/newspapers/.

"Roslindale Flyer Beats Air Crash, Japs, Jungles." *Boston Globe,* January 1, 1945, 1, 25. https://www.newspapers.com/.

Safford, Virginia. [no title]. *Star Tribune* (Minneapolis, MN), October 7, 1945, 63. http://www.newspapers.com/.

"Seacrest with Chinese Friend." *Nebraska State Journal* (Lincoln, NE), January 17, 1945, 1. https://www.newspapers.com/.

"Seattle Seems Unreal after India and Burma." *Seattle Daily Times,* February 18, 1945, 8. https://www.newspapers.com/.

"Sergeant in England [*sic*] Learns He's Father." *The Record* (Hackensack, NJ), March 29, 1944, 8.

"Sgt. Bill Earley of Allendale in India with Chenault's [*sic*] Tigers." *Ridgewood Herald-News* (Ridgewood, NJ), March 30, 1944, 15. http://www.newspapers.com/.

"Ship Jammed with Troops Writer Claims." *Great Falls Tribune* (Great Falls, MT), January 6, 1946, 3. https://www.newspapers.com/.

"Simpson Killed Countless Japs as B-25 Burned." *Flight Pattern,* October 26, 1945, 1, 3. Douglas Army Airfield, Douglas, AZ. Contributed by Larry Simpson.

Smith, 2nd Lt. James R. "Kunming." In *Night Fighter: A Memoir of the China-Burma-India Theater.* Published online by the family of James R. Smith on his behalf. 2011. http://www.nightfighter.us/Chapter02.html.

———. "Chengtu." In *Night Fighter: A Memoir of the China-Burma-India Theater.* Published online by the family of James R. Smith on his behalf. 2011. http://www.nightfighter.us/Chapter03.html.

———. "Laohokow." In *Night Fighter: A Memoir of the China-Burma-India Theater.* Published online by the family of James R. Smith on his behalf. 2011. https://www.nightfighter.us/Chapter04.html.

"Sophisticated Seniors." *Hobart Tribune* (Hobart, OK), April 15, 1940, 3. https://www.newspapers.com/.

"Stearns Promoted." *The Monitor* (McAllen, TX), July 4, 1943, 11. https://www.newspapers.com/.

Steele, N. T. "Chronic Drizzle Chills U.S. Fliers at China Base." *Chicago Daily News,* December 14, 1944. Reprinted in *Groop Poop,* 1st Bomb Group HQ, March 10, 1945, 2. https://www.newspapers.com/.

"Story of Six Fliers and an Odd Jungle Epitaph (The)." *Sunday Times Signal* (Zanesville, OH), December 31, 1944, 5. https://www.newspapers.com/.

Stoumen, Sgt. Lou. "Evacuation of Kweilin." *YANK: The Army Weekly,* November 24, 1944. https://www.cbi-theater.com/yankcbi/yank_cbi_3.html.

———. "What It's Like for Our China GIs." *YANK: The Army Weekly,* October 20, 1944. https://cbi-theater-2.home.comcast.net/~cbi-theater-2/yankcbi/yank_cbi.html.

"Superior Californians Graduate as Mechanics." *Sacramento Bee* (Sacramento, CA), February 8, 1943, 15. https://www.newspapers.com/.

Thompson, Daniel. "I Grew Up in Montezuma, KS and I Remember . . ." group, Facebook post, October 29, 2021. Credit for information and photos to Terry Healy.

"Three More War Dead Are Coming to S.E. Chicago." *Daily Calumet* (Chicago), June 17, 1949, 1. https://www.ncwspapers.com/.

"Tigers' Unspectacular Blow Neutralizes Japs' Advantages." *China Lantern,* June 8, 1945. Weidenburner 2007. https://www.cbi-theater.com/lantern/lantern060845.html.

"To Davy Jones' Locker: 195,000 Tons of Nip Ships Dispatched There by Two B-25 Squadrons." *CBI Roundup*, February 24, 1944. Weidenburner 2008. https://www.cbi-theater.com/roundup/roundup022444.html.

"T/Sgt. Robert N. Solyn with Bomber Squad in China." *The Journal* (Meriden, CT), April 11, 1945, 3. https://www.newspapers.com.

"Understanding the USA: The Flying Tigers." US embassy, Beijing, China. Managed by US Department of State. December 6, 2007. http://beijing.usembassy-china.org.cn/flyingtigers.html.

"Vet of 67 Missions Reenlists in Service." *Spokane Chronicle* (Spokane, WA), March 1, 1946, 3. https://www.newspapers.com/.

"Veteran Houston War Flier Awarded Chinese Wings." *Houston Press* (Houston, TX), July 18, 1945, 12. Contributed by John Hamilton. Email to author July 26, 2016.

Walter, Capt. Floyd. "Myitkyina." *CBI Roundup*, September 7, 1944. Weidenburner 2008. https://www.cbi-theater.com/roundup/roundup090744.html.

Washburn, Alex H. "Publisher Graves Leaves Nashville News for the War." *Hope Star* (Hope, AR), August 1, 1950, 1. https://www.newspapers.com/.

Watts, Richard, Jr. "New York Drama Critic Surveys the China Scene and Reports the Travels of Pat, Jinx & Company." *CBI Roundup*, November 16, 1944. Weidenburner 2009. https://cbi-theater-1.home.comcast.net/~cbi-theater-1/roundup/roundup111644.html.

"While Family Thought Him in Safe Job, Lt. Cantor Flew 42 Missions in China." *Herald-News* (Passaic, NJ), November 15, 1945, 29. https://www.newspapers.

White. James M. "Tiger Cubs." No title or publishing information, n.d. Contributed by Debbie McCutcheon.

"William L. Daniels" autobiographical sketch. Original publication not specified. Posted as "Bill Daniels Flying Tigers." Bob Jones, managing editor, Aircraft Technical Publishers (ATC). AskBob.aero forum for aircraft maintenance technicians. http://www.askbob.aero/special-stories/bill-daniels-flying-tigers (accessed October 20, 2020).

"With the Armed Forces." *Crowley Post-Signal* (Crowley, LA), August 3, 1945, 3. https://www.newspapers.com/.

"Word Received from Maj. Chester M. Conrad." *Sikeston Standard* (Sikeston, MO), July 11, 1944, 4. https://www.newspapers.com/.

"World Battlefronts: Battle of China; Another Paris." *Time: The Weekly Newsmagazine* 44, no. 9 (August 28, 1944): 15.

"World War II Norden Bombsight." Factsheets. Hill Air Force Base. September 25, 2007. http://www.hill.af.mil/library/factsheets/factsheet.asp?id5664.

"Yank Brings Pet Monkey from Jungle." *Los Angeles Times*, November 4, 1945, 5. https://www.newspapers.com/.

Yee, John H. "Memories of the Jing Bao Days and the Coming of the A.V.G. to Kunming in 1941." *jingbao JOURNAL* 60, no. 366 (October–December 2006): 5–7.

Books

"An Interview with Maj. Gen. Du Kai-mu." Interview by Kuo Gwan-lin. Translated by Kuo Gwan-lin and Wang Chien-chi. June 1, 2008. In *The Immortal Flying Tigers: An Oral*

History of the Chinese-American Composite Wing. Taipei, Taiwan: Military History and Translation Office, Ministry of National Defense, ROC, 2009.

Bowen, Lee. "Victory in China." In *The Army Air Forces in WWII*. Vol. 5, *The Pacific: MATTERHORN to Nagasaki, June 1944 to August 1945; Part II–Aid to China: The Theater Air Forces in CBI*. Edited by Wesley Frank Craven and James Lea Cate. Originally published by University of Chicago Press, 1950. https://www.ibiblio.org/hyperwar/AAF/V/AAF-V-9.html.

"Callan Cruises, August 1944–June 1946." In USS R. E. Callan, *WWII Navy Cruise Books*, 21. Image 301673723.

Cornelius, Wanda, and Thayne Short. *Ding Hao: America's Air War in China, 1937–1945*. Gretna, LA: Pelican, 2004.

Daniels, Ken. *China Bombers: The Chinese-American Composite Wing in World War II*. North Branch, MN: Specialty Press, 1998.

Guide to Karachi. Booklet originally published by US Army. Weidenburner 2009. https://cbi-theater.com/karachi/karachi.html.

Ilefeldt, Willard G. *Thoughts While Tending Sheep*. New York: Crown, 1988.

Johnson, Earnest Dale. *A Long Journey Home: A Memoir of Life and War in Our Times*. All references from chapter 13: "My Personal View of the War in China." Caldwell, ID: Caston, 2017. Kindle edition.

Lopez, Donald S., Sr. *Into the Teeth of the Tiger*. Washington, DC: Smithsonian Books, 1997.

Molesworth, Carl, and Steve Moseley. *Wing to Wing: Air Combat in China, 1943–45*. New York: Orion Books, 1990.

Pilot's Handbook: Karachi to Chittagong. "CBI Airfields: Supplementary Airports." CBI Order of Battle: Lineages and History. Gary Goldblatt. https://www.cbi-history.com/cbi_airfields.html.

Romanus, Charles F., and Riley Sunderland. "US Forces Organize and Prepare for New Tasks." In *US Army in WWII: Stillwell's [sic] Mission to China*. Originally published by University Press of the Pacific, 2002. https://www.ibiblio.org/hyperwar/USA/USA-CBI-Mission/index.html.

Rosholt, Malcolm. *Flight in the China Air Space, 1910–1950*. Rosholt, WI: Rosholt House, 1984. Contributed by Mark E. McCann. Grandson of James E. McCann. Message to author via Facebook Messenger, September 21, 2021.

Weaver, Herbert. "Fourteenth Air Force Operations, January 1943–June 1944," In *The Army Air Forces in WWII*. Vol. 4, *The Pacific: Guadalcanal to Saipan, August 1942 to July 1944; Part IV—China-Burma-India*. Edited by Wesley Frank Craven and James Lea Cate. Originally published by University of Chicago Press, 1950. https://www.ibiblio.org/hyperwar/AAF/IV/AAF-IV-14.html.

———. "The Pattern of India-Burma Operations." In *The Army Air Forces in WWII*. Vol. 4, *The Pacific: Guadalcanal to Saipan, August 1942 to July 1944; Part IV—China-Burma-India*. Edited by Wesley Frank Craven and James Lea Cate. Originally published by University of Chicago Press, 1950. https://www.ibiblio.org/hyperwar/AAF/IV/AAF-IV-16.html.

Documents

Aircraft Accident Report #44-64-524. "USAAF Incident & Accident Personnel List." Accident-Report.com: *Military Aviation Incident Reports*. Purchased from Michael T. Stowe and received by email. October 9, 2013.

Aircraft Accident Report #44-0704-520. Ibid. September 24, 2013.

Aircraft Accident Report #45-1022-522. Ibid. September 24, 2013.

Aircraft Accident Report #44-0710-506. Ibid. October 9, 2013.

Aircraft Accident Report #44-1106-515. Ibid. September 24, 2013.

Aircraft Accident Report, #44-1218-519. Ibid. October 9, 2013. Aircraft Accident Report #45-1022-522. Ibid. September 24, 2013.

Aircraft Accident Report #44-322-514. *USAAS-USAAC-USAAF-USAF Accident Reports, 1911–1955.* Purchased from Craig Fuller, Aviation Archaeological Investigation & Research, and received by email. February 1, 2020.

"Company Morning Report." July–December 1944 and April–September 1945. *Army Morning Reports and Unit Rosters.* National Personnel Records Center, National Archives and Records Administration, St. Louis, MO. Acquired through services of Lori Berdak Miller, professional researcher, Redbird Research. April 8, 2019.

"Core Wrapping Apparatus." US Patents. https://patents.google.com/patent/US2989430A/en.

Missing Air Crew Report #6010, *Missing Air Crew Reports (MACRs) and Related Records at the US Army Air Forces, 1942–1947.* Publication M1380, Catalog ID 305256, Record Group 92, National Archives and Records Administration.

———. #7347. Ibid.

———. #8442. Ibid.

———. #11885. Ibid.

———. #14442. Ibid.

———. #14519. Ibid.

"Papers of Edith Millican, M.D., 1943–1948: Edith Millican to Friends." Item #a022_013, December 10, 1945. Archives and Special Collections, Drexel University, College of Medicine. http://xdl.drexelmed.edu/.

"US Rosters of World War II Dead, 1939–1945." Original data from United States Army, Quartermaster General's Office, Washington, DC. 2007. https://www.ancestry.com/.

US WWII Hospital Admission Card Files, 1942–1954. National Archives and Records Administration. NAI: 570973, Record Group Number: Records of the Office of the Surgeon General (Army), 1775–1994, Record Group Title: 112. Ancestry.com, Lehi, UT: Ancestry.com Operations, 2019. https://www.ancestry.com/.

USS *Alderamin*: War Diary, 12/1/45 to 12/31/45. Micro serial #154474, serial #033, reel #A2004, from *World War II War Diaries, 1941–1945*, Record Group #38, National Archives and Records Administration, catalog ID #4697018. https://www.fold3.com/.

USS *General C. C. Ballou*. New York, Arriving Passenger and Crew Lists (including Castle Garden and Ellis Island), 1820–1957 (database). Provo, UT: Ancestry.com Operations, 2010. Original data: Passenger Lists of Vessels Arriving at New York, New York, 1820–1897. Microfilm Publication M237, 675 rolls. NAI: 6256867. Records of the US Customs Service, Record Group 36. National Archives at Washington, DC. Passenger and Crew Lists of Vessels Arriving at New York, New York, 1897–1957. Microfilm Publication T715, 8,892 rolls. NAI: 300346. Records of the Immigration and Naturalization Service; National Archives at Washington, DC https://www.ancestry.com/.

USS *General C. G. Morton*. New York, Passenger Lists, 1820–1957. https://www.ancestry.com/.

USS *General C. G. Morton*: War Diary, 10/1/45 to 10/30/45. Micro serial #131751, reel #A1739, from *World War II War Diaries, 1941–1945*. Record Group #38, National Archives and Records Administration, catalog ID #4697018. https://www.fold3.com/.

USS *General C. H. Muir*: War Diary, 11/1–30/45. Micro serial #153739, serial #07017, Reel #A1998, from *World War II War Diaries, 1941–1945*. Record Group #38, National Archives and Records Administration, catalog ID #4697018. http://www.fold3.com/.

USS *General Charles H. Muir*. New York, Passenger Lists, 1820–1957. https://www.ancestry.com/.

USS *General E. T. Collins*: War Diary, 8/31/45. Micro Serial #149845, Serial #196, Reel #A1953, from *World War II War Diaries, 1941–1945*. Record Group #38, National Archives and Records Administration, Catalog ID #4697018. https://www.fold3.com/.

USS *General George O. Squier*. New York, Passenger Lists, 1820–1957. https://www.ancestry.com/.

USS *General George O. Squier*: War Diary, 10/1/45 to 10/31/45 and 11/1/45 to 1/30/45. Micro serial #153742, serial #559, reel #A1998, from *World War II War Diaries, 1941–1945*. Record Group #38, National Archives and Records Administration, catalog ID #4697018. https://www.fold3.com/.

USS *General J. H. McRae*. New York Passenger Lists, 1820–1957. https://www.ancestry.com/.

USS *Mission Bay*: War Diary, 2/1/44 to 4/30/44. Micro serial #71424, file #A16-3, serial #0010, reel #A937. *World War II War Diaries, 1941–1945*, Record Group #38, National Archives and Records Administration, catalog ID #4697018. https://www.fold3.com/.

USS *Wake Island*: War Diary, 2/1–29 and 3/1–31/45[44]. Micro serial #115003, serial #055, reel #A1509. *World War II War Diaries, 1941–1945*. Record Group #38, National Archives and Records Administration, catalog ID #4697018. https://www.fold3.com/.

"War Diary of the 489th Bomb Squadron, February 1944." Prepared by S-2 personnel under supervision of 1st Lt. Jack A. Casper. 57th Bomb Wing Association, 2008. http://57thbombwing.com/340th_History/489th_History/transcripts/7_Hist_Transcript_Feb_1944.pdf.

Wilson, Capt. Kenneth P., Hq CACW, APO 627 (Kunming). Letter to his family dated October 11, 1944. "General Claire Lee Chennault (1890–1958)." China National Aviation Corp. (CNAC) Official Home Page. 2007. Posted by Tom O. Moore Jr. https://cnac.org/chennault01.htm.

Emails, letters, social media exchanges, and telephone conversations

Blair, Darlene. Second cousin of Loyal L. Fox. Email to author, November 10, 2013, and following. Includes photos.

Boles, Paige Conrad. Daughter of Chester M. Conrad. Email to author, September 17, 2013, and following. Includes photos and transcription of "Tiger Certificate."

Borst, Wendi. Granddaughter of Thomas H. Edgerton. Email to author, May 14, 2014, and following. Includes photos, diary, logbook, and other documents.

Bowen, Steve. Son of Francis H. Bowen. Email to author, March 27, 2014.

Brahos, Jim. Grandson of George C. Cunningham. Email to author, July 8, 2015, and following. Includes photograph.

Cantor, Ronnie. Daughter of Gerald J. Cantor. Email to author, May 1, 2017, and following. Includes photos with captions.

Chen, Edward. From Mandarin Chinese *pangzi* [胖子], meaning "fatty." Post to author on "Remembering the CBI" group, Facebook, September 24, 2013.

Colvard, Linda Peters. Daughter of Eril W. Peters. Telephone conversation and email to author, September 2, 2015, and following. Includes photos.

Cryer, Sibyl Greene. Daughter of Frederick H. Greene Jr. Email to author, September 10, 2015, and following. Includes photos.

Cunningham, George C., Jr. Son of George C. Cunningham. Telephone conversation and email to author, July 7, 2015.

Daniels, Richard. Son of William L. Daniels. Telephone conversation, October 15, 2015, and letter to author dated October 16, 2015. Includes newspaper clippings, excerpts from personal logbook, and photos.

Dent, Barbara Dorr. Daughter of Eugene H. Dorr. Telephone conversation, August 14, 2018, and email to author, August 18, 2018, and following. Includes photos, articles, and documents from scrapbook.

DiBartola, Stephen. Son-in-law of Richard C. Wellman. Post to author via Ancestry.com on July 30, 2018, and following.

Douglas, Delores Learn. Daughter of Clyde L. Learn. Email to author, April 25, 2014, and following.

Drake, Dennis K. Son of Clarence H. Drake. Telephone conversation, July 11, 2018, and email to author, July 6, 2018, and following. Includes photos, newspaper articles, Air War College bio from 1961 Annual, and eulogy.

Duffin, James. Son of William G. Duffin. Telephone conversation, September 2, 2017.

Eakes, Eleanor Hodges. Daughter of Raymond L. Hodges. Email to author, June 21, 2014, and following.

Earley, Thomas. Son of William T. Earley Jr.. Email to author, March 10, 2015.

Ewell, Barbara. Daughter of Dave H. Ewell Jr. Email to author, September 18, 2014, and following.

Faherty, Dennis. Son of John F. Faherty. Email to author, June 20, 2022, and following. Includes photos with captions and "Combat Missions Flown by 1Lt. John F. Faherty."

Garfield, Susan L. Shock. Daughter of Joseph N. Shock. Telephone conversation, October 2, 2013, and email to author same date and following.

Gong, John. Photos of banner posted on "The China Air War" Facebook group, April 9, 2018.

Grimm, Judy McCann. Daughter of James E. McCann. Telephone conversation, October 16, 2014, and following, and letter, July 11, 2015. Includes letters addressed to Jim McCann from John Hinrichs, dated December 9, 1981; Gene Dorr, dated December 21, 1981; R. C. MacNeil, dated March 27, 1982; Lou Graves, dated March 30, 1982; and Grady Fuller, dated January 1, 1988.

Grubbs, William D. Grandnephew of Chester M. Conrad. Email to author, June 18, 2013. Includes photos.

Gruber, Frederick M. Son of George Gruber. Email to author, May 9, 2022, and following.

Hall, Alvin E. Son of Alvin A. Hall. Email to author, February 26, 2014, and following. Includes photo.

Halsey, Cindy Czerniak. Daughter of Bernard J. Czerniak. Email to author, December 13, 2015.

Hamilton, John. Son of Jack M. Hamilton. Email to author, July 26, 2016, and following. Includes photos, newspaper articles, and enlistment and other records.

Hamilton, Michael. Son of Jack M. Hamilton. Email to author, July 26, 2016, and following.

Hance, Christine Ilefeldt. Daughter of Willard G. Ilefeldt. Email to author, February 3, 2014, and following. Includes photos.

Healy, Terry Godfrey. Niece of Barton L. Wherritt. Email to author, November 29, 2014, and following. Includes photo, transcript of newspaper article, and letter from Lt. Allan Mikola dated November 10, 1945.

Henry, Mary Allegretto. Daughter of Andrew R. Allegretto. Email to author, January 10 and 21, 2014, and following. Includes newspaper article and photo.

Herrick, Elizabeth Greene. Daughter of Frederick H. Greene Jr. Email to author, November 28, 2015, and following.

Hinrichs, Robert H. Son of John C. Hinrichs. Telephone conversation, June 6, 2016.

Huen, Eric F. F. President of Society of Oral History on Modern China. Email to author, December 18, 2014, and following, and meeting, January 24, 2015. Includes transcript of James H. Mills interview on January 24, 2015, in Orange, TX.

Hugel, Craig. Son of Robert G. Hugel. Telephone conversation, October 28, 2016.

Hugel, Robert G. Letter and telephone conversation on June 27, 2014. Includes photos and copy of diary.

Hughes, Barbara. Niece of Robert J. Koss. Email to author, July 18, 2017, and following. Includes photos and documents.

Jackson, Stephen. Nephew of James A. Wadlow. Email to author, August 28, 2017. Includes photos.

Jakubasz, Robert. Son of Frank T. Jakubasz. Email to author, January 24, 2014, and following. Includes photos.

Jamora, Glynis Marie Wood. Daughter of George P. Wood. Email to author, June 12 and July 21, 2014, and following. Includes photo, special orders, personal flight log, squadron personnel list, and other documents.

Johnson, Daniel P. Son of Paul R. Johnson. Email to author, October 26, 30, and 31, 2017. Includes photos, various documents, and *Memoirs: A Look Back on Our Beginnings in Jamestown*, by Paul and Betty Johnson.

Juliano, Paul A., Jr. Nephew of John J. DeFabritis. Email to author, June 8, 2016, and following.

Kasparek, Terry. Niece of Loren E. Gaffney. Email to author, December 17, 2014, and following. Includes photos.

Kimbrow, Duane. Nephew of Fred S. Stearns. Email to author, March 1, 2014, and following. Includes photo.

Kunesh, Millicent Faherty. Daughter of John F. Faherty. Letter to author dated November 3, 2015. Includes "Statement of 2nd Lt. John F. Faherty, AC, 0-743770," "Unofficial story as told to us by Dad," "The War in China, Burma and India" by Michael Faherty, and photos with captions.

Lafoy, R. Aubrey. Email to author, August 5, 2013.

Laird, Carol Trumm. Daughter of John A. Trumm. Email to author, August 18, 2021. Includes photos.

Lancaster, Kenneth. Brother-in-law of James J. Ryan Jr. Email to author, April 7 and 16, 2016. Includes photos and newspaper article by Lew Scarr.

Lim, Gerry Young. Sister of Paul L. Young. Letter to author, June 16, 2016, and email to author, June 22, 2016, and following. Includes "World War II Memories: Paul Young" and photos.

Lin, Steve. Squadron mascot "ferret" or "weasel," from Mandarin Chinese *yo shu* (鼬鼠). Post on "Flying Tigers—AVG" group, Facebook, September 24, 2013.

Logan, Katherine Aileen ("Kaki"). Email to author, June 1, 2016, and following. Includes photos.

Long, Gordon A. Son of Norman L. Long. Email to author, July 12, 2016. Includes photos.

Lyon, Kelly. Daughter of Moncure N. Lyon. Email to author, October 22, 2013, and following. Includes photos.

McCann, Mark E. Grandson of James E. McCann. Messages to author via Facebook Messenger, September 20, 2021, and following. Includes photos.

McConnell, Jarrett. Son of Jeanette Davis McConnell (widow of Donald J. Davis) by second marriage. Email to author, November 27, 2015, and following. Includes photo and copy of letters from Maj. Gen. C. L. Chennault, Capt. Otis W. Garland, Maj. James F. Smith, and others.

McCutcheon, Debbie. Granddaughter of Leo C. Baker. Email to author, September 20, 2021. Includes "Indianapolis Flyer Decorated by General" from Public Relations Office, 14th Air Force; "Tiger Cubs" article by James M. White, no publishing information; and Dave Hughes, "Flying Tigers Decorated," *Southwest Times Record*, Branch, AR, n.d., 1A, 5A.

Meehan, Beth Banger. Daughter of Robert E. Banger. Telephone conversation, October 14, 2015, and email to author, October 29, 2015, and following. Includes photos and documents, including "Statement of Captain Frederick H. Greene Jr., Pilot A/C," dated June 7, 1945.

Mondelli, Mark. Son of Leslie L. Mondelli. Email to author, June 18, 2016, and following. Includes photos.

Moore, Christine Armbruster. Daughter of Russell J. Armbruster. Email to author, March 3, 2014. Includes photos, training certificates, separation/discharge papers, and other documents.

Peng, Szu-ming (James). Email to author, April 9, 2018. Includes photos and translation of banner, gift to Capt. Robert C. MacNeil.

Pitts, Jackie Hutchinson. Daughter of Otto W. Hutchinson. Email to author, June 28, 2018, and following. Includes photos, *Angel's Harp* editions from November 29 and December 9, 1945, "Certificate of Appreciation," and other documents and memorabilia. Telephone conversation July 5, 2018.

Ragland, John. Son of Reuben Ragland. Email to author, March 27, 2015, and following. Includes photos and magazine article, "Reuben Ragland's Adventurous Spirit."

Rees, Susan Langridge. Daughter of Joseph A. Langridge. Email to author, May 12, 2014, and following. Includes photos.

Reynard, David. Son of Harley D. Reynard. Email to author, June 6, 2016, and following. Includes photos.

Rieks, Barton. Son of Maynard W. Rieks. Telephone conversation, September 28, 2013.

Rieks, Bruce. Son of Maynard W. Rieks. Email to author, September 19, 2013, and following.

Ross, Betsy Curik. Daughter of William L. Curik. Email to author, July 9, 2016, and following. Includes photos.

Schaar, Kathy Koss. Niece of Robert J. Koss. Email to author, July 19, 2017, and following. Includes photos and letters sent by Koss to family members.

Schlicher, Charles. Grandson of Robert E. Schlicher. Message to author via Ancestry.com; email to author same date. Includes photos.

Schlicher, Charles L. Son of Robert E. Schlicher Jr.. Email to author, March 17, 2015, and following.

Schroeder, John. Son of Edmund Schroeder. Email to author, September 22, 2015, and following. Includes photos.

Senecal, Gloria. Wife of Wayne H. Senecal. Telephone conversation, September 27, 2013.

Senecal, Kevin. Son of Wayne H. Senecal. Email to author, June 17, 2019, and following.

Setzer, Daniel. 57th Bomb Wing historian. Email to author, November 2, 2020. Includes photos and operational intelligence reports.

Shannahan, Jodi Libolt. Daughter of Frederick C. Libolt. Email to author, August 17, 2014, and following. Includes photo.

Simpson, Larry. Son of Thomas S. Simpson. Email to author, July 26, 2013, and following. Includes photos, diary, letters, certificates, logbook and other documents. Personal meeting with author on October 4, 2013, in Corsicana, TX.

Smith, Pamela. Daughter of Manuel C. Smith. Email to author, March 30, 2015, and following. Includes photos.

Solin, Robert N. Son of Robert N. Solyn. Email to author, June 20, 2016, and following. Includes many photos.

Thompson, Daniel. "I grew up in Montezuma, KS and I remember . . ." group, Facebook, October 29, 2021. Post describing Barton L. Wherritt's military service in honor of Memorial Day.

Ting, Cheng (David). Son of Ting Cheng-liang (Daniel). Correspondence via Facebook Messenger, March 9, 2019, and following. Includes photos and copies of silk maps of Burma.

Trumm, Robert. Son of John A. Trumm. Email to author, October 26, 2021, and following. Includes photos, flight log, and translation of blood chit.

Weinert, Ossie H. Son of Oswald Weinert. Email to author, November 19, 2013, and following. Includes photos and application letter for Distinguished Flying Cross.

Whearty, Richard. Son of William H. Whearty. Email to author, November 5, 2016, and following.

Wright, Susan M. Hamilton. Daughter of Jack M. Hamilton. Email to author, July 21, 2016, and following.

Yeager, Nancy Jackson. Daughter of Lloyd E. Jackson. Email to author, February 1 and 24, 2014, and following.

Zea, Elizabeth Fuller. Daughter of Grady B. Fuller. Email to author, February 6, 2014, and following. Includes photos and letter from Bill Dick.

Zwigard, Lynn Magyar. Daughter of Alfred J. Magyar. Email to author, January 22, 2014, and following. Includes photos.

INDEX

Boldface entries denote illustrations.

A

Allegretto, Andrew R., **20**–1, 43, 56, **60**, 78, **101**, 116, 122, 125, 150–1, 158, 166, 172, **173**–4, 176–7, 185, 188–9, 192, 204, **210**, 224, 233, 235, 238, **243**–4, 255, 260, 262–3, **280**, 282, 288–9, 298, 314, 332, 337, 339, 342–4, 350, 356, 365, 378, 393

American Volunteer Group, 7, 25, 27, 117, 129, 198, 328, 365

Anhwei (Anhui) Province, 307

Armbruster, Russell J., **284**–5, 327, 342, 349–50, 357, 360, 377, 394

Armstrong, William L. P., 30, 33, 35, 43, 56–7, 78, **89**, 100, 116, 119, 122, 125, 137, 182–3, 198, 205, 394

Arnold, Henry H. ("Hap"), 372

"Avengers" Squadron, 28–9

B

Bains, Lois G., 137, 146, 194, 279, 288, 306–7, 395

Baker, Leo C., 123, 134, 158, 162, 166, **167**–70, 172–3, 176–8, 187, 190–1, 196, **200**–1, 212, 214–8, 220, 224–5, 230, 249, 262, 380, 382, 389, 396

bamboo telegraph, 232

Banger, Robert E., 206, **207**, 210, 224, 233, 238–9, **243**, 246, 248, 255–7, 260, 262–3, 268, 270, 272–3, 277–8, 285, 287–9, **290**–91, 293–4, 297–300, **303**–4, 305, 319, 321, 324, 342, 348, 350, 354, 396

Barge, John P., 30, 41, 43, **53**, 56, **59**, 102, 114, 116, 119, 122, 125, 128, 153, 165, 179, 181, 204, 224, 233, 235, 238, **243**, 250, 262, **265**, 277, 289, 299, 310–1, 314–5, **327**, 342, 348, 350, 356, 378, 397

Barksdale Field, 18, 405

Benedict, Lawrence J., 316, 342, 350, 357, 397

Bennett, T. Alan, 27, 186, 198, 203–9, 260, 286–7, 350–1, 382

Bhamo, 84, 103–4, 108, 230

Bowen, Francis H., **312**, 334–5, 338, 340, 342–3, 345, 350, 357, 380, 398

Bradley, Everett C., 170, 172–3, 177, 199

Branch, Irving L., 26, 28, 31, 35, 70–1, 78, 94, 96, 100, 123, 148

Brown, Harry, 159–60

Burnham, Glenn, 19–20

Burton, Herman L., 35, 56, **59**–60, **101**–2, 116, 122, 125, 158, **185**–6, 224, **243**, 276, 287, 329, 378, 399

"Butcher," 347–8

butterfly bombs, 188–9, 273, 294, 309

C

Calloway, Richard, 316, 342, 349–50, 356, 365, 399

Cantor, Jerome G., 162, 173, 185, 188, 190–1, **192**, 196, **200**–1, 213, 224, 230, 233, 235, 238, **243**, 249, 252, 255, 260, 262–4, 268, 272, 279, 288–9, 291, 293, 297, 299, 305, 307, 314, 318, **319**, 324, 330–1, 336–8, 340, 342, 344, 350, 357, 360, 375, 400

"CARBANADO," 309
Carrell, Ruth, 159, **160**
Caterpillar Club, 220–1, 263, 411, 437
Chasse, Homer L., 30, 33, 56, **57**, 76, 92, **101**, 116, 122–3, 125, 139, 185, 193, 224, **243**, 321, 327, 342, 350, 357, 381–2, 400
Cheng Yung-koen "Peter," 36, 179, 238–9, 255, 374
Chengtu (Chengdu), 36–7, 56, 132, 134, 150, 179–81, 193, 195, 211, 215, 227, 230, 232, 235–6, 255, 262, 269–70, 280, 287, 296, 307, 312, 319, 321, 327
Chennault, Maj. Gen. Claire Lee, 6–7, **8**–9, 24, **25**–9, 33, 39, 55, 70–1, 117, 120–1, 125, 137, 140–1, **143**–4, 154–5, 158, 163, 196, 199, 207, 209, 232, 269, 282, 296, 321, **322**, 327–8
Chennault, Col. John S., 347
Chenoweth, Howard T., 160–2, 170, 197, 260, 262
Chiang Chue-shu, 84, 391–2
Chiang Kai-shek, Generalissimo, 6–7, 25–6, 28, 55, 93, 124–5, 127, 141, 154, 165, 204, 231, 254, 291, 353, 361, 366, 373–4
Chihkiang, 128, 158–9, 169, 173, 178, 185, 196, 200, 208–9, 212–3, 220, 222, 229, 262, 266, 275, 286, 295–6, 311, 318, 321, 323, 328–30, 334–5, 342–3, **351**–2
China Air Task Force, 7, 24, 328
Chow Chi-jou, Gen., 141–2
Chiuling Po, **128**, 153, 193, 387
Chungking (Chongqing), 25, 37, 50, 128–9, 145–6, 153, 158, 163–5, 182, 184, 194, 198, 202, 204, 209–10
Collins, Parker P., 108, 382, 401
Conrad, Chester M., 30–1, **32**, 33–4, 39–43, 56–8, **61**, 61–3, 67–71, 82, 94–6, 100–1, 103, 108–10, 113–4, 116, 119, 122, 124–9, 131, **133**, 134, 137, **142**, 150, 179, 182, 194, 198, 210–1, 224, 230–1, 275, 373, 381, 387, 402
Coury, Thomas V., 262, 275, 402
Cunningham, George C., 30–3, 56, **59**–60, 62, **83**–4, 86–90, 92–4, 96, 102, 114, 116, 119, 125, 147, 158, 162, 166–8, 170–3, 193–4, 210–1, 223–4, 375, 380, 382–3, 403
Curik, William L., 277, 282, 324, 342, 350, 359, 381, 404

Czerniak, Bernard J., 316, 318, 342, 348, 350, 356, 366, 404

D

Daniels, Kenneth W., 23–4, 81, 119, 139, 195, 227, 236–8, 252, 348, 356
Daniels, William L., 30, **33**, 34, 39–40, 44, 117, 376, 405
Davidson, Maj. Gen. Howard C., 67, 96, 105
Davis, Donald J., 249–50, 252, 255–7, 259–60, 262–4, 268, 270, 272–3, 290–3, **312**–3, 321, 369–70, 388, 406
DeFabritis, John J., 203, 210, 224, 233, 238, **243**–4, 246, 255–7, 260, 262–3, 267–8, 270, 272–3, 277–8, 285, 288–9, 291–2, 294, 298, 305, 307, 314–5, 318, 329, 338–40, 342–3, 345, 350, 357, 406
Delahoyde, Rae M., 275, 342, 348, 350, 354, 357, 360, 377, 407
Dergaon, 100–1, **102**, 105, 115–6, 122–3
Dibrugarh, 69
Dick, William H. ("Bill"), 132–3, 154, 194, 222, 288, 383
discharge points, 353
Dodd, Jimmie, 159–60
Dorr, Eugene H. Jr., 30, 33, 38, **40**–1, 56, 59, 78, **83**–87, 89, 95–6, 102, 105, 114, 116, 119, 125, 137, 146, 152, 156, 205, 375, 379–80, 382–3, 407
"DOWNFALL," 309
Drake, Clarence H., 281–2, 285, 287, 289, 291–2, 294, 298–9, 305, 307, 312, 330, 340, 345–6, 381, 408
Duffin, William G., 30, 33, 38, 41, 43, **44**, 57, 81, **101**–2, 116, 125, **130**, 146, 150, 161, 224, **243**–4, 287, 296, 342, 350, 354, 357, 360, 377, 409
Dunlap, Wilbur C., 48, 56, 116, 125, **130**, 198, 200, 206, 224, **242**–3, 310, 342, 348, 350, 356, 381, 409
Dunning, Col. John A., 158–9, 169, 186, 225, 295

E

Earley, William T., 30–1, 33, 43, **44**, 56, 80, 99, **101**, **109**, 116–7, 122, 125–6, 224, **243**, 310, 342, 350, 354, 357, 359, 378, 410

Index   505

Edgerton, Thomas H., 137, **151**, 157–8, 162, 166, **167**, 170–3, 176, 178, **185**–7, 189–90, 196, **200**–1, **212**–13, 214–21, 224–5, 230, 238, **243**, 246–8, **264**, 270, 276, 279, 282, 287, 290, 296–8, 349, 360, 375, 382–3, 411

Egdorf, Walter C., 35, 222, 411

England, John W., 43, 57, 79, 81, 100, 116, 122, **123**, 125, 137, 158, 168, 170–1, 173, 198, 224, **228**, **243**–4, 252, 256, 260, 264, 268, 272, 287, 289, 291, 297, 299, 307, 319, 321, 332, 336–7, 342, 345, 350, 357, 411

Erh Tong, 28, 31, 34–5, 40, 96, 119–21, 123–4, 127, 134

Evitts, Budd W., 35, 56, 116, 125, **130**, 206, 224, **243**, 296, 306, 342, 348, 350, 354, 357, 360, 378, 412

Ewell, Dave H. Jr., 316, **317**, 342, 348, 350, 356, 365, 376, 413

F

Faherty, John F., **48**, **51**, 56, **73**, **95**–7, 100, 107, 108, 111–3, 116, 122, 125–6, 137, **145**, 156, 161, 224, 233, 238–40, **243**, 263–5, 267–8, 272, **276**, 287, 291, 293–4, 298–9, 305, 332, 334–40, 342–3, 345, 350, 357, 360, 413

Falkenburg, Jinx, 159, **160**

Flying Skunk Squadron, 66, 286

Flying Tigers, 7, **25**–6, 121, 281, 365, 382–3

Foorman, Andrew, 316, 318, 342, 348, 350, 356, 365, 382, 414

Fox, Loyal L., 150, **151**–2, **156**, 161, 193–4, 224, **233**, 235, 238, **243**, **247**, 250 252, 255–8, 263, **264**, 267–8, 272, **276**, 278, 285, 288, 291–2, 294, 298, 371, 388, 414

Fukien (Fujian) Province, 229

Fuller, Grady B., 30, 33, 48, 56, **59**, **66**, 116, 119, 125, **138**–9, 146, 150, 179, 182, 198, 210, 224, 233, 238, **243**, 245, 282, 288, 290, 306–7, 339, 342, 348, 350, 357, 375, 381, 383, 415

G

Gaffney, Loren E., 203, **213**–4, 222, 224, 233, 238, **243**, 246, 255–6, 259, 262–3, 268, 272, 276, 288–9, 291, 293–4, 298, 307, 330–1, 334, 339, 342–3, 345, 350, 356, 377, 415

Gambay, 140, 145, 147, 241, 308, 326–7

Goeller, Howard M., 43, **44**–5, 50, 57, 81, 93, 95–6, 102, 105, 110, 375, 377, 416

Grant, Donald W., 30, 33, 48–9, 56, **59**, **101**, 116, 122, 125, 151, 186, 282, 381, 417

Graves, Louis F. Jr., 30–3, 35, 38, 40, 42–3, 56–7, 59–60, **61**–3, 65, 75, 82, 89, **94**, 100, 102–3, 108, 116, 119, 123, 125, 132, 147, 150, 157, 198, 205, 375, 378, 381, 418

Greene, Frederick H. Jr., **211**, 224, 233–5, 238, **243**, 246, 248–50, 252, 255–8, 263–4, 276–9, 287–91, 293–4, 297–8, 300–2, **304**–5, 310, 312, 329, 341–2, 348, 350, 354, **356**, 378, 388, 418

Gruber, George, 30–1, 33, 48, 54, **57**, 68, 82, 89, **101**, 116, 122, 125, 151, 206, 224, **243**–4, 296, 306, 342, 348, 350, 354, 357, 359, 419

H

Haines, Paul E., 30, 33, **41**, 43, 56, 102, 116, 122, 125, **126**, 147, 161, 224, **243**–4, 287, 342, 348, 350, 354, 357, 360, 379, 420

Hall, Alvin A., 81, **101**, 116, 122, 123, 125, 137, 420

Hamilton, Jack M., **206**, 210, 224, 233, 235, 238–40, **242**–3, 246, 249–50, 252, 255–7, 259–60, 262–4, 268, 272–3, 275, **277**, 279–80, 287, 290, 296–9, 307, 309–10, 312–4, 329, 331–2, 336–7, 339–44, 346, 350, 357–8, 361, 380–1, 421

Hanchung, 131–3, 137, 157, 161–2, 186, 193, 235–7, 239, 245, 252, 269–70, 273, 304, 323, 342, 357

Hankow, 28–9, 55, 115, 121–2, 133, 169, 174–7, 190–1, 195–6, 208, 211, 222, 229, 231, 235, 264, 275, 279, 288, 299, 306, 332–5, 337–8, 366, 371–3

Hanrahan, John P., 30, 33–4, **35**, **41**, 56–7, **66**, 91, **101**, 104, 116, 119, 122, 125, 132, 161–2, 182, 198–9, 224, 233, 235, 238–9, **243**, 246, 248–9, 256, 259, 262–4, 267–8, 276, **277**, 375, 378, 442,

Hartung, Walter E., 282, 342, 348, 350, 356–7, 366, 377, 422

Hilger, Col. John A., 26, 83

Hinrichs, John C. E. Jr., 30-3, 41, 44, 54, **57**, **58**, 62, 65, **66**, 68, 76, 78, 81-2, 100, 115, 120, 122, 125, 127, 134, 137, 151, 156, 375, 377, 381, 423

Hirohito, Emperor, 347, 349, 358

HMS *Rohna*, 60-1, 269

HMS *Sterling Castle*, 37

Ho Gei-hung, 31, **45**, 46

Hodges, Raymond L. Jr., 22, 37, 43, 46, 56-7, 59, 63, **64**-7, 79, **80**, 82, 92, 116, 119, 124-5, 131, 140, **145**, 198, 237, 282, 375, 377, 386, 389, 424

Hoke, Isadore F., 56, 60-1, 116, 122, 125, **130**, 161, 224, **243**, 321, 327, 342, 348, 350, 354, 357, 360, 377, 424

Holmes, Jack, 30, 33, **38**, 41, 57, 81, 116, 125, 150, 193, 224, **243**-4, 249, 264, **265**, 287, 289, 291, 293, 296, 306, 310, 314-5, 334, 336-9, 342-4, 350, 354, 357, 360, 381, 425

Honan (Henan) Province, 245, 247, 267, 302-3

Horner, Lawson G. Jr., 94, 194, 260

house boys, 123-4, 130, 136, 149, 152, 198, 227, 271, 323,

Hoyle, Charlie H. Jr., 30, 33, **41**, 43, 56, 78, 102, 116, 119, 122, 125, **152**, 185, 187, 189-91, 196, 201, 213, 224, 233, 235, 238-9, **243**, 246, **247**, 250, 256, 260, 262-4, 267-8, 270, 272, 276, 282, 287, 293, 426

Hsu Huan-sheng, 261, **313**

Hsu Tse-chong, 386

Hsupu, 342, 350, 352, 356

Hugel, Robert G., 10, 203, **204**, 210, 224, 238, 243, 246, 255-7, 267, 270, 273, 285, 288-9, 291, 293, 298, 300, **301**, 302-5, 321, 327, 342, 348, 350, 354, 379, 426

Hummel, Don, 28, 69, 129-30, 134

Hunan Province, 227, 235, 266, 315, 324

Hupeh (Hubei) Province, 245, 253, 321, 335

Hutchinson, Otto W., 316, **317**, 342, 348, 350, 356, 363-5, 372, 381, 427

I

Ichang, 211, 235, 238, 249, 252-4, 256-7, 263, 277, 279, 288-9, 291-3, 296, 300, 312, 321, 332-3, 339-40, 368-9, 388

Ichigo, 121, 139, 154

Ilefeldt, Willard G., 162, 179, **207**, 210, 224, 233, 235-6, 238, **243**-4, 246, 248, 250, 252, 256-7, 259, 262-4, 267, 275-6, 285, 287, 296-8, 306-7, **313**-5, 318, 334, 336-8, 340, 342-3, 350, 357-8, 360, 379, 427

Imai, Maj. Gen. Takeo, **351**-2

In Yen-san, 36, 92, 179, 193, 246, 250, 256, 262-3, 267-8, 272, 277, 285, 289, 287

J

Jackson, Lloyd E. Jr., 18, 43, 50, 56-7, 59-60, **101**-2, 107, 116, 122, 125, 158, 168, 170-2, 176-7, **185**-6, 198, 224, **243**, 280-1, 321, 327, 336, 338, 342-3, 350, 356, 365, 379, 428

Jakubasz, Frank T., 30, 33, 41, 43, 48, **51**, 54, 57, **59**, **89**, 100, 116, 122, 125, **126**, 134, 137, **138**, 179, 224, 233, 235, 238-9, 248, **265**, 272-3, **280**, 287, 291, 298, 305, 315, 321, 341, 378, 429

Jeffries, Charles W., 244, **264**, 290, 342, **344**-5, 350, 356, 365, 429

jing bao, 121, 206, 236

Johnson, Earnest D., 107, 119, 225, 231, 242, 251, 259, 306, 308, 333

Johnson, Paul R., 357-8, **371**-2, 378, 430

K

Kaifeng, 121, 248, 270, 273, 285, 287, 293

Karachi, 19, 22-4, 26, 30-3, 37-8, 40-45, 52, 54, 56-7, 78, 81, 83, 91, 106, 234, 354, 357, 359, 361-2

Keller, Albert J., 281, 342, 348, 350, 357, **372**, 378, 381-2, 430

Kelly, Edward A., 269

Kelso, James C. Jr., **114**, 116, 119, 122, 125-6, 156, 161, 182, 224, **243**-4, 280, 342, 348, 350, 354, 357, 359, 378, 431

Kiangsi (Jiangxi) Province, 235, 241

Kilian, Thomas A., 249, 264, 277, 285, 306, 320, 330-1, 360, 379, 431

King, James L., 81, 114, 116, 432

Knight, Charles B., 152, 306

Koss, Robert J., 118, **211**, 223-4, 226, **232**-5, **243**-4, **247**, 249-50, 252, 255-8, 263-4, 268, 270-2, 276, 285, 287-9, 291-2, 294, 341, 369-7, 388, 432

Kunming, 7, 24–5, 28, 31, 33, 56, 70–1, 74, 89, 113, 116–9, 122–3, 125, 134, 137, 139, 146, 151–2, 157–8, 181–2, 186, 198, 200, 204, 206, 228, 230, 266, 269, 275–7, 287, 307, 310, 319, 324, 347, 356

Kwan-Sien Rest Camp, 40, 180, 280, 327

Kwangtung (Guangdong) Province, 115, 166

Kweichow (Guizhou) Province, 192–3, 202, 219, 280

Kweilin (Guilin), 28, 30–1, 35, 92–4, 102, 108, 116, 119–27, 136–8, 157, 161

L

LaFoy, Aubrey, 58

Langridge, Joseph A., 311–2, 342, 344, 348, 350, 354, 357, 377, 433

Laohokow, 194–5, 210, 230–3, 235, 240–1, 245–9, 251–3, 255–7, 260, 264, 266, 275–6, 300

Learn, Clyde L., 43, 56, **60**, 78, **89**, **101**, 116, 122, 125, 161, **213**, 224, **243**, 327, 342, 348, 350, 356, 365, 366, 382, 434

Lee Hsueh-yen, Maj., 26, 123

Li Chan-jui (Zhanhui), 45, 79, 106, 157, 390–1

Liangshan, 36, 44, 102, 137, 150, 186, 193, 195, 206, 210–1, 222–3, 225, **226**–7, 240–1, 259, 262, 266, 308, 323, 331, 342, 348, 356, 360

Libolt, Frederick C., 30, 33, 41, 56, **59**, 116, 119, 122, 125, 155, **156**, 198, 210, 224, 230, 250, 252, 268, 287, 299, 377, 434

Lipira, Salvadore A., 166, **167**, 169, 172, **173**, 188–9, 192, 196, 200–1, 221, 262

Liu Ho-teh, 96, 256, 262–4, 267, 289, 299, 307, 314, 344, 390

Logan, Robert L., 162, 179, 182, 198, **213**, 221–2, 224, **227**, 235, **237**–9, **243**–4, 248, **313**, 319, 342, 348, 350, 352, 357, 360, 380, 382–3, 387, 435

Long, Norman L., **20**, 43, 50, 56, 79, 116, 122, 125, 137, **140**, **146**, **152**, 157, 179, 210, 224, 233, 238, **243**, 248, 255, 264, 270, **274**, 276, 299, 310, 314, 327, 342, 348, 350, 357, 377, 435

Lopez, Lt. Donald S., 54, 71, 118, 120, 258

Lucky Lady Squadron, 40, 175, 312

Lyon, Moncure N., 46, 158, 165, **166**, 168, 170–1, 174–7, 186–7, 189, 192, 196–7, **200**, 212, **213**–25

M

Ma Tian-you, 46, 391

MacDill Air Base, 17–8, 358

MacNeil, Robert C., 10, 44, 48, 56, **59**, 65, 76, 78, 82, 89, 116, 119, 125, 137, 153–4, 160, 179–80, 193, 210–1, 224, 233, 238–40, **243**, 245–6, 259, 264, 267–8, 270, 272, 276–8, 282, 287–94, 298–9, 307, 314–5, 320–1, 323, 326–7, 375, 380, 387, 436

"Magic Carpet Cruises," 359

Magyar, Albert J., 150, **151**, **161**, 178, 187, 189–91, 196, 201, 212, 221, 224, 235, 238, **243**–4, 246, **247**, 250–2, 255–8, 263, **264**, 268, 272, 276–7, 285, 287–9, 293–4, 307, 310, 315, 338–44, 350, 357, 360, 379, 437

malaria, 38, 62, 93, 96, 106, 114, 137, 146–7, 149, 152, 161, 185, 228, 241, 266, 307, 380

Malir, 23–4, 26–7, 30, **32**, 40, 42–3, 46, 50, **51**–2

Malone, Allen B. Jr., 81, **82**, 100, 116, 123, 125, 137, 381, 437

Mao Tse-tung, 25, 373

Marauders, 15, 17–8

McCann, James E., 31, 33, 50, 56, **59**, 65, 78, 83, 103, 114, 116, 125, 127, 129, 132, 134, 146, 150, 152, 156, 158, 162, **166**–7, 170–1, 173, 176, **185**–6, 224, 233, 239, **243**, 307, 353, 375, 438

McCarten, Robert D. 77, 94

McCullar, J. M., 225, 334, 340, 349

Meikle, William, 30, 33, 41, 56, 98, 100, 102, 116, 122, 125, **130**, 223–4, **243**–4, **265**, 296, 306, 342, 350, 354, 357, 360, 377, 438

Merrill's Marauders, 70–1

Mier, Isabel G., 43, 56, **58**, 78, 116, 122, 125, **156**, **161**, 179, 224, 233, 238–9, **243**, 256, 263, 287–8, 297–8, 307, 310, 332, 338–9, 342, 350, 357, 360, 439

Mikola, Allan, 203–4, 206, 210, 224, 233, 248, 250, 262–4, 267, 275–6, 292, 310, 368–9, 378, 439

Miles, Charles D., 30–1, **33**–4, 39, **40**–2, 44, 440

Millican, Aimee, 40, 280–1

Mills, James H., 12–5, **16**, **17**, **18**, 19–22, 24, 43, **45**, 46–9, 52–4, 56–62, 76, 79, 81, **91**, 98, 100, **101**–4, 107–8, 109–11, 116–7, 120–2, 125, **130**–1, 147–9, **152**, 154, 157, 163, **164**–5, 179–81, **197**, 204, 223, 228–9,

233, 235, 238–9, 243, 247, 251, 262, **265**, 269, 277–8, 286, 289, 298–9, 308, 315–6, **327**, 332, 337, 339–40, 342, 345, 347, 350, 356, 360–3, 374–6, 384, 441

Mondelli, Leslie L., 298–9, 320, 324, 334, 337–9, 342–3, 345, 350, 357, 379, 382, 442

Moran Field, 54, 56–7, 60–1, 63, 72–3, 76, 79–80

Morris, James J., Jr., 193–4, 210–1, 224, **243**–4, 248–50, 306, 334, 336–7, 339, 342–3, 350, 352, 357, 360, 443

Morse, Brig. Gen. Winslow C., 26, 31, 55, 141–2, **143**, 144, 155, 182, 186, 226, 249, 260

Mroskey, Joseph W., 35, 50, 443

Myitkyina, 28, 62–3, 68, 71–2, 75, 77–8, 102–5, 199, 230

N

Nimrod Detachment, 231–2, 241, 246, 248, 251, 387

O

O'Brien, Pat, 159–61

Office of War Information (OWI), 69, 97, **271**, 362

Okamura, Yasuji, Lt. Gen., 352

opera, 114, 202–3, 208

Operational Training Unit (OTU), 26, 31, 34, 38–9, **51**, 104, 234, 282

Outen, Raymond L., 275, 282, 360, 444

Ouyang Chun, **80**, 158, 162, 233, 246, 248, 250, 252, 255–6, 258, 287, 390

P

parachute bombs, 330–1, 334, 338, 344

Patterson, R. L., 63, 67

Peters, Eril W., 43, 56, 79, 116, 122, 125, 137, **138**, **146**, 157, 173–4, 176–8, 187–9, 191, 196, 201, 214, 222, 224, **243**, 250, 252, 256, 262–3, 279, 282, 287, 298, 300, 302, **304**, 319, 321, 332, 342, 348, 350, 354, 377, 444

Peiping-Hankow Railroad (Ping-Han), 133, 158, 229, 231, 235, 240–1, 245–6, 259, 262, 270, 278–9, 289, 296, 299–300, 306, 314, 320, 323–4, **335**–6, 339, 346, 347

Piecuch, Philip, 81, **82**, 91, **101**, 116, 122, 125, **126**, 137, 150, 162, 244, **277**, 296, 306, 327, 342, 350, 356, 377, 382, 445

Peishiyi, 50, 96, 102, 124–5, 128–31, 134, 139–40, 148–9, 155, **156**

"Pistol Packin' Papas," 35

"Pointee-Talkee," 67, 216, 218–9

Portaluppi, Charles J., 35, **166**–8, 170–2, **173**–4, 176, 178, 186–91, **200**–1, 209, 212, **213**–4, 220–2

Pulaski, Frank P., 137, 150, **151**, 155–6, 161–2, 183, 185, 187–91, **200**–1, **213**, 221–2, 224, 233, 235, 238, **243**–4, **247**, 256–8, 263, 267–8, 275, 277–9, **290**–1, 293–4, 298–300, 305, 307, 310, 318, 329–30, 336–9, 342–3, 345, 350, 357, 360, 379, 445

Purple Heart, 35–6, 49, 61, 106, 137, **142**, 144, 183, 249, 312, 345

R

Ragland, Reuben, Jr., 43, **47**, **48**, 56–7, **58**–9, 65, 67–8, 74, 78, 82, 84, 89, 90, 114, 116, 119, 124–5, 137, 158–9, 162, 165, 167, 170–4, 176, 193, 210, 223–4, 230, 233, 238–9, **243**, 246, 259, 268–9, 376, 389, 446

Ramsey, Glyn W., 269

RDX bombs, 268, 283, 297–9, 309, 318, 325, 334, 336–9

Reynard, Harley D., **293**–4, 298–301, **304**, 321, 327, 342, 348, 350, 354, 377, 446

Rich, Jack H., 186–7, 189, 190, **200**, 212, 221–2

Richards, Charles W., 30, 360, 447

Rickman, Stanley B., 35, 56, **59**–60, 102, 116, 119, 122, 125, **130**, 150, 161, 224, **243**, **265**, 275, **280**, 342, 350, 354, 357, 360, 377, 448

Rieks, Maynard W., 30, **32**–3, 43, 48, **51**, 56, **59**, 65, 78, **79**, 116, 119, 122, 125, 137, 185, 188–9, 201, 212, 214, 222, 224, 238, **243**, 256, 259, 262–4, **265**, 268, **276**, 277, 288, 307, 309, 376, 382, 448

Russell, Lt. Col. Austin J., 144, 147, 154, 157, 162, 178, 186–7, 189, 192, 194, 237, 268, 298, 338–9

Ryan, James J., Jr., **130**, 150, **151**, 161, 198, 210, 224, **243**, 248, 250–2, 255–8, 263, **264**, 268, 270, 272, 276, **277**, 285, 288–9, 291–2, 298, 341, 371, 388, 449

Ryave, Arnold H., 320, 348, 350, 356, 365, 376, 449

S

SS *Alderamin*, 365–6
SS *Marine Angel*, 363–5
Sacky, Charles J., 21
Sarver, Harold G., 35–6
Schlicher, Robert E., Jr., 162, 193–4, 224, **232**–3, 235, 238–9, **243**, 248, 256–7, 260, 262–4, **265**, 270, 276, 279, 285, 289, 291, 293–4, 307, **310**, 330–1, 336, 340, 342–3, 345, 350, 356, 366, 377, 382, 450
Schroeder, Edmund, 264, **265**, 270, 272, 275, 279, 285, 287–9, 291–2, 294, 298, 307, 314–5, 318, 334–5, 338–9, 342–3, 345, 356, 377, 451
Seacrest, Mark T., 29–30, 33–4, 39, **40**, 50, 51, 54, 58–9, 65, 71, **79**, 80–2, 89, 91, 93–4, 106–7, 111–3, 116–7, 122, 125–6, 132, 137, **142**, **143**–4, **145**, 154, 157, 161–2, 182, 185, 193–4, 198, 210–1, 224, 231, 233, 239–41, **243**, 282, 278, 286, 451
searchlights 174–7, 190–1, 202, 332
Senecal, Wayne H., 150, **151**, 158, 162, 166, 170–2, **173**, **185**–6, 198, 224, 230, 233, 235, **237**–9, **243**, **247**, 250–1, 255–6, 259, 262, 264–5, 268, 270, 272, 276, 285, 288–9, 291, 293, 297–8, 300, 302, 304–5, 313, 321, 324, 350, 354, 375, 377, 382, 387, 452
Senkbeil, Edwin A., 40
Services of Supply (SOS), 219
Seymour Johnson Field, 18, 75
Shansi (Shanxi) Province, 239
Shaw, Janet, 208
Shellback Certificate, 20–1, 316, 358
Shensi (Shaanxi) Province, 25, 37, 132
Shepard, Lyle L., 30, 453
Sheppard Field, 14–5, 91, 318
Sheridan, Ann, 161
Shock, Joseph N., 30, 33, 43, 56, **59**, 107, 116, 119, 122, 125, 137, **152**–4, 162, 185, 187, 189–90, 196, 201, 213, 224, 235, 238–9, **243**, **247**, **265**, 273, 282, 287, 319, 321, 327, 358, 377, 454
Simpson, Thomas S., 30, **32**–3, 39–42, 47, 54, 56–7, 59, 65, **66**, 68, 74–5, 77–8, 82, **83**–9, 90, 93, 95–6, 105, 108, 111, 114, 116–9, 125, 137, 144–6, 148, 150, 157, 205, 282, 375, 380, 388, 454

Sky Dragons Squadron 28–9
Smith, Lloyd S., **94**, 140, 382, 455
Smith, Manuel C., **45**, 56, **89**, **185**, 324, 378, 456
Solyn, Robert N., **21**, 43, 57, 81, **98**–9, 116, 122, 125, **126**, **136**–7, 143, 150, **156**, 198, 242, **265**, 327, 342, 348, 350, 362, 381, 456
Spray and Pray Squadron, 10, **66**, 85, 203, 294, **326**, 358, 384
Stanley, Henry A., 312, 324, 329–31
Stearns, Fred S., **297**, 299, 305, 307, 314–5, 336–9, 342–3, 350, 354, 357, 359, 378, 457
Stilwell, Lt. Gen. Joseph W., 67, 70–2, 76, 94, 105, 125, 154–5
Stockett, Marvin M., 76
Stratemeyer, Maj. Gen. George E., 69, 105, 284, 328, 353, 367
Summerville, James R., 30, 33, **49**, 56, **59**, 100, 116, 122, 125, 137, 224, **243**, 342, 348, 350, 354, 357, 360, 457
Supsic, Joseph P., 193, 210–1, 224, **243**–4, 310, 342, 348, 350, 357, 360, 378, 458
Sutley, Percy H., 154, 194, 270
Szechwan (Sichuan) Province, 227, 254

T

Thomas, B. F., Jr., **204**, 224, **243**, 287, 342, 348, 350, 354, 357, 360, 379, 458
Thompson, Elmer J., 81, **101**, 116, 122, 125, 137, 376, 459
Ting, Cheng-liang "Daniel," **36**, 79, **80**, 258, 287, 291, 299, 305, 312, 315, 334, 338, 343, 390
Trout, Jack A., 35, 54, 56, 60, 81, 102, 116, 119, 122, 125, 161–2, 182, 210, 224, 235, 238–9, **243**, 249, 252, 256, 263, 273, 277, **280**, 287, 294, 297, 299, 307, 381, 459
Trumm, John A., 329, **332**–3, 336, 338–40, 342–5, 350, 357–8, 460
Tu Kai-mu 10, **36**, **48**, 64, 170, 231, 247, 252–3, 338, 349, 353, 373, **374**–5, 387

U

USS *General C. G. Morton*, 359
USS *General Edgar T. Collins*, 358
USS *General George O. Squier*, 362
USS *General J. H. McRae*, 359
USS *General Robert E. Callan*, 316

USS *Mission Bay*, **19**–22, 43, 48, 58, 75, 81, 102, 131, 198, 228, 362
USS *Wake Island*, 19–22

V

Valley Field, 300, 302, 305, 307, 318, 344, 388
Van Zwoll, Cornelius, 222
Vincent, Brig. Gen. Clifton ("Casey") D., 125

W

Wadlow, James A., 43, 56, **59**, **92**, 100, **101**, 116, 122, 125, **135**–6, 137, 151, **185**, 187, 189, 192, 196, 201, 212, 214, 221, 224, 238, 243, 248, 255–6, 262, 272, 276, **277**, 291–2, 298, **370**, 388, 460
Wang Yung-sin, 36, 76, 84, 89, 255–6, 263–4, 268, 276, 291, 297, 386
Wanhsien, 223, 225, 230, 308, 320, 323
Wedemeyer, Maj. Gen. A. C., 154, 162–3, 181, 199, 209, 251, 284, 290–1, 309, 328, 331
Weinert, Oswald, 121, 174, **175**, 177–8, 186, 192, 195–6, 295
Wenkiang, 179, 193
Wellman, Richard C., 320, 342, 350, 356, 365–6, 377, 461
Whearty, William H., 43, 57, 91, **92**, 102, 116, 119, 122, 125, 151, **213**, 224, **228**, **243**, 248, 250, 252, 268, **277**, 288–9, 291, 297–8, 300, **304**, 310, 321, 342, 348, 350, 354, 461
Wherritt, Barton L., **203**, 210, 224, 233, 238, 240–1, **243**, 246, 248, 255–8, 260, 263–4, 267–8, 270, 272–3, 276, 285, 287–8, 291–2, 299–300, 310, 312, **313**, 368–70, 388, 462
Wilkerson, Ewell F., 30, 33, 41, 43, 48, **53**–4, 56, **59**, 76, **101**, 116, 119, 122, 125, 134, 137, **152**, 165, 179, 213–21, 224–5, **243**, 246, 267, 287, 296, 299, 314, 318, **327**, 336–40, 342–3, 345, 350, 354, 357, 360, 378, 462
Winter, Gerald J., 193, 224, **277**, 287, 290, 342, 348, 350, 357, 360, 378, 463
Wilson, Kenneth P., 147
Wood, George P., 21, 43, 56, 59, 72, **73**, **75**, 77, 90–1, 93, 95, 100, 105, 107–8, 116, 119, 122, 124–5, 151, 156, 162, 178–9, 193, 198, 223–4, **243**, 287, 290, 296, 321, 342, 350, 357, 360, 375, 383, 463
Wu Ch'ao-chen, 30, **32**, 56, 67, 116, 125, 390–1

X

X Force 71, 93

Y

Y Force 71, 93
Yangkai 28, 354, 356–7
Yao Shu-chi 45, 193, 387
Yeaton, Betty, 159, **160**
Yee, John H., 25
Yellow River Bridge, 55, 133, 247, 272, **273**, 347
Yeoh, Seou-ting, 96, 307, 375
Yen Pao-san "Paul," 36–7, 54, 252, 264, 268, 270, 277, 279, 297–8, 307, 315, 332, 339, 343–4, 374
Young, Paul L., **44**, 50, **51**, 75, 92, 96, 102–4, 106, 108, 114–6, 119–20, 125, 127, 129, 132, 134, 136–7, 139, 145, 147, 160–1, 179, 182, 185–6, 190, 193, 205, 223–4, 228, 241, 262, **265**–6, 375, 379, 382, 464
Yunnan Province, 37, 62, 71, 96, 102, 118, 134, 235, 386

Z

Zebra Club, 310